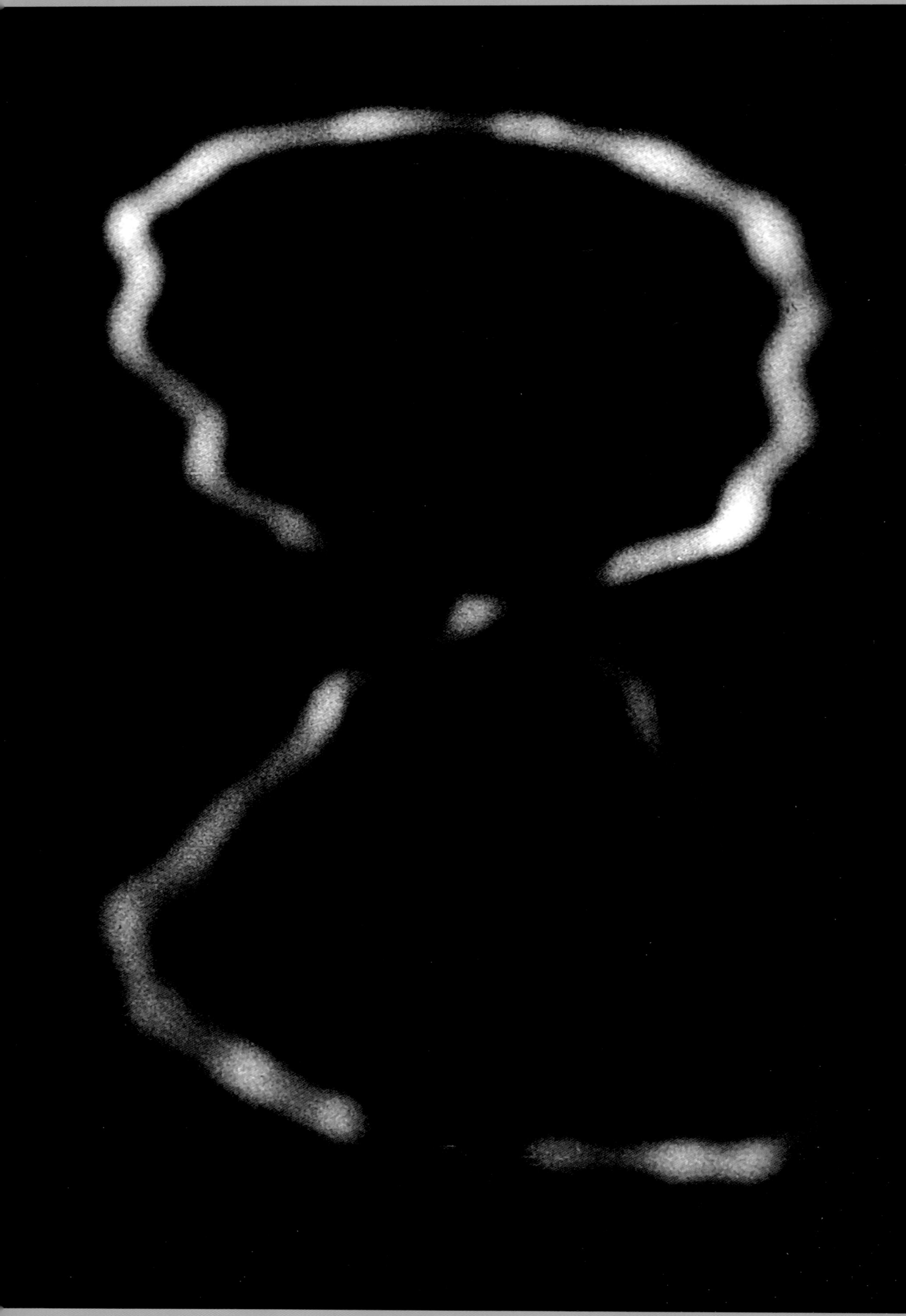

01

02

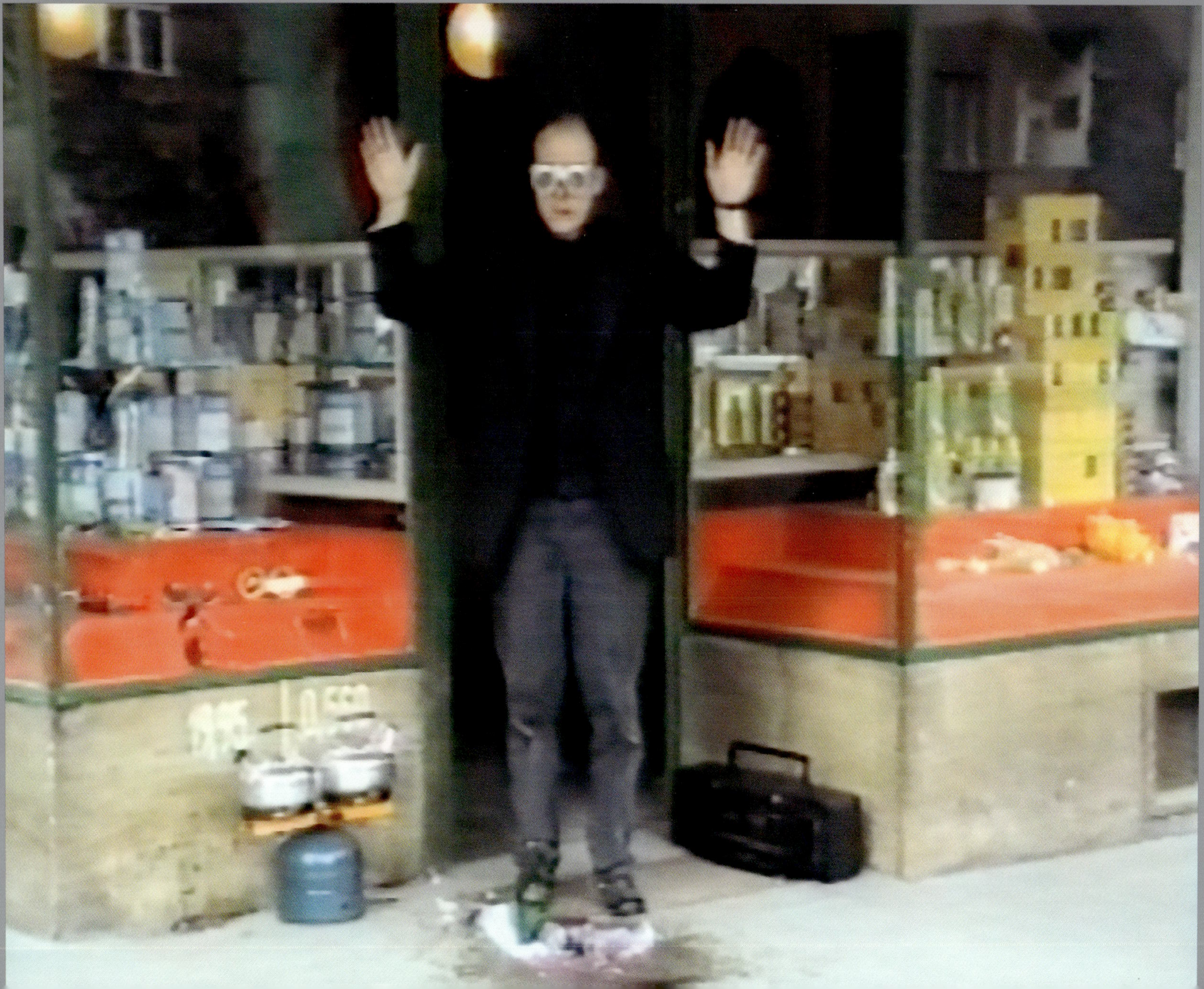

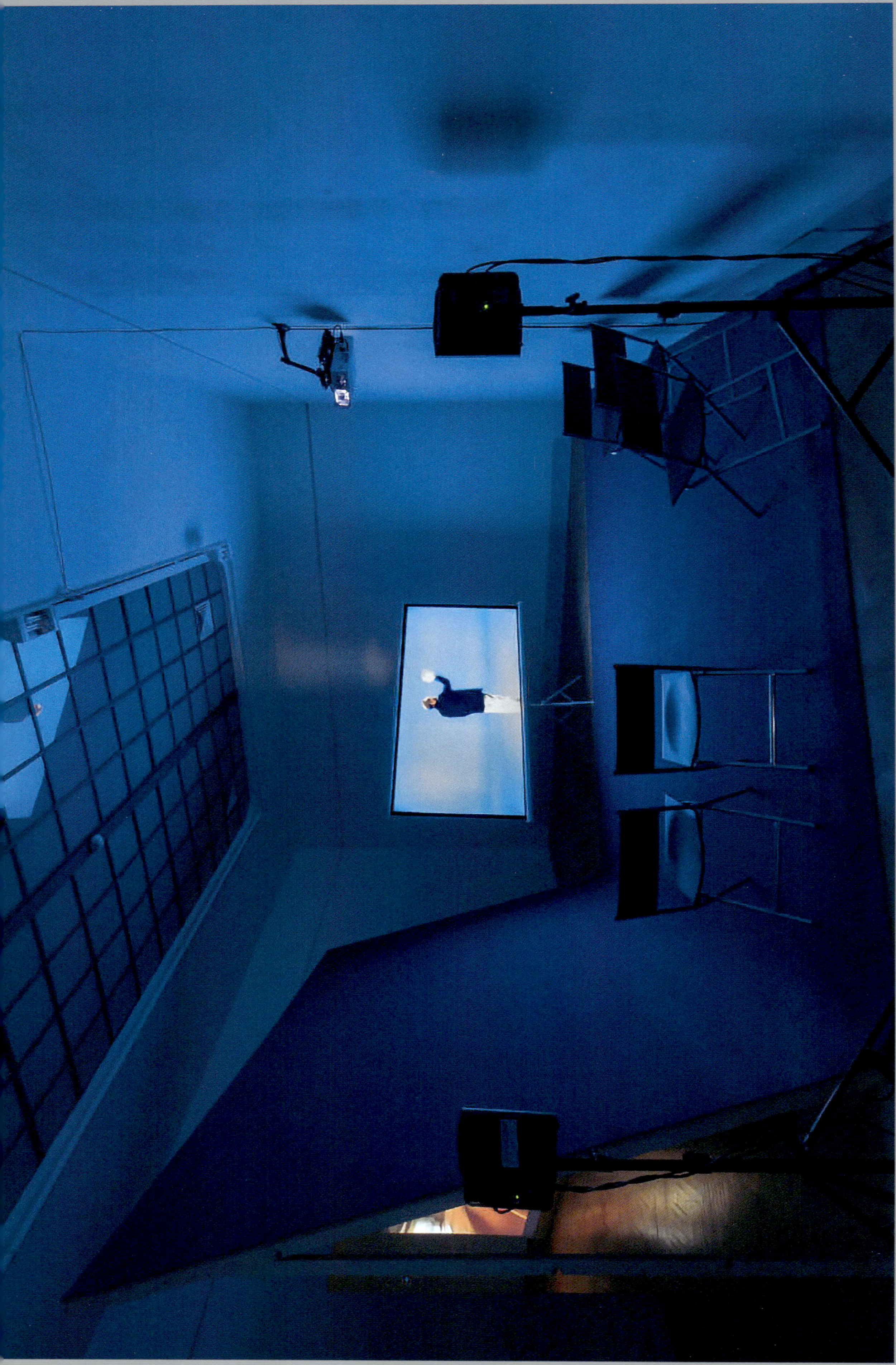

03

04

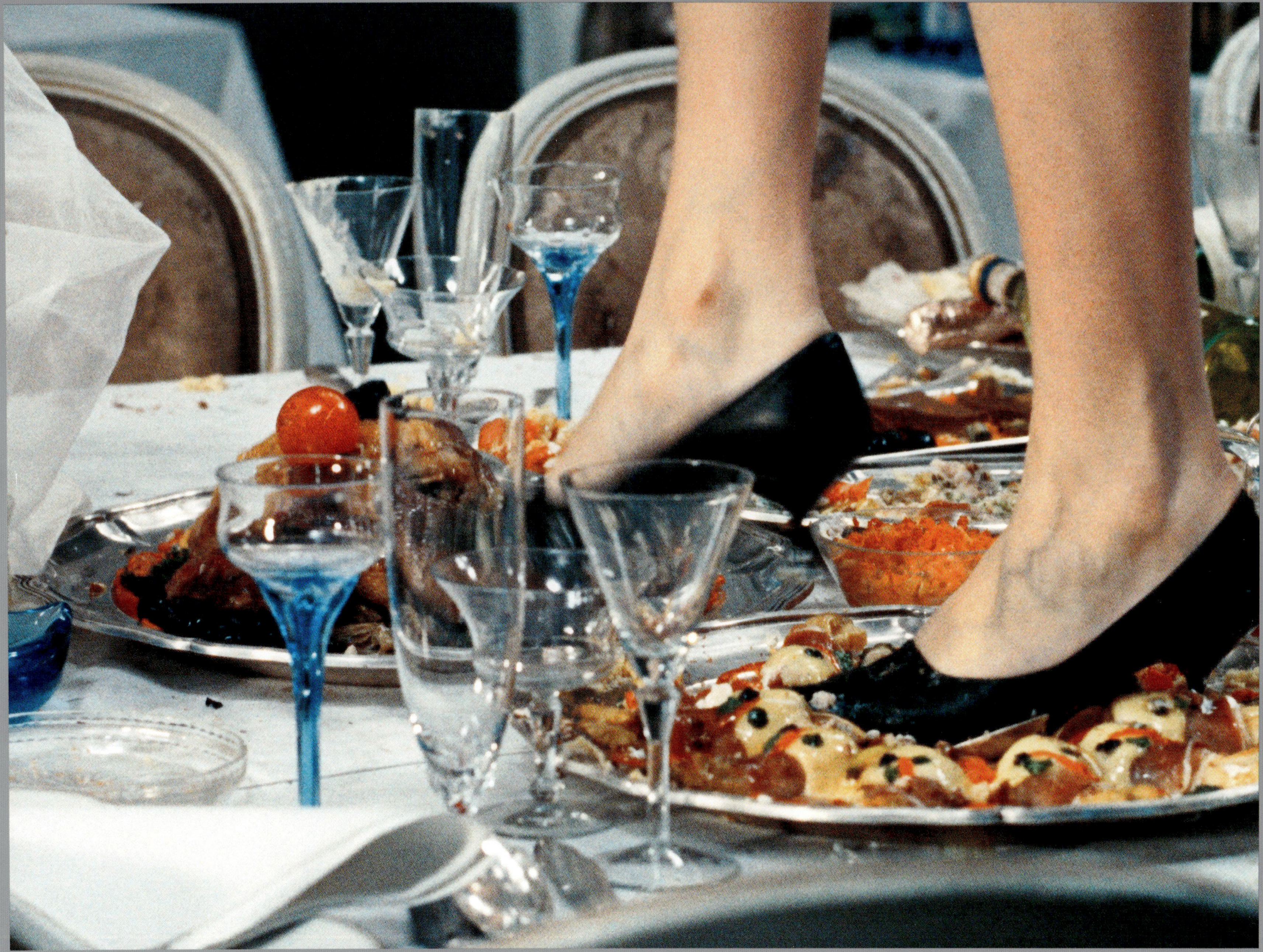

05

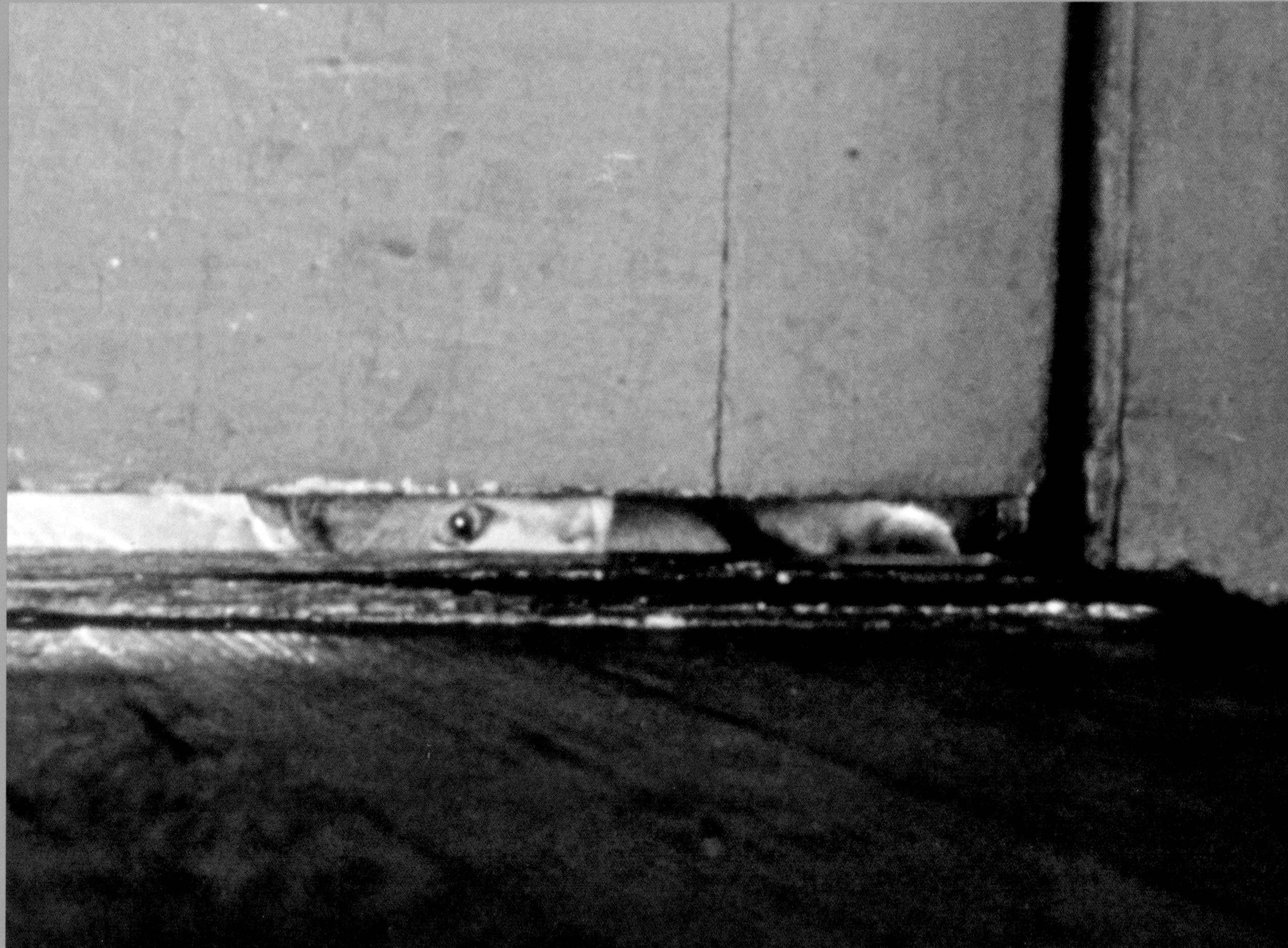

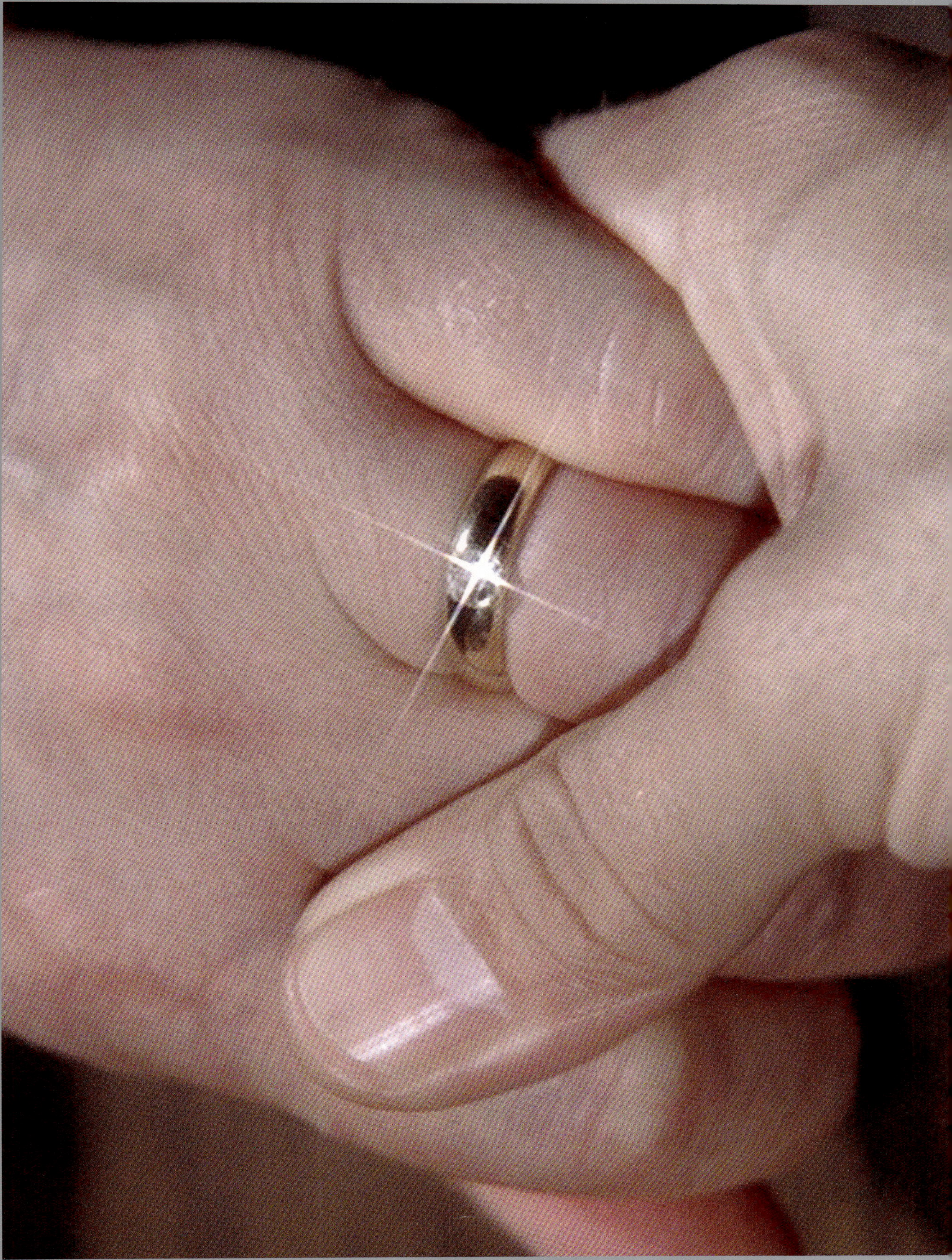

07

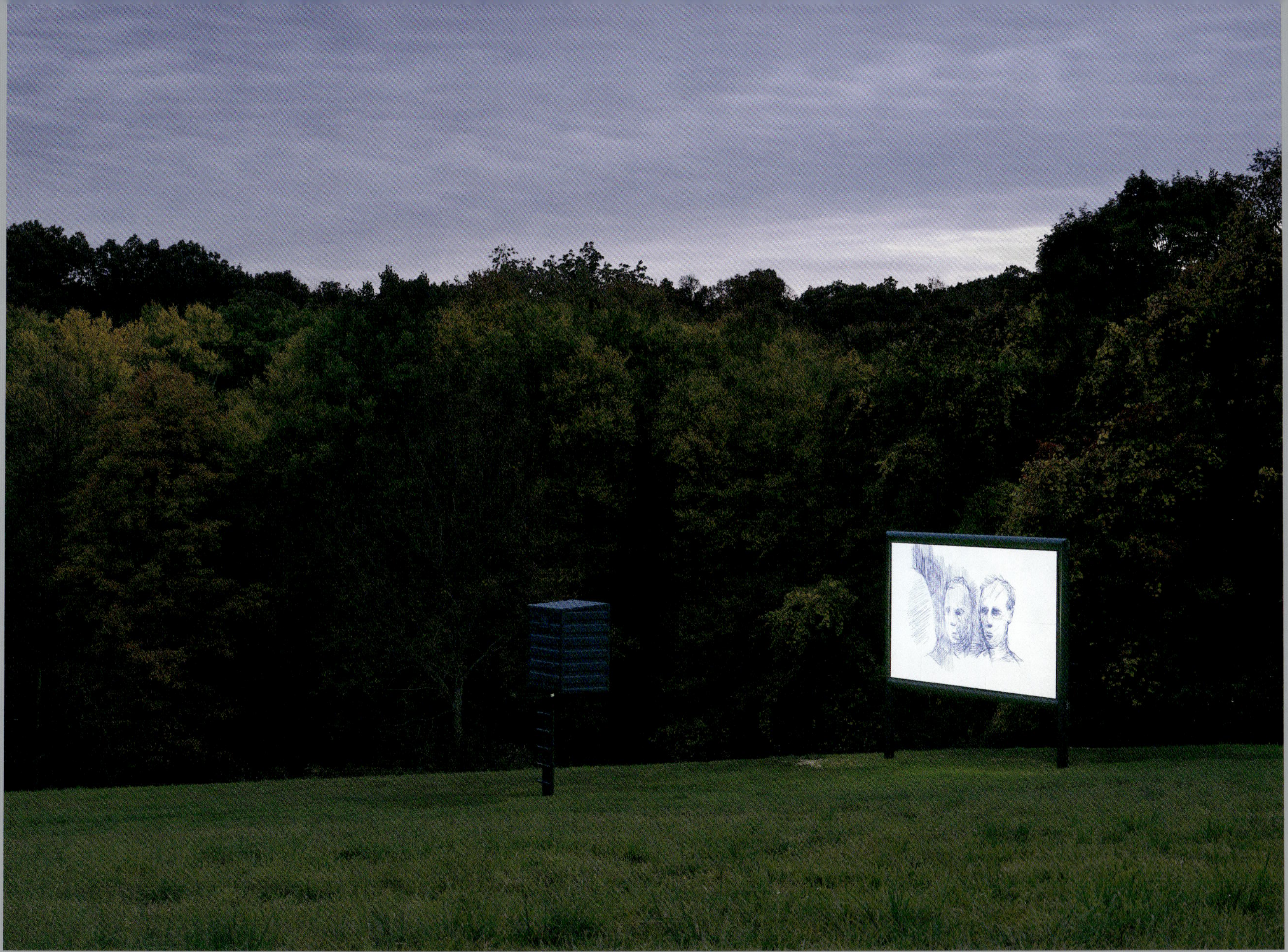

08

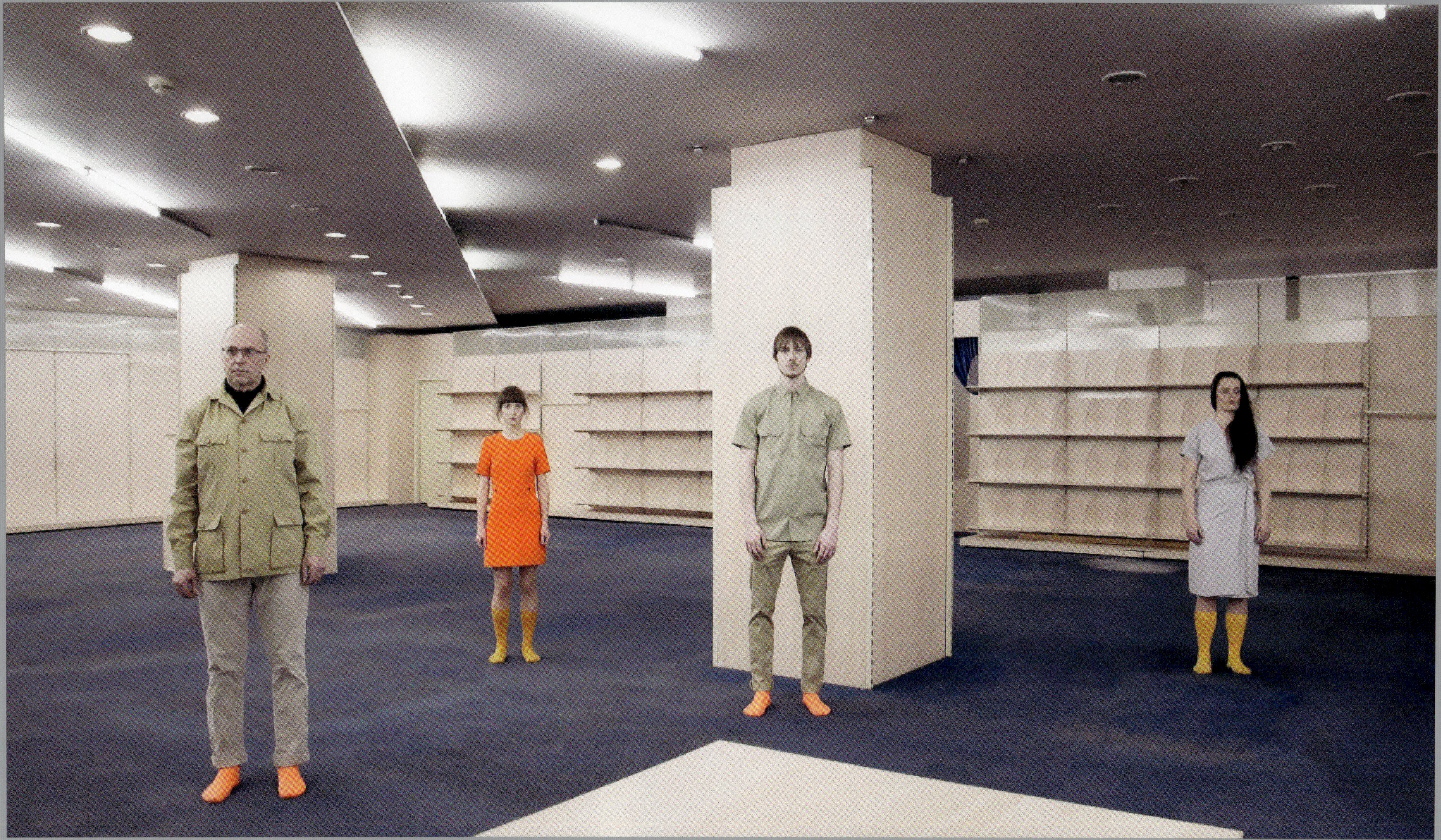

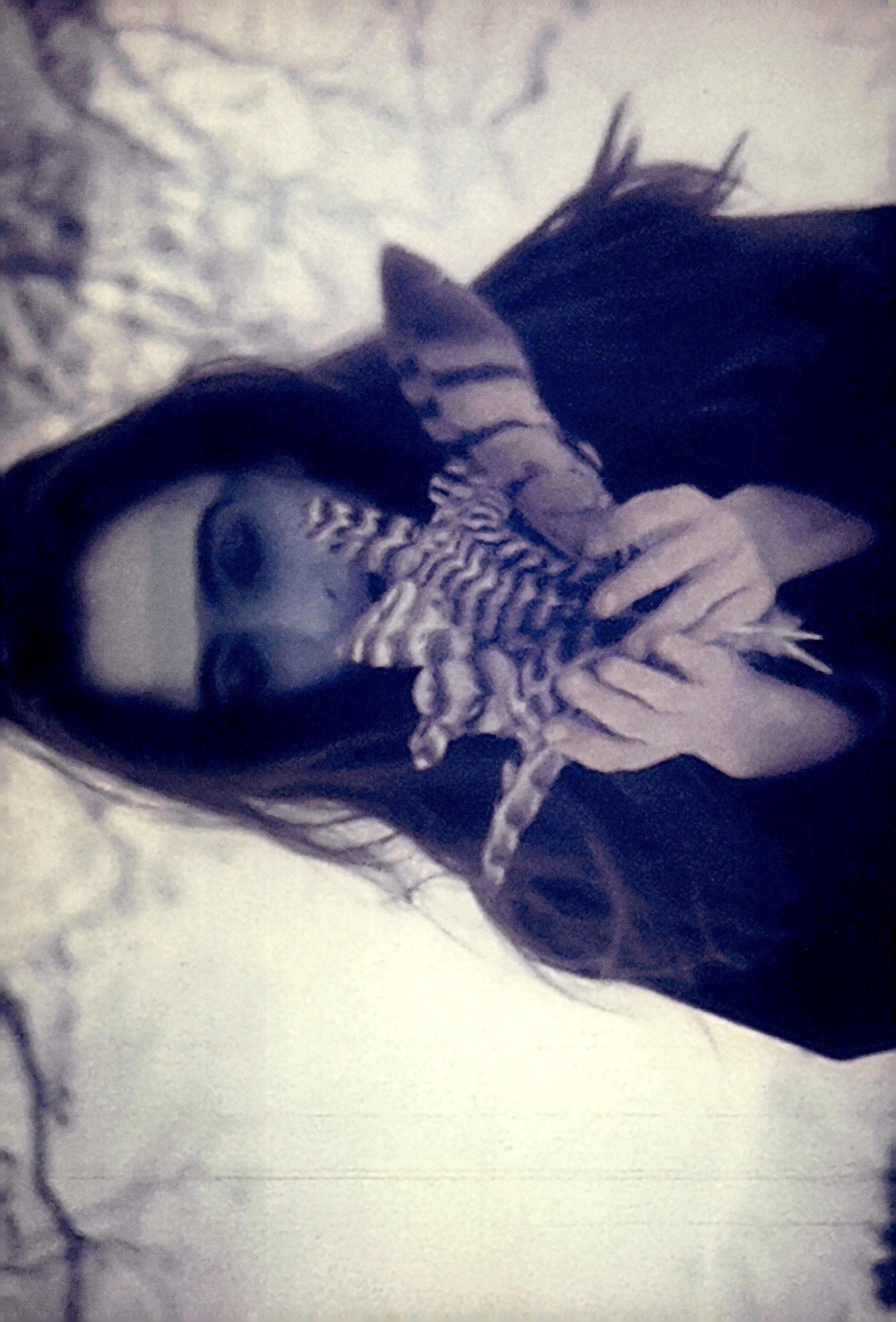

09

10

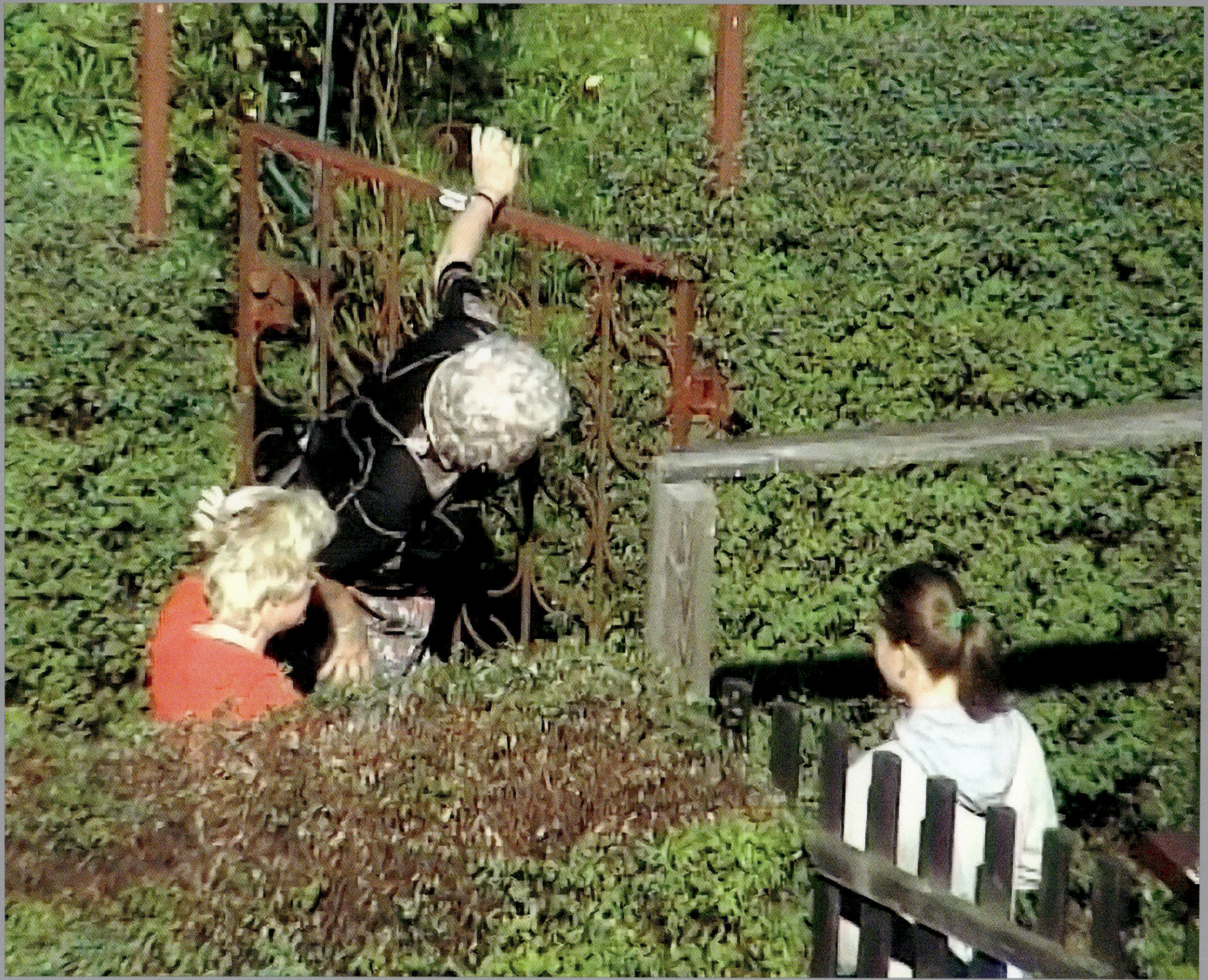

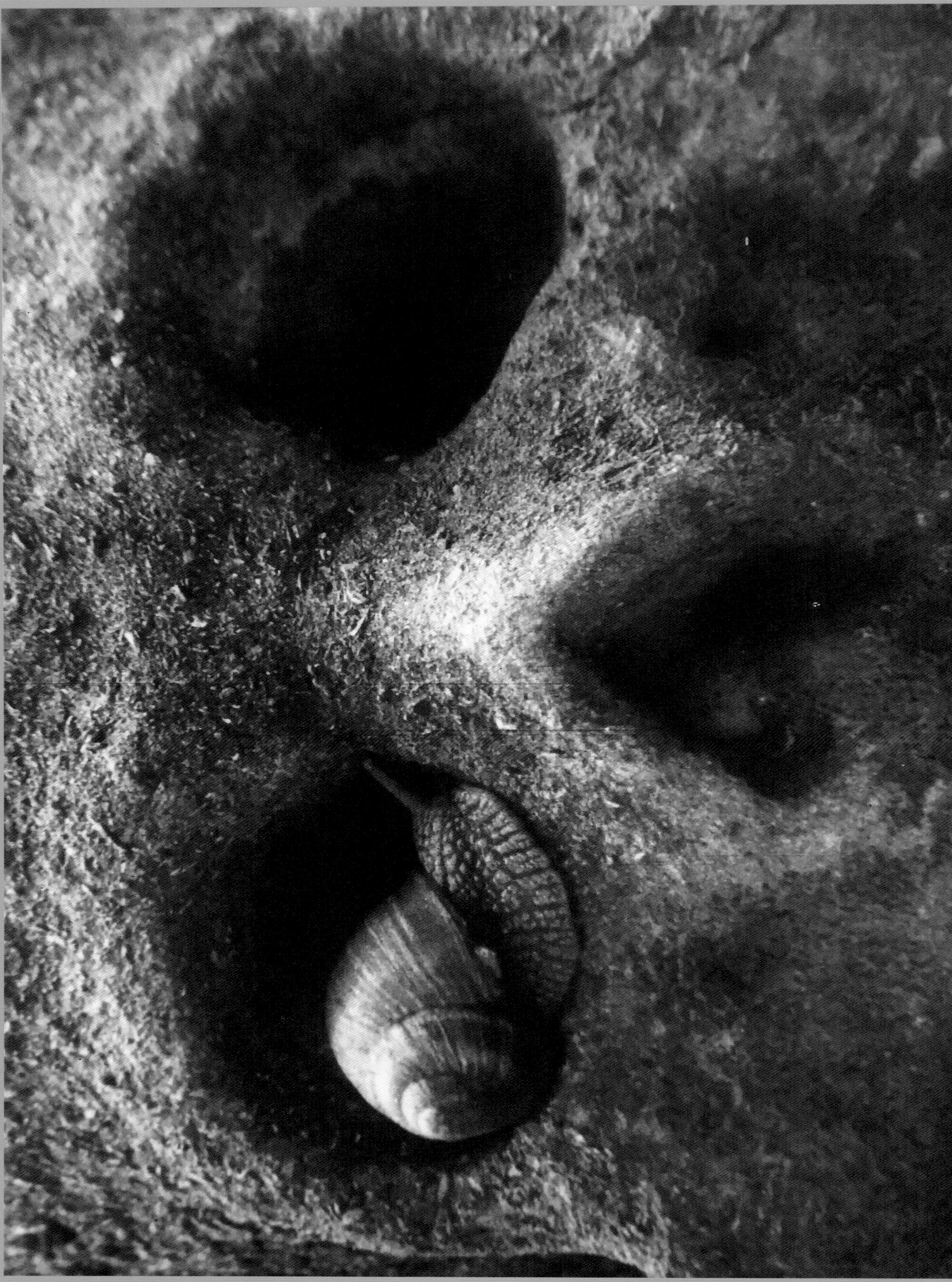

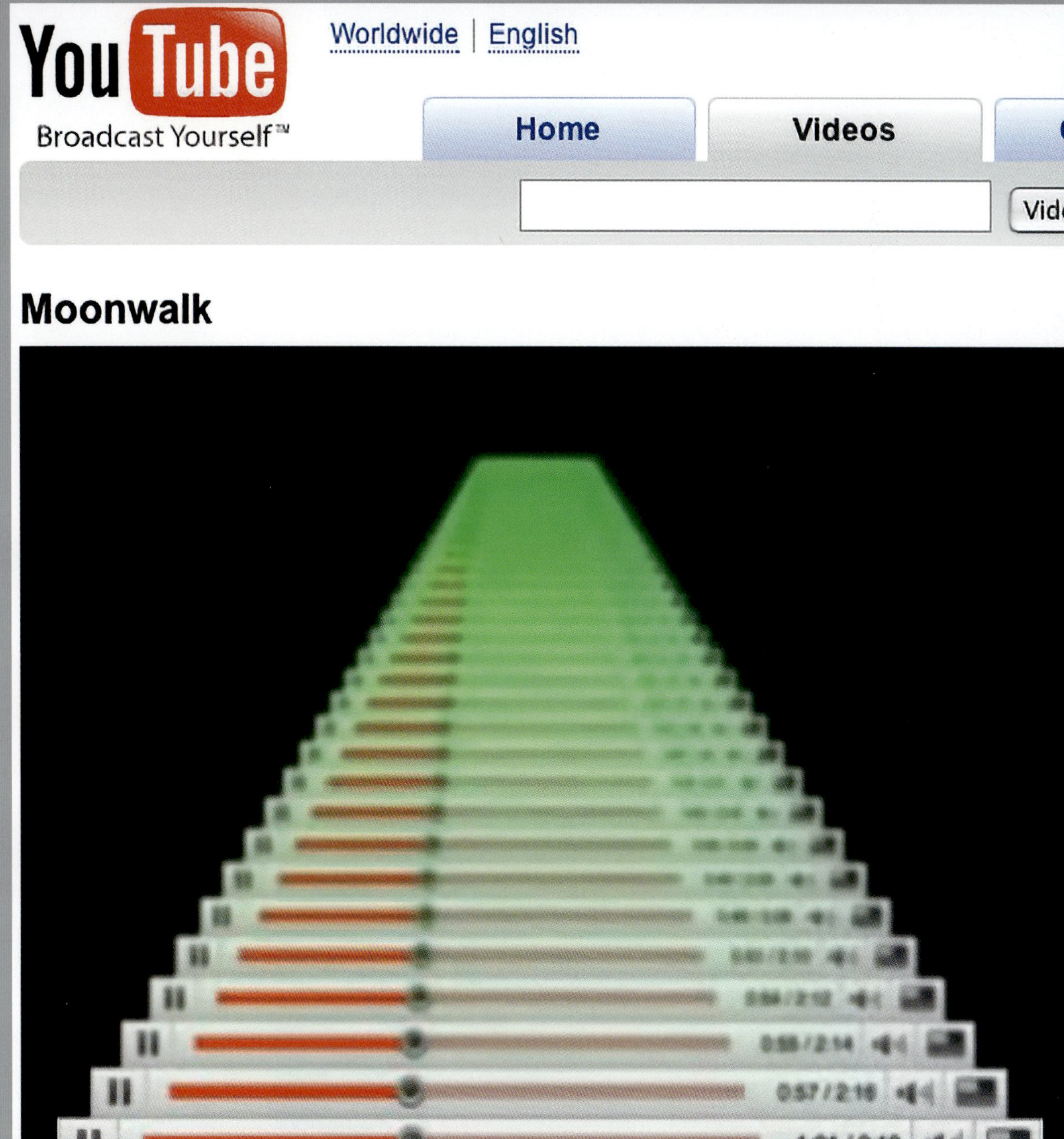
YouTube
Broadcast Yourself™
Worldwide | English
Home
Videos
Moonwalk
0:57 / 2:16
1:01 / 2:19

OBOR VIDEO SČVU

Společná schůzka rozšířené pracovní skupiny oboru videa o "Salonu 89" se koná 6.6.1989 v 18.30 hod. v salonku restaurace Mánes.

Těšíme se na setkání.

Za obor video

Radek Pilař

OBOR VIDEO SČVU

Především všem děkuji za účast při první kolektivní výstavě věnované videoartu na Salònu 89.

Jak jsme se předem domluvili, měla být tato výstava jakousi generálkou, i když technicky náročnou, pro připravovaný seminář o výtvarném umění a elektronice. Chtěl bych vás také informovat o zprávě, kterou si vyžádal předseda UP sekce od předsedů oborů a uměleckých komisí před prázdninami. Zásadním požadavkem v této zprávě je urgence služby videa, tj. technicko-administrativního zázemí oboru v ČFVU, bez kterého po zkušenostech ze Salónu 89, bude těžko obor pokračovat ve své práci. Je tam také požadavek odpovědi na náš návrh. S celým obsahem vás seznámím na schůzi oborové komise. Hlavním posláním umělecké komise musí být vytvoření existenčního prostoru pro naplňování plánu videa /experiment, videotéka, eduk.a teoretická činnost/.

Těším se na první setkání v úterý (12.9.89) od 17.30 v salonku restaurace Mánes. Tentokrát bez projekce.

Za obor

Radek Pilař

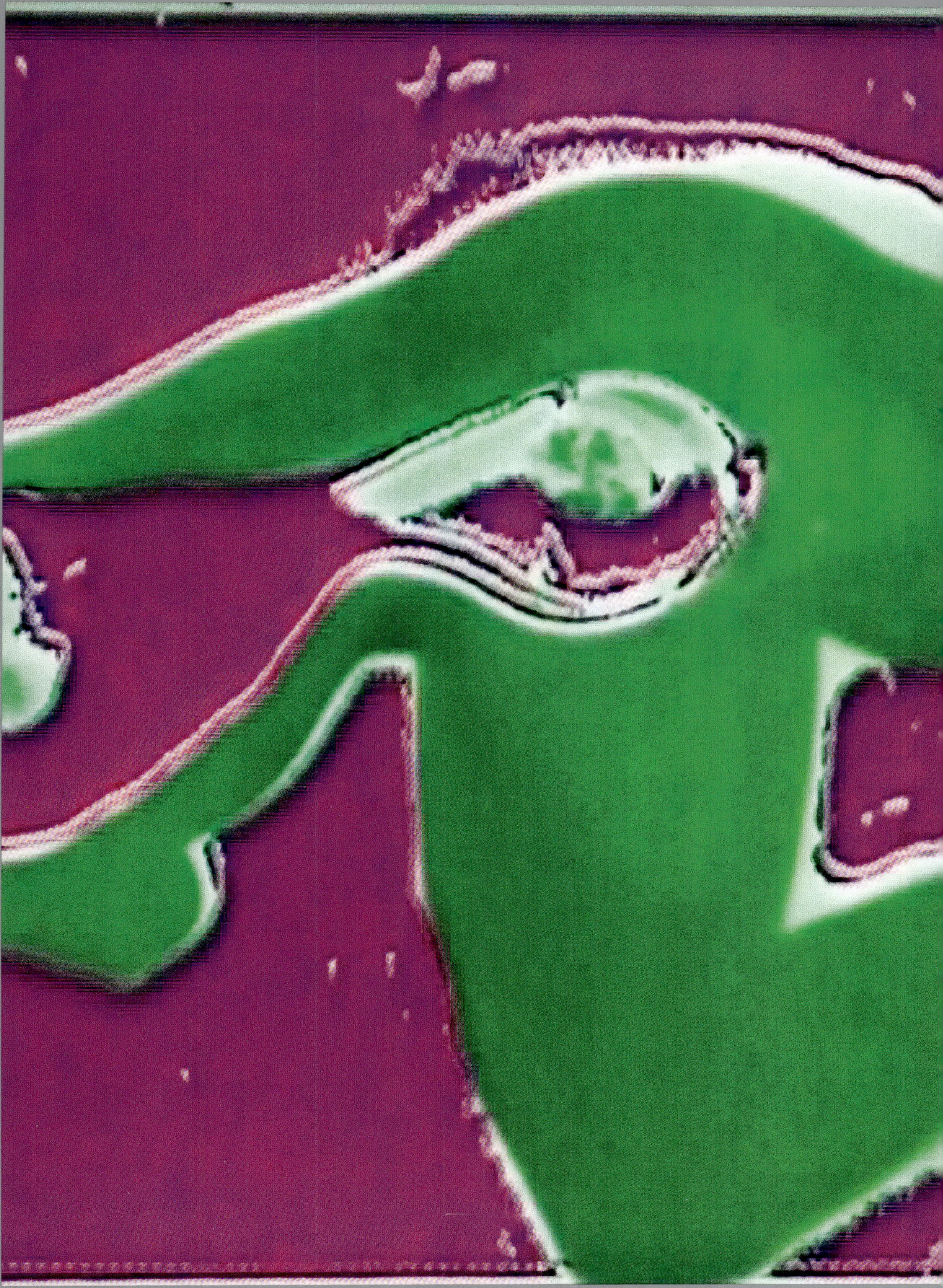

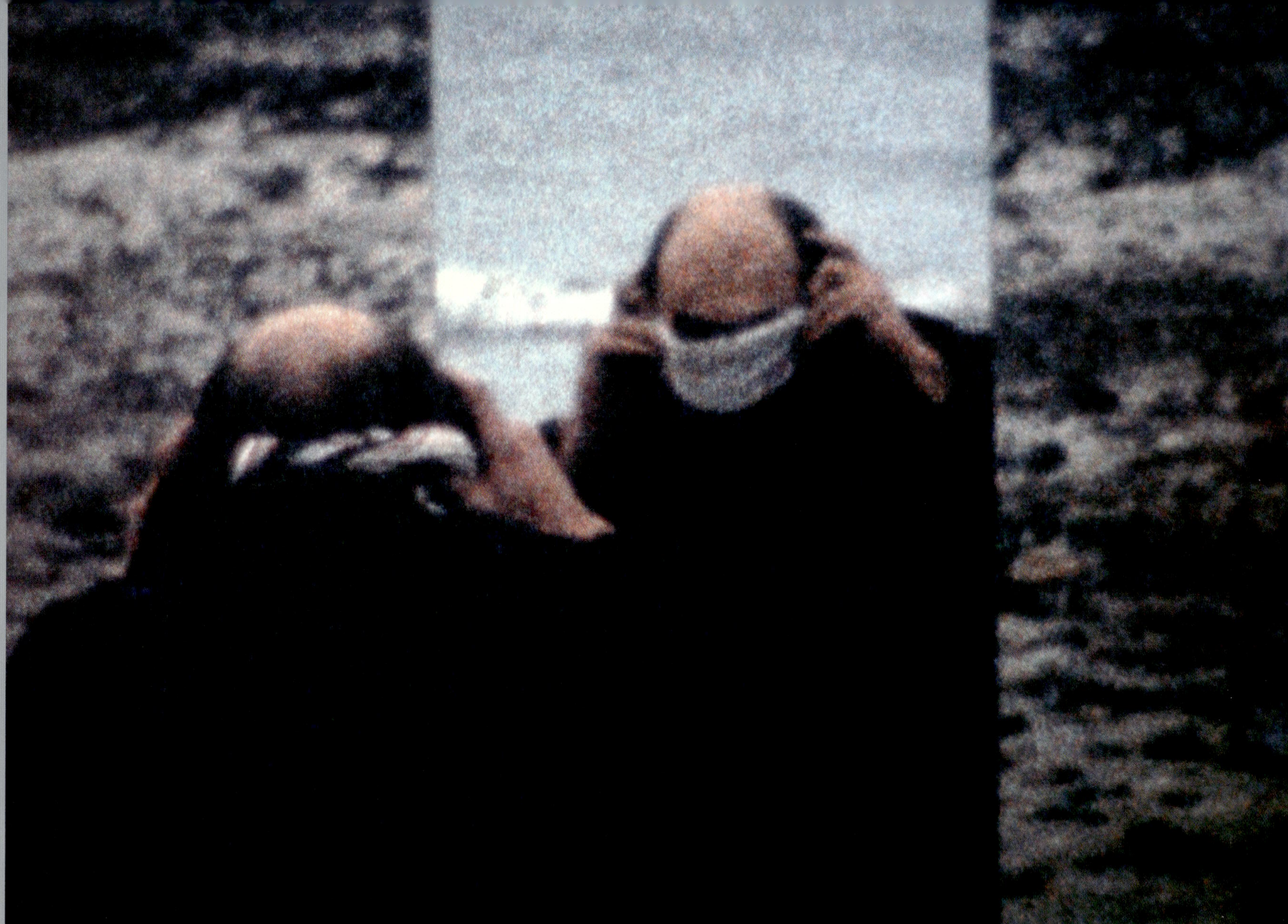

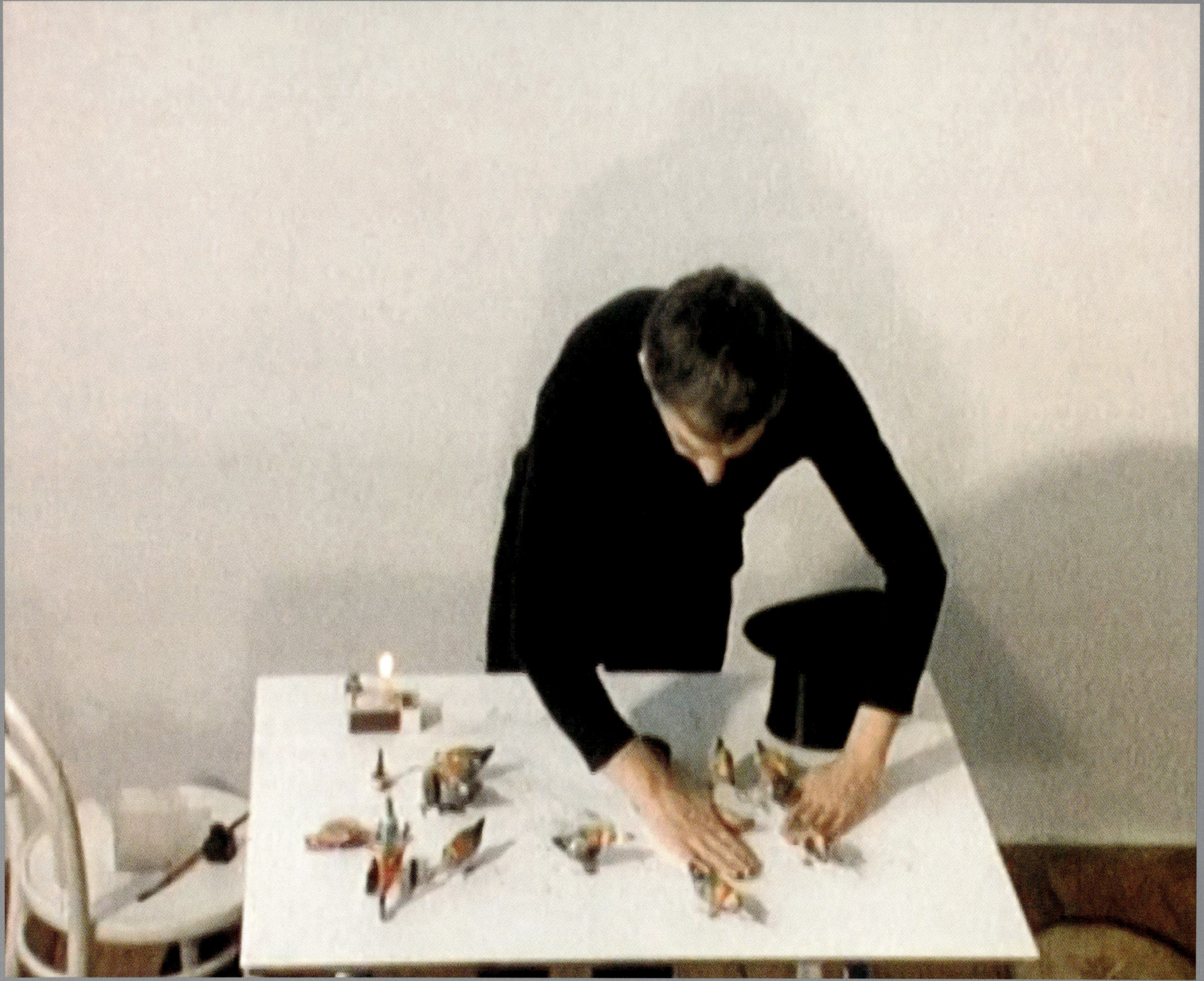

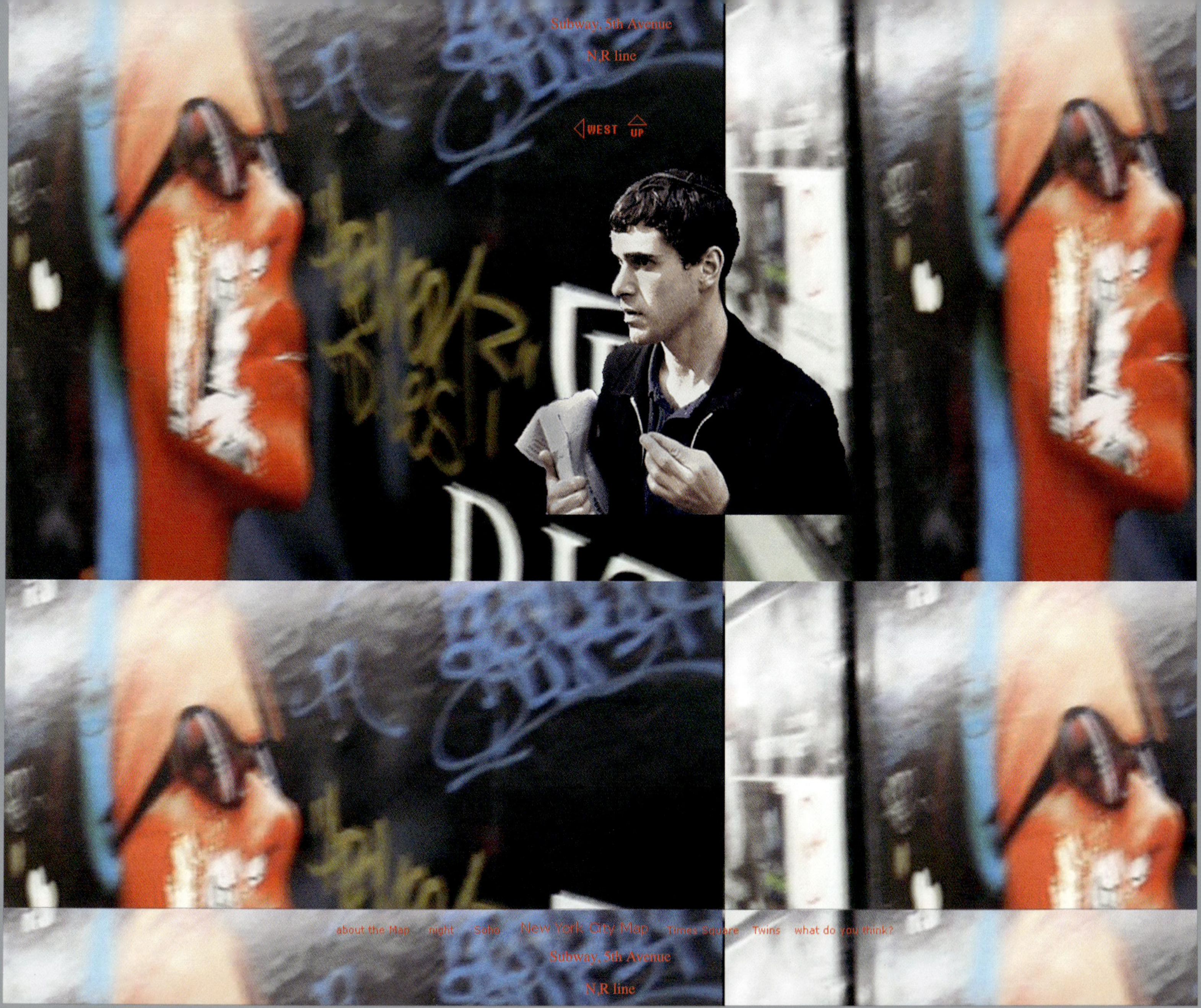
Subway, 5th Avenue
N,R line
WEST
UP
about the Map night Soho New York City Map Times Square Twins what do you think?
Subway, 5th Avenue
N,R line

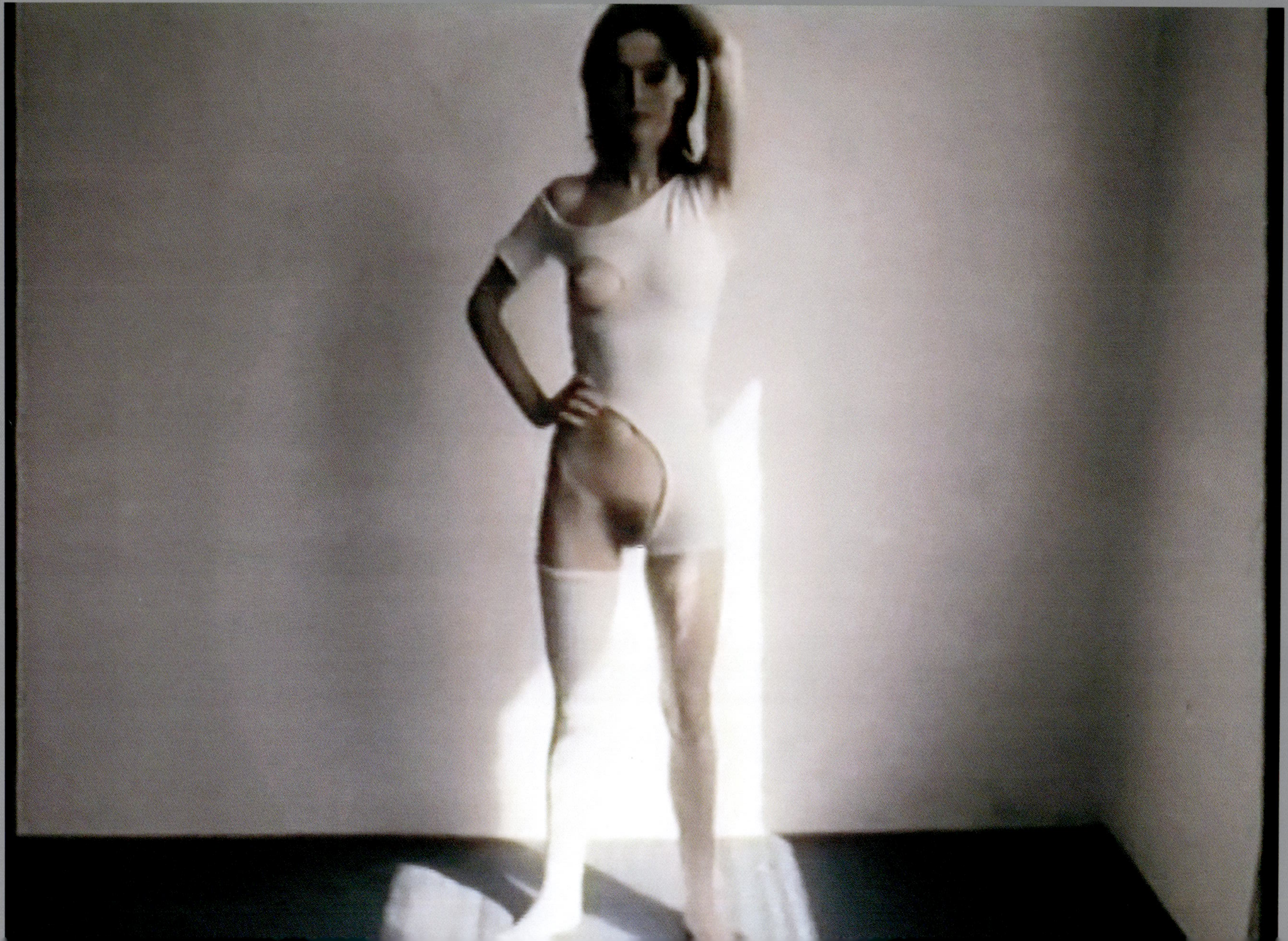

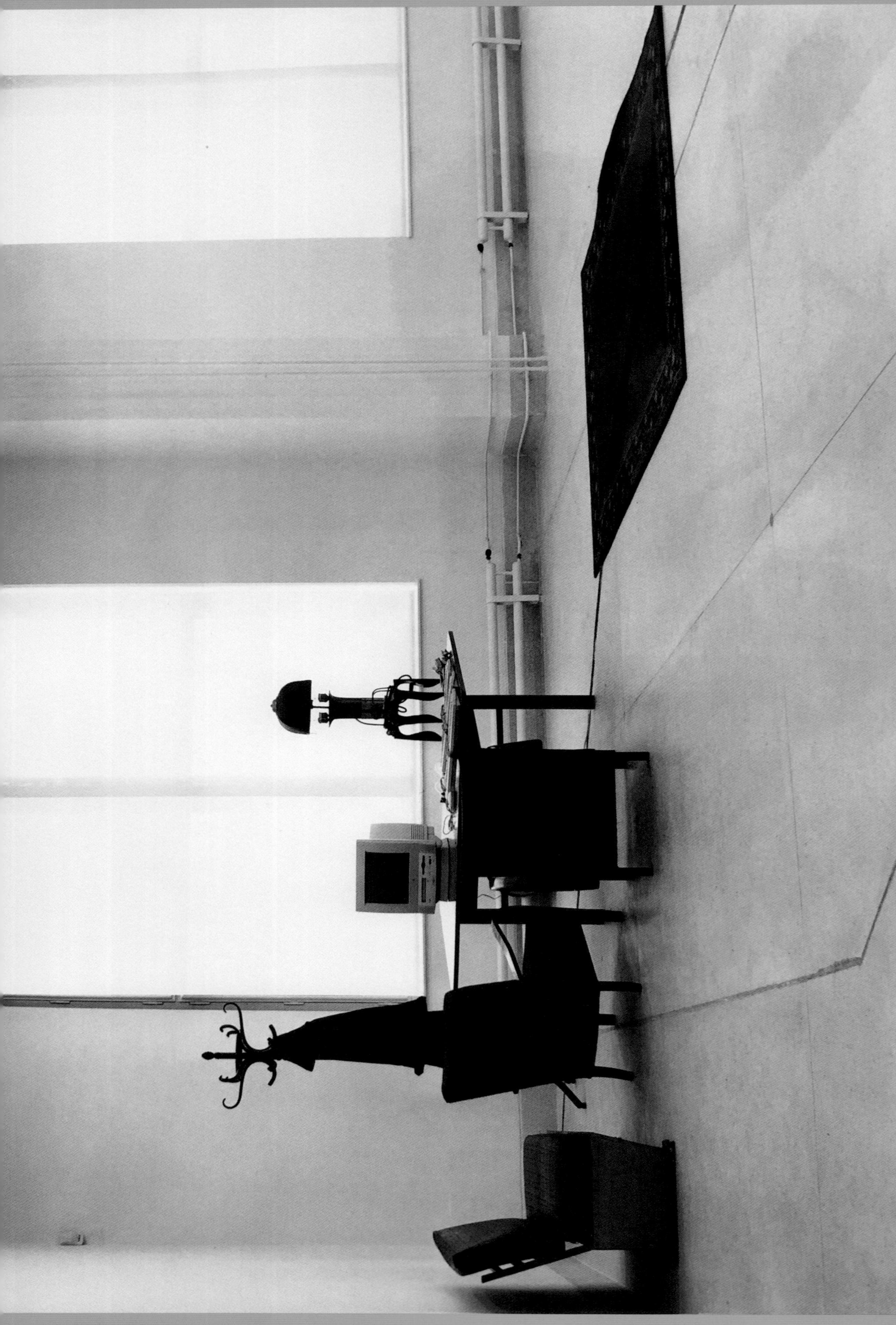

19

20

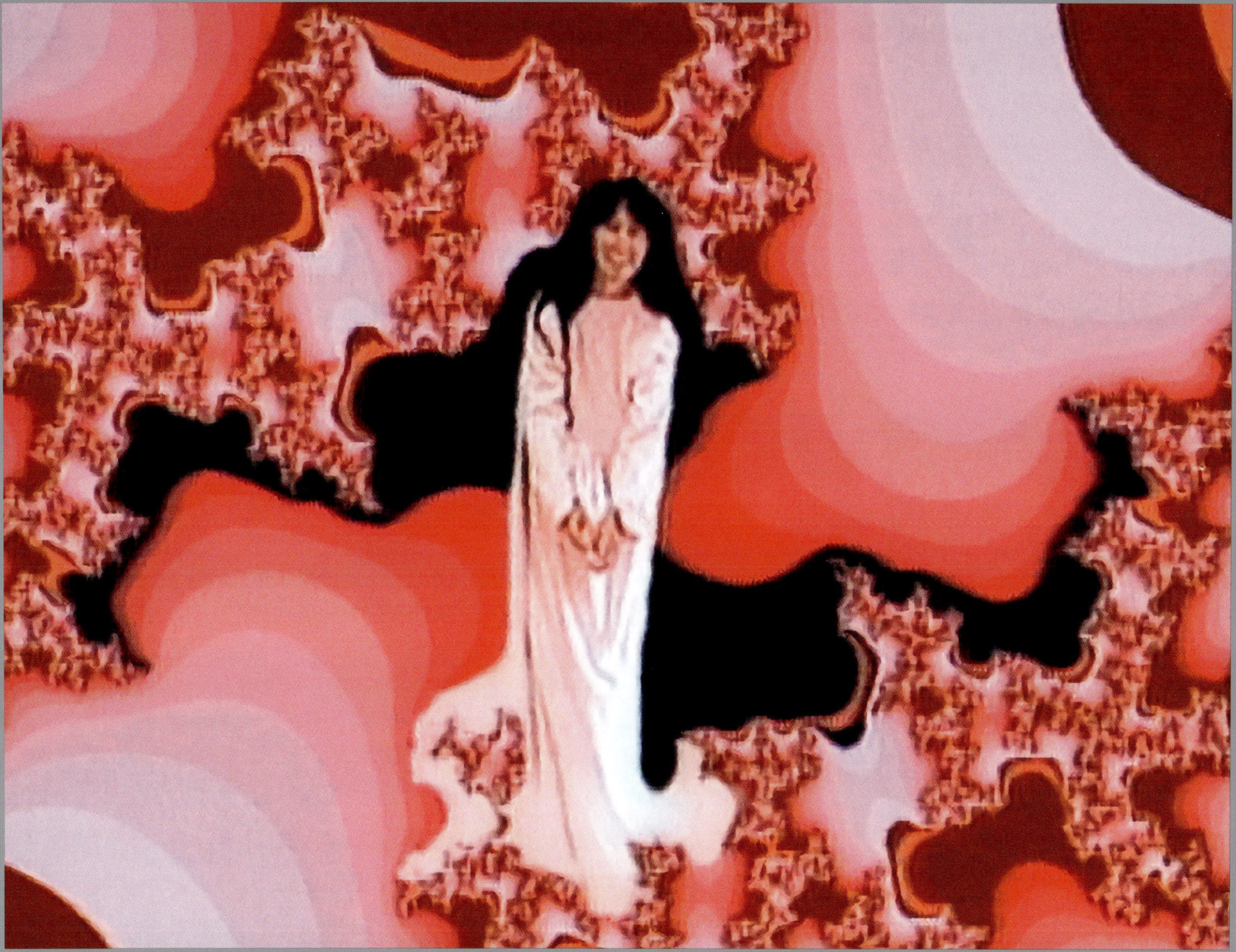

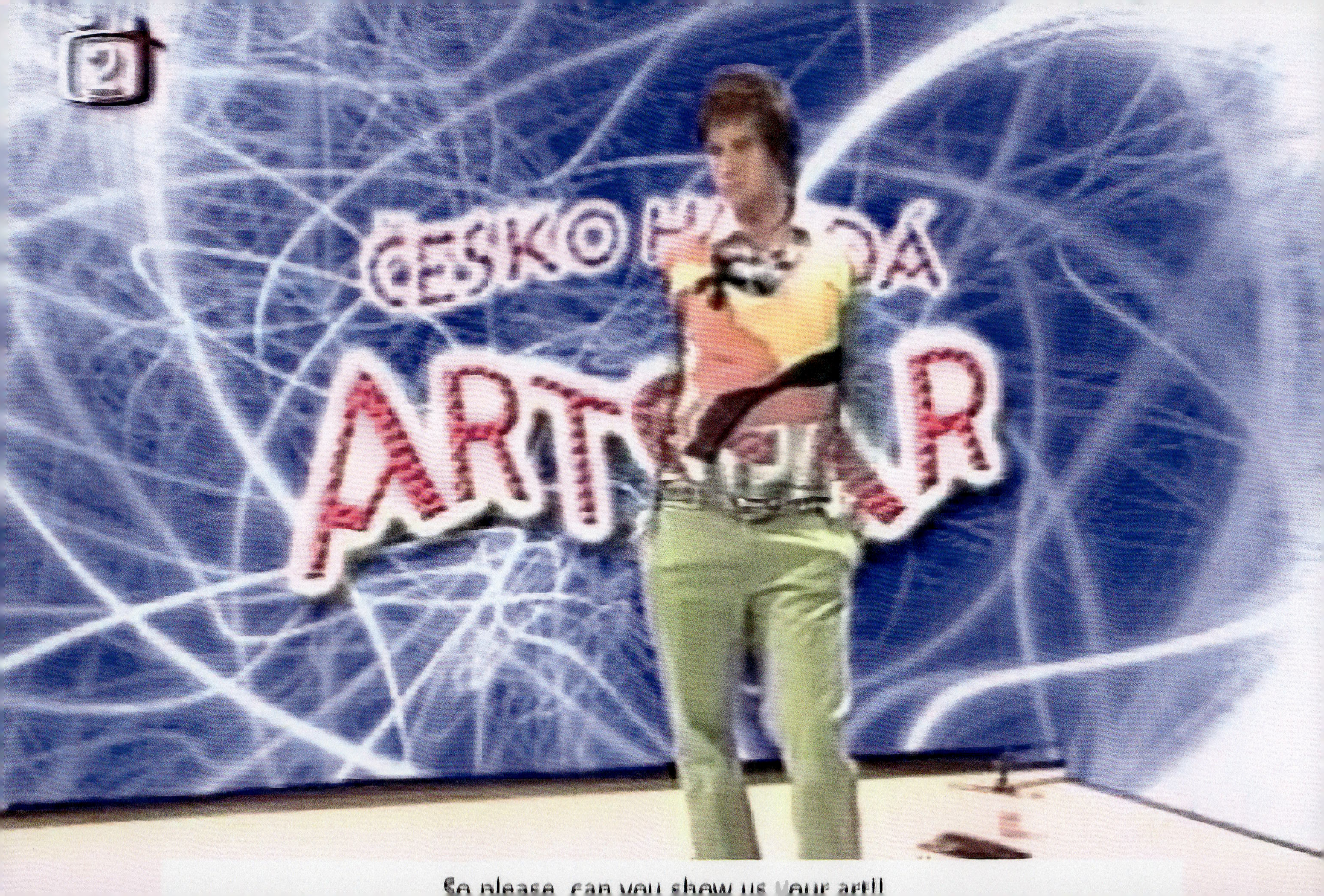
ČESKO
So please, can you show us your art!

01 **Jiří Lehovec** *Divotvorné oko* [The Magic Eye] (1939), film, 10 min
02 **Tomáš Ruller, Aleš Záboj** *Reklama* [Advertising] (1989), video, 16 min 37 s
03 **Tomáš Svoboda** *Jako z filmu: Adaptace* [Like in a Movie: Adaptation], exhibition at the House of Art, Brno, 2018
04 **Věra Chytilová** *Sedmikrásky* [Daisies] (1966), film, 76 min
05 **Alexander Hackenschmied, Maya Deren** *Private Life of a Cat* (1944), film, 22 min
06 **Roman Štětina** *Ztracený případ* [Lost Case] (2014), video, 58 min
07 **Ján Mančuška** *The Invisible* (2009), video, 19 min 18 s, installation in the private collection of Jill and Peter Kraus, Dutchess County, New York
08 **Jakub Jansa** *Spiritual Fitness* (2016), video, 6 min
09 **Pigi** *Pohádka pro šílence* [A Fairy-Tale for Madmen] (1985), film, 23 min 17 s
10 **Pavla Sceranková** *Kapusta* [Sauerkraut] (2006), video, 5 min 24 s
11 **Jan Švankmajer** *Kostnice* [Ossuary] (1970), film, 10 min
12 **Martin Kohout** *Moonwalk* (2008), video, 2 min 20 s, internet server YouTube
13 Radek Pilař's documentation for the activities of the Video Department (1989).
14 **Petr Skala** *Probuzená Sfinga* [Sphinx Awake] (1981), video, 2 min
15 **Lumír Hladík** *Moře v zrcadle* [The Mirrored Sea] (1980), film, 9 m 7 s
16 **Milan Grygar, Dobroslav Zborník** *Živá kresba* [Live Drawing] (1983), film, 5 min 38 s
17 **Markéta Baňková** *New York City Map* (1999–2001), screenshot from https://www.nycmap.com/
18 **Milan Knížák, Dobroslav Zborník** *Zab se a leť* [Kill yourself & fly] (1985), film, 15 min
19 Dawn of the Magicians? (Art, Science, Society at the Turn of the Millennium), exhibition at the Trade Fair Palace, National Gallery, Prague, 1996–1997.
20 **Zdeňka Čechová** *Kontrasty života* [Contrasts of Life] (1993), video, 6 min 20 s
21 **Ondřej Brody** *Artstar* (2004), video, 2 min 35 s

The publication was created within the research project "Audiovizuální dílo mimo kontext kinematografie: dokumentace, archivace a zpřístupnění" [The Audiovisual Work Outside the Context of Cinema: Documentation, Archiving, and Accessibility] (DG20P02OVV025) funded by the NAK II programme at the Ministry of Culture of the Czech Republic. Reviewers: Ing. and MDes. Dušan Barok, Mgr. PhDr. Marika Kupková, Ph.D.
ISBN 978-80-7004-200-7

Contents

Mapping the Moving Image. MEDIA, AGENTS, AND SITES IN THE CZECH CONTEXT

Martin Mazanec
Sylva Poláková
(eds.)

The editors would like to thank the authors of the essays, Martin Blažíček, Matěj Forejt, Eva Krátká, Marie Meixnerová, Markéta Mansfieldová, Tomáš Pospiszyl, Matěj Strnad, Lenka Střeláková, and Kateřina Svatoňová, as well as the other members of the interdisciplinary team who participated in the complex research into archival care for art of the moving image: Marie Barešová, Ladislav Cubr, Ivan David, Jakub Jirka, Michal Klodner, Lujza Kotočová, Josef Vítovec, and Jonáš Svatoš. Many thanks also to Marika Kupková and Dušan Barok for their valuable consultations and reviews, and to Miloš Vojtěchovský, Terezie Nekvindová, Jiří Anger, Pavlína Míčová, Petr Bilík, and Palo Fabuš for their detailed, expert commentary. Thanks also go to translator Ian Mikyska and the editors of the English and Czech versions Megan Bedell and Kevin B. Johnson, and Helena Černohorská and Soňa Weigertová respectively, as well as to graphic designer Petr Cabalka from Anymade Studio.

Martin Mazanec and Sylva Poláková

Introduction

Mapping the Moving Image is dedicated to the history of Czech experimental film, video art, net art, and other related disciplines on the boundaries of visual art and cinema. The art of the moving image, our general term for a diverse range of film and video media, includes autonomous yet also highly open creative expressions that can be presented in various environments and through numerous channels of communication. Connections with earlier cinematic and artistic practices, artists, or groups are so opaque that it is very difficult to reconstruct them. For a number of artists working after the year 2000, links beyond the local historical context are much clearer, while in other cases, the intergenerational bridges were only established after considerable delay. Therefore, our mapping process could not be conducted according to previously known signposts. It came across many turns and directions that did not develop further. Thus, this book does not present the narrative of the history of Czech art of the moving image in an unambiguously chronological fashion. On the contrary, this narrative is polyphonic[1] and its stories often overlap, as they take into account the interpenetration of film and video on the levels of production and presentation of moving images that led to today's notion about their fluidity and ubiquitousness.[2]

Mapping the Czech Context

The studies in this volume examine historical events, important figures, and key moments such as significant exhibitions or festivals from the perspective of various themes and research questions. The image component, which complements the chapters and essays with visual examples from archives, exhibition documentation, and sequences from the works under discussion, forms a parallel layer within the book. It was not our ambition to create a publication that strives for maximum complexity. Rather than attempting to exhaustively catalogue all the artists, we chose to prioritise studies that attempt to contextualise this artistic discipline, with particular attention to demarcating the relationship between cinematography and the art world. Considerations of other environments whose *dispositifs* also include work with moving images – particularly, for example, audiovisual production in music clubs (e.g., VJing or live processual animation) – are presented only in the form of references relevant to the central topic of

[1] For our perspective on art from the former Eastern Bloc countries, we have followed the lead of art historian Mária Orišková and her concept of a polyphonic history. See Mária Orišková, *Dvojhlasné dejiny umenia* [Art History in Two Voices] (Petrus: Bratislava, 2002) or Mária Orišková, ed., *Curating „Eastern Europe" and Beyond. Art Histories through the Exhibition* (Peter Lang: Frankfurt am Main – Veda: Bratislava 2013).

[2] Film historian Malte Hagener describes the moving image in the digital era as fluid, emphasising – in the spirit of the theory of the relocation of cinema – the significance of the location in which the given cinematic presentation takes place. See Malte Hagener, "Where Is Cinema (Today)? The Cinema in the Age of Media Immanence", *Cinéma & Cie* 11, no. 3 (2008), pp. 15–22.

the given study. The primary bearings for our mapping of the terrain were provided by events: exhibitions and festivals focused on the moving image.[3] The resultant publication offers several models for approaching the reconstruction of this medially diverse artistic discipline, which correspond to the three sections titled History, Discourse, and Practice.

The first section is introduced by Martin Blažíček's study of amateur and experimental film in late socialism and the early 1990s, a period that saw a fundamental transformation in the structures of production and distribution. Martin Mazanec's contribution about the beginnings of Czech video art reconstructs the crucial events that featured presentations of video as an artistic discipline. The moving image as a tool for documentation is explored in Sylva Poláková's essay, which focuses on the specificities of Czech performance and the strategies employed in various socio-cultural climates. Marie Meixnerová introduces the rise of the internet and the influence it had on artistic creation and the increased forms of presentation due to the more fluid character of the moving image.

The second section, Discourse, shifts the reader's attention from the historical development of media varieties and genres to curatorial practice, the implementation of the moving image in art education, and the broadening of its definitions in academic discourse. Tomáš Pospiszyl's essay points to the importance of recently established new media studios at art universities as important centres for becoming acquainted with new technologies and opening up to international developments. Presentation practices as they developed early in the new millennium are the subject of Markéta Mansfieldová's text. On the basis of specific festivals and exhibitions, her essay explores the curatorial strategies that contributed to the establishment of the moving image in the everyday art world. The last contribution of the Discourse section is Kateřina Svatoňová's reflection on the interdisciplinarisation of film studies at universities and the widespread penetration of film, in a broad array of definitions, into curatorial and dramaturgical practice.

The authors of the final four texts, in the Practice section, explore the real impact that the institutionalisation of the moving image has had on art criticism, on forms of recognition at competitions, and on practices of collecting and archiving. Matěj Forejt's contribution attempts to uncover the reasons behind the lacklustre interest in film or video put on display by state-run galleries and museums (and private collectors) dating back to the period of socialist Czechoslovakia. Eva Krátká's study offers an overview of specialised and expert periodicals where the topic of video art

[3] In examining exhibitions and other presentation events, we leaned towards the exhibition-histories methods; see Jens Hoffmann, "The Dirty Dozen. Twelve Issues of The Exhibitionist", in *The Exhibitionist. Journal of Exhibiton Making. The First Six Years*, ed. Jens Hoffmann (New York: Artbook, 2017) or Elena Filipovic, "When Exhibitions Become Form: On the History of the Artist as Curator", in *The Artist As Curator,* ed. Elena Filipovic, *Mousse* 41, č. 0 (2013), pp. 3–20.

was first introduced and where discussions about other genres, directions, and disciplines took place. Lenka Střeláková's essay describes the system of competitions and awards, including considerations of various modes of presentation, distribution strategies, possibilities for the support of further production, and the important role that they play in the circulation of works. The section and the book conclude with Matěj Strnad's text on archiving and collections, which is symbolically conceived as an epilogue summarising a number of collecting projects that compensated for lacking institutional collecting policies. The enthusiasm behind these projects – which had to run out eventually – successfully preserved historical traces of art of the moving image, albeit in an incomplete manner.

Media, Agents, Spaces

We the editors are, to a large extent, insiders, so we had to approach the legacy of the fragmentary history of art of the moving image in the Czech context appropriately. The aim was to uncover the problematic foundations of the relationship between the moving image and disciplines within visual art both in the local context and in relation to the international scene. The central task, then, was to provide facts that have been thus far neglected in historical accounts, draw attention to the agents who – whether alone, or in contact with other artists – experimented with the moving image, and analyse the environments in which this form of art was created and presented. By adhering to thorough historical research, we attempted to avoid subjectively valorising a discipline in which the authors of the essays operate as professionals. The specific perspectives that each author brings on account of their specialisation and experience in the fields of curatorship, dramaturgy, art production, teaching, writing, and archiving are also manifested in our approaches to the given terminology.

We understand an audiovisual work as technically dependent art that occurs temporally ("time-based media") and the texts in this volume operate with an expanded definition of film.[4] This open perspective allows us to examine the given practice across the entire breadth of the interdisciplinary field within which the moving image operates. The essays consider individual media varieties and their modes of presentation by means of the questions: who – what – where – how,[5] as tools for describing their unique

[4] We use the term "moving image" in its expanded definition as it has developed since the 1970s. Gene Youngblood, *Expanded Cinema* (New York: P. Dutton & Co., Inc., 1970); Stanley Cavell, *The World Viewed: Reflections on The Ontology of Film* (Cambridge, Massachusetts and London, England: Harvard University Press, 1979). And, from the 1990s, it has been discussed anew in relation to digital media: Noël Carroll, *Theorizing the Moving Image* (Cambridge: Cambridge University Press, 1996); Lev Manovich, *The Language of New Media* (Cambridge: MIT Press, 2001); David N. Rodowick, *The Virtual Life of Film* (London: Harvard University Press, 2007).

[5] I. C. Jarvie, *Movies and Society* (New York & London: Garland Publishing, Inc., 1986).

developments, which have their own prehistory, history, and structure.[6] A constant presence winding through these fields of research is what can be called the central motif in the development of Czech art of the moving image: the effort to negotiate an autonomous position. This main theme intersects with the other various topics addressed in this volume: the (un)availability of technical equipment, solitary works vs. the existence of groups, isolation and attempts to establish contacts with art worlds abroad, and the (im)possibility of presenting art of the moving image both at home and abroad. Searching for and stabilising one's own position was also a general characteristic of the art world in the developments after the Velvet Revolution of 1989, a period that saw a transformation of the institutional framing of art and art education, the establishment of an art market, and attempts at systematic preservation. Thus, it was in this period that the veneration of art of the moving image as an artistic discipline was fully realised.

We follow the art of the moving image from the late 1960s to the beginning of the third millennium. Our consideration thus begins at a time when the amateur film scene in Czechoslovakia began taking shape once again as an alternative to the local film industry, and, particularly later in the 1980s, contributed to the development of experimental films. For a short period in the 1960s, it was possible for the field to develop publication activities, associations, and galleries as well as establish relationships with the international art scene. The developments in international post-war art, which included an acceptance of non-material modes of artistic expression and an intensification of interest in new technologies, also had analogues in the artistic activities following the totalitarisation of society during the period known as "normalisation" after the Prague Spring in 1968. The early 1970s saw the creation of the first moving image documentations of action art, at first made exclusively on celluloid film. During the 1970s and '80s, on rare journeys abroad, some artists came into contact with video and, being fascinated by the new technology, began exploring the possibilities of these media in solitary seclusion. It was only in the late 1980s that videoists – as artists working with video called themselves at the time – took a more systematic interest in standing up for their common interest and began negotiating an autonomous position among the artistic disciplines. The period ubiquitously influenced by totalitarianism throughout the society was characterised by a search for gaps in the system that would allow for free expression, which required strategy, caution, and courage. The agents of unofficial culture therefore often found themselves on the fringes of the law. This can be seen in the gaining of illicit access to equipment at film studios in various state-run workplaces, in the various attempts to find spaces to present art, and in the transport or mailing of artworks or documentation abroad.

[6] Henry Jenkins, *Convergence Culture: Where Old and New Media Collide* (New York and London: New York University Press, 2006).

As a consequence of the socio-political changes in the late 1980s and early '90s, there was also a gradual transformation in cultural practice. Systemic changes in how art professionals were organised, the opening up of the free market, access to new technology, and intensive contact with the world beyond the Czechoslovak (and later Czech) borders transformed society into a turbulent, enthusiasm-powered torrent, which was as simple to enter as it was surprisingly easy to drop out from. All of this had an impact on both the production of art and its public reception. While tertiary art education was changing and becoming open to the creation of new studios, the autonomous position of art of the moving image within the art world had yet to be achieved. Crucial in this process were curatorial activities that helped to clarify and name works making use of the moving image and to include them within the context of visual art (and the context of cinema, too). Innovative exhibition concepts as well as the thematic programming of various new media festivals and other events introduced the general public to manifestations of art that had seen very limited possibilities in preceding decades. A sustained interest in the moving image began asserting itself on the pages of cultural periodicals and gradually entered academic curricula. Art of the moving image was also discovered as a cultural object that could operate within the established systems of the circulation of artworks or their conservation for future generations in the appropriate institutions.

It might seem that the legitimisation process of art of the moving image was thus concluded, yet in order for this to truly take place, we must strive for the systematic documentation of works that are – by the nature of their media – highly ephemeral and fragile. This is the impetus behind this publication, which is part of a larger research project undertaken by the Národní filmový archiv, Prague – Czech National Film Archive, which is focused on developing an archival methodology that will enable collecting institutions and smaller workplaces alike to ensure care for this segment of fine art. The historical and theoretical research for this volume was based on primary sources and elaborated acquisition documentation, all of which are available in the specialised database of the Národní filmový archiv's Videoarchiv in Prague, which can serve as an extension of this volume.

I. HISTORY

Media Varieties of the Moving Image

The Parallel Media of Late Socialism

Martin Blažíček

When we encounter, on our wanderings through the history of film, terms such as independent film, other cinema, experimental film, parallel cinema, video art, or new media art, they are usually attached to particular historical practices that are considered initiational.[1] Even though they generally reference the unique conditions of creative work, these designations result in the establishment of otherness, of aesthetic or formal exclusivity. These terms are often distributed throughout the discourse of the period, describing emergent artistic strategies unencumbered by genre expectations or industry standards. In this sense, experimental film can be understood as an attempt to bridge visual art and cinema. In the case of such works, it is not entirely clear whether they should be considered installations, objects, or films. Similarly, video art – at least in its beginnings in the 1970s – separates audiovisual production from the field of cinema and attempts to establish itself as a communication tool with an emphasis on performance, thereby blurring the lines between audiovisual works and

[1] These terms appear most prominently in the late 1960s and early 1970s as a result of the need to name the changing conditions of a broad spectrum of audiovisual work. These changes brought new technical and formal possibilities, but also changed the social roles of media art. For more detail on "other cinemas", see Sue Clayton – Laura Mulvey, eds., *Other Cinemas: Politics, Culture and Experimental Film in the 1970s* (London: Bloomsbury Academic, 2021).

the mere documentation of a performance by a camera. The artistic genres of the moving image can also be perceived as the interplay of physical media with institutions and economic, political, and social relationships. Experimental film thus represents not only a distinctive aesthetic form but also a social experiment in film cooperatives[2] – new forms of art organisations. It is a political project, based on the opposition between independent artists and large studio productions, but also an economic one, searching for new forms of "non-profit" funding through cooperative activity, subsidies, and private donors. Similarly, the term new media embodies, in the case of the 1990s, the techno-utopian potential of distribution technologies as a tool for the transformation of the world. The genres listed above can also be considered as a single, gradually transforming practice, due, for example, to the characters of individual artists, who are continually attracted to new tools of communication – film, video, computers, and new media.

In this regard, the situation in Czechoslovakia was highly specific in a number of ways.[3] The categories cited above were sometimes absent, sometimes formed according to different principles, and they developed along their own timelines.[4] Even though some works might correspond aesthetically to – for example – experimental film, it is not clear whether they should be included in this category. They might seem too divergent from the presumed social background or production methods, or else the historical period does not coincide with the standard. Other works were created as part of large

[2] The Film-Makers' Cooperative was an artistic film cooperative established in New York in 1961 by Jonas Mekas, Shirley Clarke, Stan Brakhage, Lionel Rogosin, and other artists. The idea of a film cooperative that would encompass production, distribution, promotion, and education also spread to other places in the US – e.g., Canyon Cinema (1960); Millennium Film Workshop (1964); Atlantic Filmmakers Cooperative (1974) – as well as to Europe – e.g., London Film-makers' Co-op (1962), Austria Filmmakers Cooperative (1968); Hamburger Filmmacher-Cooperative (1968), Xscreen, Cologne (1968); Das andere Kino, Munich (1968); Süd Coop, Stuttgart (1968); Paris Films Coop (1974); Cinédoc Paris (1979) – thereby becoming a sustainable form of organisation for the preservation of experimental films. Many of these cooperatives are still active, operating as archives or distributors. Films from the Film-Makers' Cooperative group are still considered canonical works that first defined the genre.

[3] The history of experimental films in other countries in Eastern Europe has been explored, for instance, by Seth Howes, *Moving Images on the Margins. Experimental Film in Late Socialist East Germany* (Rochester, New York: Camden House), 28; Ryszard W. Kluszczyński, "The Mechanical Imagination – Creativity of Machines: Film Form Workshop 1970–1977", in *The Struggle for Form: Perspectives on Polish Avant-Garde Film, 1916–1989*, eds. Kamila Kuc – Michael O'Pray (New York: Columbia University Press, 2014); Sonja Simonyi, "Artists as Amateurs: Intersections of Nonprofessional Film Production and Neo-Avant-Garde Experimentation at the Balázs Béla Stúdió in the Early 1970s", *Film History* 30, no. 1 (2018), pp. 114–137.

[4] The reasons for the various forms of development lie in a complex network of political, social, technological, and cultural relations. Although it is difficult to choose a single aspect to highlight, particularly in the normalisation era, one of the frequent arguments was a lack of contact with the West due to the "Iron Curtain" and the resulting lack of information about current global trends. Furthermore, particular pieces of equipment were either not available or came with too high price tags. The "absence of the West" is also an argument that links period critiques with later reflections following the 1989 Velvet Revolution. Additionally, we also cannot fail to mention the entirely different institutional structure of the Czechoslovak environment, in which film cooperatives, for instance, could not be established for legal reasons. State socialism, however, had at its disposal institutions of a different kind, which allowed for the realisation of "other cinema" in accordance with the possibilities and political conditions at the time.

studio productions, while others still might be too far down the path towards visual art. As a consequence, such works are generally not considered experimental films and continue to be regarded with different cultural connotations. Furthermore, these particular terms were practically never used in Czechoslovakia, and if they were, they were understood differently.[5] This is part of the reason why the current volume prefers the overarching conception of *the moving image*,[6] which – thanks to its operation above genres – allows us to bridge the media specificities of film, video, and new media. It is in this spirit that the following text will approach the culture of the moving image as a broad category that incorporates various media, environments, and creative methods. It allows us to consider the work of artists that passed through various media or genres over time, and it also enables us to identify the institutional boundaries in Czechoslovakia within which art of the moving image was produced. One of the leading arguments is that the defining impulses for creating this art were not so much the specifics of the media but the social structures in which the artists operated and the creative means and possibilities for presentation they therefore had at their disposal. The text primarily explores these creative practices in the late 1970s and throughout the 1980s, in a period known as late socialism, and in conclusion examines the transformations they underwent at the beginning of the 1990s.

Although the terms independent[7] or experimental film were not generally used in Czechoslovakia during the period known as normalisation (between 1968 and 1989), this does not mean that there were no films being

[5] In a period text reflecting on the foundation of the Svaz českých výtvarných umělců [SČVU, Union of Czech Visual Artists], *video art* is described as an "electronic paintbrush", a form of seeing that "can encompass various visual means, derivations of colour and rhythm, the tactile experience of montage structures and macrocosmic material, an artistic language enriched by visual poetry, a synthesis of art-musical perception, the defining feature of 1980s culture." (Zdeněk Pazdera, "Elektronický štětec" [The Electronic Paintbrush]. Unmarked magazine cut-out, after 1987, archive of the heirs of Radek Pilař.) This is a clear demonstration of the understanding of video as a medium of fine art that expands the possibilities of traditional techniques. The same text then emphasises video's educational, documentary, and promotional aspects. This example illustrates the difficulties the local artistic establishment had with defining the position of video almost two years after it became part of the global art scene. Still in the late 1980s, video was still understood by the Czechoslovak community of experts as an inaccessible medium of newness. The use of the term *experimental film* is explained in footnote 35.

[6] According to Noël Caroll, the term *moving image* allows us to move beyond the traditional conception of the media format serving as a formative force in order to create a specific "media language". Caroll proposes that we no longer discuss the special expressive means inherent to film, video, or digital art, since definitions of such unique qualities are no longer defensible given the mix of many forms of new media created in the second half of the 20th century. Moving image is thus a freer term that encompasses all period media, regardless of their hierarchies and historical relationships. Noël Caroll, *Engaging the Moving Image* (New Haven & London: Yale University Press, 2003).

[7] "Independent film" is understood as denoting works created outside the mainstream studios, not necessarily films of an experimental nature. In principle they are films with smaller budgets whose presentation is often limited to specialised (independent) cinemas. Independent film can also describe certain stylistic elements, but it primarily refers to limited budgets and production conditions, as well as independence from the studio system. It is not restricted temporally to the 1960s, but first emerged in the 1920s in the United States in connection with the United Artists company.

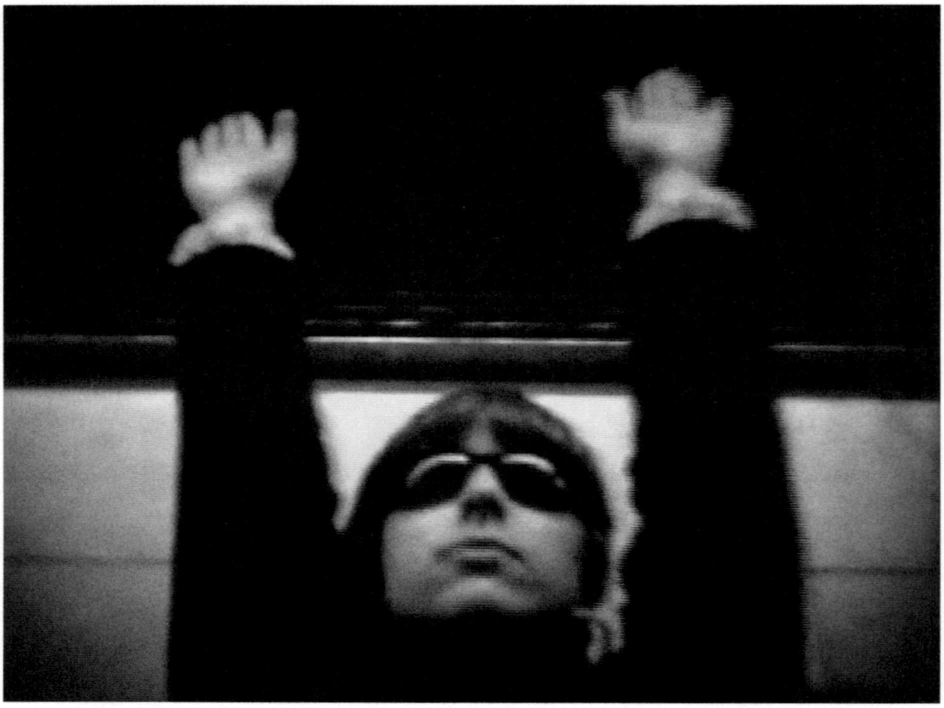

Ivan Tatíček *Metrofilm* (1984), film, 8 min 34 s

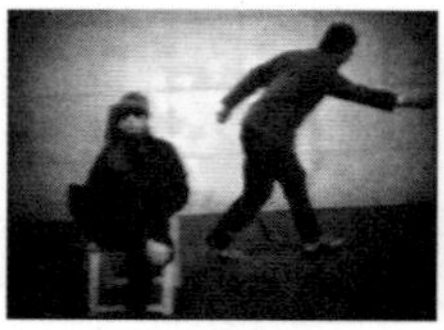
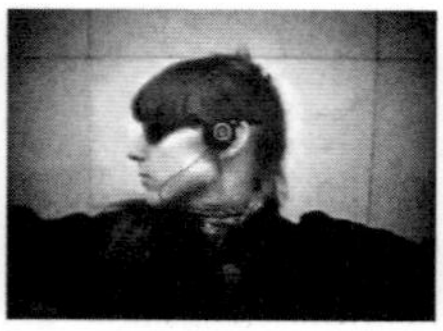
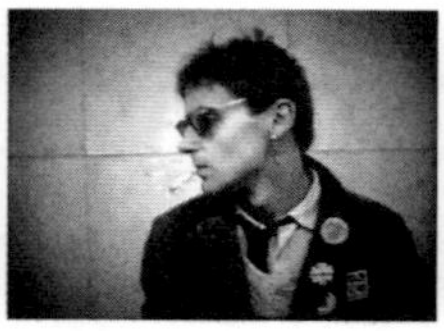
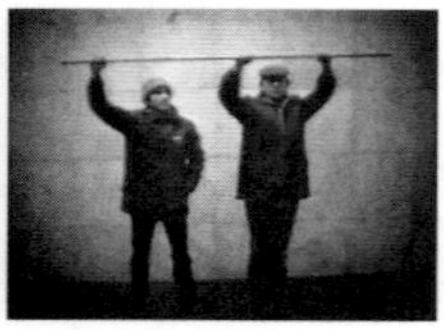

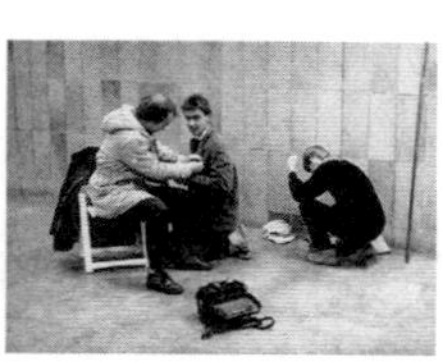

Photographs from the filming of *Metrofilm*.

made whose character corresponded to them. These works were generally thought of according to different categorisation criteria, and due to their dispersion across various production platforms, they are rarely considered a homogeneous whole. Czechoslovakia mostly operated with terms such as club film or underground film and differentiated between amateur and professional film, official and unofficial art, public and private art,[8] or art made by visual artists and by artists in the Union,[9] or underground film.[10] Two of the possible perspectives on the Czechoslovak cultural environment are particularly important here. The first is the polarity of professional and amateur art and the second is the polarity of official and unofficial art. The conditions of each of these poles result in different forms of presentation, and they also predetermine production methods and access to equipment. These criteria lie beyond genre and media specificity and are thus applicable to various genres and media practices. These polarities – particularly in the case of the latter divide between official and unofficial – are a result of the strong politicisation of normalisation-era art, with a key idea being that of a parallel society, that is of the concurrent existence of various cultural activities both at the centre and on the periphery.

Amateurs and Professionals

Art of the normalisation period is marked by attempts at systematic organisation and the grouping of art under state institutions. This is true of both visual art and cinematography, although the process was slightly different in each field. The institutionalisation of creative activity concerned not only professional art, but also amateur work – in both cases, activities in these areas e were subject to high levels of control. The opposition between amateur and professional art constitutes a dominant polarity that eclipses others, such as that between the studio system and independent practice. This is also the reason why, in this context, we do not find otherwise common institutions related to experimental film, such as cooperatives, workshops, or independent cinemas. Instead, we see a broad variety of state unions, movements, and political bodies that contribute to the creation of

[8] In the case of a number of artists, there is a clear difference between the work they presented publicly (e.g., as employees of television channels or film studios) and the work they created in the privacy of their own studios and homes without the intention of making it broadly available.

[9] Films made by visual artists are usually not grouped together with works of cinema; they are considered part of a fine art oeuvre. The films of Milan Grygar and Dobroslav Zborník, for instance – *Hmatové kresby* [Tactile Drawings] (1983), *Živé kresby* [Living Drawings] (1983), and *Prstová partitura* [Finger Score] (1982) – or the films by Dalibor Chatrný, such as *Geneze* [Genesis] and *Mříže* [Bars] (both 1969–70), were only exceptionally shown in cinemas. Even today, they are primarily presented in the context of supplementary video screenings at art exhibitions.

[10] In the second half of the 20th century, the term "underground" was used in many contexts. Unlike the American cinematic underground, which was related to artists' radical independence from the studio system (in the 1960s) or a departure from the institutionalisation of art (in the 1980s), in Czechoslovakia, the term describes activities taking place within illegal culture, often officially banned. The Czechoslovak underground describes a political position from which follow specific production strategies or aesthetic preferences.

audiovisual culture. From the artists' perspective, this did not mean that they had to become outright members of a specific union or club, though they did often rely on the activities of these organisations, e.g., by participating in official festivals. In the Czech context, the emphasis placed on the amateur environment is slightly different even from other countries of the Eastern Bloc, where experimental work mostly grew out of the film school environment[11] or was created within production units organised by the state.[12]

The amateur and professional realms each anticipated different forms of reading and a different audience, and both had specific printed journals dedicated to them. In the case of professional art, these included *Výtvarná kultura* [Fine Art Culture], *Výtvarný život* [Fine Art Life], *Film a doba* [Film and Our Times], in the amateur context *Výtvarnictvo, fotografia, film* [Fine Art, Photography, Film] or *Amatérský film* [Amateur Film]. Similarly divided were the forms of exhibiting, screening, and presenting and the specific rituals associated with them.[13] Having the status of "professional" or "amateur" predetermined the application of a particular discourse, often without any regard for the particular work in question.[14] For instance, one of the first Czech music videos, *Metrofilm* (1984) by Ivan Tatíček, was made under the influence of music videos from abroad, but within the context of an amateur festival, it was interpreted as a cinematic work containing elements of social critique.[15]

There were only very few situations in which artists from opposite sides of the amateur/professional divide could meet. For example, in rare cases the two spheres overlapped when professional cameramen

[11] In the 1970s, this included, for instance, artists from the Hochschule für Bildende Künste Dresden [Academy of Fine Arts Dresden] or the Polish Warsztat Formy Filmowej [Workshop of Film Form] at the film school in Łódź.

[12] The Balázs Béla Stúdió, for instance, which was responsible for most Hungarian experimental productions, was financed as an autonomous production unit starting in 1961 and was still active in the 1990s. An important aim of this studio was to provide a production platform for fresh film school graduates. See e.g., Gábor Gelencsér, "Continuing the Deviating Tradition of Hungarian Experimental Film Art: András Jeles's *Joseph and his Brothers – Scenes from a Peasant Bible*", *Alphaville: Journal of Film and Screen Media*, no. 9 (2015), pp. 23–37; or Simonyi, "Artists as Amateurs: Intersections of Nonprofessional Film Production and Neo-Avant-Garde Experimentation at the Balázs Béla Stúdió in the Early 1970s", pp. 114–137.

[13] Amateur film festivals, for instance, were nearly always run in a competition format, including a jury composed of professionals in the field, who would discuss the craftsmanship of the films and give the amateur artists advice. At Mladá kamera Uničov, for instance, films that did not pass through the pre-selection process were discussed as part of something known as Konzultační středisko [Consultation Centre], separate from the central screening section, where professionals would advise beginning amateurs how to make it to the main competition section the next year. This multi-levelled scheme was expected by both artists and audiences, and if there were any irregularities, these would always be criticised in the press.

[14] Journals for professional and amateur films generally defined the way in which the films would be critically assessed and the boundaries within which the discussion could even occur. While professional criticism focused on cultural and social contributions, in amateur environments, the debates often concerned mastery of craft or the achievement of a particular technical standard.

[15] Martin Blažíček – Sylva Poláková, "Ivan Tatíček – od amatérského filmu k profesionální videotvorbě" [Ivan Tatíček – From Amateur Film to Professional Video Production], *Iluminace* 32, no. 1 (2020), p. 79.

engaged in amateur or home video work;[16] likewise, amateur artists would occasionally establish themselves in professional practice.[17] The polarity of the production status is so strong that it overshadows other possible perspectives, such as that between commissioned or non-commissioned work, studio and independent productions, or experimental and commercial art. Later, historical studies of the moving image at the turn of the millennium would also be rooted in the discourse of this period.[18] This is also accented through the amateurish nature of alternative movements in art that strove to create a space for free expression within socially acceptable boundaries, often failing to take into account the activities taking place on the borders – the underground and the official contexts. It therefore seems that the division into professionals and amateurs established in the Normalisation era has outlived its protagonists and become a widely used schema for describing film culture of the 1980s, specifically for differentiating between conventional and innovative films.

Visual artists[19] were grouped under the Svaz českých výtvarných umělců [Union of Czech Visual Artists] beginning in 1972.[20] This union, however, did not represent artists working in cinema, who were instead employed by one of the state cinema production companies, such as Krátký film [Short Film]. Members of the Union of Czech Visual Artists were subdivided into sections according to their profession: painting, photography and graphics, applied and industrial art, conservation and restoration, and theory. Artists working with film and video were grouped within the section they were closest to, but until the 1980s, we probably would not find even a single artist whose practice is dominated by art of the moving image. The need to integrate art of the moving image into the Union only arose in 1987, when the creation of a video department[21] was initiated by the artist,

[16] One example is the recently published monograph on Jaroslav Kučera; see Kateřina Svatoňová, *Mezi-obrazy: Mediální praktiky kameramana Jaroslava Kučery* [Inter-images: The Media Practices of Cameraman Jaroslav Kučera] (Prague: Národní filmový archiv, 2016).

[17] For example, Pavel Dražan, a respected cineamateur (e.g., *Bravo Bravissimo*, 1989), who moved into television work soon after 1989, specifically on the Na vlastní oči [With Your Own Eyes] programme, TV Nova, 1994.

[18] E.g., Martin Čihák – Michal Bregant, "Skutečnější než realita" [More Real Than Reality], in *Alternativní kultura. Příběh české společnosti 1945–1989* [Alternative Culture. The Story of Czech Society 1945–1989], ed. Josef Alan (Prague: Nakladatelství Lidové noviny, 2001), p. 424.

[19] In the context of the fine arts, the division of professionals vs. amateurs is not as visible, but the professionalisation of art is closely tied to the constitutionally defined obligation to work. If artists were not acknowledged as professionals, they had to have a different profession – they could not officially be freelance artists. On the other hand, many Union members also had other occupations and did not make their living through art. For more on conditions in the Union, see e.g., Alena Binarová, *Svaz výtvarných umělců v českých zemích v letech 1956–1972* [The Union of Visual Artists in the Czech Lands Between 1956 and 1972] (Olomouc: Vydavatelství FF UP, 2017).

[20] The Union of Czech Visual Artists was a successor of the federalised Svaz československých výtvarných umělců [Union of Czechoslovak Fine Artists] (1956–1970). From this point on, Slovak artists were represented by the Zväz slovenských výtvarných umelcov [Union of Slovak Visual Artists].

[21] In addition to Pilař, the first members were Pavel Scheufler, Michal Pacina, Petr Skala, and Jaroslav Vančát.

animator, and video artist Radek Pilař. Since its beginnings, the department was an intermedia project that "integrates opinions and means of fine art [and unites fine artists who] are not pure video artists,[22] but continue to be sculptors, architects, graphic artists, painters, photographers, and theorists".[23] At the same time, it was not only limited to the medium of video, even though the newness of this format represented a fundamental argument for defending the department's position within the Union. In addition to the art-making itself, the role of the new department was rooted in documentation, outreach, and education, and based on interdisciplinary relations.[24] But why was it so important for audiovisual artists to become members of the video department if they were already, in many cases, members of the Union? One reason was the scarcity of video equipment in the 1980s, and the – theoretical, at least – vision that the Union could become a producer and provider of studio equipment for its members.[25] Even more important was the notion that thanks to the Union, video artists would receive important state commissions, just as other Union artists were assigned work in connection with public construction projects. In the case of video, this took the form of various logotypes, animated sequences, and jingles commissioned by the larger state companies.[26] However, activity within the Union was not a sufficient guarantee of a stable income. Most artists were employed in related fields, at museums and galleries, as lecturers and teachers, or by Czechoslovak Television and the film industry. While the Union and other professional organisations had the hallmarks of a hierarchic structure in which the rules of career advancement apply,[27] this did not manifest as a straightforward process for the artists. Many of them created their art under highly diverse

[22] The neologism *videoists* was frequently used by the group of artists associated with the department of video in the mid-1980s.

[23] From a manuscript by Radek Pilař on the occasion of the establishment of the video department (typewritten copy, undated, after 1987, archive of the heirs of Radek Pilař, 1).

[24] Shortly after the foundation of the video department, the National Gallery in Prague proposed a collaboration on documentation, educational, and promotional activities, with the notion that the department would be a supplier of these services for the needs of the gallery. See Jaroslav Vančát, "Stanovisko k plánu oboru video SČVU v souvislosti s uplatněním videotechniky v Národní galerii" [Position on the Plans of the Video Department at SČVU in Relation to the Use of Video Technology at the National Gallery] (typewritten copy, undated, archive of the heirs of Radek Pilař).

[25] In relation to this, Pilař submitted a proposal for the establishment of a "video service" that would allow members of the Union to have access to production facilities and equipment owned by the Union. Radek Pilař's speech at the Central Plenum of the SČVU (typewritten copy, undated, after 1987, archive of the heirs of Radek Pilař, 2).

[26] The discussion between the client and the creator touched on subjects such as the rate per unit of work, typically one frame or a second, which differed considerably in classical and computer animation, in favour of the new technologies. Věra Geislerová interviewed by Martin Blažíček, December 2014, recording in the archive of Martin Blažíček.

[27] Non-members or lower-ranked members were not, of course, completely denied access. In the late 1970s and early '80s, there were many exhibition opportunities, particularly at regional galleries. Among the greatest advantages that came with positions at the Union was access to more prestigious exhibition spaces. See e.g., Josef Ledvina, "České umění kolem roku 1980 jako pole kulturní produkce" [Czech Art Around the Year 1980 as a Field of Cultural Production], *Sešit pro umění, teorii a příbuzné zóny*, no. 9 (2010), p. 35.

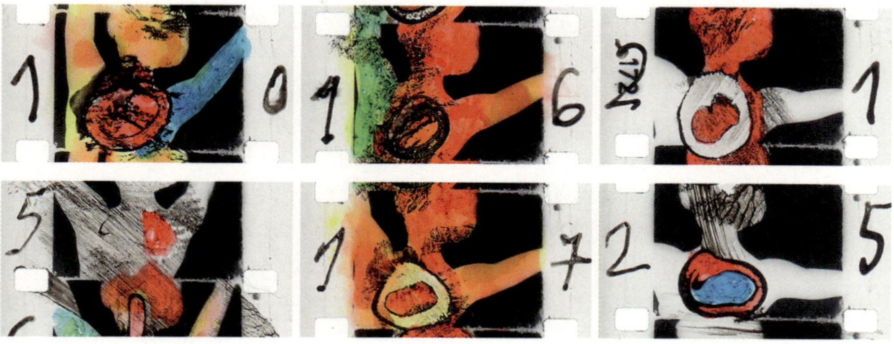

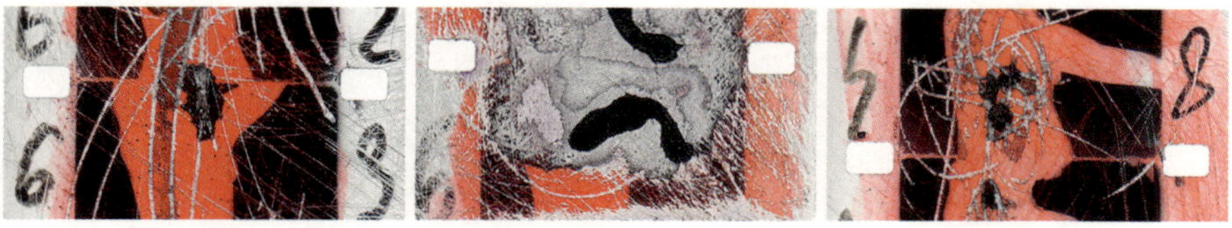

Scans of Petr Skala's manual manipulations of 16mm film, 1970s

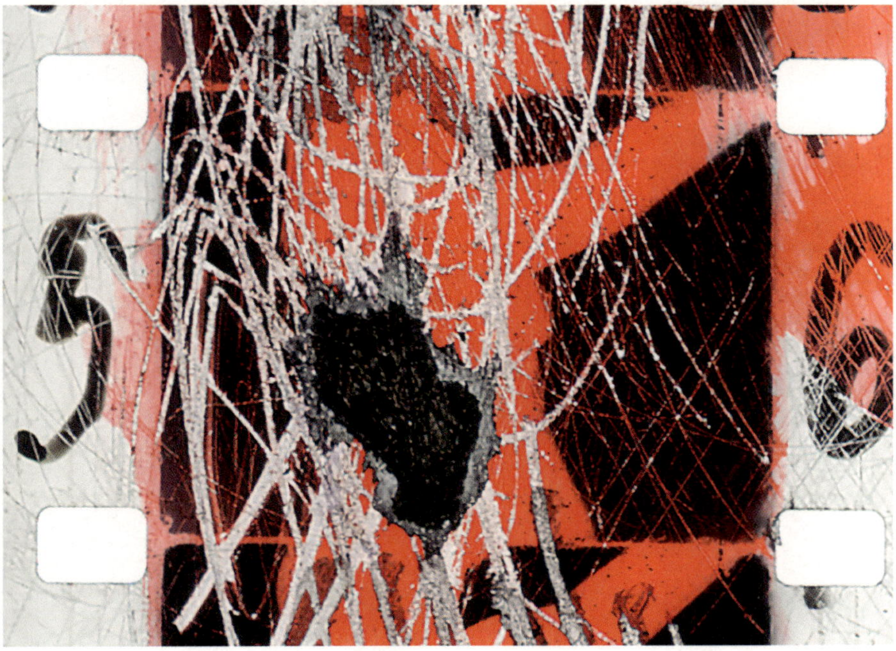

conditions. A good example is the director and animator Petr Skala, who worked independently at his home studio since the late 1960s, but, following his graduation from the documentary department at FAMU in 1975, aimed for a stable position in the film industry. He had to wait until 1986, though, when he became employed by Krátký film. Until that time, he fulfilled one-off commissions for Czechoslovak Television, Krátký film, and Czechoslovak Radio. At the same time, he was creating fine art films and video works, which he only began making public after 1987, when he became a member of the video department.[28] In part, he realised these works "illegally", by working in professional conditions thanks to his access to film and television studios.[29]

Seemingly in contrast to officially organised art was the work of amateurs, usually considered to be freer, and less subject to external influences – although in reality, it was organised with even greater complexity. Amateur cinema associational activities, whose roots lie in the 1930s, fell under the jurisdiction of the Ústav pro kulturně výchovnou činnost [ÚVKČ, Institute for Culturally Educational Activities] at the Ministry of Culture. This institute formally encompassed various forms of folk art. Its individual departments were divided by field into theatre, music, dance, and photography–film–fine art. Intended to support small organisations and coordinate their activities with regard to state policies, the Institute organised symposia and conferences, whose conclusions were relayed to the film associations in the *Zásady zájmové umělecké činnosti* [Principles of Amateur Artistic Activity].[30] ÚKVČ did not develop much organisational activity itself, since the specific associations, clubs, studios, competitions, and festivals fell under the purview of various state institutions, particularly the Revoluční odborové hnutí [ROH, Revolutionary Trade Union Movement] and the Socialistický svaz mládeže [SSM, Socialist Youth Union]. Among the most important organisers in the field of amateur film were company film clubs established within larger industrial companies.[31] The film club of the Spojený závodní klub ROH [SZK ROH, United Company Club of ROH] at the Uničov engineering works established a film festival called Mladá kamera Uničov [Uničov Young Camera] in 1975. Another important festival, the live-action competition Brněnská 16 (known as BRNO16 in English), was

[28] Bohdana Kerbachová, *Alchymie světla. Experimentální tvorba Petra Skaly* [Alchemy of Light. The Experimental Work of Petr Skala] (Písek: Prácheňské muzeum v Písku and Nakladatelství Vltavín Praha, 2017), pp. 24–27.

[29] *Ibid.*, pp. 156–157.

[30] *Zásady zájmové umělecké činnosti* [Principles of Special Interest Artistic Activity] was a document published in 1971 as a methodical output of the Národní přehlídka a konference všech oborů zájmové umělecké činnosti [National Festival and Conference of All Artistic Special Interest Groups]. Its aim was to coordinate the artistic activities of ROH, SSM, and the Český svaz družstevních rolníků [Czech Union of Cooperative Farmers]. See Hana Stavová, "Role a možnosti filmového amatéra v letech 1960–1989" [The Roles and Possibilities of the Cineamateur Between 1960 and 1989] (diploma thesis, Faculty of Arts, Masaryk University, 2016), p. 23.

[31] Veronika Jančová, "Poloprofesionál, nebo 'profesionální amatér'? Filmová tvorba mezi amatérismem a profesionalismem" [Semi-professional, or "Professional Amateur"? Filmmaking Between Amateurism and Professionalism], *Iluminace* 28, no. 2 (2016), pp. 45–60.

founded in 1960 by the Dům kultury a osvěty města Brna [House of Culture and Education of the City of Brno] and later fell under the auspices of the Městské kulturní středisko [Municipal Cultural Centre] in Brno.

The field of amateur film was not entirely homogeneous. Most of it was composed of individuals involved in company film, family film, and traditional club production. The 1980s saw the emergence of several artists whose work stepped beyond the usual format of amateur production and was repeatedly awarded prizes at the festivals mentioned above. Both festivals therefore quickly acquired the renown of being "higher level" festivals, with the work shown here being presented in the press as artistically valuable, innovative, and not only achieving the quality of official production but often surpassing it in many respects.[32] These accolades served as significant motivation for the artists to complete new films, as they could rely on them being premiered at these festivals.[33] This group of artists, which included Pavel Dražan, Petr Hvižď, Ivan Tatíček, Pavel Marek, and Pavel Bárta, operated outside the field of club activities – these were independent artists who established their own groups.

In their work, we can follow the development of a parallel, unorganised movement that fulfilled the needs of the agents themselves, without being subject to the strategic plan of the amateur movement. These artists mostly scorned the activities of amateur clubs,[34] and primarily used their infrastructure exclusively as a platform for presentation. After all, there were no other opportunities for the presentation of films during the normalisation period, barring private screenings. Paradoxically, however, their influence transformed the context of amateur festivals to such a degree that in the 1980s, both festivals mentioned above were regarded as events for the presentation of higher-quality independent art, rather than festivals presenting the activities of clubs or associations. Ultimately, amateur festivals became the site of an attempt at institutionalising experimental film. In 1985,

[32] Blažíček – Poláková "Ivan Tatíček – od amatérského filmu k profesionální videotvrobě", p. 79.

[33] Ivan Tatíček, for instance, describes what a significant impulse it was for him to "finish the film in time for Mladá kamera" when he was working on his *Metrofilm* (1984). In this sense, the deadline for festival submissions defined the timeline of filming and post-production so that it could be submitted in time. See Martin Blažíček – Sylva Poláková, "Ivan Tatíček: Pravda je jinde, to jsme všichni věděli. Rozhovor s Ivanem Tatíčkem" [Ivan Tatíček: The Truth Is Elsewhere – We All Knew That. An Interview with Ivan Tatíček], Filmový přehled, 2019, accessed 10 May 2022, https://www.filmovyprehled.cz/cs/revue/detail/ivan-taticek-pravda-je-jinde-to-jsme-vsichni-vedeli.

[34] Ivan Tatíček, one of the prominent artists of the 1980s generation, speaks of club artists as "gardeners with a camera". (Blažíček – Poláková, "Ivan Tatíček – od amatérského filmu k profesionální videotvorbě".) According to Petr Skala, the aim of the core of the amateur makers was to "imitate the official production as consistently as possible. Films that were highly conformist, with a form reminiscent of TV documentaries, were most valued." (Kerbachová, *Alchymie světla. Experimentální tvorba Petra Skaly*, p. 26.). For artists from underground circles, participation in a state-organised amateur festival was entirely out of the question. They were considered "unionised", embarrassing, and their function was entirely taken over by alternatives that underground groups created themselves. (Martin Blažíček, "Čarodějné filmy pro lid. K československému filmovému undergroundu 80. let" [Magician's Films for the People. On the Czechoslovak Cinematic Underground of the 1980s], *Iluminace* 29, no. 4 (2017), pp. 5–29.)

the Mladá kamera festival opened a competitive category called "experiment", but responses in the press at the time show that the purpose of this category was not understood.[35]

A further group of artists does not fit in either of the amateur categories discussed above: artists who worked in unofficial culture and the underground, who stood entirely outside the official institutions.[36] Nevertheless, their production is based in amateur film, or rather in family films, with which they share a number of attributes, such as a particular form of performativity for an audience informed in advance of what will happen.[37] Čaroděj OZ [Wizard OZ], one of the most prolific underground directors, expressly claims that home screenings represented a form that his creative collective consciously appropriated and transformed in their own image.[38] To a large extent, the media practice of underground film arises from its isolation – it is typical that preparations, shooting, post-production, and presentation (in the form of private screenings) all take place within the same relational network.[39] These were, in effect, private films accessible only to a limited and predetermined group of spectators.[40]

[35] The term "experiment" is understood here as a reverberation of the interwar avant-garde, but, on the other hand, also as socially critical and engaged film. Mladá kamera's programme magazine, *Informátor* [Informer], defined experimental films in the following manner: "It's either a play on form or on content. Not self-serving spitefulness or provocative reversals or a negation of the rules, but original combinations, untested or forgotten techniques, parody, paraphrase, review, or poetry. Humorous and striking joyous play. Or it can be a search. A search for a new order, a more modern form." (Anon., "Experiment", *Informátor* [Informer], no. 2, Feb–Mar 1985). Paradoxically, the experimental category was established in the same year that the organisation passed from the more "liberal" company club of the Uničov engineering works to the politically verified Ústřední výbor SSM [Central Committee of the Socialist Youth Union]. No prize was awarded, and not even a list of the participating films survived, even though there were only four of them. Based on later reflections, the experimental category did not find much sympathy. In *Amatérský film* [Amateur Film], Diviš Marek describes it as "highly problematic", considering it better to "stick to the old classification, awarding a special award for experimentalism in the documentary category" (Diviš Marek, "2x o jednom. Jaká byla Mladá kamera" [2x on One Topic. A Report from Mladá kamera], *Amatérský film*, no. 6 (1985), p. 127). Josef Chuchma noted – as found in the festival chronicles – that the category "was created because the jury did not know which categories to include certain films in during the pre-selection process, but they would have regretted not including them at all". Alena Kučerová describes that the aim was to present experimental films that "knowledgeably address the issues faced by the young generation" and "help young people spend their free time" (*Kronika festivalu Mladá kamera Uničov* [Chronicles of the Uničov Young Camera Competition], festival archive). These statements illustrate the variety with which the amateur context attempted to address the "otherness" of the selected films, for which "experimental" seemed, temporarily, like an ideal catch-all term.

[36] Blažíček, "Čarodějné filmy pro lid. K československému filmovému undergroundu 80. let", pp. 5–29.

[37] Alexandra Schneiderová, "Performance v rodinném filmu" [Performance in Home Videos], *Iluminace* 16, no. 3 (2004), pp. 69–82.

[38] Blažíček, "Čarodějné filmy pro lid. K československému filmovému undergroundu 80. let", pp. 5–29.

[39] Schneiderová, "Performance v rodinném filmu", pp. 69–82

[40] Among the works created in the context of isolated underground communities are *Pohádka pro šílence* [A Fairy-Tale for Madmen](Pigi, 1985), *My žijeme v Praze…* [We Live in Prague] (Pablo de Sax, Tomáš Mazal, 1985), *Pokušení sv. Antonína aneb víkend starého mistra* [The Temptation of St. Anthony, or The Old Master's Weekend] (Čaroděj OZ, 1984), or *Podmostní filosofická jatka* [Philosophical Abattoir Under the Bridge] (Jiří Dvorský, Milan Kohout, 1984).

The Technical Media of Normalisation

The division between amateur and professional artists also implies a different approach to period technologies. Professional contexts typically worked with 35mm film, while club and amateur film mostly used 8mm and 16mm. Amateurs mostly used reversal film, Agfa and Orwo negatives, and substantial amounts of technology that were made available thanks to the Czechoslovak producer Meopta. A developed market of amateur film formats existed mostly to meet the needs of film clubs as well as company films and – to a certain extent – television practice. For the group of artists that operated outside of the realm of amateur film competitions, 16mm technology was virtually unattainable. In the 1970s, 8mm and Super-8 were freely available formats, but nevertheless, a number of artists considered the financial demands related to the production of a film one of the greatest hurdles to overcome. This is also why practically all works created in the 1980s are on reversal film and exist only in a single copy. The use of the soundless 8mm material also led to the expansion of a practice involving asynchronous sound played back from ¼ inch tape. Even buying a camera, usually a Super-8 Quartz, was a demanding investment that saw entire groups of artists coming together to pool their resources, such as the collective of underground directors around Čaroděj OZ. Jan Ságl, too, who began filming in the early 1970s, states that he could only work with film thanks to a generous gift from poet Jiří Kolář, which he used to buy a motor controlled Eumig camera. An even greater problem was the availability of video equipment, which, until the end of the 1980s, only exceptionally made its way into private hands.[41]

It is clear that most non-professional work was financed by the artists themselves. A different economic model was not possible during the normalisation period, at least as concerns work made outside the organised film clubs.[42] At the same time, it is typical that, particularly in the 1980s, artists employed strategies involving the "grey economy", i.e., gaining access to relatively professional equipment on the basis of personal connections with employees at the appropriate institutions. Petr Skala, for instance, states[43] that he produced many of his videos "illegally"

[41] The Video 8 format, for instance, was used to produce the underground *Originální videojournal* [Original Video Journal] (1987–89). This technology made its way across the borders via dissidents living abroad, in Sweden or Vienna, in some cases as wedding gifts. Filmed materials about the situation in Czechoslovakia were published on approximately fifty VHS tapes intended for distribution both at home and abroad. *Originální Videojournal* expanded on the existing activities of the Čeněk group (Stanislav Milota, Jan Kašpar, Ivan Kyncl, Michal Hýbek, Andrej Krob), which documented events at home on 16mm material. The aim of *Originální Videojournal*, however, was primarily to document, report, and create journalism – it was not a project with a significant interest in art. Jan Ruml, "Originální videojournal – co mi uvízlo v paměti" [The Original Video Journal – What Stuck in My Memory], *Paměť a dějiny* [Memory and History] 9, no. 1 (2015), pp. 92–94.

[42] Club artists used film equipment and materials subsidised by their state founder – in the case of industrial companies, this was typically an ROH club.

[43] Kerbachová, *Alchymie světla. Experimentální tvorba Petra Skaly*, pp. 156–57.

in the studios of the Střední průmyslová škola spojů [Industrial High School of Telecommunications] in Prague, later in the Orbis studio, or during the night in the studios of Czechoslovak Television, thanks to the technicians he had befriended.[44] There were similar situations in the group of underground directors, such as when Čaroděj OZ's connections at the Filmové laboratoře Barrandov [Barrandov Film Labs] allowed him to use the ASYZ professional sound synthesiser.[45] The second most frequent economic model involved the artists standing with one foot in company or semi-professional film and the other in the independent world. Such artists typically had civic professions as cameramen or technicians at studios whose equipment they used for their own projects. Notable examples include Ivan Tatíček, who was employed at the video studio for the promotional department of the state construction company Armabeton, and Roman Včelák, cameraman of the Bulšitfilm association, in the Laboratoř vrcholové atletiky [Laboratory of Professional Athletics] at the Ústřední výbor Československého svazu tělesné výchovy a sportu [ÚV ČSTV, Central Committee of the Czechoslovak Union of Physical Education and Sport).[46] Even Radek Pilař, a representative of official art, who realised part of the work on his *Musica Picta* cycle at home and later continued the work at a professional studio – Supraphon music video.

It is clear from these examples how much the specific institutional structure of amateur and professional film formed their media practices. There was a clear qualitative distinction between the organised (both professional and amateur) environment and attempts at independent production. Not only did this distinction define which works could be presented publicly in cinemas and which would be relegated to private or domestic conditions, it also defined access to specific technology, whether due to financial limits or availability on the market. Restricted access to technology is likely the reason why Czechoslovak art of the moving image focused so little on media critique. Barring a few exceptions, there were no attempts to deconstruct or visually exhaust media. An understanding of media as mere carriers of images dominated. Later, in the case of video art, artistic approaches mostly involved an expansion of painterly space into the medium of video; the concept of a multimedia painting "coming to life". There are virtually no works investigating the structure of the film material or the video signal themselves. Similarly, we fail to find any works that would use film and video as socially engaged media, since the artists more or less rejected presentations for a broader audience.[47] Another reason for

[44] Paradoxically, this included the use of the professional PAL C tape format, which, however, could not be played back outside the studios. Masters of his works thus remained in the television studios and were eventually erased after being copied to more commonly available media: VHS and U-matic.

[45] Blažíček, "Čarodějné filmy pro lid. K československému filmovému undergroundu 80. let", pp. 5–29.

[46] Blažíček – Poláková, "Ivan Tatíček – od amatérského filmu k profesionální videotvorbě".

[47] A special case is the alternative distribution of the video cassettes of *Originální videojournal* (see footnote no. 42).

the absence of critical approaches is the late arrival of new media behind the Iron Curtain. The first works focusing on media analysis and critique began appearing (in international video art) in the late 1960s and early '70s. But video only arrived in Czechoslovakia in the mid-1980s, when video art was dominated by other themes. Furthermore, in the Czech context, new and progressive media did not function as "media of newness", inspiring artists through new forms of representation. On the contrary, this field of art was typified as first-choice, low-threshold media representing the lowest acceptable quality combined with relative availability.

Official and Unofficial Art

A second perspective of the fragmented environment of normalisation-era Czechoslovakia is a political polarity that can be described with the use of three culturally societal models: the concept of first and second culture, the notion of a parallel society, and the term "grey zone". All three describe (from different angles) an identical phenomenon: the monopolisation of state politics and its influence on the existence of cultural activities beyond the supervision of the state.

The term first culture refers to official culture, defined by the state's cultural politics and represented by a broad range of state unions. The second, unofficial culture refers to everything else, i.e., non-members of unions. However, this does not mean that the activities of the second culture were entirely illegal or anti-establishment. The plentiful and diverse group of non-members includes artists of the 1960s generation who did not pass through the sieve of political evaluations after 1968, unorganised amateur artists, and the oppositional underground. This polarisation is described in *Zpráva o třetím českém hudebním obrození* [A Report on the Third Czech Musical Renaissance] by Ivan M. Jirous, which expresses a challenge to "[...] create a second culture. A culture that will be completely independent of the official communication channels and social rewards and the hierarchy of values the establishment uses to rule. A culture that cannot aim to destroy the establishment, as that would mean running straight into its arms."[48]
At around the same time, philosopher Václav Benda formulated his conception of the parallel polis, challenging dissidents to actively create "parallel structures, capable – at least in limited terms – of supplementing the missing, generally beneficial and vital functions, and, wherever possible, making use of existing structures and 'humanising' them".[49] The bipolar notion of a dual culture was extended further with the term grey zone, popularised in the

[48] Ivan M. Jirous, *Zpráva o třetím českém hudebním obrození* [A Report on the Third Czech Musical Renaissance] (Samizdat, 1975), accessed 12 May 2022, cited in *Moderní dějiny*, https://www.moderni-dejiny.cz/clanek/ivan-m-jirous-zprava-o-tretim-ceskem-hudebnim-obrozeni.

[49] Václav Benda, "Paralelní polis" [Parallel Polis], in *Noční kádrový dotazník a jiné boje: Texty z let 1977–1989* [Night-time Cadre Form and Other Struggles: Texts from 1977–1989], ed. Patrik Benda (Prague: Agite/Fra, 2009), pp. 56–66.

late 1980s by sociologist and dissident Jiřina Šiklová.[50] The grey zone refers to a broad field between official culture and oppositional dissent. Šiklová considered these two groups to be marginal and small, while she described the space between them as the "silent majority", espousing apolitical and pragmatic positions.

All three of these conceptions attest to the division of society with the official production of the unions on the one hand and a number of unorganised activities, most often without mutual communication or cultural exchange on the other, existing as individual production units with their own audiences. The practical realisation of the second culture led to the growth of second cultures, plural – various disconnected activities by isolated, relatively small groups. The conception of a parallel and second culture is a response to state cultural policy at a time when it was clear that the cultural sphere could not contribute to societal transformation. Furthermore, existence outside the mainstream did not simply mean the creation of a cultural space, but also a physical space – most activities in the second culture were pushed outside the centre, often to villages and abandoned farms. This dystopian dimension of culture resulted in a position of resignation regarding positive social developments, but also the will to develop independent, parallel institutions.

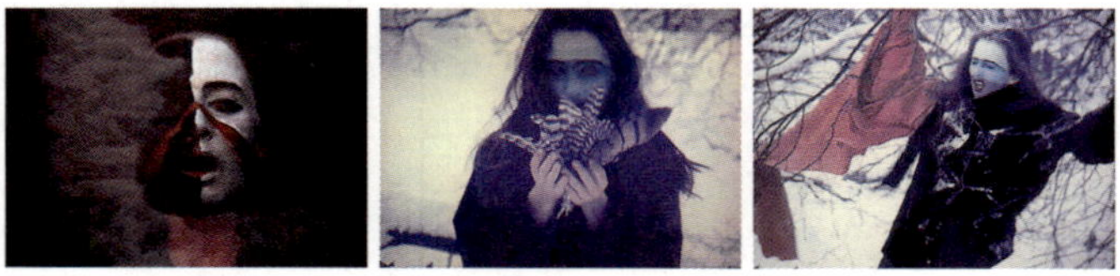

Pigi *Pohádka pro šílence* [A Fairy–Tale for Madmen] (1985), film, 23 min 17 s

The philosophical stances of the protagonists of the second culture are also mirrored in the themes of their films that capture the life stories of absolute individuals in confrontation with society, often supplemented with elements of surveillance and the potential for conflicts with state power. Čaroděj OZ's film *1984* (1984), for instance, translates Orwell's novel into 1984 Prague, with the film's protagonist followed by the camera surveillance systems of the state police and subjected to repeated interrogations. In the underground films *Nirvana* (Čaroděj OZ, 1982), *Pohádka pro šílence* [A Fairy-Tale for Madmen] (Pigi, 1985), and *Titaniku zkáza* [Doom of the Titanic] (Jiří Dvorský, Milan Kohout, Miroslav Čapek, 1982), we find protagonists in conflict with society, their hopeless lives ending in suicide or death. Although Jan Ságl's *Underground* (1972) consisting of a long static shot of travellers on an escalator can seem like a formalist or structural film, the real reason for its creation was the need to capture the hopelessness of early normalisation, invoked here in the way the bodies are unceasingly pushed forward. Proof that this message was not limited to underground circles can be found in

[50] Jiřina Šiklová, "The 'Gray Zone' and the Future of Dissent in Czechoslovakia", *Social Research* 57, no. 2 (1990).

highly acclaimed films from amateur circles. *Mat* (Pavel Bárta, 1983), which shows the subjective perspective of a surveillance device, or the dystopian dramas *Jarmareční bouda* [Market Chalet] (Pavel Dražan, 1982) and *Bravo Bravissimo* (Pavel Dražan, 1989).

Works from the cultural underground were highly engaged and appellative, but they were directed inwards, towards their own community. The need to capture an authentic experience and mediate it to a narrowly defined audience might be part of the reason why these are mostly live-action films with minimal interest in the visual component. This approach is almost an anti-artistic conception, foregoing artistic form or content in favour of one's own engagement and the demand for an authentic "capturing of life". The strong fluctuation of genres is also related to this aspect. Parallel culture tended towards a replication of all the institutions of official culture, which is why it includes genre films, such as grotesques (*Zlato* [Gold], Milan Kohout, 1983), parodies (*Easy Rider OZ*, Karra, Čaroděj OZ, 1984), travesties (*Queen of China Town*, Čaroděj OZ, 1981), and horror films (*Za spásu duší* [For the Salvation of Souls], Pablo de Sax, Pigi, 1986), in so far as these genres are perceived as authentic by their audience. Artists from this milieu generally rejected purely visual content, including abstract films, as insufficiently authentic and, in their view, insufficiently "cinematic".[51]

By contrast, approaches based on visuality dominate "official" films, such as the surrealist films produced by Krátký film, e.g., *Kostnice* [Ossuary] (1970) and *Leonardův deník* [Leonardo's Diary] (1973) by Jan Švankmajer or *Botička* [Little Shoe] (1988) by Radek Pilař, as well as the work of video artists from the group Independent video art Prague beginning in 1972,[52] and the video department at the Union beginning in 1987. A major portion of this official art has not yet been subject to broader research or preservation; today, the majority of the films are virtually unavailable or lost. Even so, we can assume that many films of an experimental nature were made by Krátký film during the normalisation era, as well as by the artists at the Union, making use of the professional and television studios of the time.[53] Furthermore, their distinguishing feature seems to be an emphasis on an artistic use of the medium as an attempt to avoid potential politicisation, not only

[51] Blažíček, "Čarodějné filmy pro lid. K československému filmovému undergroundu 80. let", pp. 5–29.

[52] The group existed under the auspices of the Institut průmyslového designu [Institute of Industrial Design] and its members included Miroslav Klivar, Jaroslav Pavelka, or Zdenka Čechová. See e.g., Miroslav Klivar, *Nová umění v Čechách* [New Art in Bohemia] (Prague: Regulus, 2001) or Martin Mazanec, "Výzkumný projekt český videoart. Od programu k formě" [The Czech Video Art Research Project. From Programme to Form], *A2*, no. 49 (2008).

[53] While production groups such as Krátký film held more potential for cinematic experiments, overall, they created a broad spectrum of films of various standards: animated, instructional, reportage, children's, and educational, mostly on the basis of state commissions. Although we can consider these an Eastern parallel to film cooperatives, an important difference is the broad focus on production of various types and qualities. The studio also lacked a cultural manifesto, which is always the foundation of a film cooperative. By contrast, socialist production groups applied period production standards and the formal or artistic possibilities of the realised films were subject to internal negotiation.

protect against suspicions of "anti-establishment" activities, but also as a way of sidestepping political commissions. Věra Geislerová, one of the video artists of the generation of the 1980s, for instance, describes how state political commissions such as art pieces for new construction projects were usually realised in highly abstract forms whereby the original setting was hardly recognisable.[54] Even though these works were created within the official domain, they were not accepted unconditionally and were often criticised for their formal invention. Their distribution was sometimes limited, as in the case of Jan Švankmajer.[55] Although Radek Pilař's VHS edition *Musica Picta* (1985–1991) was made in the professional facilities of the JVC Supraphon broadcasting vehicle, the publisher withdrew from the project after its completion.[56]

The Networked and Disconnected Parallel Society

The dual culture and high level of state organisation within the cultural sector in normalisation-era Czechoslovakia created highly specific conditions. It discursively divided cultural agents and predetermined their movements to restricted groups with limited reach. While antagonism to the hegemony of the film industry or state regulations is a general feature of experimental film, in Czechoslovakia, these groups strove to negotiate with the state and achieve their goals through non-systemic means. The large number of concurrent cultural activities existing in plurality and diversity resulted in a strong sense of individualism and only a limited need to construct more permanent institutions such as cooperatives or art centres.[57] That which is usually described as experimental film, independent film, film made by artists, or video art did not find a common platform at the time of its birth, which is why these works remained ungrouped, isolated in their own circles, and are still perceived separately today. Although we can find trends and common

[54] "I made art in architecture. [...] All these realisations were damaged by socialism. I would usually make it abstract, but the name might have been 'Letting Out the Doves' or 'Garden of Peace'. [...] I think everyone is a little ashamed of this, as various things happened during the sessions of the committee. The competitions were awful. Who would want to seriously apply themselves to documenting this period... I don't know. It was based on lies. Everyone knew they didn't want to 'let out the doves'. I stopped doing art for architecture very quickly, 1986, '87. It finished then. And then I basically floated right into the world of computers." Věra Geislerová interviewed by Martin Blažíček, December 2014.

[55] A number of Švankmajer's film were censored (e.g., *Kyvadlo, jáma a naděje* [The Pendulum, the Pit, and Hope], 1983) or their screenings banned (*Zahrada* [Garden], 1986; *Žvahlav* [Jabberwocky], 1971). Between 1972 and 1977, Švankmajer was completely unable to produce films officially.

[56] Pilař's *Musica Picta* series was conceived as a VHS edition for commercial distribution. For this reason, Supraphon demanded a significant prolongation of the running time to two hours, which was an adequate running time for a marketable product. In the version that survives on U-Matic tape, there is a final credit for "Bohemia video art, 1991", referring to the joint-stock company that took over the operation of the Supraphon studio after the publisher was privatised following the revolution in 1989.

[57] We can speculate whether the lack of non-state institutions was not a starting point from which emancipated video artists could step out towards strongly individualistic tendencies after 1989. Many of them considered "starting to work for oneself" a crucial step in their lives, leaving television and company studios and establishing their own studios operating on commercial foundations.

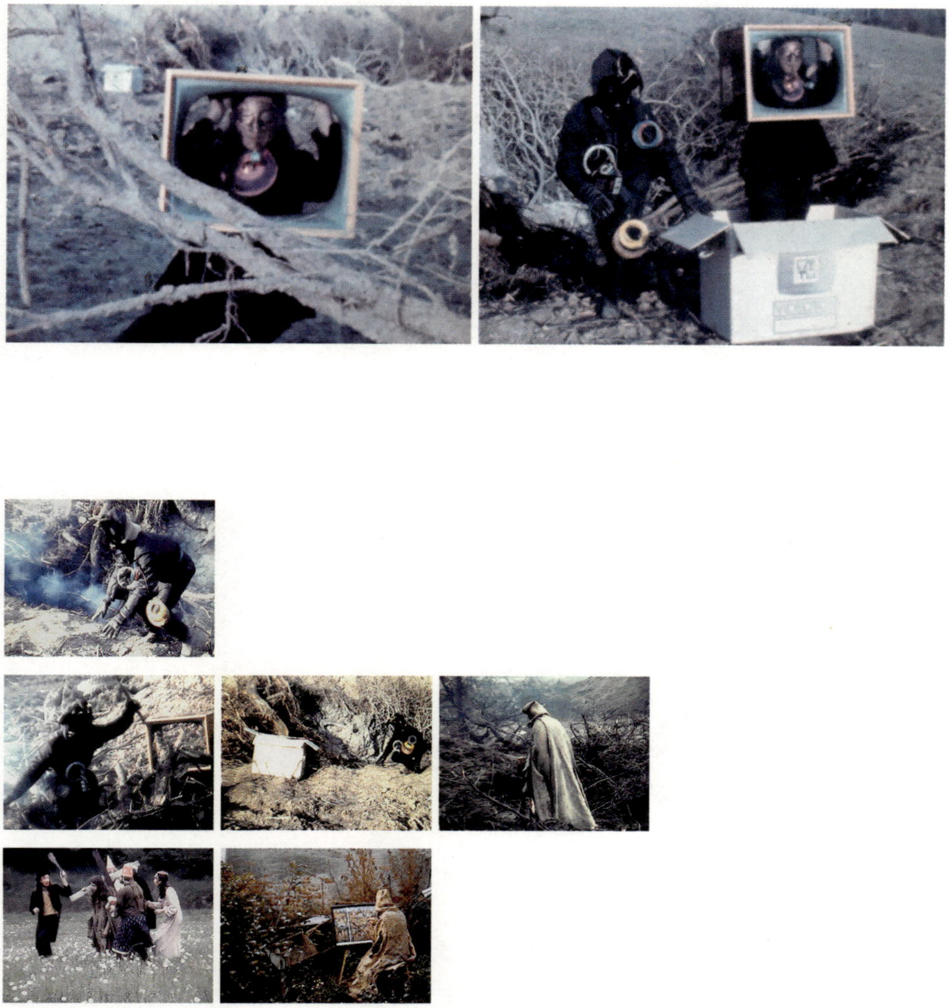

Čaroděj OZ *Pokušení sv. Antonína aneb víkend starého mistra*
[Temptation of St Anthony, or Weekend of an Old Master] (1984), film, 30 min

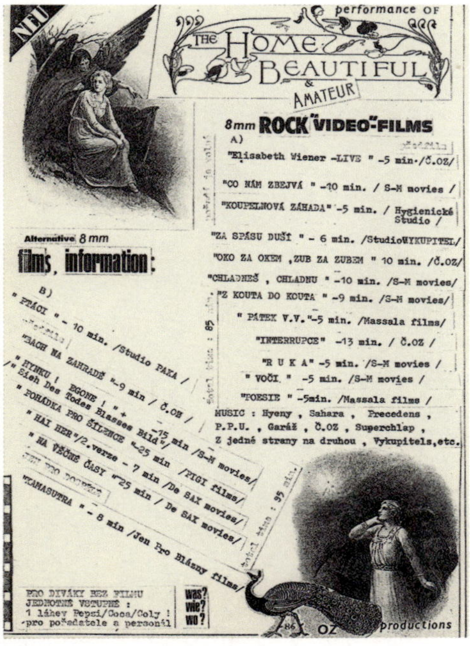

Poster for a film screening by Čaroděj OZ, 1980s

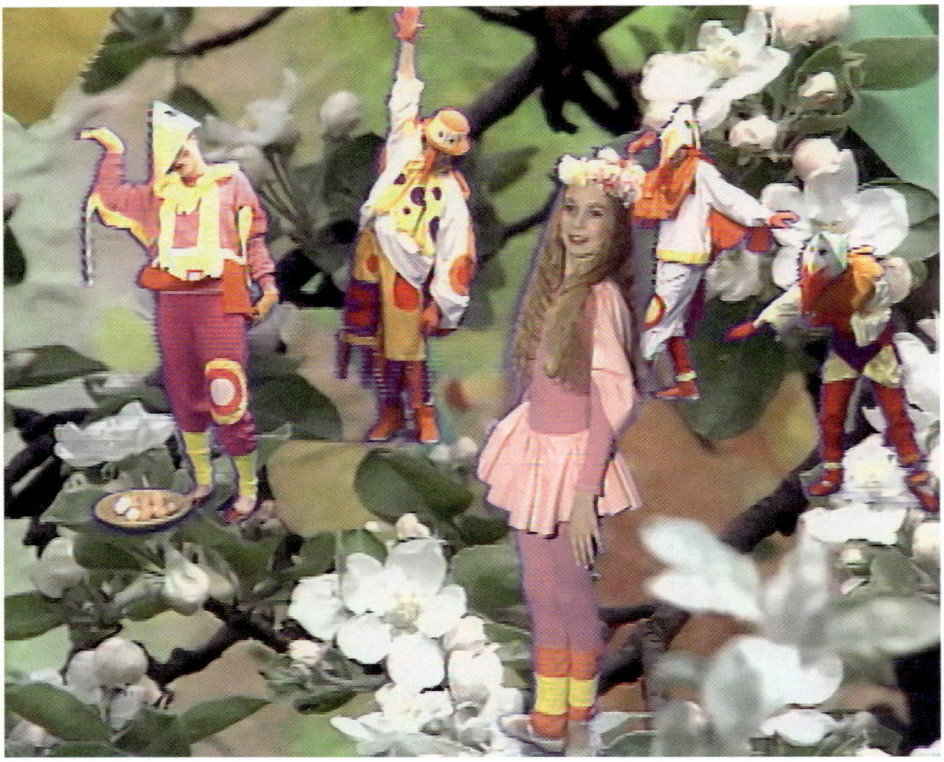

Radek Pilař *Musica Picta – Čas radování* [Musica Picta – Time of Mirth] *(1985–1991), video, 4 min 13 s*

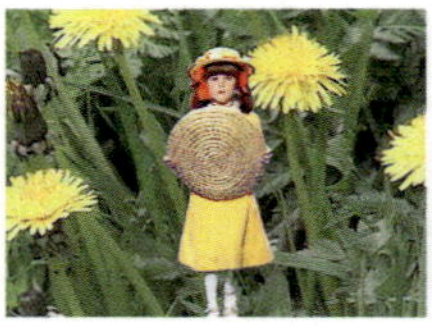
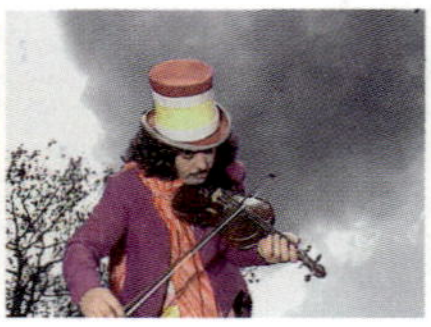
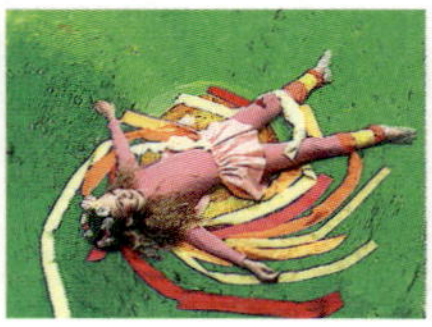
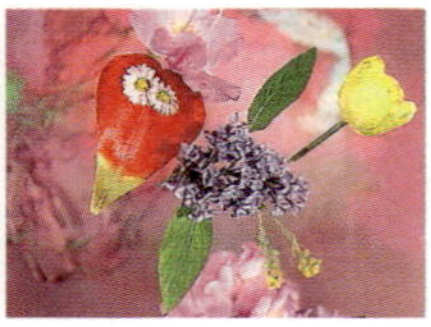

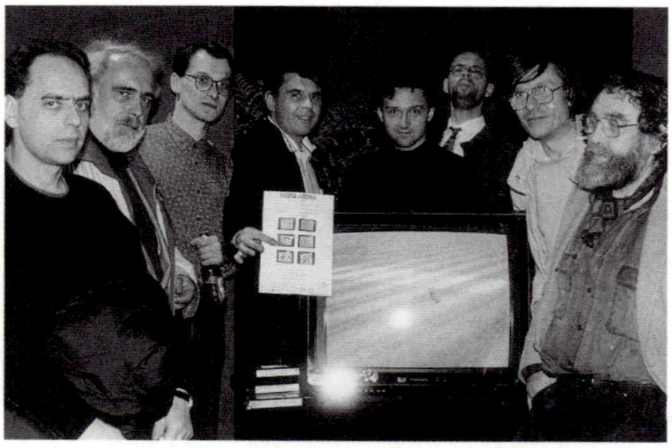

Photographs from the establishment of Media archiv, Prague, 1992. Left to right: Michael Bielický, Petr Skala, Michal Pacina, Petr Vrána, Pavel Zvolenský, Pavel Scheufler, Milan Vobořil, Radek Pilař.

features at the turn of the 1970s and '80s, in truth, the artists responsible for these works had no idea about each other. Petr Skala and Radek Pilař, for instance, were making art films since the 1960s, but they did not meet each other until 1985 and even then knew nothing about one another's work. Similarly, the filmmakers from underground circles often existed in parallel enclaves despite the fact that their films use similar forms to capture the same basic life experience. On the other hand, temporary networks did occasionally emerge – particularly on the underground scene – bringing together individuals (and sometimes dozens of artists) and ensuring the circulation of their works, at least in these limited circles.[58] These networks, however, served only for distribution, never for production. Amateur festivals also often generated networks, but they were temporally limited to the duration of the event. Visual artists that used film, such as Miloš Šejn, Dalibor Chatrný, Ľubomír Ďurček, and Vladimír Havrilla understood their film pieces from an intermedia position and had no ambitions to enter the world of cinematography. Their works were therefore not presented in cinemas – neither when they were created nor later, in the 1990s, when their work could have been recognised as instances of experimental film. Instead, these artists consistently presented their film work as a complement to their (static) visual art exhibitions.

The '90s – Transforming the Network and Putting an End to the Past

The absence of a unified video art or experimental film "scene", as well as institutions for their production, publication, and distribution, is a phenomenon that passed freely into the 1990s. Although the post-revolutionary transformation period opened possibilities to create new professional associations or special interest groups, we once again discover here a disconnected mass of activities whose shared feature is an attempt to put an end to the past and adapt to the new conditions. Existing institutions, such as the video department at ČSVÚ or regional cultural centres that brought amateur clubs together slowly died out and were for the most part not transformed into new institutions.[59] One consequence of their dissolution was that there was no need to preserve or historically describe the audiovisual production of the normalisation period, nor to critically revise it under the new conditions.

[58] Attesting to the networked nature of underground culture is the 1984 Meliés samizdat catalogue, containing dozens of films made by numerous real or virtual production groups. Given the practice of changing names and nicknames, it is not entirely clear how many independent productions truly existed at the time, but they probably numbered in the dozens.

[59] In the 1990 edition of Mladá kamera's festival magazine, *Informátor*, for instance, there are many expressions of justified concerns about the continued existence of clubs supported by trade union or state organs, which were now left without the amateurs who had already built corresponding facilities at home. One of the projects aiming for further sustainability in the amateur movement was a not entirely successful initiative called Iniciativa 100, whose aim was to establish an independent amateur film union whose guarantors would be a hundred "leading" amateurs (*Informátor*, no. 2, 1990, p. 5).

The influence of the revolutionary activities in November 1989 also led to the decline of socially political projects in the underground network. The very concept of parallelism in close relation to an understanding of a dual culture became dysfunctional under the new circumstances – therefore the activities of most underground collectives ceased almost immediately. However, this does not mean that the second cinematic culture automatically became the first. Activities founded on an oppositional relationship to mainstream society did not generally find an adequate extension in official institutions. Many thus remained in seclusion and were, over time, forgotten as part of the supposed legacy of the "old world".[60] The transformation of the underground into the mainstream never took place. Quite the opposite: in the 1990s, a need arose to quickly come to terms with an onslaught of international influences. Artists who had spent years living in relative isolation had to quickly catch up with many new impulses, the availability of contemporary and historical works, and new technological possibilities as well. This period, in fact, is marked not only by a societal transformation, but also by a medial one: from film and analogue media to the digital world.

Many artists who had previously emigrated returned to their homeland during this period. Michael Bielický began teaching in Czechoslovakia (and later Czech Republic), as did, for a short time, Woody Vasulka.[61] Their influence was crucial for 1990s video art. The new generation of students at art schools, where multimedia programmes were soon established, no longer turned to the artists in the video department, but to figures coming from abroad, from an entirely different cultural context. In 1990, the department of video transformed into the Asociace videa a intermediální tvorby [AVIT, Association of Video and Intermedia Art] and, for several years, organised lectures, exhibitions, and presentations of video art. Its activities peaked with the retrospective exhibition Český obraz elektronický [The Czech Electronic Picture] (Mánes, 1994) and then gradually died down. Artists represented by the video department also set out on their own careers as commercial audiovisual producers and, given the relative accessibility of equipment, established their own studios, such as Stanislav Miler's Trimedia, Věra Geislerová's Art Impression, Martin Hřebačka's Prograf, Vít Komrzý's UPP, or Ivan Tatíček's DADA. For these artists, this development represented a significant emancipatory step from amateurs to professionals, but also from the uncertain existence of free

[60] November 1989 seems like an easily identifiable transition, but underground film festivals peaked around the year 1986. In the last two years of the normalisation era, we note a general decline of the entire underground film scene, which we can speculate is rooted in the penetration of new cultural currents into Czechoslovakia in the late 1980s, but also in a certain exhaustion in the community that created its most mature works between 1984 and 1986.

[61] Michael Bielický emigrated to Germany with his parents in 1968, later studying at the academy in Düsseldorf with photographer Bernd Becher and video artist Nam June Paik. Bohuslav (Woody) Vašulka graduated from the documentary film department at FAMU in Prague in 1965, after which he departed for the United States accompanied by his wife and collaborator Steina, from Iceland. They settled in New York and began working with video.

artists to media producers. These studios did not necessarily specialise only in art production, they were open to a broad range of commissions for television and private clients. At the time, Petr Vrána attempted to systematically collect video art,[62] establishing the Media Archiv on Prague's Národní třída in 1992. The Archiv's activity, however, ceased by the mid-90s. The Center for Contemporary Arts Prague, established in 1992, played an important role in the field of art video. The project, financed by George Soros's Open Society Foundations, with the patronage of historian Ludvík Hlaváček, which had a medialab[63] managed by Miloš Vojtěchovský, was an important centre for new media beginning in the 1990s, as well as an open studio that allowed artists to use technologies that were otherwise unavailable.

Along with the development of new media art, the 1990s also saw the gradual establishment of experimental film in the form in which it is usually understood in the Western context. A relatively small group of artists concentrated around pedagogue Martin Čihák[64] proceeded from the foundations set by the canonical experimental works from other parts of the world at the turn of the 1960s and '70s, which slowly made their way into Czech cultural space in the form of VHS tapes. The work of these Czech artists, however, was also made in the context of a new wave of interest in experimental film in the form of the DIY practice of small film labs in Europe and the USA. Furthermore, it was also motivated by the gradually declining importance of film as a medium as it was being progressively replaced by video and digital media. For this group of film experimentalists, film was important as a medium with specific properties of visualisation. They were brought together by an often almost alchemical approach to work in the laboratory, optical copying, and other experimental techniques. The Czech group quickly became part of a European experimental film network and its works were presented internationally, albeit only for a short period in the late 1990s.[65]

The 1990s are marked by attempts to create a "new world" that would be unencumbered by the experience of the normalisation era.

[62] Petr Vrána was another one of the returning emigrants after 1989. He participated in the activities of AVIT, exhibited at their group exhibitions, and was also a commercially successful designer of television graphics. He is responsible for TV Nova's graphic design in the 1990s, as well as the introductory sequences for popular TV shows including Eso, Občanské judo [Civic Judo], and Volejte řediteli [Call the Director].

[63] The medialab project was only officially inaugurated in the year 2000, though preparations stretch back to 1997. After several months under the direction of Petr Svárovský, Miloš Vojtěchovský took over during the first year of operation. The lab, called The New – digital – Media Laboratory, built with the support of the Open Art Institute and Silicon Graphics, supported a broad range of artistic activities, including the creation of 2D and 3D graphics, interactive media, and internet radio. "Center for Contemporary Arts Prague, Annual report 2000", accessed 17 May 2022, https://cca.fcca.cz/fileadmin/user_upload/CENTRUM/O_centru/Vyrocni_zpravy/2000.pdf.

[64] In addition to Martin Čihák and Jan Daňhel (*Naše zahrádka* [Our Garden], 1993), see also e.g., Martin Blažíček (*Test*, 1997, *NP55*, 1997), Alice Růžičková (*Pozitivní negativ* [Positive Negative], 1998), Martin Ježek (*Folklor* [Folklore], 1999), and František Wirth (*In Nuce*, 1999).

[65] E.g., Álommásolatok Közép-európai filmavantgárd, Balázs Béla Stúdió, Budapest, 1998; Lux Center, London, 1998; OFF/OFF Copenhagen, 2000; Kurzfilmtage Oberhausen, 2000, and others.

This meant not only a rejection of official culture, but also a distancing from underground circles, which were subconsciously perceived as one of the symptoms of the "old world".[66] Although this period is often discussed in terms of transformation, the changes that occurred did not typically mean a true transformation of the old into the new – rather, the process was one of the abolishment of normalisation-era institutions and the creation of new ones from the ground up. Although their aim was to mark a clear break between themselves and the past and to construct a new future unencumbered by the past, this effort would later be seen as unsuccessful. The active protagonists of the transformation process were primarily artists who were already active during the normalisation period, whose own life experiences were truly undergoing fundamental changes, and this was the case in all areas – official, amateur, and underground.

There was also a new generation of art school graduates, which included Janka Vidová, Elen Řádová, Filip Cenek, and Jiří Havlíček. This group had not been significantly influenced by the normalisation experience and mostly directed its attention to international influences and their own peers. A consequence of the dual institutional transformation – first removing any traces of normalisation and then sidelining those who effected the transformation – thus led, paradoxically, to an erasure of the historical traces of the 1980s as well as any documentation about the institutions of transformation. It is precisely such absence of reflection across long periods of time that is the major cause of the sense of vacuum we now have when relating to this period.

[66] In a 1992 interview for *Lidové noviny*, literary critic Jan Lopatka described the dislike of dissident circles as part of a general trend of forgetting the late 1980s as a traumatic experience. As part of a strategy that could be described as "snatch what you can and forget everything", the end of the normalisation period was dismissed across the board in favour of the future, without any attempts to focus in greater detail on the recent past. Cited according to Michael Špirit, "K nedožitým narozeninám Jana Lopatky" [On What Would Have Been Jan Lopatka's Birthday], *Bubínek Revolveru*, 2020, accessed 6 Feb 2022, https://www.bubinekrevolveru.cz/k-nedozitym-narozeninam-jana-lopatky.

Hours, Days, and Weeks of Video Exhibitions. "Conditions for the Creation of Video in the Czech Lands"[67]

Martin Mazanec

Video technology has been a part of visual art since its introduction to the market in the 1960s. The specifics of the electronic image define the historical period of video art, the beginnings of which are most commonly dated to 1965.[68] During the course of its analogue and

[67] Radek Pilař, "Podmínky pro vznik videa v Čechách" [Conditions for the Creation of Video in the Czech Lands], typescript, 1990, archive of the heirs of Radek Pilař.

[68] In addition to Nam June Paik, artists who worked with video technology in artistic practice at that time included Ira Schneider, Andy Warhol, Frank Gillette, Les Levine, and others. With regard to the television screen as a symbol and object of video art, we can also discuss the work of Wolf Vostell. Cf. Hanne Mugaas, "The Year Video Art was Born", *The Take*, 15 Jul 2010, accessed 24 Jul 2022, https://www.guggenheim.org/blogs/the-take/the-year-video-art-was-born.

digital development, video became a technical medium for art projects and, consequently, also the subject of discussions on the presentation and archiving of the moving image. In the Czechoslovak context, the beginnings of its use in artistic practice came two decades later due to the political and socio-economic situation in the country.

The title of this text refers to problems connected to the establishment of video first in socialist Czechoslovakia and later in the first exhibitions where the field of art of the moving image was developed curatorially in the context of video art, new media, and the more general category of media art. The historical position of video can be traced according to a selection of exhibitions as well as through a consideration of the role of television broadcasting and the manner of disseminating information in Eastern Europe. Exemplary exhibitions from the 1980s to the early 2000s retrospectively define the course of Czech art of the moving image. The chosen timeframe can be approached via two possible reading levels: one focused on the meaning of communities, societies, and specific figures; and the second as a history of exhibitions of art of the moving image. In order to describe the history of the moving image within the world of art it is necessary to break away from the interpretation of individual works, and to focus instead on the context of these events. Transformations in the modes of presentation for projections, installations, or live performances were also influenced by the availability of the technology in question. More so than the Czech tradition of film and art practice, it was the international context that substantially contributed to the current position of the moving image in art.

The subtitle of this study, "conditions for the creation of video in the Czech lands", comes from the title of a typescript written by artist and videoist Radek Pilař in 1990. Pilař prepared this research summary for the Japanese curator Keiko Sei,[69] who lived in Eastern Europe from the late 1980s to the early 2000s and was also active in the Czech Republic. The contributions of these two figures to the growing acceptance and dissemination of video as an art discipline in the Czech Republic are presented in this study according to two elementary positions: the Czech experience and the international experience. Pilař had the ability to connect his own work to the production of large amounts of texts, which focused, for instance, on the critical analysis of television and the efforts to establish a new field dedicated to video. Keiko Sei was probably the first person to consider – from a curatorial position – developments in the Czech Republic and Slovakia in the broader context of Eastern Europe, while most other artists and curators tended towards comparisons with the Western art world.

[69] Radek Pilař used the Czech neologism "videoist" mostly in texts written in the 1980s. The typescript prepared for Keiko Sei served – according to a handwritten note under the signature – as the foundations for a meeting of videoists that took place in Paris in 1990.

Televisions and Video Cassettes

In Western Europe and the USA, the first television programmes or satellite channels exclusively dedicated to the artistic production of videos were first introduced in the late 1960s.[70] In Czechoslovakia, the significance and role of the easily copyable medium of video were defined by the availability factor, as in other countries living under repressive regimes. Until the 1980s, the social and political contexts here made it more difficult to acquire any video equipment (portable video cameras, video players, video recorders, etc.) as private property, since these were tools useful for the dissemination of content and information. This reality circumscribed the spectrum of possibilities for the circulation of video until the 1990s. Making video works available in collaboration with the state television channels was virtually impossible in the Czech context, although in other countries of the Eastern Bloc there are examples of video activism that – when compared to television dramaturgy in democratic countries – often appeared to be anti-establishment.

Video activism and community, or guerrilla television in the Western world were conceived as alternatives to official broadcasting and – particularly in the USA – also as a critique of mass television production. These television and information strategies[71] were motivated by a need to define oneself against the political situation and draw attention to various social problems. Rooted in political, aesthetic, and economic foundations, documentarists and activists in the US focused on questions related to the struggle for human rights. "Street tapes" made on Portapaks often made it directly into television broadcasts. The connection between television production and the work of activists and artists arose primarily from the availability of technology in these countries. In some cases, the impulse also came from the generally available television broadcasting and the resulting possibility of mediating information directly into households. In Western societies, discussions about understanding media as extensions of societal developments and human existence were complemented by a critique of the inequality between the originators and

[70] From 1967 to the mid-1970s, some television stations (especially in the US, but also in Europe) dedicated some of their screen time to the developing phenomenon of video art. In 1969, the WGBH station (supported by the Rockefeller Foundation) presented the first programme made by video artists. Titled *The Medium is the Medium*, it was prepared by six artists using WGBH technology (Nam June Paik, Allan Kaprow, Otto Piene, James Seawright, Thomas Tadlock, and Aldo Tambellini). Swedish artists Ture Sjölander, Lars Weck, and Bengt Modin created *Monument* in 1967, a programme intended for experimental television. The essence of this programme consisted of a combination of pre-taped films with diapositives and videos in a process of image distortion that took place during the broadcast. For more on this topic, see Martin Mazanec, "Video art, umění pohyblivého obrazu" [Video Art, Art of the Moving Image] (Diploma thesis, Faculty of Arts, Palacký University, Olomouc, 2006) p. 75.

[71] In 1993, a conference took place in Amsterdam titled The Next Five Minutes (N5M), which used the term "tactical television" to describe various activities from around the world (the Eastern European examples were Hungary and Romania). Cf. Jeroen van Bergeijk, Geke van Dijk, Karel Koch, Bas Raijmakers, eds., *The Next Five Minutes. Zapbook* (Amsterdam: Paradiso, 1993).

receivers of media information.[72] The principles related to the democratising potential of this new medium were highly developed – video recording allowed for almost immediate presentation both in private and via television network broadcasts.[73]

Thus, for several decades, the technology of video and television broadcasting was considered in the West as a possible tool for cultural or pan-societal change. Countries within the Soviet sphere of influence only experienced the possibility of using this emancipatory potential at the end of the communist totalitarian era. One dramatic example was that of the studios of TVR – Romanian state television – which were occupied by protesters during the December 1989 revolution, which was violently suppressed by the regime. The continual stream of the protesters' broadcasts were described by German visual artist Hito Steyerl as a transformation of the history and function of the televised image: "Broadcasts from occupied TV studios became active catalysts of events – not records or documents."[74] Soon after this, in April 1990, the technological and civic role of television and video during the revolutionary days of the late 1980s and early '90s in Eastern Europe was the focus of an international symposium in Budapest whose programme was curated by Keiko Sei.[75] Philosopher Vilém Flusser characteristically noted that "the effect of the information revolution consists of the fact that we have to stay at home when we want to be informed".[76] This was a period of political and economic transformation in Eastern Europe, and, according to Steyerl, "televised images began literally

[72] As with radio, which Bertolt Brecht described in the 1930s as a tool of dialogic and equal communication, artists of the 1960s saw hope in video and television broadcasting, just as later artists did the same with information dissemination on the internet. Concepts related to television and video as extensions of human communication were explored by media theorist Marshall McLuhan as well as the pedagogue and utopian architect Buckminster Fuller, whose theoretical concepts were often a source of inspiration for artists working in the United States during the 1960s. The impulse was the utopian desire to broaden human perception through new technologies of the electronic image, i.e., television and video. In Western Europe, the texts that were crucial for artists were authored by representatives of the Frankfurt School, particularly Herbert Marcuse, and Hans Magnus Enzensberger, who explored the centralised structure of radio and television, which limits the individual manifestations of both the spectator and listener and of the individual employees of the station in question. For more on this topic, see Mazanec, "Video art, umění pohyblivého obrazu", p. 76.

[73] The development of communication processes in the USA was the subject of works from groups including Raindance (1969–1970), Ant Farm (1968), TVTV (1972), and Videofreex (1969–1971). In France, art groups were established in the early 1970s based on similar approaches to those in the US (e.g., Immedia, Vidéo Out, Vidéo OO, and others). Ibid., p. 75; Chris Hill, "Attention! Production! Audience! Performing Video in its First Decade, 1969–1980", 1996, accessed 10 Jul 2022, www.vdb.org/sites/default/files/attention.pdf.

[74] Hito Steyerl, "Too Much World: Is the Internet Dead?", *e-flux* 6, no. 49 (2013), accessed 10 Jul 2022, https://www.e-flux.com/journal/49/60004/too-much-world-is-the-internet-dead/.

[75] The symposium was called The Media Are With Us!: The Role of Television in the Romanian Revolution (Mücsarnok, Budapest, 6–7 Apr 1990), with speakers including Vilém Flusser, Peter Weibel, Geert Lovink, and many others. The Romanian TV revolution is also the subject of the video essay *Videogramme einer Revolution* (Harun Farocki, Andrej Ujica, 1993).

[76] Tjebbe van Tijen, "A context for collecting the new media", 1993, accessed 10 Jul 2022, https://monoskop.org/images/d/d9/Van_Tijen_Tjebbe_1993_A_Context_for_Collecting_the_New_Media.pdf.

walking through screens, right into reality" and the dissemination of information became accelerated in a manner very similar to what would take place several years later with the onset of the infrastructure of the internet.[77]

In Czechoslovakia, television broadcasts were not the medium that contributed to the circulation of information as part of the activities of a parallel culture – it was the distribution of video tapes among domestic environments, a network operating outside official state politics. In 1984, the playwright, dissident, and – from 1989 – also president Václav Havel wrote that parallel culture:

> does not aim to or cannot or should not impact the public through the media controlled by the power of the state, which, in a totalitarian state, means all publishers, printers, exhibition halls, concert halls, theatres, scientific institutes, etc. This culture then uses only what is left: typewriters, private studios, apartments, barns, and so on. It is clear, then, that 'parallelness' is defined entirely externally and nothing else follows from it directly – no quality, no aesthetic, nor an ideology.[78]

Video as a technology well suited to journalistic activities and the spread of information was consulted and requested by Havel in correspondence with friends living in exile.[79] The Sony Video 8 camera he acquired, for instance, was then used by members of the group Čeněk, who had, until then, mostly filmed on 16mm film and sent images of anti-communist activities to émigrés abroad. "Čeněk had to be reorganised, with new equipment, so that it would be able not only to film the material but also edit it and turn it into completed programmes", adds Jan Ruml, one of the co-organisers of the future video-periodical, a dissident, and – after 1989 – also a politician.[80]

Attempts to create a new video-periodical that would be disseminated not only abroad, but also in Czechoslovakia led to the concept of *Originální videojournal* or *OVJ* [The Original Video-Journal], which was first

[77] The gradual closure of open access to information within the monopolised internet is the subject of an essay by Hito Steyerl. Cf. Steyerl, "Too Much World: Is the Internet Dead?".

[78] Václav Havel, "Šest poznámek o kultuře" [Six Notes on Culture], in *České umění 1938–1989* [Czech Art 1938–1989], eds. Jiří Ševčík – Pavlína Morganová – Dagmar Dušková (Prague: Academia, 2001), p. 377.

[79] Václav Havel mostly communicated about the need for video equipment required to create an alternative news channel with the physicist František Janouch, who lived in Stockholm, and historian Vilém Prečan, who had settled in Hanover. Cf. Alice Růžičková, "Český dokumentární film v 80. letech: 'Originální Videojournal'" [Czech Documentary Film in the 1980s: "The Original Video Journal"] (Diploma thesis, FAMU, AMU, 2000), pp. 3–4.

[80] Ruml, "Originální videojournal – co mi uvízlo v paměti" [The Original Video Journal – What Stayed in My Memory], pp. 92–94.

distributed on the accessible medium of VHS tape in 1987.[81] One inspiration was the format of the *Videomagazín* [Video Magazine], released quarterly from 1985 in England by the exiled journalist Karel Kyncl using a traditional model of reports and commentaries.[82] The word "original" in the title ironically paraphrased the impossibility of officially copying and disseminating content in communist Czechoslovakia. The title sequence of *OVJ*, created by Joska Skalník with animator Milan Rychetský and featuring the motif of clouds and commentary by Andrej Krok, drew attention to the regular sections and dramaturgy of *OVJ*. The aim was to follow a broad conception of alternative culture in the form of portraits and interviews with scientists, artists, and philosophers. There were reports about literary samizdat publications and the musical underground; ecological problems were also thematised.[83] The reports were produced in small teams not dissimilar from those typical of television production, and when there were dangerous situations, all roles were doubled. In terms of content, *OVJ* was close to the samizdat *Lidové noviny* [The People's Newspaper], which were first published in the same year. Until 1988, the members of *OVJ* had only a single video camera, the editing process took place in secret on state-owned equipment, and the copying onto video tapes was done at various homes. Several copies would be sent abroad, and the rest were distributed in Czechoslovakia, most often as part of meetings at private apartments.[84]

[81] The editorial team included not only Olga Havlová and Jan Ruml but also the amateur filmmaker (and Havel's fellow inmate), cameraman Michal Hýbek; director Pavel Kačírek; actor Jan Kašpar; theatre director and actor Andrej Krob; artist and graphic designer Joska Skalník; and poet Andrej Stankovič. The broader circle of collaborators included many other people tied to the activities of the dissenting Charter 77, and the activities of parallel culture in other cities. In addition to film and video news reports, the Czechoslovak environment also had several other centres of unofficial video work – in Brno, for instance, there was a group gathered around the theatre dramaturg Petr Oslzlý and artist Rostislav Pospíšil, who, among other activities, initiated the filming of exhibition openings and video portraits at the unofficial Galerie Drogerie Zlevněné zboží [Discounted Goods Drug Store Gallery]. For more on this topic, see Sylva Poláková's contribution to this volume.

[82] It is apparent from Havel's correspondence with František Janouch and Vilém Prečan that the idea of a news report video project was first formed at the turn of 1983–1984. Cf. Růžičková, "Český dokumentární film v 80. letech", Appendix I.

[83] The animated title sequence was shot on 35mm film material and transferred to video. The sections of *OVJ* included: Malý zpravodaj [Little Reporter], Náš host [Our Guest], Dokumenty [Documents], Reportáž [Report], Společenská kronika [Social Chronicle], Interview, Dílna [Workshop], Fotogalerie [Photo Gallery], Slovo pro Jiřího Kantůrka [A Word for Jiří Kantůrek]. Cf. Růžičková, "Český dokumentární film v 80. letech", pp. 14–17.

[84] Copies were made at first by Michal Hýbek in his apartment on tape recorders borrowed from his friends. Between 1987 and 1989, *Originální videojournal 0–7* were published, along with two monothematic programmes. Director and researcher Alice Růžičková wrote the following about the preparation of the individual episodes in her diploma thesis on *OVJ*: "Although the individual editions are composed of many different types of material of different qualities and durations, thanks to the work of Pavel Kačírek, who gave them a definitive form, they seem like compact, unified works." Nine editions were prepared during the Velvet Revolution, labelled *Originální videojournal: zvláštní vydání 1–9* [Original Video Journal: Special Editions 1–9], wherein these "documents serve the primary function of documentation and are often filmed in a single long shot with varying transfocation. We sometimes see the date in the bottom right corner, which further supports the raw archival feeling", says Růžičková of these special editions of *OVJ*. The final issue of 1989 is a report from the revolutionary events taking place in Romania, where the *OVJ* team filmed at the end of December in the former presidential palace. For more on this topic, see Růžičková, "Český dokumentární film v 80. letech", pp. 16–17.

The output of the parallel culture stepped beyond the shadow of socialism and into the international limelight mostly thanks to emigrants and their network of samizdat distribution. By contrast, contact with video activists in neighbouring countries where platforms similar to *OVJ* existed was completely absent. The Hungarian video magazine *Black Box* began in 1987, recording everything concerning alternative culture and social or political topics in the country. These activities often involved professional filmmakers and support came from the foundation of the Hungarian-born American philanthropist George Soros, established in 1985 with the aim of championing the notion of an open society. Different content and a different model of approaching the works in terms of selection and thematic focus were the hallmarks of another Hungarian video magazine: *Infermental* (*Internation-Fermentum-Mental*), established in 1980 by the experimental filmmaker and screenwriter Gábor Bódy and his wife Vera. Between 1982 and 1991, ten international editions were published. The individual episodes contained experimental films and video art from across the West and East, with an emphasis on introducing one particular region in each edition. One of the experts invited to participate was Keiko Sei, who worked on the Japanese edition (*Infermental 8*, 1988) and later on the Yugoslavia edition (*Infermental 10*, 1991). Only one Czech film was included in *Infermental* – this was in the 1989 edition, which was prepared by an Austrian editorial team. This episode was introduced by media critic Ilse Gassinger and the artist duo Graf+XYZ as a "mix of the tastes of the West and East, not unlike gastronomy in the Viennese metropolis".[85] The Czech representative was the amateur film *Narozeniny v parku* [Birthday in the Park] (1987) by the Bulšitfilm association, included in a section titled "Explosives in the Hand Baggage". The fact that the Austrian curators selected a Czech amateur film and not video art points to the importance of amateur film in socialist Czechoslovakia; a direct precedent of local video work.[86]

Videoists and Video Artists and their Limited International Contacts

In the 1970s, Miroslav Klivar, a fine art critic and historian, painter, graphic artist, poet, and political functionary of the Communist Party, made the first pioneering attempts at using video.[87] Beginning in 1972 Klivar established and led the Independent video art Prague group

[85] *Infermental 9* presented forty-five works from five countries divided into five sectors. The supervisor of the edition was American video curator Chris Hill. See "Infermental 9 (1989)", accessed 10 Jul 2022, https://zkm.de/de/infermental-9–1989.

[86] For more on Czech amateur film, see Martin Blažíček's contribution to this volume.

[87] Miroslav Klivar most likely cooperated not only with the StB, the secret police, but also with other components of the communist apparatus, e.g., the foreign department. His file, however, was shredded shortly after the revolution, in December 1989. Cf. Miroslav Vodrážka, *Výtvarné umění a jeho subverzivní role v období normalizace: demytologizační a detektivní příběh* [Visual Art and Its Subversive Role in the Normalisation Period: A Detective and Demythologising Story] (Prague: Centrum pro dokumentaci totalitních režimů, 2019).

at the library of the Institut průmyslového designu [Institute of Industrial Design], which also presented an exhibition by Klivar titled Video situace [Video Situation]. The group operated between 1972 and 1990 at the Institute of Industrial Design and later under the auspices of Masarykova akademie umění [Masaryk Academy of Art] in Prague. Members included Klivar, architect Jaroslav Pavelka, and artist Zdeňka Čechová, a representative of computer art and author of several videos and multimedia projects in public spaces, including a programme for a singing fountain in Mariánské Lázně and Křižíkova fontána [Křižík Fountain] in Prague. Although Klivar had the option of travelling abroad and maintained contacts in the Western art world, it was mostly his graphic and painterly work that represented him in the international field.[88] Video can be considered one of the many (new) media formats the artist focused on.[89]

Asynchrony with the international video art scene arose not only due to the highly limited availability of video, but also the atomisation of the situation in Czechoslovakia, and was further intensified by the limited information coming in from abroad. If news and materials from the field of art existed, they were distributed along the lines of individual communication channels, such as those available, for example, to Miroslav Klivar. The professional trips abroad that were made possible by the regime influenced the work of individuals, or, at most, a narrow circle of their friends.[90] A different example of contact with international developments were the state approved export productions. These included presentations of economic and technological development at world fairs, where Czechoslovakia amazed the international community with the ingenuity of

[88] With his interest in poetry, lettrism, and, generally speaking, new forms of art (such as "stamp art", which he established), Klivar's work also entered several international art collections. His name flows through various international symposia and conferences (his specialist field was 20th century French art) as well as exhibitions at which he presented his own art, thanks to which he was often connected to representatives of what was known as unofficial culture, i.e., artists who did not cooperate with the regime. There is a mention of Klivar in a 1976 issue of the Italian magazine *Flash Art*, in an article by Helena Kontová titled "Czechoslovakia: Information". Helena Kontová, "Czechoslovakia: Information", *Flash Art* 10, no. 66–67 (1976), pp. 18–22. Klivar is listed in the article alongside Milan Knížák, Petr Štembera, Vladimír Ambroz, and Dalibor Chatrný. See Klara Kemp-Welch, *Networking the Bloc. Experimental Art in Eastern Europe 1965–1981* (Cambridge: MIT Press, 2018), p. 375

[89] The emphasis on Klivar's video work was, to a certain extent, also cultivated by the artist himself. In his own publication, he considers himself a pioneer of video art. Klivar's position is also confirmed in an article by his colleague from the Institut průmyslového designu [Institute of Industrial Design], author of several videos, and architect Jaroslav Pavelka. Cf. Miroslav Klivar, *Nová umění v Čechách* [New Arts in Bohemia] (Prague: Regulus, 2001); Jaroslav Pavelka, "K dějinám českého videoartu" [On the History of Czech Video Art], *Ateliér* 8, no. 26 (1995), p. 6.

[90] Radek Pilař, a graduate of the Academy of Fine Arts in Prague, was introduced to the work of the neo-avant-garde group Cobra in the Netherlands in 1961, and two years later, he participated in the third biennial of young artists in Paris (Bienal de Paris 1963), where he first saw pop art collages and was introduced to several other art movements. The festival, based on the model of the Biennale in Venice, invited artists from various countries around the world. Another example is the visual artist Milan Knížák, who was a member of the Fluxus international art movement. He was invited to the United States in 1968 and became a delegate of the Eastern European fraction of Fluxus. He also owned a collection of experimental films by this group. For more on Milan Knížák, see Sylva Poláková's contribution in this volume.

its interactive and scenographic projects making use of the moving image, such as Laterna magika (1958) or Kinoautomat (1967). These were produced by professionally diverse and plentiful teams whose work consisted of artistic collaboration and synthesis. By contrast, artists experimenting at home with film material or with video at selected workplaces mostly knew nothing of each other until the 1980s, such as in the case of Radek Pilař and Petr Skala.[91]

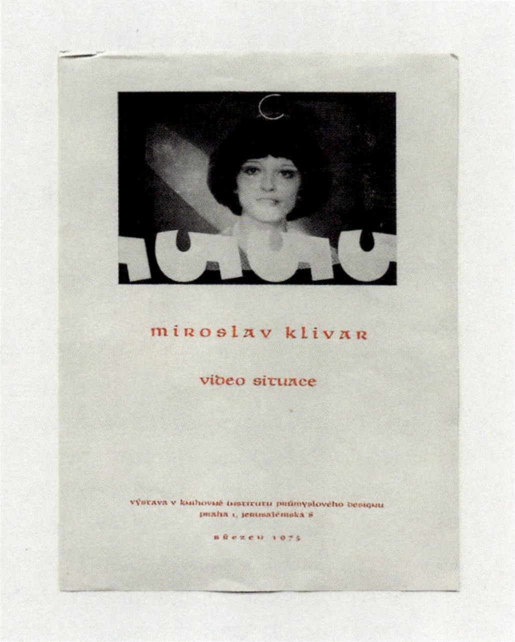

An invitation to Miroslav Klivar's exhibition Video situace, library of the Institute of Industrial Design in Prague, 1975.

Rare one-off presentations took place at the unofficial level, realised in apartments or studios. Radek Pilař only met filmmaker and documentarist Petr Skala, a graduate of FAMU, in 1985, at a private presentation of Skala's experimental films. Their meeting led, among other things, to the initial conception of and eventual establishment of the video department at the Svaz českých výtvarných umělců (SČVU) [Union of Czech Visual Artists]. The purpose of this initiative was to facilitate an official means by which to organise and acquire access to equipment, as well as to open a discussion on the new artistic discipline of video that fascinated both artists. The fragmentary films that both Skala and Pilař made using drawn-on-film animation at home in the 1960s later became the objects of creative interventions during their first video experiments. Like Skala, Pilař began gradually transforming (or archiving) his film works, often short film loops, which began a process of authorial remediation and led to the future existence of several variations of the individual

[91] See Martin Blažíček's contribution in this volume.

works.[92] Skala's and Pilař's experiments attest to their experiences with film material, which partially sets them apart from the artists who used video for its more characteristic features, such as the technical possibilities of immediate recording and presentation.

The very material of film mediates the physical possibility of a divided perspective in which one sees the individual film frames and the soundtrack. Video, on the other hand, is a purely audiovisual medium. "In the sense of its method or type of inquiry, video is more closely connected to sound arts than to film",[93] says Keiko Sei of the differences between film and video. Given its elementary technical foundations, video is an electronic signal channelling information both visual and sonic. The signal

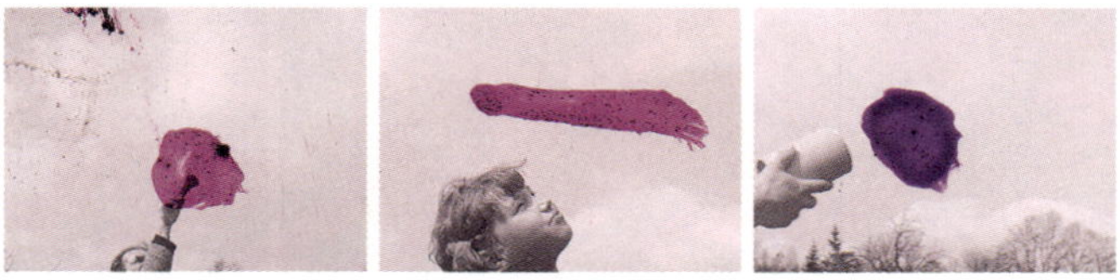

Radek Pilař *Malování do vzduchu* [Painting in the Air] (1965–1990), film, 2 min. In 1984, the artist transferred the original 16mm film to video and experimented with it further.

is constantly in motion, both when the image is broadcast in real time and when it is reproduced. Work with this "fluid pictoriality",[94] as historian of video Yvonne Spielmann describes the beginnings of video art, appears in canonical works in which artists – and often musicians, too – focused on exploring the natural essence of the electronic image, which is said to be "unstable, flexible, unfixed".[95] In contrast to film, the use of video allows for the immediate presentation of the recording as well as working with the simultaneity of an immediate broadcast of the image in the presence of the event recorded (the present tense). These possibilities were explored by one artist a generation later: Tomáš Ruller, a graduate of sculpture at AVU. For his underground events in the 1980s, he used not only documentation but also immediate video broadcast, thus expanding the possibilities of performance.

[92] Thanks to a DIY optical copying machine, Skala was able to process hand-drawn and scratched 16mm film loops. During the 1970s, he began using the first TV title machine available at Czechoslovak Television workplaces to test out chroma keying effects. Film fragments and loops then became the material for live performances with which the artist accompanied musical or pantomimic performances. 1982 saw the beginnings of experiments with video by the painter and illustrator Radek Pilař, who had until then used 16mm film in his non-commissioned and homemade works. The problem of the existence of several variations and media generations of individual artworks is a topic of discussion among curators and archivists. Cf. Martin Blažíček, "Trable s Rumcajsem aneb co počít s českým videoartem 90. let" [Troubles With Rumcajs, or What To Do With Czech '90s Video Art], *Cinepur*, 6 Jun 2017, accessed 10 Jul 2022, http://cinepur.cz/article.php?article=2479; Martin Blažíček, "Mediální pohyby v experimentální animaci Radka Pilaře" [Media Movements in Radek Pilař's Experimental Animation], in *PAF Reader Nr. 1*, eds. Alexandr Jančík – Nela Klajbanová – Martin Mazanec (Olomouc: PAF, 2021), pp. 90–94.

[93] Petr Szczepanik, "Média mezi kulturami a žánry. Rozhovor s Keiko Sei" [Media Between Cultures and Genres. An Interview with Keiko Sei], *Cinepur* 12, no. 23–24 (2002), pp. 16–19.

[94] Yvonne Spielmann, *Video – The Reflexive Medium* (Cambridge: MIT Press, 2008), p. 4.

[95] This type of piece, for instance, also appears in the tests and experiments by Woody Vašulka and his wife Steina. Other artists abroad include Nam June Paik and Ed Emshwiller. Cf. ibid.

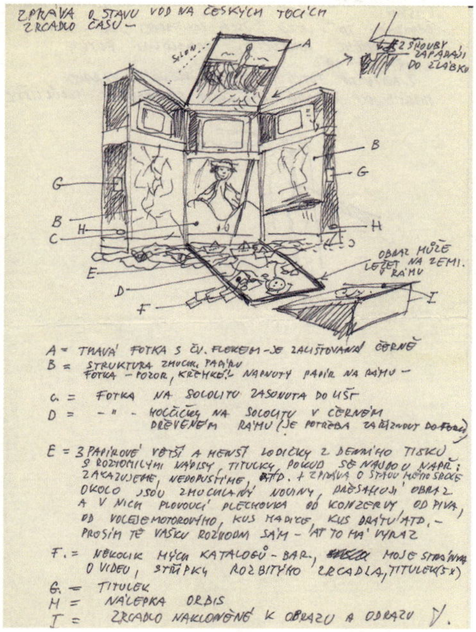

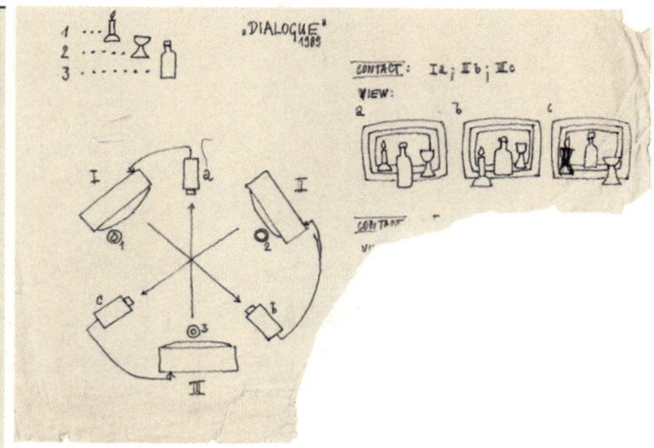

Radek Pilař *Zpráva o stavu vod na českých tocích* [A Report on the State of the Water in Czech Watercourses] (1989), notes and diagram for the video installation
Jaroslav Vančát *Diskuse* [Dialogue] (1989), diagram for the video installation

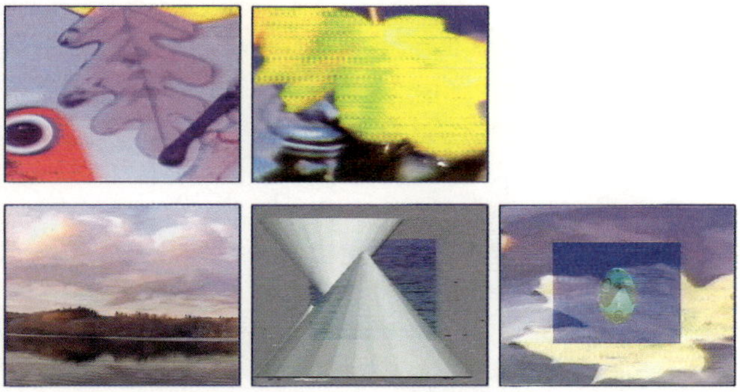

Radek Pilař *Zrcadlo času* [The Mirror of Time] (1985–1992), video, 10 min

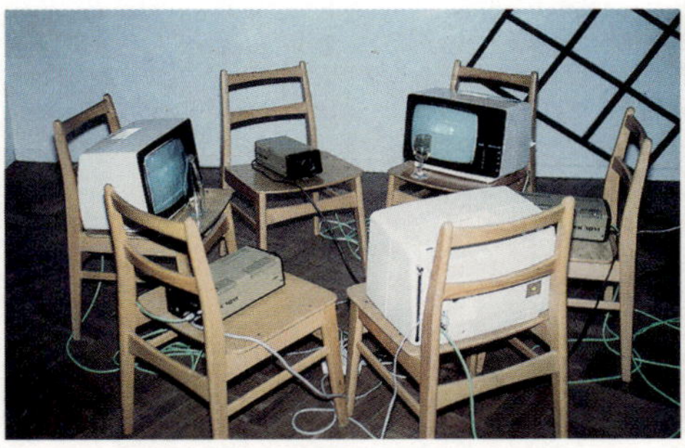

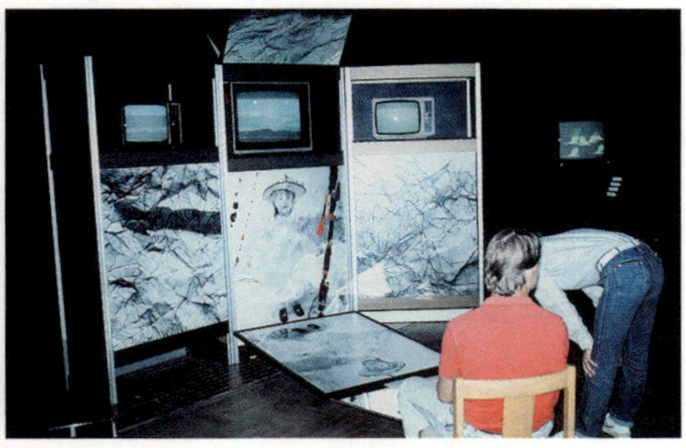

Jaroslava Vančát and Radek Pilař's video installation at the Day of Video Exhibition, Salon of Applied Art '89 by the Fine Artists of Prague, Congressional Palace, Prague, 11 Jul 1989.

Of all Czech artists working in this field, Ruller was probably the closest to the understanding of video art in the international context at the time. His works were determined not so much by a fascination with the technology of video, but rather by the conditions of its use within the space, stage, or the work as a whole and its documentation.[96]

In the Czechoslovak context, there was no video art that explored the modulation of electronic signal or reflections of this technology as we know it from the experimental work of Woody Bohuslav Vašulka and his wife Steina, who emigrated from Czechoslovakia to the United States in the 1960s. Nor do we encounter pieces that deconstruct or critique the cinematic apparatus with video used by artists as a part of the non-programmatic international expanded cinema movement, as seen in Europe or the United States. Instead of a conscious broadening of the media specificities of photography, film, sculpture, or painting through video, Czechoslovak work is marked rather by an illustrative use of the newly available technology. Here is a similar description of this local particularity from the pen of art historian and curator Jiří Zemánek:

> Initial approaches to the medium of video in our lands therefore took on the characteristics of making noble; of subordinating to relatively unambiguous artistic aims. This led to aesthetic methodologies from other fields (particularly painting and animated film) being imported into video on the one hand, and on the other to a certain disregard of the material and structural qualities of the video image itself.[97]

A Plan for Video

In the Czech context, arguments about the uniqueness of video were mostly rehearsed in texts by Radek Pilař, who submitted a proposal for the establishment of a video department at the Union of Czech Visual Artists. Part of his reasoning was rooted in the possibility of future availability whereby the Union would be able to guarantee purchases. The establishment of a separate department was part of Pilař's strategy to protect video from attempts at restrictive monopolisation such as that

[96] Ruller's exclusive approach to video was described in 1990 by art historian and member of the video department, Jaroslav Vančát: "It seems that Tomáš Ruller's conception – which is less determined by the medium during the creation itself, but is defined by the necessity of its presence – is closest to what we know of the use of video in art abroad. Unlike the understanding of video present at the video department, their use is much more direct, independent, less constricting, just as in these societies, the medium itself is not only an exclusively accessible means, instead representing an indelible component of the civilisational equipment both in the area of recording and the area of reception." Jaroslav Vančát, "První kroky videoartu" [The First Steps of Video Art], *Panorama*, no. 2 (1991), p. 5. For more on Tomáš Ruller's performances, see Sylva Poláková's contribution in this volume.

[97] Jiří Zemánek, "Od luminodynamismu k médiu videa" [From Luminodynamism to the Medium of Video], in *Dějiny českého výtvarného umění 1958–2000 VI / 2* [The History of Czech Visual Art 1958–2000 VI / 2], eds. Rostislav Švácha – Marie Platovská (Prague: Academia, 2007), p. 548.

afflicting the art of animation.[98] He wrote the proposal with Petr Skala and handed it over to SČVU in 1987.[99] The department was approved the following year and its members began meeting regularly at the Mánes gallery in Prague. The activities were to include non-commissioned work as well as a variety of services for the other departments of the Union, such as the documentation of exhibitions, artist portraits, educational activities, and a video archive, all of which would also confirm the position of video as a craft.

The actual contents of the document and the language Radek Pilař chose in the project text *Plán oboru video* [Plan for the Video Department] (1987) demonstrate freethinking and emphasise the possibilities for the presentation of the new medium within the crumbling communist apparatus: "In a sense, video can be understood as a form of art that is capable – to a greater extent than some other forms of art – to become the bearer of a democratisation of culture and a cultivation of humanity."[100] Pilař accented the importance of freedom in the sense of ideological and creative independence in the production of art. According to him, video – like film – was "a discovery and an exemplary case of art in the age of technical reproducibility",[101] a reference to the iconic text by Frankfurt school philosopher Walter Benjamin written in the 1930s. Pilař also saw technology of the electronic image as a tool for future work with the moving image, including computer art:

> The specifics of video are determined by electronics. They lie, therefore, in its speed, in the possibility of immediately searching and previewing the files and information about them, the limitless possibilities of combination bordering on the freedom of the imagination and dreams, realised thanks to computer technology Possibilities of immediate representations of three-dimensional concepts, the simulation of narratives, tests, changes, phases.[102]

[98] In the document "Historie výtvarné elektroniky v České zemi" [The History of Art Electronics in the Czech Lands], Radek Pilař recapitulates attempts at establishing the field of video. In 1985, he submitted *Návrh studia obrazového výzkumu* [A Proposal for a Studio of Image Research] as an invitation for collaboration with the animated film department at ČST, but the proposal was rejected. Radek Pilař, "Historie výtvarné elektroniky v České zemi" [The History of Art Electronics in the Czech Lands], typescript, 1990, archive of the heirs of Radek Pilař, p. 1.

[99] The text made its way to the director of the National Gallery in Prague, Jiří Kotalík, and also to a technical worker at the National Gallery, Jaroslav Vančát, who later became one of the members of the newly established department of video.

[100] Radek Pilař, "Plán oboru video" [Plan for the Department of Video], typescript, undated, probably 1987, archive of the heirs of Radek Pilař, p. 1.

[101] Ibid., p. 1.

[102] Ibid., p. 4.

Video Finally Has Its Day

The first joint presentation of the video department – which was also the first group video exhibition in Czechoslovakia[103] – was an exhibition retroactively known as Den videa [Day of Video], which took place on 11 July 1989 as part of the Salón užitého umění '89 [Salon of Applied Art '89] at the Park kultury a oddechu Julia Fučíka [Julius Fučík Park of Culture and Recreation].[104] The event only lasted for a single day due to the lack of available equipment – for financial reasons, the equipment could not be rented for a longer time. This was the first time video was exhibited in the context of applied (i.e., craft-based) work rather than among set pieces of the art world.[105] The unified exhibition architecture within the environment of the Salon was made from black cloth (400 metres of it) and black plastic film, which the architect – and video department member – Miro Dopita used to demarcate and separate the space of the videoists from the other departments presenting at the event. The literal screening out of the videoists' exhibition was not only practical as the drapery made from cloth and plastic also covered up the design of the screens intended for home use. The exhibition presented sixteen autonomous works of art[106] – blocks of computer animations and short videos screened in blocks on monitors and four multi-channel video

[103] The individual exhibition Pokus o portrét 5 D Studia [An Attempt at a Portrait of 5 D Studio] (Tomáš Kepka, Michal Pacina, Marta Karoliová), which featured an eponymous video installation, took place a year earlier at the Fotochema exhibition spaces (Prague, 13–31 Jul 1988).

[104] Den videa [Day of Video] (Salón užitého umění '89 pražských výtvarných umělců [Salon of Applied Art '89 by the Fine Artists of Prague], Sjezdový palác [Congressional Palace], Prague, 11 July 1989), exhibiting artists: Ondřej Černý, Věra Geislerová & René Slauka, Václav Hodan, Roman Milerský, 5 D STUDION (Tomáš Kepka, Michal Pacina, Marta Karoliová), Radek Pilař, Pavel Scheufler, Petr Skala, Lucie Svobodová, Lenka Štarmanová, Ivan Tatíček, Petr Trojan, Jaroslav Vančát. In accordance with texts by Radek Pilař, including an assessment of the event, this Oborový den [Department Day], as the group exhibition was labelled within the organisation, was simplified to Den videa [Day of Video]. The exhibition was repeated under the title Den videa 1989/2018 [Day of Video 1989/2018] at the same location on 4 September 2018. The reconstruction process – in which the author of this text participated as a curator – included discussions with the participating artists. The event took place as part of the filming of Adéla Komrzý's documentary *Viva video, video viva* (2019).

[105] The department of video and the list of artists was not even a part of the catalogue of the Salón, which presents lists of artists in other departments, including the departments of photography, animated and film work, and set design and puppetry. This was partly due to the fact that the presentation of the video department took place in a single day, while the Salón itself lasted for almost two months (1 Jul – 20 Aug 1989). Cf. *Salón užitého umění ,89 pražských výtvarných umělců* [Salon of Applied Arts '89 of the Fine Artists of Prague] (Prague: Svaz českých výtvarných umělců [Union of Czech Visual Artists], 1989).

[106] Computer animation – or "computerové grafiky" [computer graphics] in the language of the period – was introduced by artists working with the interfaces of Amiga computers, namely UMPRUM graduates Lucie Svobodová (*Obrázky* [Pictures], 1989) and Věra Geislerová, as well as René Slauka and Roman Milerský. Single-channel projections of short videos were introduced by photography historian Pavel Scheufler, amateur filmmaker and videoist Ivan Tatíček (*Motýl v tunelu* [Butterfly in the Tunnel], 1989), architect Václav Hodan, as well as Ondřej Černý, and Lenka Štarmanová. Other artists mentioned in connection to the exhibition include those making applied art, specifically the documentation of SČVU exhibitions: Dagmar Kučerová, Zdeněk Raiser, and František Lukáš.

installations.[107] In a text assessing the exhibition and the operation of the department, Pilař said of the various interdisciplinary collaborations and the intermedia nature of the videoists themselves:

> It follows from the work of the members that this is integrated creation, there are no specialised videoists, every participant instead being a painter, sculptor, photographer, graphic artist, architect, or theorist. Attempts to exclude a department member from membership in other departments is in direct opposition to the video department's programme and also with the current state of visual art – both at home and abroad.[108]

The joint ethos of the heterogeneous sample of works presented was, to a certain extent, a critical position in opposition to mass media, particularly television, as well as a belief in the potential of video as a progressive artistic discipline. Radek Pilař's short introductory text for the exhibition makes this critique of television broadcasting explicit: "The ubiquitousness of the television screen and the constant stream of information that flows from it have brought about a deterioration of the image and its perception."[109] Pilař believed that video art, on the other hand, should be a protest "against the consumerist character of television production, against the devastation of the image and the deterioration of the spiritual process that takes place during its perception".[110] These ideas seem to foreshadow the importance and reach of mass media in the 1990s, when video was shortly in use as a democratising medium, although market interests in establishing new media channels soon prevailed.

Several months after the video department's first presentation, the political regime in Czechoslovakia changed. During the Velvet Revolution, video joined photography as a useful tool for disseminating information, replacing – at least in the streets of Prague – official television broadcasts. Students at FAMU and some creative artists prepared journalistic material for an exhibition titled Československý listopad 1989 [November 1989 in

[107] Radek Pilař created an installation titled *Zpráva o stavu vod na českých tocích* [A Report on the State of the Water in Czech Watercourses] (1989), a "visual-musical composition for three monitors and three players", a triptych combining photographic assemblages, and a video titled *Zrcadlo času* [The Mirror of Time] (1989). Petr Skala installed his video *Obrazy noci* [Images of the Night] (1989), a two-channel installation on two televisions placed one on top of the other, accompanied by a live performance by clarinettist Lukáš Matoušek. For his installation *Diskuse* [Dialogue] (1989), Jaroslav Vančát placed three cameras and three televisions on chairs and in the still life presented that arose from the dialogue of camera and television within the closed circuit of live broadcasting he explored the concept of a shifted perception of reality. Michal Pacina and Tomáš Kepka installed a social probe titled *Pokus o portrét* [An Attempt at a Portrait] (1989).

[108] Radek Pilař, "Bez názvu" [Untitled], typescript, August 1989, archive of the heirs of Radek Pilař.

[109] Radek Pilař, "Bez názvu (průvodní text k výstavě oboru videa)" [Untitled (Accompanying Text for the Department of Video Exhibition)], typescript, July 1989, archive of the heirs of Radek Pilař.

[110] Radek Pilař did not personally participate in the exhibition, as he had a heart attack during its preparation, so he effected a "performance in the intensive care unit of Bulovka Hospital, with my heart connected to a Tesla monitor". Pilař, "Historie výtvarné elektroniky v České zemi", p. 1.

Czechoslovakia], which responded to current events and included a series of photographs presented at three locations in Prague. Anna Fárová, a student of art history at the time, was approached with the offer of selecting the photographs for the exhibition at Mánes. The installation also included a video prepared by Radek Pilař, which – period critics agree – made present the atmosphere in Prague in these turbulent days.[111] In a short published text titled *Viva video*, Pilař drew attention to the transformation in the role of official television and the sharing of journalistic content between individuals: "In the first days, video replaced television, which did not participate, and the contents of televised broadcasting were in comical – tragicomical, in fact – conflict with the reality of the desirous crowds on Wenceslas Square, so full of conviction."[112] Keiko Sei characterised the period during the revolution as one of the most interesting moments in the application of video in Czech society, describing, for instance, the number of televisions distributed across city streets. In Czechoslovakia, technology did not play a reserved, ornamental role, instead becoming a semi-natural component of events during the revolution.[113] Retrospectively, Keiko Sei reflected on the events that took place in Czechoslovakia through a series of questions about the local conditions and the use of video: "What importance did video installations have for people in the Czech Republic? What did the term 'video installation' mean to them? Were these ways of more precisely depicting their life, or were they aware of the artistic aspect? Did video artists help in preparing these exhibitions? Or did these installations represent a rare form of art, the spontaneous result of the people's desire and the remarkable circumstances, not influenced by an enforced history of art?"[114] In terms of media, the author

[111] The exhibition Československý listopad 1989 [November 1989 in Czechoslovakia] took place in Prague, instigated by Marcel Deyl. In addition to the Mánes halls, it also took place in Fotochema (coordinated by Vladimír Birgus) and the gallery of Svaz českých fotografů [Union of Czech Photographers] (coordinated by Ján Šmok). The exhibitions were realised by the Radost [Joy] student agency, which was acting under the auspices of the strike committee of FAMU in Prague. Comp. Eva Kúnová, "Československý listopad 1989" [November 1989 in Czechoslovakia], *Ateliér* 2, no. 26 (1989), p. 7. In Radek Pilař's text, we learn about the technical and personnel obstacles that arose during the preparations for the exhibition at Mánes: Many people are working on copying and distribution, especially Michal Caban, who has assumed responsibility for the technical aspects of the matter. [...] Since December 3rd, we have been trying in vain to set up a contract obligation for the professionalisation of its operation and supervision, the player has been arranged so that it runs throughout the day as a loop. [...] As could have been expected, the students did not arrive on December 20th, as they are dealing with more important problems at the faculty. The video went out. The spectators were disappointed. In its broadcast of December 20th, O.F. [Občanské fórum; the Civic Forum] demands a professionalisation of labour, so we demand the same. Signed "Video Mánes". See Radek Pilař, "Bez názvu (text o průběhu výstavy Československý listopad 1989)" [Untitled (Text on the Progress of the Exhibition November 1989 in Czechoslovakia)], typescript, 21 Dec 1989, archive of the heirs of Radek Pilař, p. 2.

[112] Radek Pilař, "Viva Video", *Ateliér* 2, no. 26 (1989), p. 7.

[113] Comp. Keiko Sei, "Po stopách médií" [On the Trail of Media], in *Orbis Fictus. Nová média v současném umění* [Orbis Fictus. New Media in Contemporary Art], eds. Ludvík Hlaváček c– Marta Smolíková (Prague: Soros Center for Contemporary Art, 1995), pp. 148–149.

[114] Keiko Sei, "Solidity in Flux – Video Installation, Media Art and Media Landscape in Eastern Europe during the Transition", in *TRANSITLAND: Video Art from Central and Eastern Europe after the Fall of the Berlin Wall /1989–2009/*, ed. Alina Ignatova (Moscow: Centr kultury i isskustva "MediaArtLab", 2010), p. 43.

of these questions holds exceptional regard for the video installations created for a 1990 exhibition titled Historie československé demokracie [The History of Czechoslovak Democracy], hosted at Dům U Hybernů in Prague. It consisted of a reconstruction of the television screen installations from the Velvet Revolution days. According to Keiko Sei, this exhibition concluded the phase of the 1980s, presenting "journalism and art as the two fields that use video most prominently",[115] by which she was referring to the atomised activities of the samizdat, art societies, and individuals.

With the political transition in November 1989, there was also an immediate demand from Československá státní televize [Czechoslovak State Television] (ČST) for a new title sequence to respond to the changes in the content of the news coverage. The title sequence was put together by several members of the video department and the version used in December broadcasts was completed by Lucie Svobodová and René Slauka. Material selected from sources made available by the television were combined with video effects and geometric computer animation and accompanied by a newly selected typography. This vanguard example of the art of video and computer animation in public broadcasting was accompanied by negative reactions from the general public – complaints were addressed in writing to the station's management and were also accompanied by a satirical song.[116] Another symbolic connection between ČST and the video department was the format of the television weekly. This regular thematic show by the totalitarian TV station, which drew attention to social or cultural topics during the Perestroika period, changed its programming. Petr Skala began preparing the last weekly – on the topic of video art – in 1988, however, it was only broadcast shortly after the Velvet Revolution due to the protracted approval process.[117] Radek Pilař celebrated the presentation of Skala's programme with the words: "The expression video art is filled with content, the department of video and intermedia art exists, images created by electronic means are accepted as equal to other media. The last Czech film weekly popularises video art."[118]

The Interfaces of Video and New Media

After 1989, the art world in Czechoslovakia had to redefine both the relationship between the state and public institutions, as well as its position in relation to the private entities that began to form. The system of financial support changed: the Ministry of Culture established a new methodology for grants intended for individuals, and the position of associations,

[115] Sei, "Po stopách médií", p. 149.

[116] Lucie Svobodová, "Vidíš, tedy jsem Lucie Svobodová" [You See Therefore I Am Lucie Svobodová] (presentation as part of the PAF Spring festival, Olomouc, 26 Mar 2022).

[117] For more on this topic, see Bohdana Kerbachová, "První schůzky naplňovalo snění. Rozhovor s Petrem Skalou" [The First Meetings were Filled with Dreams], *Iluminace* 18, no. 2 (2006), p. 191.

[118] Pilař, "Historie výtvarné elektroniky v České zemi", p. 2.

societies, and foundations in the non-profit sector was gradually defined.[119] The entry of agents and organisations from abroad into the post-socialist territory also bore a considerable influence on the development and support of visual art. The newly developing commercial sector formed an entirely separate segment of financing – in the case of the moving image, this mostly concerned the opportunities for and attraction of new technologies in connection with the ongoing processes of digitisation and the development of the internet.[120] Artists working with the electronic image before the regime change often found work opportunities in the nascent audiovisual industry[121] or at universities.[122] Systematic changes led to the abolishment of SČVU in 1990. The department of video was renamed Klub videa [Video Club] and existed as part of the newly established Unie výtvarných umělců [Union of Visual Artists].[123] The aim of Radek Pilař within Klub videa was to organise a future distribution network,[124] and events organised by the club soon began hosting international guests – some of the first being the Austrian artist and curator Peter Weibel and the American video artist Steve Fagin. For the isolated Czech environment, encounters with artists from abroad – as well as with the emigrants who began returning to Czechoslovakia – meant an introduction to contemporary international developments in the fields of experimental film, video art, and new media.[125]

Radek Pilař described leading representatives of international video art Woody and Steina Vašulka as "apostles of the electronic faith

[119] The position of foundations was gradually adjusted; their legal status was unclear throughout most of the 1990s, making them untrustworthy given how easy it was to take advantage of them in applications for support.

[120] For more on the rise of the internet in the early 1990s, see Marie Meixnerová's contribution to this volume.

[121] Some of these artists established graphic, animation, and special effects studios during the course of the 1990s. The journalist group Originální videojournal was adapted to a production company. As for examples of private studios, we could mention Lucie Svobodová's Factory Art and Ivan Tatíček's Studio DADA. In 1994, Vít Komrzý – Radek Pilař's son-in-law – established the post-production and special effects studio UPP, which is still active today.

[122] Radek Pilař was active at FAMU in Prague. At FaVU in Brno, Pilař's first assistant was Tomáš Ruller, while at AVU in Prague, the new media studio was led by Michael Bielický, a graduate of the Kunstakademie Düsseldorf, since 1991. For more on art universities, see Tomáš Pospiszyl's contribution in this volume.

[123] The same year also saw the production of another group exhibition titled Výtvarníci sekce video [Artists of the Department of Video] (Sokolov, 6–30 Sep 1990), which, in many respects, followed on from the video installations at the Day of Video exhibition at the 1989 Salon of Applied Art. Exhibiting artists were: Radek Pilař, Kateřina Scheuflerová, Petr Skala, Jaroslav Vančát, 5 D studio – Tomáš Kepka, Michal Pacina, Marta Karoliová, and Pavel Jasanský, a photographer and artist working with video sculpture, an unusual form for the Czech context, which was not presented at the first video department exhibition.

[124] "I believe in the proposed Klub videa [Video Club] as a non-commercial distribution network that will allow for the work to be made public. I believe in the young and free art of video." Pilař, "Podmínky pro vznik videa v Čechách", p. 2.

[125] The first international exhibition of video art in Czechoslovakia was a travelling exhibition put together by the Dutch platforms Rijksdienst Beeldende Kunst and Montevideo. The exhibition, titled Imago: Fin de Siècle in Dutch Contemporary Art drew attention to the grasp of new technologies in contemporary Dutch art and was presented in Czechoslovakia in Bratislava (30 May 1991–13 Jun 1991).

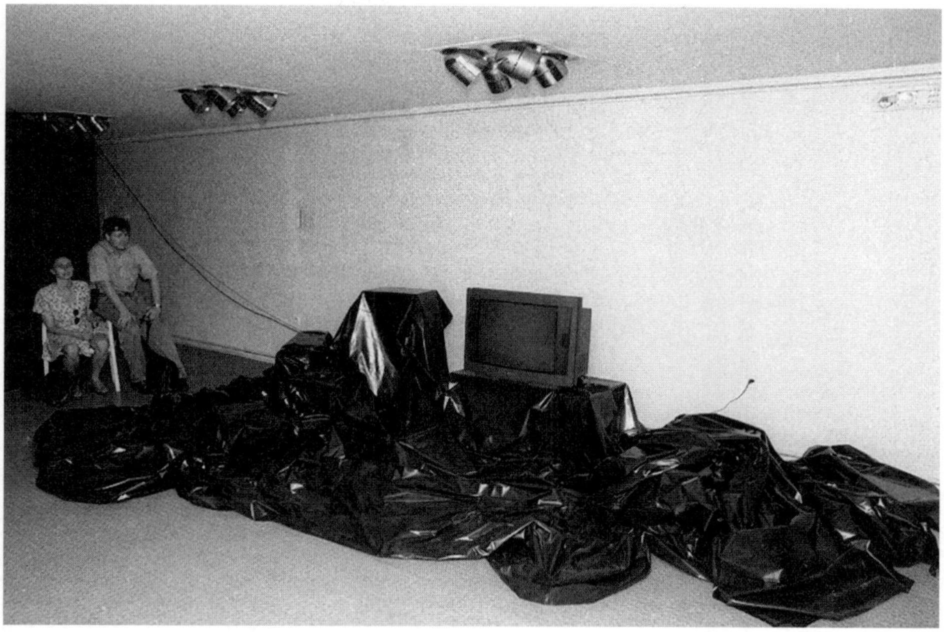

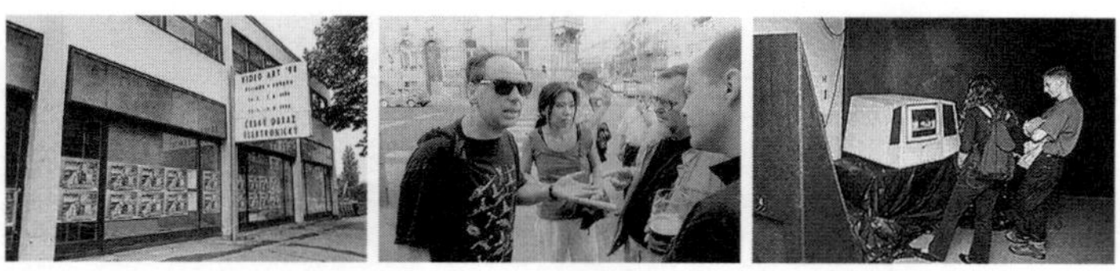

Český obraz elektronický – [The Czech Electronic Image – The Inner Sources], show opening, Mánes, Prague, 12 Jul 1994.

The Czech Electronic Picture – The Inner Sources, exhibition in the underground spaces at Mánes, Prague, 1994.

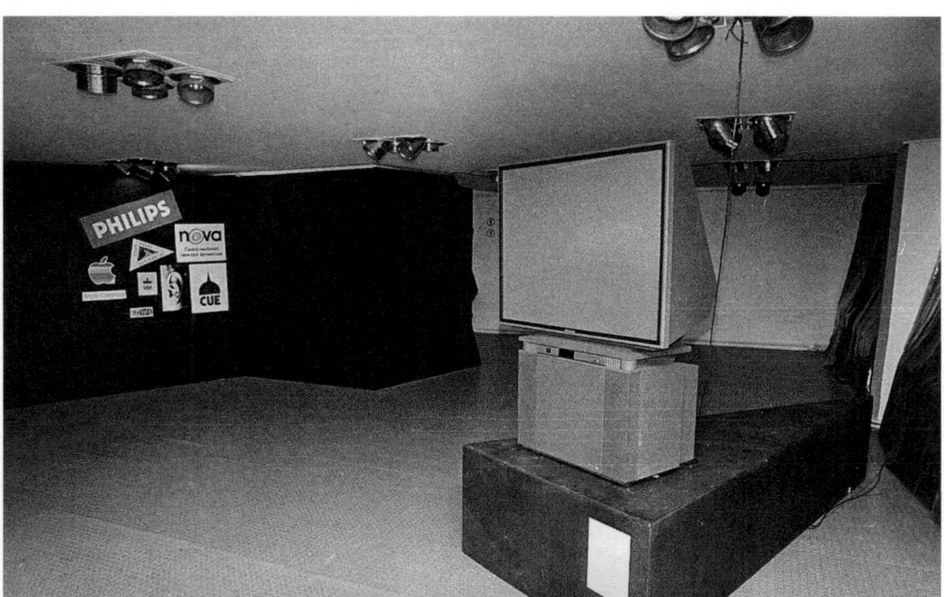

and discoverers of new worlds".[126] The Vašulkas returned to the Czech context with incomparable experiences from the United States. Their video monument *Art of Memory* (1987) was broadcast on the OK3[127] channel of Czechoslovak Television (ČST). This personal reflection on art and historical trauma was "a bang, with which video art entered Czechoslovakia from above", as Pilař describes the "sudden and brutish entry into broadcasting, which, on our channels, so likes uniting with verbalism and variety revues".[128] The Vašulka's presence became an indelible component of symposia and new media exhibitions in Czechoslovakia and the Czech Republic during the course of the 1990s that responded both to the informational gaps that were now being filled in as well as to current developments in the field of the moving image, particularly the use of technology in art. Their activities were closely tied to the Faculty of Fine Arts at the Brno University of Technology, located in Vašulka's home city, and to a collaboration with Tomáš Ruller, who, after Radek Pilař's unexpected death in 1993, took over as studio leader.

Examples of other returning émigrés who were creatively and organizationally active in Czech video art in the early 1990s are Michael Bielický and Petr Vrána. After working as an assistant to Nam June Paik in Düsseldorf, Bielický became the leader of the New Media Studio at the Academy of Fine Arts in Prague (AVU) in 1991. Vrána returned from Kassel to co-initiate the foundation of the Media archiv in 1992, which functioned for several years as a gallery, a cinema, and a gradually developing library of international video art.[129] An overview of video art was presented at the

[126] Radek Pilař used these words to describe the Vašulkas after visiting their seminar at the Klub videa Mánes [Mánes Video Club] with his students from FAMU. Radek Pilař, "Do Prahy a Brna přijeli ze Santa Fe Steina a Woody Vasulkas, zakladatelé světového videoart" [Founders of International Video Art Steina and Woody Vasulka Come to Prague and Brno from Santa Fe] (typescript, 1990), archive of the heirs of Radek Pilař, p. 1.

[127] OK3, the third channel of Czechoslovak Television (referred to as the "Open Channel") broadcast from 14 May 1990 to the dissolution of Czechoslovakia on 31 Dec 1992. It broadcast on a frequency originally intended for pro-Soviet television. The contents of OK3 were mostly foreign-language programmes in their original languages, which the TV company acquired free of charge from satellite stations and productions abroad. The broadcasts also included news, language courses, and works by independent creators. See: Filip Rožánek, "Před 30 lety začala vysílat stanice OK3, přinesla nejen Tutti Frutti" [The OK3 Station Began Broadcasting 30 Years Ago, Bringing More Than Just Tutti Frutti], *lupa.cz*, 14 May 2020, accessed 10 Jul 2022, https://www.lupa.cz/aktuality/pred-30-lety-zacala-vysilat-stanice-ok3-prinesla-nejen-tutti-frutti/.

[128] From the manuscript of a speech by Radek Pilař on the occasion of the opening of the Media archiv, typescript, undated, probably 1992, archive of the heirs of Radek Pilař, p. 2.

[129] The Media archiv was attached to Rock Café in Prague as a gallery and projection hall, also offering the possibility of access to a library containing video cassettes with video art from around the world. The founders of Media archiv included not only Petr Vrána, but also Michal Pacina, Václav Kučera, Michael Bielický, Stanislav Müller, Ivan Tatíček, and members of the association of the Ústav výtvarných umělců (ÚVU) [Institute of Visual Artists]. For more on the role of the Media archiv in the context of Czech attempts at collecting art of the moving image, see Matěj Strnad's contribution to this volume.

exhibition Český obraz elektronický – Vnitřní zdroje[130] [The Czech Electronic Picture – The Inner Sources] (Prague, 1994), which took place in the basement of Mánes. It introduced art made by video artists, underground figures, émigrés, and also works by the first students of the recently established new media studios. The exhibition's curator Jaroslav Vančát described the influence of the characters who entered the local scene after November 1989 and the growing number of students who began working in this field. He drew attention to the "rise in interest in digital media" and also noted that a "divergence in plurality of interest in all the fields these tumultuous developments bring up is gradually taking shape".[131] Twelve televisions and one projection space presented loops of both monographic[132] and group-based screening blocks. The breadth of works was stunning, which many critics at the time perceived as disorganised and hard to digest.[133] The exhibition also included a presentation of technology in the Media archiv and a lecture series in the library of the National Technical Museum,[134] which focused on the international development of the electronic image and the Czech multimedia tradition of the cinematic avant-garde. Jiří Lehovec – an avant-garde film director between the wars, lecturer at FAMU, and later also a member of the

[130] Český obraz elektronický – Vnitřní zdroje [The Czech Electronic Picture – The Inner Sources], Prague, Mánes, 12 Jul – 7 Aug 1994, exhibiting artists: Michael Bielický, Petr Bradáček, Zdeňka Čechová, Lubomír Čermák, Miro Dopita, Jennifer De Felice, Věra Geislerová, Radek Hanák, Pavel Hart, Martin Hřebačka, Pavel Jasanský, Tomáš Kepka, Aurel Klimt, Světlana Kulíšková, Marek Mařan, Tomáš Mašín, Roman Milerský, Michal Pacina, Marian Palla & Petr Váša, Dominika Randlíková & Patrik Pašš & Ondřej Nývlt & Michaela Pohořelá, Radek Pilař, Tomáš Ruller, Kateřina Scheuflerová, Petr Skala, René Slauka, Josefína Slezáková, Lucie Svobodová, Ivan Tatíček, Vladimír Vaca, Tomáš Veškrna, Petr Vrána, Woody Vašulka, Janka Žáčková. The exhibition was partly organised by Ivan Tatíček and the exhibition architecture was designed by Miro Dopita. The exhibition was organised in 1994 by the Asociace videa a intermediální tvorby (AVIT) [Association of Video and Intermedia Art], a subsection of ÚVU.

[131] Comp. Jaroslav Vančát, "Český obraz elektronický" [The Czech Electronic Picture], in *Český obraz elektronický „vnitřní zdroje“* [The Czech Electronic Picture "The Inner Sources], ed. Ivan Tatíček – Ivo Jebousek (Prague: DADA, s.r.o., 1994), p. 14.

[132] Individual monitors presented the work of Radek Pilař, Petr Skala, Lucie Svobodová, Michael Bielický, and Tomáš Ruller.

[133] The editor of the cultural section, Lenka Lindaurová, said the following about the exhibition in the newspaper *Lidové noviny* [The People's Newspaper]: In the lower spaces of Mánes in Prague, the first collective exhibition of Czech multimedia art, Český obraz elektronický, attempts to map video art in the Czech lands. This form is in its infancy and the exhibition is more of an overview than a curatorial project. [...] The high attendance makes this hunger for visual information clear, and it also suggests a fascination with the medium of television. At the beginning of the exhibition space, in which televisions are placed in separate cubicles, there is an electronic menu. The visitor can move freely around a kind of 'table of contents' of the exhibition, and select for themselves which items on the video menu caught their eye. Because walking around the individual screens, which feature up to ten loops of two to six minutes – and process their message as well – is virtually impossible. Lenka Lindaurová, "Naše elektronická budoucnost" [Our Electronic Future], *Lidové noviny* [The People's Newspaper] 7, 2 Aug 1994, p. 11.

[134] It included the following contributions – Jiří Lehovec: Filmová avantgarda 30. let [Avant-Garde Film of the 1930s], with a lecture accompanied by film screenings; Radúz Činčera: Multimédia 50. a 70. let [Multimedia of the 1950s and '70s]; Jaroslav Vančát: Gnoseologické a komunikační aspekty zobrazování [The Gnoseological and Communicational Aspects of Imaging]; Michael Bielický: Nová média v komunikaci [New Media in Communication]; Woody Vašulka: Koncepty a instalace [Concepts and Installations].

department of video – also made a contribution to this series. He was one of the few figures in the Czech context to connect the tradition of avant-garde cinema with the interest in contemporary video.[135] The exhibition lasted only two weeks and was above all a notable attempt to present an exhaustive overview of Czech art of the moving image and catalogue it.[136] An anthology was published to accompany the show, which included factographic information about the artists including contact information, thus partially playing the part of a distribution catalogue. At the same time, the main hall of the Mánes exhibition space hosted an exhibition related in both theme and personnel: a curatorial project by Vlasta Čiháková-Noshiro and Keiko Sei titled Video art '94: Příroda v pohybu [Video Art '94: Nature in Motion]. Unlike the exhibition in the basement, which was built purely on the moving image and presentation of Czech work, the curators of Nature in Motion worked more extensively with the intermedia overlap between the individual installations, as well as with the international context, which functionally broadened the interpretive framework of both the exhibitions taking place in the building.[137]

That same year saw the opening of an exhibition in Slovakia titled Video – vidím – Ich sehe: Slovenské, české a švýcarské videoumění [Video – I See – Ich sehe: Slovak, Czech, and Swiss Video Art].[138] The grand-scale exhibition project was the work of curators Eshter Marii Jungo, Maria Smolenická, and Katarína Rusnáková and defined the position of contemporary video art with examples of installations from these three countries. According to reviews from the time, the curatorial trio managed to step beyond the framework of a facile dialogue between the eastern isolation of Czech and Slovak video art with a country (Switzerland) whose video art tradition had an extra twenty years in which to develop. A catalogue was published to accompany the exhibition, in which Vlasta Čiháková-Noshiro introduced the Czech-Slovak context (also in connection with the Mánes exhibition) and Keiko Sei discussed the situation in Eastern Europe in the pan-European context. The latter text drew attention to the shared experience in Europe after the fall of the Iron Curtain and the opening up of information

[135] Petr Skala is one of those who describe Jiří Lehovec as an inspiring pedagogue and an active participant in discussions at meetings of the department of video. For more, see Kerbachová, "První schůzky naplňovalo snění. Rozhovor s Petrem Skalou", p. 190.

[136] The selection of works also served as a foundation for the TV programme *Antologie českého umění videa* [An Anthology of the Czech Art of Video] (1996), produced for Czech Television by Petr Skala.

[137] Video art ,94: Příroda v pohybu, Mánes, [Video Art '94: Nature in Motion], Prague, 14 Jul – 7 Aug 1994, exhibiting artists: Michael Bielický, Bettina Gruber, Gary Hill, Tomáš Mašín, Vladimír Merta, Jiří Příhoda, Peter Rónai, Tomáš Ruller, Christa Sommerer & Laurent Mignonneau, Woody Vašulka, Peter Weibel, Jana Želibská.

[138] Video – vidím – Ich sehe: Slovenské, české a švýcarské videoumění [Video – I See – Ich Sehe: Slovak, Czech, and Swiss Video Art], Považská galéria umenia v Žiline [Váh Region Art Gallery in Žilina], 14 Sep – 30 Oct 1994, exhibiting artists: Marie José Burki, Alexander Hahn, Simon Lamunière, Muda Mathis, Tomáš Mašín, Peter Meluzín, René Pulfer, Peter Rónai, Tomáš Ruller, Anna Wienteler, Jana Želibská. The exhibition was also presented at Dům umění města Brna [Brno House of Arts] (Brno, 15 Dec 1994 – 22 Jan Jan 1995), Galérii mesta Bratislavy [Bratislava City Gallery] (Bratislava, 10 Feb – 26 Mar 1995), and Kunstmuseum Thun (Thun, 27 Apr – 5 Jun 1995).

channels: "As concerns the art scene in the 1990s, there is no real difference between the G7 countries and Eastern Europe."[139] During the preparations for this Czech-Slovak-Swiss project, some of the participating artists responded to the particular exhibition possibilities in the individual cities, adapting their works to the various spatial conditions. The exhibition at the Dům umění [House of Art] in Brno significantly contributed to Czech critics' perception of art of the moving image as an autonomous artistic practice.[140]

In the 1990s, an intermedia approach to technology and new media at art universities was demonstrated not only in pedagogical conceptions but also in the frequent participation of international guests in teaching or in the preparation of exhibitions and symposia. In Brno, examples of the latter included the international new media festival Hi-Tech / Umění [Hi-Tech / Art] (1992–1997), which took place at the same time as the Invex computer trade fair. On the side of FaVU, it was co-organised and curated by Tomáš Ruller with the participation of his students. One of the individuals who participated in conceiving the festival was Michal Klimeš, who was a representative of Silicon Graphics, the company that sponsored the festival.[141] AVU in Prague, along with the studio led by Michael Bielický, participated in the programme in the form of a series of symposia dedicated to the legacy of philosopher Vilém Flusser, picking

[139] With the fall of the Iron Curtain, Western countries provided those from the former Eastern Bloc with many television and radio programmes, since, according to Keiko Sei, "there was a general conviction that there was a hunger for information in Eastern European countries. The information mania of Eastern Europe thus led to the collapse of the image of a relatively calm Europe". Keiko Sei, "Za všetkými hranicami" [Beyond All Borders], in *video vidím ich sehe: slovenské, české a švajčiarske videoumenie*, eds. Esther Maria Jungo – Katarína Rusnáková – Maria Smolenická (Bern, 1994), pp. 59–61.

[140] The series of recent video art exhibitions has culminated with exceptional quality with this travelling international project titled Video-vidím-ich sehe [...] Unlike the exhibitions that did little more than provide information on video art, here, this exhibition is a well-conceived whole – something that cannot be said about the thematic summer exhibition Příroda v pohybu [Nature in Motion] at Mánes in Prague. [...] Thanks to its accessibility to visitors and an excellent catalogue, it is also an act of 'agitation' that clearly emphasises what an important and natural component of art video represents today. Radek Horáček, "Výstava videoartu s lidskou tváří dorazila do Brna" [An Exhibition of Video Art with a Human Face Arrives in Brno], *Mladá fronta,* 22 Dec 1994.

[141] The festival programmes included presentations, screenings, or exhibitions by artists from abroad working with new technologies. Discussions were held on the transformations in the field of communication as a consequence of the spread of new media and the internet, including the idea of virtual symposia. In 1996, a festival titled Allvision took place at the Brno House of Arts, which included an extensive retrospective of the work of Steina Vašulka. Artists participating in or presenting their work at the festivals in Brno included Stelarc, Gideon May, or historian of video Chris Hill. The presence of artists and researchers from abroad was often contrasted with student works. This was a unique platform in the Czech environment, initiated in 1992 by a presentation by the Vašulkas and continually developed by curators and invited researchers and students until 1997, when the festival took place for the last time, curated by Jennifer De Felice.

up the thread of his influential 1991 lecture in Prague.[142] Both regular events in Brno and Prague influenced the new media discourse of the time to a considerable extent.[143] Also grouped with the series of symposia in Prague is the conference titled Umělé životní prostředí jako umělecké dílo [The Artificial Environment as a Work of Art], which was realised at the Valdštejnská jízdárna [Waldstein Riding School][144] in close connection with an extensive exhibition project, Orbis Fictus, whose subtitle was Nová média v současném umění [New Media in Contemporary Art] (Prague, 1995–1996). The exhibition was produced by Sorosovo centrum pro současné umění [Soros Centre for Contemporary Art] (SCSU), which was led by art historian Ludvík Hlaváček, who curated the exhibition together with Marta Smolíková. A number of consultants and participating artists were also involved in producing the project, with many artists creating brand new works for the show. Keiko Sei states that the works that were closest to the original intention were projects that engaged directly with scientific knowledge and technology – where the interdisciplinary ties between fields could be applied – as well as civic applications of new technologies.[145] A pervasive theme in both the conference papers and the exhibition catalogue was the new media tradition of Czech art, which was to be found in avant-garde film, polyvision, kineticism, and computer art. This historicising layer in the interpretation of new media, however, did not appear at the exhibition itself, which presented contemporary works from the Czech environment. Although this exhibition is considered historically to be a pivotal moment in the debate on new media elements in Czech art, for most of the participating artists (barring a few exceptions) the exhibition was more of an opportunity for isolated artistic experiments that were not further developed.

[142] The initiatory moment that retroactively formed post-revolutionary debates on new technology and the role of computers and media in Czechoslovakia was a lecture titled "Masová komunikace, elitní komunikace a změna paradigmat" [Mass Communication, Elite Communication, and Paradigm Change], delivered by Prague native and philosopher Vilém Flusser, at the Goethe Institut in 1991. Further symposia under the patronage of the same institution dedicated to Flusser's legacy took place in 1992–1997, 2001, and 2007. These conferences were conceived between 1992 and 1997 by Andreas Ströhl, partly in cooperation with Michael Bielický, who visited the Flussers in 1991 at their home in Robion in the south of France. In 1994, Bielický edited the video material he filmed there and presented the resulting documentary, *Vilém Flussers Fluß*, at the symposium.

[143] Art historian, artist, curator, and pedagogue Miloš Vojtěchovský states that: "the 'Prague new media symposia' were framed by the optimistic atmosphere of the newly connected regions of Western and Eastern Europe and were also the expression of dialogue in the fields of media studies and digital art. Flusser's ideas about technical images, the apparatus, and communicology generated lively responses not only among theorists but also among artists". Miloš Vojtěchovský, "Předpoklady budoucnosti: Mediální archeologie" [Prerequisites of the Future: Media Archaeology], April 2017, accessed 10 Jul 2022, https://agosto-foundation.org/cs/predpoklady-budoucnosti-medialni-archeologie.

[144] Orbis Fictus, National Gallery in Prague, Valdštejnská jízdárna [Waldstein Riding School], Prague, 30 Nov 1995 – 1 Jan 1996, exhibiting artists: Lubor Benda, Veronika Bromová, David Cajthaml, Lubomír Čermák, David Černý, Federico Díaz, Vojta Dukát, Friedrich Förster, Michal Gabriel, Milan Guštar, Martin Janíček, Monika Karasová, Pavel Kopřiva, Tomáš Mašín, Robert Novák, Tomáš Ruller, Ester Řádová, Šárka Sedláčková, Silver, Lucie Svobodová, Zdeněk Sýkora, Jan Trnka, Tjebbe van Tijen, Janka Vidová Žáčková, Miloš Vojtěchovský.

[145] These included projects by Lubor Benda that made use of the Tamara radar system, Pavel Kopřiva's collaboration with the Czech Meteorological Institute, and a multimedia installation by Miloš Vojtěchovský and Tjebbe van Tijen, "Oživený Orbis Pictus" [Orbis Pictus Brought to Life]. Comp. Sei, "Po stopách médií", pp. 154–155.

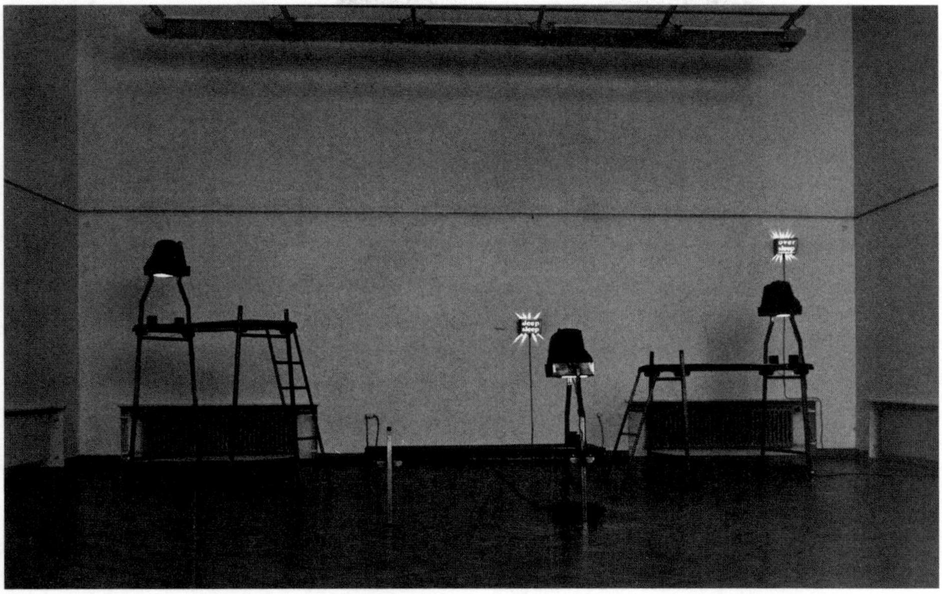

Video – I See – Ich Sehe: Slovak, Czech, and Swiss Video Art, exhibition at the House of Arts, Brno, 1994.

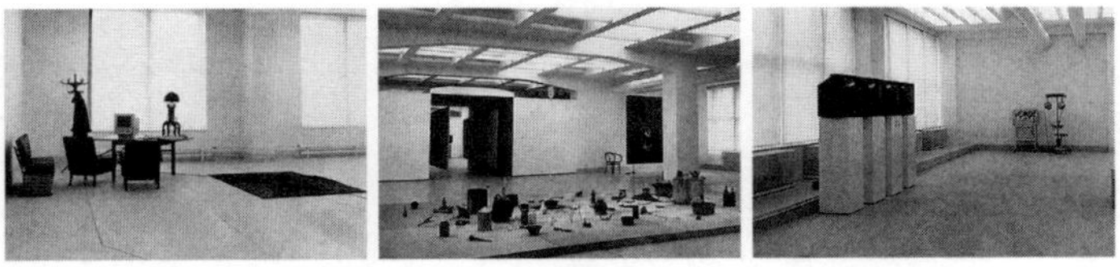

Dawn of the Magicians? (Art, Science, Society at the Turn of the Millennium), exhibition at the Trade Fair Palace, National Gallery, Prague, 1996–1997.

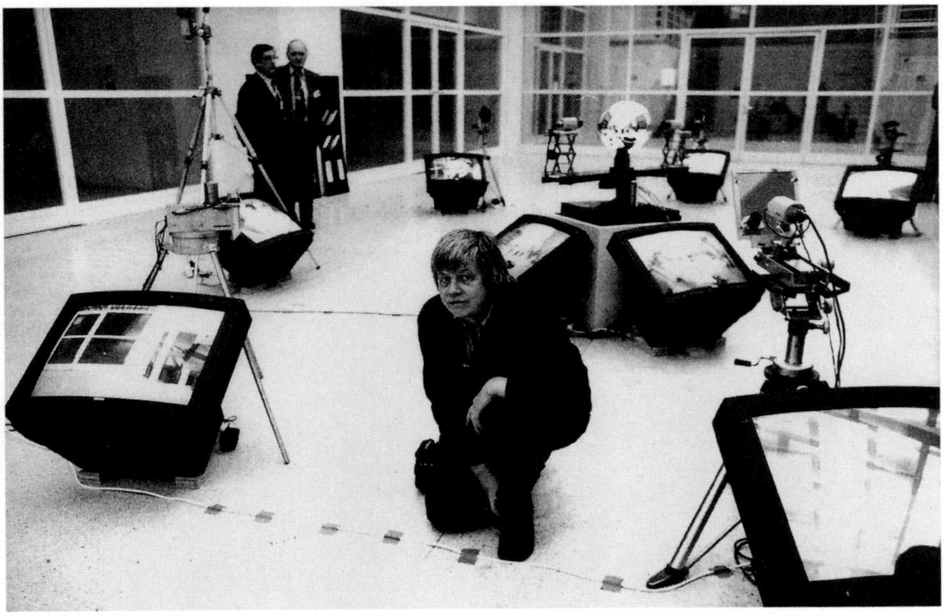

Steina Vasulka in her installation at the exhibition Dawn of the Magicians? (Art, Science, Society at the Turn of the Millennium).

Not long after Orbis Fictus, a series of exhibitions was initiated by the National Gallery. The conception of these exhibitions was oriented toward thinking about video and the possibilities of new media in the broader context of contemporary art and its operation. The cycle of exhibition chapters titled Jitro kouzelníků? (Umění věda společnost na přelomu tisíciletí) [Dawn of the Magicians? (Art, Science, Society at the Turn of the Millennium)] was organised in 1996 and 1997 by the newly established director of the modern and contemporary art collection at the National Gallery in Prague, Jaroslav Anděl, together with curators Miloš Vojtěchovský and Ivana Raimanová. The concept of the exhibition was an open laboratory system initiated by a series of questions aimed at the position of scientific research in art and society and also at the transformation of the role of the museum during the course of the 20th century. Jitro kouzelníku? also involved many performances, audiovisual and sound-based presentations, as well as lectures and conferences that contributed to the overall laboratory concept. The original plan was to prepare four chapters over the course of two years. These chapters would be based on a reflection of the "transitional and uncertain in the twilight and red skies of the millennium",[146] as Miloš Vojtěchovský described the project. In the end, only two chapters were ultimately produced: Od mediálních kreseb ke kyberprostoru [From Medium Drawings to Cyberspace][147] and Ztracené a nalezené [Lost and Found].[148] Parallels between the artists were sometimes criticised for being too loose, almost random,[149] but this does

[146] See Miloš Vojtěchovský, "Jitro kouzelníků. Umění, proutkaři a hrozivý konec milénia" [Dawn of the Magicians? Art, Diviners, and the Terrifying End of the Millennium], *Vokno 2000* 1, no. 1 (1997), p. 34.

[147] Jitro kouzelníků? (Umění věda společnost na přelomu tisíciletí) [Dawn of the Magicians? (Art, Science, Society at the Turn of The Millennium)], I. Od mediálních kreseb ke kyberprostoru [I. From Medium Drawings to Cyberspace], Fair Trade Palace, National Gallery in Prague, Prague, 18 September 1996–28 September 1997, exhibiting artists: Michael Bielický, Lubor Benda, Pavel Brázda, Ladislav Čarný, Jiří Černický, Paul DeMarinis, Rudolf Dzurko, Peter Fischli & David Weiss, Martin Janíček, Jan Jedlička, Beneš Knüpfer, Vladimír Kokolia, Jiří Kornatovský, Matej Krén, František Kupka, Karel Malich, Frank Josef Malina, Julius Mařák, Jiří Matoušek, Ilona Németh, Petr Nikl, Jiří Příhoda, Roman Signer, B. K. S., Martin Spanjaard, Zdeněk Sýkora, Miloš Šejn, Josef Váchal, Janka Vidová, Martin Zet. See also Jitro kouzelníků? (Umění věda společnost na přelomu tisíciletí) [Dawn of the Magicians? [Art, Science, Society at the Turn of The Millennium], Agosto Foundation, accessed 10 June 2022, https://www.agosto-foundation.org/cs/jitro-kouzelniku-umeni-veda-spolecnost-na-prelomu-tisicileti.

[148] Jitro kouzelníků? (Umění věda společnost na přelomu tisíciletí), II. Ztracené a nalezené [II. Lost and Found], Fair Trade Palace, National Gallery, Prague, 11 Apr – 28 Sep 1997, exhibiting artists: Jiří Bartůněk, Barbara Benish, Pavel Brázda, Peter Campus, Atilla Csörgő, Jiří David, František Drtikol, Gerco de Ruijter, Arnold Dreyblatt, Eye Scratch, Daniel Fischer, Graham Harwood, Nan Hoover, Dalibor Chatrný, Joan Jonas, Pavel Kopřiva, Otis Laubert, George Legrady, Jiří Příhoda, Tennessee Rice Dixon & Jim Gasperini, Tomáš Ruller, Cindy Sherman, Andres Serrano, Surrealistická skupina [the Surrealist Group], Vladimír Škoda. See also ibid.

[149] Art critic and curator Marek Pokorný, for instance, in his review for *Lidové noviny*, pointed out the imbalance present in the exhibition in terms of work selection and contexts highlighted, describing the former in the following manner: "as if you were to say 'water' and then place next to each other a boiler, a view of a river by Chittussi, Křižík's Fountain, and a video by Pipilotti Rist". Marek Pokorný, "Po jitru kouzelníků nastává úplně banální den" [After the Magicians' Morning Comes an Utterly Banal Day], *Lidové noviny*, 1996, accessed 10 Jul 2022, https://www.agosto-foundation.org/cs/jitro-kouzelniku-umeni-veda-spolecnost-na-prelomu-tisicileti.

not diminish the importance of the conception that brought together the selected examples and media, with video assuming an entirely post-media position, related not only to video art or new media tendencies but to contemporary art more generally.

Reconstruction of History: The Traces Lead to Animation

Early in the third millennium, leading international visual art institutions decided to organise thematically related symposia whose subject was the history of video art and also the position of moving image art in the gallery more generally. The questions were aimed at both the transformations of the moving image as a consequence of its presence in galleries – the so-called "white cubes" – and at the positions of cinematography and visual art themselves. During the course of the 1990s, the supply of projection systems (data beamers) was complemented by television monitors, which were closely connected to gallery forms of presentation for video art. The use of projections reached a peak on the international scene at contemporary art festivals in the early 2000s,[150] where the projection possibilities of video brought the moving image closer to spectators' experience of the movie theatre. Another common element of these symposia is that they demarcated the end of the golden age of video art in the early 1990s, when video art was still connected to the analogue nature of the recording and the dual form of presentation at exhibitions or as televised broadcasting.[151] From the beginning of the new millennium, the field of the moving image in Europe and America was understood as part of the artistic

[150] In his dissertation, film historian Petr Szczepanik analyses "spaces between the images" using the conceptual framework of French film theorist Raymond Bellour, whose:commentary on the Venice Biennale detailed how certain exhibitions of media artists (e.g., Doug Aitken, Pipilotti Rist, Bill Viola, Douglas Gordon) are in direct competition with film by decomposing and redistributing the dispositifs of cinema and the heritage of film history: they distribute projections of various forms, sizes, and genre conventions in the spaces of the gallery, composing projection screens into architectural forms and inviting the visitor to walk among them, enter them and depart, gleaning a new form of quasi-cinematic experience from these passages. Petr Szczepanik, "Filmy, které vidí vlastní vidění. Strategie intermediality a reflexivity v současné kinematografii" [Films That See Their Own Seeing. Strategies of Intermediality and Reflexivity in Contemporary Cinema] (Dissertation, Masaryk University, Brno, 2002), p. 27. When putting together documenta 12 in Kassel in 2007, curator Ruth Noack and artistic director Roger M. Buergel invited Alexander Horwath, a curator from the Austrian Film Museum in Vienna, to assist them on the issue of the moving image in the gallery. Horwath situated film at the festival within the programmatic grid of the Gloria cinema in Kassel, by which he attempted to avoid the artificial relocation of certain cinematic works into unnatural installation forms that, when attempted in galleries, seems more like remakes (or parodies) of the works grouped under the expanded cinema banner, for instance. See: Paolo Cherchi Usai, David Francis, Alexander Horwath, Michael Loebenstein, "Curatorial Values: Two Case Studies", in *Film Curatorship. Archives, Museums, and the Digital Marketplace*, eds. Paolo Cherchi Usai – David Francis – Alexander Horwath – Michael Loebenstein (Vienna: SYNEMA, 2008), p. 132.

[151] Curator Bill Horigan mentions in particular the symposium Moving Image as Art: Time-Based Media in the Art Gallery (Tate Modern, London, 2001) and an event dedicated to the history of art organised by the Art Institute of Chicago and MoMA in New York. The symposium did not ultimately take place due to a strike, but the structure and thematic areas were presented in materials available in advance. Comp. Bill Horrigan, "Five Years Later", in *Art and the Moving Image: A Critical Reader*, ed. Tanya Leighton (London: Tate – Afterall, 2008), pp. 293–294.

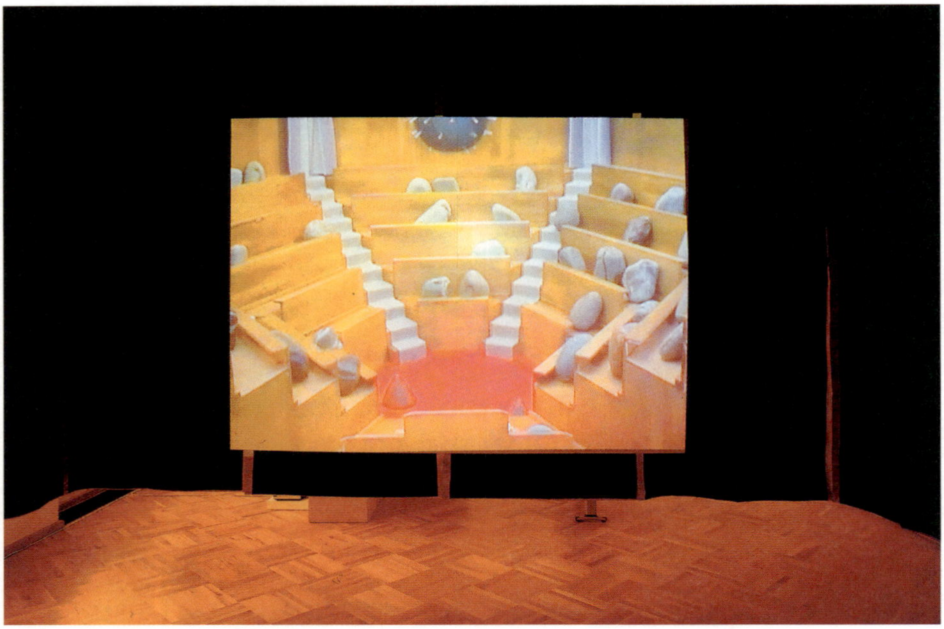

Eva Marisaldi *La Legenda* (2002), installation at the exhibition Movies Without Cinema: The Animation and Contemporary Art.

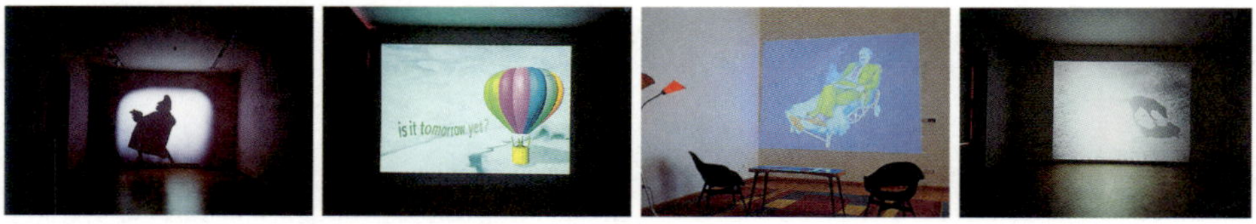

Movies Without Cinema: The Animation and Contemporary Art, exhibition at the Brno House of Arts, 2003.

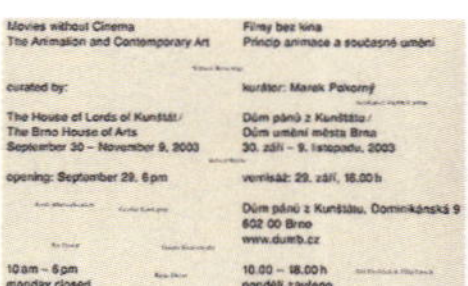

Movies without Cinema
The Animation and Contemporary Art

curated by:

The House of Lords of Kunštát /
The Brno House of Arts
September 30 – November 9, 2003

opening: September 29, 6 pm

10 am – 6 pm
monday closed

Filmy bez kina
Princip animace a současné umění

kurátor: Marek Pokorný

Dům pánů z Kunštátu /
Dům umění města Brna
30. září – 9. listopadu, 2003

vernisáž: 29. září, 18.00 h

Dům pánů z Kunštátu, Dominikánská 9
602 00 Brno
www.dumb.cz

10.00 – 18.00 h
pondělí zavřeno

springsia

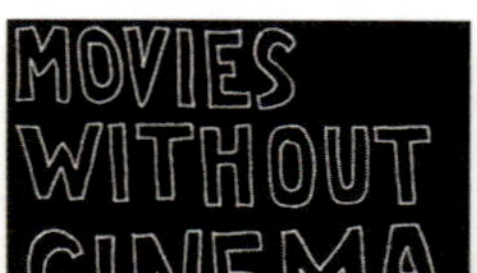

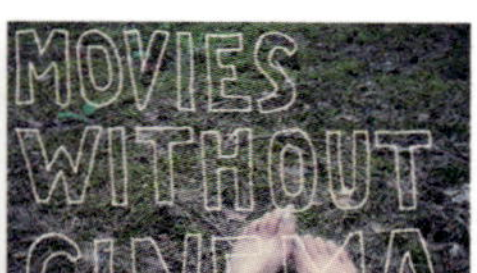

canon. The process of legitimation is also corroborated by the number of exhibitions abroad that focused on historical connections and particular moments in various historical periods of experimental film and video art, as well as their future.[152]

The interchangeability or interpenetration of video film takes place at a time when both practices of the production of moving images are being digitised. This effect is well illustrated by the transformation in perceptions of the category of animation not only as a spectrum of techniques, but also as an overarching form for the moving image. Animation was the subject of a 2003 issue of *Cinepur* magazine. The Olomouc-based PAF festival began at the same time, which curator Marek Pokorný links to the conception of the exhibition Filmy bez kina: Principy animace a současné umění [Movies Without Cinema: The Animation and Contemporary Art],[153] which he produced for the House of Arts in Brno.

> Both the festival in Olomouc and *Cinepur* primarily focused on animation as a phenomenon of cinema, while my own approach was tied to the transgression of artforms and a transferral of principles between individual fields. And, in contrast to the extensive and comprehensive Animations[154] festival, I had intended from the start to use a selected system of references to various animation traditions, especially in relation to the environment in the Czech Republic and the local paradigm of considering animation a specific/autonomous art form.[155]

Part of the title of the exhibition, "movies without cinema", was based both on a paraphrase of one of *Cinepur* magazine's regular sections, "mimo kino" ("outside the cinema")[156] and on the thesis of the interwar film critic Siegfried Kracauer, who did not consider animation to be a part of cinema, instead

[152] From this period, I would mention the exhibitions Into the Light: The Projected Image in American Art 1964–77 (Whitney Museum, New York, 2001), Future Cinema: The Cinematic Imaginary after Film (ZKM, Karlsruhe, 2002), and X-Screen. Film Installations and Actions (MUMOK, Vienna, 2003).

[153] Filmy bez kina: Principy animace a současné umění [Films Without Cinema: Principles of Animation and Contemporary Art], Brno House of Arts, 30 Sep – 9 Nov 2003, exhibiting artists: Katja Davar, Havlíček & Cenek, Robert Hlůže, William Kentridge, Avish Khebrehzadeh, Tamás Komoróczky, Cecilia Lundqvist, Eva Marisaldi, Vít Pancíř, IN / OUT 2003.

[154] The exhibition was curated by Carolyn Christov-Bakargiew in cooperation with Larissa Harris, Animations (P.S.1 Contemporary Art Center, New York, 14 Oct 2001 – 13 Jan 2002; Kunst-Werke Berlin, 8 Feb – 6 Apr 2003). It took place in a gallery, but it also had a separate programme in a web interface which emphasised the phenomenon of net art. Also part of the exhibition were screening blocks by invited experts. Animation historian Giannalberto Bendazzi included in his section, titled "Hits of the 1990s in the World of Animation", Michaela Pavlátová's film *Repete* (1995).

[155] Marek Pokorný, "Film / animace / umění" [Film / Animation / Art], in *Filmy bez kina: Princip animace a současné umění*, Marek Pokorný – Radim Peško (Brno: Brno House of Arts – Prague: Kant, 2003), p. 50.

[156] For more on *Cinepur* magazine, its establishment and focus, see Kateřina Svatoňová's and Eva Krátká's contributions to this volume.

theorising it as "a broadening of contemporary art into the dimension of movement and time".[157]

The exhibition drew attention to the role of animation within the realm of contemporary art both in the Czech Republic and abroad. Thanks to a broader conception of this phenomenon, animation at the exhibition became a guide for film and video across visual culture. But in the Czechoslovak environment, animation, with its cinematic prestige, can be understood as one of the hindrances to the development of video art in the 1970s and '80s. As Keiko Sei noted, the lack of interest on the part of organised animated film productions – as well as on the part of individual filmmakers and animators – in the technology of video, which they saw as a form of image that was "too technical, raw, and allowing for the manipulation of images and time", could have been a contributing factor that made video as such so difficult for Czech artists to access.[158] The situation was similar in the case of future exhibitions and events titled "movies without cinema", which used the phenomenon of animation to engage in a more extensive dialogue with artists in the international context. In some cases, the labels "film" or "video" even seemed to lose all relevance, although these designations often still said much about the means of production, presentation, or distribution. And video itself became, in some cases, a sort of technical support for works in various media, a ferryman between environments, or a layer in the post-production process. Given its rising availability, art of the moving image began permeating galleries, cinemas, clubs, festivals,[159] the internet,[160] and, thanks to the Czech "tramping" tradition, sometimes even tents.[161]

[157] Comp. Marek Pokorný, "Film / animace / umění", p. 56, or Kamila Boháčková, "Úvod k tématu: animovaný film" [Animated Film – An Introduction], *Cinepur* 13, no. 27 (2003), accessed 10 July 2022, http://cinepur.cz/article.php?article=16.

[158] "Video is fast, it allows for simple manipulation both with the equipment and with time; its image is raw, more real than surreal. People feel that you can manipulate real images, sounds, and times in video too easily, even before you properly master the 'craft'. And that's something Czech artists are sceptical of." Keiko Sei, "Jak lépe porozumět médiím reálného času" [How to Better Understand Real Time Media], in *Video art '94 – Nature in Motion / Příroda v pohybu* (Prague: Mánes, 1994), p. 9, or Zemánek, "Od luminodynamismu k médiu videa", p. 548.

[159] For more on film festivals and galleries, see Lenka Střeláková's contribution to this volume.

[160] For more on forms of art of the moving image on the internet, see Marie Meixnerová's contribution to this volume.

[161] For more on the entry of the moving image into the art world, including site-specific festivals, see Markéta Mansfieldová's contribution to this volume.

From Recordings to Video Performance. Between Life and Documentation

Sylva Poláková

One of the most important art practices to exert an influence over the development of the moving image in the artistic context is performance. In this genre – or, more generally, this expressive means – of live art (or action art), the specificity of the cinematic medium, which allows one to record a unique event in time, was newly recognised and put to use. As soon as documentation became accepted within the conception of artistic performance, artists started to employ the moving image in addition to texts and photographs. In 1970s Czechoslovakia, performances and happenings were first recorded onto celluloid. The growing access to other technological possibilities of capturing the moving image multiplied the possibilities for convergence between this medium and other artistic practices, which invites a discussion of – among other phenomena – expanded cinema.[162]

The aim of this essay is not to capture all the possible media intersections of artistic practices that make use of live action and film. For example, I leave to the side the entire field of light kinetism or live cinema, where an emphasis on technology is foregrounded. With a knowledge of the existence of artists and collectives who are unambiguously performers in their actions, taking on a considerable part of the presented event during their art productions, I will focus my attention on art performance and its survival and ongoing manifestations that employ film as a technically reproducible, time-dependent art. I thus withdraw from considerations of live art performances that are realised (and can be repeated) on the basis of a theatrical situation in which spectators interact directly with the performance.[163] Rather, I focus predominantly on works that are presented to spectators through the use of film recording (for the purposes of this text, this includes video and digital film) thereby creating something akin to the experience of a cinematic spectator, which, thanks to the expansion of the moving image into everyday life, has become established not only in the environment of the cinema (black box), but also in galleries (white cube) and public spaces. The principal aim of this text is not to provide an overview of representatives of this practice, but rather to name and characterise the central dynamics that had an influence on bringing together the art world and cinematography.[164] The study aims to contribute to our understanding of how the documentation of art

[162] In this essay, I work with Noël Carroll's general term *moving image*, which allows us to untether the medium of film from its ontological photographic roots; see Noël Carroll, *Theorizing the Moving Image* (Cambridge: Cambridge University Press, 1996). However, by employing Gene Youngblood's older term *expanded cinema*, I bring attention to an understanding of film as a heterogeneous practice of working with the moving image; see Gene Youngblood, *Expanded Cinema* (New York: E. P. Dutton, 1970). The integration of other media and technical equipment allows for the relocation of the cinematic experience, discussed early in the new millennium by film theorists in relation to the question *where is cinema?* (e.g., Francesco Casetti, Malte Hagener, Philippe Dubois, David N. Rodowick). Along with the film relocators, I respect various historical terms whose definitions arise from technological determination and practice (e.g., film, video, video art). The term *film*, however, is mostly used in the sense of a cultural interface (Rodowick, Lev Manovich), thus acknowledging my own academic position, which is based in film studies. In the Czech academic press, the question of cinematic relocation was the subject of a special edition of *Iluminace* magazine: "Film je jinde / Mimo prostor kina" [Film is Elsewhere / Outside the Cinema]; see *Iluminace* 23, no. 1 (2011).

[163] The aim of this study is not to present theoretical frameworks that include the relationship between spectator and artist, a basic differentiation between live action and staging, or the historical motivations for the expansion of these artistic strategies in relation to the art world, as they are discussed in publications focused on (video)performance as such. Comp. Kathy O'Dell, "Performance, Video, and Trouble in the Home", in *Illuminating Video: An Essential Guide to Video Art*, eds. Doug Hall – Sally Jo Fifer (New York: Aperture/Bay Area Video Coalition, 1990), pp. 135–151; Christine Ross, "The Temporalities of Video: Extendedness Revisited", *Art Journal* 65, no. 3 (Fall, 2006), pp. 82–99; Adrian Heathfield, *LIVE Art and Performance* (London: Tate Publishing, 2004).

[164] In this essay, I understand the connection between the art world and cinema at the level of the dispositif – that is, institutional wholes that include the systems of production, exchange, and consumption – as the concept was discussed within film studies and ideology in the 1970s; see, for example: Jean-Louis Baudry – Alan Williams, "Ideological Effects of the Basic Cinematographic Apparatus", *Film Quarterly* 28, no. 2 (Winter, 1974–1975), pp. 39–47.

events gradually became emancipated as a factor of socio-cultural changes (politico-ideological, legislative, or technological) as well as due to the contribution of specific artistic communities and individuals.

The beginnings of Czech video art (or, more generally, the moving image) as an expressive means in visual art were influenced by the prevailing totalitarian social conditions. These led, among other things, to a marginalisation of art forms that were not in agreement with the ideological demands of the communist regime, which consequently pushed them outside the production and distribution networks of the art world. Those who transgressed in terms of content and form or simply did not fit into the "curricula" were cut off from all support, including the possibility of using media equipment owned by state companies. According to the official doctrine, art, like film, was to follow traditional forms and genres. Barring a few exceptions, experimentation and interdisciplinarity were not supported and attempts in these directions could well be perceived as manifestations of elitist formalism.[165] This situation led to the development of varied strategies to access the needed equipment.[166] Such artists and their works were precluded from official avenues of public presentation, which applied to galleries, film distribution, and, of course, televised broadcasts. Searching for and creating supplementary presentation environments demanded, at various times during communist rule, various levels of creativity and risk which the artist, curators, and other organisers took upon themselves. But it was this emancipation from the formative institutional influence on the creation of art that allowed for the development of creative approaches that incorporated the everyday, the quotidian, chance, and ephemerality into the autonomous genres of action, performance, and happening.

Action art, which was less limited by technical equipment, was one of the possible lines along which Czech post-modern art could develop.[167] It was precisely these events – actions (whether in the form of performances or happenings) – that played an important role in establishing

[165] One of the few exceptions was the work of Laterna magika – staged productions that brought together elements of live theatre and dance performances with media interventions including moving images, all adapted into a revue format. The reasons behind the acceptance – even support – of Laterna magika by official cultural institutions in communist Czechoslovakia despite the fact that it extended trends in avant-garde theatre are explored in Lucie Česálková – Kateřina Svatoňová, "Laterna magika jako experiment v socialistické společnosti" [Laterna Magika as an Experiment in Socialist Society], in *Diktátor času: (De)kontextualizace fenoménu Laterny magiky* [Dictator of Time: (De)contextualising the Laterna magika Phenomenon], eds. Lucie Česálková – Kateřina Svatoňová (Národní filmový archiv and Charles University – Faculty of Arts, 2019), pp. 20–31.

[166] See the contributions by Martin Blažíček and Martin Mazanec in this volume.

[167] The first to write of postmodern art in the Czech context, and specifically in connection to action art, was Věra Jirousová in 1970; see Věra Jirousová, "Příklad post-moderny" [The Example of Post-modernity], *Výtvarná práce* 18, no. 5 (1970), pp. 1–6. The term post-modernism became part of the terminology of art studies in the 1980s, primarily in connection with painting; see Ludvík Hlaváček, "Postmoderna a neoexpresionismus" [Postmodernity and Neoexpressionism], in *Dějiny českého výtvarného umění VI/2* [The History of Czech Visual Art VI/2], eds. Rostislav Švácha – Marie Platovská (Prague: Academia, 2007), pp. 715–728.

film and video in the artistic environment, partly because they were valorised in the 1990s, at which time they were described as one of the connections with post-war developments in Western modern and postmodern art. Czech action art approached – within its specific local context – the ideas present in minimalism, land art, or conceptualism. Particularly the latter also significantly influenced later generations of students who began working with the moving image in the 1990s during their studies at art schools, at the newly established studios and at departments that engaged with so-called new media.

In the 1960s, as the result of a partial cultural thaw, it became possible to organise artistic events that included the presentation or outright creation of art works or activities that stood outside the confines of the declared aesthetic and ideological framework of official culture.[168] It was only a matter of time before one of these events would be documented on film. In 1960s Czechoslovakia, film equipment provided the only opportunity for such visual documentation, since video technologies (which already became available in the second half of the decade in the technically advanced regions of Western countries or in Japan) only made their way to the Eastern Bloc countries with a considerable delay. The reason for this delay was not merely due to differences in the market. The security services of the totalitarian regime considered owning a camera to be suspicious and sufficient grounds to *a priori* presume the dissemination of anti-regime content.[169]

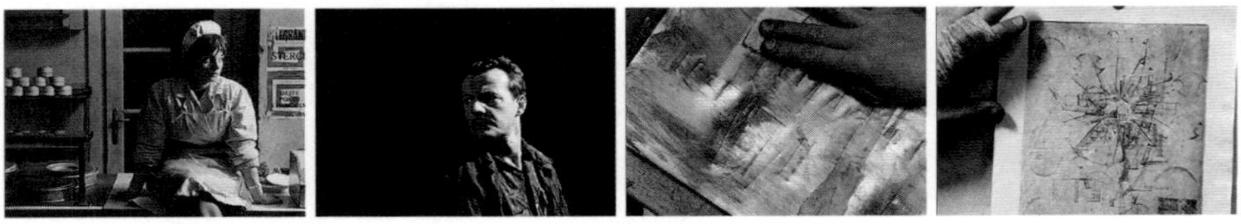

Věra Chytilová *Automat svět* [The World Café] (1965), film, 23 min

The first recordings of action art were made predominantly on narrow 8 and 16mm film, formats that were popular with film amateurs. In several cases, the artists also collaborated with film professionals, particularly cinematographers who had access to equipment at FAMU or other state-run professional film workplaces. These film recordings were later, under various conditions and employing the methods of the times, copied onto video cassettes (from the mid-1980s and especially in the following decade) or

[168] This thaw resulted in a change in the management of the Svaz československých výtvarných umělců [Union of Czechoslovak Visual Artists] in 1964. A secret selection process saw the appointment of historians, theorists (e.g., Jindřich Chalupecký), and artists (e.g., Jan Kotík) who were interested in the development of modern art and the establishment of contacts with Western artists and institutions; for more, see e.g., Alena Binarová, "Svaz výtvarných umělců v českých zemích v letech 1956–1972. Oficiální výtvarná tvorba v proměnách komunistického režimu" [The Union of Visual Artists in the Czech Lands 1956–1972] (Diploma thesis, Faculty of Arts, Palacký University, Olomouc, 2016), p. 184.

[169] Jaroslav Vančát – media theorist and one of the first "videoists", to use the term promoted by Czech video art pioneer Petr Skala – retrospectively compared owning a video camera to owning any samizdat tool; see the documentary film *Viva video, video viva* (Adéla Komrzý, 2019).

digitised (from the early 2000s), allowing for easier dissemination within the art community. In most cases, however, the process also meant a decrease in technical parameters. Film recordings of action art can be considered as predecessors of video performances, however, from the perspective of their historical context, we should not confuse the technologies used to create both forms. Not only do these technologies generate differences in terms of aesthetics and expression, they also operate within different networks of dynamic relationships between production and distribution. In the case of documentation made on film, we must take into account cinematographic specificities as well as methods characteristic for specific generations of filmmakers. We can also then recognise nuanced differences between the work of professional cinematographers and amateurs.

The investigation into first recordings of art events leads us to Vladimír Boudník, whose conception of art events, graphic art, and public space interventions influenced future generations of artists who endorsed action art as one of the important offshoots of conceptualism.[170] In 1956, camera operator Jaromír Pergler made a film titled *Akce v ulicích Prahy*

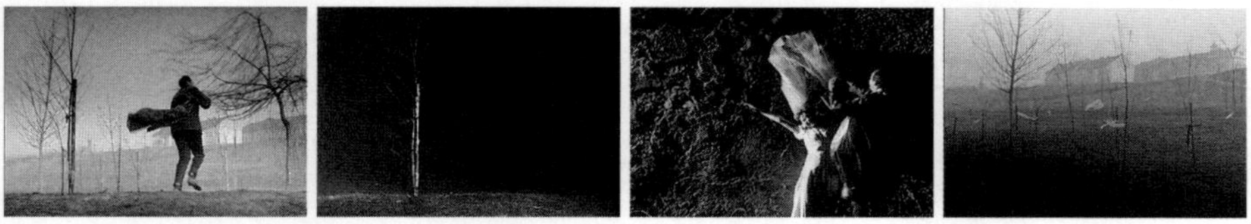

Věra Chytilová *Automat svět* [The World Café] (1965), film, 23 min

[Events on the Streets of Prague], in which he followed Vladimír Boudník in the company of his friends, who, inspired by the patina of the facades in the historical centre of Prague, set visual associations in motion.[171] As a social outsider, Boudník embodied the desire for the avant-garde tendencies of Czech interwar art, which had been violently eliminated during and after

[170] For more on Vladimír Boudník as a predecessor of action art, see e.g., Mahulena Nešlehová, "Informelní projevy" [Informel Discourses], in *Dějiny českého výtvarného umění VI/1* [The History of Czech Visual Art VI/1], eds. Rostislav Švácha – Marie Platovská (Prague: Academia 2007), p. 127. Probably the first acknowledgement of Vladimír Boudník as the Czech precursor of the happening comes from art critic and historian František Šmejkal; see František Šmejkal, *Vladimír Boudník* (exhibition catalogue, Prague: Galerie na Karlově náměstí, 1965), unpaginated. At around the same time, Jindřich Chalupecký also wrote of Boudník in connection with the happening; see Jindřich Chalupecký, "Umění, šílenství, zločin" [Art, Madness, Crime], *Sešity pro mladou literaturu* [Notebooks for Young Literature] 2, no. 11 (May 1967), p. 47. In 1966, Chalupecký wrote a text on contemporary genres; see Jindřich Chalupecký, "Experimentální umění. Happeningy, events, dekoláže" [Experimental Art. Happenings, Events, Décollage], *Výtvarná práce* 14, no. 9 (1966), pp. 1–7.

[171] According to the records of the Academic Research Centre of the Academy of Fine Arts in Prague, the film made by Jaromír Pergler was later screened at a number of underground events. A VHS copy was made in the 1990s and a digital version was created later, since which time it has been part of the permanent exhibition of Czech art at the National Gallery in Prague. The original film material is now lost; see "Vladimír Boudník – Akce v ulicích Prahy" [Vladimír Boudník – Events in the Streets of Prague], Videoarchiv VVP AVU, accessed 20 Feb 2022, https://vvp.avu.cz/videoarchiv/2454/?table=artvideoarchiv. The film was included on a DVD of Czech action art; see Pavlína Morganová – Terezie Nekvindová – Sláva Sobotovičová, eds., DVD *České akční umění: Filmy a videa 1956–1989* [Czech Action Art: Films and Videos 1956–1989].

World War II, and for a parallel to post-war developments abroad. His legendary status – which was cultivated across the fine art, literary, and film environments – was also aided by the live-action short *Automat svět* [The World Café] (Věra Chytilová, 1965) from the anthology film *Perličky na dně* [Pearls of the Deep], inspired by a collection of short stories by Bohumil Hrabal.[172] In her contribution to this film, director Věra Chytilová introduced several characters that are differently anchored to the world: from an experienced innkeeper capable of listening to an artist-lathe operator – played by Boudník performing, to some extent, a version of himself – to a frolicsome bride whose indifference towards what takes place around her prefigures the arbitrary hedonism of Chytilová's iconic *Sedmikrásky* [Daisies], Chytilová's iconic film.[173] In *Automat svět*, Boudník describes his first exhibition, Hmatový prožitek fabriky [A Tactile Experience of the Factory], which took place at the factory where he worked while flashbacks show us both the creative process and installation of his prints, creating a sort of docu-fictional moment.

What are considered to be the first true recordings of art events were created by an informal group of visual artists, writers, theorists, and other characters that began to form in the mid-1960s at the U Křížovníků pub in Prague, from which they derived the group's name: Křižovnická škola čistého humoru bez vtipu [The Crusader School of Pure Humour Without Jokes]. Its self-named directors were sculptor Karel Nepraš and conceptualist and draughtsman Jan Steklík. During the 1960s and '70s, its members included theorists Ivan Jirous and Věra Jirousová; happening-makers, poets, and writers Eugen Brikcius, Olaf Hanel, Petr Lampl, and Andrej Stankovič; photographer Helena Wilsonová; and painters Otakar Slavík, Zbyšek Sion, and Rudolf Němec.

Film Etudes, Friendly Excursions, or Action Art?

There is no consensus as to the nature of the events realised by the Křížovnická škola čistého humoru bez vtipu, neither in the community of experts nor among the members of the group. Conceptual thinking

[172] Bohumil Hrabal, "Automat svět" [The World Café], *Literární noviny* [Literary Newspaper] 12, no. 24 (1963), p. 7. The five short stories were adapted by representatives of the up-and-coming generation of the so-called Czech New Wave: Jiří Menzel, Jan Němec, Evald Schorm, Věra Chytilová, and Jaromil Jireš. All five short films were shot by cinematographer Jaroslav Kučera. Boudník's work in film is the subject of research in: Vladislav Merhaut, "Explozionalista Vladimír Boudník očima kamery" [The Explosionalist Vladimír Boudník in the Eyes of the Camera], *Kritická příloha Revolver Revue* [Revolver Revue Critical Supplement], no. 14 (1999), pp. 133–136.

[173] With its use of collage and a Dadaist conception of action extended ad absurdum, the film *Sedmikrásky* [Daisies] (Věra Chytilová, 1966) was a stark contrast to other, more subdued New Wave films. The film has mostly been discussed in relation to feminist themes. Formally and thematically, however, it resonates with artistic movements that made use of collage, even prefiguring bricolage: the scenes in which both protagonists (two girls named Marie) destroy both themselves and the environment they find themselves in are only a step away from the Dadaist conception of action, performance, and happening.

about art events, performance, and happenings took place spontaneously, and included the need to extricate oneself – even if only as part of a small community – from the categories of quotidian socialist experience. In the mid-1970s, under the influence of normalisation-era restrictions, the group's activities culminated in several happenings that ensured their position in the history of art, in no small part thanks to the surviving documentations and testimonies, which include film recordings. Painter Rudolf Němec, who owned an 8mm camera, filmed the excursions by members of Křížovnická škola and invited guests as active participants in these "patriotic trips". These events were initiated and organised by painter, photographer, and performer Olaf Hanel, who – according to contemporary witnesses – acted as the director of Křížovnická škola's travel agency. Such titles, however, were part of a game playing at a parallel society rather than designations for serious positions. At the time, Hanel was already familiar with the Fluxus movement and its conception of action art. At the same, as American art historian Amelia Jones argues, action art was often a continuation of modernist approaches that the artists themselves called postmodern.[174] While Jones uses this observation to analyse Western action art in relation to the legacy of Jackson Pollock and Allan Kaprow, it is also relevant in the Czech (or rather Czechoslovak) context, where the alternative scene maintained the severed links to modernist artistic ideas and processes, as well as the modernist art aesthetic. While it is very difficult to interpret the images in Němec's recordings of the so-called patriotic trips, which have no sound track,[175] the identification of the agents and sites they present can inform

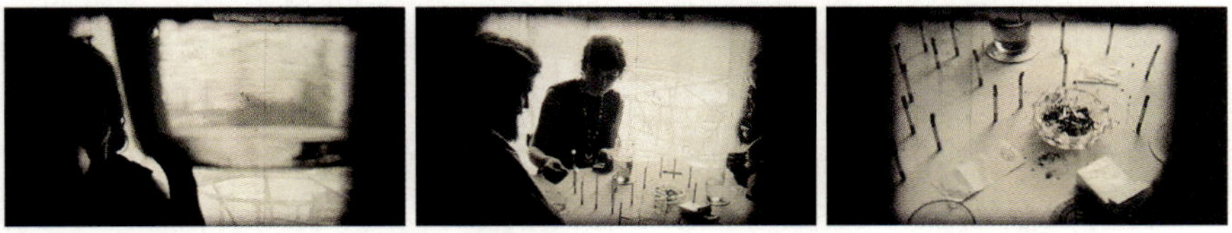

Rudolf Němec *Bez názvu* [Untitled] (1971), film, 3 min 9 s

Czech research on action art and allow us to compose an image of this episode in Czech art. Recordings of events, and particularly happenings, which generally included more participants, are a rich source of authentic shots of figures who influenced the particular cultural milieu at the time.

[174] Amelia Jones, *Body Art / Performing the Subject* (Minneapolis: University of Minnesota Press, 1998), p. 16.

[175] The film *Bez názvu* [Untitled] (Rudolf Němec, 1971), which records an artistic interpretation of a pilgrimage from Prague to Stará Boleslav (a city approximately thirty kilometres north-east of Prague), was loaned to the Academic Research Centre of the Academy of Fine Arts in Prague for digitisation by Němec's partner Alena Taschnerová. The original 8mm film was returned to Mrs. Taschnerová. The digital copy made at AVU was presented on DVD (Pavlína Morganová – Terezie Nekvindová – Sláva Sobotovičová, eds., DVD *České akční umění: Filmy a videa 1956–1989*) and on AVU's platform for contemporary art, Artyčok TV ("Bez názvu" [Untitled], Artyčok TV, accessed 29 March 2022, https://artycok.tv/28697/krizovnicka-skola-cisteho-humoru-bez-vtipu).

The film recordings thus acquire further value: capturing a historical moment and co-creating a trace of history.[176]

A more compact form of happening was on offer at the events organised by Zorka Ságlová, who was in contact with Křížovnická škola as well as other communities outside the official structures, particularly the circle surrounding the Jirous family and music groups such as The Plastic People of the Universe and The Primitives Group.[177] In the 1960s, Ságlová contributed to a transformation in the medium of the exhibition with interactive, site-specific events that her husband Jan Ságl documented (as he also did for her land art happenings) first with photographs and later also with film. The photographic sequences from events like *Seno – sláma* [Hay – Straw] (1969) or *Kladení plín u Sudoměře* [Laying Down Diapers Near Sudoměř] (1970) belie an interest in the temporality of these events. The choice of film as recording medium was thus a logical next step, despite the fact that photographic cycles were easier to distribute. In 1972, Jan Ságl filmed his wife's land art event, *Pocta Fafejtovi* [A Homage to Fafejta]. The performance was dedicated to a Prague-based chemist renowned for rhyming advertising slogans he used to sell condoms, which Ságlová had her friends blow up and release from the first floor of an abandoned fort called Vřísek near the town of Česká Lípa, where the rest of the happening also took place.

Today, diapers, condoms, or reminiscences of forking hay in Ságlová's events invite a gender-based reading of history, which, in the 1960s and '70s, involved the general debate about a revision of the women's question in relation to what was known as the "second shift", that is, taking care of children and the household. In hindsight, her work also reflected the difficult position of female artists in art communities that were (like Křížovnická škola) often full of machismo and sexism.[178] Female artists had to defend their position as authors, and quite often, life circumstances (typically connected

[176] The importance of photography (and, by extension, film recordings) of art events are explored by Hana Buddeus in her study comparing the legends of Boudník and Pollock, legends that were, in both cases, considerably aided by film and photography; see Hana Buddeus, "Fotografické podmínky happeningu" [Photographic Conditions of the Happening], *Sešit pro umění, teorii a příbuzné zóny* [Notebook for Art, Theory and Related Zones], no. 16 (2014), pp. 17–37. In the booklet that accompanies the DVD *České akční umění: Filmy a videa 1956–1989*, there is an emphasis on the list of people appearing in Němec's film: "The film contains rare portrait shots of Jiří Boreš, who later worked in theatre in emigration, poet and critic Vladimír Burda, action artist Eugen Brikcius, and man of letters and historian Josef Kroutvor." See Pavlína Morganová – Terezie Nekvindová – Sláva Sobotovičová, eds., DVD *České akční umění: Filmy a videa 1956–1989.*

[177] On the connections between the intellectual communities in which Zorka Ságlová took part and which were interwoven with familial and friendly connections, as well as on their interdisciplinary thinking about art, music, literature, and creativity in general, see Lenka Dolanová, ed., *Nejedna rodina: Jirousovi, Padrtovi, Ságlovi* [Many a Family: the Jirous, Padrt, and Ságl Families] (Humpolec: Nadační fond 8smička, 2020).

[178] The reminiscences of female artists who formed part of some underground groups – including Křížovnická škola čistého humoru bez vtipu – are the topic of research by Marianna Placáková, an art historian with a focus on gender, e.g., Marianna Placáková, "Jedna rodina: Ludmila Padrtová, Zorka Ságlová, Věra Jirousová, Juliana Jirousová" [One Family: Ludmila Padrtová, Zorka Ságlová, Věra Jirousová, Juliana Jirousová], in *Nejedna rodina: Jirousovi, Padrtovi, Ságlovi*, pp. 132–141.

with care for the family) often resulted in a temporary or total decline in their creative work. In Ságlová's case, however, an ingenious permeation of both spheres took place, as she managed to transfer both the themes and artefacts from one to another. According to historian and poet Věra Jirousová, *Pocta Fafejtovi* was not only a provocative event on sexual topics, as the work could easily be reductively described, but more so an ironic commentary on the natalist politics of the socialist state.[179] The continuity of Ságlová's work was also aided by the support of and collaboration with her husband Jan, who, among other things, was employed as a photographer at the *Výtvarná práce* magazine from 1963 until its demise in 1971.[180] In the years that followed, which saw the "normalisation" of gallery life, the mass cancellation of associations and clubs, and the elimination of field-specific magazines, artistic activities once again shifted outside institutional grounds, which paradoxically strengthened the position of action art and once again brought to light the question of documentation.

It was also at this time that a recording was made (and, in this case, not an "insider" recording) of one of the Křížovnická škola's repeated events: a game called Fando nezlob se (Fanda, Don't Get Angry), a variation on a popular board game called Člověče nezlob se (Man, Don't Get Angry, from the German name Mensch ärgere Dich nicht). Fanda was the name of the bartender at the group's local pub. Shots of liquor were used in place of game pieces. A version of the game played during a group picnic was filmed by Dobroslav Zborník as part of his work on a graduation film at the documentary film department at FAMU.[181] At this school, creating a portrait of an artist was a frequently set exercise, so this film did not particularly deviate from the norm. Dobroslav Zborník decided to introduce two figures and characterise them through their differences. Following period conventions at FAMU, the film included music and an explanatory commentary.[182]

[179] Věra Jirousová, "Velký malý králík Zorky Ságlové" [Zorka Ságlová's Great Little Rabbit], *Výtvarné umění* 17, no. 1 (1993), p. 25.

[180] During these years, *Výtvarná práce* existed as one of four professional periodicals published by the Ústřední svaz československých výtvarných umělců [Central Union of Czechoslovak Visual Artists]. In 1964, the editorial staff was reorganised after Adolf Hoffmeister became the new chairman of the union. This reorganisation allowed for broader reflections of abstract art and current events both internationally and at home. One of the new members of the editorial board, for instance, was Jindřich Chalupecký, who, in the second half of the 1960s, introduced the Fluxus movement and also wrote about the Czech "experimental art" of Milan Knížák and Vladimír Boudník. The editorial staff – which filled the pages of *Výtvarná práce* with the first texts on international developments in video art and electronic art – included art historian, curator, and Japanologist Vlasta Čiháková Noshiro and art critic Miroslav Klivar, who founded Independent Videoart Prague (1972–1990) and was also active as a video artist himself (see also Martin Mazanec's contribution to this volume). His active membership in the Communist Party of Czechoslovakia and collaboration with the secret service (StB) allowed him to travel abroad and become acquainted with international artistic developments.

[181] *Antinomie* [Antinomy] (Dobroslav Zborník, 1973).

[182] On the DVD *České akční umění: Filmy a videa 1956–1989*, however, it was presented without sound, which considerably changed the impression of the film, which was created under conventional conditions (Pavlína Morganová – Terezie Nekvindová – Sláva Sobotovičová, eds., DVD *České akční umění: Filmy a videa 1956–1989*).

After graduating from the school, Zborník began working in the standard, monopolised film industry as an assistant director at the Barrandov Studios, but he never severed his contacts with the unofficial and underground art environment.[183] In the second half of the 1970s and the early 1980s, he made cinematic documentations of art events for Milan Knížák and Milan Grygar. These are notable for their professional work with film equipment and use of cinematic language. Milan Knížák recalls that it was Zborník who introduced the idea of film documentation, while at the time, Knížák himself had no concept of how to document his own happenings.[184] And this despite the

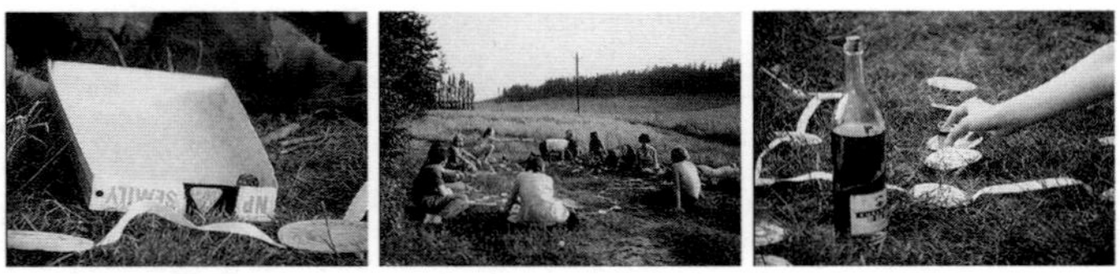

Dobroslav Zborník *Antinomie* [Antinomy] (1973), film, 17 min

fact that he had learned of the use of film on the art scene during his stay in the United States at the turn of the 1960s and '70s as a member of the Fluxus movement. In 1968, his performance *Ležící obřad* [Lying Ceremony] was filmed in New Jersey, and he also had the opportunity to try his hand at filmmaking with the creation of a short film about New York and the uninhabited Ginger Island (part of the British Virgin Islands).[185] Four years later, Dobroslav Zborník recorded a reconstruction of Knížák's happening *Kamenný obřad* [Stone Ceremony] on 8mm black-and-white material. In 1977, together they realised a documentation of the *Materiálová events* [Material Events] performance, and, in the mid-1980s, a short film on fashion titled *Zab se a leť* [Kill Yourself and Fly].[186]

[183] In the 1990s, he also made a number of documentaries produced by *Originální videojournal* or for Olga Havlová's Nadace dobré vůle [Committee of Good Will]. After 1989, it came to light that he had collaborated with the secret police from 1971 to 1989 (ABS, f. MV-KR, volume of secret collaborator Dobroslav Zborník, reg. č. 10399, arch. č. 808985 MV, cover name Sýkora). This made Zborník's reputation as a film professional in the service of artistic experimentation highly problematic. Until recently, his contribution to the creation of film documentations of events by Milan Grygar and Milan Knížák was rather overlooked – e.g., the Národní filmový archiv's *Filmové ročenky* [Film Yearbooks] only listed Dobroslav Zborník as a film assistant or director of television documentary.

[184] Milan Knížák interviewed by Sylva Poláková, 8 Jun 2021, Národní filmový archiv, Orální historie collection. Knížák also discusses documentation in Milan Knížák, *Akce po kterých zbyla alespoň nějaká dokumentace 1962–1995*[Events that Left Behind at Least Some Documentation] (Prague: Gallery, 2000), pp. 9–12.

[185] The film *Ležící obřad* [Lying Ceremony] (Milan Knížák, Paul Ryan, 1968) is kept at New York's MoMA, where it was donated as part of the Gilbert and Lila Silverman Fluxus Collection, see Milan Knížák "Lying Ceremony from Performance Files 1968", MoMA, accessed 4 Apr 2022, https://www.moma.org/collection/works/178953. According to Knížák, the second film in particular had more of an advertising character; a kind of video guide. He shot it on an 8 mm Kodak film camera. The reason Knížák went to the island was the interest of his friend George Maciunas in purchasing an island for the Fluxus movement. The footage was later included in the film *George: The Story of George Maciunas and Fluxus* (Jeffrey Perkins, 2018). Milan Knížák interviewed by Sylva Poláková, 8 Jun 2021, Národní filmový archiv, Oral History collection.

[186] *Kamenný obřad* [Stone Ceremony] (Milan Knížák, Dobroslav Zborník, 1972), *Materiálová events* [Material Events] (Milan Knížák, Dobroslav Zborník, 1977), *Zab se a leť* [Kill Yourself & Fly] (Milan Knížák, Dobroslav Zborník, 1985).

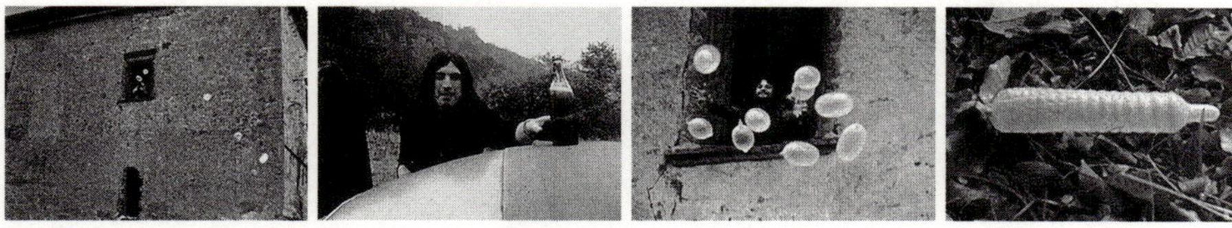

Zorka a Jan Ságlovi *Pocta Fafejtovi* [Homage to Fafejta] (1972), film, 20 min 18 s

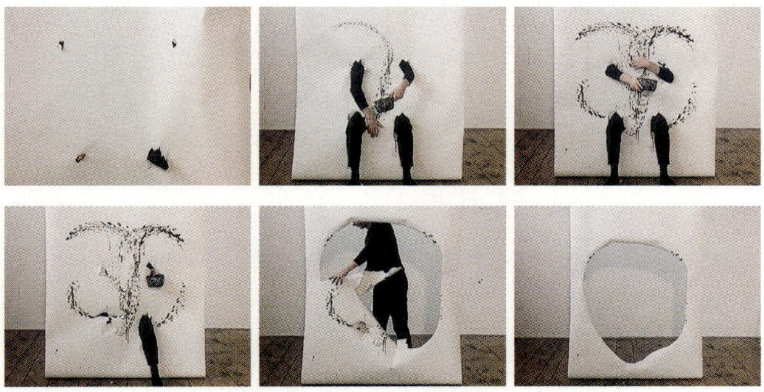

Milan Grygar, Dobroslav Zborník *Hmatová kresba* [Haptic Drawing] (1983), film, 6 min 18 s

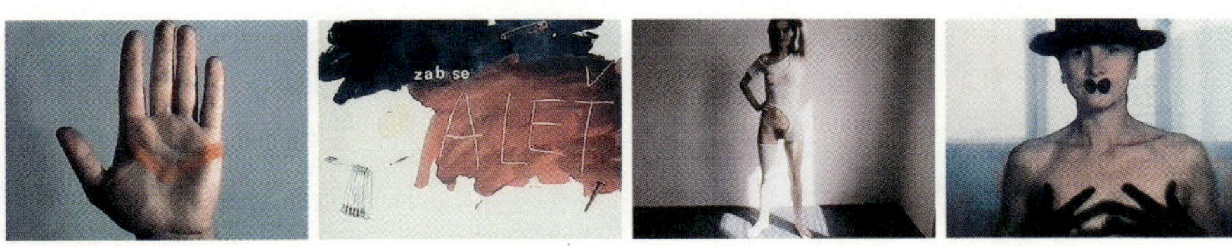

Milan Knížák, Dobroslav Zborník *Zab se a leť* [Kill yourself & fly] (1985), film, 15 min

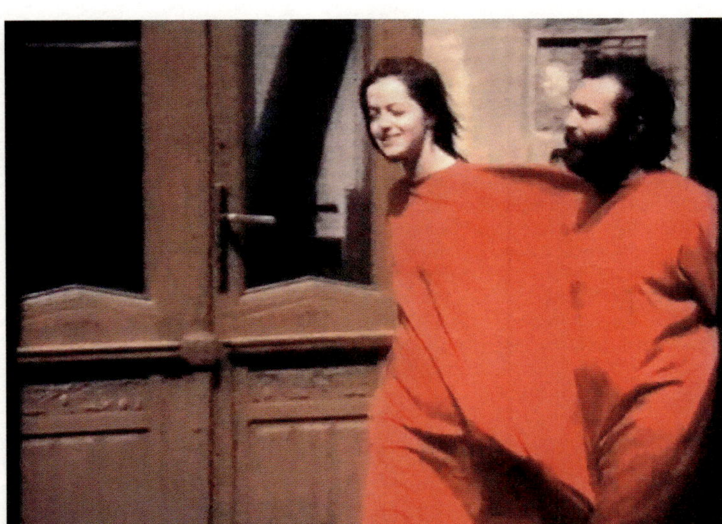

For Milan Grygar, a Czech audiovisual artist whose work is typified by experiments with the connections between graphic art and sound (and, by extension, music), Zborník created two performances in 1982 and 1983 respectively: *Prstová partitura* [Finger Score], *Hmatová kresba* [Haptic Drawing] and *Živá kresba* [Live Drawing] (all on 16mm film).[187] Both Knížák and Grygar's documented performances were events staged for the camera, not authentic documentations in the sense of capturing the temporality of unique, unrepeatable events. This staged approach allowed Zborník to consider the composition and inner dramaturgy of the films, emphasising the aesthetic and conceptual strength of these art events, thereby also influencing how these artists were perceived both abroad and on the domestic scene, where it was not only the films that circulated, but also individual stills from the film, which were used in lieu of photographic documentation. With the figure of Dobroslav Zborník, the theme of cinematic documentation of performances and happenings is enriched by the issue of authorship, which clearly highlights disparities between the systems of the art world and cinema. Neither of these media *dispositifs* has clear rules by which to determine authorship in this form of creative practice. In the art world, authorship is typically tied to the artist creating the event, although there are also efforts to list the names of photographers or videographers or to present the pieces as products of equal co-authorship.[188] In the film sphere, authorship is commonly tied more closely to the figure of the director. In practice, however, individual solutions to the problem of authorship abound, often considerably influenced by curatorial, archival, and cataloguing decisions.[189]

[187] *Prstová partitura* [Finger Score] (Milan Grygar, Dobroslav Zborník, 1982), *Hmatová kresba* [Haptic Drawing] (Milan Grygar, Dobroslav Zborník, 1983), *Živá kresba* [Live Drawing] (Milan Grygar, Dobroslav Zborník, 1983).

[188] The theme of the documentation of live art in the Czech environment, including the historical debt to photographers and camera operators documenting their friends' events, was the subject of the Konference Dokumentace umění [Art Documentation Conference], hosted by the Faculty of Art and Design at Jan Evangelista Purkyně University in Ústí nad Labem, 5 Dec 2012; see "Konference Dokumentace umění", accessed 10 Feb 2022, https://performance.ffa.vutbr.cz/konference-dokumentace-umeni/. Papers were presented (and later edited for publication) by historian of photography Hana Buddeus and significant representatives of Czech performance such as Vladimír Havlík, Jiří Kovanda, Jan Mlčoch, Tomáš Ruller, and Miloš Šejn. In addition to these conference papers, the book also included an introductory text by art historian Tomáš Pospiszyl, who situated the Czech scene within an international context in terms of the creation, distribution, and reflection of documentation; see Jan Krtička – Jan Prošek, eds., *Dokumentace umění*[Art Documentation] (Faculty of Art and Design at Jan Evangelista Purkyně University in Ústí nad Labem, 2013).

[189] In the case of film recordings of the patriotic trips organised by Olaf Hanel and created organically by all participants, the Academic Research Centre of the Academy of Fine Arts lists Rudolf Němec as the author of these films. A telling comment on the problematic nature of listing authorship is provided by a comparison of several funds or distributors, each of which lists different authors for the same work. *Pocta Fafejtovi* [A Homage to Fafejta], for instance, which Jan Ságl made as the documentation of an event by his wife, Zorka Ságlová, is listed by the Academic Research Centre as a work by Ságlová (see "Zorka Ságlová – Pocta Fafejtovi", Videoarchiv VVP AVU, accessed 5 Apr 2022, https://vvp.avu.cz/videoarchiv/2462/?table=artvideoarchiv), while the documentary portal DAFilms mentions only Jan Ságl as an author (director) (see "Pocta Fafejtovi", dafilms, accessed 5 Apr 2022, https://dafilms.cz/film/10190-pocta-fafejtovi).

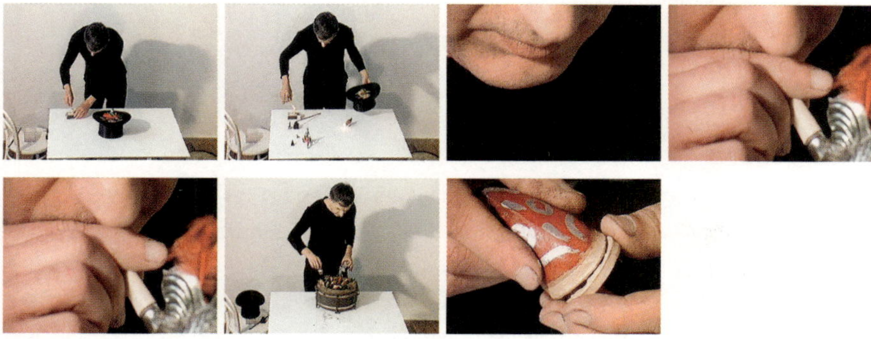

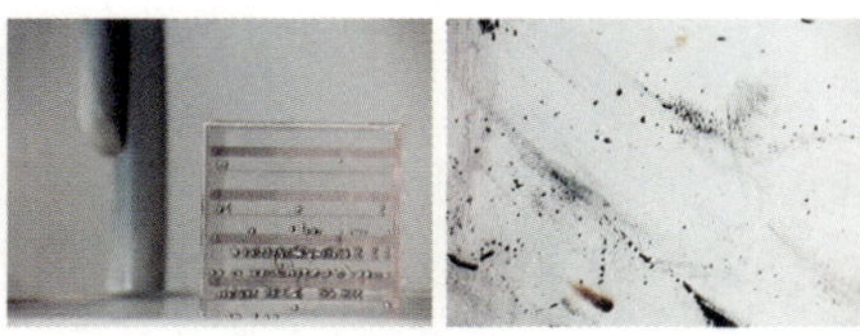

Milan Grygar, Dobroslav Zborník *Živá kresba* [Live Drawing] (1983), film, 5 min 38 s

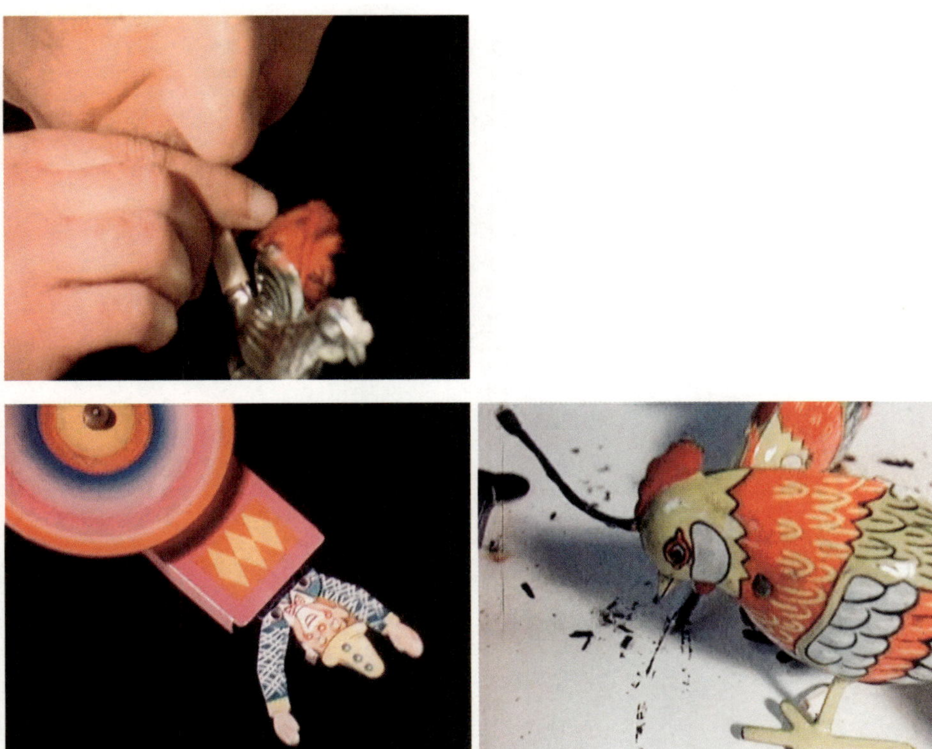

As soon as the artists themselves were convinced of the importance of documentation and began treating it appropriately, they secured a ticket into the annals of art history. The inclusion of the happening and performance in the history of art was conditioned by photographic documentation, as historian of photography Hana Buddeus aptly summarises in a recent study.[190] The artists themselves were also well aware of this factor.[191] These strategies had potential in the West, but in the Czech context, we must remember the socio-political situation, which virtually eliminated the possibilities of dissemination for this kind of art. Its mediation therefore took place primarily as mail art directed abroad. This was not the case of all artists, however. In the case of film recordings, distribution was even more complex than in the case of photographs. These works were often first presented several decades after they were created, as in the case of Lumír Hladík, whose performance recordings were only introduced in the Czech context through the work of art historian Pavlína Morganová.[192] Hladík's 1970s events, created within a circle of action artists (Jiří Kovanda, Petr Štembera, Karel Miler, or Jan Mlčoch),[193]were mostly made without an audience presence and with the participation of Hladík's friend and amateur film-maker Petr Soukup. Between 1976 and 1981, Soukup filmed seven of Hladík's performances on 8 mm colour film, which he later edited, adding several titles separating the individual events. In 1981, Hladík emigrated to Canada, where he only received these film recordings a decade later. They turned out to be one of the most unified period sources of Czech action art. *Moře v zrcadle* [The Mirrored Sea] (1980), *Můj osobní „nekonečný“ vektor* [My Personal "Infinite" Vector] (second half of the 1970s), *Už nikdy*

[190] "Photography was present very strongly in the happening, as it was through photography that the happening became connected to the history of art and became a part of it. Retrograde commercialisation and institutionalisation not only of the happening but also of a large portion of so-called dematerialised art through documentary photography then appears to be not a random paradox, but rather a natural consequence of the fact that photography allowed for this type of art to be connected to the world of fine art – after all, Milan Knížák openly admits this himself, unlike the existence of any precedents." Buddeus, "Fotografické podmínky happeningu", p. 35. Hana Buddeus dedicated her next publication not only to the relationship between performance and photography but also photographic documentation as a tool for the reception of dematerialised art; see Hana Buddeus, *Zobrazení bez reprodukce: Fotografie a performance v českém umění sedmdesátých let 20. století* [Representation without Reproduction: Photography and Performance in Czech Art of the 1970s] (Prague: UMPRUM, 2017).

[191] Milan Knížák said of documentation: "The happenings of the 1960s did not need documentation as much. There was documentation, but it was marginal, a message for our successors, as pre-prepared pages from an art history book." See Milan Knížák, "Performance jako vývoj i jako degenerace" [Performance as Development and as Degeneration], *Vokno*, no. 4 (1981), p. 44.

[192] Pavlína Morganová, *Lumír Hladík* (Galerie SVIT, Prague, 2011). Pavlína Morganová began searching for Hladík's work after she found a mention of his event *Moře v zrcadle* [The Mirrored Sea] in Petr Rezek's book on period reflections on action art; see Petr Rezek, *Tělo, věc a skutečnost v současném umění* [The Body, The Thing, and Reality in Contemporary Art] (Prague: Jazzová sekce, 1982).

[193] Not only this circle of action artists, but also the conceptualists working in Olomouc and Brno including Vladimír Havlík, Vladimír Ambroz, Josef Daněk and Blahoslav Rozbořil, or Jiří Sozanský, and the film and video documentation of their events were the focus of art historians Pavlína Morganová –Terezie Nekvindová – Sláva Sobotovičová, eds., DVD *České akční umění: Filmy a videa 1956–1989.*

tenhle balvan [The Never Boulder] (1978), and *Zmenšil jsem průměr Země* [I Reduced the Diameter of Earth] (1977) thematise the borders of personal freedom and perception of space (particularly landscape), which Hladík explored through conceptual limitations whose execution and impression are close to a personalised ritual: "The ritual as a thought process helped me, in my performances, to construct the situation of a new kind of unknowing, a conflict taken to absurdity that had to be carried out in order for it to be fulfilled. That's what's so beautiful about action art. I spent weeks or even months thinking about how to establish such a situation."[194]

Hladík did not interfere with the processing of the film material. The manner in which it was shot and edited (and, in some cases, complemented by rudimentary titles informing the viewer on the process or site of the event) was entirely in the hands of Hladík's friend Petr Soukup. After the reels made their way back to Hladík, the artists had them digitised several times (with the resulting digitisations always reflecting the technical possibilities of the period), and thus allowing his semi-forgotten work from the late 1970s to enter into the history of Czech action art and presented in publications, exhibitions, and festivals.[195]

"The Discounted Generation"

The film medium allowed artists to record the temporality and processuality of live events, and, in some cases (like that of Milan Grygar), to maintain the intermedia connection between the sonic and visual components of the work. Recording the progress of an event is only a step away from creating narrative, which is a conscious component of the work of intermedia artist and performer Miloš Šejn, for instance. In the 1970s, Šejn made several experimental films on 8 mm film (first on a borrowed camera, then on his own).[196] In the 1980s, after one of the events (*Na vrcholu – Zebín* [At the Peak – Zebín]) was filmed on video by an acquaintance of his, Ivo Sehnoutka,[197]he decided to record his further performative pilgrimages through the landscape on video, given the medium's practical advantages.

[194] Sylva Poláková, "Ztratit hlas, abych dostal nohy. Rozhovor s Lumírem Hladíkem" [Losing My Voice in Order to Get My Legs. An Interview with Lumír Hladík], *Dok.revue*, 1 Nov 2020, accessed 17 May 2022, www.dokrevue.cz/clanky/ztratit-hlas-abych-dostal-nohy.

[195] Hladík first had the films digitised and fitted with explanatory titles and music during his time in Canada. It was in this form that his most famous event, *Moře v zrcadle* [The Mirrored Sea] was presented, for instance, at a joint exhibition with Jiří Kovanda called 35 let 7000 kilometrů [35 years 7000 kilometres] (SVIT, Prague, 8 Sep – 27 Oct 2011) or as part of the online exhibition project Okno do videoarchivu VVP AVU [A Window into the AVU Academic Research Centre] (2013), accessed 6 Apr 2022, https://artycok.tv/20466/more-v-zrcadle-1980. Later, the artist gravitated toward a more authentic period version without music and text explication of the image. This version was included on the DVD *České akční umění. Filmy a videa 1956–1989*. In 2020, *Moře v zrcadle* [The Mirrored Sea] was presented along with six other events at a screening block titled Filmové záznamy akcí Lumíra Hladíka / 1976–1981 [Film Documentation of Events by Lumír Hladík / 1976–1981] (Jihlava IDFD, 2020).

[196] For more on these films, see Martin Blažíček's contribution to this volume.

[197] *Na vrcholu – Zebín* [At the Peak – Zebín] (Miloš Šejn, 1988). The camera operator's name was specified by Miloš Šejn in email correspondence with the author.

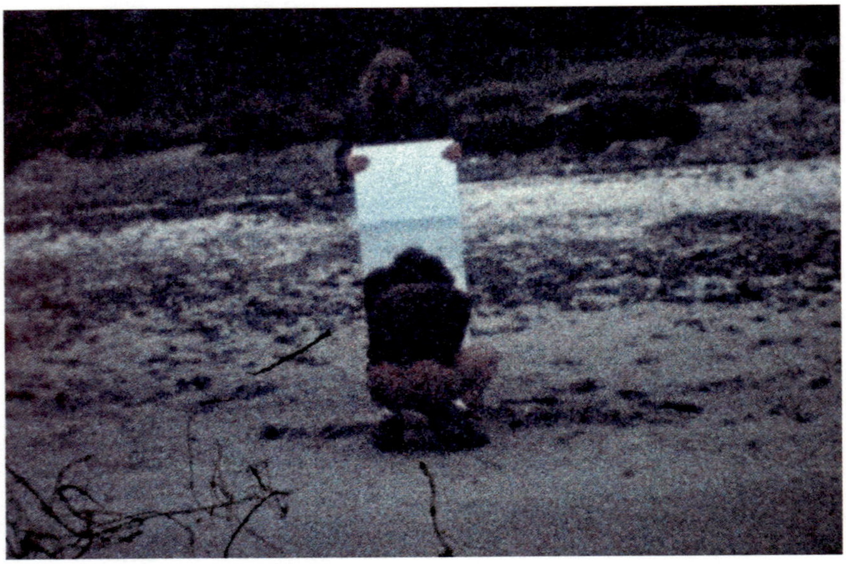

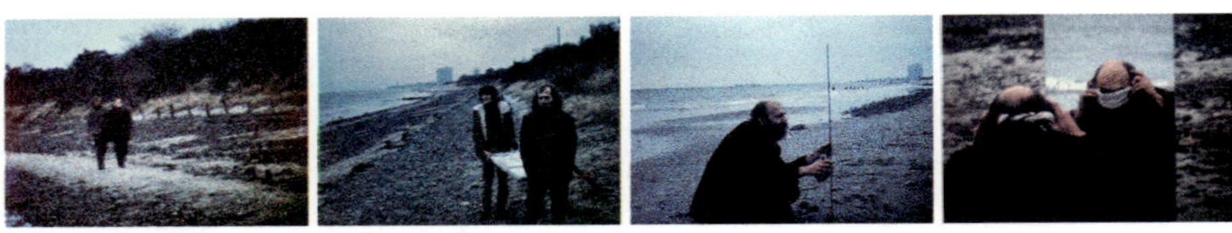

Lumír Hladík *Moře v zrcadle* [The Mirrored Sea] (1980), film, 9 min 7 s

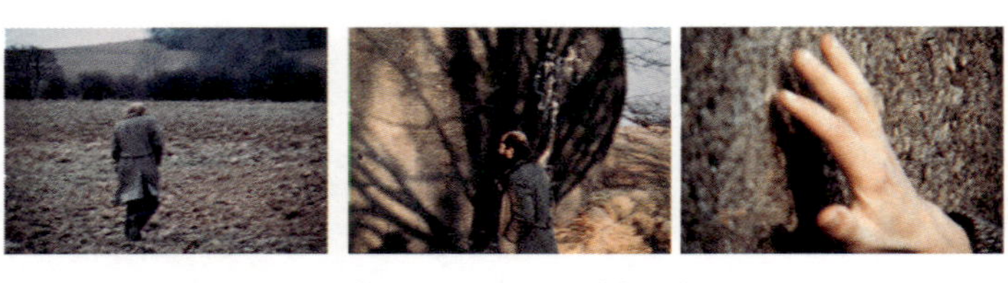

Lumír Hladík *Už nikdy tenhle balvan* [The Never Boulder] (1978), film, 2 min 1 s

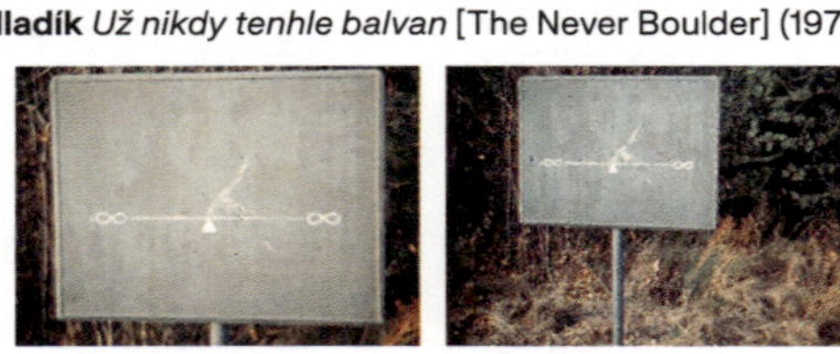

Lumír Hladík *Můj osobní „nekonečný" vektor* [My Personal "Eternal" Vector] (second half of the 1970s), film, 18 s

In the case of this performance, Šejn could make it present again shortly after its original performance, at his exhibition Práce z let 1984–1988 [Works from 1984–1988 (Malá výstavní síň, Liberec, 1988),[198] where the original 30-minute recording was played back on a television screen.[199] Video technology allowed artists working with action art and its documentation a faster and easier processes for the creation and presentation of their works. Prior to this, in the case of Miloš Šejn and others, film screenings at exhibitions were special events organised during the opening or as accompanying programmes. The use of television monitors and VHS players to present art of the moving image in a loop was also better suited for the gallery (until the spread of digital technology). Thanks to video, exhibitions – and in particular show openings – whose character had been growing closer to happenings or art performances since the 1970s, could be documented. Today, in the cases where they survive, these recordings are valuable historical sources and have, in some cases, acquired the status of stand-alone artworks.[200]

Among such surviving recordings is the documentation of the activities of the Brno-based Drogerie Zlevněné zboží [Discounted Goods Drug Store] and Tomáš Ruller. In the 1970s and '80s, there were several parallel developments in the art world, which all arose from the local possibilities of specific socio-cultural communities. In addition to the rather exceptional opportunity to exhibit contemporary art in official galleries, other possibilities for the realisation of events or exhibition projects included apartment seminars[201] or temporary repurposing of public spaces, such as youth clubs or even shops. In all cases, it was down to the specific constellation of participants if a suitable situation would arise and how long it could remain under the radar of the state organisations.

At the end of the 1980s, an initiative by theatre historian Petr Oslzlý and artist Rostislav Pospíšil led to the establishment of Galerie Drogerie Zlevněné zboží [Discounted Goods Drug Store Gallery]. Since

[198] Miloš Šejn discusses the production of the documentation in an interview with Martin Blažíček: "Miloš Šejn: V mé práci jde v podstatě o vytržení" [My Work Is Essentially About Rapture], *Filmový přehled*, 31 Jan 2020, accessed 6 Apr 2022, https://www.filmovyprehled.cz/cs/revue/detail/milos-sejn-v-me-praci-jde-v-podstate-o-vytrzeni.

[199] Later, in 2009, Miloš Šejn shortened the original digitised recording to a seven-minute version.

[200] The later exhibiting of documentation as an autonomous work was the subject of a debate at the Art Documentation conference featuring Jiří Kovanda, Tomáš Ruller, Jan Mlčoch, Jennifer De Felice, and others; see Krtička – Prošek, eds., *Dokumentace umění*, pp. 58–66.

[201] E.g., the joint apartment events by artists Josef Daněk and Blahoslav Rozbořil. A restaging of the event *Ambrož, svátek svátků* [Ambrose, Feast of Feasts] (1988) was filmed by Aleš Záboj in Rozbořil's apartment. An eponymous recording forms part of the DVD *České akční umění: Filmy a videa 1956–1989*. Aleš Záboj received a video camera from the Vzdělávací nadace Jana Husa [Jan Hus Educational Foundation], which, beginning in 1980, systematically supported apartment seminars in communist Czechoslovakia and still has branches in Great Britain, the United States, Germany, and France. The foundation supported Petr Oslzlý's apartment seminars from 1984 on, and starting in 1985, the foundation developed a project to disseminate video technology with the aim of apartment screenings and the production of recordings of events and figures of Czechoslovak independent culture; see "Historie nadace" [The Foundation's History], accessed 6 Apr 2022, https://www.vnjh.cz/o-nadaci/historie-od-1980/.

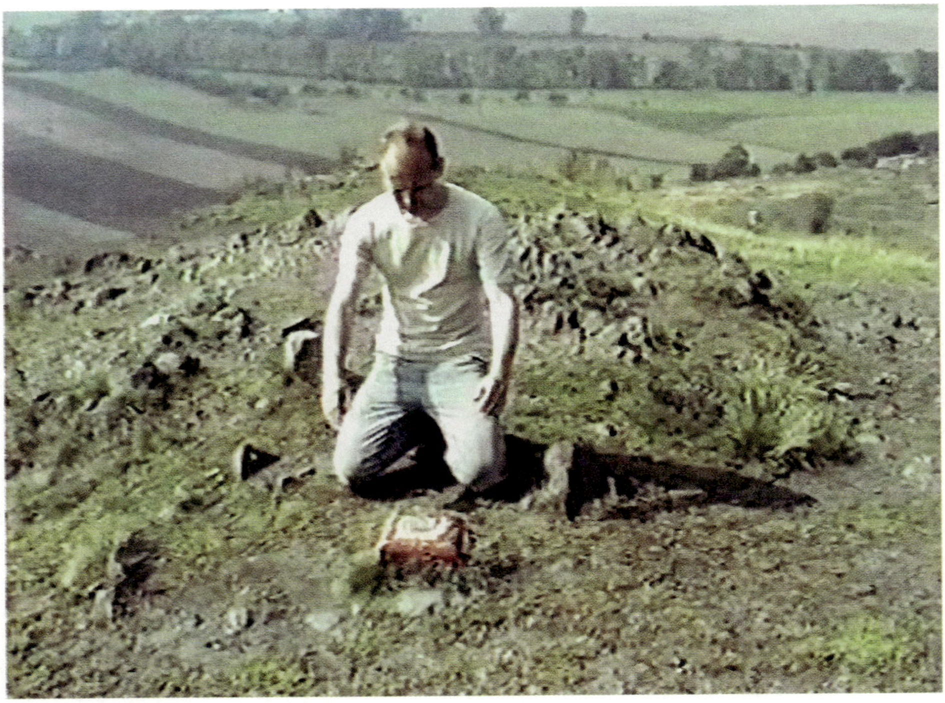

Miloš Šejn *Na vrcholu – Zebín* [At the Peak – Zebín] (1988), video, 7 min

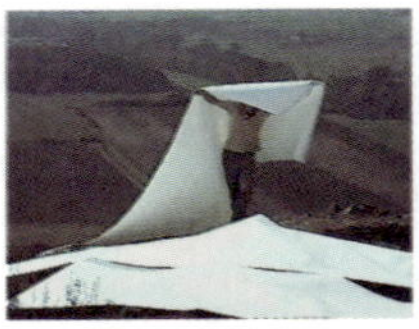

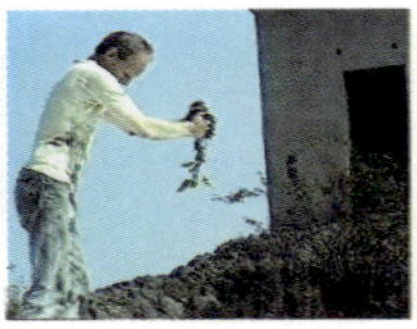

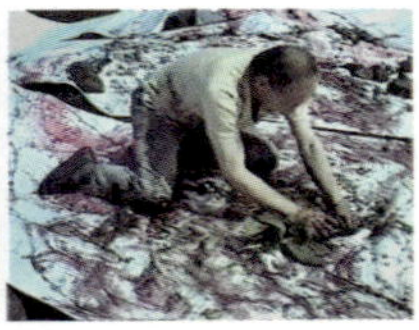

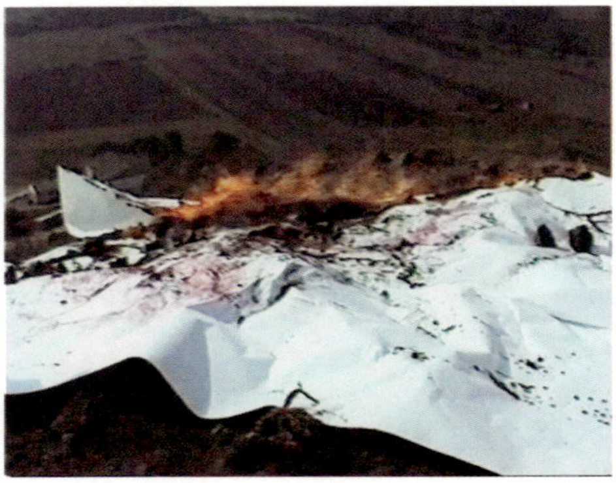

the 1970s, Oslzlý and Pospíšil had been active in the Brno theatre scene, particularly in connection with the activities of the Husa na provázku [Goose on a String] Theatre. The concept of the open theatre and inspiration from street theatre that characterised Husa na provázku were also inherent in the art events produced by Oslzlý and Pospíšil's new project. Galerie Drogerie Zlevněné zboží was located in a real drug store selling discounted goods in Brno, on the corner of Bayerova and Kotlářská streets. Part of the exhibition included the creation of a video portrait of the exhibiting artists including Zorka Ságlová and Tomáš Ruller, whose event *Reklama* [Advertising] concluded the gallery's operation in April 1989. These portraits, created over the course of a single day, were filmed by Aleš Záboj, the videographer for a number of socially cultural events taking place during the end of the communist period in Czechoslovakia and later studio leader at the Studio of Audiovisual Art and Theatre at the Janáček Academy of Performing Arts in Brno (JAMU). The exhibition opening had a performative form, and afterwards, the group moved to the adjacent beer house, Praha, where the artist's video portrait was screened in the salon.[202]Works exhibited at Drogerie Zlevněné zboží were available to the public during the store's opening hours for a month after the show opening, but, unlike the rest of the objects on display, were not for sale. On the contrary, legend has it that the openings were a huge help for the sales of the shop's goods. It was on this basis that Petr Oslzlý used the term "discounted goods" to describe artists who were banned from exhibiting at official exhibition platforms, later also extending the term to call them the "discounted generation".[203]

A knowledge of the consequences of "expulsion" from the official art world, and the accompanying absence of financial valuation and preclusion of a place in the history of art was a constant factor in the practice of performance and happening in the Czech environment, but one which is only rarely discussed. A debate at the 2012 conference Dokumentace umění [Art Documentation] opened the topic, with some artists expressing their favour for a circulation of their events in the form of documentation, particularly for two reasons. Tomáš Ruller drew attention to the fact that when the events in the 1970s and '80s were created, there was not much interest

[202] Writers on the operation of Galerie Drogerie Zlevněné include Hana Pospíšilová, "Galerie Drogerie Zlevněné zboží: Neoficiální prezentace výtvarného umění v 80. letech v Brně" (bachelor's diploma thesis, Masaryk University, Faculty of Arts, Department of Musicology, Theory of Interactive Media, Brno, 2012); Marcela Macharáčková ed., *Brněnská osmdesátá* [80s Brno] (Brno: TT klub výtvarných umělců v Brně [TT Club of Visual Artists in Brno], 2010), p. 52; Jiří Valoch, "Brněnský okruh: Památce Gerty Pospíšilové, bez níž by mnohé nebylo tak, jak bylo" [The Brno Circle: To the Memory of Gerta Pospíšilová, Without Whom Much Would Not Be As It Was], in *Zakázané umění I* [Forbidden Art I], eds. Milena Slavická – Marcela Pánková (Prague: Občanské sdružení pro podporu výtvarného umění [Civic Association for the Support of Visual Art], 1995), p. 162.

[203] These are the words Petr Oslzlý uses to discuss period presentations of the gallery; see "Aleš Záboj (režisér). O Galerii-Drogerii Zlevněné zboží" [Aleš Záboj (director). On the Gallery Discounted Goods Drug Store], accessed 6 Apr 2022, https://artycok.tv/19695/o-galerii-drogerii-zlevnene-zbozi-1987.

in documentation and the emphasis was on the personal experience.[204] Even so, his personal archive contains much documentation, including film. Copies of his film documentations transferred onto various generations of video cassettes allowed him to present his work abroad, when he would participate in art festivals and exhibitions. The presentations took the form of single screenings followed by a discussion. It was only in the new millennium that Ruller began exhibiting period recordings in the gallery, accompanied by other forms of documentation (e.g., plans and blueprints, pieces of correspondence, or legal documents regarding censorship) or objects he calls relicts.[205] The artist, who has participated in a number of events on the borders between public and private space since the early 1980s[206] – in the presence of a kindred community of members of the unofficial cultural scene as well as random passers-by[207] – absorbed into his work a sculptural understanding of material with an interest in experimental theatre, specifically street theatre. Beginning in the 1990s, his work began manifesting an interest in new media, which was also influenced by encounters with international artists whom he invited to lectures and other events as a lecturer at FaVU.[208] His interest in technologies that can lead to a new-media conception of the Gesamtkunstwerk is also demonstrated by his membership in the Via Lucis group. This group was established in 1976 by Jan Doubek, whose focus was the integration of the laser in art, thus extending the work in light kinetism begun by the interwar pioneer Zdeněk Pešánek. The other members of Via Lucis were influenced by their collaboration with Ruller at the

[204] In a discussion, Tomáš Ruller referred to Allan Kaprow, drawing attention to the fact that "there were also times, when documentation was in fact denied entirely as something impure"; see Krtička – Prošek, eds., *Dokumentace umění*. Personal reminiscences of filming with TV and film professionals make it clear that Ruller considered the presence of the crew (which would sometimes request that the filming be stopped for technical reasons) highly disruptive – the *Trikolora* event, for instance, was realised by cameraman Jaroslav Göbl as part of a film shoot produced by Krátký film [Short Film]. In the 1990s, Göbl gave Ruller a copy on a U-matic cassette which the artist then had digitised. Nevertheless, he never returned to recording events purely for the camera, without an audience present. This information was provided to Sylva Poláková by Tomáš Ruller during an identification screening and form part of the acquisition documentation, 1 Apr 2022, Národní filmový archiv.

[205] The largest comprehensive presentation of the documentation of Ruller's events was a double exhibition titled Perform-Made in Brno (Perform-Made / Odolné okamžiky [Resistant Moments], 13. 9. 2017–12. 11. 2017, Dům umění města Brna [Brno House of Arts]) and in Prague (Perform-Made / Udržitelné záblesky [Sustainable Glimmers] 27. 6. 2018–14. 10. 2018, Galerie hl. města Prahy [Prague City Gallery]).

[206] E.g., the cultural events and symposia Malechov (1980 and 1981), Malostranské dvorky [Malá Strana Courtyards] (Prague, 1981), Setkání na tenisových dvorcích [Meeting on the Tennis Courts] (Prague, 1982) or Chmelnice [Hop Field] (Mutějovice, 1983). See also Jitka Hlaváčková, ed., *Tomáš Ruller: PERFORM-MADE. Udržitelné záblesky* [Tomáš Ruller: PERFORM-MADE. Sustainable Glimmers] (Prague: GHMP, 2018), unpag.

[207] After his exhibition at Kulturní dům Opatov [Opatov House of Culture] in 1988 was banned, he effected, on the day of the opening, a performance near the House of Culture, in a former concrete mixing plant. It is said that the attention of the police was drawn to the event – during which Ruller ultimately set himself on fire – by people looking out from the windows of panel houses. Participants supposedly succeeded in persuading the police that the entire event was a film shoot, so they left soon after. See "8.8.88", accessed 6 Apr 2022, http://vvp.avu.cz/videoarchiv/2476/?table=artvideoarchiv, or Pavlína Morganová – Terezie Nekvindová – Sláva Sobotovičová, eds., DVD *České akční umění: Filmy a videa 1956–1989* (DVD booklet), unpag.

[208] He repeatedly invited the Czech-Icelandic artistic couple Woody and Steina Vasulka to Brno. For more on Tomáš Ruller's position at FaVU, see Tomáš Pospiszyl's contribution to this volume.

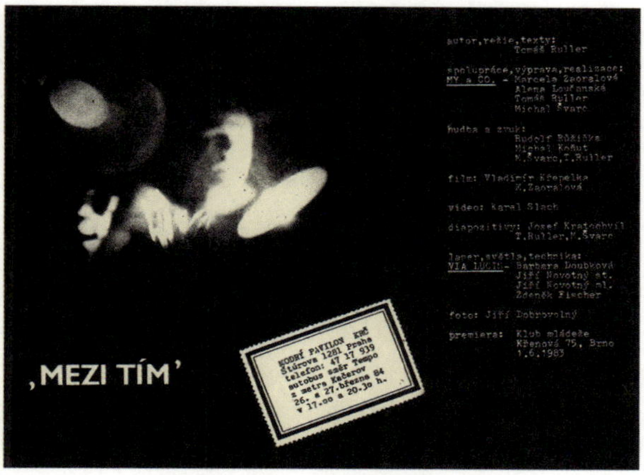

Poster for a screening of a film by Tomáš Ruller and Via Lucis *Mezi Tím* [In Between] (1983) at Modrý pavilon, Prague, 26 and 27 Mar 1984.

turn of the 1970s and '80s, who introduced the theme of the human body as a central concern. Together, they created the multimedia performances *Oslava přeletu ptáků* [A Celebration of a Crossing of Birds] (1981) and *Mezi Tím* [In Between] (1983).

In Czechoslovakia, there were also attempts at integrating technological media in performance, which occurred not only on the level of documentation, but also within the process itself, whether that meant the use of video or other technologies like lasers and, in later years, computers. Such attempts were made by individuals or collectives such as the Syntéza [Synthesis] group (1964–1970), Via Lucis (1977–1981), or Independent Videoart Prague (1972–1990), which strove for multimedia and interdisciplinary connections between art, music, theatre, dance, and new technology, a field that was "monopolised" by Laterna magika, an institution well anchored not only in socialist culture but also in its economy. During their existence, the output of these groups of the "discounted generation" remained marginalised, with expert circles only expressing an interest in them in relation to reconstructing the history of normalisation-period art and a mapping of the historical trajectories of new media.[209]

[209] Several diploma theses have been written on the subject of these groups, e.g., Vít Havránek, "Český kinetismus 1956–1970 a skupina Syntéza" [Czech Kineticism 1956–1970 and the Syntéza Group] (diploma thesis, Faculty of Arts, Charles University, Prague, 1997); Andrea Sloupová, "Syntéza po Syntéze: české kinetické umění 60. let a pozdější tvůrčí postupy jeho protagonistů" [Synthesis after Syntéza: Czech Kinetic Art of the 1960s and Its Protagonists Later Creative Approaches] (diploma the-sisDepartment of Art History, Faculty of Arts, Charles University, Prague, 2008); Denisa Přichystalová, "V zajetí světla: užití laseru v české scénografii a umění 20. století" [Captivated by Light: The Use of the Laser in Czech Set Design and Art of the 20th Century] (bachelor diploma thesis, Theory of Interactive Media, Department of Musicology, Faculty of Arts, Masaryk University, Brno, 2020).

The Multimedia and the Interdisciplinary Blurring Boundaries

In the 1990s, the situation changed across cultural spheres. Artistic disciplines that were developed as alternatives to the official possibilities of presentation began to develop fully. In the spirit of the French philosopher and sociologist Michel de Certeau, we could say that tactics gradually became strategies as soon as they were institutionalised on – or rather beyond – the border of legality.[210] As the art community left the "grey zone" and exiled artistic and intellectual figures returned home, the artistic canon was broadened to include action art[211] and teaching bodies at art universities (which were undergoing their own transformations) were expanded.[212] There was growing interest in disciplines that had not, until then, been taught or analysed within the academic sphere – the interest was so great, in fact, that it surpassed what the existing studios could offer. Students of traditional programmes such as sculpture or drawing would make use of exchanges in the new studios, but even the openness of the study programmes themselves allowed students to work in an interdisciplinary fashion.[213] Soon, therefore, art of the moving image in various media variants (including those tied to performance) appeared in the portfolios of a number of artists who studied at Czech art universities (both in local centres and on the periphery) in the 1990s. There were also essential changes taking place in the field of cinema, brought about by the disintegration of previous restrictions and certainties. With the privatisation of the state film industry, the enthusiasm of newly established film and graphic studios, and the opening up of television programming to include new material, particularly documentary films, the unofficially established connections between film and art practice were temporarily allowed.[214] Video technology made working with the moving image possible even without professional training. The need to share experiences with these new tools also led to a strengthening of collaboration between studios. At FaVU in Brno, performance as a discipline was led by Tomáš Ruller along with Peter Rónai,

[210] Michel de Certeau wrote an entire book on this topic: *L'invention du quotidien, 1: Arts de faire* (Paris: Union générale d'éditions, 1980). Although this was originally a sociological study that took place between 1974 and 1978, the publication had an impact across multiple disciplines, particularly in art studies.

[211] Beginning in the late 1990s, these disciplines were gradually valorised, and their representatives such as Jiří Kovanda, Milan Knížák, Zorka Ságlová, Tomáš Ruller, and others became iconic artists for the younger generation whose modus operandi also arose from an extended interest in new media and particularly the interface of film.

[212] See Tomáš Pospiszyl's contribution to this volume.

[213] In the late 1990s, Ján Mančuška graduated from AVU, having studied at Jitka Svobodová's drawing studio, Vladimír Kokolia's graphic studio, and Vladimír Skrepl's painting studio. His work explored the deconstruction of media and the authorial position, to which ends he used both performative methods and the moving image from early in the new millennium.

[214] In the field of documentation of performance and happening, for instance, this professional shift can be exemplified in the example of photographer and amateur film-maker Michal Hýbek, who was actively filming for *Originální videojournal* in the 1980s and then worked mostly on international travel reportage after 1989. See Jan Bernard, *Filmaři disentu – Michal Hýbek v paměti archivů a přátel* [The Film-makers of Dissent – Michal Hýbek in the Memory of Archives and Friends] (Prague: AMU Press, 2020).

Petr Váša, and Marian Palla. At AVU in Prague, it was mostly represented by then-Rector Milan Knížák[215] and, later, multimedia artist and performer Veronika Bromová, who led the New Media Studio 2 (photography and the digital image) from 2002 to 2011, enriching the theme of the body to include confrontation with the apparatus.

Crucial for the development of action art in the 1990s was the performance scene in Ostrava, which was characterised to a large extent by the Malamut performance meeting festival. The founding figures were artist and lecturer Jiří Surůvka, who, beginning in 2004, led a studio at the Ostrava University Faculty of Fine Arts and Music originally titled Video – multimedia – performance, and artists and curators Petr Lysáček and Stanislav Cigoš. The festival was originally conceived as an international event, which was an effective weapon against perception of the Ostrava art scene as provincial. Beginning with the first edition of the festival in 1994, it was profiled as an important Central European event focused on performative art and contributing to a strengthening of relationships with the Polish art world in particular.[216] Graduates of the Ostrava faculty then continued in the activities of their teachers Jiří Surůvka a Petr Lysáček (who together formed a duo called Předkapela Lozinski),[217] creating performance groups such as Kamera skura (since 1996), Record (since 2002), and I love 69 pop gejů (since 2001) and thereby extending the possibilities of performance as provocation accepted by society.

[215] The atmosphere at AVU in the 1990s is apparent in the period documentaries by director Jiří Věrčák: *AVU – AVU na Chmelnici* [AVU – AVU at Chmelnice] (1991) and *dejAVU* (1994), created in co-production with Czechoslovak and later Czech Television. In 2014, this thread was picked up by art historian and AVU lecturer Tomáš Pospiszyl and AVU graduate Mark Ther, see *AVU – AVU to má ale šmrnc!* [AVU – AVU's Got Flair!] (2014), who attempted to point out not only the somewhat more stable climate at the school a decade after the original documentaries, but also the exceptionally open television programming of the 1990s.

[216] A short history and overview of all the festival editions is available in the VVP AVU database; see "Malamut", accessed 8 Apr 2023, https://vvp.avu.cz/archivy/i-datum/54/?table=vystavy.

[217] Which was later joined by František Kowolowski, with the group becoming František Lozinski o.p.s.

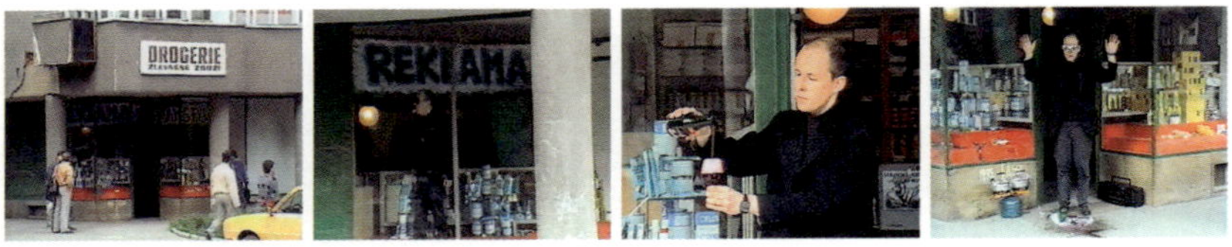

Tomáš Ruller, Aleš Záboj *Reklama* [Advertising] (1989), video, 16 min 37 s

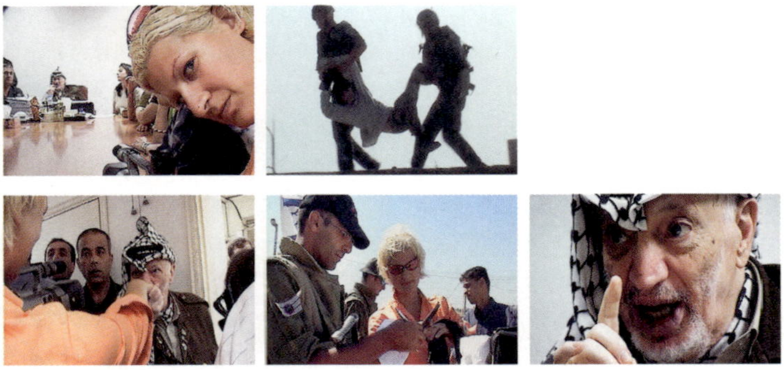

Tamara Moyzes *Me and Arafat* (2003), video, 3 min 24 s

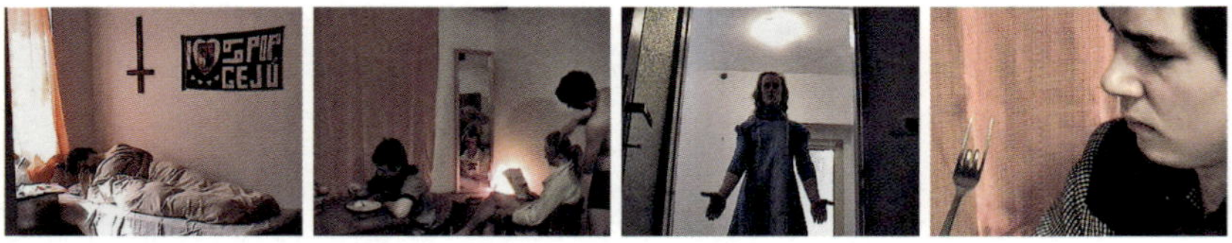

I Love 69 Popgejů *Flaming Lips and The Monster* (2005), video, 5 min 55 s

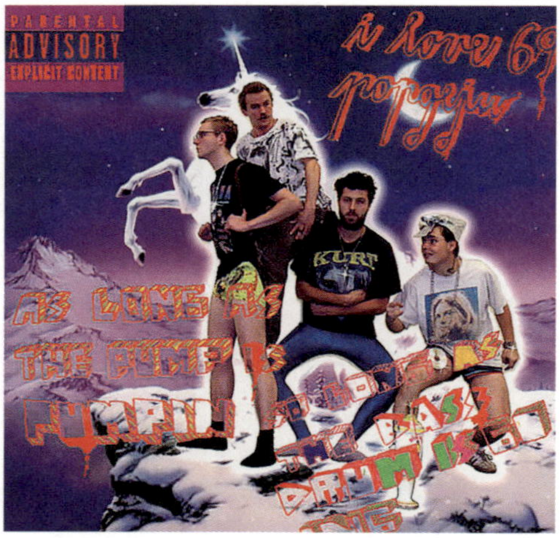

Cover of an EP by I Love 69 Popgejů, As long as the Pump is pumpkin, so long as the Bassdrum is going (2006).

A Dissolution in Place of a Conclusion

In the digital era, any medium can be simulated, themes and artistic intentions can grow freely through galleries, theatre stages, or cinemas, and, with an unprecedented degree of naturalness, also public and private spaces. For artists working with such ephemeral artistic expression as performance or happening, art is, in the words of theorist Boris Groys "identical to life, because life is essentially a pure activity that does not lead to any end result".[218] If we follow Groys, we will perceive that "art documentation as an art form could only develop under the conditions of today's biopolitical age, in which life itself has become the object of technical and artistic intervention".[219] It is characteristic of this "biopolitical age" that by narrating its origins (Groys uses the term "making of"), we can construct a narrative and thereby a history for anything "artificial".[220]Today, we struggle to distinguish between what is authentic and what is edited, simulated, or outright fake. Performative events can be live but already count on future presentations from recordings, just as they can integrate staged or simulated elements. It is possible, at least, to suggest the lines that run from earlier practices as described above, including: conceptual tendencies with subthemes of deconstructing media, institutions, and ideologies; the development of environmental and body art disciplines that allow for the articulation of themes of intimacy and our relation to the environment that surrounds us (whether this means the landscape, the urban environment, or private spaces); and, last but not least, a tendency toward narration that exhibits the clearest relationship to cinematography, reflecting the need for a confirmation of one's right to exist through one's own narrative.

The theme of deconstruction was present in the activities of the Display gallery, which were expanded in 2002 by the tranzit.cz initiative to include international connections with Austria, Slovenia, Hungary, and Romania. Through their activities at the tranzitdisplay gallery in Dittrichova Street, as well as through screenings of crucial films from abroad and publications, the team – led by curator Vít Havránek, art historian Vjera Borozan, and artist Zbyněk Baladrán – contributed to the development of conceptualism in contemporary Czech art, a reflection of the transformational period in Czech culture (the 1990s and 2000s), and a more intimate knowledge of themes that resonate abroad, such as the archival turn, post-colonialism,

[218] Philosopher and media theorist Boris Groys has explored the topic of documentation in texts such as "Kunst im Zeitalter der Biopolitik. Vom Kunstwerk zur Kunstdokumentation", in *Documenta 11Plattform 5: Ausstellung. Katalog*, eds. Heike Ander – Nadja Rottner (Ostfildern-Ruit: Hatje Cantz, 2002), pp. 107–113. Groys draws attention to varying perceptions of the autonomy of the artwork under the influence of the broadening of the practice of artwork presentation as documentation. The text was published in Czech under the title "Umění ve věku biopolitiky. Od uměleckého díla k dokumentaci umění", *Sešit pro umění, teorii a příbuzné zóny*, no. 4–5 (2008), p. 116. Available in English in *Biomediale. Contemporary Society and Genomic Culture*. ed. Dmitry Bulatov (Kaliningrad: The National Centre for Contemporary Art, 2004).

[219] *Ibid.*

[220] *Ibid.*, p. 120.

or feminist institutions.[221] tranzit.cz, for instance, supported artist Barbora Klímová in her artistic research into the personal archives of Czech action artists Vladimír Havlík, Jiří Kovanda, Karel Miler, Petr Štembera, and others. With her *Replaced* project (2006), in which she re-staged the events of these performers from the 1970s and '80s, Klímová contributed to a valorisation of documentation as well as the aestheticisation of the tools of its presentation, and drew attention to the changed status of the autonomous work.[222]

The relationship to public themes was particularly articulated in events by artists who chose to assume the central position of the protagonist along with methods involving body art or public space interventions. One's own corporeality and the intimacy derived from it is one of the tried and tested ways to mediate for the audience the tension between the individual and the collective, the private and the public, thereby establishing an effective mode of communication. These artistic strategies contain an emancipatory potential that can have various degrees of engagement. Gender politics are a frequent theme of the above-mentioned Veronika Bromová, as well as Slovak artist Anna Daučíková, the duo composed of Anetta Mona Chişa & Lucia Tkáčová, Radim Labuda, Darina Alster, and Tamara Moyzes, who often works with specific socio-cultural affairs regarding racial and national conflicts. Eva Jiřička also enters a polemic with social convention through her urban interventions: she films her delicate disruptions of street furniture, rules, and established models of behaviours in order to then be able to present them in various contexts. The practice of event recording has become for these artists an eminently commonplace part of their performances, making use of a static camera or another person to operate the camera without particularly specific demands as to the form of documentation.

A number of artists who hold on to the performative role also work with narrative – and it is the telling of stories that brings art of the moving image in the context of the art world closest to cinema. Artist Michal Pěchouček confesses to an admittedly naive penchant for traditional cinematic genres, having also performed in some videos, photo-novels, and short films.[223] Also fans of fictional narration and the use of symbolism reminiscent of fairy tales are Veronika Vlková and Magdalena Bažantová, two artists who bring together live action footage and animation. In 2009, they made *Snow Queen,* a joint introspective fantasy film. An interest in audience mechanisms in the porn industry led the work of Ondřej Brody to a series of

[221] An overview of exhibitions, publications, lectures, and screenings is available on the tranzit.cz website, accessed 8 Apr 2022, https://cz.tranzit.org/cz/.

[222] The same year, Barbora Klímová became a laureate of the Jindřich Chalupecký Award for this project.

[223] Sylva Poláková, "Méně tvořit a více makat. S Michalem Pěchoučkem o „kulátolství" a kolektivní terapii"" [Create Less, Work Harder. With Michal Pěchouček on "Culatolship" and Collective Therapy], Kulturní týdeník A2 4, no. 49 (2008), pp. 14–15.

explicit erotic video performances: *Noise Pictures* (2005), *Dominik* (2007), and *Carpe Diem Picture* (2008). With more complex narrative works came the need for collaboration with film professionals. Beginning with the second decade of the new millennium, the demands (and possibilities) of cinematic treatment became more professional, and these pieces are therefore also often intended both for exhibition spaces and film screenings. We find a similar duality in the cinematographically more sophisticated products on the borders of documentary film, fiction, and activist art that appear in the work of artists who have a background both at art universities and in film education. Vladimír Turner, creator of a number of environmental films – both documentaries and stylised performances – is a graduate of FAMU, as is artist Lea Petříková, who bases her work on artistic research, thus giving rise to works on the borders of reality and fiction.

Rather than assembling a catalogue of names representative of particular approaches, I tend towards mapping developments in art through the question of *where*[224] the event in question takes place, both in the sense of the process (if it is a live event) as well as in terms of presentation. The environment in which, and for which, the event is effected is crucial for uncovering the dynamic relationships that influence its concept, form, interpretation, and contextualisation. The live component of a video performance, which can be documented and then circulate as a virtually autonomous work in the form of a recording, is best used in an exhibition (in the case of performances, particularly exhibition openings) [225]or festival model,[226] both of which contribute to the establishment of interaction with the spectator. Interventions into public urban space can take the form of direct action in a physical environment, with the artists counting on film documentation as an independent form of output.[227]Artists, however, are not only limited to physical, material space. The original reasons for the development of temporary artistic interventions such as performances

[224] See footnote no. 162.

[225] A good example is Radim Labuda's site specific installation *Tihle – Sociální situace: pět svázaných mužů* [These – Social Situation: Five Men Tied-Up] (2008) for the finalists' exhibition of the Jindřich Chalupecký Award. The installation was composed of five television screens with performances recorded during the exhibition opening. The second performative component, which consisted of internet communication with another protagonist, only took place for the duration of the exhibition. For more on exhibition practice, see Markéta Jonášová's contribution to this volume.

[226] Today, performative interventions making use of the moving image appear at almost all Czech art and film festivals, as they form part of the festivals' strategies for targeting audiences and promotion. Performative interventions in public spaces help appeal to broader audiences and can also be used as part of the organiser's branding campaign. A specific example is screenings onto the facades of buildings, including projection mapping, creating a light-kinetic environment (e.g., the Macula group's projection mapping on the facade of the Aeroport festival building, Karlovy Vary International Film Festival, 2008–2010). For more on festival practice, see Lenka Střeláková's contribution to this volume.

[227] E.g., events by Mark Ther and Ondřej Brody, who, at the beginning of the millennium, tested the thick skin of passengers in public transport by cutting reeking foodstuffs – *MHD* (Mark Ther, Ondřej Brody, 2002).

and happenings – to extricate art from its ties to the art world in order for it to become living art – can be applied today, in this era of communication, to public spaces, which can be broadened to include the virtual domain. The current generation is well aware of the specificities and reach of television and the internet.

In the case of the older medium of television, which, as a public service, falls under greater control, the character of the interventions was dependent on whether the event took place within television programming or outside it. In 1993, when director Michal Caban approached Tomáš Ruller to include his performance *Nehybnost* [Immobility] in the Czech Television programme Možné cesty pohybu [The Possible Paths of Movement], the request to perform the piece live was refused and a recording was broadcast instead.[228] If artists wanted to avoid dramaturgical limitations or even restrictions, they had to resort to the strategy of the "moment of surprise" or camouflage, as in the case of Ondřej Brody on the Artóza programme, where he surprised the other guests (Michal Pěchouček, Jiří Surůvka, and Vlasta Čiháková Noshiro) by wetting himself.[229]At the turn of the millennium, the artist Tomáš Svoboda, whose work involves a deconstruction of the cinematic experience, infiltrated the programming of commercial televisions Nova and Prima: during the Kotel [Cauldron] discussion programme, the guest of which on that occasion was the minister of health, Svoboda stood in the audience holding up a banner that claimed "art heals" (*Umění léčí* [Art Heals], 1999). Six years later, he participated in the cooking show Prima vařečka [Prima Wooden Spoon], where he prepared recipes named after famous painters (*Prima vařečka*, 2005). His gentle actions took place without any interven-

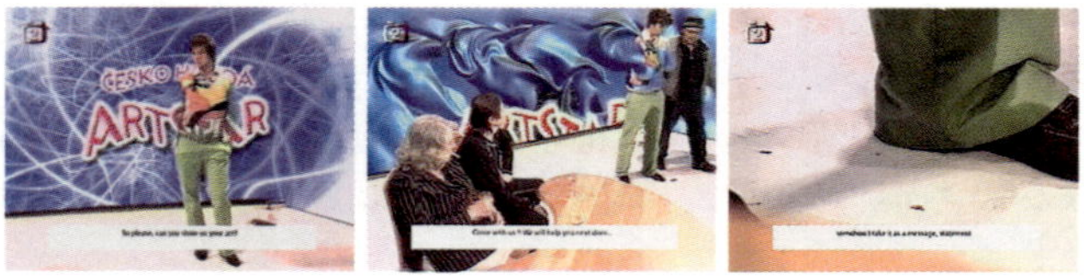

Ondřej Brody *Artstar* (2004), video, 2 min 35 s

tion from the TV stations. At the other extreme is an event called *Atomový výbuch* [Atomic Explosion] by the Ztohoven group, which resulted in its members being taken to court on charges of scaremongering. On June 17th 2007, Ztohoven, which at the time also included Vladimír Turner,[230] hacked into Czech Television's morning broadcast. Suddenly, amongst the online webcam shots of Czech mountains and cities, an atomic mushroom cloud appeared. The scaremongering lawsuit was ultimately dropped. Artistic interventions in communication media offer a broad range of strategies to

[228] This information was provided to Sylva Poláková by Tomáš Ruller during an identification screening, acquisition documentation, 1 Apr 2022, Národní filmový archiv.

[229] *Artstar* (Ondřej Brody, 2004).

[230] Vladimír Turner interviewed by Barbora Aradská (not only) about the *Atomový hřib* event, 29 Feb 2022, Národní filmový archiv, Orální historie [Oral History] collection.

communicate with users of media outside the scheme of control. An even greater range is available on the internet, although here it is also problematic to judge the origins of the published content or the ratio between living and artificial relationships, and to achieve a complex grasp of identity.[231] The possibilities of realising deinstitutionalised communication with the help of networked connection are enticing and unanchored, but they also carry great risks, perhaps even greater than the risks faced by action artists in public spaces in the 20th century. Video performance, in the sense of action captured by the moving image, is dissolved among other genres, with the term gradually losing its ontological justification, similarly to the process undergone by the term video art itself.

[231] For more on art created in the internet environment, see Marie Meixnerová's contribution to this volume.

Net Art as Art of the Moving Image: Foundations and Presentation

Marie Meixnerová

What were the conditions for the creation and presentation of internet art in the Czech Republic from 1989 to the present, seen from the particular perspective of the moving image? It seems that a crucial role is assumed by mutually influential transforming technologies, their development and availability, the situation in education and institutional support, and opportunities to exhibit (and, by extension, purchase) art. This essay first explores the establishment of the internet and the availability of crucial technologies in the Czech Republic, describing the first experiments with the moving image on the internet in the global context (GIF, web films, ASCII). It takes into account the restructuring of art universities – which was so crucial for the creation of Czech new media art – and their connection to key figures in Czech net art who were active shortly after the introduction of the internet to the Czech Republic and attained an international reputation during this time of technological optimism. Their success was often thanks to unique institutional support provided by the Soros Center for Contemporary Art Prague, the Linhart Foundation, the Goethe-Institut, or commercial sponsors, particularly the multinational company Silicon

Graphics. It is only because of the foundation of these systemic dynamics – technology, education, and production – that we can sketch the thematic content that characterises various generations of artists. Against the backdrop of the expansion of the internet into everyday life, the study introduces a second wave of artists born after 1980, active at a time when internet platforms allowed for the relatively simple sharing of audiovisual content. The text concludes with a description of our current, "post-internet" or "post-digital" situation, when the relationship between art and the internet has entirely dissolved into the category of contemporary art.

Transformations of Internet Art

The exploration of the internet within the context of contemporary art, the attempt to mirror in audiovisual form its structural, socio-political, historical, or "just" visual specificities has been part of artistic practice in the Czech Republic since the spread of the internet in the 1990s. The formal transformations of what we now call internet art are, to a large extent, brought about by the technological development of the medium of the internet itself.[232] The first phase, known as the age of the pioneers, is of a primarily digital character, and can be perceived quite unproblematically as part of the superordinate category of new (or digital) media. Even so, net art in this period cannot be considered something media specific or formalist – on the contrary, a broad spectrum of works was created at this time. The pioneers of internet art at the turn of the 1980s and '90s explored the potential of the medium in an experimental and self-reflective manner,[233] but there were also art projects exceeding digital space in both the material and social sense.[234]

After the introduction of the World Wide Web, and especially after its mass dissemination in the mid 1990s,[235] this specific interface and greater access to technology opened up the internet to the public, which

[232] For more on the changes in development and the stages of the internet in art, see e.g., Katarína Rusnáková, "Digitálne umenie na Slovensku v prvej dekáde 21. storočia: perspektívy a frustrácie, I. čas" [Digital Art in Slovakia in the First Decade of the 21st Century: Perspectives and Frustrations, Part 1], *Profil súčasného výtvarného umenia* [Profile of Contemporary Visual Art] 19, no. 3 (2012), pp. 8–25; Marie Meixnerová, ed., *#mm Net Art—Internet Art in the Virtual and Physical Space of Its Presentation* (PAF, z. s. and Link Editions, 2019).

[233] See e.g., Dieter Daniels – Gunther Reisinger, eds., *Net Pioneers 1.0. Contextualizing Early Net-Based Art* (Berlin – New York: Sternberg Press, 2010).

[234] E.g., works and projects including *history of net.art carved in stone* (Blank & Jeron, 1999), ** FuckU-FuckMe* (Alexej Šulgin, 1999), *[V]ote-auction* (Ubermorgen, 2000), *Biennale.py*, (0100101110101101.ORG & [epidemiC], 2001), *Nike Ground* (0100101110101101.org, 2003). As concerns societal themes, I focus – with a view to the Czech context – on cyberfeminism, which has been explored in detail by informatics researcher Petra Jedličková, see e.g., Petra Jedličková, "Ženy na drátech aneb český kyberfeminismus / Women on the Wires, or Czech Cyberfeminism", *Jedním Okem / One Eye Open* 1, special edition (Spring 1998), pp. 95–102; Petra Jedličková, "Kyberfeminismus tady a teď" [Cyberfeminism Here and Now], in *Nové čtení světa. 1./ feminismus devadesátých let českýma očima* [A New Reading of the World. 1./ Feminism of the 1990s Through Czech Eyes], eds. Marie Chřibková – Josef Chuchma – Eva Klimentová (Prague: Marie Chřibková, 1999), pp. 260–272.

[235] See Marie Meixnerová, "Web 1.0", in *#mm Net Art—Internet Art in the Virtual and Physical Space of Its Presentation*, p. 12.

also led to the appearance of a number of net art projects. In this essay, I define "net art" – one of the period's terms for art working with the internet or its context – in accordance with the American organisation Rhizome, active at the New Museum in New York, as: an expansive, hybrid set of artistic practices that overlap with multiple media and disciplines. In order to name such a diversity of practices, Rhizome conceives of net art as "art that acts on the network, or is acted on by it".[236]

As software and hardware specifications changed, computer – and, particularly, internet – technologies underwent crucial changes between 1995 and 2022, allowing for greater inclusion of the moving image. Connection speeds, the relative financial availability of the internet, and advances in resolution brought about an ever-increasing incorporation of audiovisual content on the internet, attested to by the growing number of videos uploaded to the net. The first YouTube video was uploaded on 23 April 2005, at the beginning of an era we call "web 2.0", during which it became much easier to include the moving image. The era was ushered in by the creation of platforms such as the open encyclopaedia Wikipedia (2001; its Czech version in 2002) and MySpace (2003) and came into full fruition with the introduction of YouTube (2005; Czech version in 2008), Facebook (2004, available worldwide in 2005; Czech version in 2008), Tumblr (2007), and others.

The Beginnings of the Internet

The spread of the internet in the 1990s coincides with the breakdown of the Soviet Union. The work of the generation of internet artists working in the 1990s was thus inevitably influenced by the fall of the Iron Curtain between East and West. The year 1989 brought great political, social, and technological changes to Czechoslovakia. New technologies entered the market, including the personal computer. In 1992, Czechoslovakia became the thirty-ninth country to connect to the internet, whose original aim was to allow for the transfer of information between research centres and universities and connect existing workplaces in such a way that they could efficiently and quickly share information and data.[237] The internet only became available to

[236] Rhizome had a crucial influence on the presentation, presentation, and theory of digital art. Their definition of net art is from 2016 and was formulated on the occasion of the Net Art Anthology project, whose outputs included: a website in the form of a catalogue, launched in 2016 and gradually supplemented until 2019 and an exhibition – The Art Happens Here: Net Art's Archival Poetics – introducing sixteen crucial works in the history of net art. For more, see Michael Connor – Aria Dean – Dragan Espenschied, eds., *The Art Happens Here: Net Art Anthology* (New York: Rhizome, 2019).

[237] In order for the network to fulfil its role, individual institutions had to be connected first. In the Czech and Slovak Federative Republic (1989–1992), the Ministry of Education supported the construction of a core network (i.e., a system serving for the transfer of information between the individual nodes) between Prague and Brno. This project was first called FERNET (Federal Educational and Research Network) and later renamed to FESNET (Federal Educational and Scientific NETwork). It was to connect academic institutions across the federation and serve as a network for experts. After the dissolution of the Czechoslovak federation in 1993, the project split into two: SANET (Slovak Academic Network) and CESNET (Czech Educational and Scientific Network), the latter of which began operation on 15 March 1993 and still serves as the e-infrastructure for research and development in the Czech Republic. For more, see https://www.cesnet.cz/sdruzeni/.

general users several years later, thanks in part to the clearly demarcated borders defined by legislature, which had, until then, been an obstacle in its development. The sole licence-holder for operating a public data network (and, therefore, the internet) within Czech(oslovak) borders was, until 1995, Eurotel, which offered access through a dial-up connection whereby users paid for the specific amount of time they spent on the internet.[238] At the time, connecting (at a speed of 76 kbps) was a very expensive affair. A milestone for the development of the internet in the Czech Republic came in the year 1995, which saw a liberalisation of the internet take place; the network licence was awarded once again to Eurotel, only this time the licence was not exclusive and allowed private providers to enter the market by mid-1995.[239] Up to this point, it had been mostly students at selected art universities that had an opportunity to encounter internet art (internet access was established at AVU and FaVU in 1994). Visiting the Orbis Fictus exhibition (30 Oct 1995 to 1 Jan 1996), which included a computer connected to the internet, was, for many visitors, one of the very first opportunities to personally try using the internet. In 1995, the first internet café opened in the Czech Republic – in fact, the first in all of Eastern Europe.[240]

Communicating Vessels: Technology, Education, and Acquisition Opportunities

The conditions for the creation and presentation of internet art from 1989 to the present are determined primarily by three mutually influential variables: technology, education, and opportunities for exhibitions and acquisitions. Developments in the internet and other technologies influence their availability: for the development of new media on the Czech scene, a crucial moment was the transition from analogue to digital computer code and getting connected to the internet in the mid-1990s. An important role was played by the availability of highly developed Silicon Graphics

[238] For more on how this historically conditioned situation came about, see Jiří Peterka, "Historie naší liberalizace – I." [The History of Our Liberalisation – I.], 8 Oct 2001, accessed 9 Nov 2023, www.earchiv.cz/b01/b1008002.php3.

[239] "Nevertheless, even before this date, internet services were offered on a commercial basis, but not publicly, only to a closed circle of customers. In actual fact, it was more a circumvention of Eurotel's nonsensical exclusivity (the company did not itself offer access to the internet)," states Jiří Peterka, a lecturer at the Faculty of Mathematics and Physics of Charles University and a member of the Board of the Czech Telecommunication Office (from 6 June 2020 to the present) in his 2001 series on the liberalisation process in the Czech Republic for the ISDN server. The academic CESNET, for instance, provided internet connection to collaborating institutions, COnet to the members of the CSUUG organisation – see Jiří Peterka, "Historie naší liberalizace, díl III: Liberalizace Internetu v ČR" [The History of Our Liberalisation, Part III: The Liberalisation of the Internet in the Czech Republic], 23 Oct 2001, accessed 9 Nov 2023, www.earchiv.cz/b01/b1023001.php3.

[240] "Před 25 lety do Česka oficiálně dorazil internet. Byl pomalý a drahý" [Twenty-five Years Ago, the Internet Arrived in the Czech Republic. It Was Slow and Expensive], ČT24, 13 Feb 2017, accessed 16 Jun 2022, https://ct24.ceskatelevize.cz/veda/2033584-pred-25-lety-do-ceska-oficialne-dorazil-internet-byl-pomaly-a-drahy.

computers that allowed for the first animation projects to be created. The company also supported schools and exhibition activities.[241]

In the 1990s, education at art universities was being restructured. New media and internet approaches permeated into the work of the students at newly established studios.[242] The connection between exhibition and acquisitional activities was characterised, on the one hand, by an enthusiasm for new media, and on the other by the limits arising from the conventions and technical possibilities of the art world and collecting conceptions. In the new millennium, this situation led to the creation of often short-lived specialised galleries and scattered presentations at festivals with an interdisciplinary focus. While the creation of new works and the realisation of exhibitions in the 1990s was significantly supported by entities such as George Soros's foundation and the Goethe-Institut, at the time of writing, Czech institutions are still struggling with fundamental issues such as acquisition strategies, storage methodologies, and the capacity to exhibit net art and keep an installation functional throughout the duration of the exhibition.

First Attempts at Moving Images on the Internet – GIF, Web Films, ASCII

Working with the moving image on the internet was practically unimaginable in the 1990s, nevertheless, attempts at this form did assert themselves online, first in the form of simple animated gifs.[243] The GIF format was the first format in the internet environment that was able to capture and present moving images in the form of an infinite loop. This time-based art can be related to flip books or pre-cinematographic inventions such as the kinetoscope. Inspired by Sergei Eisenstein's film theories, Alexey Shulgin and Olia Lialina, Russian pioneers of internet art who have a knowledge of avant-garde cinema, applied the principles of parallel montage to computer screens and interactivity.[244] Olia Lialina's first web works were based on her experiences as a film critic and founder of Cine Fantom, a film club in Moscow. These works, based on animated GIFs, worked with the possibilities of juxtaposition and the renowned Kuleshov effect.

[241] In this text, I mention the granting of technology to FaVU VUT in Brno and the financial and technological sponsorship, between 1994 and 1997, of the Hi-Tech / Umění v Brně [Hi-Tech / Art in Brno] festival (the director of the Czech branch of Silicon Graphics and also a VUT graduate Michal Klimeš was also its co-curator). The company is also listed in the catalogues of other important exhibitions, such as Orbis Fictus (Waldstein Riding School, 30 November 1995–1 January 1996).

[242] See Tomáš Pospiszyl's contribution to this volume.

[243] GIF, or The Graphics Interchange Format, was defined by the CompuServe development company in the late 1980s.

[244] For more detail on this topic, see Katarína Rusnáková, "Internetové umění a jeho formáty" [Internet Art and Its Formats], in *#mm Net Art—Internet Art in the Virtual and Physical Space of Its Presentation*, p. 15.

Alina Matějová[245] attempts to define the GIF in relation to the moving image as a "short animated silent film created primarily for consumption in private spaces". Lialina and the American artist and critic Tom Moody describe it as an "ubiquitous minicinema".[246] Animated GIFs had been a technical possibility since 1987, when the so-called 87a version of the GIF was introduced – this new format allowed for the creation of compressed animations using timed delays. Web browsers made by the Netscape company, which, at the beginnings of the internet, defined today's form of the web, made animated loops possible in their interfaces in 1995.[247] The possibility of automatically looping animated GIFs was later adopted by rival browsers. In only a few months, the face of the internet changed due to the enormous increase in animations.

In 1997, shortly after the introduction of the GIF, the web film format appeared, which has been explored in more detail by Slovak researcher Katarína Rusnáková and the American novelist, writer, and internet project producer Nora Barry.[248] These are short films intended to be watched on the internet, defined by the digitality, interactivity, and bidirectionality of the medium. In order for web films to be viewed via dial-up internet connections, which were unstable and slow, the image had to be small. At the same time, the internet's interactivity did not limit filmmakers to a single narrative structure.[249] This genre experienced a great upswing around the year 2000, with the dominant centres of Canada and the USA

[245] GIF art – its transformation or continuation of preceding media and art forms including the moving image (film, video, etc.) – and a more precise definition of its position in relation to net art is the subject of a master's thesis by graphic designer Alina Matějová. Alina Matějová, "GIF art: Od grafického formátu až po etablované umění" [GIF art: From a Graphic Format to Established Art] (Diploma thesis, Faculty of Arts, Masaryk University, Brno, 2014), p. 50, p. 71.

[246] Olia Lialina, "Ubiquitous Minicinema", Guggenheim, 20 Aug 2010, accessed 16 Jun 2022, www.guggenheim.org/blogs/the-take/ubiquitous-minicinema. In another text, however, Lialina adds an important note: "If it had been possible to distribute video online from day one, there would be no web as we know it today. Instead, during the long wait for shareable online video, artists developed a distinctive language that we still value today, applying clever montages, modular visuals constructed from reusable, repeatable elements, and minimal activity." Olia Lialina, "Early Experiments Online", Guggenheim, 22 Jul 2010, accessed 16 Jun 2022, www.guggenheim.org/blogs/the-take/early-experiments-online.

[247] The first graphical browser was Mosaic (1993, later renamed to Mosaic Netscape), and it was the first to offer the possibility of including images in websites using the programming language known as HTML (HyperText Markup Language). Its 2.0 version (1996) included Application Extension Blocks – the possibility for the automatic looping of animated GIFs.

[248] Barry uses the term "web cinema". For more on the history, development, and genealogy of web film and its formal specificities, see Nora Barry, "Rozprávanie príbehov na obrazovkách: dejiny webového filmu" [Telling Stories on Screens: The History of Web Film], in *V toku pohyblivých obrazov. Antológia textov o elektronickom a digitálnom umení v kontexte vizuálnej kultúry* [In the Flow of Moving Images. An Anthology of Texts on Electronic and Digital Art], ed. Katarína Rusnáková (Bratislava: Academy of Fine Arts and Design in Bratislava, Afad Press, 2005), pp. 165–179.

[249] Rusnáková, "Internetové umění a jeho formáty", p. 17; Barry, "Rozprávanie príbehov na obrazovkách: dejiny webového filmu", p. 166. These moving images are based on computer games and works made in the early 1990s in QuickTime for CD-ROM. Its existence was conditioned by the introduction of the necessary tools in 1997 (Flash 1.0 by the Macromedia company; RealVideo 1.0 by Real Networks; the internet version of QuickTime by Apple) and the arrival of modem speeds of 28 kb/s.

being followed by Europe (thanks to a reduction in internet prices). In the Czech context, however, the format was not significantly used in art.[250] The ensuing crash of the dot-com bubble brought about a rapid draining of investors and a general stagnation in the field.[251]

In the 1990s, GIF formats were mostly animated with transparent backgrounds, which made them useful in many graphic contexts – e.g., as part of websites, where they became an indelible component of many net art projects. In the Czech environment, this also included Markéta Baňková's hypertext novels *Město.html* [City.html] (1997–1999), *New York City Map* (1999–2002), and others.[252] The latter is composed of fictional interactive maps in HTML composed of texts, hypertext links, original sound recordings, animations, and documentary photographs, and includes over two hundred and thirty-five websites in total.

The GIF format was also popular on blogs (made available since 2007 by the American microblogging platform Tumblr) and is currently experiencing a massive boom in the era of smartphones and phone apps, where GIFs appear without the use of a computer. The aesthetics of the GIF, with the glittering effects and small, simple animations in low resolution typical of the 1990s, have infiltrated contemporary art where they have been identified by a broad range of terms including post-internet, sea punk aesthetics, vaporwave, and others. The GIF became part of the discourse of art and has also established itself in art of the moving image. In the Czech Republic, these methods and formal elements could be observed primarily in student works and works by young artists in the second decade of the 21st century.[253]

Digital Technologies and Art Universities

Crucial for the development of new media art in the Czech Republic was the gradual equipping of art university labs with the appropriate technologies throughout the 1990s.[254] Tomáš Ruller's Video and Multimedia Performance Studio at FaVU succeeded with its first funding

[250] It was in this period that Ivana Košuličová wrote her diploma thesis at Masaryk University in Brno, which explores the topic from the perspective of animated film and analyses, among other elements, the basic traits that characterise the aesthetics of animated film in cyberspace and its distribution. She also does not mention any Czech artists. Ivana Košuličová, "Animovaný film v kyberprostoru" [Animated Film in Cyberspace] (Diploma thesis, Faculty of Arts, Masaryk University, Brno, 2001).

[251] See Barry, "Rozprávanie príbehov na obrazovkách: dejiny webového filmu", p. 174.

[252] The first web work on which Baňková began working during her studies at the graphic art and new media studios at the Academy of Fine Arts in Prague was a hypertext novel – the fictional diary of Růžena Šetková titled *Město.htmll*. This multimedia work was composed of forty-two web pages comprising texts, images, animations, and sounds. In its visuality and conception, *Město.htmll* fully explored the possibilities of the internet in the 1990s. After concluding her studies at AVU, she spent a year in New York. This was where she made her best known and most extensive work, *New York City Map*.

[253] For more on this topic in the global context, see Olia Lialina, "All that Glitters", 14 Sep 2010, accessed 16 Jun 2022, www.guggenheim.org/blogs/the-take/all-that-glitters.

[254] For more on this topic, see Tomáš Pospiszyl's contribution to this volume.

applications for "Multimedia Interaction in the Digitised Environment" and "Integration of Modern Technology and Eco-culture", using the funds to develop a local computer network and build several PC 486s as a foundation for the shift to digital technologies.[255] Woody and Steina Vasulka provided part of their own equipment from their Santa Fe laboratory.[256] For its Multimedia Laboratory, FaVU acquired the first SGI Indy station as a server and an optical internet connection. "The equipment at the Silicon Graphics workstation was exceptional. They had a camera, CD-ROM drives, storage arrays onto which you could digitise video – with very low resolution, but at the time, it was something exceptional (before then, the studio had used an analogue cutting room – author's note)".[257] This made possible the realisation of web projects and network streams, laying the technological foundations for internet art projects at Czech art universities. One of the longest running (since 1997) interdisciplinary projects taking place under the patronage of a studio is a multimedia internet broadcast titled Filum Terminal by Filip Cenek and Zdeněk Mezihorák in collaboration with Tomáš Ruller and Luděk Skočovský.[258] Their activities were then the basis for the collective project InterVision Lab and their "net art streaming", a live multimedia internet broadcast (1999–2004).[259] Under the guidance of Tomáš Ruller, many web-based projects were created at FaVU in the 1990s, mostly of a conceptual nature.[260] Emphasis was placed on expanding contact with the international scene, which took the form of collaborations with external lecturers and trips to international new media festivals.[261] In the late 1990s, the studio was

[255] The "Protohistory" of FaVU is summarised exhaustively from a participant's perspective by lecturer, artist, and performer Tomáš Ruller in his text "Příběh ateliéru" [The Story of a Studio]. Tomáš Ruller, "Příběh ateliéru", 2002, accessed 20 May 2022, http://performance.ffa.vutbr.cz/ARCHIV/CDROM/inner/sub/pribeh.html.

[256] See Jana di Lenardo, FaVU, "Historie a současnost" [History and the Present], accessed 20 May 2022, https://www.favu.vut.cz/fakulta/historie-soucasnost.

[257] Barbora Šedivá, "Vlastně ani nevím, jestli se za tu dobu utvořil nějaký smysluplný způsob, jak novomediální umění učit. Rozhovor s umělcem a pedagogem doc. MgA. Filipem Cenkem nejen o vývoji na FaVU VUT v Brně, ale i o rozličných přístupech k tvorbě a výuce" [I Don't Really Know If We Managed to Find a Meaningful Way of Teaching New Media Art in All That Time. An Interview with Artist and Pedagogue doc. MgA. Filip Cenk About the Developments at FaVU in Brno and Diverse Approaches to Art and Teaching], accessed 20 May 2022, https://monoskop.org/images/a/ad/Rozhovor_s_Filipem_Cenkem.pdf.

[258] For more on this topic, see Lustigová, "Umění nových médií v České republice do roku 2000", p. 83.

[259] "InterVision Lab", *ABART*, accessed 20 May 2022, https://cs.isabart.org/group/4665/members. According to the archived studio website, the project, led by Robert Mořkovský, realised a number of live multimedia internet broadcasts and also prepared for online streaming the video archive of students of VMP. Video Multimedia Performance, "Web-projekty" [Web-projects], accessed 20 May 2022, http://performance.ffa.vutbr.cz/ARCHIV/CDROM/inner/www.html. From 2000 to 2001, the project was presented at the House of Arts in Brno and at the Rudolfinum and AVU in Prague. Ibid.; for more, see also Ruller, "Příběh ateliéru".

[260] For a list of student web works, see "Web-projekty".

[261] Lecturers took students to the MultiMediale in Karslruhe, to Ars Electronica and the Offenes Kulturhaus Oberösterreich in Linz, and to others. They regularly participated in symposia dedicated to new media at the Goethe-Institut with workshops at AVU in Prague or the Hermit alternative international metamedia symposia, organised by Miloš Vojtěchovský at the convent in Plasy. See Ruller, "Příběh ateliéru".

restructured and the faculty expanded. The Video Studio was then led by Japanese theorist Keiko Sei (1998–2001), who brought in her wake a significant shift in thinking about new media.[262]

AVU also acquired Silicon Graphics computers and connected them to the internet network in 1994 (the same year as FaVU in Brno). The manner in which the New Media Studio at AVU was equipped with communication technology has been described by artist and then studio leader Michael Bielický as crucial for the joint studio projects: "The year 1992 was all about communication projects: our studio was invited to [d]ocumenta in Kassel to collaborate on a project by a group of artists called 'Van Gogh TV'. We represented 'Piazzeta Prague' – from our studio, we could, with the help of an 'image telephone', create several broadcasts that were then beamed via satellite throughout the world. [...] This interactive television experiment was then taken over from the satellite programmes by the OK television programme who broadcast it along the normal terrestrial television network. [...] That same year, the New Media Studio participated in a communication project titled 'IPI' (International Painting Interactive), in which artists from sixteen countries used phones and top-quality Silicon Graphics graphic computers to paint a painting together. The result could then be observed in real time during Seagraph (sic)[263] in Chicago on 16 HDTV (High Definition Television) monitors that formed an enormous video screen. This project confronted the participating artists with the question of the individuality of the artwork, but also with the new opportunity for an artist who works in real time: to experience the feeling of omnipresence."[264]

Projects at art universities in the 1990s mostly took the form of videos and interactive or telematic projects, realised at first through satellites, terrestrial television broadcasts, telephone, and fax, and only later through the internet, in the form of timid, initial attempts to explore this newly arriving medium. Art universities and their lecturers participated in the organisation of other public activities associated with the development of the production and presentation of new media art. FaVU played an

[262] For more on this topic, see Martin Mazanec's contribution to this volume.

[263] What is being referred to here is in fact SIGGRAPH (Special Interest Group on Computer Graphics and Interactive Techniques), which has organised an annual conference on computer graphics since 1974.

[264] Michael Bielický, "PRAHA, – NOVÁ MÉDIA, – AKADEMIE VÝTVARNÝCH UMĚNÍ / PRAGUE, – NEW MEDIA, – THE ACADEMY OF FINE ARTS", in *Orbis Fictus: nová média v současném umění / New media in contemporary arts* (catalogue of the second annual exhibition of the Soroc Center for Contemporary Art Prague, 30 Nov 1995 – 1 Jan 1996), ed. Ludvík Hlaváček (Prague: Soros Center for Contemporary Art, 1995), pp. 157–159.

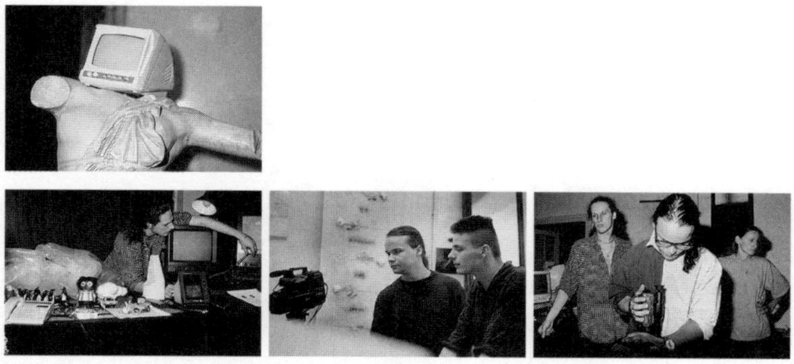

Documentation for the Piazzeta Prague project, broadcast from AVU Prague
as part of Van Gogh TV, [d]ocumenta, Kassel, 1992.

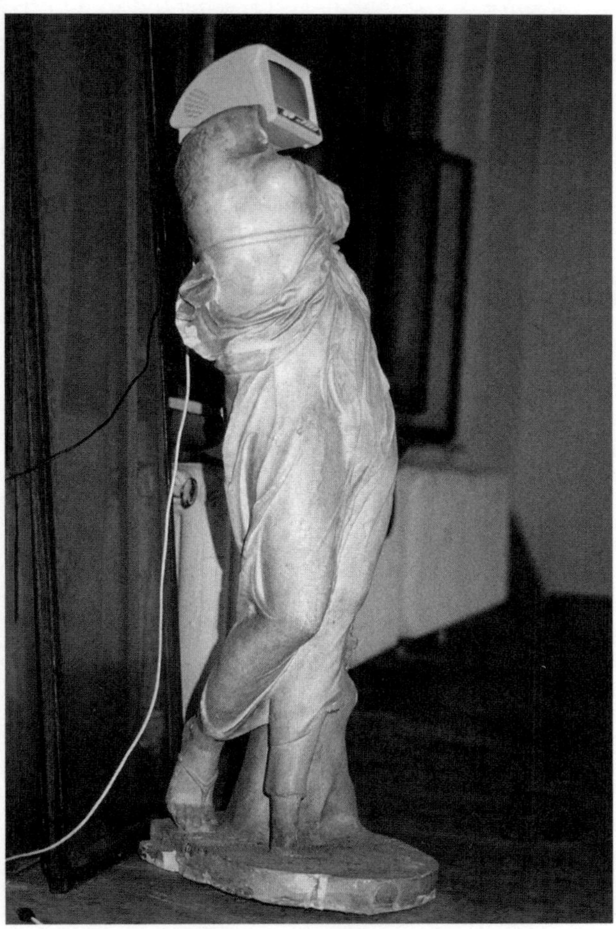

important role in establishing a regular yearly festival, Hi-Tech/Umění.[265] In addition to leading the New Media Studio at AVU, Michael Bielický was also active in Prague as an adviser to the Soros Center for Contemporary Art[266] and collaborated with the Goethe-Institut. In the 1990s, both institutions played a crucial role for the presentation of new media art in the Czech Republic, as well as in other countries of the former Eastern Bloc.

Indispensable Support

The nationality of many of the artists that are today respected as pioneers of internet art – such as Olia Lialina, Alexej Shulgin, Vuk Ćosić, Michael Bielický, and others – suggests that in the 1990s, the former Eastern Bloc was one of the most active regions with regard to net art, partly due to the support of media laboratories financed by the American billionaire with Hungarian roots George Soros.[267] "Soros's laboratories were openly involved in the American post-war plan, which was to connect the former Eastern Bloc with the democratic principles of open access and freedom of speech, the free market, electronic superhighways, and a single superpower."[268] The central aim of George Soros, the founder of the Open Society Foundations and the network of Centers of Contemporary Art, was to support liberal civic societies of the Western type and so-called "open societies". In the Czech Republic, pieces of net art and exhibition opportunities for them were also created thanks to the support of Soros's centre. Founder and former director of the Prague centre, art theorist Ludvík Hlaváček, described the situation at the time as follows:

> Art that works with media, and particularly with so-called new media, such as television, video, satellites, optical cables,

[265] This was a series of international festivals and symposia dedicated to new media art with a belief in the contribution of the commercial sector. Typical of the period, this significantly techno-optimist event was realised in close collaboration with the director of Silicon Graphics, Michal Klimeš, between 1994 and 1997. In 1995, students Petr Bradáček and Zdeněk Mezihorák introduced their new media art, which is close, in some respect, to net art – performances involving software errors. For more on this topic, see e.g., Eliška Fajkusová, "Výstavy a symposia 'Hi-Tech umění' v Brně v letech 1992–1997" [The "Hi-Tech Art" Exhibitions and Symposia in Brno Between 1992 and 1997] (Diploma thesis, Faculty of Arts, Masaryk University, Brno, 2012); Radka Bobčíková, "Brněnské přehlídky a festivaly digitálního umění v 90. letech" [Brno's Festivals of Digital Art in the 1990s] (Bachelor's thesis, Faculty of Arts, Masaryk University, Brno, 2015), p. 13; Ruller, "Příběh ateliéru".

[266] The Soros Center for Contemporary Art was established in 1992. The support from George Soros ended in 2002. Nadace pro současné umění Praha [Foundation for Contemporary Arts Prague], which served as an organisational component for the Soros Centers of Contemporary Art after 1999, took over the funding programme and established the Center for Contemporary Arts Prague, which assumed patronage over the remaining projects.

[267] Frani O'Toole, "The New Museum Hits 'Save' on Net Art", *Hyperallergic*, 20 Feb 2019, accessed 20 May 2022, https://hyperallergic.com/485466/the-new-museum-hits-save-on-net-art/. Net art pioneer Olia Lialina, for instance, first encountered the internet in 1995 on a computer which her Moscow-based experimental club Cine Fantom received thanks to a grant from the Soros foundation; see Net Art Anthology, "My Boyfriend Came Back From the War", 2019, accessed 20 May 2022, https://anthology.rhizome.org/my-boyfriend-came-back-from-the-war.

[268] O'Toole, "The New Museum Hits 'Save' on Net Art".

> computers, the Internet, and other technological means, is now the frequent subject of exhibitions across the entire network of the Soros Centers for Contemporary Art active in formerly socialist countries. This has to do, it seems, with the hopes that are placed in art, and particularly media art, with the desire these countries have for the reestablishment of democracy.[269]

One of the four central project tasks given to each national centre in the network was the so-called annual exhibition, whose goal was to present to the public a genre of contemporary art that was not well established in the country due to the totalitarian conditions that had existed there in the past. The centre in Prague chose the theme of new media and public art.[270] Thanks to a collaboration between the Soros Center and the International Studio & Curatorial Program in New York – and their financial support – artist Markéta Baňková could realise her best-known piece of net art (and also probably the best-known Czech piece of this kind), *New York City Map*, which, in its day, boasted millions of visits. As its second annual exhibition, the Soros Center in Prague realised Orbis Fictus: nová média v současném umění [Orbis Fictus: New Media in Contemporary Art] and published a catalogue, which also became the first publication on new media in the Czech Republic. The centre also supported selected artists financially.[271] Other institutions such as the Linhart Foundation and the Goethe-Institut also supported free artistic activity by providing artists with financial and marketing support. The Goethe-Institut, for example, organised regular symposia on the work of Vilém Flusser (international events on topics involving new media)[272] and invited a number of renowned theorists and artists to Prague, who gave lectures and workshops in collaboration with AVU. In the spirit of the technological optimism of the time, the presentation of new media

[269] Ludvík Hlaváček, "Umění, technika a otevřená společnost. Komunikace jako transcendence / Arts, Technology, and Open Society. Communication as Transcendence", pp. 8–12, here p. 8.

[270] For more details, see Ludvík Hlaváček, Atlas transformace [Atlas of the Transformation], "Sorosovo centrum současného umění" [The Soros Center for Contemporary Art], 2008–2010, accessed 20 May 2022, http://www.monumenttotransformation.org/atlas-transformace/htmll/s/sorosovo-centrum/sorosovo-centrum-soucasneho-umeni.htmll. See also Open Society Fund Praha, "10 let Nadace Open Society Fund Praha" [10 Years of the Open Society Fund Praha Foundation], 2002, accessed 20 May 2022, https://osf.cz/wp-content/uploads/2015/08/OSF_10let.pdf.

[271] At the end of 1995 (30 Nov 1995–1 Jan 1996), the Soros Center for Contemporary Art Prague organised (in collaboration with the Goethe-Institut, the National Gallery in Prague, the commercial TV station TV Nova, and Silicon Graphics) an exhibition in the Czech Republic dedicated to new media, held at the Waldstein Riding School. An international conference was also organised at the Goethe-Institut in connection to the exhibition: "Umělé životní prostředí jako umělecké dílo" [The Artificial Environment as an Artwork]. The catalogue published along with the Orbis Fictus exhibition (30 Nov 1995–1 Jan 1996) was the result of two years of research and represented an attempt to present Czech new media art in the international context, particularly its historical contextualisation within the Czech environment. Ludvík Hlaváček, *Orbis Fictus: nová média v současném umění: new media in contemporary arts*.

[272] Bielicky, "PRAHA – NOVA MEDIA – AKADEMIE VYTVARNYCH UMĚNI / PRAGUE – NEW MEDIA – THE ACADEMY OF FINE ARTS", p. 160.

art was also sponsored by commercial subjects, such as TV Nova, Philips Lightings, s.r.o., TIS Apple Computers, a.s., Siemens, s.r.o., Tesla Television, and the multinational company mentioned above, Silicon Graphics.[273]

The Ubiquitous Internet and the First Generation of Artists

In the Czech Republic, the year 1998 marked a turning point in the financial availability of dial-up connections thanks to a public consumer event known as "Internetem proti monopolu" [The Internet Against Monopolies]. That year, Czech Telecom announced a spike in the prices of dial-up connectivity, planned for January 1999. As a consequence of "Internetem proti monopolu", the market ended up offering much friendlier prices. In the late 1990s, then, dial-up connections were considerably cheaper at night (between 9 p.m. – changed to 11 p.m. a year later – and 7 a.m.), on weekends, and on state holidays, while the most expensive prices were during work hours. At the time, however, dial-up connectivity as such was in decline – many internet providers who entered the market after 1995 were offering internet as part of a monthly package and prices were pushed down to an acceptable level. During the course of the 1990s, the internet gradually displaced the Bulletin Board System (BBS) in the Czech Republic, which was most active between 1983 and 1995.[274] The year 2002 brought the first Wi-Fi connection to the country, facilitated by the CZFree. Net non-profit community network, which used its own finances to allow anyone to connect to the internet. The first fast ADSL connection in the Czech Republic was offered by SkyNet in 2003, and the same year saw the introduction of an offer from Eurotel for unlimited connection for a monthly rate. Also at this time, Web 2.0 gradually set in, introducing the period in which common users are no longer simply consumers of content created by a handful of professionals but also become active producers ("prosumers").

In 2004, 24% of households owned computers, and only 15% had internet connections – and only a tenth of these were high-speed. The internet was most used by the age 15–24 demographic (72%). By 2010, 50% of Czech households were connected, and in 2012, an LTE mobile network running at a speed of 60 Mb/s became available. According to data from the Czech Statistical Office, in 2015, three quarters of all people above the age of 16 used the internet, i.e., 6.6 million people. According to the VNICTP (Výbor nezávislého ICT průmyslu [The Independent ICT Industry Committee], vnictp.cz), an association that brings together

[273] For more on the support of individual exhibitions and festivals, see Bobčíková, "Brněnské přehlídky a festivaly digitálního umění v 90. letech".

[274] The BBS system preceded the mass use of the internet at a time when users would connect to BBS using a dial-up phone line and a modem. These were the first centres where groups of enthusiasts were formed – they would exchange all kinds of information, although predominantly things related to computers. Wikipedie – The Free Encyclopedia, "Bulletin Board System", 16 Jul 2020, accessed 20 May 2022, https://cs.wikipedia.org/wiki/Bulletin_Board_System.

regional operators, internet unavailability was lower than 1% in 2018; 81% of Czech households were connected to the internet and a similar share of households owned a computer. 95% of people between the ages of 16 and 24 used a smartphone. In 2020, 98.2% of people aged 16 to 34 used the internet, with 81.7% of all households connected. Today, the number of internet users is larger than the number of computer users (primarily due to the rise of smartphones). The internet has long ceased to be a space that artists need to explore and bring the threshold of its possibilities closer to users through net art. It has become the living environment of the current generation, one of whose natural components is art.

In the 1990s and the first half of the 2000s, several Czech artists worked with the internet as a distinctive creative tool. We can use their selection of themes and presentation environments as well as how they are preserved to examine the difficult position of this ephemeral art. Despite the difficulties, however, all those named below achieved a certain level of renown both at home and internationally. In addition to Michael Bielický, they include Markéta Baňková, the Silver virtual unit, and a group of artists centred around FaVU in Brno (Zdeněk Mezihorák, Filip Cenek, and the InterVision Lab). From today's perspective, we can label them representatives of the older or first generation of Czech internet artists. They are artists who were active in the Czech Republic in the 1990s and the first half of the 2000s (i.e., in the time before web 2.0). Most of them then left the country or began working in other fields of art, often as a consequence of a logical extension of internet art into other spheres.[275] They were influenced by their teachers and the educational context (its open atmosphere, interdisciplinary approach, multimediality, and technical facilities) that these pedagogues – particularly Tomáš Ruller and Michael Bielický – helped develop at FaVU and AVU. In contrast to Ruller, whose work examined the possibilities of live action (though in connection with new media), Bielický's was inclined towards the use and creation of multimedia works and projects. In addition to many video installations, video sculptures, and new media projects, Bielický also worked on teleperformances in which he initiated artistic research into virtual communication on the network.[276] At the turn of the millennium, virtual reality caught his attention.[277] In the interactive installation *Tento rok v Jeruzalémě* [This Year in Jerusalem] (2006) for

[275] I have described these artists' activities in detail elsewhere; Marie Meixnerová, "A Note on the Older Generation of Czech Net Artists", in *#mm Net Art—Internet Art in the Virtual and Physical Space of Its Presentation*, pp. 25–30

[276] E.g., the projects *Inteligentní pošťák* [Intelligent Postman] (1992) and *Exodus* (1995), in which he made use of GPS technology. For more on this topic, see Jiří Zemánek, "Od ideologie reality k pluralitním modelům. České umění elektronických médií v devadesátých letech" [From the Ideology of Reality to Pluralist Models. Czech Electronic Media Art in the 1990s], in Rostislav Švácha – Marie Platovská (eds.) *Dějiny českého výtvarného umění VI / 1, 2. 1958–2000* [History of Czech Art VI / 1, 2. 1958–2000] (Prague: Academia, 2007), p. 910.

[277] E.g., projects such as *Delvauxův sen* [Delvaux's Dream] (1996–1999) and *Pokoj s výhledem* [A Room with a View] (*Das Zimmer mit Aussicht*, 1999–2000).

the Robert Guttmann Gallery in Prague, he connected Prague and Jerusalem in real time using motion sensors and webcams. An interest in bringing physical spaces together with the use of communication technologies – and, by extension, virtual space – and the issue of creating public media content have been present in his work since his time at AVU until today.[278]

Typical for Markéta Baňková's internet works was a propensity towards the literary and text as a bearer of information with the use of sound. Her net art pieces take the form of interactive websites, mostly created in the HTML language, in contrast to works intended for presentation in physical spaces, such as that of Bielický or certain contemporary young artists. In this sense, her work is net art *per se*: art about the net, created on the net, and intended for the net, examining and critically commenting upon its possibilities. In 2001, the American digital artist and computer scientist Martin M. Wattenberg included *New York City Map* in his representative IDEA LINE, a timeline of crucial pieces of net art that he prepared for the Whitney Museum of American Art in New York.[279] Baňková's final work of net art is the website *Čáranice – CNN více v obraze(ch)* [Scribble] (2005), in which the artist "used" CNN's global news website, covering it up with a collage of drawings automatically responding to the contents of the main article and its most important links. This created a considerably unpredictable yet eloquent commentary on world news, which the artist described as a "visual commentator". Shortly after this work was published, Baňková explained in an interview for *Hospodářské noviny* her decreasing motivation to devote the time needed to create another web project as a consequence of the difficulty in commodifying new media artworks. She cited the then prevailing impossibility of trading internet art and the obstacles to circulating it in the gallery world in comparison to other forms of art.[280] Baňková's rational distancing from net art projects points to the unique challenges in asserting this practice within the art world, which was unable to provide this internationally known artist adequate valuation. She never finished her next piece, *Initialnews.com.* As late as 2002, however, as one of the five finalists of the Jindřich Chalupecký Award, a prestigious prize for Czech artists under thirty-five, she presented

[278] He continues to create projects that have the character of monumental net art installations connecting physical and virtual spaces. Projects such as *Falling Times* (with Kamila B. Richter and D. Reinbold, 2007) and *Columbus 2.0* (with Kamila B. Richter, A. Jungnickel, D. Reinbolda A. Siefert, 2008) interactively thematise world news. His installation *Garden of Error and Decay* (*Zahrada omylu a úpadku*, with Kamila B. Richter, 2011) and his proposal for a site-specific project at the cathedral in Ulm (*Passage*, 2013) are receptive to activities on Twitter; the silent film *Why Don't We* (with Kamila B. Richter, 2013) drew tweets from Twitter in real time, using them as film titles. The creative duo describes this form of narration as "Data Driven Narratives". For more on Bielický, his net art, and his work in the present, see my text Meixnerová, "Poznámka ke starší generaci českých internetových umělců", pp. 25–31; and Michael Bielický's profile in *Net art* (Šobáňová, *Net art*, pp. 120–130.)

[279] See Martin M.Wattenberg, IDEA LINE 2001, accessed 20 May 2022, whitney.org/exhibitions/idea-line.

[280] Magdalena Čechlovská, "Markéta Baňková: 'Žádné technologie nenahradí mejdan'" [Markéta Baňková: 'No Technology Will Replace a Party'], *Hospodářské noviny*, 21 Jan 2005, accessed 4 Sep 2015, http://kultura.ihned.cz/index.php?p=J00000_d&article[id]=15529680.

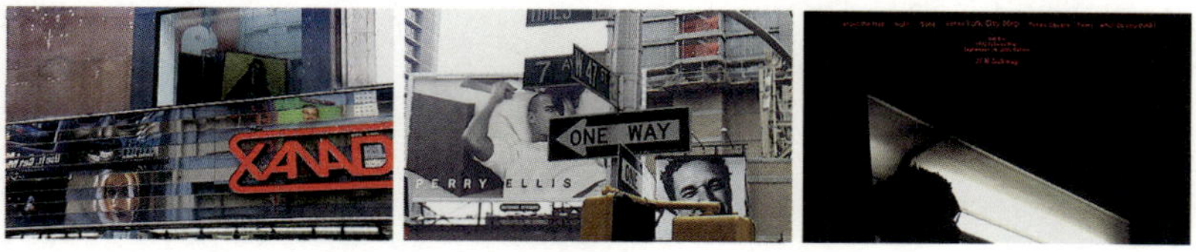

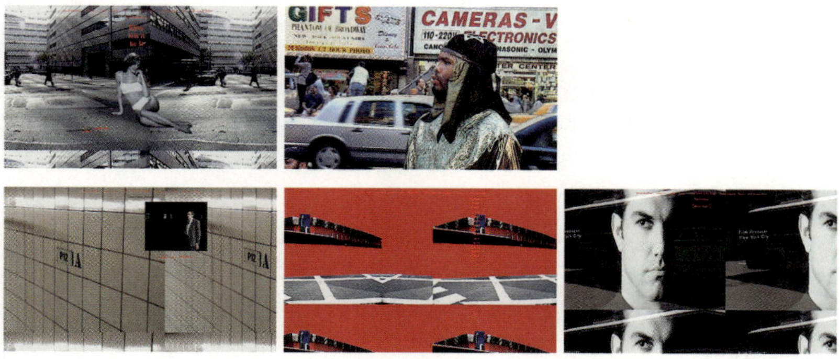

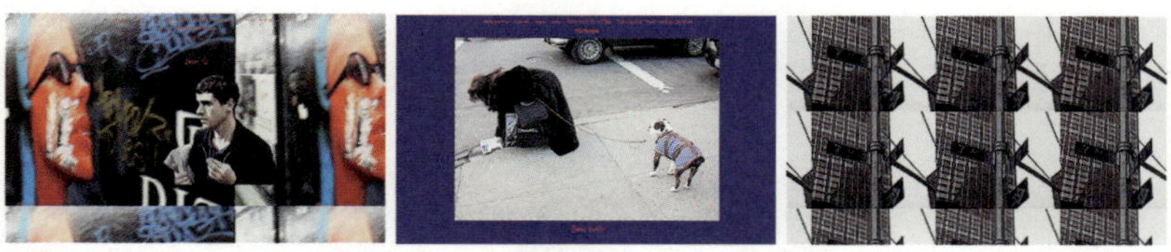

Markéta Baňková *New York City Map* (1999–2002),screenshots from https://www.nycmap.com/

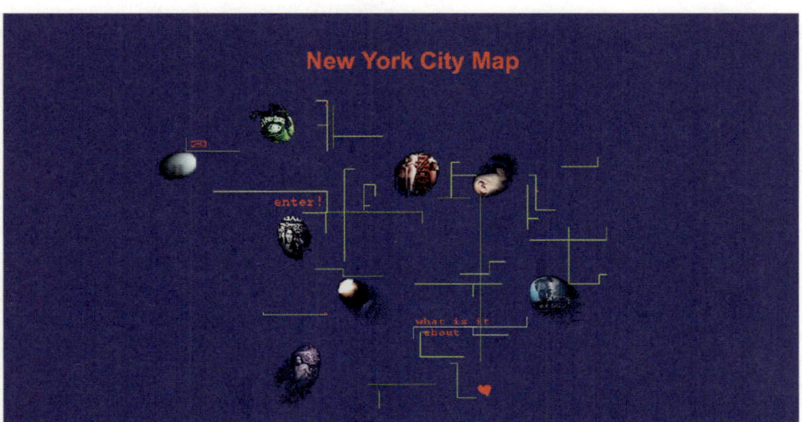

the net art piece *New York City Map* at the House of Arts in Brno in a manner typical of the 1990s[281] and also adapted her older web project *Město* for the purposes of a gallery exhibition.[282]

Other artists made their first net art pieces as students at art universities. Petr Svárovský studied at AVU and, following his graduation, became an assistant to Michael Bielický in the New Media Studio. In 1994, he established the Silver group, which presented itself as a *visual artist*. It was a variable entity, a virtual, fictional identity operating on the borders of art, science, and technology. For each project, an implementation team was assembled, responsible for the creation of the work, with the core of the group consisting of Svárovský himself, who participated in most of the projects (and with whom Silver is often mistaken).[283] The group first worked on interactive sound installations, later moving to virtual reality, the internet, and code art, and, finally, to the technological possibilities and uses of mobile phones and collaborative strategies as a form of pushing the boundaries of art. Like many pieces of internet art, some of Silver's older pieces were impossible to maintain on the web due to quickly changing technical specifications. Today, they are no longer available and survive only in the form of period descriptions by spectators and the authors. Among the best-known works, now included in the historical canon of art of the 1990s, are the interactive project *Rose* (1995) or *E-Flowers* (1996), a work at the intersection of computer animation and net art.[284] Towards the end of the decade, Svárovský added to his pedagogical activities an attempt to mould the local new media scene (including internet art) as a curator. In 1998, he curated an exhibition of Czech new media artists who had realised their projects in the New Media Laboratory of the Soros Center for Contemporary

[281] When installing *New York City Map* (1999–2002) for the finals of the Jindřich Chalupecký Award in 2002 at the House of Arts in Brno, a "literal" principle for the exhibition of internet art was used – this approach was inoperative and had been vocally criticised since its first and best known use at the 1999 documenta X international festival in Kassel and is now considered outdated since it is entirely inappropriate for internet works: A table with a computer is placed in the exhibition space, with the website – the piece of net art – loaded up. Two chairs are added and peripherals allowing for audience interaction – a keyboard or mouse. Furthermore, at the House of Arts, the computer screen was also projected onto a wall in the same room. As part of the exhibition and the competition presentation, her work was described as an "interactive computer project". See Lenka Lindaurová, ed., *MEZERA. Mladé umění v Česku 1990–2014* [GAP. Young Art in the Czech Republic 1990–2014) (Prague: Jindřich Chalupecký Society, Yinachi, 2014), pp. 255, 289.

[282] Her presentation at the exhibition of the finalists of the Jindřich Chalupecký Award also included a video titled *Smysly života* [Senses of Life] (2002).

[283] Among the artists who participated on some of Silver's projects are sound engineer Pavel Rejholec; Jan Stehlík; organologist and composer Milan Guštar, who works with electronic and electro-acoustic instruments that can be used by visual artists in the field of new media; web designer Petr Hejda; Monika Karasová, a graduate of Michael Bielický's New Media Studio who focuses on multimedia stage productions; and Alena Kupčíková from Milan Knížák's studio of Monumental Art, who explored the use of multimedia tools in the field of care for dyslexic children. The group also had several international members, especially from Norway, with whom Petr Svárovský has collaborated on the creation of multiple, variously focused virtual environments, e.g., Martin Havnør, Hanne Rivrud, True Solvang Vevatne, and Henrik G. Sundt.

[284] Petr Svárovský interviewed over email by Marie Meixnerová, 18 Aug 2014.

Art in Prague.[285] The Laboratory concluded its activities in 2002 when it lost financial support from the Soros Centre. In the new millennium, the artists who had often been associated with net art in the 1990s, who often used the facilities of art universities or the Laboratory, directed their creative and professional paths towards better established practices connected to set design, cinema, or graphic design. Markéta Baňková used her skills in popular science to write prose.[286] Petr Svárovský has lived in Norway since 2003, where he works on "connection aesthetics" or "geolocation aesthetics". His works such as *Trolley Singers*, the *Some Evil Is Good* series (*Visitor*, *Visitor Beta*, *Intrigue*, *Intrigue E*), and *Flirtman* can be seen as a continuation of net art. "Unlike net art, however, this is not a fascination with the new aesthetics of the web browser, nor a political message, but precisely connection aesthetics."[287]

The Artists of the New Millennium: Czech Net Art Before the Post-Internet

For the new generation in the new millennium, a crucial event where net artworks or pieces influenced by the internet could be presented and reflected upon was the Přehlídka animovaného filmu [Festival of Animated Film] in Olomouc, later renamed Přehlídka filmové animace a současného umění [Festival of Film Animation and Contemporary Art], PAF for short, which is primarily focused on art of the moving image. In 2008, at the Other Visions competition, Martin Kohout – then a student at the camera department at FAMU in Prague and also at the fine arts faculty at Universität der Künste Berlin – presented his net art piece *Moonwalk*, which was included in the competition screening section. The work was also presented in an installation version and published freely on the internet, specifically on YouTube.[288]

Four years after *Moonwalk* was presented at PAF, I served as a dramaturg for this festival and produced a programme section dedicated to net art. Its aim was to focus attention on Czech net art and attempt to contextualise current approaches to this discipline in the Czech scene.

[285] Participating artists: Jakub Dolejš, Kateřina Fojtíková, Jolana Kuchařová Kalounová, Alena Kupčíková, Františka Ševčíková, Petra Vargová, Aleš Veselý, Janka Vidová. See "Galerie Jelení", accessed 9 Nov 2023, https://www.galeriejeleni.cz/1999/lab-scsu98/.

[286] In 2010, she published a book of short stories, *Straka v říši entropie* [The Magpie in the Realm of Entropy] (Prague: Petr Prchal, 2010), followed in 2015 by a novel, *Maličkost* [A Little Thing] (Prague: Argo, 2015), which popularised genetics.

[287] Petr Svárovský interviewed over email by Marie Meixnerová, 18 Aug 2014.

[288] The *Moonwalk* video was selected as part of the YouTube Play Bienale as one of the twenty-five most creative videos uploaded to YouTube, and was then presented at the Guggenheim Museum in New York. In 2009, it was presented at the Brazilian biennial of contemporary art (7a Bienal do Mercosul, Porto Alegre, Brasil) in an installation version for which Kohout made use of projections onto an object and mirror reflections, giving the internet environment a 3D dimension. The video works with the graphical elements of YouTube, as do works by Constant Dullaart, Ben Koolis, and other net artists from this period, and is included with "site-specific" screenings within the interface of this platform. For more on Kohout's net art period, see Marie Meixnerová, "Martin Kohout (Pash*)", MEDIABAZE.CZ, 12 Oct 2013, accessed 22 May 2022, https://web.archive.org/web/20161029082628/http://mediabaze.cz/page.php?artist=8.

Represented in the net art section were intermedia projects that brought together virtual and physical space. One notable example was the installation *Loginlogout* by Kristýna Lutzová, then a student at the Supermedia Studio at UMPRUM in Prague, which brought together sculpture, video, and a web interface to virtually connect the U Mloka gallery in Olomouc with the conceptual online part of the project, exhibited in the festival press centre.[289] Others projects implemented live projections of flash animations in public spaces – this was the approach chosen by the members of the

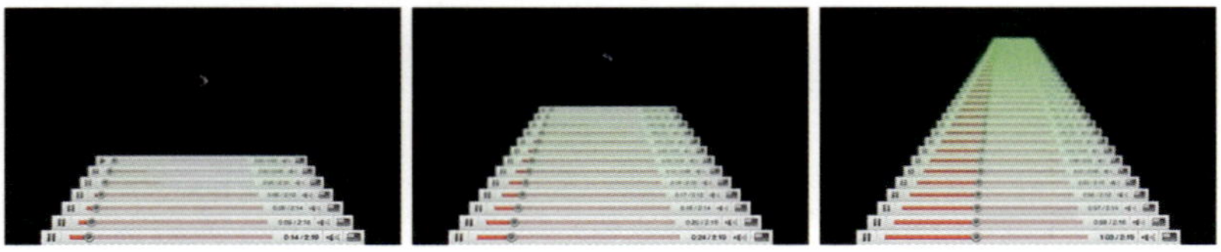

Martin Kohout *Moonwalk* (2008), video, 2 min 20 s

MANIPUL group, which was formed for the occasion of the festival by students of Richard Loskot (who himself authored several works making use of flash animation – *Peříčka* [Feathers], *Káva* [Coffee], *Padání do pole* [Falling Into a Field]) at the Department of the Electronic Image at Jan Evangelista Purkyně University in Ústí nad Labem. Some of the exhibited artists continue to work in the realm of net art. Given the insufficient time that has passed, it could be misleading to attempt to characterise these artists as a particular artistic generation with common features. For now, though, it is possible to outline what art schools they come from and what their experiences are with exchanges abroad that focused on new media. Zdeněk Svejkovský, for instance, followed his master's studies by entering the doctoral programme at the Faculty of Art and Design at Jan Evangelista Purkyně University in 2021 and in addition to his creative practice, which is focused on net art, he also works on web design and in other disciplines connected to new media technologies.[290] The creative duo & (Barbora Trnková and Tomáš Javůrek) has worked consistently on net art since 2010, when, as part of their studies at FaVU in Brno, they participated in an initiatory exchange at the new media studio of the Accademia di Belle Arti di Brera in Milan, led by Mauro Folci and the important theorist, critic, and pedagogue of net art, Domenico Quaranta. At PAF, they introduced their existing net art pieces and a Wi-Fi installation titled *Anna Marie* (annamarie.metazoa.org) in a deconsecrated Baroque chapel.[291] The programme section also included projects by (c) merry (the author of this study), who a year later, during a residency on the Facebook profile of Los Angeles-based

[289] For more on the project, see "www.loginlogout.cz", KRISTÝNA LUTZOVÁ, supermedia sculptor, accessed 25 May 2022, http://www.kristynalutzova.cz/wwwloginlogoutcz.

[290] For more on Zdeněk Svejkovský, see "O mně" [About Me], Zdeněk Svejkovský, accessed 25 May 2022, http://www.zdeneksvejkovsky.name/cv/.

[291] For a profile of Trnková and Javůrka's net artwork, see Marie Meixnerová, "ScreenSaverGallery (2013–Present)", in *The Art of Screensaver*, ed. Marie Meixnerová (Olomouc: PAF & BUT, 2020).

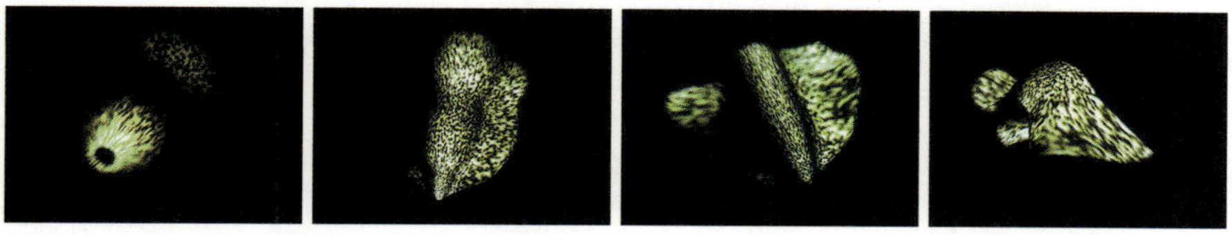

Silver *REZIDENT* (1995), interactive installation

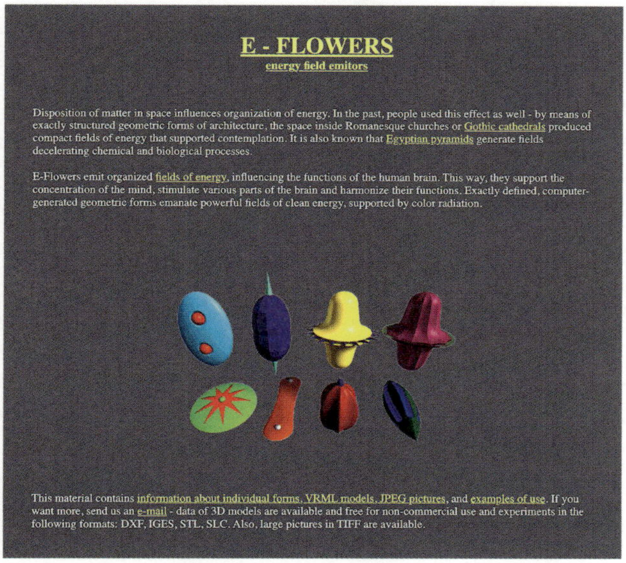

Silver *E-FLOWERS* (1996), internet project

Silver *SIRENES* (1993), documentation from an interactive sound installation, Nová síň, Prague, 1993

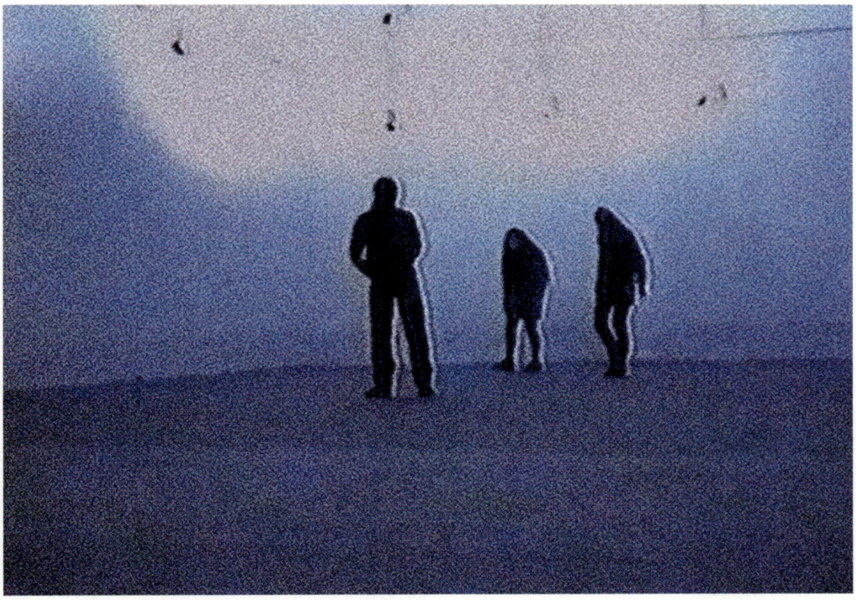

curator Chloë Flores, realised a long durational performance following from the works of the structural filmmakers of the 1950s and '60s.[292]

Martin Kohout also introduced his work in a performative lecture he presented along with new media theorist Palo Fabuš. The variety of art working with the internet was complemented by a number of other artists who are also active in different artistic disciplines. Their projects thematised the internet experience as part of a programme block titled Možná je tma, ale já ji nevidím [Maybe there is darkness, but I can't see it]. Another thematic block, Po stopách současného českého net artu [On the Trail of Contemporary Czech Net Art] featured Stanislav Abrahám, 2046 (Jan Mucska), Trancelater (Tomáš Kořínek), Kristýna Lutzová, Michal Kindernay, The Rodina, and MANIPUL. It can be said that self-representation is a significant feature of the Czech scene (and others): it can take the form of a performance experimenting with one's own identity as a central theme through which the internet environment is examined. Unlike the early days of the internet, web 2.0 allows one to act anonymously or under an untraceable nickname.

The fact that net art is treated as an artistic discipline and therefore exceeds the demarcation of a "mere" artistic period is also attested to by the slow yet extant response of the Czech art market and collecting activities. One example can be the success of the Brno-based artistic partnership & (Tomáš Javůrek and Barbora Trnková) who continue to work in net art (specifically app art and the moving image as part of augmented reality). & mostly exhibits in Czech galleries and is less known abroad, but since 2017, their works have been represented in the collection Od moderny po současnost 1945–2013 [From Modernism to the Present 1945–2013] at the Museum of the City of Brno. This is one of the few acquisitions of net art by a collecting institution – an exceptional case in the Czech Republic due to the lack of methodologies and human or financial resources.[293] Since 2013, & have used their original net artwork, a gallery existing entirely through screensavers called ScreenSaverGallery, to present the work of other artists. Originally an art project, it gradually became a regular online exhibition space whose content consists in large part of art of the moving image: in addition to net art and digital art, there is also video art, particularly performative videos. The programme combines the work of local artists (mostly graduates of FaVU in Brno) and artists from abroad, aiming for an international audience.

[292] "FACEBOOK SCULPTURE", 2013, accessed 20 Jul 2022, https://sites.google.com/site/facebooksculpture/.

[293] See "ZPRÁVA O ČINNOSTI Muzea města Brna, příspěvkové organizace za rok 2017, Brno, únor 2018" [REPORT ON THE ACTIVITIES of the Museum of the City of Brno, Contributory Organisation, for the year 2017, Brno, February 2018], accessed 25 May 2022, https://www.spilberk.cz/wp-content/uploads/Vyrocni-zprava-2017-1.pdf. The work was acquired as part of a series of purchases of artworks by contemporary artists from Brno and Moravia.

The Moving Image and the Post-internet in the Czech Environment

It seems that on the local scene, "internet influences", following an initial boom at the turn of the millennium, only began to appear in greater numbers after the year 2010, with the arrival of the concept of post-internet. In the Czech context, the term became important for the debate around the year 2013,[294] when it was mostly art students who took an interest in the post-internet, dedicating artworks and diploma theses to it as well as initiating public discussions[295] and specialised "white-cube" galleries that operated in Prague. Galerie Plevel [Weeds Gallery] was run by Petr Hošek, Luis Artemio De Los Santos, and Kateřina Cepáková from 2013 to 2014, and Kurzor Gallery by Kristýna Lutzová and Kateřina Cepáková in 2015–2016.[296] The post-internet period, which is approximately dated as 2010 to 2015, emerged as the result of a generational trend and broader socio-cultural contexts and became an expression of a repeated reappraisal of the possibilities of technology. It arose from the post-internet condition, which is characterised by the ubiquitousness of the internet and an erasure of borders between "offline" and "online" events. The artists' critical position also arose from this condition, reflecting their own experiences with the internet.[297] Typical elements of post-internet art include: a return to the gallery space (which the art of the pioneers of net art in the 1990s attempted to escape through a transition to online space); a characteristic mode of visual representation and new aesthetics; a critical position on topics such as information sharing, participation, corporate identities, and self-reflection that mirrors a permeation of the roles of artist, curator, and theorist. Visually, the post-internet can be characterised by paraphrases of elements related to 1990s computer culture (e.g., hardware, elements of the Windows 95 and Mac OS operating systems) that are juxtaposed with classical statues and appropriations of logos and brand names as symbols of the contemporary

[294] See the results of Veronika Sellnerová's research for her bachelor's thesis: Veronika Sellnerová, "Reflexe českého post-internetového umění" [A Reflection of Czech Post-internet Art] (Bachelor's thesis, General Theory and History of Art and Culture / Theory of Interactive Media, Faculty of Arts, Masaryk University, Brno, 2016), p. 41.

[295] Participants in a panel discussion titled Já bych ty post-internety zakázala [I Would Ban Those Post-internets] (Prague, Café Jedna, 28 May 2014), led by Marina Poliačková and Lumír Nykl, included Richard Nikl, Martin Kohout, Palo Fabuš, and David Kořínek. It was held in Prague in 2014, and included the participation of Richard Nikl, Martin Kohout, Palo Fabuš and David Kořínek participated, for example. See "Já bych ty post-internety zakázala", Facebook, accessed 20 Jul 2022. https://www.facebook.com/events/499236446870532/.

[296] https://kurzorkolektiv.wordpress.com/, https://www.facebook.com/kurzorgallery/; the Galerie Plevel Manifest is available at Luis Artemio De Los Santos, "Manifest Galerie Plevel", PAF Olomouc, accessed 20 Jun 2022, https://www.pifpaf.cz/cs/manifest-galerie-plevel; for a presentation of the gallery's activities, see "Legenda o Galerii PLEVEL" [The Legend of Galerie PLEVEL], vimeo.com, 5 Dec 2014, accessed 20 Jul 2022, vimeo.com/140757688.

[297] For more on this topic, see e.g., Omar Kholeif, ed., *You Are Here: Art After the Internet* (Manchester: Cornerhouse and SPACE, 2014); Melanie Bühler, ed., *No Internet, No Art. A Lunch Bytes Anthology* (New York: Onomatopee 102, 2015); Ed Halter – Lauren Cornell, eds., *Mass Effect. Art and the Internet in the Twenty-First Century* (Cambridge, Massachusetts – London: The MIT Press, 2015).

world (Google, Facebook, The Pirate Bay, and others). The subgenres of this aesthetic (seapunk, vaporwave, plantwave) that reference – often in deliberately kitschy ways – the 1980s and '90s, were exhausted relatively quickly.[298] In the work of Czech artists, we can more often trace post-internet tendencies in the conceptual rather than the aesthetic component of the work. Attention is focused on the ontology of the artwork, authorship, being engulfed in technology, or the self-presentation of both individuals and artists on social media.[299] We could say that the only Czech participant in the global post-internet scene is Martin Kohout, who was involved with the Berlin-based Future Gallery as both an artist and curator. This gallery was focused on the post-internet and presented, among other projects, an exhibition and publication crucial for this stage of net art: *Post Internet Survival Guide* by Katja Novitskov.[300]

In the mid-2010s, attempts appeared at more comprehensive presentations of Czech post-internet art. In 2015, curators and artists David Kořínek and Milan Mikuláštík curated an exhibition called Generation Smart, whose subtitle was První výstava českého postinternetového umění [The First Exhibition of Czech Post-internet Art] at the NTK Gallery in Prague, which presented works by over twenty artists including established figures as well as and students at art universities.[301] The Virtual Modality exhibition by curator Veronika Zajíčková presented the youngest artists working directly with the medium of video and post-internet motifs.[302] However,

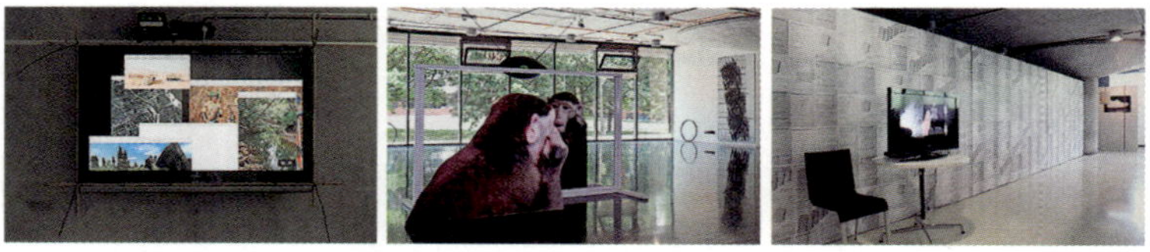

Generation Smart. First exhibition of Czech post-internet art, Galerie NTK, Prague, 2015.

[298] For more details including a description of the individual subgenres, see Veronika Sellnerová, "Post post-internet: Mapování vývoje české umělecké scény" [Post Post-internet: Mapping the Development of the Czech Art Scene] (Master's thesis, Theory of Interactive Media, Faculty of Arts, Masaryk University, Brno, 2018).

[299] Ibid.

[300] Better Brain: Projected Manifestations of Futurity (Charles Broskoski, Martin Kohout, Oliver Laric, Rafaël Rozendaal), 29 Jan – 7 Feb 2010; Martin Kohout: Solo Show, 25–27 Jun 2010; Moving Image. An Art Fair of Contemporary Video Art, New York, 3–6 Mar 2011. On the individual presentations, see "Projects Archive", FUTURE GALLERY, accessed 22 May 2022, http://thefuturegallery.org/index.php?/ongoing/archive/. Also as part of the exhibition of the originally Estonian artist Katja Novitskova Post Internet Survival Guide (Future Gallery, Berlin, 2011), ibid.; for more on this topic, see Katja Novitskova, *POST INTERNET SURVIVAL GUIDE 2010* (Berlin: Revolver Publishing, 2011).

[301] GENERATION SMART. První výstava českého postinternetového umění (Galerie NTK, Prague, 13 May – 13 Jun 2015), exhibiting artists: Kryštof Ambrůz, Filip Dvořák, Jakub Geltner, Katarína Hládeková, Ondřej Homola, Martin Kohout, Martin Kolarov, Adéla Korbičková, David Krňanský, Ladislav Kyllar, Martin Lukáč, Kristýna Lutzová, Black Media, Andrea Mikysková, Richard Nikl, Olbram Pavlíček, Julius Reichel, The Rodina, Lucie Rosenfeldová, Barbora Švehláková, Ladislav Tejml, and Nik Timková.

[302] Virtual Modality (Video NoD, Prague, 19–28 Feb 2016), exhibiting artists: Kryštof Ambrůz, Andrea Mikysková, Anna Sláma, Ladislav Tejml.

only some of the participating artists subscribe directly to the post-internet aesthetic, due in part to the critical distance of the Czech environment, in which the post-internet is reflected more "retroactively".[303]

The alternative, somewhat more accurate term "expanded internet art" appeared briefly towards the end of the 2010s.[304] Contemporary internet art is "expanded", meaning that it takes on various forms, a priori counting on the fact that it will not only be presented on the internet, but also in galleries and that it will exist as photo-documentation, etc. Over time, net art and post-internet art are gradually dissolved in the thematic categories and questions addressed by contemporary art. Curators and theorists abroad attempt to describe this situation using elusive terms and nonce labels of which perhaps the most pertinent is "post-digital practice".[305] We are arriving at a point where it is no longer defensible to single out net art within the context of contemporary art. Today, net art is not definable through the specificity of the medium, it does not arise from the "netizenship" of its creators, nor can it be described on the basis of an "inspiration" from the internet – at most, we can discuss the mutual influence of art and the internet or discuss art *about* the internet. The separation of art and internet is, however, a purely thematic division.

[303] Veronika Sellnerová came across this feature (and described it in greater detail) during her research into and interviews with Czech post-internet and post post-internet artists; see Sellnerová, "Reflexe českého post-internetového umění" or Sellnerová, "Post post-internet: Mapování vývoje české umělecké scény".

[304] Ceci Moss, *Expanded Internet Art. Twenty-First-Century Artistic Practice and the Informational Milieu* (New York: Bloomsbury, 2019). For a definition of the post-internet, see also Meixnerová, *#mm net art – internetové umění ve virtuálním a fyzickém prostoru prezentace*, pp. 109–112.

[305] The topic of the impotence and redundancy of terms attempting to describe or pigeon-hole the relationship between the internet and art was the focus of a panel discussion of curators and researchers with Michael Connor, artistic director of Rhizome, at Art Basel, 9 Dec 2017. A recording is available on YouTube, accessed 22 May 2022, https://www.youtube.com/watch?v=tqdjbXovLqM.

01 **Niké Papadopulosová** *Polednice* [The Noonday Witch] (1999), video, 6 min
02 Archival newspaper article on the legacy of Vilém Flusser, Goethe-Institut, Prague.
03 **Lea Petříková** *Godiva, from the series V hodině Schrödingerovy kočky* [In the Hour of Schrödinger's Cat] (2014), video, 4 min 44 s
04 **Eva Koťátková** *Žaludek světa* [Stomach of the World] (2017), video, 46 min
05 **Filip Cenek** *Po Atentátu (3 fragmenty)* [After the Assassination (3 Fragments)] (1998), video, 6 min 10 s
06 **Pavel Ryška** *Cheesy Change* (2006), video, 7 min
07 Installation as part of the Videokemp festival (2011).
08 **BCAA system** *No~one Is an Island* (2019), video, 26 min
09 **Eva Jiřička** *360°* (2006), video, 6 min 48 s
10 New media studio, Academy of Fine Arts in Prague, first half of the 1990s.
11 **Michal Pěchouček** *Sběratel* [Collector] (2003), video, 7 min 26 min
12 **Elen Řádová** *Wet Video* (1993), video, 1 m 24 s

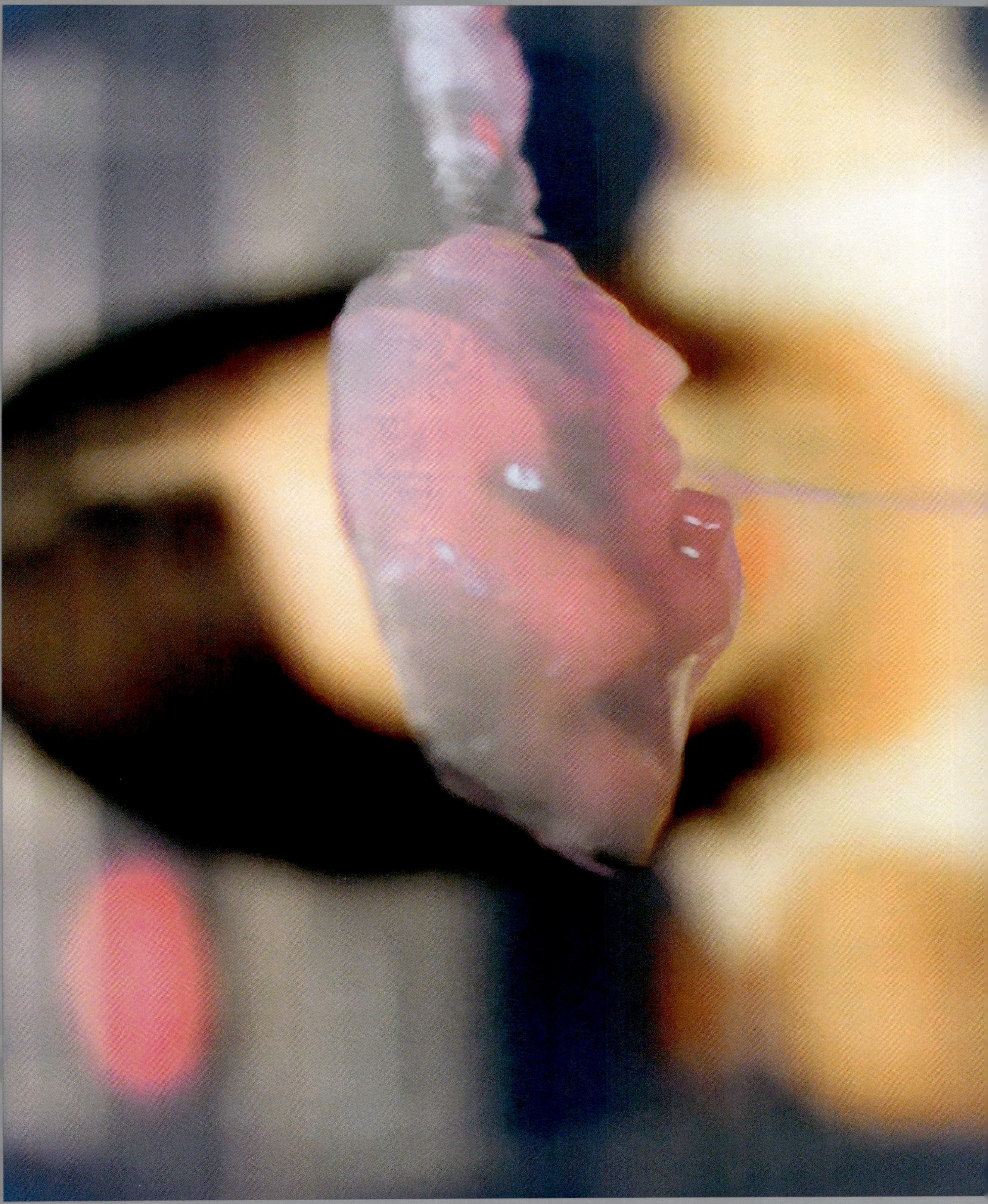

01

Gespannte Oberfläche

taz 4.12.97

Sechs Jahre nach seinem Tod erlebt der Philosoph Vilém Flusser eine Renaissance. Das Karlsruher ZKM zeichnete ihn mit dem Siemens-Medienpreis aus. Eine Tagung in Weimar untersuchte „Design und die Philosophie der Lebensformen" ■ Von Ulrike Baureithel

Die „kopernikanische Wende" von der Schrift- zur Bildkultur liefert ihr Krisenphänomen gleich mit. Denn im Zuge ihrer Digitalisierung verschiebt sich der alte philosophische Streit um die urteilsbildende beziehungsweise täuschende Kraft der Bilder eindeutig zugunsten ihrer instabilen, virtuellen Potenz. Die medial gebundenen, substanzlosen, in doppeltem Sinne „flüchtigen" Bilder verweigern sich der „rationalen" Linearität der Schrift. Im Bild-Punkt fällt – wie im Zeit-Punkt – Aktualität und Möglichkeit zusammen. Die „verflüssigten" Bilder präfigurieren, wie der Weimarer Medienwissenschaftler Lorenz Engell am vergangenen Wochenende in Rekurs auf Deleuze meinte, eine neue Zeiterfahrung, die sich jenseits ihrer linearen Abfolge konstituiert.

Bereits vor über 30 Jahren sandte der damals noch ziemlich unbekannte Marshal McLuhan eine Flaschenpost aus, in der er behauptete, daß die „elektrische Implosion" und ihre entstörten Bildoberflächen die Gesellschaft in einen der deutschen Intellektuellengeschichte.

Eben diese historisch-biographische Verortung muß mitgedacht werden, wenn man Flussers Feier des Nomadischen, seine theoriestiftende Flucht aus den (ursprünglichen) Bindungen, seine radikale Vernunftkritik und sein Einverständnis mit der Medienkultur thematisiert. Auschwitz bildet den Flucht- und Umkehrpunkt des Überlebenden, in Auschwitz hat die westliche Kultur, wie Flusser in seiner autobiographischen Sammlung „Bodenlos" formuliert, „ihre Maske abgeworfen". Das in der liberalen Denktradition als „Unfall" deklarierte Ereignis ist in Flussers Geschichtsbild ein dem „Programm" inhärenter „Zufall", nicht Entartung also, sondern (wenn auch: extreme) Möglichkeit und insofern „Utopie" westlicher Zivilisation.

Was jedoch, wenn sich Geschichte in ein laufendes „Programm" verabschiedete? Wenn Auschwitz tatsächlich die zu sich selbst gekommene Vernunft ist? Vergänglichkeit: „Das eigentliche Ziel aller Körperentwürfe", erklärt Flusser im Band mit dem sprechenden Titel „Vom Subjekt zum Projekt", „ist, den Körper so zu gestalten, daß man sich seiner bedienen kann, statt durch ihn den Objekten unterworfen zu sein. Sollte dies gelingen, wäre man nicht mehr Subjekt und könnte aufrecht und aufrichtig leben."

Die schöne neue Medienwelt, eine schöne neue Männerwelt? Gewiß kein Zufall ist es, daß immer, wenn Flussers „Projekt" eines dialogisch gestalteten und geschalteten Netzes, in dem wir künftig als punktuelle „Knoten" floaten, auf seine sozialen Bedingungen hin untersucht wird, Ernüchterung Platz greift. Die „Wohnmaschinen", die uns Flusser andient, stammen bekanntlich aus Bauhaus-Zeiten. Schon damals haben sich die avanciertesten Architekten Gedanken über die Wechselwirkung von Gebäuden und zwischenmenschlichen Beziehungen gemacht. Doch bei Flusser geht es, es sei d[illegible] erinnert um [illegible]

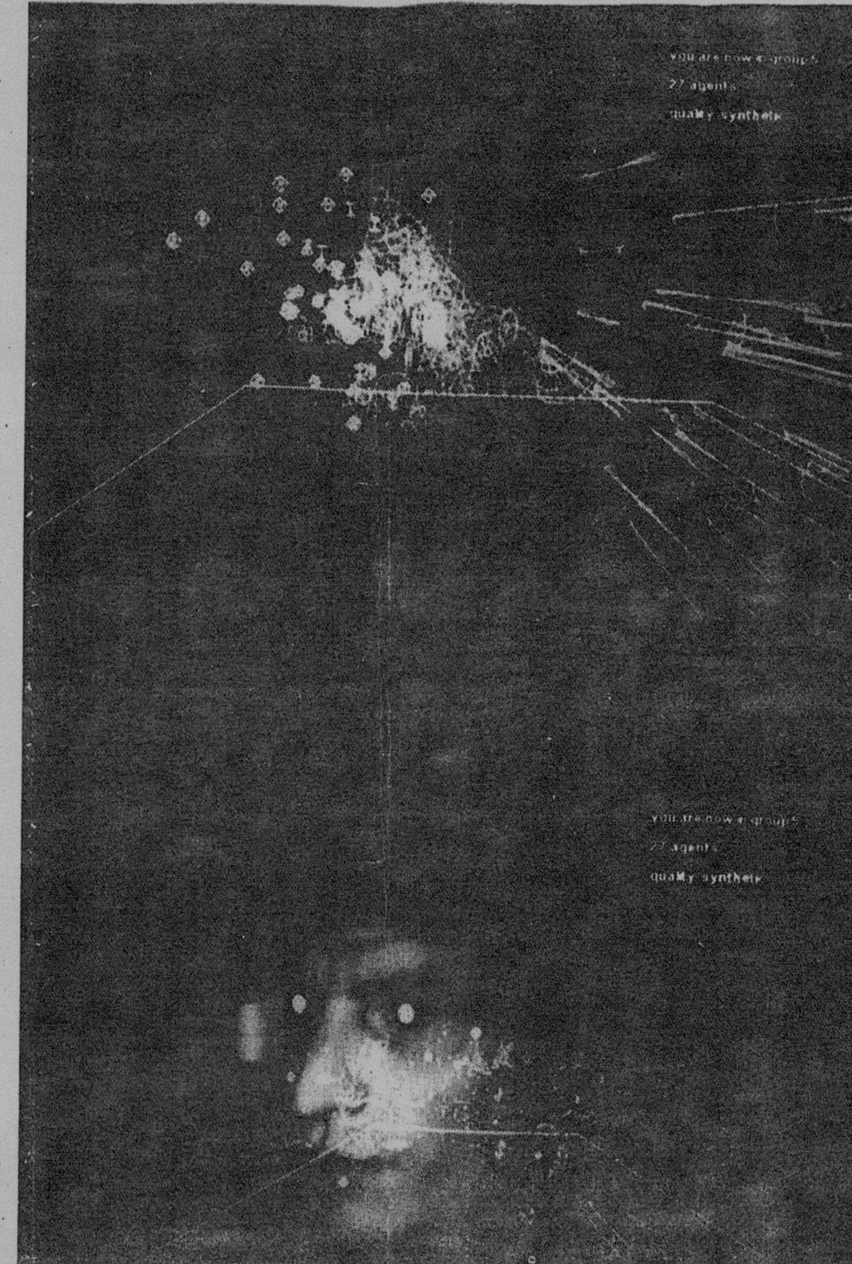

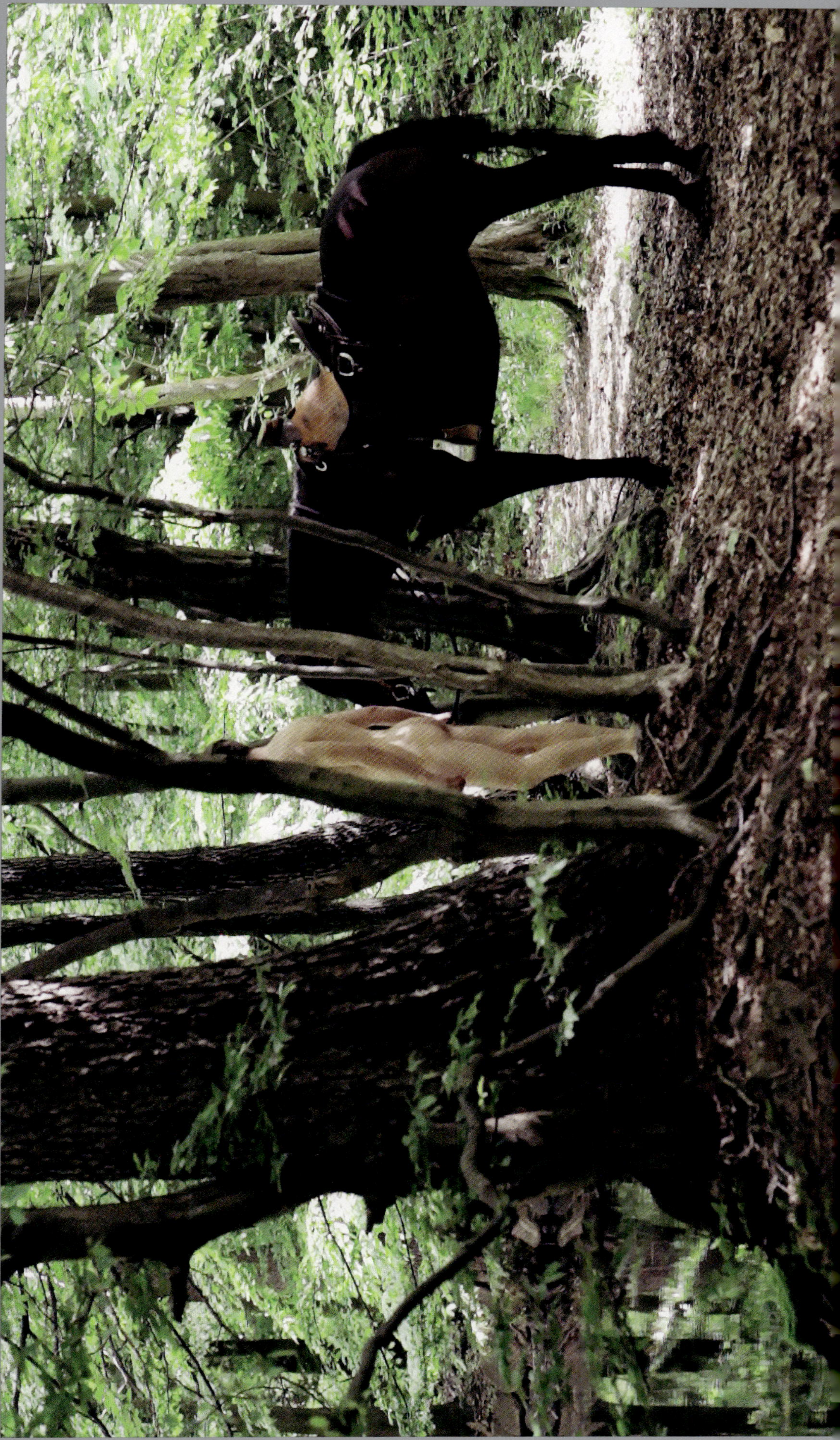

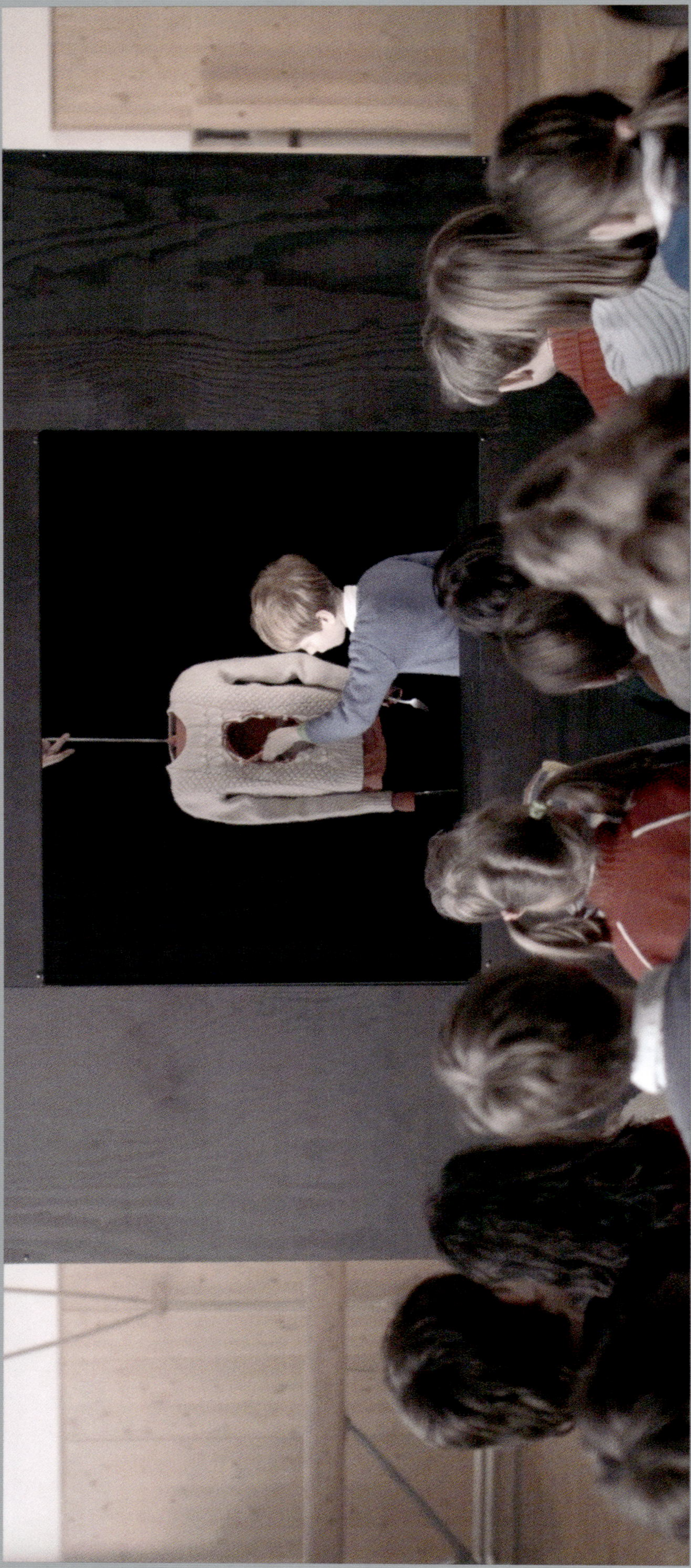

04

05

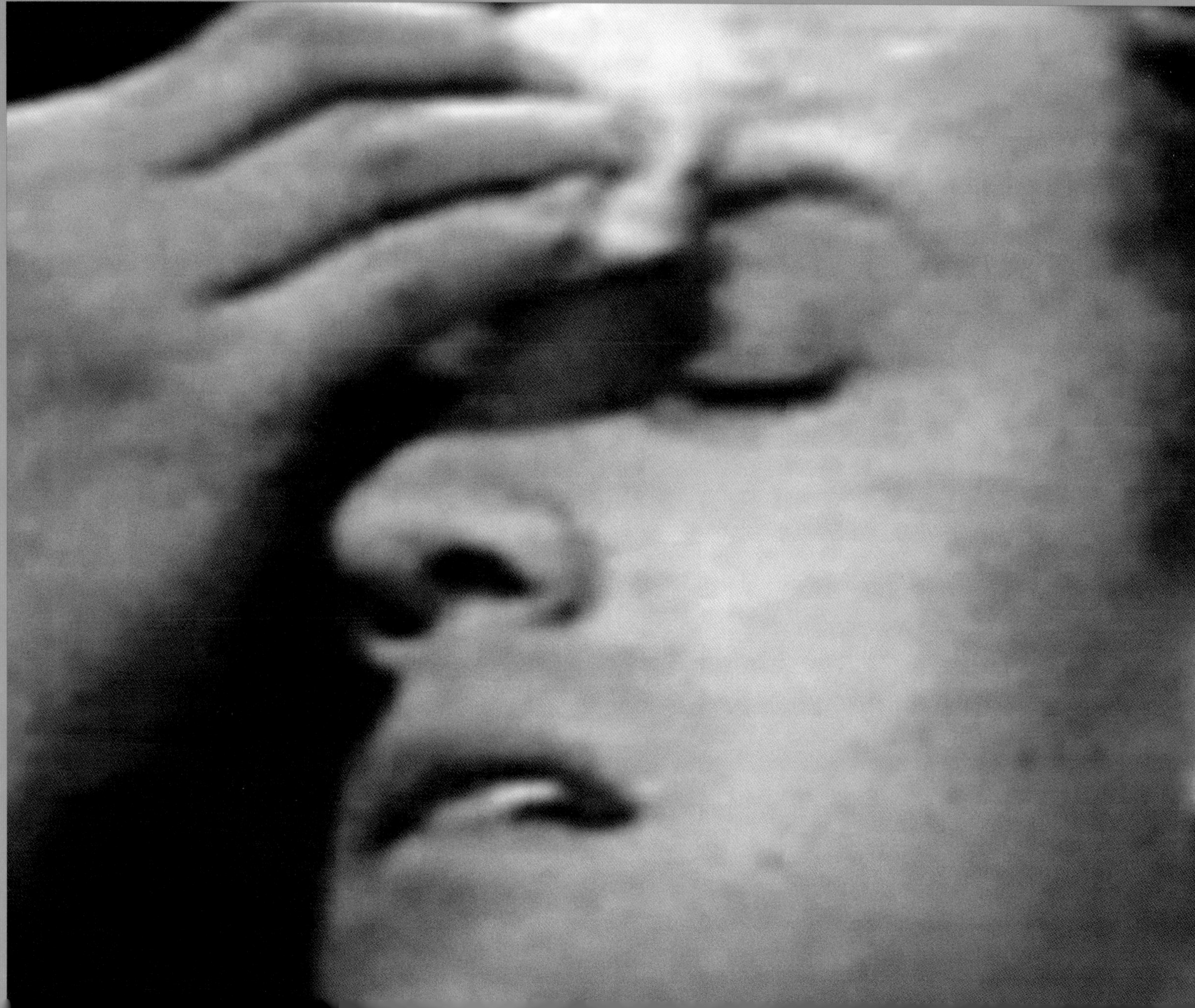

06

07

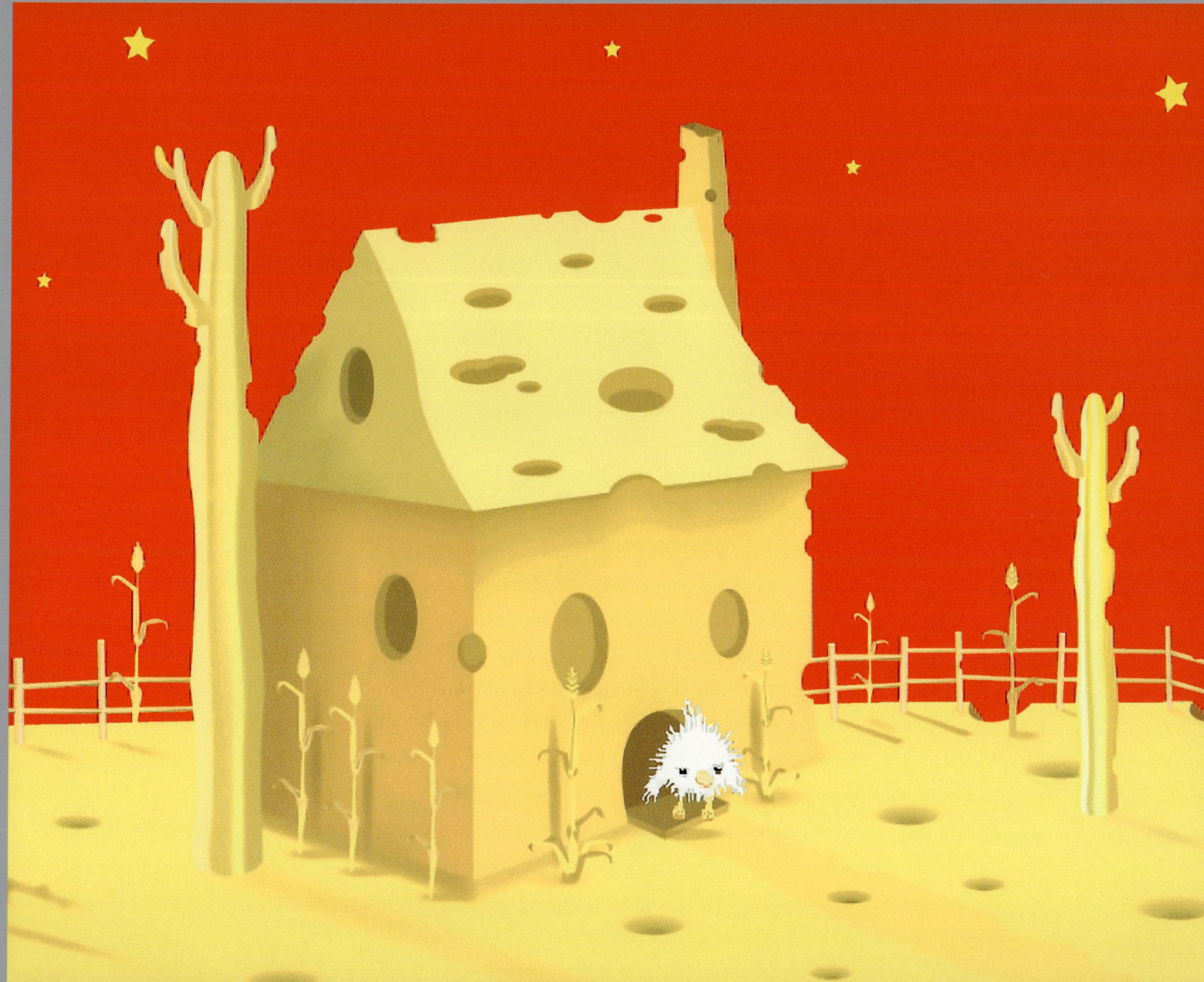

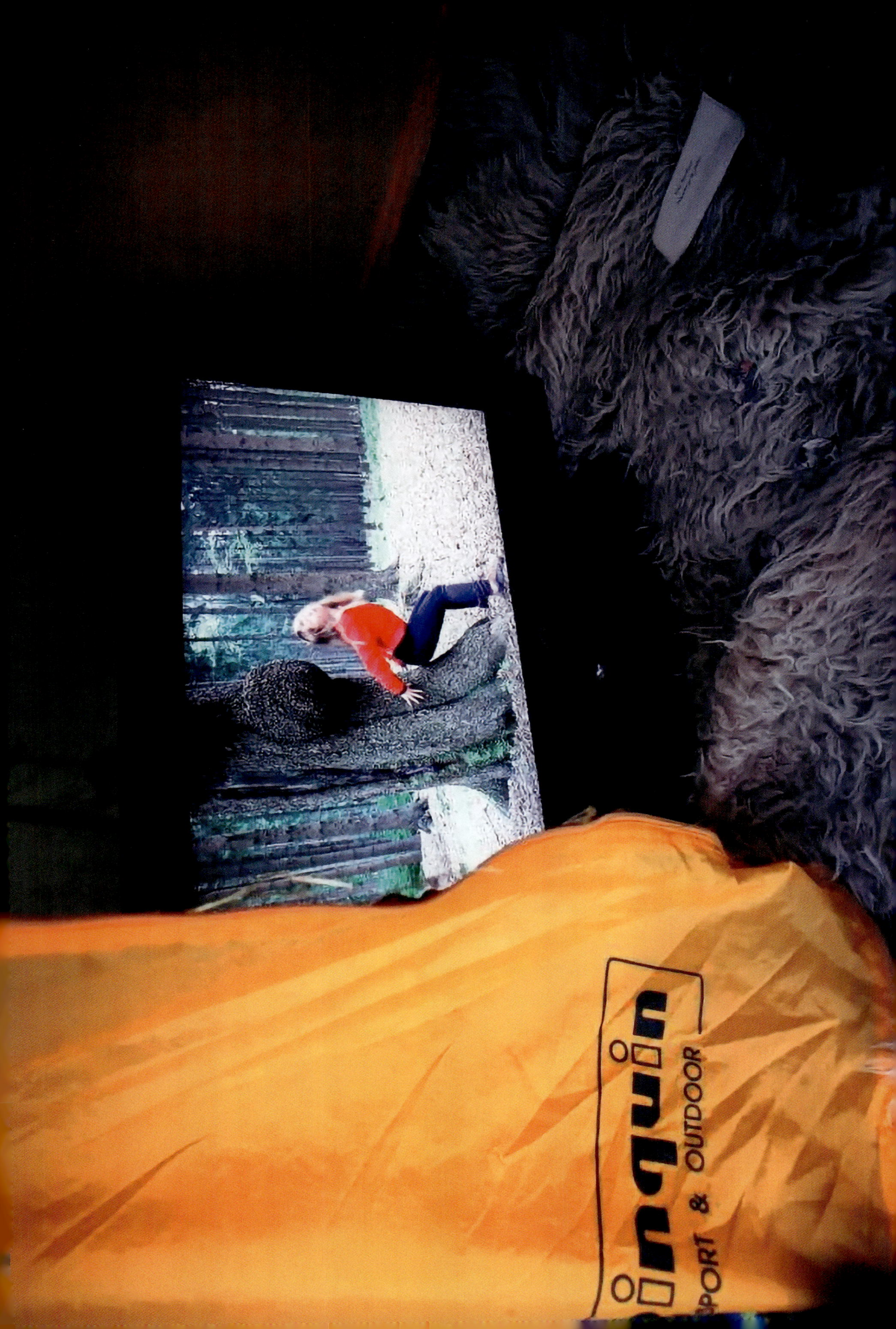
PORT & OUTDOOR

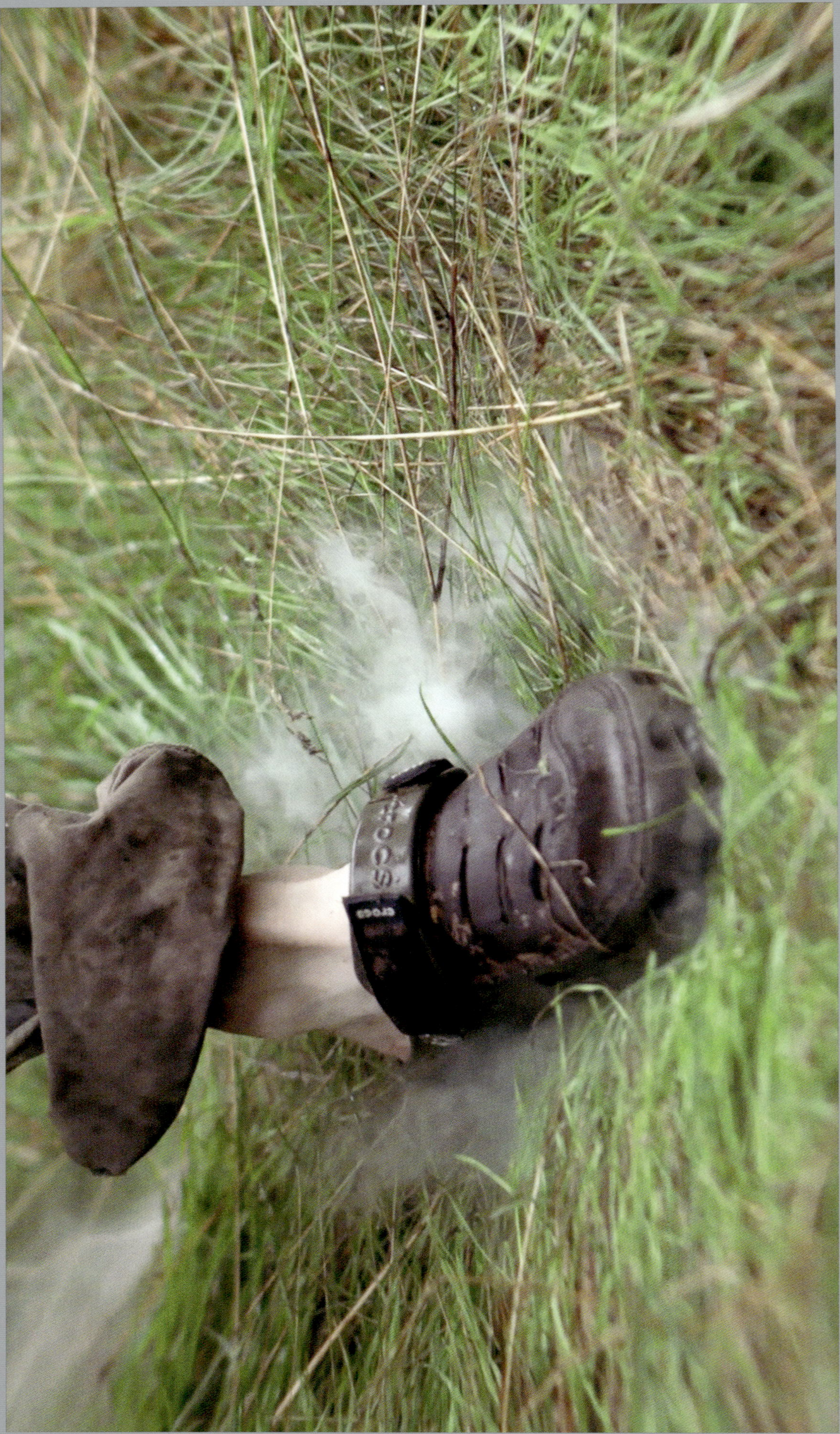

08

09

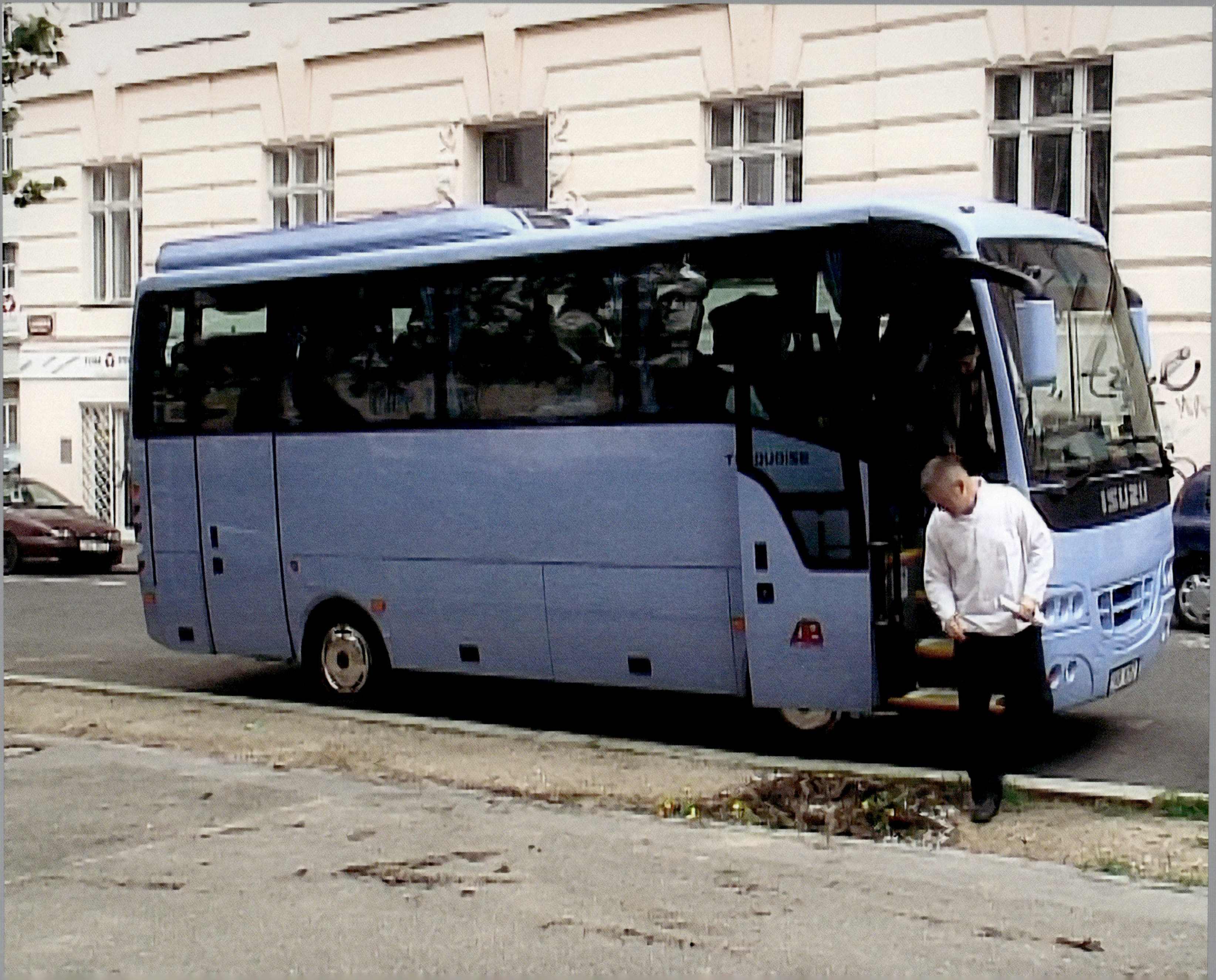

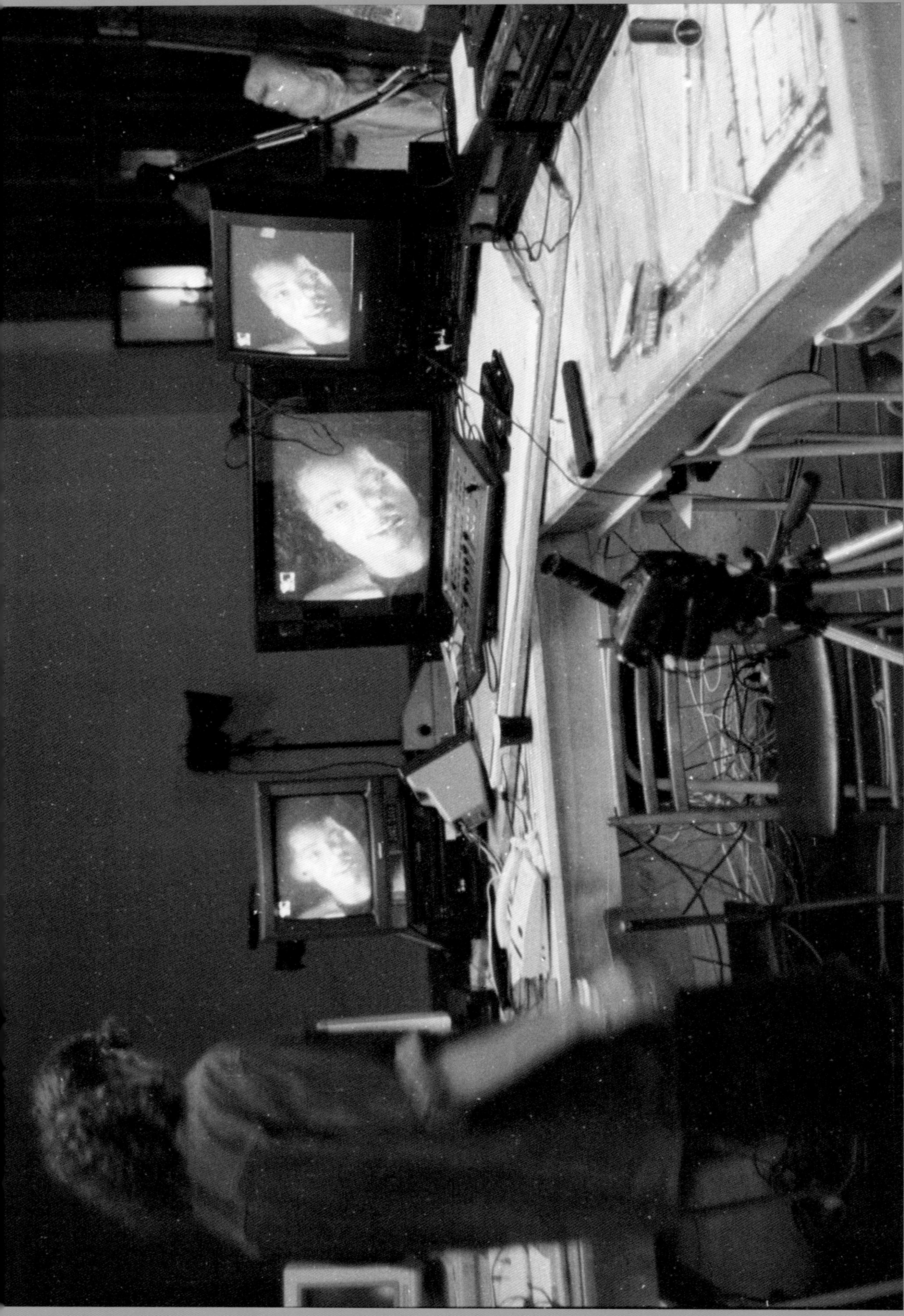

10

11

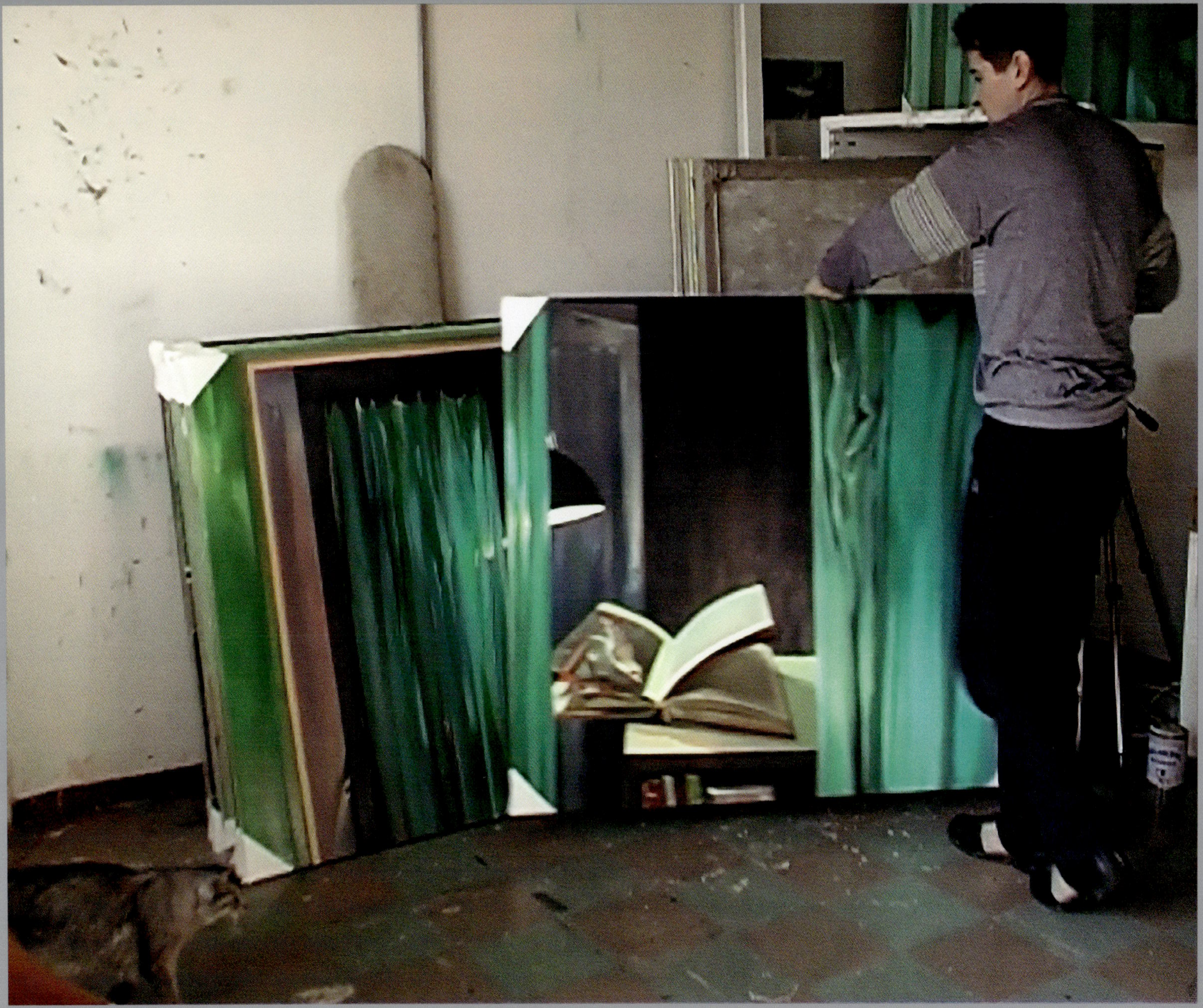

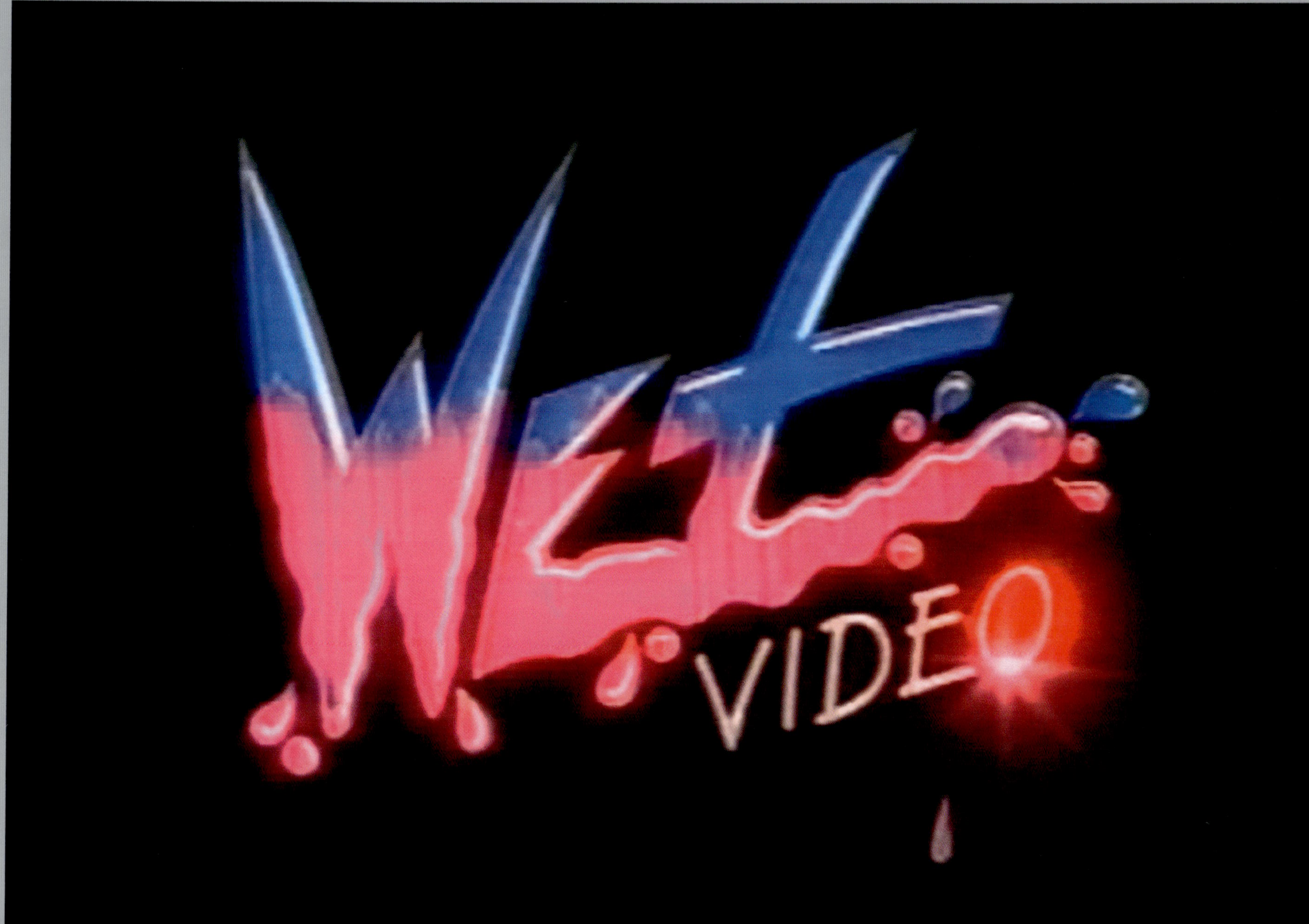
Wet
VIDEO

II. DISCOURSE

Negotiating the Moving Image

(157–211)

Digital, Intermedia, and International Confrontations: Presentations of Art of the Moving Image at the Beginning of the New Millennium

200

Markéta Mansfieldová

"I Am Here!" The Dawn of the Moving Image at Czech Art Schools

Tomáš Pospiszyl

Academic courses focused on video art and new media were created in Czechoslovakia (and later the Czech Republic) shortly after 1989.[1] In the first wave, this involved the Department of Animated Film and Video at the Film and TV School of the Academy of Performing Arts in Prague (FAMU). A year later, the New Media Studio was established at the Academy of Fine Arts in Prague (AVU). 1993 saw the establishment of the Faculty of Fine Arts at the Brno Technical University (FaVU) with a specialised course in electronic multimedia art (i.e., video art). These departments generally had no precedent to follow – both lecturers and students started from nothing. They attempted to institutionalise fields that were not sufficiently

[1] In the 1990s, video art and new media were the most common forms of art of the moving image on the Czech art scene. In this essay, the term art of the moving image is understood to signify the area between fine art, film, and other forms of art including not only video art but also experimental film, multimedia theatre, interactive art, computer art, or internet art.

established in either the educational or artistic contexts, and they needed technology that was not readily available.

The second wave of establishment – and, to a small extent, dissolution – of similar courses at art universities in the Czech Republic occurred over ten years later, in a different historical situation with different motivations and results. After the year 2000, computers and video cameras entered most fields of art. The use of audiovisual material outside the traditional film and television industries also expanded. Schools responded to this trend by innovating existing courses or establishing new ones. The curricula of traditional artistic disciplines were enriched by the addition of instruction in the use of audiovisual equipment, while new specialisations such as multimedia art, game design, and others were established.

Despite the relatively late development of art of the moving image in the Czech Republic, the beginnings of institutionalised education in this field were not dramatically delayed in comparison to the rest of the world. Only a few exceptional schools abroad can boast a significantly longer history.[2] There were numerous experiments with video technologies at Western European and American art schools in the 1970s and '80s, but specialised departments and institutions only began forming at the turn of the 1980s and '90s. As early as 1989, British artist and lecturer David Hall noted that art schools were important for the development of art of the moving image not as spaces for focused theoretical and practical instruction but primarily as sources of equipment that was otherwise difficult to access. The high-end portion of this equipment was developed for particular professional aims, but in the environment of the art schools, it came into the hands of students unencumbered by a curriculum aimed at preparing them for a career in the audiovisual industry. According to Hall: "The occasional use of professional equipment is enticing but economically untenable, particularly if you need to spend a longer period experimenting".[3]

Art schools – unlike film schools – thus became crucial to the development of art of the moving image in the Czech context. We find

[2] The Department of Media Study at the State University of New York in Buffalo was founded in 1967 by Gerald O'Grady. Figures such as Tony Conrad, Hollis Frampton, Paul Sharits, Peter Weibel, and Steina and Woody Vasulka collaborated with O'Grady after 1973. British art schools such as Central St. Martins and the Royal College of Art in London or the Maidstone College of Art in Brighton had video equipment at their disposal since the first half of the 1970s. The first Time Based Media programme at Maidstone College started in 1975. Nam June Paik became a lecturer at the Kunstakademie Düsseldorf in 1979, while the artist and theorist Peter Weibel taught at the Universität für angewandte Kunst in Vienna from 1976. The first Time Based Media Department in the Netherlands was established in 1980 by Elsa Stansfield at the Jan van Eyck Academie in Maastricht. The Zentrum für Kunst und Medien (ZKM) in Karlsruhe was founded in 1989 with the ambition of becoming an electronic Bauhaus, i.e., to invoke the spirit of the legendary art education centre of the 1920s and '30s, which emphasised connections between craft and technology on the one hand and the ideas behind the art on the other. The Institut für Neue Medien at the Städelschule in Frankfurt began its activities in 1987, the Medienakademie in Cologne in 1990, etc.

[3] David Hall, "Video Art – The Significance of an Educational Environment", in *Video Positive*, ed. Lisa Haskel (London: Foundation for Art and Creative Technology, 1989), p. 47.

similar experiences across Eastern Europe. During the rule of socialist regimes, works in the field of art of the moving image were created in the grey areas of state-controlled or semi-state-controlled platforms – television, film studios, and amateur clubs, as well as promotional and educational departments at state companies – without which they would be extremely difficult to realise in terms of technology and production. Only a few of these environments, however, were directly connected to the education sector. The Warsztat Formy Filmowej at the Państwowa Wyższa Szkoła Filmowa, Telewizyjna i Teatralna (the National Film School in Łódź) was in operation between 1970 and 1977, and allowed for the creation of a number of important works, particularly in collaboration with artists from the Akademia Sztuk Pięknych w Warszawie (the Academy of Fine Arts in Warsaw).[4] 1985 saw the establishment of a video department at the Magyar Képzömüvészeti Egyetem (Hungarian University of Fine Arts), and a year later, a post-graduate video program began at the Eötvös Loránd Tudományegyetem (Eötvös Loránd University) – both located in Budapest. The intermedia department at the Magyar Képzömüvészeti Egyetem (Hungarian University of Fine Arts) was established in 1990.

Socialist Czechoslovakia had a distinctive tradition of audiovisual art: a successful film school (FAMU), a functioning film industry, and experimental projects such as Laterna magika or Kinoautomat. These institutions and projects could not have been established without the framework of state support and the related ideological control. The workers of Czechoslovak film were excellently trained. During their countless attempts to step beyond the established rules of the Czechoslovak audiovisual industry, however, they generally encountered institutional problems, or, at the very least, a lack of understanding. This state of affairs, together with Czechoslovakia's long-term isolation from global cultural developments, created an environment that failed to motivate local artists working in film to experiment beyond established techniques and genres. The absence of such attempts was incomprehensible to some international figures, even to Woody Vasulka, who had more than a little knowledge about the situation in Czechoslovakia: "I met my Czech colleagues after years and listened to their long complaints about the impossibility of working creatively. I tried to motivate them to get a 16 mm camera and shoot something themselves, with their own eye, from their own hand. All I got was cold looks of disbelief."[5]

We must realise that in 1980s Czechoslovakia, even standard music videos produced abroad were only available in those parts of the

[4] For more on this topic, see Tomáš Pospiszyl, *Asociativní dějepis umění; Poválečné umění napříč generacemi a médii: koláž, intermediální a konceptuální umění, performance a film* [An Associative Art History: Post-war Art Across Generations and Media: Collage, Intermedia and Conceptual Art, Performance, and Film] (Prague: tranzit.cz, 2014), pp. 156–160.

[5] Woody Vasulka, "Galerie: místo pro pohyblivý obraz" [The Gallery: A Space for the Moving Image], in *Orbis Fictus; Nová média v současném umění* [Orbis Fictus; New Media in Contemporary Art], eds. Ludvík Hlaváček – Marta Smolíková (Prague: Sorosovo centrum současného umění, 1995), pp. 130–131.

country that could be reached by the signal of Austrian TV. There was no functional infrastructure that would allow for the dissemination of new forms of art. Film amateurs found themselves in a position that was no better, limited by the character of the official distribution networks and, most importantly, by a lack of equipment. Video equipment was not available for purchase by private citizens up until the mid-1980s. Even after this, the exorbitant prices made the equipment practically unattainable.[6] In contrast to the West – and some other countries of the socialist bloc – the various forms of art of the moving image took a long time to establish themselves, which also meant that the appropriate technology remained absent from art institutions. Those who wished to use such technology had to search elsewhere, such as in semi-official or outspokenly alternative communities.[7]

The First Wave – Institutions and Key Agents

The system and form of art schools as they were established in Czechoslovakia after World War II had not changed much by the late 1980s. AVU (the Academy of Fine Arts), in Prague, continued teaching classical fine arts subjects and continuity was ensured by rather artistically conservative and socially conformist lecturers. The Academy of Art, Architecture and Design (VŠUP, also known as UMPRUM) became a university in 1946, and in 1951, the Special Studio of Animated and Puppet Film was established there, later known as the Animation and Film Studio. Given the school's spirit of emphasising the applied or practical value of the work, however, the studio did not become a space for interdisciplinary explorations of new technologies.[8] In 1945, the Academy of Performing Arts (AMU) was formed in Prague, which included the newly established Film and TV School (FAMU). The Architecture Faculty at the Brno University of Technology (VUT) also had a tradition in both drawing and modelling.

[6] The Czech state company Tesla began producing a videocassette recorder in 1985. The production for the Czechoslovak market was at first sold predominantly in Tuzex shops (*state-run shops that provided luxury items in exchange for vouchers that could only be purchased with foreign currency – translator's note*). One of these devices cost 20,000 Czechoslovak crowns, i.e., around seven average monthly salaries. Video cameras could be imported from abroad, and were also available in Tuzex stores by the late 1980s.

[7] As professionals working with official institutions, Radek Pilař and Tomáš Kepka had access to the equipment of Czechoslovak Television and the Supraphon label, while Petr Skala could use that of the Střední průmyslová školy sdělovací techniky (Secondary School of Communication Technology). Independent artists working outside the socialist institutions were much worse off. In December 1980, a video camera, recorder, and monitors belonging to the Janáček Academy of Performing Arts were secretly used to record a performance by Vladimír Ambroz, Petr Štembera, and Milan Kozelka in Brno, see Tomáš Pospiszyl, *Vladimír Ambroz, Mediaman* (Prague: BiggBoss, 2017), pp. 118–120. In the 1980s, Tomáš Ruller made video documentation of his performances using equipment borrowed from his friends, or from institutions such as the Goose on a String Theatre, Svazarm (the state-run association for collaboration with the army), Originální video-journal (Original Video-journal, an independent media network), and the like.

[8] Graduates of the studio included Lucie Svobodová, later active in video art and computer animation. Věra Geislerová, another pioneer of computer animation, also studied painting at VŠUP and later taught computer animation at the school.

The teaching of video in the Czech Republic is tied to the establishment of the independent Department of Animated Film and Video at FAMU in 1990.[9] At that time, the word "video" in its name mostly referred to the activities of Radek Pilař, with the department soon acquiring the status of a separate offshoot studio of electronic animation. However, Pilař died unexpectedly on February 7th, 1993. He was succeeded at the studio by Petr Vrána (from 1994 to 1995), after which Tomáš Kepka took over and turned it into a separate programme in Multimedia Art, which existed – with some changes – until 2002. Among its lecturers in the mid-1990s were Lucie Svobodová, Věra Geislerová, Jaroslav Vančát, and – for the longest of all – Petr Skala. All of the above (except Vrána and Kepka) had previously participated in the activities of the video department at the Union of Visual Artists of the Czech Republic, initiated in 1988 by Radek Pilař.

In Brno, there was a movement to transform the Institute of Drawing and Modelling at the Faculty of Architecture of VUT to an independent art school, which opened its doors on 1 January 1993. Its founders, architect Ivan Ruller and sculptor Vladimír Preclík, invited Pilař to apply for the position of lecturer in a programme devoted to electronic and multimedia art (i.e., video art). Pilař's application was successful, and he selected Tomáš Ruller and Peter Rónai to join him as teaching assistants. Due to his premature death, however, he was not able to leave a significant mark on the programme. Following the first semester, Tomáš Ruller assumed leadership of the studio, changing it to a more broadly conceived studio of video–multimedia–performance. In 1998, now as dean of the school, he succeeded in dividing the components into independent studios. A number of pedagogues taught in these studios – in addition to those mentioned above, lecturers included figures such as Jaroslav Vančát, Miloš Vojtěchovský, and Keiko Sei.[10]

AVU also went through a considerable transformation after 1990. A New Media Studio (also described in the earliest surviving documents as the Studio of Video Art or Video Sculpture) was already under consideration at AVU as early as 1990.[11] An open call was put out to establish the studio, and Radek Pilař was one of the applicants. The jury, however,

[9] As early as 1985, Břetislav Pojar, Jiří Kubíček, Jiří Jaroš, and Radek Pilař established a studio of animated art at the documentary film department at FAMU. At the time, Pilař attempted unsuccessfully to establish a study programme for artists in animated film and video; see Bohdana Kerbachová, "Počátky českého videoartu" [The Beginnings of Czech Video Art], *Iluminace* 18, no. 2 (2006), p. 134. At around the same time, Pilař also played an active role in the creation of the experimental department of Czechoslovak Television. From today's perspective, he used unusual terminology: he presented the output of the proposed department to the station's director Jan Zelenka as "animated image material making use of contemporary technology". Radek Pilař, undated letter to the management of Czechoslovak Television, Radek Pilař's family archive, Prague.

[10] For materials on the history of the studios mentioned here, see https://performance.ffa.vutbr.cz/ARCHIV/CDROM/inner/sub/pribeh.html.

[11] Discrepancies concerning the name of the studio are also found in the annual reports and the school's official correspondence, both from the side of the school's administration and by the studio leader himself, at least until 1993. Even later, however, there are often variants such as the New Media Studio or the New Media School.

selected Michael Bielický, under whose leadership the new studio was first opened to students in the 1991/1992 academic year.[12]

The lecturers and students of these first study programmes knew each other. Some were active in Pilař's circle of video artists, for others, experiences from abroad were essential.[13] The establishment of new study courses was aided by the mythology that greats of world art were patrons: Nam June Paik in the case of AVU and Woody Vasulka at FaVU. These myths, however, were not entirely unfounded. Although Nam June Paik never visited Prague, his influence on new media at AVU was felt as soon as Bielický informed him of his appointment: "So I went to see Paik and I told him about it and he said that's great and just pulled five thousand German marks out of his pocket. He put the money on the table in front of me and told me to use it to buy equipment."[14] Woody Vasulka met Tomáš Ruller at the emerging art school in the autumn of 1992. Brno, specifically the FaVU spaces in Květná Street, became one of his European bases for the next three years. At first, he was a guest at the school, although he did later sign a contract for the position of laboratory manager. His name was used in the school's advertising materials, but he never took part in regular teaching. He did, however, use the school's facilities to create and complete his artworks. Students could meet him at various gatherings or follow the germination of his works as they became available in Květná Street.

The students and lecturers of the first wave of education in art of the moving image experienced an unusual situation. They educated themselves in fields that had no local tradition or appropriate facilities. In hindsight, it is clear that many of them would later prove successful in an extremely broad range of occupations.[15] The first wave symbolically culminated in 1996 with Orbis Fictus – a costly festival of auratic works in the prestigious exhibition spaces of the Wallenstein Riding School (Valdštejnská jízdárna) in Prague, discussed in detail in Martin Mazanec's contribution

[12] In May 1990, Michael Bielický visited Prague for the first time after a number of years spent in exile. He contacted Milan Knížák, then rector of AVU, and lectured at the school for the first time. By 1 October 1991, he had signed an employment contract and was also named a docent by the rector on the same date. Michael Bielický's personal file, AVU Archive.

[13] Petr Vrána, Michael Bielický, and Miloš Vojtěchovský had lived abroad for years, acquiring experience in the contexts of contemporary art, the audiovisual industry, or education. Vrána worked for West German TV stations and also operated in the world of experimental animation and new media art. In 1992, he opened the Media archiv (Media Archive) in Prague, assembling diverse examples of video art on VHS tapes. Michael Bielický was a student of Nam June Paik at the Kunstakademie in Düsseldorf and later became his assistant. Miloš Vojtěchovský ran a gallery in Amsterdam that specialised in video works. Keiko Sei was a respected video art curator in Japan and she personally knew the leading international figures in the field. In the Czech context, Tomáš Ruller also had above standard relationships with the international scene.

[14] Michael Bielický, *ARCO – Aneb český videoart proniká do světa* [ARCO – Or Czech Video Art Penetrates the World] (Ivan Tatíček, 1993), video documentary, Prague, 1994. The 1991 contract between Michael Bielický and AVU shows that in reality, the figure was twice as large, i.e., 10,000 West German marks.

[15] The occupations included those in the fine arts, film, advertising, television, the video game industry, theatre, education, programming, popular and experimental music, literature, politics, social activism, etc.

to this anthology. Many of the exhibiting artists were pedagogues at the departments mentioned above, or their students. A number of the presented works thematised the very newness of new media in the Czech context. The protagonists of the first wave also shared the experience of moving from linear to non-linear editing and from an analogue to a digital environment. Towards the end of the study period of the first wave of students, the dissemination of the internet became a crucial phenomenon. Among other possibilities, it opened the doors to appropriation, database film, and artworks created in and for the internet environment.

Technical Facilities and Teaching Methods

Technical equipment played a key role in the teaching of video and new media art. None of the schools of the first wave had this, except for the TV studio at FAMU, which was disliked by students and lecturers alike. The electronic animation studio at the same school was based on Radek Pilař's conception arising from classical art pedagogy: still-life drawing, considered composition through various visual techniques, etc.[16] With this experience, students went on to work with film and video. Pilař's surviving lesson plans and requests for supplies addressed to the school's administrator's reference a broad variety of materials and tools: oil paint, canvases, dispersant, card, 16 mm film, an HI8 camera, an Amiga computer, a Silicon Graphics computer, and Wavefront software. Pilař was unsatisfied with the material and spatial conditions at FAMU. He did not want to be dependent on the professional but bulky equipment that was part of the school studio. He approached the dean at the time, Josef Pecák, with an offer: the students could use his own private studio and equipment. Thanks to this document, we have a detailed list of Pilař's technical facilities, which he was willing to allow students to access upon contractual confirmation.[17] "I believe that in a time of an audiovisual revolution, we need a fast and direct approach without delays and references to better equipment in the future and without a sentimental approach to manufacturing habits in animated art, acting instead in direct relation to the artistic tradition of animated film".[18]

After the death of Radek Pilař, Petr Vrána took over his position, but given his workload both at home and abroad, Vrána spent little time at FAMU. He equipped the department with super VHS technology, paid for from his own pocket. Silicon Graphics computers were also purchased relatively quickly. As Vrána himself says, he only used the FAMU Studio once,

[16] Students regularly attended life drawing classes at VŠUP. Longin Wdowiak interviewed by the author, 18 May 2021.

[17] The studio in Slezská Street, with an area of 110 metres square, contained a special effects table, a separate darkroom, a film projector, a Bolex film camera, a Mamyia RB 65 photo camera, a SORD 5 computer with graphic software, a Sony HVC 4000 P video camera, a JVC VHS HR D 150 E videocassette recorder, and other equipment. Letter to Josef Pecák, 18 Jun 1990, family archive of Radek Pilař, Prague.

[18] *Ibid.*

in connection with a workshop involving Zbigniew Rybczyński in 1997.[19] He concentrated teaching into blocks. Within these, he focused mostly on relaying the history of and various innovations in international cinema, television, and the fine arts.[20] His aim was not merely to prepare students for a smooth entry into the audiovisual industry – he also strove to support their varied artistic ambitions. FAMU, with its established system of lectures and compulsory exercises, however, provided precious little space in which to operate. The results of student works overseen by Vrána, therefore, were often music videos.

In the first half of the 1990s, FAMU students were taught electronic animation by Věra Geislerová, a pioneer of computer-processed moving images in the Czech Republic. Between 1993 and 1995, students were introduced to the possibilities of computer technologies by Lucie Svobodová, who used them in her practice as an artist to create works based not only on computer animation but also involving 3D modelling, virtual reality, and interactivity. The experimental film-maker Petr Skala spent

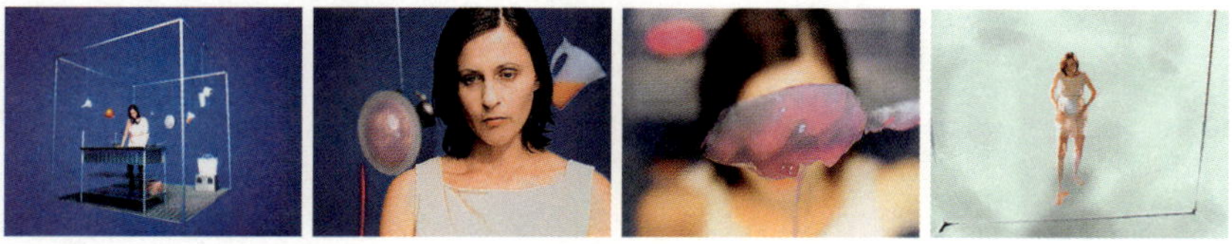

Niké Papadopulosová *Polednice* [The Noonday Witch] (1999), video, 6 min

the longest period at FAMU, influencing students between 1993 and 2006 not only through his work, but also through his charismatic personality, befitting of an independent artist.

In 1996, Petr Vrána was replaced as studio head by Tomáš Kepka, who transformed the department into an independent programme called Multimedia Art. The content shifted from electronic animation to a distinctive form of cinematic works whose expressive means were still fundamentally rooted in narration and cinematic language.[21] Emphasis was

[19] Petr Vrána interviewed by the author, 21 May 2021.

[20] It was characteristic of Petr Vrána that he barely differentiated between his activities at FAMU and in the Media archiv. He introduced students to materials from exhibitions and festivals. The range of these events attests to Vrána's position astride both the artistic and commercial spheres: Berlinale, Documenta, Osnabrück, Montreux, etc.

[21] "This was no longer just computer animation, it was a field that used live action, documentary footage, and hand-drawn and puppet animation, teaching students to search for a new stylised form of film not just through digital animation and post-production but throughout the process of shooting, dramaturgy, etc. Since the very beginning, then, this was neither video art nor pure computer animation, but a synthesis of the expressive possibilities of modern film; a search for new means and a new style of cinematic language, a modern dramaturgy. For instance, students would film an acted etude in virtual space with 3D set design, a live-action sequence with actors in a green screen studio in combination with puppets, and so on. The aim was to demonstrate the possibilities of film in cooperation with theatre, the dance scene, interactive art exhibitions, etc." "Anyone Who Has Anything to Say Can be a Film-maker or Photographer – Interview with Mgr. Tomáš Kepka, Film-maker and Teacher of Adult Courses", accessed 2 May 2021, https://epale.ec.europa.eu/cs/blog/filmarem-fotografem-muze-byt-kazdy-kdo-ma-co-rici-rozhovor-s-mgr-tomasem-kepkou-filmarem.

placed on top-class post-production, often realised outside the school. In Kepka's line of thinking, Pilař, Svobodová, and Skala taught students how to draw but not how to make films.[22] Neither were students of the department interested in experiments outside of cinematic language and film technology. They were fully integrated into the world of the film school, and, strictly considered, their work fell short of the criteria of authorial art of the moving image.[23] A number of graduates later found work in the film industry – in the first wave of students, this included Longin Wdowiak, Jan Zajíček, and Niké Papadopulosová. An exception in this respect is Ondřej Anděra, a musician who went on to apply his multimedia education to direct *Graffiti* (2002), a theatre piece performed at the New Stage of the National Theatre in Prague.

Equipment was also important for the establishment of the New Media Studio at AVU. As early as the summer of 1990, i.e., a year before the studio was actually established, Rector Milan Knížák gave Michael Bielický an official letter with which to approach potential sponsors.[24] Bielický used Nam June Paik's monetary contribution to purchase Blaupunkt monitors, cameras, analogue editing machines, Amiga computers, and other equipment. He established a partnership with the Goethe-Institut, as well as various technological companies, which enabled the acquisition of Silicon Graphics computers in 1994, after which the new media studio was completely digitalised. In addition to regular innovations in terms of equipment, Bielický was aware of the need to anchor new technologies in theory. He took his students to the legendary Prague lecture by Vilém Flusser in November 1991, and later also took part in the various Flusser conferences that posthumously established this theorist a seminal interpreter of the language of new media art in the Czech Republic.[25]

Since Michael Bielický's career as an artist was mostly developed abroad, he spent most of the year beyond the borders of the Czech Republic. He did not consider himself a classical teacher[26] and did not waste time setting tasks or working out detailed teaching plans.[27] In his *Programme*

[22] Tomáš Kepka interviewed by the author, 24 Jun 2021.

[23] This situation was partly brought about by the school's subjects in the fields of film theory and practice. Apart from computer animation, taught by Lucie Svobodová and Věra Geislerová, and courses offered by Tomáš Kepka and Petr Skala (seminar of electronic directing, analysis of animated and multimedia works, electronic montage, multimedia directing), students were essentially offered the same curriculum as students of live-action directing.

[24] See the letter from 24 Aug 1990, Michael Bielický's archive.

[25] The first of these conferences was Vilém Flusser – Prehistorik historie [Vilém Flusser – Prehistorian of History], which took place at the Goethe-Institut in Prague from the 1st to the 3rd of December 1992. Michael Bielický presented at the annual Flusser symposia that followed in 1993, 1994, 1995, 1996, and 1997.

[26] Michael Bielický interviewed by the author, 11 May 2021.

[27] This also led to tense relations with the school's management. Bielický received a number of formal warnings in writing from Rector Milan Knížák, usually around three a year. The reasons included the absence of the pedagogue or his assistant at meetings or the school sports day, a failure to supply the appropriate materials, or the absence of students at the school of new media at the evening classes of life drawing (see, e.g., the letter from 25 Jan 1993, Michael Bielický's archive).

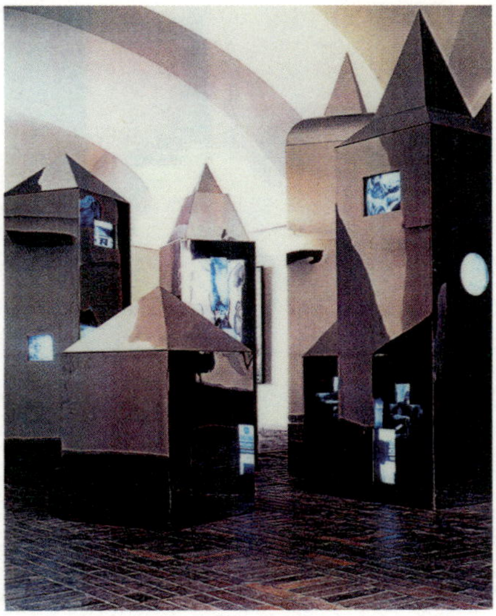

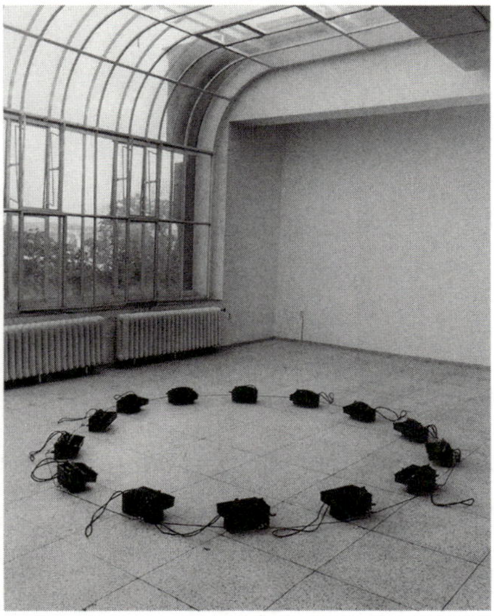

Installation of student works at AVU,
first half of the 1990s.

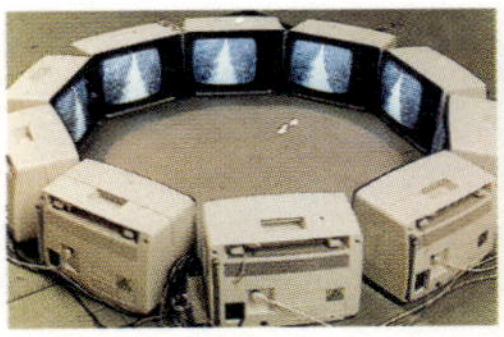

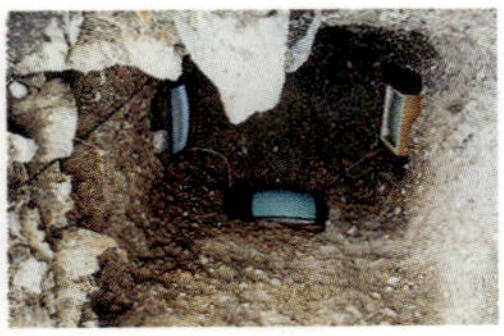

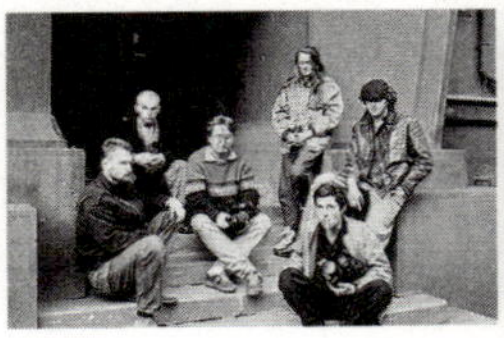

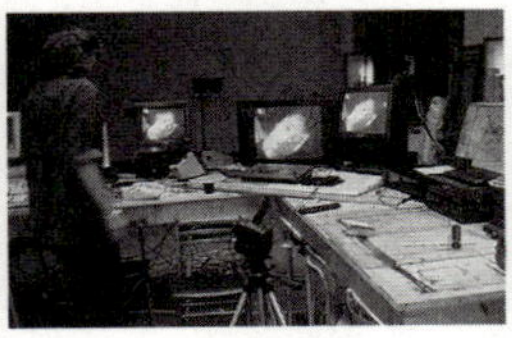

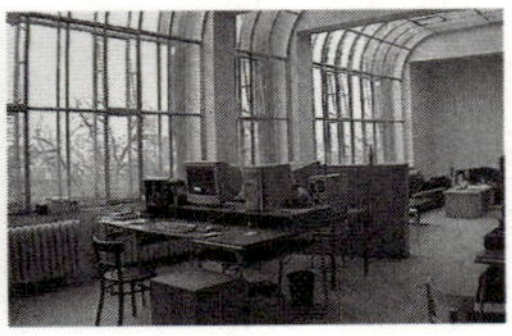

for the New Media Studio, he simply sketched an overview of foundational skills that the students would develop over time.[28] In his own words, he aimed to be a partner with whom the students could develop their particular projects, whereby he would secure the necessary technology, involve students in international projects, and relay his own artistic know-how and contacts.[29]

Bielický's first students were inherited from other studios, but they later became an important group of artists working with the moving image in the Czech Republic (including Janka Vidová Žáčková, Tomáš Mašín, and Elen Řádová). Some of them would gravitate towards more complex spatial works, or virtual pieces with elements of interactivity or artificial intelligence (e.g., Petr Svárovský, Markéta Baňková, Kamila Richterová, Petra Vargová, Krištof Kintera, Jakub Nepraš). In later years, there were also students interested in documentary approaches, the edges of cinematography, and related areas (e.g., Mark Ther, Radim Labuda, Adéla Babanová). Michael Bielický's students appreciated the fact that whatever they came up with was usually approved of by their teacher, who motivated them to work individually. This open approach was part of the reason many students migrated to his studio for shorter periods.[30] By the year 2000, only ten students had graduated from the new media studio. During the past thirty years, there were relatively few students who spent their entire time at the school exclusively in this studio. Many more students, however, passed through this inspiring environment.[31]

Radek Pilař did not have sufficient time before his death to practically develop his teaching approach at FaVU in Brno. We do, however,

[28] The students at the studio were to master the camera, electronic editing, digital effects, and methods of integrating video software into sculptures and installations. See *Program ateliéru pro nová média* [Programme of the New Media Studio], 26 Jun 1991, AVU Archive. Later documents include computer technologies (and individual programmes) or work with VR and AI.

[29] Michael Bielický interviewed by the author, 11 May 2021. As studio leader, he organised a trip to New York to see Nam June Paik. He took his students to the Ars Electronica festival and established collaborations with ZKM. In 1992, his studio joined the *Piazza Virtuale* project, part of the Documenta IX festival. It was based on interactive connections using television satellites, phone lines, faxes, and modems. Participants – including those from AVU – thus experienced virtual global interconnectivity. The astonishment at the new technologies was so extensive that most of them made do with a simple transmission: "I am here!"

[30] Another reason for the high rate of visiting students was their belief that experience with the field of new media would increase their prospects on the job market. This was the motivation behind Markéta Baňková's transfer from the graphics studio. She did not have a computer and she wanted to learn to work with graphic software. She was planning to make a live action film for her diploma work, but when Bielický found out she was working on a hypertext novel, *city.html*, he convinced her to use that as her graduation piece – something she had previously considered impossible. Bielický, however, was proud that there was a diploma work in his studio that existed in the internet environment. (Markéta Baňková interviewed by the author, 28 May 2021).

[31] Following their graduation, some students at AVU (Jiří Příhoda, Michal Pěchouček, Ján Mančuška, and the present director of the new media school, Tomáš Svoboda) also began engaging in art of the moving image without having come into contact with Michael Bielický's studio. The rising interest in new media led to the establishment of a new studio in 2002, the School of New Media II, which was led by Veronika Bromová until 2011. Michael Bielický was at AVU until 2011. He was succeeded as head of the new media school by Markus Huemer (2011–2015), after which Tomáš Svoboda took over.

Intersubjectivity: media metaphors, play & provocation

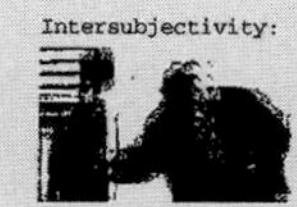

6th international Vilém Flusser symposium
& event series

march 15-19 1997 budapest hungary

Previous International Vilém Flusser Symposia

- (1) Vilém Flusser - Anticipating Post-History
  Goethe-Institut Prague
  1-3 December 1992
- (2) Vilém Flusser Symposium
  Koninklijk Palais Antwerpen
  28-31 October 1993
- (3) Experience and Innocence - Flusser Symposium
  (Steirischer Herbst)
  Palais Attems Graz
  1-2 October 1994
- (4) Telepolis (Burda Academy on the Third Millennium)
  Action-Forum Praterinsel
  October 1995
- (5) Total digital? Reality and Virtuality Post-Flusser
  Evangelical Academy Tutzing
  18-20 October 1996

Vilém Flusser Archive

The archive contains more than 2,000 publications: books, printer's proofs, anthologies, newspapers, journals and catalogues. The archive also contains Vilém Flusser's lectures in Portuguese and French, interviews, discussions, audio-video recordings and speeches in four languages.
There are files according to language, in alphabetical order, containing manuscripts of essays, published and unpublished, originals or carbon copies, with keywords (up to eight).
There is correspondence with artists, students, friends, publishers, regarding symposia.
Each document has a document number in the computer database.
There is a subject catalogue.
There are reviews before and after 1991 (obituaries).
The archive also comprises the remains of the former library, including rare Brasilian books with dedications, and special prints. There is text and audio-video material from various sources.
There is correspondence from after 1991, following the establishment of the archive.

Donnerstag, 11. März 1999

GOETHE-INSTITUT PRAG
Masarykovo nábřeží 32
CS-111 21 Praha 1
P. O. B. 1118
Tel.: (00422) 299551-4
Fax: (00422) 299421

VILEM FLUSSER - VORDENKER DER NACHGESCHICHTE
TRANSDISZIPLINÄRE WERKSTATT

VIDEO WORKSHOP: 26.11. - 03.12.92
mit Michael Bielicky, Egon Bunne, Woody Vasulka sowie Studenten aus Prag und Karlsruhe
Ausstellungseröffnung: 03.12.92, 16.00 Uhr, Technisches Museum

SYMPOSION:

01.12., 9.00 Uhr: Dr. Jochen Bloss, Edith Flusser: Eröffnung
Prof. David Flusser: Willy Flusser als Mensch und als Philosoph
Dr. Stefan Bollmann: Die Vorgeschichte der Nachgeschichte
14.30 Uhr: Dr. Florian Rötzer: Vom Subjekt zum Projekt
Prof. Friedrich Kittler: Geschichte der Kommunikationsmedien

02.12., 9.00 Uhr: Prof. Irmgard Zepf: Die Geste des Zeichnens
Raimund Stecker: Ein Versuch über die Fotografie bei Flusser
Josef Moucha: Uloženo v paměti (Abgespeichert)
14.30 Uhr: Fred Forest: Les gestes du professeur (Die Gesten des Professors)
Louis Bec: Petite promenade zoologique avec Vilém (Kleiner zoologischer Spaziergang mit Vilém)
Prof. Michael Bielicky: Piazza virtuale
Vilém Flussers Fluß

03.12., 9.00 Uhr: Dr. Petr Rezek: Bild/Bildschirm/Live-Übertragung
Prof. Peter Weibel: Künstliche Welten: Die Welt der kontextgesteuerten Variablen
Diskussion
Národní Technické Muzeum, Kostelní 42, Praha 7
15.00 Uhr: Dr. Ing. Ivo Jancušek: Muzeum budoucnosti (Das Museum der Zukunft)
16.00 Uhr: Egon Bunne: ERÖFFNUNG DER AUSSTELLUNG
Videovorführung
Schlußdiskussion
Empfang

Conferences dedicated to Vilém Flusser's legacy, Goethe-Institut, Prague (1992–1997, 2001, 2007), printed programmes.

Neue Medien und Ethik

Donnerstag, 08.12.94	Goethe-Institut Prag (Masarykovo nabrezi 32)	
11.00 Uhr	Pressekonferenz	
Sonntag, 11.12.94	Media Archiv (Narodni trida 20)	
20.00 Uhr	Videovorfuehrung - Moderation: PhDr. Jaroslav Vancat	Das tschechische elektronische Bild
Montag, 12.12.94	Goethe-Institut Prag	
9.00 Uhr	Prof. Michael Bielicky	Auf dem Weg ins Immaterielle
	Keiko Sei	Medienscheinheiligkeit
	PhDr. Jaroslav Vancat	Multimedia und der Beruehrungspunkt mit der Wirklichkeit
14.00 Uhr	Prof. Dr. Peter Glotz	Neue Medien und Ethik
	PhDr. Miroslav Petricek	Die Frage der Darstellung
	Prof. Dr. Norbert Bolz	Medienevolution und humane Kompensation
19.00 Uhr	Videovorfuehrung	Deutsche Video-Kunst 1992 - 1994: Ausstellung zum 6. Marler Video-Kunst-Preis
Dienstag, 13.12.94	Goethe-Institut Prag	
9.00 Uhr	Thomas Kaulmann	Internet
	Rudi Stoert	Computergestuetzte Kommunikation und virtuelle Gemeinschaften
	PhDr. Antonin Kosik	Die uebertragene Wirklichkeit
14.00 Uhr	Ing. Jan Fikacek	Virtuelle Realitaet und einsteinsche Aesthetik
	Juergen Linke	Offene Kanaele
	PhDr. Petr Rezek	Narziss im Medium - Zur Zirkularitaet der Ethik in politischen Medien
	Schlussdiskussion	Weiterfuehrende Fragestellungen
	Media Archiv	
20.00 Uhr	Prof. Petr Vrana	Zbigniew Rybczynski: Retrospektive & Analyse

SOROSOVO CENTRUM SOUČASNÉHO UMĚNÍ PRAHA

Einladung zum Internationalen Symposion

GOETHE-INSTITUT

"Künstliche Umgebungen als Artefakte"

am Goethe-Institut Prag, Masarykovo nabrezi 32, 111 21 Praha 1, Tel.: (0042-2) 24915725, Fax: 299421, in Zusamm
mit dem Soros Center for Contemporary Art - Prague, Staromestske namesti 22, 110 01 Praha 1, Tel.: (0042-2) 2422745
24227451

4.-7. Dezember 1995

Donnerstag, 30. November 1995
13.00 Uhr Pressekonferenz zur Ausstellung und zum Symposion in der *Waldstein-Reitschule*
19.00 Uhr Eröffnung der Ausstellung Orbis Pictus (in der *Waldstein-Reitschule*)

Sonntag, 3. Dezember 1995
19.00 Uhr Informelles Treffen der Teilnehmer im *Soros Center for Contemporary Art*, Staromestske namesti 22

Montag, 4. Dezember 1995
9.00 Uhr Begrüßung im *Goethe-Institut* (Jochen Bloss/Ludvik Hlaváček)
Der Historische Kontext
Michal Bregant: Zwei Wege zur Abstraktion
Jiří Zemánek: Zdeněk Pešánek und die Anfänge Kinetischer Kunst in der Tschechoslowakei
11.00 Uhr Jiří Valoch: Kunst und Computer in den Sechziger Jahren
Radúz Činčera: Zur Vorgeschichte der Interaktivitaet
Gerald O'Grady: Die Historische Rolle von Tschechen in den Internationalen Medienkünsten
13.00 Uhr Imbiß im *Goethe-Institut*
Kuenstlerforum (Moderatorin: Keiko Sei)
14.00 Uhr Einführung: Ludvík Hlaváček und Marta Smolíková
Einige der ausstellenden Künstler sprechen über ihre Arbeiten.
17.00 Uhr Podiumsdiskussion: Warum setzen Künstler Neue Medien ein?
19.00 Uhr Besuch der Ausstellung *Orbis Pictus*

Dienstag, 5. Dezember 1995
9.00 Uhr Olga Shishco: Kunstgeschichte der Neuen Technologien in Rußland
Ekaterina Andreeva, Elena Kolovskaya: Zeitgenössische Videokunst. Über die Ausstellung *Video-Vidente* i
Petersburg
Marko Peljhan: Die Kunst der Intelligenz oder Die Kunst der Kriegführung
Siegfried Zielinski: Für eine Heterologie des Symbolischen
14.30 Uhr Ventsislav Zankov: Fleisch und Blut und Virtualitaet
Tjebbe van Tijen: Orbis Pictus, Überarbeitet (1991-1995)
Axel Wirths: Wie vertreibt man Medienkunst?
Dieter Daniels: Die Krise des Kunstobjekts im Zeitalter der Kommunikation
17.00 Uhr Hilmar Hoffmann: Zur Zukunft des Kulturellen Lebens angesichts der Medienentwicklung
19.00 Uhr Brian Springer präsentiert sein Video *SPIN* im *Goethe-Institut*

Mittwoch, 6. Dezember 1995
9.00 Uhr Antya Umstätter: Die Ewige Gegenwart - *Ping*, ein sich selbst Generierender Film im Visuellen Datenraum
Margaret Morse: Du, Ich und Es: Vom Spiegel und dem Ersetzen zum Künstlichen Leben in Ausgewählten
Beispielen Elektronischer Kunst
Richard Schütz: Logos - Logik - Logistik
Jaroslav Vančát: Sehen als Aneignung der Welt
14.30 Uhr Paul DeMarinis: Verspielte Mechanik: Künstler schließen Medien kurz
Sergius Golowin: Künstliche Wirklichkeit
Antonín Kosík: -
Nebojsa Vilic: Ästhetische Kategorien angesichts der Neuen Technologien
17.00 Uhr Nebojsa Vilic präsentiert ein CD-ROM Projekt im *Goethe-Institut*.
19.00 Uhr Empfang im *Goethe-Institut*

Donnerstag, 7. Dezember 1995

have a rough outline of the curriculum.[32] The first year was focused on visual expression and the principles of images in time, followed by the forms of hand-drawn and puppet animated films. The second year was to continue with animation, extending it via electronic transformations of the image. However, in a different set of manuscripts intended for Ivan Ruller, Pilař gives precedence to the teaching of video art, video sculptures, video dance, video performance, followed by applications of these fields into television advertising, jingles, and music videos.[33]

After teaching started in practice, under Tomáš Ruller's direction, the Video–Multimedia–Performance Studio shifted towards performance, which was determined both by the personnel and the lack of equipment. Nevertheless, video did form a part of some of the exercises. These were based in traditional fine art tasks – still lifes, portraits, objects in motion or in a field, etc. – that were processed using various means, just as Radek Pilař had indicated in his own materials. VHS technology

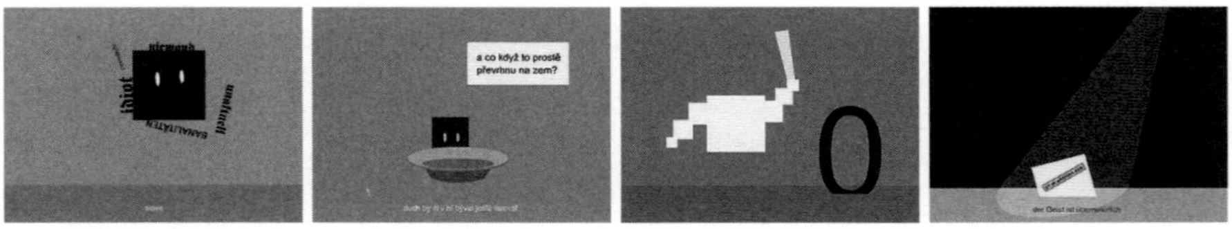

Pavel Ryška *Ursonáta, stará švýcarská legenda* [Ursonate, An Old Swiss Legend] (2004), video, 4 min 45 s

was available, later complemented by V-8, HI8, and other formats. The Video–Multimedia–Performance Studio was located in a building that was also home to the Davay post-production studio, equipped with a U-matic editing machine. The students had access to it, although only in a limited manner: they were required to work together with a studio technician, whose experiences in television influence the work.[34] They could also follow what Woody Vasulka and his assistants were working on. The department soon acquired new technology, including an RGB projector (rare and precious at the time). Tomáš Ruller organised the acquisitions and attempted to bring as many international guests to Brno as possible, whether for the festivals and exhibitions he organised, or as guest lecturers at the school.[35] The first generation of students included Marek Mařan and Naďa Slováková, who achieved the best results with simple but meaningful and powerful manipulations of images. A short time later, a new generation of artists matured at FaVU, represented by artists such as Filip Cenek, Jiří Havlíček, Pavel Ryška, Petr Strouhal, and Magdalena Hrubá. They had a more developed

[32] Radek Pilař, undated sketches for the curriculum, family archive of Radek Pilař, Prague.

[33] *Ibid.* Pilař presumed the workplace would be financially independent and therefore involved in the commercial sector.

[34] Filip Cenek interviewed by the author, 14 May 2021.

[35] These included Paul DeMarinis, Stelarc, Phill Niblock, and Kristine Stiles. In 1995, curator Chris Hill donated a collection of ten VHS cassettes to the school, presenting an overview of American video art titled *The First Decade*. The studio also travelled extensively around the country and internationally.

relationship with audiovisual technology and software for working with the moving image. Thanks to collaborations and mutual influence among the students, a distinctive school of computer animation was established there.

If they had the means, students in the second half of the 1990s would buy their own video cameras and computers. The development of the internet was also important, since beginning in 1995/1996, it allowed students to overcome information barriers and acquire an overview of developments around the world. There were some technologies, however, that were unavailable to students on their own – only to schools. Thanks to the efforts of network manager Luděk Skočovský, Silicon Graphics computers allowing for non-linear editing appeared at FAVU in 1996, 1997, and 1998.[36] Students not only consulted each other regarding technology, they also shared information about remarkable works, developing an interest in hypertext, and the expanded possibilities of narration that the world of electronic media offered.[37] Theorists acted as welcome partners in discussions. Between 1997 and 2000, this role was taken up by Jaroslav Vančát, who taught directly in the video studio, while Miloš Vojtěchovský taught at the department of art theory and history from 1995 to 2004. Japanese media theorist and curator Keiko Sei led the video studio from 1998 to 2002. However, she had no interest in remaining at the school for longer:

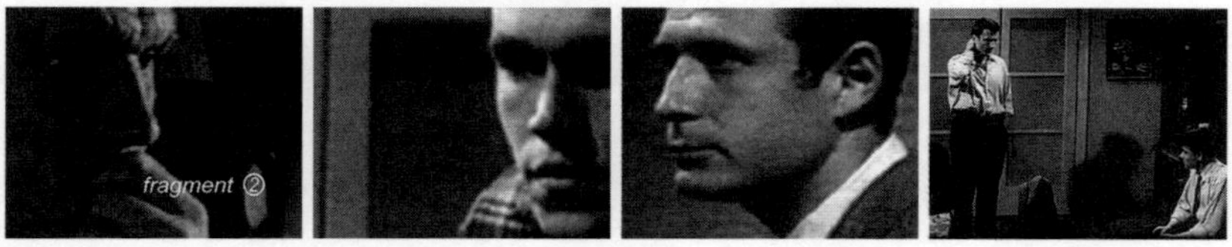

Filip Cenek *Po Atentátu (3 fragmenty)* [After the Assassination (3 Fragments)] (1998), video, 6 min 10 s

> I never really believed in academic study. [...] I was the worst student of all my students at FaVU, agitating amongst them along the lines of 'what are you going to do here for such a long time'. It's a problem at schools like this – which also includes

[36] As Filip Cenek recalls, the students essentially appropriated the new equipment: "We immediately knew all the equipment acquired while we were students better than all the rest of the staff, because we spent time with it. That was crucial." See "Vlastně ani nevím, jestli se za tu dobu utvořil nějaký smysluplný způsob, jak novomediální umění učit. Rozhovor s umělcem a pedagogem doc. MgA. Filipem Cenkem nejen o vývoji na FaVU VUT v Brně, ale i o rozličných přístupech k tvorbě a výuce" [I Don't Really Know If We Managed to Find a Meaningful Way of Teaching New Media Art in All That Time. An Interview with Artist and Pedagogue doc. MgA. Filip Cenek], interview by Mgr. Barbora Šedivá PhD. in 2013, transcription by *Monoskop*, https://monoskop.org/File:Rozhovor_s_Filipem_Cenkem.pdf. For Cenek and his colleague Zdeněk Mezihorák, an important discovery was when they found a Videomachine graphics card in one of the school computers. It allowed for new ways of manipulating audiovisual material. In 1998, now-classic works were created that include *13. revír* [13th District], *Po stopách krve* [On the Trail of Blood], or *Spejbl a Hurvínek* [Spejbl and Hurvínek] by Zdeněk Mezihorák or Filip Cenek's *Po atentátu (3 fragmenty)* [After the Assassination (3 Fragments)]; the latter piece also involved Adobe After Effects software. These works, which re-edited classic works of Czech cinema, were not the result of a school task to re-cut an existing cinematic work (a common task at certain film schools), but the product of the students' independent experimentation.

[37] After concluding his studies, Zdeněk Mezihorák found success in the gaming industry at an international level.

FAMU – that students can learn technique, but they learn very little about real society, as they spend such a long time in a kind of moratorium.[38]

The Second Wave and its Specifics

The second wave of programmes that allowed students at Czech art universities to study art of the moving image only appeared after the turn of the millennium. The situation had changed since the 1990s in several important respects. International experience was no longer limited to that of the lecturers but became part of the regular curriculum. The moving image became commonplace and achieved a certain level of institutionalisation. It entered the gallery, the cinema, the internet, festivals, and public spaces. Technology and access to information were both dramatically democratised. New media were no longer "new", and the term video art definitively became historical, while digital cameras and projectors gradually

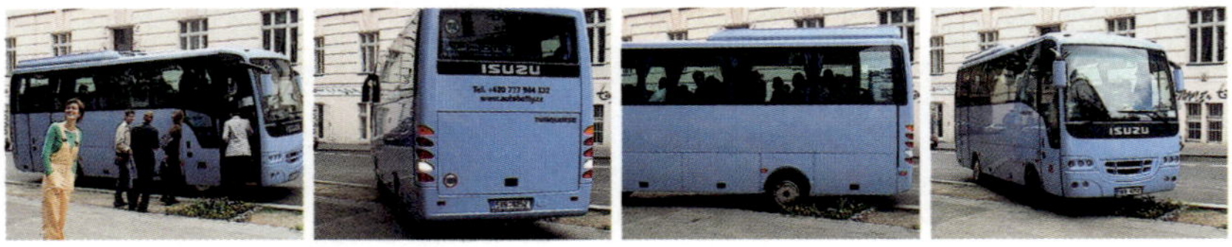

Eva Jiřička *360°* (2006), video, 6 min 48 s

became standard equipment at art schools. The second wave occurred in a world saturated with technology – technology no longer intended exclusively for narrowly focused professionals and specialised distribution platforms. At some level, anyone could use this equipment. This availability led to a wave of projects that could be grouped under the headings of expanded cinema, live audiovisual performance, or works making use of VR and AI. Mastering technology became an optional foundation for a broad range of creative practices, leading more to a thematic differentiation and structuring of the individual schools. The lead pedagogue remained a decisive figure for the profile of the schools. The following part of this essay therefore does not aim to present a complete overview of all the schools at which students can study new media art, but instead presents a more detailed perspective on selected departments.[39]

In 2001, the Institute for Art Studies was established at the Ostrava University. It also included a New Media Studio, led from

[38] Petr Szczepanik, "Média mezi kulturami a žánry. Rozhovor s Keiko Sei" [Media Between Cultures and Genres. An Interview with Keiko Sei], *Cinepur* 10, nos. 23–24 (2002), p. 19.

[39] According to vysokeskoly.cz [universities.cz], there are nineteen schools and faculties in the Czech Republic offering an education in the arts. Vysokeskoly.com [universities.com] even lists thirty-one. Among the departments with a history of interesting lecturers and graduates that could not be included in this text for reasons of brevity are the Multimedia and New Media Studios at the Ladislav Sutnar Faculty of Design and Art at the University of West Bohemia in Plzeň, where teachers have included Dušan Zahoranský, Michal Pěchouček, and Milena Dopitová, the Audiovisual Art studio at the Faculty of Multimedia Communications of Tomáš Baťa University in Zlín, and many others.

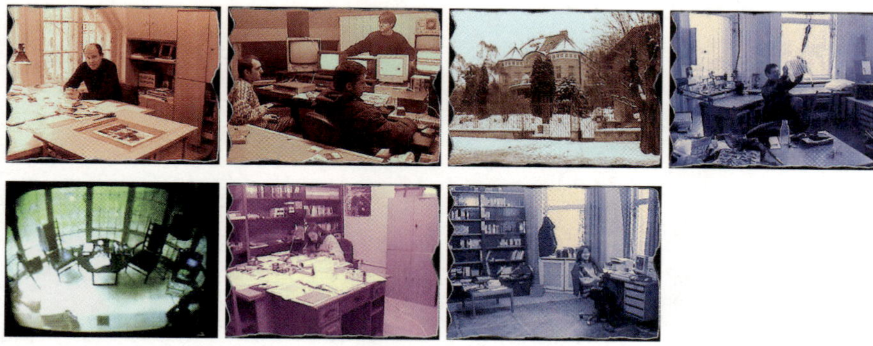

Landing page of Květná, the first webpage of the video and multimedia performance studio, Faculty of Fine Arts, Brno University of Technology, 1996.

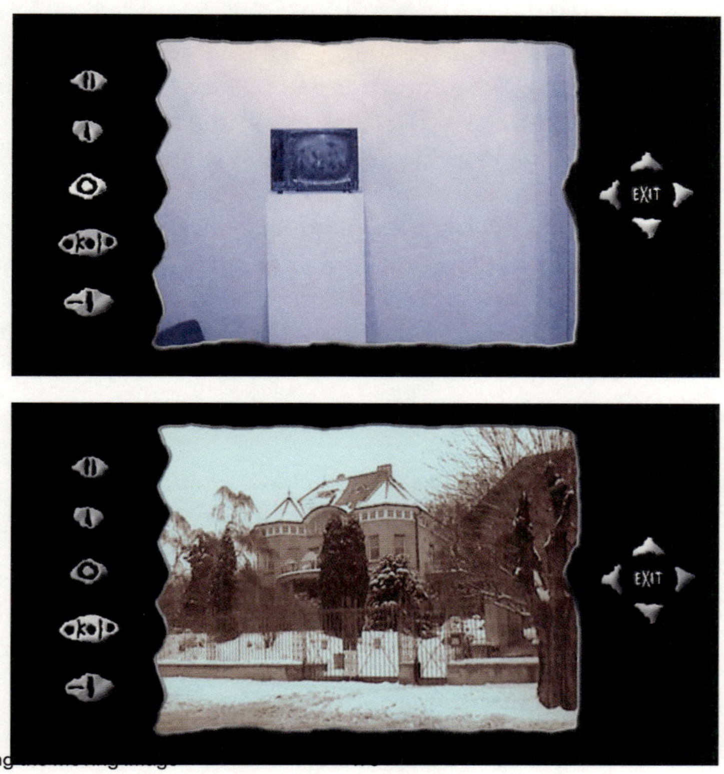

2004 by Jiří Surůvka, who gave it a more fitting name: Video–Multimedia–Performance.[40] In 2007, the studio became part of the Department of Intermedia at the newly established Faculty of Fine Arts and Music of the Ostrava University. The studio is not limited to one particular form of art or technology, rather, it introduces students to various forms of visual expression ranging from drawing, painting, collage, objects, art in public spaces, digital graphics, and video. The curriculum partially overlaps with the Concept–Object–Installation Studio at the same faculty. This is not a question of disagreements about jurisdiction or competence – rather, it reflects the reality of the breadth of media used by contemporary art. More specialised equipment and know-how is provided by a close collaboration with Denisa Jánská's Animated Art Studio and external companies such as the QQ post-production studio. According to Surůvka and his teaching assistant Barbora Mikudová, the aim of the instruction is to produce original artists who can also find employment in the television industry.[41]

The Center for Audiovisual Studies (CAS) was established at FAMU in 2004. Its aim was to bring together the teaching of historical and theoretical subjects at the school whilst also opening a new study programme. This programme was to operate between theory and creative practice, and also between various forms of the moving image that do not fit into any of the traditional categories of the cinematic and television industries. The original concept for CAS was created by Vít Janeček and Michal Bregant, while the teaching staff, of considerable size, included Miloš Vojtěchovský, Martin Blažíček, Eric Rosenzveig, and the author of this text. The loosely conceived centre was long an outlier at FAMU, a school otherwise clearly delineated by profession. In comparison to other departments the centre has modest facilities and (at first) limited access to the school's technical equipment. The original assumption – that the programme would attract theorists – proved to be inaccurate. Creative instruction is structured – like at other departments at FAMU – according to studios headed by core or visiting lecturers. The works created in these studios vary broadly, ranging from classical or experimental film to art installations, activist projects, or works using elements of computer animation or AI. In 2007, CAS was one of the co-founders of the Institute of Intermedia, run jointly by the Faculty of Electrical Engineering of the Czech Technical University in Prague and AMU (the Academy of Performing Arts).[42]

Teachers and students at the Academy of Art, Architecture and Design in Prague (VŠUP/UMPRUM) were already using video in the

[40] Jiří Surůvka interviewed by the author, 21 May 2021.

[41] Among the most interesting graduates working in the field of art of the moving image are Kateřina Sudolská and Jan Vytiska.

[42] See https://www.iim.cz/cs/. Graduates of CAS include Kryštof Pešek, Vladimír Turner, Alma Lily Rayner, Lea Petříková, and František Fekete. For more on the first ten years of CAS, see Tomáš Pospiszyl – Eric Rosenzveig, eds., *CAS, Co je to?* [CAS, What Is It?], (Prague: AMU Press, 2013).

1990s, but a studio specialising in new media was only established in 2008. Federico Díaz and David Kořínek were primarily responsible for the conception of this new department. They called it the Supermedia Studio: they wanted to work with new media, but they also considered this term to be depleted.[43] They were interested in the relationship between the real and the virtual, cyberculture, and the beginnings of post-internet art. From the very beginning, they had a clear concept for the technical facilities of the department, and they managed to convince the school of its necessity whilst also securing external subsidies. However, they did not understand the purpose of the studio as systematically teaching individual technologies – but rather, to consult on specific projects. The lecturers of the Supermedia Studio felt a need to present the work of their students beyond the school – David Kořínek considered the PAF festival in Olomouc an ideal platform.[44] However, after several years of activity, they began to feel personal fatigue and an exhaustion of ideas. Federico Díaz left the school in 2014, while David Kořínek and Milan Mikuláštík continued for a few more years. In 2018, ten years after the studio began, they decided to conclude its activities without replacement.[45]

In 2008, the same year as the Supermedia Studio, the Time-Based Media (TBM) Studio was established at the Faculty of Art and Design of Jan Evangelista Purkyně University (UJEP) in Ústí nad Labem. This was

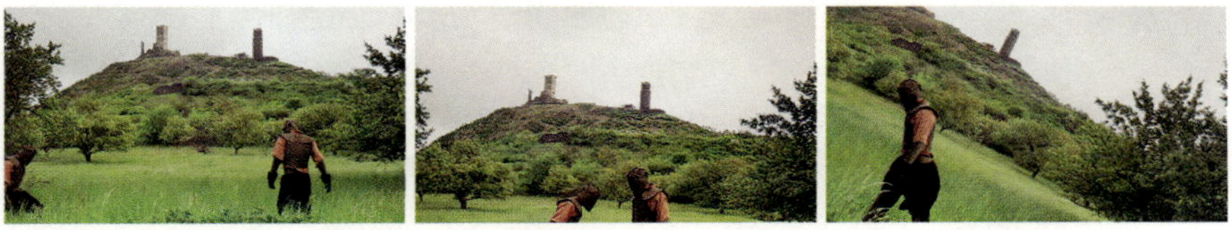

Lea Petříková *Rytířsko* [The Knight's Fee], from the Animalia trilogy (2017), video, 4 min 49 s

not the first department at UJEP to work with various forms of art of the moving image. These were already being taught in 2002 in the studios of Michaela Thelenová and Pavel Kopřiva, which is now grouped together with the TBM studio under the Department of the Electronic Image. The aim of the faculty administration was to avoid copying what was being taught elsewhere. The dean at the time, Michal Koleček, therefore invited Pavel Mrkus and Daniel Hanzlík to expand the offering of studios by creating one focused on technology.[46] Their conception was based on an exploration of temporality in the context of audiovisual works, whereby prospective

[43] David Kořínek interviewed by the author, 12 May 2021.

[44] Ibid.

[45] Graduates include 3D modelling and VR specialist Jonáš Strouhal, conceptual artist Jakub Jansa, and multimedia artists Jan Nálepa, Jan Hladil, and Marie Lukáčová. The history of the Supermedia Studio is summarised in Radim Labuda – David Kořínek, eds., *Supernova, katalog Ateliéru supermédií* [Supernova, A Catalogue of the Supermedia Studio] (Prague: AAAD Publishing House, 2019). This history is supplemented with programmatic texts by Claire Bishop, Hito Steyerl, and Nick Land.

[46] Pavel Mrkus and Daniel Hanzlík interviewed by the author, 12 May 2021.

students search out various forms of bringing sound and image together. Mrkus's semestral exchange at the Rhode Island School of Design had a considerable influence on the form of the studio, as did his experiences with schools in Japan. From the very earliest days, Mrkus and Hanzlík had a clear idea of the technology needed and they gradually acquired it: workspaces for sound equipped with Pro Tools software, a CAVE immersive environment, a room for creating and listening to multi-channel sound, and other facilities. Teaching does not focus on mastering specific tools – what they are interested in is nurturing autonomous artists. Most students are interested in sound production, interactive installations, live audiovisual performances, or video mapping.[47]

In Place of a Conclusion

If we were to attempt to grasp the beginnings of the teaching of art of the moving image at Czech art schools as a story, its narrative arc would trace from tough early days to an attainment of stability, as well as from exclusivity to standardisation. The first wave of study courses was established with no previous foundations, in the stormy atmosphere of societal changes following the Velvet Revolution in 1989. These were accompanied by a no less significant technological transformation in the form of digitalisation and the advent of the internet. Both social and technological changes, however, were perceived with great optimism.

If someone wanted to pursue video or new media in the last decade of the preceding century, the best conditions – or, indeed, even the possibility of making work – were to be found at art schools. The corresponding departments (perhaps with the exception of FAMU) were clearly divergent from the rest of the school, which was noticeable already at first glance. They used different tools and they had different, seemingly unclassifiable outputs. What's most important is that they developed without the constricting (or anchoring) influence of an immediately influential tradition: here, everything was new. The specific character of each individual department was considerably defined by the leading pedagogue; by the artistic, pedagogical, and managerial skills that they applied in acquiring astronomically expensive (and rapidly obsolescent) technologies.

This is no longer true today. Equipment that was once inaccessible is now available at art universities at comparable standards to the other studios and workplaces. Individual courses are more and more permeable in terms of the media they use. Teaching styles are changing too, moving from the master-pupil model of the studios to various alternatives.

Will we even be able to discuss the specialised teaching of art of the moving image in a few years? I believe we will, in some form or

[47] Graduates include sound artists Iva Polanecká and Polina Khatsenka, musician Ondřej Mikula (Aid Kid), and František Pecháček, who regularly works in theatre.

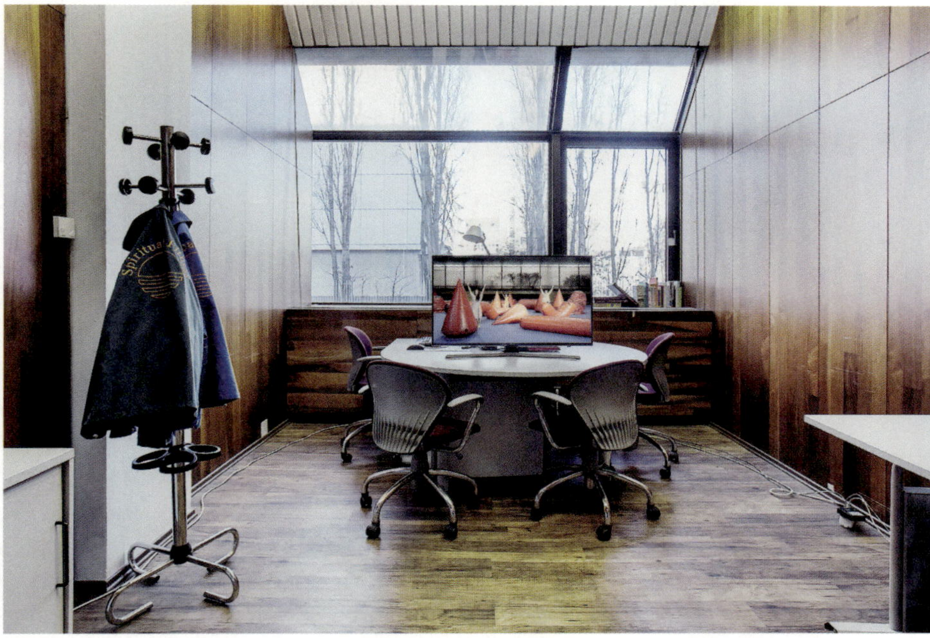

Jakub Jansa *Spiritual Fitness* (2016), installation at the Healing exhibition, Czech Centre, Berlin, 2018

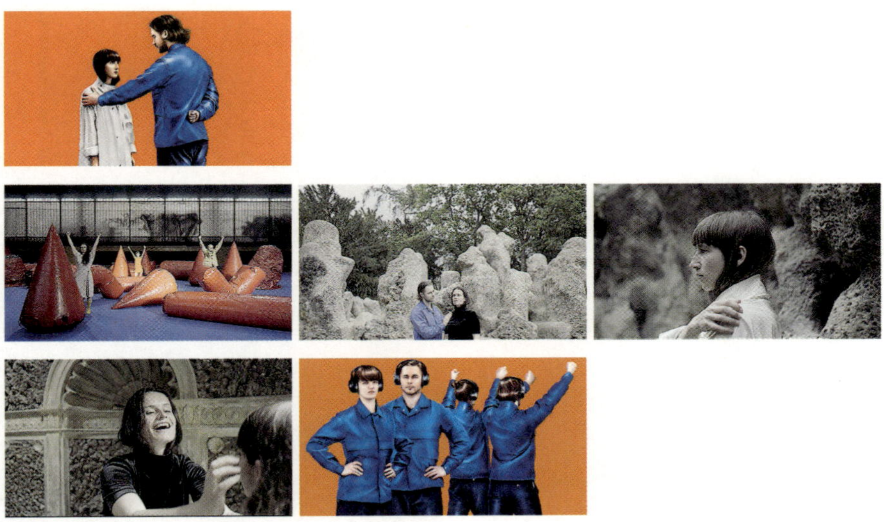

Jakub Jansa *Spiritual Fitness* (2016), video, 6 min

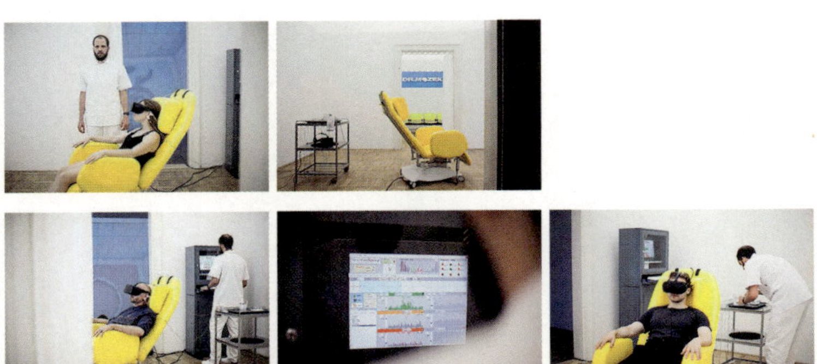

Jonáš Strouhal *Dr. Mozek* [Dr. Brain] (2017), exhibition at the Nau Gallery, Prague, 2017

other. In recent years, we have had the opportunity to observe a rise in professional standards in the teaching of audiovisual technologies, as well as the creation of new fields in which professionals in this area can find employment. Schools will have to come to terms with similar challenges, employing more and more specialists. I believe the importance of the central role of studio leaders will gradually diminish while block teaching will lead to the creation of collective forms of collaboration. Most important is the need for artists to put new technologies to creative use and develop them. It is the students themselves who step beyond the established confines of practical and theoretical instruction, thereby introducing something new. Optimism has been replaced by a critical approach, thus closing the circle. If the pioneers of the video art of the 1960s and '70s were aiming to create an alternative to the effects of mass media, we are now witnessing a similar process in the relationship between young artists and social media. Let us hope that they are successful!

Film Studies in Motion

Kateřina Svatoňová

In this text, I will attempt to trace various deviations, detours, and meanders in the curricula of Czech academic film studies. For over half a century, this field has sought to develop a history of cinematography and film theory, cultivate critical thinking, and teach students tools with which to analyse the medium of film. In contrast to other academic disciplines that focus on specific art forms (e.g., art theory, musicology, or theatre studies), film studies is relatively young and is marked by a certain fluidity. Just like the medium of film itself, it has a broad range, establishing varied relationships with other artforms, from literature through theatre to architecture and fine art (and thereby gradually making its identity more and more uncertain). It also has the potential for "flitting", adopting, accepting, establishing dialogues, and questioning its object of study. I will therefore focus primarily on how this fluidity and dynamism is fulfilled; examine the extent to which there are transformations taking place in the discourse that surrounds teaching and research in the field; follow the extent to which the focus has been broadened to include various kinds of moving and static image; and explore the gradual acceptance of interdisciplinary topics in pedagogy, in students' works, and in dialogues within the field as they play out on the pages of Czech journals.

This essay follows in the footsteps of a memoire-styled study by film historian and one of the founders of the only Czech film studies journal, *Iluminace*, Ivan Klimeš, which maps the establishment of the field during the period known as normalisation (the 1970s and '80s). In my exploration of whether and how film studies discourse is expanding, I follow the lead of Klimeš's study not only in terms of content but also in my manner of working: my essay, too, is a combination of personal recollections and an attempt to reconstruct historic reality. I find myself in a similar insider situation to Klimeš, who said of himself: "The author is a contemporary witness of the dawn and the true birth of the field, which is at once an advantage and a handicap."[48] I also invoke Jiří Brabec, who theorised the writing of history in which the historians themselves participated, whereby he drew attention to their transformed evaluating position. Particularly at the moment when we participate in the stories of our time, Brabec emphasises, we have a tendency to explain more, to defend, objectivise, or elide.[49] For these reasons, I focus more on description than on trying to theoretically assess the situation at hand, or alternatively attempt to use it to deduce a "story" about the transformation of discourse.

The final introductory note is purely terminological – my text focuses (unless stated otherwise) on the opposition between "film" or "cinema" – understood as the traditional product of a film crew screened in a (home) cinema and intended for concentrated viewing from beginning to end regardless of its narrative or otherwise – and "the moving image". I consider the second term to refer to a technological image that takes place in time but is not bound to one particular materiality – I include within it film, video, and digital images of an experimental nature, filling the gaps in the history of "classical" cinematographic practice; it is, according to Raymond Bellour, "between", "other", and hard to grasp or describe.[50] For these reasons, it can be variously relocated, it can make use of film language or serve as a reflection of it, entering different contexts and initiating a debate of an interdisciplinary nature. Given its plurality (which is manifested in form, media, and materiality, as well as interpretation), it is problematic (and often finds itself outside the scope of individual disciplines) but also exciting. In 2003, Lenka Dolanová published a text in *Iluminace* titled "The Entry of 'Moving Images' into the Gallery", in which she discusses the vague designation of video art and also expresses her surprise at the fact that "in art history practice, relationships to the history and theory of film and media are often suppressed [...]".[51] Seven years later, Sylva Poláková drew attention to Dolanová's essay: "The diffidence of theoretical reflection not only of video art but also of other extensions of the moving image, and the suppression of relationships to the history and theory of film and media perpetuated by historians and theorists of art history, still survives in the Czech context, even

[48] Ivan Klimeš, "Filmová studia v předsálí svých zdejších dějin" [Film Studies in the Waiting Room of Their Local History], *Slovo a smysl* [Word and Sense] 17, no. 35 (2020), pp. 139–147.

[49] Jiří Brabec, *Panství ideologie a moc literatury: Studie, kritiky, portréty (1991–2008)* [The Dominion of Ideology and the Power of Literature: Studies, Critiques, Portraits (1991–2008)] (Prague: Akropolis, 2009), p. 161.

[50] See Raymond Bellour, "The Film Stilled: Unspeakable Images", *Camera Obscura* 8, no. 3 (1990), pp. 98–124; Raymond Bellour, *Between-the-Images* (Zurich: JRP/Ringier, 2012).

[51] Lenka Dolanová, "Vstup pohyblivých obrazů do galerie" [The Entry of Moving Images into the Gallery], *Iluminace* 15, no. 4 (2003), p. 99.

seven years after Lenka Dolanová's paper was published".[52] Now, eleven years after Poláková's text, I consider the changes that have taken place, and it is I who is diffident – there are intersections between these media, whether in the form of lectures, composed screening programs, or curatorial practice, interchange takes place in both directions, yet these processes are not a matter of course.

The Enclosed Openness of Film Studies

Film studies, as a new discipline in the humanities, first began appearing at universities around the world in the 1960s. At that time, various film theories were established, and their capabilities and potentialities tested on films (such as feminist or ideological theories), and this was also a time when filmmakers began participating in political struggles. In addition, there were crucial technological developments that gradually disrupted the unequivocal status of the medium of film and its specificity. The institutional foundation of film studies was thus born in a turbulent time of many debates, a broadening of the field of cinema, and a gradual interpenetration of theory and practice. As a consequence of these movements, it was not only the thinking about film that changed – on the one hand, approaching its epistemological and ontological levels (and their social consequences), on the other hand towards the very possibilities of the media as a new form of thought – but also the aesthetics of film as such; film began "slowing down" and offering more space for philosophical and aesthetic reflection.[53]

Film studies mirrored this dynamic, leading, on the one hand, to the establishment of theoretical departments at art schools that aimed to create an informed background to film production, and, on the other hand, to increased support of various methodological and research lineages, with departments established at universities alongside other fields of art

[52] Sylva Poláková, "'Současný český videoart' jako výzva filmovým studiím" ["Contemporary Czech Video Art" as a Challenge to Film Studies], in *Současný český a slovenský film – pluralita estetických, kulturních a ideových konceptů* [Contemporary Czech and Slovak Film – A Plurality of Aesthetic, Cultural, and Ideological Concepts], ed. Luboš Ptáček (Olomouc: Palacký University, 2010), p. 122.

[53] It would be appropriate to broaden the scope of this text to include another study that would compare the development of film studies departments in various fields, and it must be noted that it is often defined by the political and economic situation and the preferences of local strategic priorities. Taking a particular field of study as one's own brings not only institutional and state support, along with the related subsidies, but also an adoption of terminology and establishment of discourses. In Germany, for instance, film studies transformed into media studies, thereby automatically integrating non-cinematographical audiovisual forms and practices. The 1990s complicated the situation, as media studies began asking what a medium, in fact, is (and whether it even exists in its "pure" form). Media studies thus split into a branch that ignores this question and studies specific media (film, image, text) and a branch that studies mediality as such. The German line of thought is significantly differentiated from Anglo-American media studies, as we know it in the Czech Republic. This school does not concern itself with the philosophical dimension of media, instead focusing on empirically and sociologically focused research, particularly of mass media. See also Kateřina Krtilová – Kateřina Svatoňová, "Česko-německý 'Medienwissenschaft'" [Czech-German "Medienwissenschaft"], *Iluminace* 26, no. 2 (2014), pp. 185–189.

studies, literature, or culturally focused fields. In the Czech context, this development was not significantly different from elsewhere in the world. The department in Prague, for instance, passed through all these levels: it was established as part of FAMU (the Film and TV School of the Academy of Performing Arts in Prague), moving to the Faculty of Arts at Charles University in 1968, where it spent an extended period fighting for an autonomous position (having been typically grouped together with theatre studies). A separate film studies department was only established at Charles University in 1996. Film studies at the Masaryk University in Brno appeared in the 1960s, at first paired with Slavic literature and theatre studies, before migrating across various faculties as a dual subject with theatre studies in a process of repeated dissolution and restoration. In 1993, film studies at the Masaryk University gained independence as a field of study, and an autonomous Department of Film Studies and Audiovisual Studies was established ten years later. Film studies at Palacký University in Olomouc arose from the study programme of Czech language and literature – art theory, transformed into an ideologically focused cultural theory department in 1980 and changing again after 1990 when students were allowed to choose one field of art studies to focus on (the choices being literature, theatre, film, fine art, and music). Two years later, however, the Department of Art Studies was split into three departments, one of which was the department of dramatic arts, which also included film studies. To this day, the department in Olomouc has close ties to theatre studies (the department was renamed the Department of Theatre and Film Studies in 2014), currently extending to include television and radio studies.

What is important for the theme at hand is that despite relatively strong relations to other fields, film studies – unlike the older discipline of art history – never looked back to the intellectual structures of the 19th century, instead considering its material through the prism of topical concepts and methods, whilst also observing what was happening to film, including constant reflections on its "death".[54] The debate has remained open to include various possibilities and disciplines, but certain elements have

[54] The death of film began being discussed in broader film studies around the mid-1990s, while in the Czech context, it was not thematised until the 2000s. Susan Sontag's article "The Decay of Cinema" (New York Times Magazine, 25 Feb 1996, published in Adéla Sušická's translation in Cinepur 73, nos. 1–2, 2011, pp. 60–62), which links this death to the end of cinephilia, is well known in Czechia. There are also those (such as Malte Hagener) who are of the opinion that cinema is, to a considerable degree, losing its (textual and economic) stability, dispersing into many (material and intangible) fragments. Furthermore, there have been those who welcome the end of classical cinema (such as Peter Greenaway, who was interviewed in the same magazine). This process is often connected to digitalisation – D. N. Rodowick, for instance, discusses the possible disappearance of film (and the survival of "cinema", as the narrative structure we recognise as a classical narrative film will, he, claims, survive, firmly rooted in our media subconscious). See Malte Hagener, "Kde je (dnes) film? Film ve věku imanence médií" [Where is Film (Today)? Film in an Age of the Immanence of Media], *Iluminace* 23, no. 1. (2011 [2008]), p. 79; Petr Szczepanik – Jakub Kučera, "Rozhovor s Davidem Normanem Rodowickem" [An Interview with David Norman Rodowick], *Iluminace* 15, no. 2 (2003), p. 94; the Death of Film as the topic of *Cinepur* 73, nos. 1–2 (2011).

become subservient to other fields – namely the study and accreditation plans of the individual film studies departments. The central axis at all departments in the country was (and is) the history of world and Czech cinema and the development of theoretical thought. Curricula were complemented (again, at all departments) with courses on the foundations of critical thinking, (formal or narratological) analysis, and academic research. Later, elective courses were added that explored the dynamics of film as a medium or the stratified nature of debates about film – this was the entry point for courses that examined film in relation to fine art or literature, or modules informed by various gender-based, sociological, or aesthetic theories. Curricula include traditional profiles of national cinematographic traditions or artists, themes related to classical film, or – in recent years – courses on creative industries or the economic and institutional foundations of cinematic production and distribution.

The turning point at which film studies began to expand to include other media, and when the essentialist approach to film began to be disrupted, came at the turn of the millennium. More and more students began to appear who had an interest in the broader contexts of film, or in various specific manifestations of it – this included the moving image, as well as popular culture. Some reasons for this development were the inspirations coming from researchers and their scholarly texts working abroad,[55] lectures by striking interdisciplinary figures (specifically the philosophical-cinematic connections of Miroslav Petříček[56] or Martin Čihák's idiosyncratic lectures on avant-garde film[57]), and spectator's experiences with various art practices. Another reason was the attempt to revise the field and expand it beyond the rigidly defined borders of cinema. Rather than a systematic expansion of film studies' field of interest, this took the form of individual constituent works (particularly

[55] The Brno film studies department hosted crucial, subsidised visits by researchers from abroad (e.g., Andrzej Gwóźdź, Thomas Elsaesser, and Sean Cubitt).

[56] Philosopher Miroslav Petříček regularly writes and lectures about overlapping areas between philosophy, film, literature, and fine art. He has also translated many works that are crucial for film theory as well as for the theory and philosophy of media, e.g., May Ann Doane, *Zrození kinematografického času: Modernita, nahodilost, archiv* [The Emergence of Cinematic Time: Modernity, Contingency, the Archive] (Prague: Karolinum, 2021). His monograph *Myšlení obrazem* [Thinking Through the Image], subtitled *Průvodce současným filosofickým myšlením pro středně nepokročilé* [A Guide to Contemporary Philosophical Thinking for the Moderately Non-advanced] (Prague: Herrmann & synové, 2009) is a crucial contribution to the relationship between philosophy and the image.

[57] Martin Čihák is a graduate of the Faculty of Mathematics and Physics at Charles University and the editing department at the Film and TV Faculty of the Academy of Performing Arts in Prague (FAMU), where he is currently a lecturer. Beginning in the 1980s, he shot 8mm films, experimented with various cinematic and photographic materials and techniques, and made documentary films. He wrote *Ponorná řeka kinematografie* [Subterranean River of Cinematography] (Prague: NAMU, 2013), a book primarily focused on the compositional principles of various cinematic avant-garde movements. His idiosyncratic and to a large extent performative lectures on avant-garde and experimental film, along with his considerable erudition, have influenced a number of students throughout all departments of the Film and TV School.

those by Petr Szczepanik[58]) and later a series of lectures on the moving image: video art (Marika Kupková, Pavlína Míčová, Sylva Poláková, Martin Mazanec); film beyond the cinema (Lucie Česálková); the relationship between photography, fine art, and film (Petra Hanáková,[59] Miroslav Petříček); and (amateur) experimentation (Martin Blažíček) – I myself also lecture on these last two areas. A certain level of systematisation (but one achieved more in hindsight and artificially) can be observed in how dissertations were supervised. It was under the guidance of these lecturers that graduate theses were written that mapped the entry of the moving image into the gallery as well as the art world they are a part of.

A similar process then took place in writing about film, which is the subject of Eva Krátká's essay in this publication and the reason I limit myself here to emphasising only the crucial film studies magazines. The journals *Cinepur* and *Film a doba* [Film and Our Times] began including partly interdisciplinary topics reflecting a broader conception of the moving image, but were, again, connected to figures who had backgrounds in film studies or art studies departments or who were themselves lecturers at these departments (such as Helena Bendová, Jan Kolář, Martin Blažíček, Martin Mazanec, Tomáš Pospiszyl, Sylva Poláková, Kamila Boháčková, Lucie Česálková, Marika Kupková, or Matěj Nytra). The articles in *Cinepur* focus on topics such as Czech experimental film and films at exhibitions, with most of the other texts being reviews or interviews. Nevertheless, the dominant discourse has remained subject to the cinephile tradition, monographic writing, and primarily historical texts related to classical cinema. All this despite the fact that since the beginning of the new millennium, the academic journal *Iluminace* has published theoretical texts in Czech translation that offered different perspectives and new tools, drawing attention to crucial transformations of film, cinematography, and their discourses, both in relation to video art and other gallery formats (see, for instance, Noël Caroll[60]); the relationship between film and other art forms (e.g. Pascal Bonitzer[61]); and

[58] Under the influence of foreign-language theoretical texts, Petr Szczepanik began attempting to conceptualise non-cinematographic practice. In 1998, he defended his diploma thesis in Brno on the topic of music videos, titled "Videoklip – změna modelu diváka a elektronická tělesnost: Pragmatický obrat v teorii filmu a populární kultury" [The Music Video – A Change in the Model of the Spectator and Electronic Corporeality: The Pragmatic Turn in Film Theory and Popular Culture], and in 2002 he completed his doctorate with a dissertation on intermediality: "Filmy, které vidí vlastní vidění: Strategie intermediality a reflexivity v současném filmu" [Films That See Their Own Seeing: Strategies of Intermediality and Reflexivity in Contemporary Cinema].

[59] Petra Hanáková was one of the first to connect the teaching of film studies with a broader conception of visual culture – she taught courses with titles such as Vizuální slast [Visual Pleasure] or Je to ještě film? [Is this Still Cinema?], whereby she collaborated with art historian Václav Hájek and invited many guests from other fields.

[60] Noël Carroll, "Definování pohyblivého obrazu" [Defining the Moving Image], *Iluminace* 13, no. 2 (2001 [1996]), pp. 5–32.

[61] Pascal Bonitzer, "Odrámování" [Deframing], *Iluminace* 15, no. 4 (2003), pp. 31–34.

digitalisation (e.g. John Belton[62]).[63] In this context, interviews with theorists such as David N. Rodowick or Raymond Bellour led by Petr Szczepanik (often with Jakub Kučera) played a very important role. These interviews allowed the thinkers' theoretical conceptions to be thoroughly expressed, explained, and related to the environment in the Czech Republic, therefore providing impetus for valuable new discussions (although this seldom occurred). There were also texts that were outspoken in their ambition to broaden film studies discourse, such as Lenka Dolanová's essay mentioned above, "The Entry of 'Moving Images' into the Gallery".[64] A crucial feat that changed the discourse of film studies was the publication of an anthology of translations of texts by international researchers on the method known as new film history, edited by Petr Szczepanik and published in 2004.[65] These essays helped change the dominant mode of thought about historical research methodology and expanded local knowledge about the pre-cinematographic and the earliest stages of film. Film began to be considered a component part of a broader media landscape and a complex socio-cultural practice. This book – and the activities of its editor – were crucial in shifting film studies from cinephilic and essayistic writing to more complex research on the history of cinema. What is significant for us is that film itself began to be analysed from more than one perspective, and the moving image as such (along with short films) proved itself to be a much more complex practice than had been previously thought when it was considered within the closed space of the cinema.

One of the few systematic scholarly publications dedicated to the moving image was (and still is) a section on experimental film in the internet journal *25fps*, created by the Olomouc film studies department. Since 2007, this section has been edited by Marie Meixnerová, who was at that time a student at the faculty and is currently a curator at the PAF festival and the ScreenSaverGallery, one of the few exhibition spaces focused on net art (with contributors including Meixnerová as well as Veronika Zýková, Jiří Neděla, Tatiana Rusnáková, and Milan Kroulík). Tracing the development of this periodical's texts over time also maps the development of the art of the moving image and film experiments in the Czech Republic – at first, the articles mostly discussed the global history of these phenomena, later moving on to Czech art, and finally focusing on internet art and digital media.

[62] John Belton, "Digitální technologie ve filmu: Nepravá revoluce" [Digital Cinema: A False Revolution], *Iluminace* 19, no. 4 (2007), pp. 43–59.

[63] This was, of course, also determined by the fact that around the turn of the millennium, the editorial board was interdisciplinary – it included philosophers Miroslav Petříček and Karel Thein, aestheticist Vlastimil Zuska, linguist Petr Mareš, and literary theorist and historian Petr Málek.

[64] Dolanová, "Vstup pohyblivých obrazů do galerie", pp. 85–99.

[65] Petr Szczepanik (ed.), *Nová filmová historie: Antologie současného myšlení o dějinách kinematografie audiovizuální kultury* [New Film History: An Anthology of Contemporary Thought on the History of Cinematography and Audiovisual Culture] (Prague: Hermann & synové, 2004).

The Escape Beyond Academia

The figures discussed above often oscillated between teaching and curating, gradually abandoning the cinema, or instead importing various formats into the cinema that receded from the relatively precise definitions of classical cinematography in various directions. Marika Kupková, for instance, a graduate of film studies in Brno, has had sustained success in escaping traditional cinema.[66] She is active as a curator, focusing primarily on video art and art of the moving image in gallery spaces. Between 2015 and 2018, she was also the artistic director of the BRNO16 International Short Film Festival, where she has stayed on as a dramaturg. In her 2009 exhibition *Bad Filming*, she created a firm bond between the "impure" media

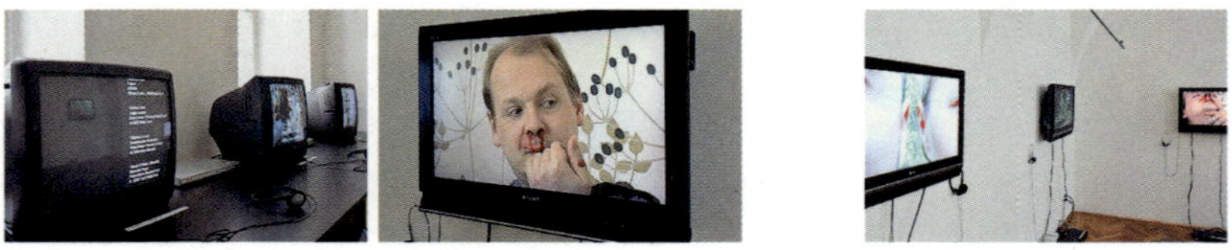

Bad Filming, exhibition at Galerie U Dobrého pastýře, Brno, 2009.

formats of film and video art. She demonstrated the extent to which video creators make use of cinematic conventions, dividing the individual pieces into sections conceived along cinematic terms (following various genres, the cinema of attractions, narrative, direct references to classical film, and construed authorship). She used a similar methodology in putting together Tomáš Svoboda's exhibition *Jako z filmu: Adaptace* [Like in a Movie: Adaptation] at the House of Arts in Brno in 2018. The exhibition was based on multiple transfers between cinematic and fine art formats and the constant oscillation between the experience of a cinema goer and a gallery visitor. *The Process of Adaptation*, the subtitle of Svoboda's exhibition, is not only typical of Marika Kupková's work but also presents a highly stimulating impulse toward broadening the discourse within the field of film studies.

Students that sought to escape academia often established festivals, some of which are still running today, including Zlatý voči (Golden Eyes), Ji.hlava, or PAF. The former was created in 1988 as an alternative, avant-garde, and satirical idea by the Bulšit group (Pavel Marek, Roman Včelák, Dalibor Fencl), Táňa Slánská, Martin Mička, David Černý, and others. In 1994, practical reasons forced the festival to move from the Delta club in Prague to the film studies department at Charles University. In recent years, it has been organised by students from the department in various spaces including cafés, cinemas, and cultural centres.[67] The Ji.hlava International

[66] In 2001, she graduated with a thesis titled "'Zakázaná' sexualita v českém meziválečném filmu" ["Forbidden" Sexuality in Czech Interwar Cinema]. Her advisor was Jiří Voráč.

[67] The festival is characterised by the fact that it presents films by students of audiovisual art, enthusiastic theorists, and historians without a practice in cinema – very often, the core of the programme is composed of theory-supported moving images, experiments of all kinds, as well as audiovisual essays and attempts at found footage works. The originally local festival has grown to an international scale.

Documentary Film Festival was established in 1997 thanks to the efforts of students from the Jihlava academic high school. The festival, headed by Marek Hovorka along with Petr Kubica and Andrea Slováková, with its motto of "thinking through film", focuses on auteur documentary films. From its inception, the festival has provided an important space for various forms of moving image, cinematic essays, and experimental film. In 2000 – partly thanks to the work of Petr Bilík, a doctoral student at and employee of the film studies department at Palacký University in Olomouc – the Ji.hlava festival was also the site of the "0th edition" of the Přehlídka animovaného filmu [Festival of Animated Film], later known as PAF. In 2002, PAF moved to Olomouc and now uses the facilities of the local film and theatre studies department. Throughout its existence, the specificity of this survey has rested not only in its thematically focused yearly editions, but also in the fact that animation is conceived in very broad terms, which means that the programme includes a large amount of art videos from around the world.[68] What all these festivals have in common is not only the fact that they were created "bottom up" by students of film studies, or that they branch out into public spaces, but also that it is paradoxically at these events that film studies discourse has broadened considerably. The festivals featuring diverse films are all accompanied by workshops, lectures, and exhibitions. Many guests are invited, as well as curators for individual blocks or series, regardless of their field-specific affiliations. Informal interdisciplinary encounters thus broaden the field of cinema to include numerous border areas and inter-art overlaps, devoting equal attention to traditional cinematic formats and various forms of the moving image that go beyond these.

A similar need for "escape" was felt by the former student of film studies in Prague, Sylva Poláková, one of the co-founders of the Audiovisual project, which was realised between 2005 and 2008 at the Světozor cinema in Prague.[69] These were "regular encounters with audiovisual projects in the fields of video art, advertising, music videos, animated, experimental, and student films, complemented by lectures and discussions with artists, critics, theorists, and other guests". The lecturers were film studies colleagues and pedagogues: Aleš Stuchlý, Kamil Fila, and David Čeněk. This format, which operated on a friendly basis, provided opportunities both for academic lectures (e.g., Iva Baslarová's discussions of gender topics or Kamil Fila's talks on genre), artistic performances (e.g., presentations of friendly cinema led by the duo of Martin Mazanec and Michal Pěchouček or performances by Aleš Stuchlý and Mark Ther), collections of works from art schools (e.g., by Pavlína Míčová), and presentations on the relationships between film and other art forms (such as the regular

[68] The current director of PAF is Alexandr Jančík, with Martin Mazanec, Marie Meixnerová, Nela Klajbanová, and Jiří Neděla serving as permanent curators.

[69] Sylva Poláková founded it along with her classmates Jindřiška Bláhová and Eliška Děcká.

music video screenings with commentary by Pavel Klusák). Non-cinematic formats were re-situated within the cinema, film analysis and interpretation were popularised, and relationships were tested including those between film and video, the cinema and the gallery, and artists and theorists.

Events that included art of the moving image began to proliferate after 2008, e.g., at the Béla studio, at the tranzitdisplay gallery space in Dittrichova Street, or the Školská 28 Gallery.[70] Now, they are most prominently migrating online (e.g., in the form of the curated selections of DAFilms) or to festival programmes. Festivals, supported by research into new film history, have revealed a specific trait of atypical moving image formats: it has become apparent that they can be much more easily "included" in the history of documentary or animated film than among feature films (and no less remarkable is the fact that these films are often absent from curricula, as if they were separate genres with no relation to the dominant stream of cinema).[71] The visual aspects of animation, as well as works that test the possibilities of documentation, lead to more open ideas about what film can be; how its borders can be pushed; and how film material and (digital) methods can be experimented with. We can observe the way in which festivals like PAF or the Ji.hlava International Documentary Film Festival gave rise to a different conception of film; to a multiplication of curatorial selections; to a development of interdisciplinary collaborations; and also how the festivals have expanded into the internet and various periodicals, archives, and databases, which can be found either on the festival website or in more systematic collections such as *dok.revue*, which contains contributions not only by film scholars, but also aestheticians, philosophers, or researchers in literary studies.[72]

A highly specific element is the expansion beyond the field of film studies to departments that generally had no interest in film or the moving image. In this respect, the most progressive is the Department of Musicology at the Masaryk University in Brno. Since 2006, it has been home to a programme called Theory of Interactive Media, which focuses on various forms of digital art, net art, video art, the relationship between music and the moving image, experiments, and curatorial practice, thanks to modules taught by Jana Horáková, Marika Kupková, Pavlína Míčová, or Martin

[70] Activities related to the moving image were summarised by the *Katalog událostí pohyblivého obrazu I.* a *II.* [Catalogue of Events of the Moving Image 1 and 2], which were published by the Mediabaze project on the occasion of the curatorial competition Jiné vize [Other Visions] as part of the PAF festival in Olomouc in 2010 and 2011.

[71] It was new film history that allowed us to consider the moving image *beyond* established cinematic genres, and to include it among other information-communication practices. This is also part of the reason why the "margins" of film – experimental film or video art – became more acceptable for festival dramaturgs.

[72] The Imagina section of programming was established at the Karlovy Vary International Film Festival in 2013, aimed at introducing films with unconventional approaches to narrative and style, with an idiosyncratic and radical visions of cinematic language. The curators of the first edition were Pavlína Míčová and Viktor Palák.

Flašar. It is quite surprising that it is here that we find the kind of thought that is so rarely present in the Czech context and that the texts mentioned above challenge us to adopt.[73]

Art of the Moving Image as Part of Visual Studies

Lectures and discussions at Czech and – crucially – international conferences and symposia have exerted a considerable influence on the transformation of thinking about film in the broader field of visuality. The participation of students and lecturers at international forums opened the opportunity for participation in an international project dedicated to spoken versions of silent films, with the participation of historians from Amsterdam, Bremen, Locarno, Milan, Pisa, Paris, Udine, and Valencia. Every year, this team organised not only a conference in the Italian city of Udine, with participants including leading specialists in the field, but also a week-long workshop for students in Gradisca. Both events have transformed traditional perceptions of film and opened new horizons for the Czech environment, offering methods of historical research undertaken in accordance with new film history, and increasing awareness of various film formats that were known since the very beginnings of cinema. The project concluded in 2006, yet that very same year an extensive European platform for film studies was established: NECS (European Network for Cinema and Media Studies), which is still one of the largest film conferences in the world today. Other influential debate forums involved in the expansion of the traditional conception of film included the Paris Spring School and the conferences organised by Media Art History. It was at these events that new formats of art of the moving image were discussed, blurring the boundaries between film and visual art and between theory, history, and practice. New themes also included those related to the relocation of the cinematic image – thanks to the fact that films gradually abandoned the cinema to a greater and greater extent, permeating into various kinds of public spaces, the question "what is film?" ceased to be asked and was replaced with questions about where and when a work is a film, opening up the field for forms of art of the moving image such as video mapping. The international debate gradually infiltrated the Czech environment, with experts from abroad invited to lecture in the Czech Republic on the basis of personal connections to mediate some of these topical themes to Czech audiences.[74]

Since around the mid-2000s (i.e., some ten years after these topics first became relevant internationally), the Czech environment began to be infiltrated – particularly through the work of film historian Petra Hanáková and art historian Václav Hájek, later also through my own

[73] A list of works can be found here, accessed 5 Nov 2021, https://is.muni.cz/vyhledavani/?agenda=th&search=Teorie+interaktivn%C3%ADch+m%C3%A9di%C3%AD.

[74] Important figures in this respect include Petr Szczepanik, Petra Hanáková, Tomáš Dvořák, Vít Janeček, Miloš Vojtěchovský, and others.

research – discussions about the possibility of visual studies as a new space in which to explore (not only) moving images that step beyond existing academic frameworks.[75] This gave rise to a neutral field – or, in these times, more of a fluid structure – that follows not only artistic images but also visualisation techniques and methods across culture and society. This approach considers advertising next to medical diagrams, landscape views with technical visualisations, film side by side with computer generated images, video art alongside Vj-ing. The methodology is broadening too, drawing on various fields from film studies through art history and literary studies to sociology and cultural studies. Following debates about whether visual culture has its place in academia, given how unfocused it is both in its object of study and its methods, Hanáková and Hájek defined the field as "the study of the cultural construction of visual experience in everyday life, or as a certain interface between all the disciplines that inquire into visuality".[76]

Visual studies thus became another possibility for escape on those occasions when academics or students wished to engage moving images outside the framework of traditional film or the relationship between film and other media. Introductions to visual studies, as well as the need to expand visual literacy became part of the curricula (especially in doctoral programmes) at both the film studies department at Charles University in Prague and the art history department at the Masaryk University in Brno, as well as at art universities such as the Academy of Art, Architecture and Design in Prague (VŠUP) or the Faculty of Fine Arts (FaVU) at the Brno University of Technology. While this trend has so far failed to find a stable position among the academic disciplines, it has allowed the academic community to bridge the chasm between art history and film studies, and between theory and practice.

In addition to producing various publications (including in translation[77]) focused on visual studies, this specialisation also stepped beyond academia, mostly thanks to the Fresh Eye project, organised since 2011 under the leadership of Andrea Průchová Hrůzová, a graduate of the Faculty of the Humanities of Charles University and now a theorist and lecturer on visual culture. Fresh Eye presents regular evening discussions

[75] And again, this was preceded by an interview published in *Iluminace* in 2003, in which D. N. Rodowick discusses the fact that visual studies can offer film studies an interdisciplinary framework that can be highly productive, effective, and successful. Petr Szczepanik – Jakub Kučera, "Rozhovor s D. N. Rodowickem, Virtuální život filmu" [An Interview with D. N. Rodowick, The Virtual Life of Film], *Iluminace* 15, no. 2 (2003), pp. 89–106.

[76] Petra Hanáková – Václav Hájek, "Film v době vizuálních studií" [Film in the Age of Visual Studies], *Iluminace* 21, no. 1 (2009), p. 37.

[77] Particularly the anthology, edited by Marta Filipová and Matthew Rampley, *Možnosti vizuálních studií* [Possibilities of Visual Studies] (Brno: Barrister & Principal 2008) and translations of works by Lisa Cartwright and Marita Sturken – *Studia vizuální kultury* [Studying Visual Culture] (Prague: Portál 2010) – and Nicholas Mirzoeff – *Úvod do vizuální kultury* [An Introduction to Visual Culture] (Prague: Academia 2012) and *Jak vidět svět* [How to See the World] (Prague: Artmap 2019).

for the general public featuring specialists from various fields. The first evenings were devoted to the relationship between image and text, with further instalments developing various topics related to visual culture, introducing new projects, and following current (social and political) problems. These events also aim to map developments in experimental moving images and the gallery environment. This interdisciplinary popularising platform, which is open to diverse approaches and types of images, enables discussions that go beyond the framework of institutionally and definitionally codified media and art forms, and is thus a functional "escape" that allows us to reflect on all that is missing in official academic activities.

The Freedom of the Moving Image

It is perhaps paradoxical that those responsible for an essential expansion of film studies discourse and an adaptation of the moving image into its framework are, in large part, not filmmakers, but rather artists, who have a higher degree of creative autonomy due to their position outside the industry. By contrast, those working in the film industry have defined and continue to define themselves against theory – symptomatic of these positions are the long-standing conflicts at FAMU, where each new dean seems to alternate in siding with theory or with professional craft that can make do without theory.[78] One of the few departments that was always open to theoretical and conceptual thought (sometimes to the extent that it was so open that its direction became unclear) is the Center for Audiovisual Studies (CAS), established in 2002, which focuses on the forms of moving image that this volume addresses.[79] The creative output of students from CAS appears in cinemas, galleries, at film festivals, and at exhibits of experimental work.

Most credit for disrupting the cinematic monolith, however, lies with visual artists, particularly those close to art schools – namely, FaVU in Brno or VŠUP and the Academy of Fine Arts (AVU) in Prague– who are discussed in greater detail in this volume by Tomáš Pospiszyl. Projects at these

[78] In 2017 and 2018, this conflict escalated, particularly due to the involvement of dean Zdeněk Holý, whose programme involved returning to the craft of filmmaking and limiting the teaching of theory, which he believed to be excessive. Taking a stand against these steps were several lecturers at FAMU, particularly at CAS (the Center for Audiovisual Studies). Because of this conflict, which also spilled over into the media, the question was open once again about the course of the entire school, as well as the orientation of individual deans. Their activity was thus polarised on the theory–practice axis (with statements claiming that "theory for practice" is what's needed notwithstanding), although this duality had been refuted since the very beginnings of the institution, with theorists attempting to erase it entirely since the 1990s. For more on this topic, see Vít Janeček, "FAMU jako zážitková agentura" [FAMU as an Experiential Travel Agency], *Cinepur* nos. 106 and 107 (2017) and responses to it, or Jindřiška Bláhová, "Teorie kontra řemeslo: Akademický senát navrhuje odvolání děkana Holého" [Theory Against Craft: The Academic Senate Suggests Dean Holý be Called Off], *Respekt*, accessed 8 Jul 2021, https://www.respekt.cz/tydenik/2018/22/teorie-kontra-remeslo.

[79] The graduate profile emphasises that former students are "prepared for an independent artistic career in the field of working with audiovisual media such as video, film, internet, computer-generated images, etc.". O centru [About the Center], accessed 12 Jul 2021, https://www.famu.cz/cs/katedry/centrum-audiovizualnich-studii/.

schools are rooted in the discourse of art history, but they are oriented towards other fields, including the moving image, whether in gallery spaces, cinemas (such as the Videotime evenings, organised by Pavlína Vogelová and Filip Cenek from 2009 to 2020)[80] or DVD (the Vida DVD edition published by the AVU Academic Research Centre). Václav Krůček is a good example of interdisciplinary and intermedia practice as well as a rich interplay of academic discourse and art. This academic painter and conceptual artist who works on the materiality of the image, its structure, and the network that captures it, as well as its dissolution and disappearance, applied to the doctoral programme at the film studies department in Prague in 2013 (where the author supervised his dissertation on the phenomenon of film stasis). In 2020, he defended a thesis titled "The Intuition and Vacuum of Film Imaging" whose approach is closest to media philosophy. The thesis examines various forms of encroachments into the stability and continuity of the medium of film (particularly art films) that are marked by the pressure of the field beyond the frame, which stimulates the relationship between the visible and the sensed – the movement of elementary structures in time and instigate a particular form of perception. Krůček analyses the moments in cinematic narration that disrupt the whole and turn the spectator's attention from the fictional world to the surface of the image, i.e., the same moments that he is interested in when making art.

At this point, I would like to engage in a more thorough consideration of what can happen when the specific artistic thinking that connects cinematic and art-historical discourse without abandoning the latter is applied to the creative process. In this regard, the artists I consider to be essential hail from a generation that has an "awareness of the camera",[81] for whom it is no longer a particular "effect" with which to make their artistic expression more special, but rather a form of image that grows through our quotidian existences as well as through the art scene. Artists such as Tomáš Svoboda, Adéla Babanová, Marek Meduna, Zbyněk Baladrán, Ján Mančuška, Daniel Pitín, Eva Koťátková, Marek Ther, Martin Zet, Filip Cenek, and Pavel Ryška have integrated cinematic means into their artistic vocabulary, thereby achieving new meanings.[82] For these artists, intermediality is not a goal but a norm, a starting point that media specificity is

[80] Since 2013, these can be watched under the Videogram heading on the internet. Videogram, accessed 17 Sep 2021, https://videogram.favu.vut.cz/archiv.

[81] I am building here on the ideas of Anne Friedberg, who claims that film definitively changed our perception and seeing, or rather, that we are now privy to "the consciousness of the camera" and are incapable of thinking and perceiving in any other mode than the cinematic. Anne Friedberg, *Window Shopping. Cinema and the Postmodern* (Berkeley, CA: University of California Press, 1993). According to Malte Hagener, film is now (in human perception) indistinguishable from reality: "we live in images permanently and images live in us". Hagener, "Kde je (dnes) film?", 79.

[82] On some of these, see my text "Život v obrazech a odchylující se vidění: Úvahy nad medialitou pohyblivých obrazů v souladu s německou teorií/filosofií médií" [Life in Images and Diverging Sight: Reflections on the Mediality of the Moving Image in Accordance with German Theory and Philosophy of Media], *Sešit pro umění, teorii a příbuzné zóny* 10, no. 22 (2017), pp. 83–106.

derived from. These artists regularly work with conceptual media transpositions and theoretical foundations (often involving film theory), without aiming to decompose the dispositif of the film down to its foundational elements. For me, then, their work represents perhaps a (not exhaustive) exploration of the knots of the media chiasma, which have the ability to show different perspectives of the mediality and materiality of film; different ways of thinking about film and video.

In order to set in motion the borders of the moving image, film studies discourse, and the cinematographic dispositif, an excellent model seems to be the work of Tomáš Svoboda, one of the guests of the Audiovisual series in Prague, where he narrated the story of the 1996 film *Independence Day* on an open stage.[83] His work was already mentioned above in connection to the curatorial activities of Marika Kupková and her adaptive processes. Since 2008, Tomáš Svoboda has worked on exhibition projects that use diverse non-cinematic practices to evoke the medium of film.[84] He often uses the crossing of two media (the works being infused with references to film and the cinematic imagination, their rhythm structured by film stills) or the blending of projection and reconstruction (creating architectural imitations of a cinematic mise-en-scène inside the gallery). Also typical of his work is the substitution of media codes, most often inverting the function of words and images (moving images are accompanied by text, even occasionally transformed into text, while the text takes on the cinematic format). Through these medial shifts, Tomáš Svoboda achieves a dual effect: on the one hand, he employs artistic strategies to achieve the effects of medial reflection, on the other, he returns to the initial transfer by which the film enters the gallery in part also to dismantle the absorbing cinematic narrative, distribute it in space, and draw attention to the ideological nature of this seamless medium. While works conceived in this manner represent the migration of a visual artist into the field of film, they still adhere to the gallery tradition, intermedial thinking remains tied to the limits of the individual media, thus essentially copying the demarcations of two different forms of discourse.

While these projects still follow the logic of the physical transfer of film into the gallery, with the process of uncovering what film is and where it is located most often making use of the media practices of fine art, Svoboda's entry into the cinema and the feature-length format with *Like in a Movie* (2016) reflects the second possibility – an internal change,

[83] *Independence Day* (Roland Emmerich, 1996).

[84] At the *Imagine Psycho* exhibition at Berlin's Antje Wachs Gallery, for instance, they used a reproduction of the set design from Hitchcock's famous horror film (a replica of the motel in which the murder took place was built and placed behind a glass wall), with the accompanying screening of the cinematic image replaced by projected texts that dryly described the plot and spaces of the film's narrative. *Imagine Psycho*, Berlin: Antje Wachs Gallery, 2008. Cf. Sylva Poláková, "Tomáš Svoboda: Dekonstrukce a (re)imaginace" [Tomáš Svoboda: Deconstruction and (Re)Imagination], *Fotograf* 11, no. 19 (2012), pp. 68–71. Svoboda used similar methods in his exhibition *Like a Movie*, which was a nearly exhausting display of possible media transformations. *Like a Movie*, Prague: tranzitdisplay, 2015–2016.

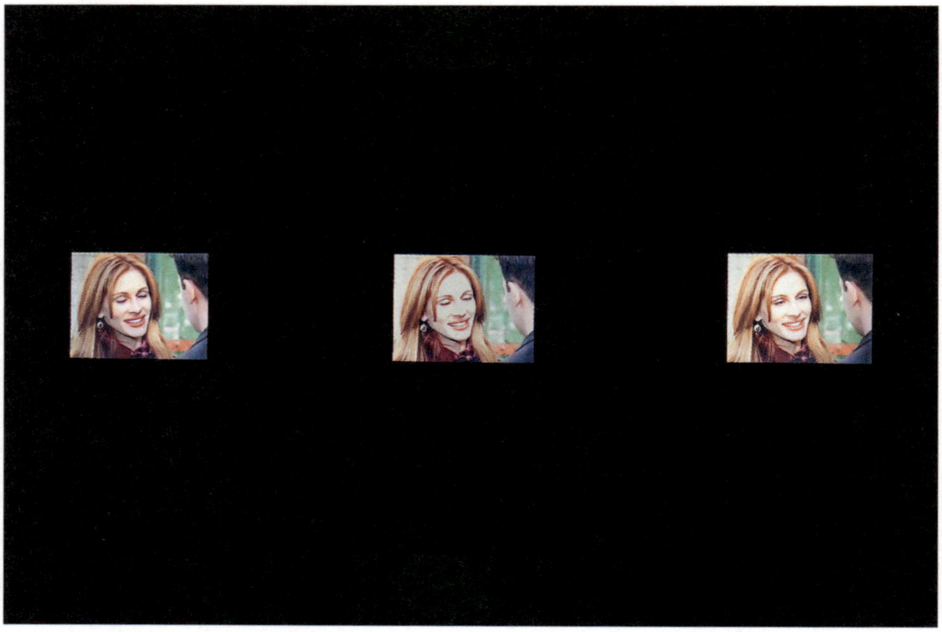

Tomáš Svoboda *Jedna vteřina života Julie Roberts* [One Second in the Life of Julia Roberts] (2012), installation of twenty-four photographs

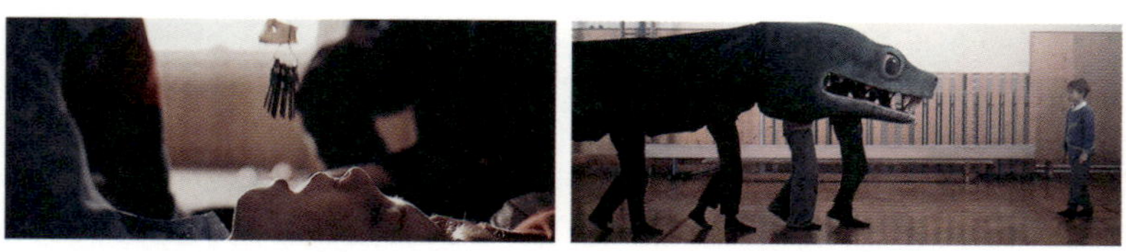

Eva Koťátková *Žaludek světa* [Stomach of the World] (2017), video, 46 min

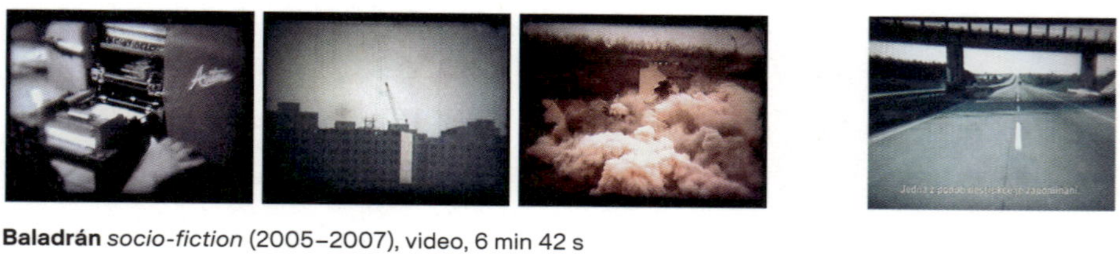

Zbyněk Baladrán *socio-fiction* (2005–2007), video, 6 min 42 s

a transformation of perspective (meaning both a view and a position), no longer thinking merely *about* film, but also *with* film; *through* film. The question of *what* film is becomes an investigation of when something can seem *like* a film. Svoboda then expanded on this theme by writing a theoretical dissertation which he defended at AVU. For the dissertation, he created a compilation text of contemporary theories considering the role of the cinematic image in society, supplying as proof various forms of material he has encountered as a viewer of film and television or as a user of the internet. He then transferred the individual theses, examples, and theories into cinematic form. This is why *Like in a Movie* can be understood as a theoretical work (and a specific adaptation of theory), which examines not only how our reality is permeated by cinematic visuality and how we are constantly surrounded by moving images, but also how we identify with cinematic seeing and cinematic narrativity, becoming film actors, accepting the cinematic apparatus as our living space, and dissolving in it. We follow various forms of life in films, films in life, film as life, and life as film via diverse formats and genres. The idea of a film is mediated to us in the form of a manifesto, a feature film, narrated film plots, or collages of trailers and short videos on YouTube, wherein the transformation of the cinematic form is accompanied by constant revelations of the cinematic illusion (filming in front of a blue screen; the narration of the essential plot line by the director of the film, the construction of a camera track used to film horizontal camera movements). This systematic de-construction constantly reminds us of conceptions focused on the ideological effects of new media, as well as philosophical reflections of the human situation in the world-image.

Tomáš Svoboda is one of the examples of how (my) generation of artists responds to film, making use of it and abusing it, calling it into question and loving it at the same time. Cinematography and video art are thus beginning to crumble from the inside, changing their narrative methods, their locations, their technical and stylistic means, and exchanging audiences. Film has broken into the gallery while video art has entered the cinema. Digitalisation has unified diverse formats at the level of code, thus completing the process of media fusion and making unclear everything that had previously been clear. The aesthetics of computer games and internet art has merged with the moving image permeating both cinema and fine art. And it is perhaps thinking through images (which I attempted to demonstrate in one particular example), not through text, that allows for this multiple reflection and that will facilitate a true expansion of discursive fields.

From Cinematographic Seeing to Digital Thinking

It is only the up-and-coming generation – now concluding their courses in film studies or working towards a doctorate – that has grown up in this fully heterogeneous environment, accepting it as their own. Only in the present can we discuss the fact that we are beginning to come to terms with the fact that the theoretical/film studies discourse has expanded in following the model established by artistic practice. It is only now that we are rising to Noël Carroll's challenge, expressed in the mid-1990s, to be more precise and speak of the moving image rather than film, as it "advertises this deep feature of the artform".[85] Carroll thus defines himself against media specificity (among other things), which, though it defined the beginnings of film as an art and formed early and avant-garde thinking about film, has now come to exist entirely at odds with reality. The moving image has outgrown its frame and framework, with works often even diverging from their own medium. In this environment, art historians have stopped defining themselves in opposition to film studies scholars and accusing these scholars of invading their (artistic) space when they write about the moving image in the gallery, instead, academics from both fields contribute to journals that do not pertain to their field and enter directly into artistic or gallery practice.

The experimental moving image allows us to respond to the indescribable and elusive nature of various forms of moving images (*unspeakable images*),[86] thinking about the moving image through the movement of the image itself. Media mediate without being capable of mediating themselves,[87] not providing any space for reflection on their own, as they already contain the embryo of another medialisation. Therefore, if we write about the moving image, particularly when it is of an abstract character, which forfeits the narrative, word-based component, we are in essence receding from the essence of what we are writing about. But if we are able to remain within the logic we aim to approximate, we might discover unexpected dimensions and meanings, similarly to those suggested by Tomáš Svoboda's works.[88]

Another possibility for the future of film studies discourse exists thanks to interdisciplinary collectives such as BCAA system, two members of which, Noemi Purkrábková and Jiří Sirůček, are also film studies PhD candidates. This poly-functional collective operates on the borders between alternative music production, curatorial practice, art practice,

[85] Noël Carroll, *Theorizing the Moving Image* (Cambridge: Cambridge University Press, 1996), p. 65.

[86] I am borrowing this term from Raymond Bellour, who uses it to describe the impossibility of grasping film, particularly in the moment when film and its history are being aesthetically revised. Raymond Bellour, "The Power of Words, The Power of Images", in Unspeakable Images, eds. Raymond Bellour – Elisabeth Lyon, *Camera Obscura* 8, no. 3 (1990), pp. 7–9. Jiří Anger focuses primarily on the found footage effect.

[87] Dieter Mersch, in his text "Tertium datur", writes: "Media hide their mediality only to the extent to which they create medial effects – if they manifest something, they pay for it by becoming visible. Their presence has the characteristics of absence." Dieter Mersch, "Tertium datur: Úvod do negativní mediální teorie" [Tertium Datur: An Introduction to Negative Media Theory], in *Medienwissenschaft. Východiska a aktuální pozice německé filozofie a teorie médií* [*Medienwissenschaft* [Foundations and Present Positions of German Philosophy and Theory of Media], eds. Kateřina Krtilová – Kateřina Svatoňová (Prague: Academia, 2016), p. 338.

[88] Jiří Anger, currently a doctoral candidate at the film studies department in Prague, is among those working with audiovisual essays, both in his teaching and in his own practice, in collaboration with the artist Jiří Žák or with Adéla Kudlová at the Národní filmový archiv [National Film Archive].

and theoretical thought. They are unique not only in forsaking authorship and individuality in the interest of the whole, but, from the perspective of the topic at hand, particularly in how they manage to operate across (and despite) clearly defined areas and fulfil the possibilities of new thinking – thinking through the moving image, as attested to by their well-received "theoretical" film *No~one Is an Island* (furthermore the fact that BCAA system first produced an exhibition, then a short film, and then a musical compilation attests to the extension of their thinking). Their projects attempt to open entirely new perspectives, conducting a polemic against the anthropocentric perspective and position, and striving for a more ethical approach to making art. This is also why they make extensive use of randomness and a sense of belonging with technology, which they allow to exert a considerable level of influence on the creative process itself. In addition to various digital applications, they also use video game engines in order to escape the human perspective. Their efforts, which exist on the margins of film, music, and exhibition practice, are based not only on activism but primarily on theory, building upon numerous concepts that approach polemically the existing dualistic and anthropocentric course of society.

In these examples, it is possible to recognise the important shift in thought and perception – this is no longer a cinematic consciousness as was the case for the previous generation, but a digital seeing and consciousness. Up-and-coming scholars of film studies are steadfast in their approach to working in the field of the moving image and broader visual culture, abolishing many borders and dualities, and stepping beyond or abandoning a mode of perception that is "cinematographic", image-based, and representational in favour of coded thought.

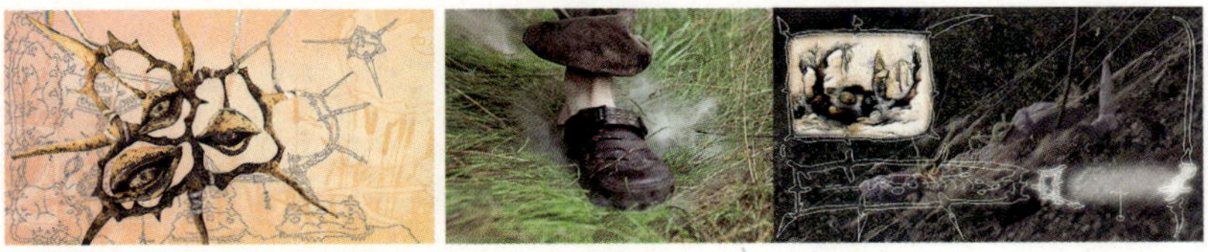

BCAA system *No~one Is an Island* (2019), video, 26 min

Digital, Intermedia, and International Confrontations: Presentations of Art of the Moving Image at the Beginning of the New Millennium

Markéta Mansfieldová

"Video is a tumultuously developing, progressive art form" – it was with this statement that members of the video department at the Union of Czechoslovak Visual Artists introduced the first exhibition of Czech video art, which took place shortly before the Velvet Revolution in

1989.[89] Their visionary prediction only began to be fulfilled on the Czech art scene some fifteen years later. During the 2000s, many new exhibition and dramaturgical projects were initiated across the local art and film scene, linked by an interest in presenting art of the moving image. In established fine art galleries, independent galleries, at festivals, in cinemas, but also in music clubs and in public and online spaces, exhibitions and screenings were held that were dedicated to video art, media art, and experimental film.[90] Curator Viktor Čech, one of the co-founders of the Videokemp video art festival, described this development as the transition of Czech art of the moving image from puberty to middle age, during which time video became a universal means of expression for virtually every artist belonging to the young generation.[91] The creation of new exhibition formats thus cannot be reflected without considering the expansion of the medium of the moving image itself on the local art scene of the late 1990s and early 2000s, which was determined by an historical confluence of technological, geopolitical, economic, and ideological conditions. This essay explains the manner by which the increasing availability of digital technology, new possibilities for international collaboration, and an expansion of intermedia approaches to making art have influenced the form of art of the moving image and formats of its presentation on the Czech art scene.

Digital Democratisation

In socialist Czechoslovakia, the availability of audiovisual equipment in the 1970s and '80s was regulated by the state and was limited mostly to equipment for film and television studios, educational institutions, and workplaces, or else to illegal imports from abroad.[92] The transition of post-socialist countries from a centrally planned economy to a free market led to a broader availability of video cameras, television screens, and computers in the early 1990s. This unprecedented availability of audiovisual equipment in Czech society was heightened by the rise of digital video, which began in the West with the introduction of the DV format in the mid-1990s. The introduction of the Digital Versatile Disc (DVD format)[93] was a turning point, as this was a distribution format that made it

[89] DEN VIDEA 1989 / 2018 (2018). Den videa 1989 / 2018: První skupinová výstava českého videoartu [Day of Video 1989 / 2018: The First Group Exhibition of Czech Video Art]. Exhibition text.

[90] For an overview of these events, see Martin Mazanec – Sylva Poláková (eds.), *Katalog událostí českého pohyblivého obrazu I., II.* [Catalogue of Events of the Czech Moving Image I, II] (Olomouc: Pastiche Filmz, 2011).

[91] Viktor Čech, "Videokemp 2007", accessed 10 Jul 2021, https://videokemp.wordpress.com/2007-2/.

[92] The approach of Czech and Slovak video artists to audiovisual technologies is well documented in the film *Viva video, video viva* (Adéla Komrzý, 2019).

[93] David M. Lang, David M. Switzer, Brandon J. Swartz, "DVD sales and the R-rating puzzle", *Journal of Cultural Economics* 35, no. 4 (2011), p. 269.

easier to disseminate auteur editions and watch films in high resolution.[94] In addition to new digital media, the market also began offering cheap handheld cameras and post-production software for editing audiovisual recordings, such as Final Cut Pro, Adobe Premiere, or Adobe After Effects, which made non-linear video editing methods available directly on one's computer screen.[95] The user-friendly interface, economic availability, and simple distribution of digital video all contributed to the fact that digital formats gradually began replacing analogue video recordings. In the Czech environment, this development was characterised by a different dynamic than in the West due to the professional backgrounds of the local art and film schools. While at the Film and TV School of the Academy of Performing Arts in Prague (FAMU), it was still common in the early 2000s to use analogue film, which was then edited using digital post-production tools of increasing quality,[96] fine art universities often lacked professional equipment and artists typically used commercially available digital cameras and post-production software.[97]The exception in this regard was the New Media Studio at AVU in Prague and the video–multimedia–performance studio at FaVU in Brno, where students had access to professional technical equipment.[98]

The first large-scale exhibition of art of the digital image in the Czech Republic was the In Out festival in 2003, whose first instalment was initiated that year by Ivan Mečl and Pavel Vančát in collaboration with David Korecký. In comparison with the international festival of art and new technology ENTER multimediale, which had taken place three years earlier, introducing multimedia installations and works from the field of video art and experimental film, the curatorial conception of the In Out festival focused primarily on audiovisual works produced and distributed by means of the digital image.[99] According to curator Pavel Vančát, the main difference between the two events consisted primarily in the democratisation of audiovisual art brought about by the expansion of the digital image. While the ENTER multimediale introduced a number of technically complex works, the curators of the In Out festival also introduced the art by the up-and-coming

[94] Chris Meigh-Andrews, *A History of Video Art* (London: Bloomsbury Academic, 2014), p. 7.

[95] Ibid., pp. 316–317.

[96] Jan Zajíček interviewed by Markéta Jonášová, 25 Oct 2021, Národní filmový archiv, Oral History collection.

[97] Tomáš Hrůza interviewed by Markéta Jonášová, 26 Oct 2021, Národní filmový archiv, Oral History collection.

[98] For more on the technical equipment available at art schools, see Tomáš Pospiszyl's contribution to this volume.

[99] The first ENTER multimediale festival was in 2000, with future instalments only taking place in 2005 and 2007. The organisers of the first edition were Asociace Film & Sociologie AfiS [AfiS Film and Sociology Association], the Profil Media PR agency, and CIANT – Mezinárodní centrum pro umění a nové technologie [CIANT – International Centre for Art and New Technologies] in collaboration with the organisations Prague – European City of Culture 2000, Správa Pražského hradu [Prague Castle Administration], Palác Akropolis, and Divadlo Archa [Archa Theatre], which administered the festival locations.

generation of artists from art academies who did not work with audiovisual material at a professional level using expensive equipment, instead working with commonly available digital cameras and computers. The artists working in the Czech Republic included Jesper Alvaer, Michal Pěchouček, Markéta Baňková, Sláva Sobotovičová, Mark Ther, and Ondřej Brody. New digital formats not only made the production of audiovisual works easier – they also simplified their distribution, which meant that the In Out curators could introduce over a hundred artists from various countries in both Eastern and Western Europe.[100] The significant international dimension of the project and its realisation in the prestigious spaces of the historical centre of Prague were supported by a private sponsor, namely the PPF investment group, which provided a generous budget in the order of millions of crowns.[101] The core of the expensive production was a large-scale projection screen on Old Town Square, which made the programme available not only to a small artistic community but also to the local and international public on the go in the centre of Prague.[102]

The In Out festival was not the only event at the time to introduce audiovisual art in urban public spaces. A similar idea became part of the curatorial conception of another significant project created around this time, the Videokemp festival, founded in 2005 by a team that included curator Lenka Sýkorová, intermedia artist Milan Salák, and curator Viktor Čech, who was already mentioned in the introduction. In many respects,

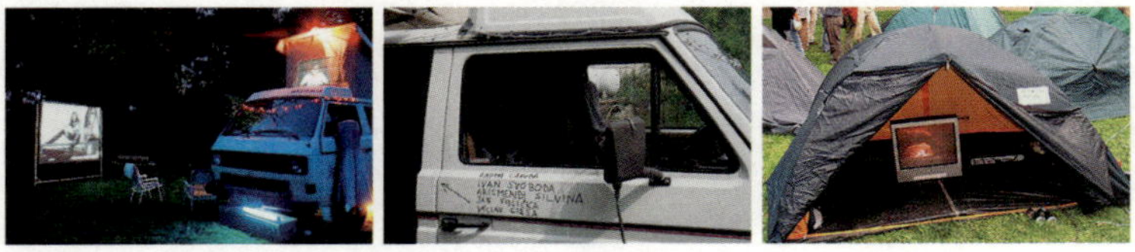

Videokemp, 2005–2011, 2013, 2015, 2019, various locations.

Videokemp represented a notional antipole to In Out. The festival's conception worked with newly available technologies for the presentation of art of the moving image, which corresponded with the idea that the festival should operate on DIY principles. The idea of creating a temporary exhibition space that breaks free from the mechanisms of institutional control and allows participants to co-create the form of the event while the event itself takes place had its foundations in the theory of autonomous temporary zones as formulated by philosopher Hakim Bey,[103] whose writings were first published

[100] Pavel Vančát interviewed by Markéta Jonášová, 30 Sep 2021, Národní filmový archiv, Oral History collection.

[101] Festival digitálního obrazu In Out v Praze [In Out – Festival of the Digital Image in Prague], accessed 30 Aug 2021, https://www.ireport.cz/352-festival-digitalniho-obrazu-in-out-v-praze.

[102] Novinky z festivalu In Out [News from the In Out Festival], accessed 30 Sep 2021, http://web.archive.org/web/20031219012435/http://www.inout.cz/indexFrame-c.html.

[103] Videokemp, 2006, accessed 30 Aug 2021, https://videokemp.wordpress.com/2006-2/.

in Czech a year before the first Videokemp took place.[104] Rather than arising from an expensive technical and production background, it was mostly the artists themselves who organised the festival. During the one-day event, they presented their pieces on television or computer screens in tents or simple shelters that could easily be put up and made available to visitors. This de-centralised form of organisation ensured the event's independence from grant subsidies or commercial sponsorship, which, curator Viktor Čech claims, contributed to the flexibility of the project.[105] The realisation of

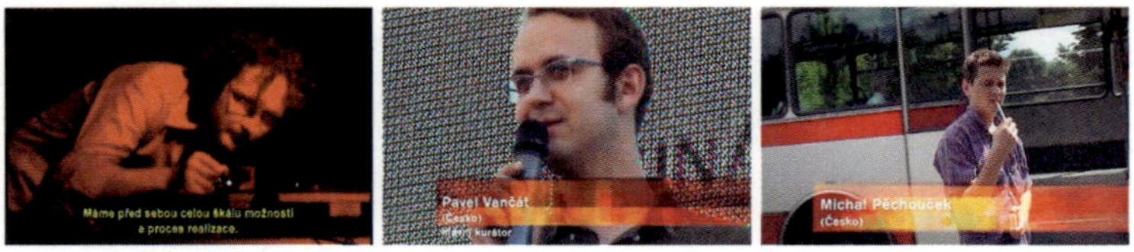

In Out, Prague, 18.–29. 7. 2003.

Videokemp thus relied primarily on the personal contributions of the organisers and participants, which, while providing autonomy, also prevented any degree of professionalisation.

Thanks to this level of flexibility, the Videokemp festival was held in many public locations throughout Prague and in other Czech cities.[106] Since the festival took place in parks or gardens, it did by nature open the event to the general public, however, playing back audiovisual works in tents was something beyond the normalised forms of presentation of art in public spaces, such as those that the curators of the In Out festival worked with, and ordinary spectators would thus seldom visit the Videokemp. However, this only added to the long-term importance of the festival for sharing creative methodologies in the field of video art and creating relationships within the artistic community itself.[107] Despite the significantly different form of organisation, both festivals were connected by their international dramaturgical framework, which allowed for the parallel introduction of art by both local and international artists. In the case of the In Out festival, this was one of the curatorial starting points of the project, made possible by the luxurious budget and international contacts of curator Ivan Mečl.[108] The work of local and international artists such as film-maker Oliver Pietsch, media

[104] Hakim Bey, *Dočasná autonomní zóna* [Temporary Autonomous Zone] (Prague: tranzit.cz, 2004).

[105] Lenka Sýkorová, "Jedná se o nekonečný den" [It is an Endless Day], *A2*, no. 17 (2013), accessed 30 Aug 2021, https://www.advojka.cz/archiv/2013/17/jedna-se-o-nekonecny-den.

[106] The Videokemp festival took place in 2005 (Altán Klamovka, Prague), 2006 (Altán Klamovka, Prague), 2007 (Chateau Třebešice, Třebešice u Čáslavi), 2008 (Letná, Prague), 2009 (Letná, Prague), 2010 (Central Bohemian Gallery, Kutná Hora), 2011 (Brno House of Arts, Brno), 2013 (Břevnov Monastery gardens, Prague), 2015 (Altán Klamovka, Prague), and 2019 (Convent of St. Agnes, Prague). Videokemp, accessed 20 Feb 2022, https://videokemp.wordpress.com/2011-2/.

[107] Martin Blažíček, "Klášter videoartu / Videokemp 2013" [Monastery of Video Art / Videokemp 2013], *Flash Art*, nos. 28–29 (2013), accessed 30 Aug 2021, https://flashart.cz/2013/10/11/klaster-videoartu-videokemp-2013/.

[108] Pavel Vančát interviewed by Markéta Jonášová, 30 Sep 2021, Národní filmový archiv, Oral History collection.

artist Andreas Müller-Pohle, and director Margaret Salmon, was brought together in individual screening blocks based on the concepts of body, fear, illusion, observation, time, and space.[109] Such general themes were also common at other presentations of art of the moving image, such as the ENTER multimediale festival.[110] An intention shared by the curators of these festivals was to introduce a broad spectrum of audiovisual works, thus allowing both artists and spectators to compare various creative approaches. Curatorial conceptions were thus often based on overarching frameworks that did not arise from the theoretical discourse focused on art of the moving image, but instead sought connections in theme and genre across a spectrum of works. This rising interest in the presentation of various formats of audiovisual works reflected the growing importance of the digital medium of the moving image not only on the Czech and international art scenes but also in the broader social and cultural context.

International Festivals

The development of the possibilities of international artistic collaboration was closely tied to the rise of the use of the internet and digital technologies in the early 2000s, as well as the fact that the Czech art scene was situated in the post-socialist geopolitical space. The globalised reality of the local media culture was reflected not only in the dramaturgy of various exhibition projects, but also in the subject matter of the audiovisual works presented, as a number of artists transformed pop-culture images taken from mainstream film and television productions created abroad, particularly in the United States. In the early 2000s, the term "postproduction", introduced by art theorist Nicolas Bourriaud, began to be used to describe this phenomenon. In an eponymous publication, Bourriaud applied the concept of postproduction to characterise artistic strategies that transform existing cultural forms.[111] At local festivals and exhibitions, spectators had the opportunity to encounter this phenomenon in the works of Jiří Surůvka, Tereza Velíková, Jan Nálevka, and the politically oriented group Guma Guar. Reflections of the adoption of media forms in the post-socialist context also appeared in a work by Dušan Zahoranský titled *Skutočný príbeh*: *Verzia Láska* (*True Story: Version – Love*, 2001–2002), in which the artist transforms a scene taken from the popular American TV show JAG. The dramatic dialogue between Major Rabb and a woman close to him first take place in Slovak, but after a short time, the conversation passes into Hungarian, Polish, and Rusyn. The foreign-language dialogue alienates the well-known protagonists from local audiences, inviting

[109] In Out festival programme, accessed 30 Aug 2021, https://web.archive.org/web/20030807145619/http://www.inout.cz/indexFrame-a.html>.

[110] Ivan M. Havel, Jarmila Poláková, Jana Semerádová, Pavel Smetana, Markéta Uhlířová, *enter-multimediale* (Prague: ENTER multimediale, 2000).

[111] Nicolas Bourriaud, *Postprodukce: kultura jako scénář: jak umění nově programuje současný svět* [Postproduction: Culture as Screenplay: How Art Reprograms the World] (Praha: tranzit.cz, 2004), p. 4.

them to reflect critically on the local meaning of a crime soap opera set in an American military prosecutor's office.[112]

The geopolitical location of the Czech art scene between East and West is also reflected in the exhibition dramaturgy of newly established projects. New works by audiovisual artists from Poland, Hungary, Romania, and the countries of former Yugoslavia were often presented here, but much greater space was devoted to established artists from Western countries – the first instalment of ENTER multimediale, for instance, featured a retrospective of media artist Bill Viola.[113] Both local and international audiovisual art was also significantly represented in the Audiovisual project, which organised screenings focused on audiovisual work in the broader context of visual culture at the Světozor cinema in Prague between 2005 and 2008. The dramaturgy of the project included series focused on American and British audiovisual art, but there were also thematic programs that introduced works by artists from Eastern Europe or the Global South, such as the work of the Brazilian film avant-garde, the Hungarian experimental movement Béla Balázs Studio, or contemporary Croatian video art.[114] A focus on the Western video art scene was determined by the activities of Czechoslovak artists in Western countries[115] as well as the hegemonic position of the Western artistic canon in post-communist cultural reality, which is characteristically illustrated by Bourriaud's work, his theory having been established in the Czech context despite the fact that it completely omits the work of artists from Eastern European countries.

While events organised by Audiovisual focused on both local art and productions from abroad, foreign works would only rarely permeate into the individual blocks of programming. This was not unique to Audiovisual, since despite new possibilities of international collaboration, many exhibitions were still organised under the concept of national art. Frisbee, for instance, an extensive exhibition of audiovisual works that took place in a number of galleries both in Czechia and abroad, presented local artists as representatives of "contemporary Czech video art".[116] It was a similar case with the Punctum exhibition, held in 2007 at the Futura Centre for Contemporary Art, which aimed to be – in the words of curator Václav Magid – "a representative selection of contemporary Czech art of the

[112] Toma Bačić, "Tema Roma u suvremenoj umjetnosti", accessed 20 Apr 2022, http://www.zarez.hr/clanci/

[113] Havel, Poláková, Semerádová, Smetana, Uhlířová, *entermultimediale.*

[114] Audiovisual programme for January and February 2005; January and February 2006; November and December 2006, Světozor Cinema archive.

[115] This primarily involved artists Petr Vrána, Michael Bielický, and Woody and Steina Vasulka, whose extensive archive was transported to the Czech Republic, see Miloš Vojtěchovský (ed.), *Vašulkova kuchyňská kniha #1: texty k médiím: první & poslední = Vasulka kitchen cooking reader #1: beyond media texts: primal & final* (Brno: Vašulka Kitchen Brno, 2020).

[116] Markéta Jonášová, "Globalizované krajiny českého audiovizuálního umění: Studie výstavního projektu Frisbee" [The Globalised Landscapes of Czech Audiovisual Art: A Study of the Frisbee Exhibition Project], *Sešit pro teorii, výtvarné umění a příbuzné zóny* 15, no. 30 (2021), 94–125.

moving image, without making any claims to objectivity".[117] Although curators were primarily motivated to organise overviews of "Czech" audiovisual art by the need for reflecting on and representing the increasing importance of the medium of the moving image on the local art scene, an unintended consequence of exhibitions conceived in this manner was a problematic tendency to introduce groups of works based primarily on national origin or the artists' geographical location.[118] The national definition of these exhibitions was also supported by the curators' education in art history, as the period methodology of art history did not call into question art historical narratives that defined the identity of the art of a particular nation or in a space demarcated by national borders.[119]

The national foundations of art history canons were also

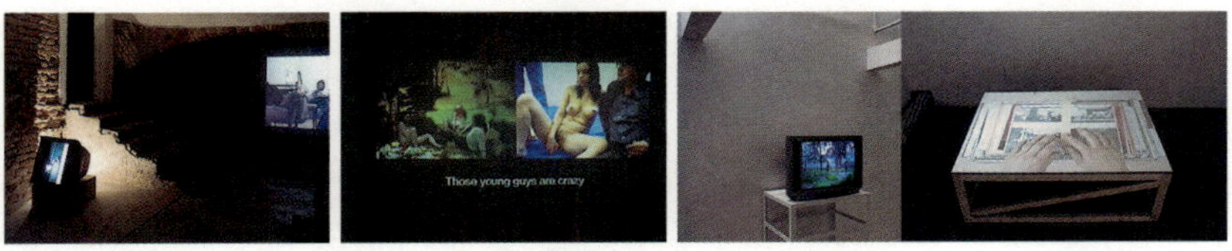

Punctum, exhibition at the Center for Contemporary art FUTURA, Prague, 2007.

evident in festivals dedicated to historical forms of audiovisual art, such as the presentation of post-war American video art organised in 2006 by the curators of the Audiovisual programme in collaboration with the tranzit art initiative.[120] The aim of this historicisation of video art, however, was not to demonstrate the differences between individual national traditions, but rather to introduce local audiences to the historical development of audiovisual art as an autonomous art form. Curator and pedagogue Pavlína Míčová describes the limited knowledge that local audiences possessed about the history of video art in her reminiscences of the presentation of the Contemporary Czech Video Art cycle for film studies students at Masaryk University in Brno in the mid-2000s, which was accompanied by debates about whether the works of Dušan Zahoranský, Radim Labuda, or Guma Guar were, in fact, still art at all. During screenings of audiovisual art at the Světozor cinema, Míčová continues, one could easily follow the difference between positive reactions from students of intermedia, for whom the programme was an opportunity to contextualise their own work, and reticent reactions from spectators accustomed to classical cinematography.[121] It fol-

[117] Exhibitions, Futura Gallery, Prague, Punctum, accessed 20 Oct 2021, http://artservis.info/archiv/brezen/pages/vystavy_brezen_Punctum.html.

[118] František Kowolowski, "Talíř, který přilétne a zase odlétne" [A Plate That Flies in and then Flies Away], *Literární noviny* 17, no. 8 (2006), p. 15.

[119] Milena Bartlová, *Naše, národní umění: Studie z dějin dějepisu umění* [Our – National Art: Studies from the History of Art History], (Prague: Společnost pro odbornou literaturu – Barrister & Principal, 2009), p. 106.

[120] Audiovisual programme for May and June 2006; Světozor Cinema archive.

[121] Pavlína Míčová interviewed by Markéta Jonášová, 29 June 2021, Národní filmový archiv, Oral History collection.

lows from this that the theoretical analysis of audiovisual art in traditional art studies lagged behind the manner in which these forms were progressively taught at practical art schools.[122]

The Limits of Installation

The establishment of new intermedia courses at Czech universities during the course of the 1990s was essential for the development of audiovisual art on the local art scene, and naturally also entailed the creation of new formats for the presentation of a broadening spectrum of audiovisual works.[123] The accessibility of digital video also deepened the reach of the cinematic medium as a creative means that enables artists to capture or unify elements of various artistic media including painting, sculpture, performance, or photography.[124] In place of a specific art form, students of intermedia courses would use an idea or concept for a work as a starting point, with its realisation being possible in various media. This intermedia turn can be illustrated well with the example of Michal Pěchouček, who studied at the Academy of Fine Arts in Prague in the early 1990s – first in the more traditional graphics studio and later in the intermedia studio of visual communication. At one of his first solo shows, titled *Sběratel* [The Collector], 2003, Pěchouček introduced a series of paintings depicting a storyboard for a fictional thriller accompanied by the music from Alfred Hitchcock's *Psycho.*[125] The exhibition installation then served as a foundation for the creation of an eponymous audiovisual work in which the artist composed one painting after another in front of the eyes of the notional spectator, creating an animated film from the oil paintings. Pěchouček also adapted the presentation formats of this playful approach to the possibilities of narration: audiences could see *The Collector* in the public spaces of the cinema as well as in private, since the work was published in 2009 along with other films by the artist on a special edition of the DVD catalogue *Pater Noster Video Stories*. Pěchouček then donated this edition, along with the series of paintings and a list of installation instructions, to the collection of the Moravian Gallery in Brno.[126]

The intermedia turn thus influenced not only the audiovisual artworks themselves, but also the formats of their distribution, which

[122] See Kateřina Svatoňová's contribution to this anthology.

[123] See Tomáš Pospiszyl's contribution to this anthology.

[124] Alice Jedličková, "Jak Perseus osvobodil Andromedu nebo osvobození Andromedy?" [How Perseus Liberated Andromeda, or the Liberation of Andromeda?], in *Vybrané kapitoly z intermediality* [Selected Chapters from Intermediality], Lenka Krausová, Jan Schneider (eds.) (Olomouc: Univerzita Palackého, 2008), pp. 67–68.

[125] Michal Pěchouček – Sběratel [The Collector], accessed 10 Jul 2021, http://www.moravska-galerie.cz/moravska-galerie/vystavy-a-program/aktualni-vystavy/2003/michal-pechoucek-sberatel.aspx.

[126] Jan Press, Výroční zpráva Moravské galerie za rok 2014 [Annual Report of the Moravian Gallery for the Year 2014], accessed 20 Oct 2021, https://invenio.nusl.cz/record/200696/files/nusl-200696_1.pdf.

diverged considerably in the individual exhibition contexts. In the case of the Videokemp, transferring responsibility for the installation of the works to the artists themselves led to separate playback of the pieces on classical TV screens or computer monitors in the confined spaces of tents, while the installation conditions of the In Out festivals were closer to a traditional spectator's experience watching large-format projections at film festivals. Group exhibitions in galleries usually presented series of works in a darkened exhibition room, as well as individual works on television screens connected to DVD or VHS players, which placed great demands on spectators' attention.[127] Despite considerable differences in the quality of sound and image, group exhibitions of audiovisual art mostly introduced works on screens or in the form of single-channel projections. Given the existing technical limitations, multi-channel projections, object installations, or multimedia works were either introduced in simplified form or else not included in group selections at all.[128]

Artists found the opportunity to implement intermedia projects in the installation environment primarily in the context of solo shows at gallery institutions, thanks to close collaborations with curators, greater space in which to realise their plans, and a concentrated production framework. At the Punctum exhibition at the Futura gallery, the artist Pavla Sceránková – whose work is marked by an intermedia approach to objects and performance – was only represented by her short film *Kapusta* [Sauerkraut], 2006; two years later, for her solo exhibition Alles wird gut at Galerie G99 in Brno, she created a site-specific projection titled *Modelová situace* [*Model Situation*], 2009. Having entered the gallery, visitors were directed to interact with a circular wooden spool with a diameter of three meters, which their steps and weight could set in motion in such a way that they found themselves inside a screening room. The film screened there depicted the gallery space filmed by means of a miniaturised model of the spool.[129] The concentrated format of the solo exhibition allowed the artist to explore the intermedia character of the work, with the audiovisual component not limited to serving as a recording, but instead becoming an autonomous element related to the object installation and the performative movement of the visitors.

Pavla Sceránková's early audiovisual works represent one of the many examples of art influenced by the dissemination of digital technologies in the early 2000s that supported the use of audiovisual means of expression not only at film schools, but also among students of intermedia courses who suddenly had at their disposal simple tools for producing, editing, and presenting moving images. The growing popularity of the moving

[127] Archive of the Brno House of Arts, documentation of the Frisbee exhibition, "Technika pro FREE-František".

[128] František Kowolowski interviewed by Markéta Jonášová, 14 Sep 2020, Národní filmový archiv, Oral History collection.

[129] Projeďte se výstavou [Take a Ride Through the Show], accessed 10 Oct 2021, https://artalk.cz/2009/10/04/projedte-se-vystavou/.

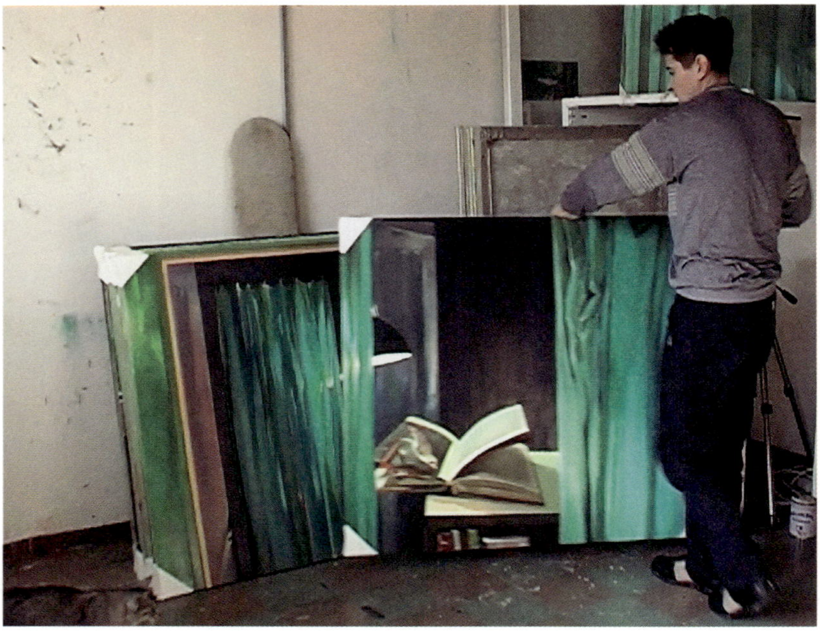

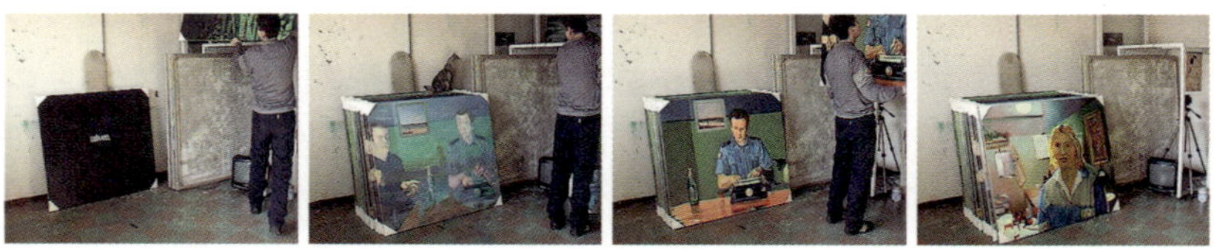

Michal Pěchouček *Sběratel* [Collector] (2003), video, 7 min 26 s

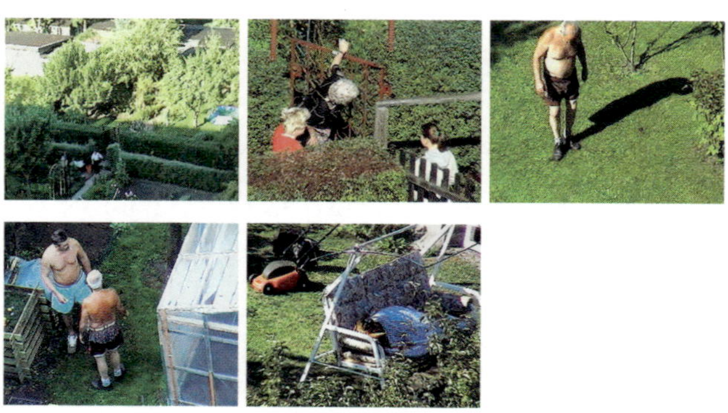

Pavla Sceranková *Kapusta* [Sauerkraut] (2006), video, 5 min 24 s

image as a means for recording conceptual art or creating autonomous artworks did not escape the attention of curators – they responded by organising exhibitions and festivals at both established institutions and new spaces. The availability of technologies for presenting digital video aided the realisation of audiovisual festivals in public spaces, thus supporting a broader expansion of audiovisual art beyond the narrow circle of spectators from inside the artistic community. Newly established festivals of audiovisual art would often turn away from the traditional frameworks of art studies and curatorial approaches, such as the concept of the nationally delineated art exhibition. This concept was typically used to frame the presentation of both historical and contemporary forms of audiovisual art within galleries and museums, even in the case of festivals realised abroad or with a focus on art created beyond the borders of the Czech Republic. The increasing possibilities for international exhibition projects were limited by the inclusion of the Czech art scene in the context of the post-socialist cultural dynamic, which was characterised by a balance between "catching up" with the Western European art canon and a sense of belonging with the post-socialist, Eastern European cultural environment. In the early 2000s, these circumstances began converging in the development of presentational forms of art of the moving image on the Czech art scene, prefiguring the increasing importance of audiovisual art in the decades to come.

01 **Mark Ther** *Mitsu* (2019), video, 14 min
02 Playback conference (1996), webpage screenshot.
03 **E. F. Burian, Čeněk Zahradníček** *Máj* [May] (1936), film, 9 min
04 **Alžběta Bačíková** *Talk & Twerk* (2014), video, 35 min 57 s
05 **Ján Mančuška** *Notion in Progress* (2010), installation at the exhibition Everything that really is, but has been forgotten, Meyer Riegger gallery, Berlin, 2010
06 **Lucie Svobodová** *Obrázky* [The Pictures] (1989), video, 5 min 58 s
07 **Dalibor Chatrný** (1969–1970), planfilm
08 **Oskar Helcel** *It's Buildable* (2020), video, 7 min 59 s
09 **René Slauka** *Hlavolam* [Brain Teaser] (1994), video, 2 min
10 Other Visions CZ, competition section of the PAF Olomouc festival, exhibition in the atrium of the Artistic Centre of Palacký University in Olomouc, 2017
11 **Petr Váša, Marian Palla** *Větev – Prorážení televize větví* [Branch – Smashing Through a Television with a Branch] (1994), video, 11 min
12 **Adéla Babanová** *Rozhovor se Sylvií Plath* [Interview with Sylvia Plath] (2006), video, 10 min 31 s

01

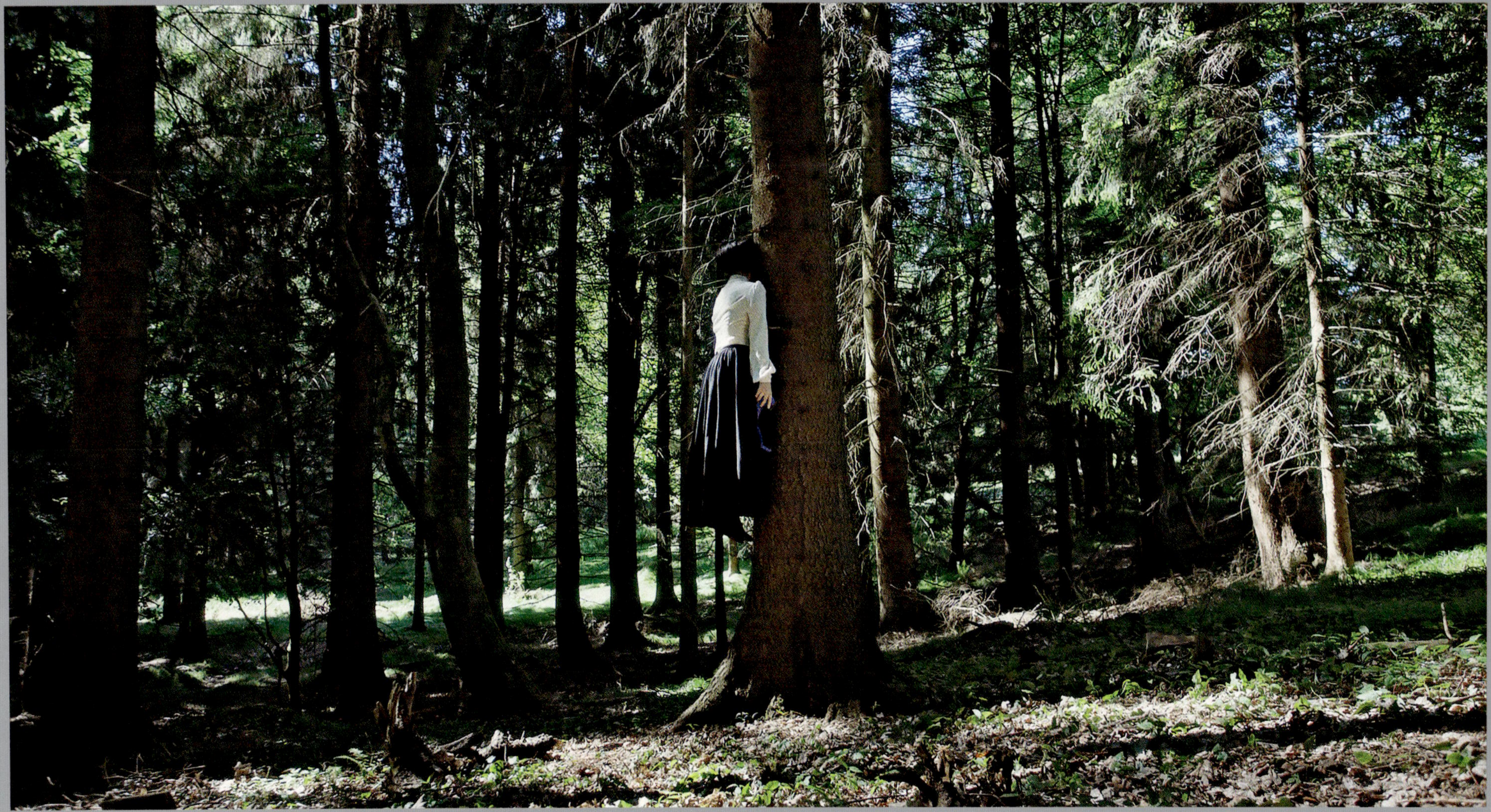

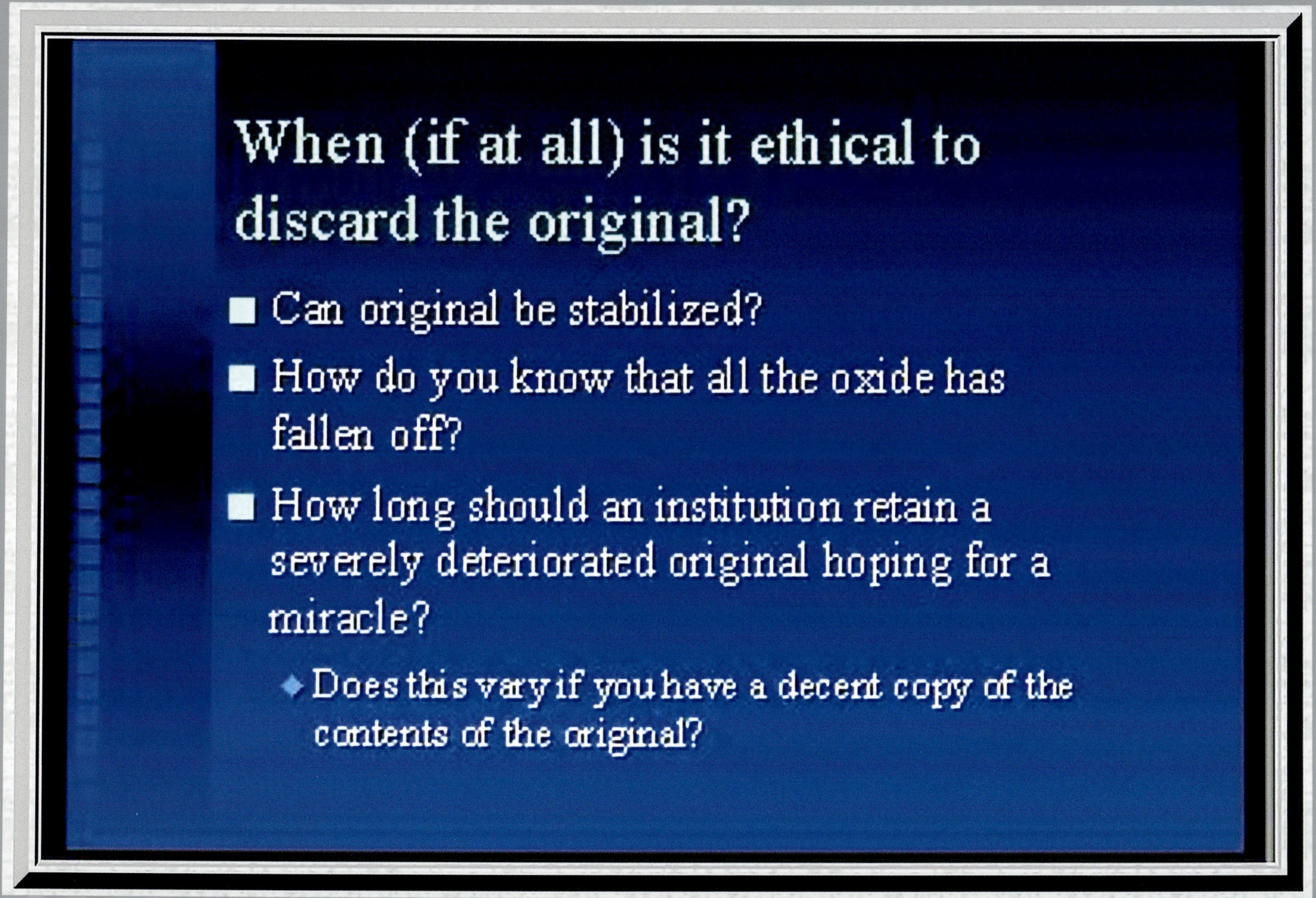
When (if at all) is it ethical to discard the original?
Can original be stabilized?
How do you know that all the oxide has fallen off?
How long should an institution retain a severely deteriorated original hoping for a miracle?
Does this vary if you have a decent copy of the contents of the original?

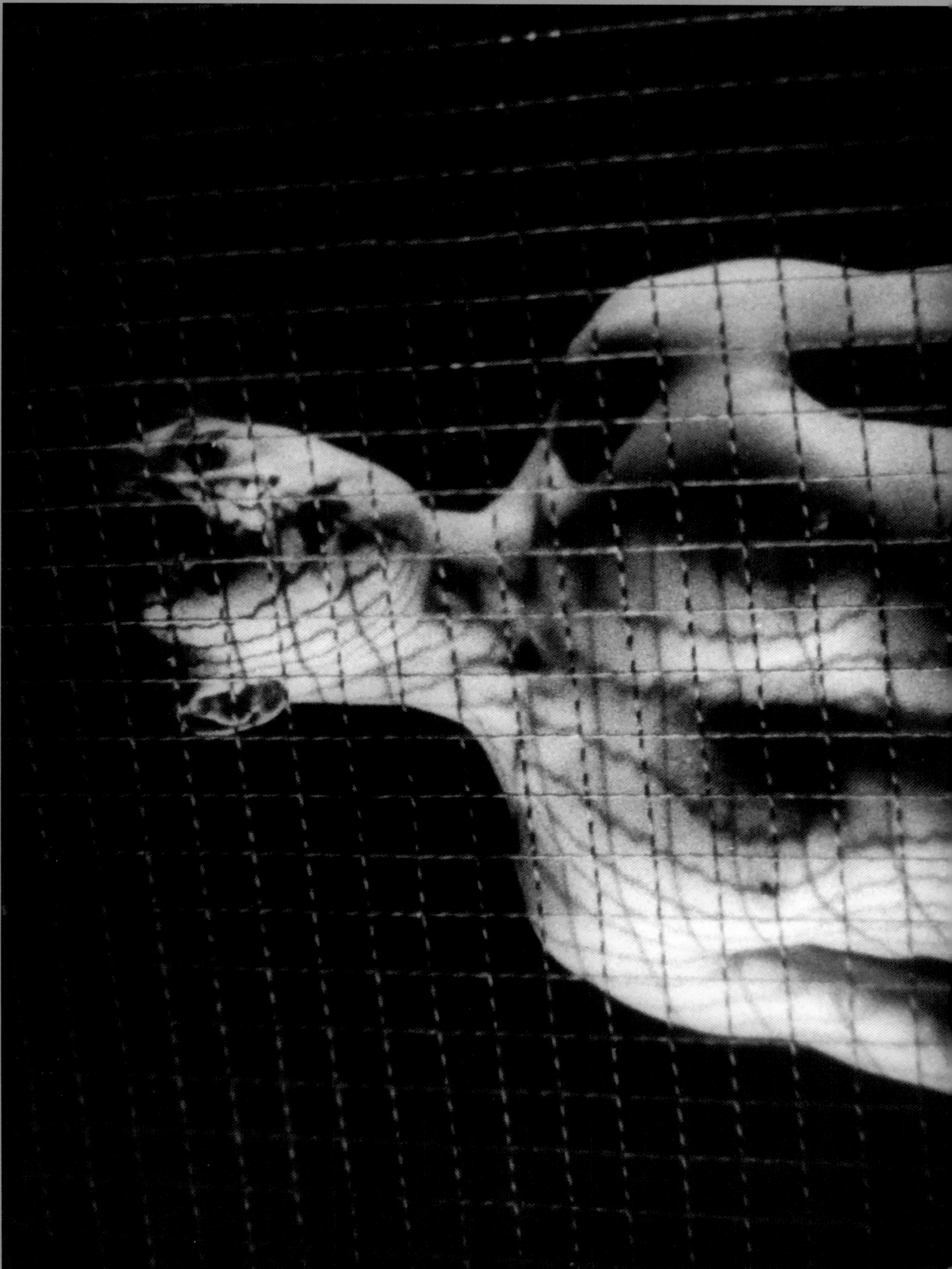

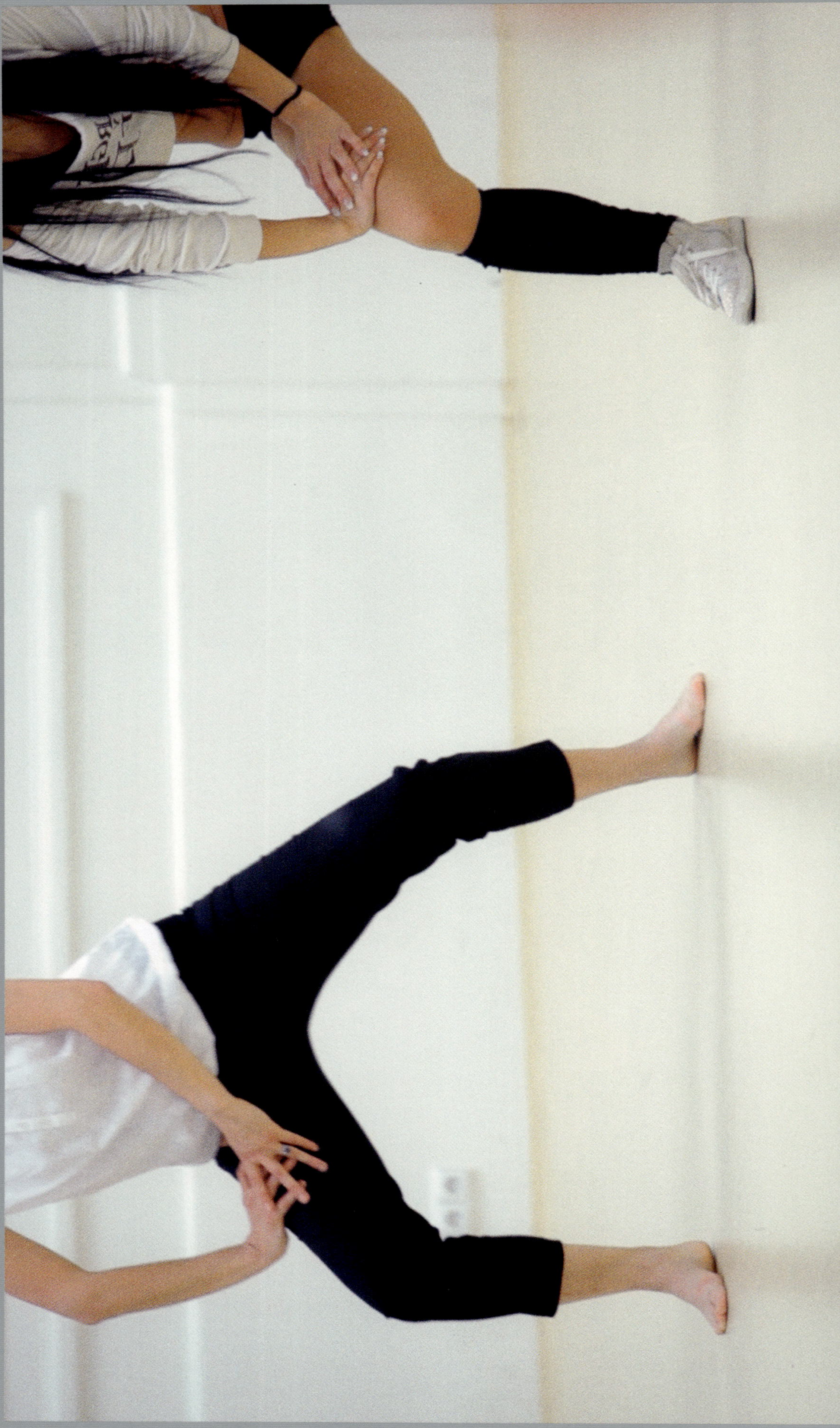

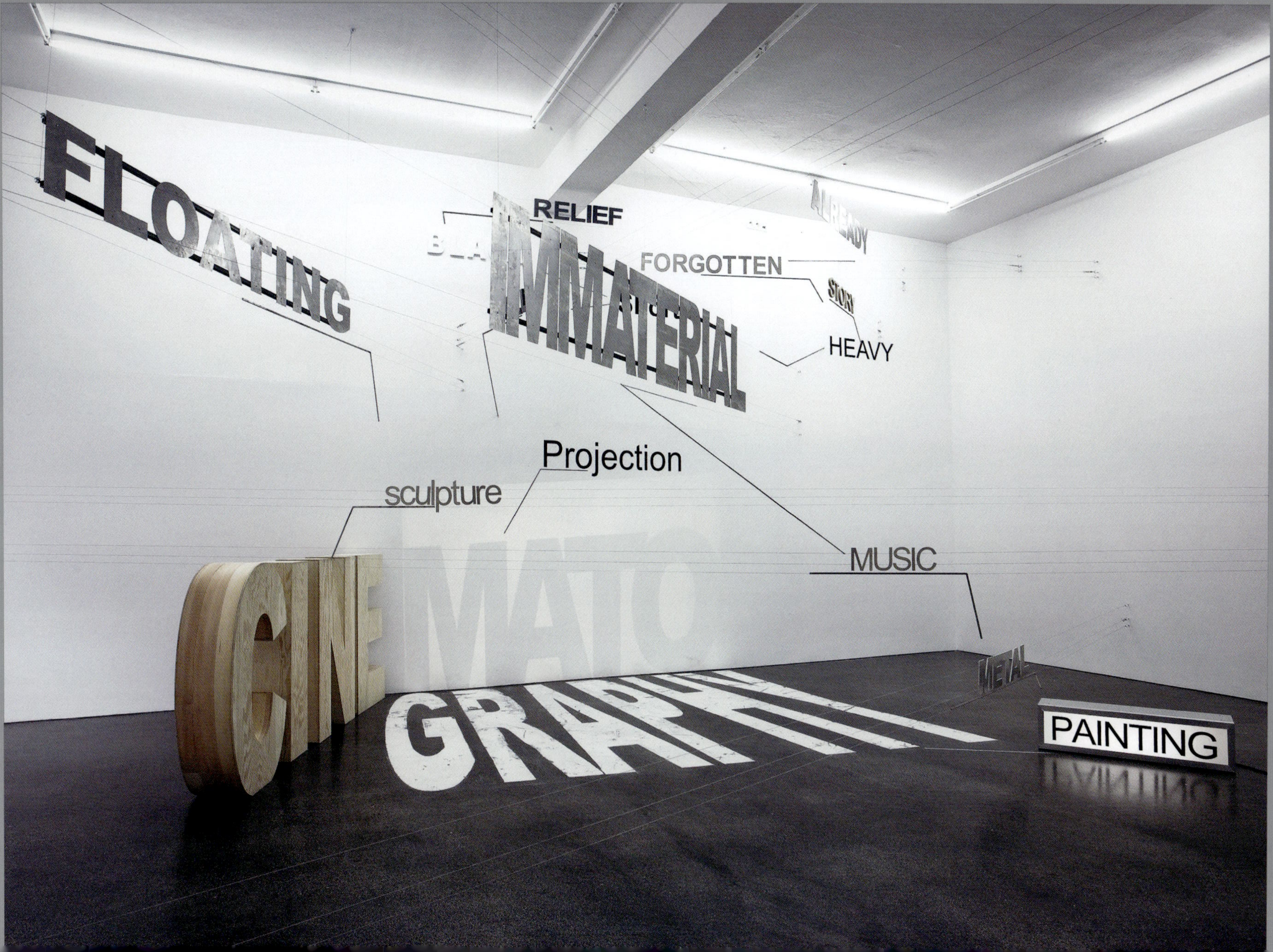
FLOATING
RELIEF
IMMATERIAL
FORGOTTEN
ALREADY
STORI
HEAVY
Projection
sculpture
MUSIC
CINE
MATO
GRAPHY
METAL
PAINTING

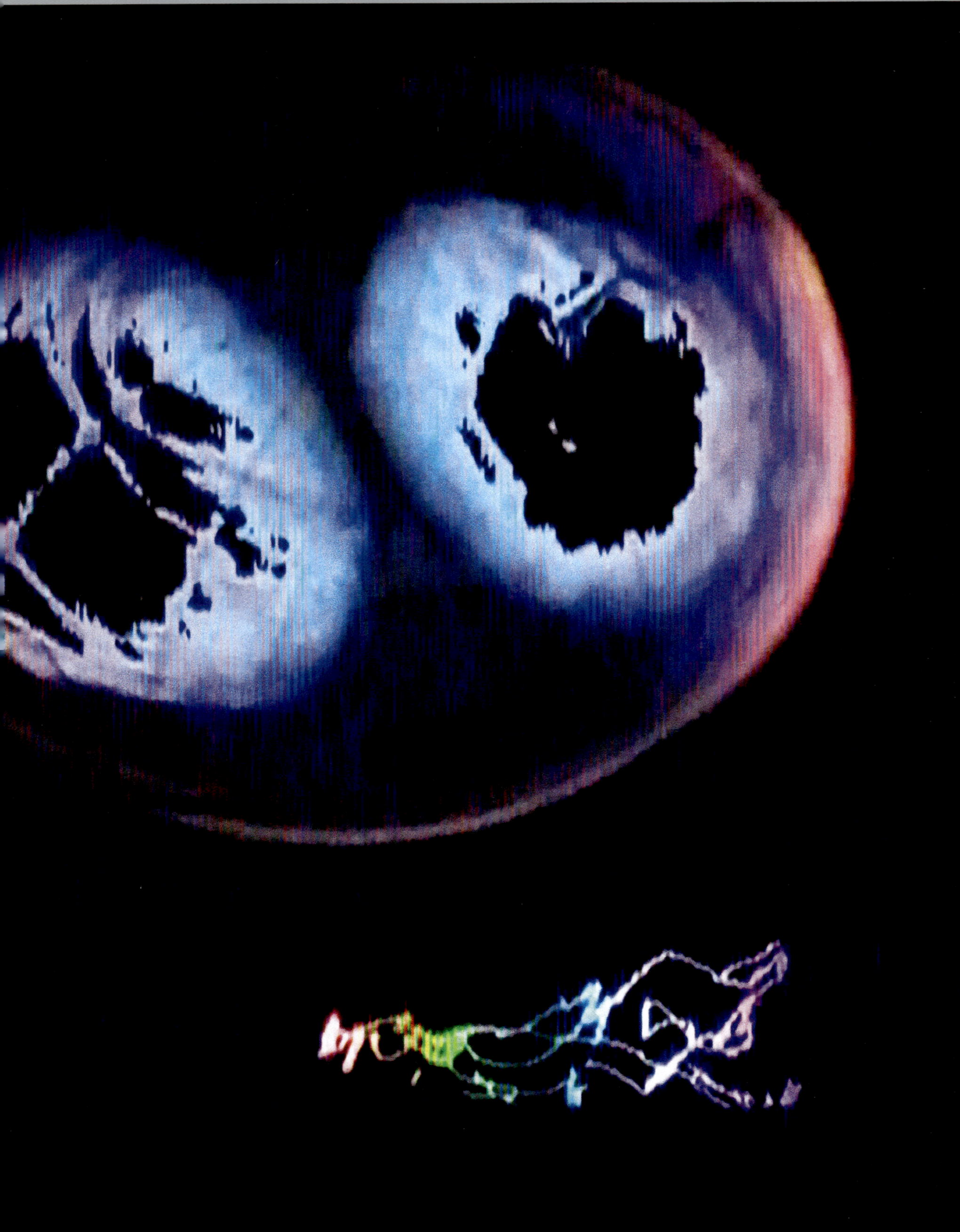

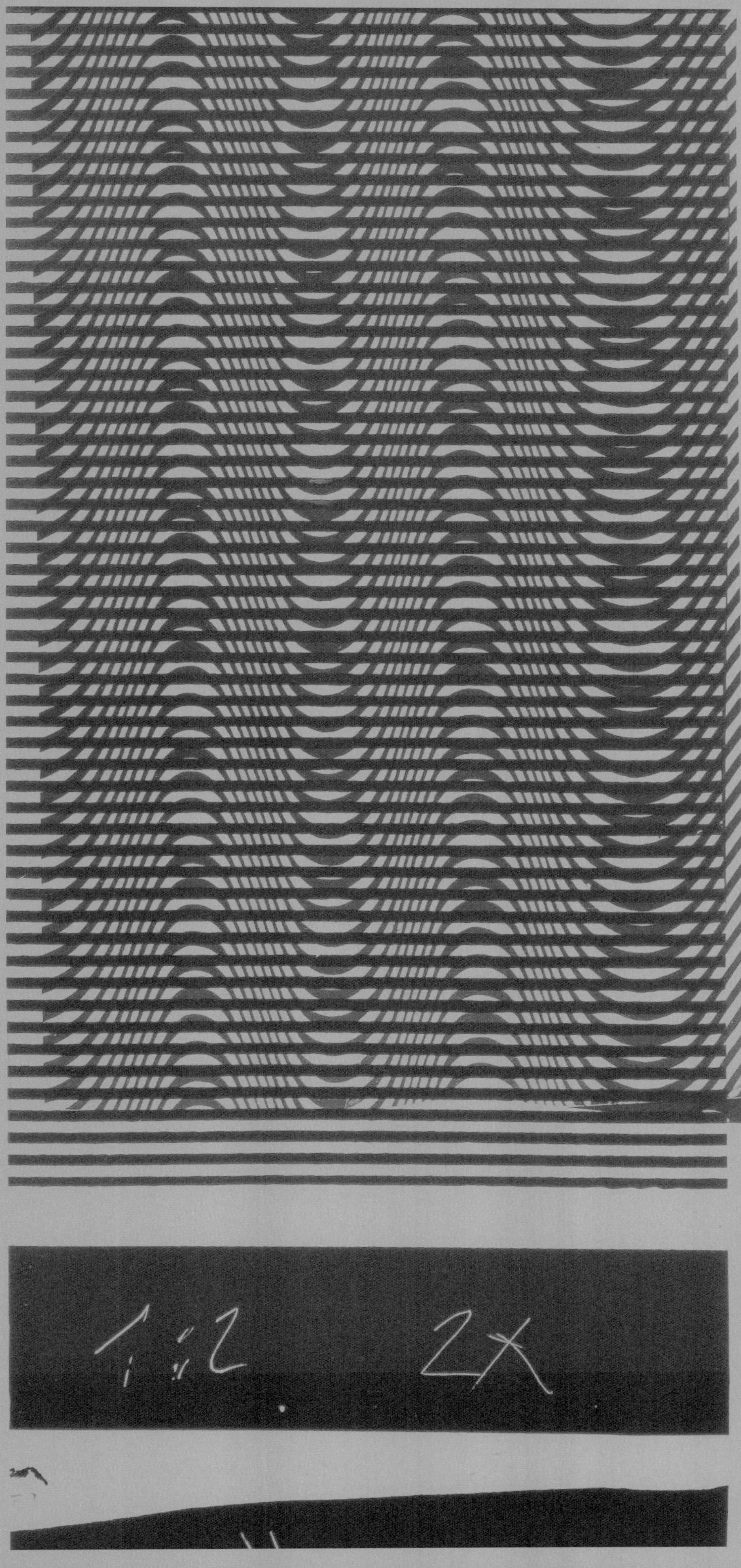
1:2
2X

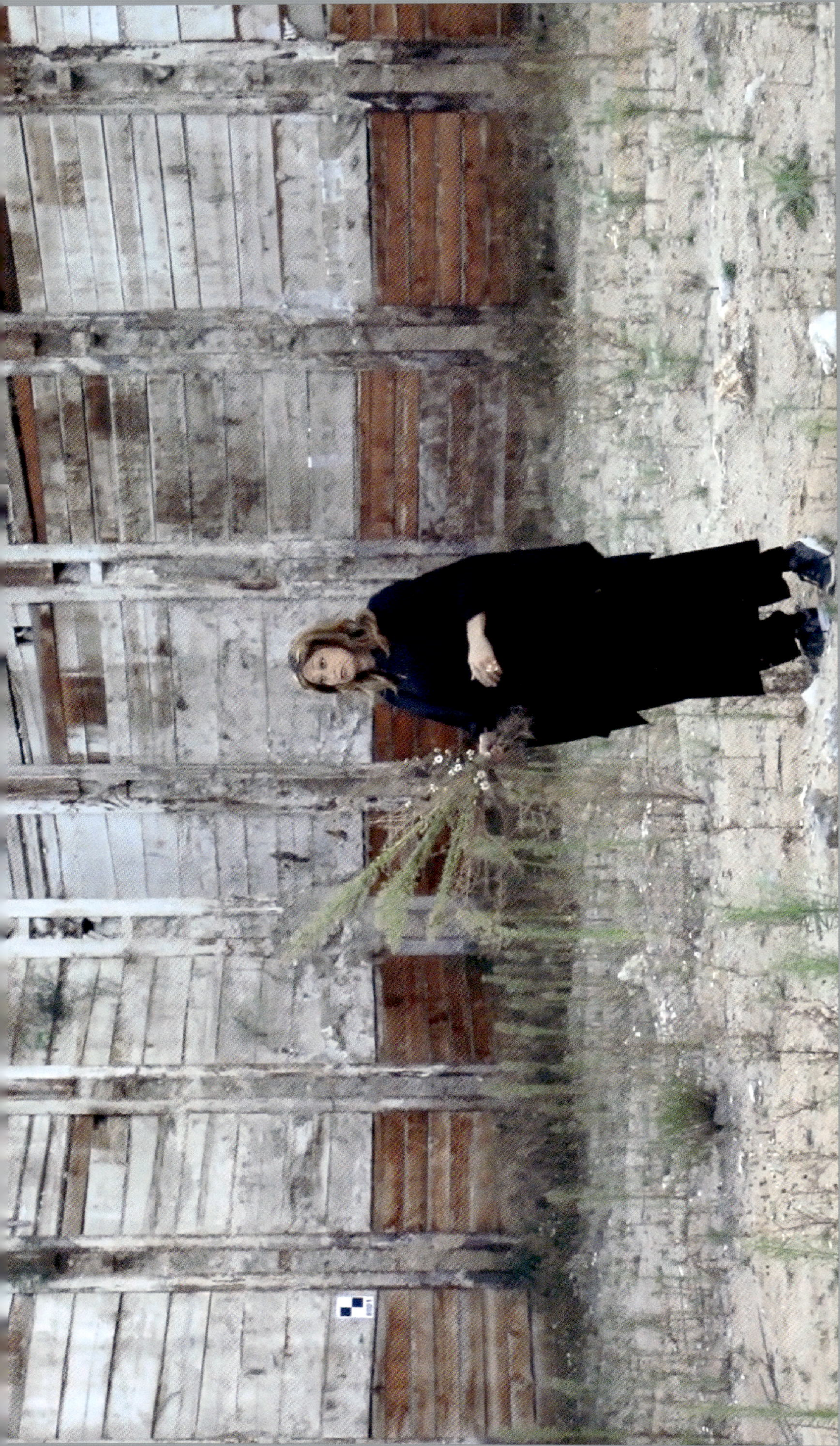

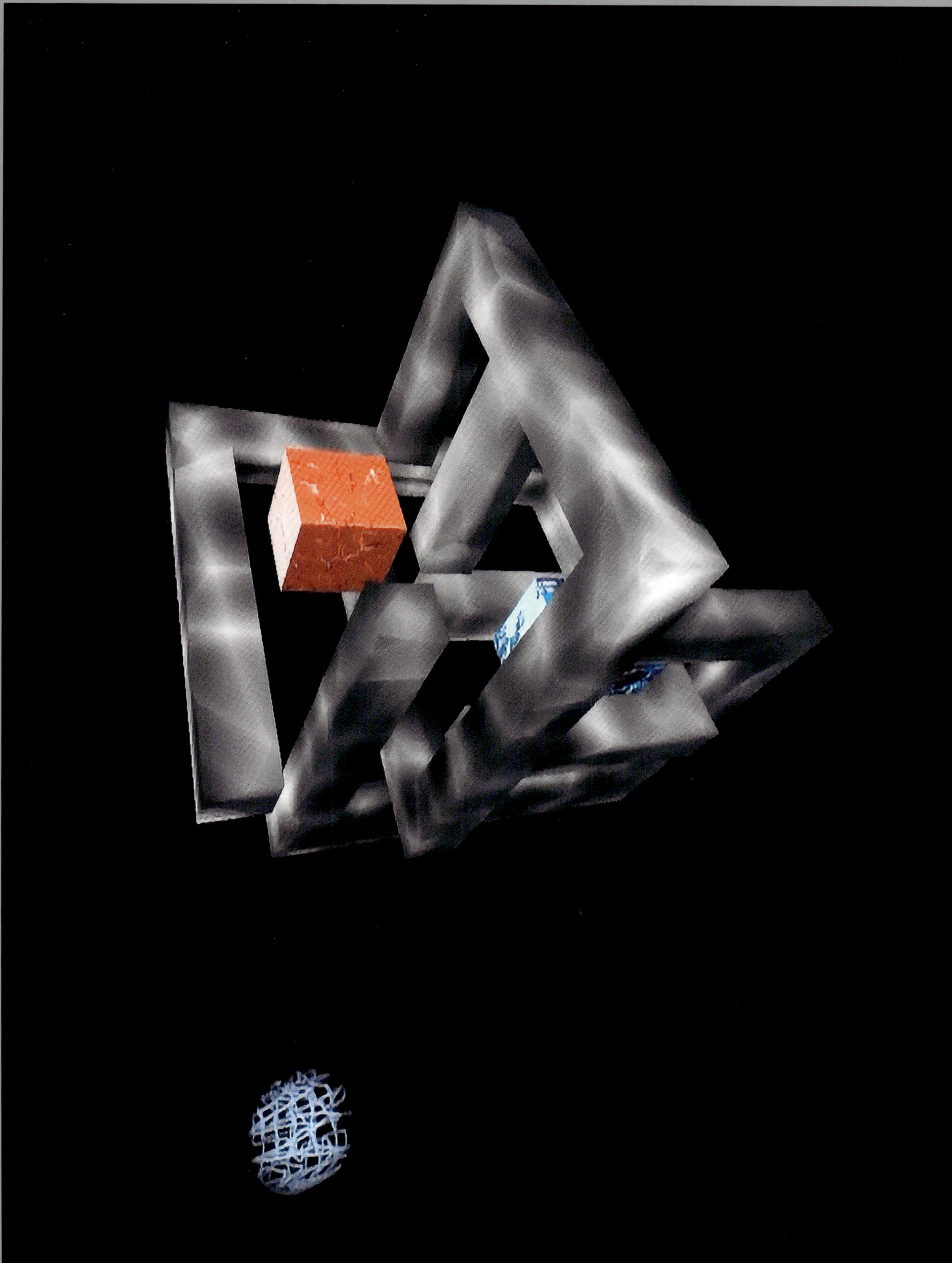

08

09

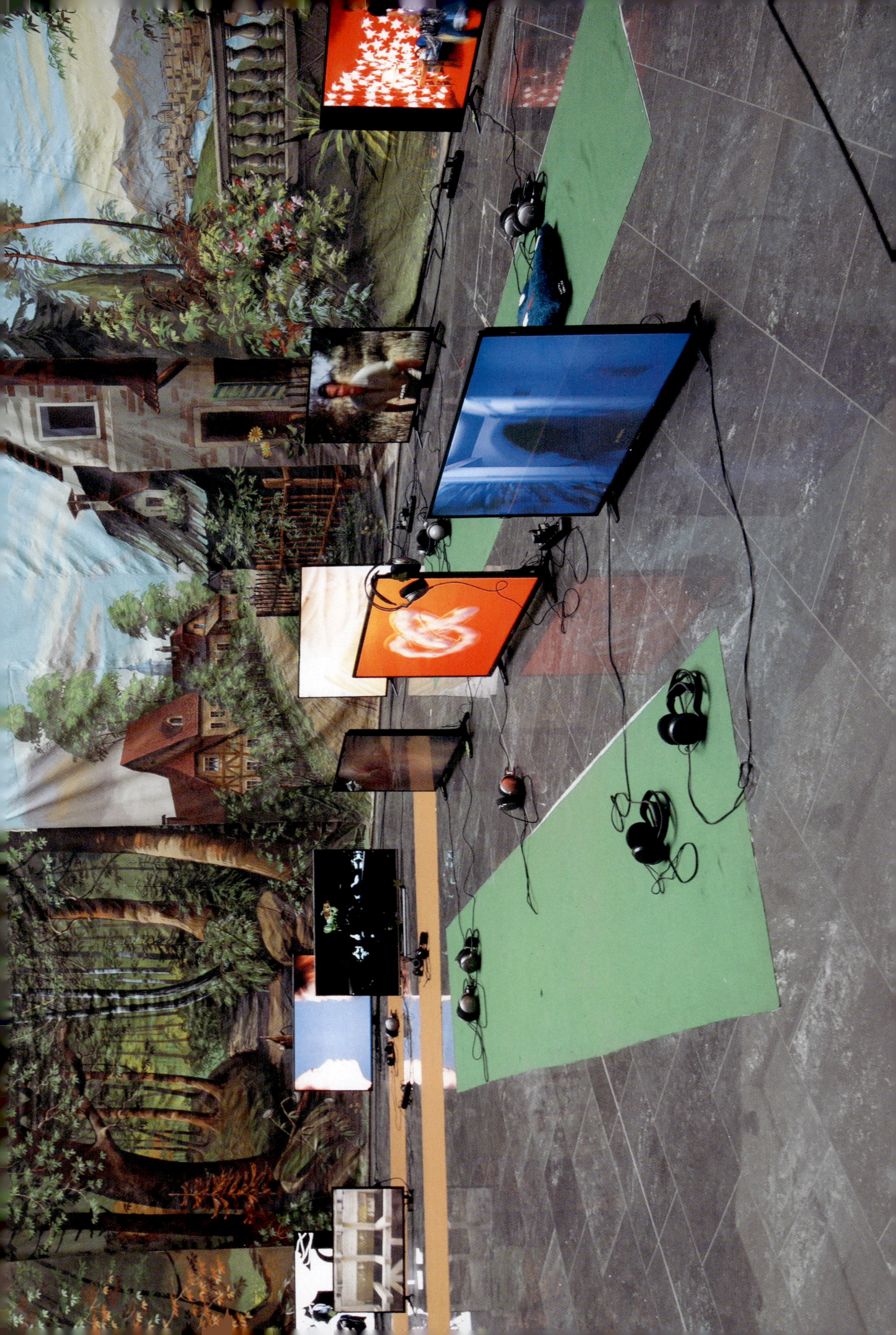

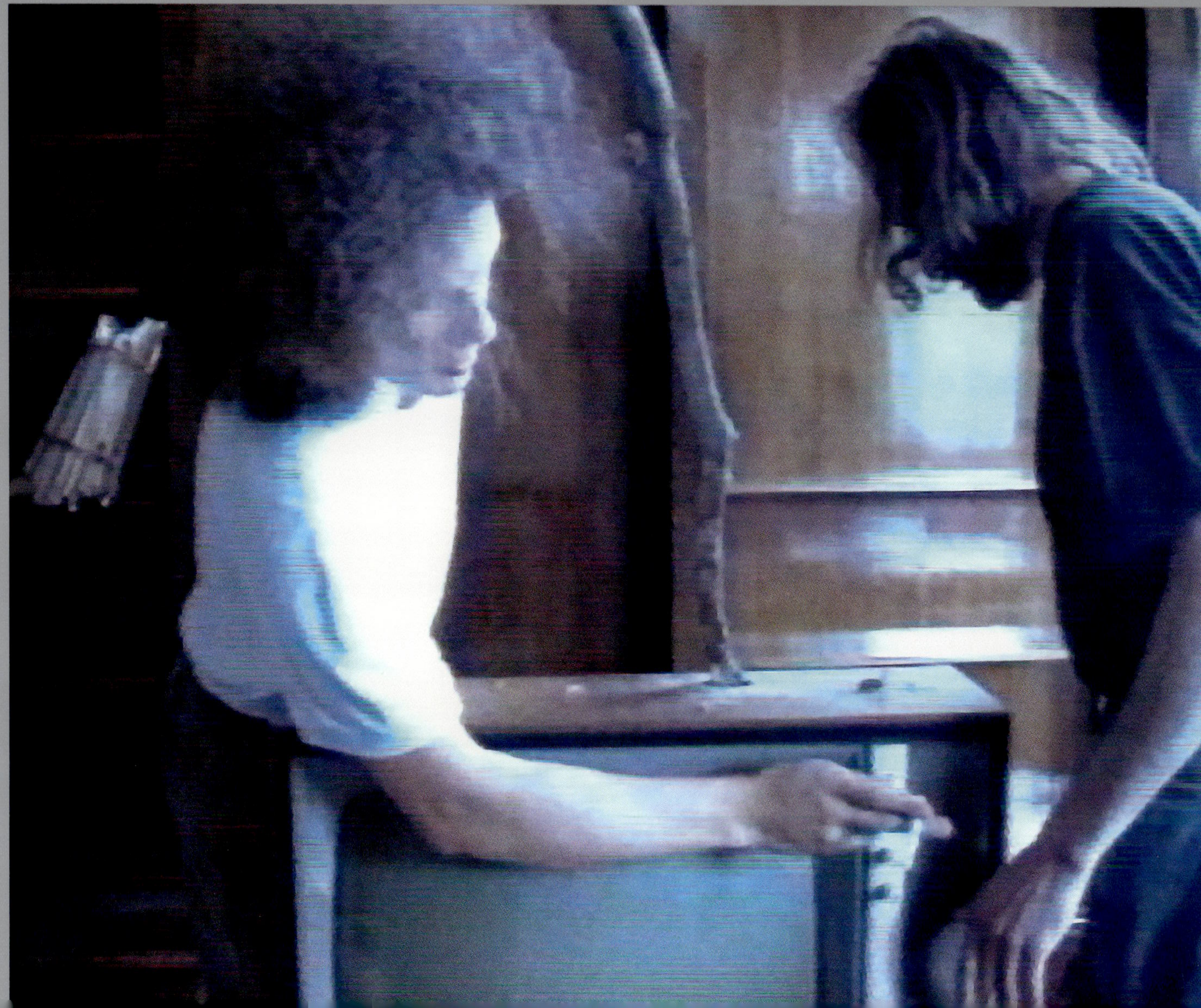

12

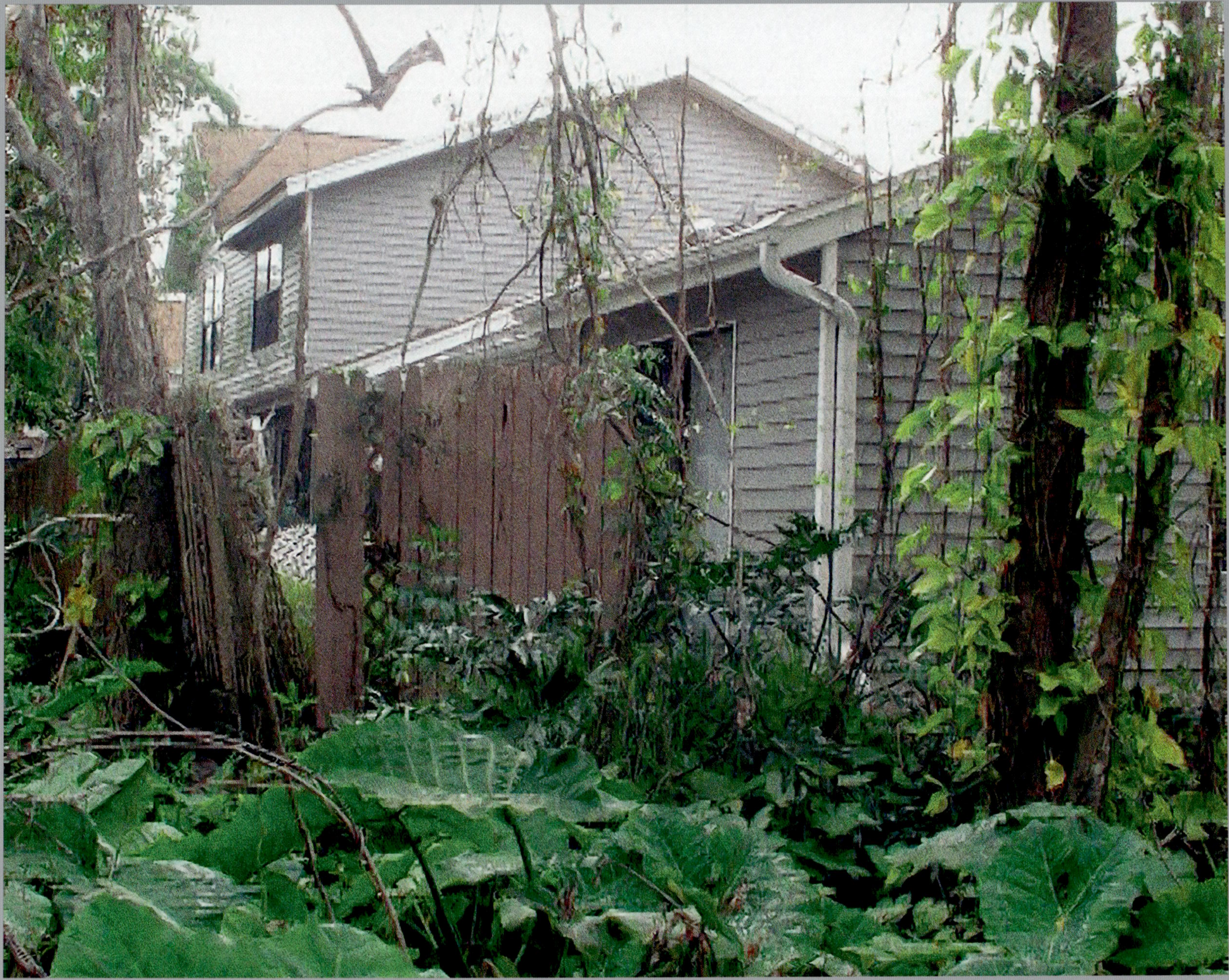

III. PRACTICE

The Circulation of the Moving Image

(225–302)

From the Cinema to the Gallery and Back Again? On the Circulation of the Moving Image in the Context of a (Post) Socialist Country and its Theoretical Framework

Matěj Forejt

Terminological Maturation. The Construct of the Moving Image and Its Resonance in Czech Artistic Periodicals

248

Eva Krátká

Competition Cages and Enclosures for the Moving Image

 Lenka Střeláková

A Collection is Not a Project (Epilogue). On Attempts To Collect and Preserve Art of the Moving

Image in the Czech Context

From the Cinema to the Gallery and Back Again? On the Circulation of the Moving Image in the Context of a (Post)socialist Country and Its Theoretical Framework

Matěj Forejt

A more complex historical assessment of Czech experimental film of the post-war period, existing on the blurred line between cinematography and the art world, is in its early days. The current volume focuses on artists that do not fit squarely in the fine arts or cinematic canon alone, who are interested in cinematic works that are often located in the margins of artistic biographies, and it also does not exclude strategies for treating audiovisual heritage existing outside the film industry. As a consequence, this book also uncovers the existing absence of operational theoretical concepts to have risen from the regional reality of Central Europe. It is highly appropriate to ask about the true motivations for the migration or expansion of the moving image beyond the border demarcating film and fine art; about the motivations to create audiovisual art outside the framework of the film industry; and about the motivations to search for alternative means for making works available. These questions, however, cannot be satisfactorily answered by simply adapting existing concepts that were created on the basis of a different historical experience, regardless of their quality.

The convergence of film and fine art – or at least a desire for it – can be observed, in various forms, from the early days of cinematography. This involves not only historical attempts to establish film as a new form of high art,[1] but also the inverse fascination with the mass nature of film, which we can trace to the interwar left-wing avant-gardes. Moreover, it is in the activities of the avant-garde that we can locate both the pre-historic context of the later exhibition practices of the moving image[2] and the early stages of the expansion of the cinematic medium outside the usual format of projection onto a single screen. We can identify here also cinema's integration into broader multimedia arrangements or even its mere reflection through non-cinematic means, as noted in the early 1970s by the German experimental filmmaker, artist, and writer Birgit Hein, who wrote about expanded cinema in the context of interwar modernism:

> The beginnings of expanded cinema lie in the 1920s, e.g., in the first three-part projection by Abel Gance, but particularly in the light concerts created by Baranov-Rossiné, László, Hirschfeld-Mack, and others, who also included film in their precisely

[1] A pioneering figure in this respect is Ricciotto Canudo, who published a lecture in 1911 titled *The Birth of the Sixth Art*. In Czech, see Ricciotto Canudo, "Teorie sedmi umění" [The Theory of the Seven Arts], *Iluminace* 4, no. 1 (1992), pp. 19–21.

[2] See Franziska Stöhr, *endlos. Zur Geschichte des Film- und Videoloops im Zusammenspiel von Technik, Kunst und Ausstellung* [Endless. On the History of Film and Video Loops in the Interplay of Technology, Art, and Exhibitions] (Bielefeld: Transcript Verlag, 2016).

programmed performances featuring colour pianos or light organs. Then there were the theatre performances making use of film, such as those in Piscator's theatre in Berlin. Ruttmann and Moholy-Nagy made films for him, while Gropius proposed the concept of total theatre:[3] "If we use a system of lights and film projectors, we will transform the walls into a living image, the entire house will come to life through three-dimensional means in place of the flat image effects of normal stages."[4]

In seeking to identify relatives of Birgit Hein's conception of "expanded cinema" in the Czech context, we can mention Alfréd Radok and his Laterna magika [Magician's Lantern] concept, which was created on commission for the Czechoslovak presentation at the Expo 58 in Brussels.[5] With Laterna magika, Radok extended his earlier forays into combining film and theatre, which began in the late 1930s and the first half of the 1940s in connection with his collaboration with theatre director and composer E. F. Burian. The experiments that were realised in Burian's theatre survive in a film sequence created in 1936 by Čeněk Zahradníček and Burian himself for the stage adaptation of Karel Hynek Mácha's *Máj* (*an tragic epic poem written in 1836, a central work in the Czech literary canon – translator's note*). Also contemporary to the period when Gropius's designs were created, the visual artist Zdeněk Pešánek was engaged in similar intermedia projects in the Czech context. Pešánek began his explorations into kinetism and colour music in the 1920s and also applied them in commissioned public art pieces, such as those

[3] Although Birgit Hein originally used the term *totales Theater*, Gropius himself described the term as *Total-Theater* (or, in accordance with the Bauhaus's distaste for capital letters, *total-theater*). Although in German (and all the more so in Gropius's times), the semantic distinction between a hall used for theatre performances and film screenings is not as sharp as in Czech (the cinema can also be called a *Filmtheater*, or, more archaically, *Lichtspieltheater*), so while we could probably speak of "total cinema" in this concept, such a term in Czech would not be appropriate for Gropius's multimedia concept. Gropius's schematic plans for total theatre, dated 1927, are stored by the Harvard Art Museums and are gradually being made available online. See Harvard Art Museums, accessed 29 Jun 2021, https://harvardartmuseums.org/art/219479.

[4] Birgit Hein, *Film im Underground* [Film Underground] (Frankfurt a. M.: Verlag Ullstein, 1971), pp. 98–99. Walter Gropius is cited by Birgit Hein following Jud Yalkut, "Understanding Intermedia", *Arts Magazine* (May 1967).

[5] On Laterna magika, see especially: Lucie Česálková – Kateřina Svatoňová, eds., *Diktátor času: (De)kontextualizace fenoménu Laterny magiky* [Dictator of Time: A (De)Contextualisation of the Laterna Magika Phenomenon] (Prague: Národní filmový archiv, 2019).

created for the Elektrické podniky [Electrical Company] in Prague, with whom he began collaborating in 1928.[6]

Technical Reproducibility and the Issue of Mass Culture

It comes as no surprise that two of the innovators working in Erwin Piscator's theatre – namely László Moholy-Nagy and Walter Gropius – were also important representatives of the Bauhaus, despite the fact that film was never taught at this school (unlike theatre). Bauhaus belonged to the domain of traditional applied art educational institutions whose aim was to train artists and designers to create high-quality mass production. The Bauhaus was attempting to reform the institution, allowing it to face the new challenges of the times.[7] Furthermore, the idea of making conveniences for the modern lifestyle broadly available intersected with left-wing politics of social justice, which the Bauhaus also tended towards. So, while the medium of film is not among the most important themes for the Bauhaus, the attempt to make art available with the use of the methods of mass entertainment is symptomatic of this school.

However, the mass production and distribution of moving images (images that, by the late 1920s, also became speaking and singing images), as well as photographs or musical recordings, meant not only increased availability of visual and sonic experiences – the flood of various modern image formats also began devaluing the concept of the original, which had been of primary importance, particularly in fine art. The problem

[6] See Lucie Česálková – Kateřina Svatoňová, "Na světelné křižovatce: Vzájemné zrcadlení města a filmu jako reklamní strategie" [At the Traffic Lights: The Mutual Mirroring of the City and Film as Advertising Strategy], in *Divadlo ulice: Reklama a aranžérství výkladních skříní v kontextu modernismu 1918–1938* [The Theatre of the Street: Advertising and Shop Windows in the Context of Modernism 1918–1938], ed. Lada Hubatová-Vacková (Prague: Academy of Art, Architecture and Design, 2021), p. 165. On the work of Zdeněk Pešánek, see his own volume *Kinetismus* [Kinetism] (Prague: Česká grafická unie, 1941) and Sylva Poláková, "Konvergence filmu a architektury. Případ Prahy" [Convergences of Film and Architecture] (doctoral thesis, Faculty of Arts, Charles University, Prague, 2015). On later activities that built upon Pešánek's ideas, see Vít Havránek, "Český kinetismus 1956–1970 a skupina Syntéza" [Czech Kinetism 1956–1970 and the Syntéza Group] (doctoral thesis, Prague: Charles University Faculty of Arts, 1997), and also Andrea Sloupová, "Syntéza po Syntéze: české kinetické umění 60. let a pozdější tvůrčí postupy jeho protagonistů" [Syntéza After Syntéza: Czech Kinetic Art of the 1960s and the Later Creative Methods of Its Protagonists] (doctoral thesis, Prague: Charles University Faculty of Arts, 2008).

[7] Also not without interest is the fact that László Moholy-Nagy was a guest lecturer at the Škola umeleckých remesiel [School of Applied Arts] in Bratislava in 1931. Zdeněk Pešánek, the Czech creator of light and kinetic objects mentioned above, was also a guest lecturer there at the time. Also, this same school in Bratislava was the first in interwar Czechoslovakia to open a film programme, co-initiated by Karel Plicka, who later took part in establishing FAMU. Pešánek also emphasised the need to teach novel approaches to applied art, advertising, and light technologies at applied art schools. See Lada Hubatová-Vacková, "Siluety plátěných nevěst: Aranžérství výkladních skříní v kontextu modernismu" [Silhouettes of Linen Brides: Shop Window Arranging in the Context of Modernism], in *Divadlo ulice: Reklama a aranžérství výkladních skříní v kontextu modernismu 1918–1938*, ed. Lada Hubatová-Vacková (Prague: Academy of Art, Architecture and Design, 2021), p. 137. Cf. Pavel Coufalík – Lada Hubatová-Vacková, "Neonová záře: Elektrická světelná reklama, kinetické a reflektorické hry" [Neon Lights: Electric Light Advertisements, Kinetic and Reflectional Games], ibid., p. 283. Cf. Václav Macek – Jelena Paštéková, *Dejiny slovenskej kinematografie 1896–1969* [The History of Slovak Cinematography] (Bratislava: Slovenský filmový ústav, 2016), pp. 101–103.

of the loss of the aura of a single (and unique) original was articulated in 1936 by the German philosopher and critic Walter Benjamin in his essay "The Work of Art in the Age of Mechanical Reproduction".[8] Less than a decade later, the Swiss film theorist and founder of the Swiss film archive Peter Bächlin[9] wrote his dissertation on film as merchandise, in which he too explored film as a "mass product" in the theoretical portion of his paper, considering the "character of the cinematic product as an object of exchange".[10] Bächlin writes:

> Film can serve to educate, entertain, and relax, as well as to provide artistic experiences. Every film thus addresses a large number of people. The spiritual needs of these people are markedly different. For producers the question then arises as to which needs their cinematic product is to satisfy. Capitalist film production and its endeavour to be profitable demands that the cinematic product considers primarily those needs that are shared by as many consumers with the appropriate purchasing power as possible.[11] [...] If film wants to make good on its technical and financial conditions, it must inevitably address broad strata of the public.[12]

A mass character and the absence of an original seemed to be the indisputable genetic building blocks of film and other modern media, and not only at the philosophical level but also economically. However, with the onset of new forms of temporal or performative art – including experimental film – the art world of the capitalist West also had to gradually come to

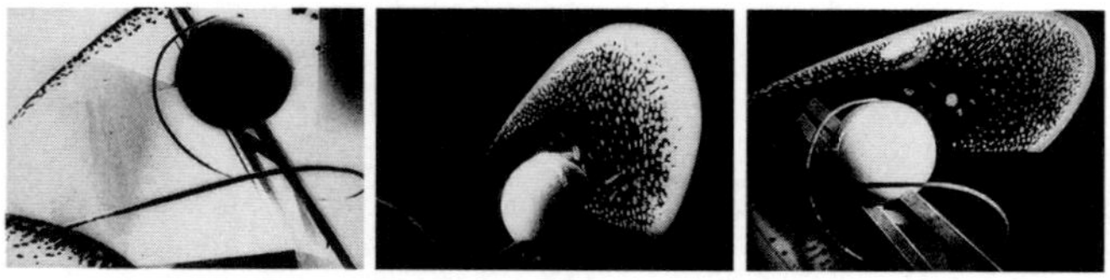

Otakar Vávra, František Pilát *Světlo proniká tmou* [The Light Penetrates the Dark] (1930), film, 4 min

[8] *Das Kunstwerk im Zeitalter seiner technischen Reproduzierbarkeit.* In English: *The Work of Art in the Age of Mechanical Reproduction* (London: Penguin Books Limited, 2008).

[9] Historisches Lexikon der Schweiz [Historical Lexicon of Switzerland] – Peter Bächlin, accessed 29 Jun 2021, https://hls-dhs-dss.ch/de/articles/009131/2012-11-20.

[10] Peter Bächlin, *Der Film als Ware* [Film as Commodity] (Basel: Burg-Verlag, 1945), p. 155.

[11] Ibid., p. 188.

[12] Ibid., p. 211.

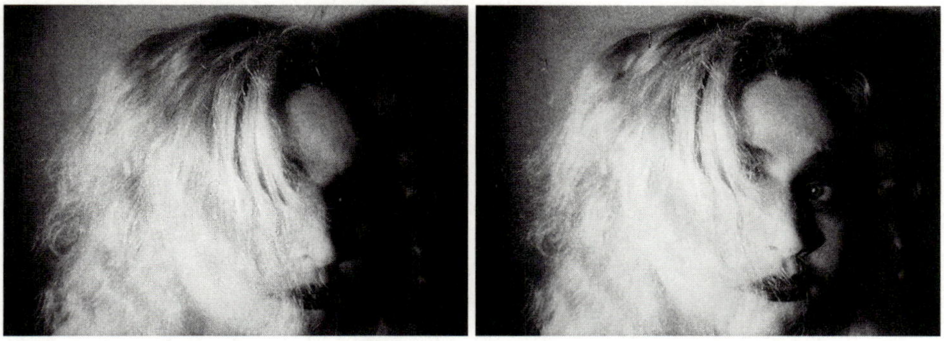

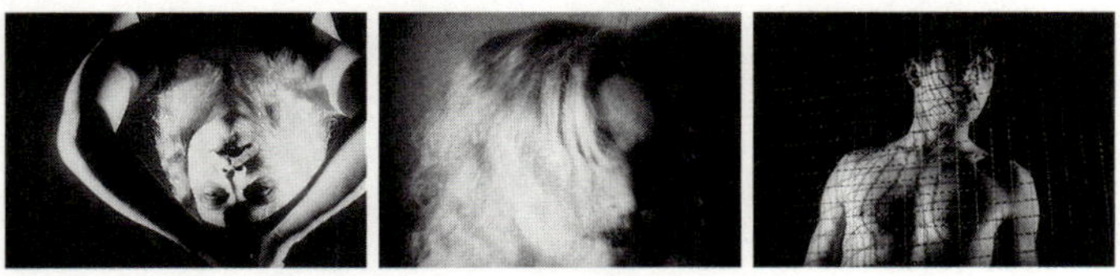

E. F. Burian, Čeněk Zahradníček *Máj* [May] (1936), film, 16 min

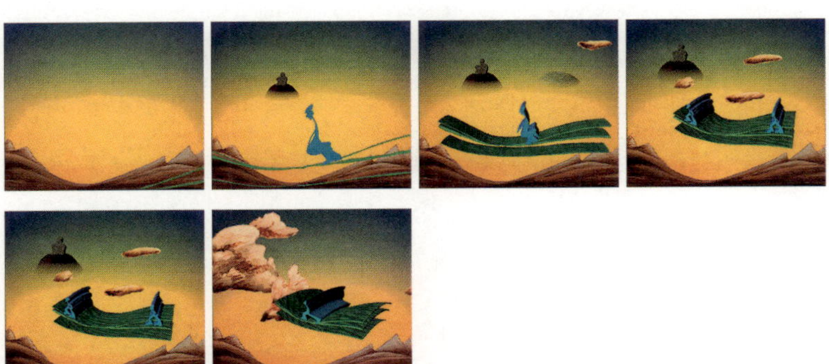

Lucie Svobodová *Cesta* [Journey] (1993), video, 4 min 35 s

terms with such works entering the market, their tradeability, and the possibility of their being integrated into artistic collections.[13]

Present conceptions of the theoretical understanding of elementary motivations for the existence of film and the moving image in the sphere of fine art are derived precisely from these practices of the capitalist art market. A crucial starting point for theoretical and critical reflections on gallery presentations of moving images was to take into consideration the market mechanisms of the art world. If we focus on the cinematic medium as existing within this framework, and if we keep in mind the possibilities of various forms of temporal art being traded or collected, the practices of collectors and the market will no longer seem all that surprising. Nevertheless, this has only come to be critically assessed in recent years, with one of the most important theoretical works on the practice of the cinematic medium in the gallery context and its impacts written by Erika Balsom, a theorist of film and fine art active in Great Britain. In a 2013 text, she emphasised that:

> [q]uestions concerning the sale and pricing of art are frequently left out of scholarly discourse; they are presumably thought to be vulgar and tasteless, a disavowed part of a business that never wants to recognize itself as such. However, as the following will show, such practices in fact have an intimate relationship to the symbolic value attached to a given art object, as well as a direct impact on how that object may be collected and archived.[14]

Balsom reminds us that as early as the 1930s, New York gallerist Julien Levy introduced the idea to "sell film prints as art objects", sharing his passion for the medium of film with the surrealist artists in whose work he specialised.[15] However, at a time when the convictions about the indis-

[13] Today, the resulting practice is no longer something that takes place after the creation of an autonomous art work, but something that can even transform into an integral part of the authorial gesture: The Berlin-based conceptual artist Tino Sehgal, for instance, who makes what he calls constructed situations, entirely denies the practice of authorised documentation of the work or certificates of ownership by strictly prohibiting any recordings of his performances, arranging purchases with collectors or museums exclusively in person. In part, this makes impossible the usual form of exhibiting performances, based on the presentation of video documentation. However, at the 2018 exhibition *Welt ohne Außen – Immersive Räume seit den 60er Jahren* (World Without an Outside – Immersive Spaces Since the 60's) at Berlin's Martin-Gropius-Bau, which Sehgal co-curated, the artist did not even include his performance in the orientation map. In this manner, he provides a subversive commentary not only on the practices of buying and selling certain forms of art, but he primarily adopts them as artistic practices, making this commentary on market practices indivisible from the other aspects of his artwork. For more on this topic, see Simone Miller, "Never Ending Story. Zum musealen Umgang mit wiederholbarer Kunst", in *Art Handling. Partituren der Logistik*, eds. Lucie Kolb – Christoph Lang – Wolfgang Ullrich – Judith Welter (Zürich: JRP – Ringier / Migros Museum für Ge≠genwartskunst, 2016), pp. 51–58.

[14] Erika Balsom, "Original Copies: How Film and Video Became Art Objects", *Cinema Journal* 53, no. 1 (2013), p. 100.

[15] Ibid., p. 97.

putable mass character and non-auratic nature of film were at their peak, his concept did not succeed. We have no proof of the sale of even a single copy from his limited series.[16] Balsom considers this failure one in a long historical lineage that began in the late 19th century with limited editions of bronze statues and art prints that were to be different from the predominant practice of unlimited series of reproducible artworks. The lineage continues with American artist Bruce Conner, who – even before making his very first film, *A Movie*, in 1957 – suggested to his gallerist that he should consider selling original film reels, and the West German gallerist Gerry Schum, who, at the beginning of the 1970s, "issued videotapes in both limited and unlimited editions, complete with signed and numbered certificates of authenticity, as well as a precisely formulated pricing model". In March 1973, financial troubles led him to close his gallery and commit suicide.[17] Not even Leo Castelli, with his brand Castelli-Sonnabend Tapes and Films Inc., the very first in the USA to focus on selling art of the moving image, succeeded in overturning this trend in the 1970s and early '80s – instead, he registered more interest in loans of the limited editions of films than in sales.[18] The strategy of rental copies of experimental film, which was established by the late 1940s,[19] continued to thrive (and still survives today as a relic on several distribution platforms). A strong argument to abandon this model and replace it with a limited-edition arrangement was the rising frustration of experimental filmmakers at the minimal possibility to generate income. Erika Balsom discusses the example of the experimental film-maker Kenneth Anger, who produced a series of limited-edition films in the late 1970s that were aimed exclusively at private collectors and were not screened publicly.[20]

Balsom situates the anchoring of the limited-edition strategy in the 1990s, i.e., a period of growing interest in working with the medium of film outside the film industry. She describes three factors whose confluence allowed for the creation of a viable market, contributing to the rise of limited editions of film and video "[a]fter roughly sixty years of existence at the margins of the art market". First, the economic factor, which points to the lower expenses for presenting video and other alternative formats. Second, the factor of "technological innovation and changes in the speed and facility of image reproduction and circulation". One consequence of this was that "[a]t a time when images were more mobile than ever before, the limited edition provided a way of guaranteeing that the work would circulate only within authorised channels and would be seen only in the proper setting". And, finally, the third factor, and the most important in Balsom's opinion: the

[16] Ibid.

[17] Ibid., p. 106.

[18] Ibid., pp. 106–107.

[19] Ibid., p. 104.

[20] Ibid., p. 108.

interplay of technological changes and the policies of particular institutions. "The moving image might have once challenged the traditional museum, but in the 1990s, endowed with a new, large-scale mode of display, it was recruited by museums to secure relevance in an increasingly competitive market- place demanding breathtaking, immersive experiences. And where institutions go, the market follows".[21]

Erika Balsom's research[22] not only focuses on the history of the practice of limited editions of art of the moving image, but also explores a much broader range of themes including critical responses to the currently dominant model of trading this form of art, the issue of exhibiting in the gallery cinematographic works originally intended for other forms of presentation,[23] and other aspects involving theoretical approaches to forms of the cinematic medium existing as part of the art world and presented in gallery spaces. All

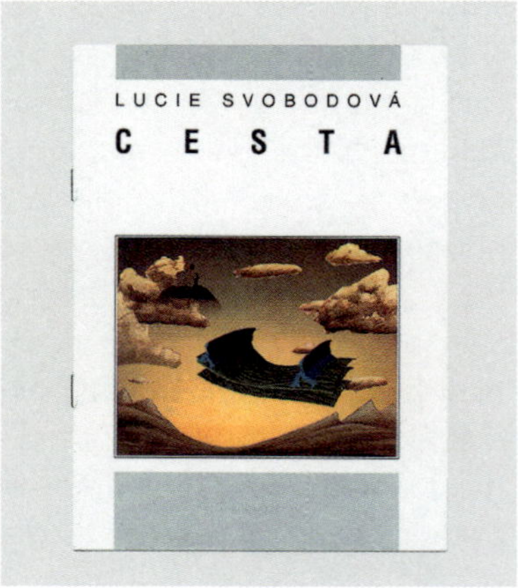

Catalogue for Lucie Svobodová's exhibition at Galerie Radost, Prague, 1993.

[21] Ibid., pp. 109–111. In a practice established since the 1990s, Erika Balsom summarises the market for art of the moving image in the following basic practical outline: "When purchasing a video edition, the collector usually receives an archival master (often Digital Beta); exhibition copies in a current format; digital files; a signed and numbered certificate of authenticity; and a contract specifying the rights to exhibition, duplication, and format shifting. In the case of film, the collector usually acquires a master in the form of an inter negative; a number of prints; a digital preview copy of the work; a signed and numbered certificate of authenticity; and a contract specifying the rights to exhibition, duplication, and format shifting. In some cases, the technological support required to display the work might be included as a part of the edition, though such a practice is relatively rare. Editions sometimes also include ancillary materials such as still photographs or sculptural packaging, included so as to endow the work with objecthood, but more commonly such objects (when they do exist) are sold separately from the edition. When one buys an edition, one purchases a rather curious combination of rights, content, and technical support – the specifics of which are all closely regulated by the contracts accompanying the acquisition. This makes the accession of film or video into a museum collection distinctly more complicated than would be the case with most traditional artworks. Though moving-image media do possess a kind of objecthood, it is crucial to recognize that what is for sale is less this object per se than a set of permissions, privileges, and responsibilities concerning the exhibition and guardianship of a given work over time." Ibid., p. 99.

[22] In addition to the study cited above, this mostly concerns the books *Exhibiting Cinema in Contemporary Art* (Amsterdam: Amsterdam University Press, 2013) and *After Uniqueness: A History of Film and Video Art in Circulation* (New York: Columbia University Press, 2017).

[23] See, for example, her critique of the gallery presentation of Fassbinder's series *Berlin Alexanderplatz* (1980), prepared in 2007 by Klaus Biesenbach for Kunst-Werke in Berlin and MoMA PS1 in New York. Balsom, *Exhibiting Cinema in Contemporary Art*, pp. 41–42.

these lines of thought, however, rely considerably on concepts derived from the dynamics operating within art markets in capitalist countries.

What is probably the first Czech example of a limited VHS edition of artistic video is dated to the period following the end of the socialist regime. It was published in 1993 on the occasion of an exhibition at Galerie Radost by the artist Lucie Svobodová, who made a series of tapes containing her four-minute animation *Cesta* [*Journey*], which was presented at the exhibition in an original spatial installation. Her idea to create an edition of fifty numbered tapes, however, was apparently not inspired by models from abroad, but rather by the practice of limited editions of graphic prints or photographs. In Svobodová's words, the VHS tape, stored in an original case and signed by the artist, was an experiment with the possibilities of presenting a new media work to the public. It was also intended to create a path by which such a work could be allowed to exist in the spectator's home, on the screen of their television. However, not a single one of the tapes available at the exhibition was sold.[24] So, while this endeavour is already part of the period when the Czech market environment was being formed, as well as a period when VHS players were more widely available, we can assume that its failure is connected to the lack of preparation among Czech audiences and a lacking infrastructure in the art market. The situation did not change with the new millennium, and interest in buying and distributing art of the moving image remained virtually absent in Czechia. While the activities of private galleries brought about copious presentations of art of the moving image created by both Czech and international artists starting in the 1990s and increasing in intensity in the new millennium, they did not produce an immediate awareness of video collecting, the video market, or video distribution.[25]

Katherine Kastner, owner of the established hunt kastner gallery in Prague, uses her exhibition programme to directly draw attention

[24] Lucie Svobodová interviewed by Matěj Forejt, January 2022.

[25] Galerie Jiří Švestka, for instance, which has been active on the art market since 1995, prepared an exhibition of videos by the American artist Doug Aitken, and its portfolio has also included Michal Pěchouček, Jiří Černický, and Krištof Kintera, as well as Adéla Babanová after 2010. Babanová's film *Návrat do Adriaportu* [Return to Adriaport] (2012) was presented by the gallery at the LOOP 2013 moving image trade fair in Barcelona and at other events. In 2005, the American curator with Czech roots Katherine Kastner and the Canadian artist Camille Hunt established a private gallery, hunt kastner, whose portfolio includes moving image works by Eva Koťátková, Zbyněk Baladrán, Jan Šerých, Tomáš Vaněk, Daniel Pitín, and Josef Bolf. Since 2000, artists working with the moving image have also been represented by younger galleries such as Polansky Gallery (established in 2012), Lucie Drdova Gallery (since 2012) or Nevan Contempo (since 2014). The Sbírka Marek [Marek Collection] has maintained an uncommonly strong interest in the area of film, video, and new media (for the Czech context) since 2007. The collection was established by the Marek brothers in 2000 and today operates, quite uncommonly, in the form of a cooperative. The collection's focus is determined not only by its founders but also by their friends and cooperative members, such as film historian and curator Marika Kupková and her husband, visual artist Milan Houser. See Sbírka Marek – O sbírce [Marek Collection – On the Collection], accessed 29 Jan 2022, https://marekcollection.cz/cz/o-sbirce. As a representative of the cooperative board of Sbírka Marek, Marika Kupková also participated in round tables organised by Other Visions, see Pohyblivé obrazy a Jiné vize [Moving Images and Other Visions], accessed 1 Mar 2022, https://artycok.tv/29890/pohyblive-obrazy-2.

to the particularities of the purchasing, circulation, and technical provisions for art forms such as installations or sound art. The gallery hosted expert panels on the subject of maintenance of moving images on the boundaries of fine art and cinematography that were organised by the PAF festival in Olomouc and also included reflections on the contemporary practice of limited editions.[26] Their foundations lay in the experience with the international market, where attempts at video editions are conceived following the models of limited editions of photographs or prints. One subject to take a clear position against the limited-edition system in Czech institutional practice was the Gallery of Modern Art in Hradec Králové, which in 2019 became the first institution in the Czech Republic to establish a separate collection of art of the moving image. František Zachoval, the gallery's director, is an advocate of purchasing art of the moving image on the basis of exclusive licences, which he believes will boost the corresponding segment of the art market. This system, however, would ultimately lead to a practice of loans, reminiscent of the model of licensing monopolies well known from standard cinematic distribution.[27] Zachoval is practically solitary in his position in the context of local institutions with an interest in acquiring art of the moving image.[28]

Migration or Expansion?

Arising from similar premises as the work of Erika Balsom is that of German journalist and curator Lars Henrik Gass. However, having spent years as the director of the short film festival in Oberhausen,[29] one of the most important institutions for independent cinema in Europe, Gass does not consider the existence of the cinematic medium in the world of fine art at the level of theoretical or historical research, but focuses instead on critical journalism arising from his own professional experience. The most extensive formulation of his ideas to date was published in 2017 in the second, extended edition of *Film und Kunst nach dem Kino* [Film and Art After Cinema].[30] Similarly to Erika Balsom or others who have theorised the

[26] Pohyblivé obrazy a Jiné vize, [Moving Images and Other Visions], accessed 1 Mar 2022, https://artycok.tv/29890/pohyblive-obrazy-2.

[27] See Anežka Bartlová – Anna Remešová, "František Zachoval: Pohyblivý obraz se sbírá jen minimálně" [František Zachoval: Moving Image is Barely Collected], *Artalk*, 8 Mar 2021, accessed 28 Sep 2021, https://artalk.cz/2021/03/08/frantisek-zachoval-pohyblivy-obraz-se-sbira-jen-minimalne/.

[28] See Magdalena Juříková, "Vyjádření GHMP k akvizicím pohyblivého obrazu" [A Statement by Prague City Gallery on Acquisitions of Art of the Moving Image], *Artalk*, 10 Dec 2021, accessed 2 Mar 2022, https://artalk.cz/2021/12/10/vyjadreni-ghmp-k-akvizicim-pohybliveho-obrazu/.

[29] He has been part of the management of the Internationale Kurzfilmtage Oberhausen since 1997.

[30] Lars Henrik Gass, *Film und Kunst nach dem Kino* (Köln: Strzelecki Books, 2017). The book is also available in the author's English translation: Lars Henrik Gass, *Film and Art After Cinema* (Zagreb: Multimedijalni institut, 2019). In Czech, see my review, which serves as a partial foundation for this section: Matěj Forejt, "O kině po kině" [On Cinema After Cinema], *Iluminace* 30, no. 3 (2018), pp. 130–135.

relocation of film,[31] Gass too traces the reasons for the shift of the medium of film outside the cinema, its traditional arena, into various other areas – a move that he discusses in terms of *migration*.

On the one hand, Gass describes the technological developments thanks to which "video installations were then able to be shown not only on small monitors, but on large screens too, without the technical complexity and noise of film projection".[32] On the other hand, Gass also considers the dark side of advances in technology – today, rather than screening in a cinema, it "has already become more efficient to sell a film on DVD or release it on demand for smart TVs or on the internet".[33] Additionally, Gass posits the disappearance of the "liminal experience" "which entails certain collective obligations (punctuality, sitting still, keeping quiet, etc.)" as a crucial consequence of the *migration* of film outside the space of the cinema.[34] Under the influence of TV and the internet, he claims, films modify their forms of use and must be made with smaller and smaller players in mind.[35] As a proper cinephile, for whom the cinema represents an "Arcadian place",[36] he emphasises that "film is something else beyond the screen and collective perception".[37] Reading these reflections by Gass, which often critique the presentation of films in galleries, we must always keep in mind his connection to the cinephile tradition, which is rooted in classical cinema culture. In his essays, Gass adopts the position of a sworn (and highly authentic) advocate of this tradition, refusing to accept that film has become a standard medium in the art world.

However, it does not follow from this that Gass would be reluctant to draw critical attention to weak points in the exploitation of the medium of film in classical cinemas and at film festivals.[38] It is precisely in connection with one of these weak spots that he sees the source of other impulses for the filmic medium's move outside the confines of the cinema when he describes the contemporary system of film subsidies as dysfunctional, claiming that "in today's Europe, film funding [...] contradicts its

[31] For a fuller context, see also Francesco Casetti's reflections on the relocation of film. The processes described by Gass could also be considered as belonging to this phenomenon. Francesco Casetti, "The relocation of cinema", *Necsus* 1, no. 2 (2012), pp. 5–34. In Czech, see also: Malte Hagener, "Kde je (dnes) film? Film ve věku imanence médií" [Where is Film (Today)? Film in the Age of the Immanence of Media], *Iluminace* 23, no. 1 (2011), pp. 79–88.

[32] Gass, *Film und Kunst nach dem Kino*, p. 96.

[33] Ibid., pp. 21–22.

[34] Ibid., p. 28.

[35] Ibid., p. 27.

[36] Ibid., p. 54

[37] Ibid., p. 25.

[38] On the basis of this critique, he also proposes new forms of support for film, with a greater role for film festivals. See Lars Henrik Gass, "Vom Markt zur Marke" [From Marketplace to Brand], *Schnitt* 14, no. 2 (2009), p. 44. Cf. Gass, *Film und Kunst nach dem Kino*, [Film And Art After Cinema] p. 60.

historic mission".[39] On the other hand, "the art world promises filmmakers new attention and exclusivity, and is keeping its promises in part. Every short film in a large-scale exhibition today reaches a greater number of spectators and receives greater recognition there than it could ever attain in cinemas".[40] Gass also warns us of the price film must pay in order to exist in the art world. In the case of experimental film, whose makers are sometime discovered only after decades of working outside the art world, the adoption of film by the art world also demanded a new format for the medium, which "can sometimes have an almost exorcising effect on film history and the cultural practice of cinema, which is denied its standing as a fundamental technique and genuine mode of perception of film".[41] Although these films were not presented exclusively in classical cinemas, often shown at private salons or in temporary screening spaces, they were not, historically, presented in exhibition arrangements with several films being screened at once, often with their soundtracks overlapping – and where the visitor, to a considerable extent, determines the dynamics of their own experience.

Although the "elevation of film to an art form on the condition of its scarcity (limiting the number of copies and screenings) was gratefully accepted by many filmmakers, because this offered them the recognition, sometimes also financially, that the cinema had refused them so far",[42] Gass also draws attention to the fact that "exclusivity in the art scene [...] is a privilege awarded only to the happy few".[43] It is clear that the author conceives the fundamental problem of the *migration* of film into the art world as rooted in the different foundations of the public presentation and economic valuation of film and fine art. He then explores further the concept of "scarcity" mentioned above (Verknappung), which he posits as a cardinal principle for the art market. In opposition to it, he posits multiplication as a principle intrinsic to cinematography:

> films must be shown as often as possible under any circumstances in the film world to refinance themselves, while a film on the art market should be exhibited as little as possible under very specific conditions. [Any film must be screened in the cinema as often as possible in order to recoup costs.] The film's print has purely material value, not sentimental value. The art market, however, which still clings to the idea of the original, considers only a limited edition – exclusivity, a certain

[39] Gass, *Film and Art After Cinema*, p. 88.
[40] Ibid., pp. 89–90.
[41] Ibid., pp. 92–93.
[42] Ibid., p. 95.
[43] Ibid., p. 96.

inaccessibility, sometimes almost culminating in invisibility – as guaranteeing the value of a certain work.[44]

According to Gass, "[a]s a result, it is not just well-known paintings that sometimes disappear from the public view after auctions, but films too – for instance those of British artist Gillian Wearing, which are now rarely exhibited".[45] Gass calls such practices, with which the art market supposedly attempts to correct the fundamental tension between technically reproducible cinematic images and artworks based on the author's original, "reauratization" (doubtless in reference to Walter Benjamin's concept of the aura). Its dangers, he claims, lie in the fact that "this kind of 'reauratization' of works lies in losing an audience and the increased privatization of art, as it prioritizes the market value of a limited-edition object".[46]

Despite the delayed development of private collections in the Czech Republic, we can still trace similar "disappearances", such as in the case of pieces by Ján Mančuška. However, it would be unfair to speak only of private collections, as these "disappearances" also take place in the case of works acquired by public institutions – despite the fact that Gass's thesis on the privatisation of art is not valid in this particular case. Only a few Czech public galleries make acquisitions of art of the moving image[47] and these lack platforms for broadly available presentation. This is due to the fact that the operation of such platforms is technologically even more demanding than digitising and making available static media – and Czech museums are not doing particularly well in that regard, either.[48]

Although the articles and books by Erika Balsom and Lars Henrik Gass are among the most significant to be found in the theoretical literature and expert journalism on the topic, their thinking cannot automatically serve as a theoretical foundation for the reflection of the local history of the moving image in the Czech Republic. The application of Western European ideas and concepts on post-war Central European experimental film often fails – and this is no exception. Particularly in the field of post-war art history, there is a lively discussion on the need to perceive these two regions as belonging to two separate paradigms. This discussion has developed furthest in respect to the art of the former

[44] *This sentence is not included in the author's English translation and is here translated from the German original – translator's note.* Gass, *Film und Kunst nach dem Kino*, p. 96.

[45] Ibid., p. 125.

[46] Ibid., p. 126.

[47] Among the most important are the collections of photography and new media at the Prague City Gallery and the Moravian Gallery, the collection of art of the moving image at the Gallery of Modern Art in Hradec Králové, and the new media collection at the Vysočina Regional Gallery in Jihlava.

[48] See *Otevřené sbírky* [Open Collections], accessed 26 Sep 2021, http://www.otevrenesbirky.cz/.

German Democratic Republic and its acceptance into the narrative of reunited Germany after 1990.[49]

The central problem does not lie in the isolation and reclusiveness of the Central European scenes of experimental film and video. After all, a group of filmmakers from Łódź known as the Warsztat Formy Filmowej [Workshop of Cinematic Form] made an appearance at the documenta 6 exhibition in Kassel, West Germany as early as 1977.[50] The fundamental obstacle in applying theoretical frameworks created in the Western European environment is their starting point, which supposes the existence of an art market. Although even in Czechoslovakia, pioneering activities in the fields of video art, experimental film and video, and the cinematic underground are marked by their break with the official production of the film industry, we do not see here an escape of cinematic experimentalists into the waiting arms of private gallerists. And it also cannot be turned into a different, substitutive, generally valid rationale. For Czechoslovak artists of the 1970s and '80s, the motivations for working with experimental forms of the moving image aimed at presentation

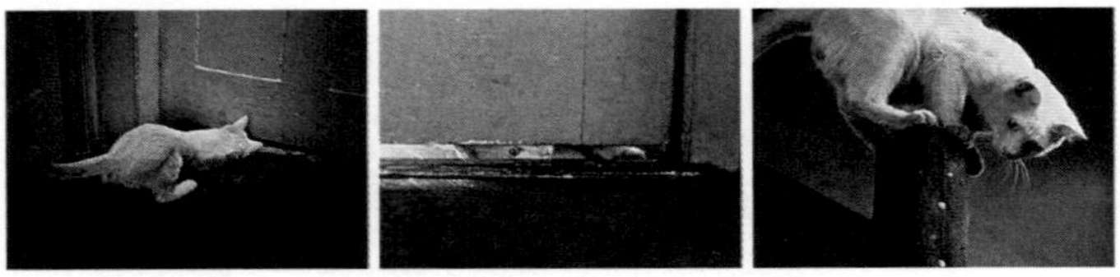

Alexander Hackenschmied, Maya Deren *Private Life of a Cat* (1944), film, 22 min

outside official film distribution were not necessarily inspired by the need to produce part of their output outside the dramaturgical oversight of the state cinematographic institutions, as we can identify in the case of the Czech video art pioneer Petr Skala.[51] Also important here is the access to

[49] In Czech, see Joachim Fischer – Dana Giesecke, "Umění distinkce a umění inkluze – K sociologii umělecké komunikace v SRN a v NDR" [The Art of Distinction and the Art of Inclusion – On the Sociology of Artistic Communication in the FRG and the GDR], in *Umění z NDR. Dědictví na obtíž?* [Art from the GDR. A Heritage – A Burden?], ed. Matěj Forejt (Prague: Galerie Rudolfinum, 2021). Cf. Tomáš Pospiszyl, "Úkoly pro dějiny umění východní Evropy doby socialismu" [Tasks for the Art History of Eastern Europe Under Socialism], *Sešit pro umění, teorii a příbuzné zóny* 13, no. 27 (2019), pp. 17–24.

[50] For the general context of cultural relationships between East and West, it is worth mentioning that this was the year when East Germany was first invited to participate in documenta with its own official contribution. For more on this topic, see Kathleen Rosenthal, "'DDR-Stars' in Kassel – The GDR's Official Contribution to documenta 6", in *Umění z NDR. Dědictví na obtíž?*, ed. Matěj Forejt (Prague: Galerie Rudolfinum, 2021), pp. 92–96. Birgit Hein, quoted above, an important figure in West German experimental film, also participated in the preparations for the experimental film section at documenta 6. See *documenta 6 – Band 2: Fotografie, Film, Video* [documenta 6 – Volume 2: Photography, Film, Video] (exhibition catalogue, Kassel: Paul Dierichs KG & Co., 1977).

[51] See Jan Křipač, "Petr Skala", Filmový přehled [Film Overview], accessed 24 Jul 2021, https://www.filmovyprehled.cz/cs/revue/detail/petr-skala.

film and video equipment via the Czechoslovak cine-amateur movement.[52] In the form it took at the time, this movement can be considered regionally specific, and it played an important role – among others – in the work of Ivan Tatíček.[53]

Likewise, the beginning of the 1990s and the end of the state monopoly on cinematography in Czechoslovakia was not an essential breaking point. Although Erika Balsom emphasises the 1990s as the moment when the weight of experimental film shifted towards the practice of limited editions and private and public collections, the Czech environment lacked the necessary institutional infrastructure, as we saw with the example of Lucie Svobodová's VHS tape edition. Furthermore, the gradually developing Czech art market was (and still is) considerably conservative in its choice of media, with art of the moving image still existing at the margins of interest.[54] This media conservatism of the Czech collecting world was also manifested into the modern canon of post-war Czech art, the form of which was considerably influenced by the activities and collecting preferences of Jan Mládek and Meda Mládková.[55] Although we have evidence that their circle of friends and occasional visitors during their period of exile in Washington DC included filmmakers, the collection of the Mládeks was focused on traditional media that do not arouse any doubts regarding the aura of originality.[56] A greater interest in work made outside the borders of traditional artistic media can be observed in the

[52] The cinematic work of amateurs is traditionally connected to what's known as narrow film formats. In Czechoslovakia, this history reaches back to 1932, when Čeněk Zahradníček, whom we have already mentioned, became an important figure in the cine-amateur movement. In the second half of the 20th century, socialist Czechoslovakia boasted a lively and active cine-amateur scene, composed of several regional amateur film-maker clubs, who organised their members' access to cinematic equipment. At the time, several cine-amateur competitions and festivals existed in Czechoslovakia, and specialised magazines and books for cine-amateurs were published. Even though the amateur cinema film scene changed after 1989 in connection with the onset of digital technologies, some specialised festivals and competitions still exist.

[53] See Martin Blažíček – Sylva Poláková, "Ivan Tatíček – od amatérského filmu k profesionální videotvorbě" [Ivan Tatíček – From Amateur Film to Professional Video Art], *Iluminace* 32, no. 1 (2020), pp. 77–92.

[54] Also telling is the fact that the yearly *Art+* survey, which presents a summary of activities on the Czech art market, has so far devoted virtually no attention to the market for art of the moving image. Although the moving image does not, of course, play a dominant role on art markets abroad, the situation on the Czech market is even less advantageous, as the Czech market is more distinctively focused on old art and interwar art.

[55] Jan Mládek and Meda Mládková turned their family homes in Washington, DC into a centre for meetings of the Czech cultural elite in exile, situating artworks they bought from Czechoslovak and other Central European artists directly in their living quarters. After 1989, the existence of such an extensive collection of non-official art certainly contributed to unofficial art production becoming the central pillar of the new artistic canon. For more on this topic, see Pavel Liška – Robin R. Mudry, *MEDA Ambassador of Art* (exhibition catalogue, Prague: Museum Kampa, 2019).

[56] The relationship of the Mládeks to the medium of film is aptly demonstrated by the discovery of a film reel of *The Private Life of a Cat*, a 1944 film by Alexander Hackenschmied and Maya Deren. I witnessed this discovery in 2019, when I participated – as a representative of the NFA – on preparations for the *MEDA – Ambasadorka umění* exhibition at Museum Kampa. Unlike the artworks presented to the public at exhibitions, this film reel – perhaps given to the Mládeks by Hackenschmied directly – remained in a box with old home movies during Meda Mládková's move from Washington to Prague, where it lay unnoticed until 2019. Its owners clearly did not consider it part of their art collection – rather, it was a curiosity from the family archives.

activities of Polish collector and champion of Czech art Janina Ojrzyńska, who is not as well known in the Czech Republic as the Mládeks, although her activities form an interesting parallel to theirs. Yet not even Ojrzyńska included the moving image as a medium in her exhibitions of Czechoslovak art, instead using it (as far as we can tell from the information available) mostly as illustrative material, particularly when, as early as 1974, she included a 1971 documentary film by Josef and Jaroslav Kořán, *Černobílé kontrapunkty* [Black and White Counterpoints], in her exhibitions of Milan Grygar's pieces.[57]

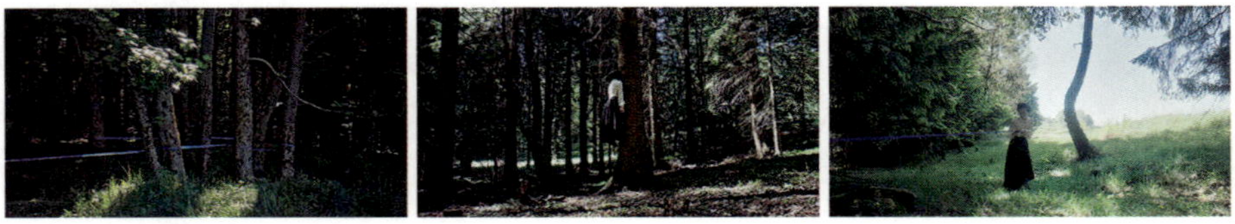

Mark Ther *Mitsu* (2019), video, 14 min

The absence of an art market, or rather its delayed establishment and continuing conservative focus ultimately do not complicate the adoption of Western European concepts as a theoretical framework for events taking place in the second half of the 20th century (either before the year 1989 or after). Different histories of the art world in (post)socialist countries and different dynamics operating between the art world and cinema at the time ultimately also led to different institutional foundations of today's experimental film and art of the moving image scenes. If, therefore, Lars Henrik Gass calls for more efficient support of short and experimental films in order to prevent a situation whereby experimental film and its creators would adapt to the art world, the present situation in the Czech Republic can be described as precisely the opposite. The transparent subsidy policy of the Státní fond kinematografie [Czech Film Fund], which, since 2014, has also supported the production of short experimental films, brings artists into areas of the film industry that might already have years of experience working with the moving image, but have primarily operated within the art world, presenting their works in galleries. The first results of this strategy of cinematic support were *Jako z filmu* [Like in a Film] by Tomáš Svoboda (2017), *Neptun* by Adéla Babanová (2018),[58] and *Mitsu* by Mark Ther (2019). All these films demonstrate that support for films can, through the availability of more professional equipment, influence stylistic

[57] Pavla Rousková, "Sbírka Janiny Ojrzyńské – náhradní institucionální rámec českého umění v období sedmdesátých a osmdesátých let 20. století" [The Collection of Janina Ojrzyńska – A Surrogate Institutional Framework for Czech Art of the 1970s and '80s] (diploma thesis, Prague: Academy of Art, Architecture and Design, 2019), pp. 25–28. Other film recordings of Grygar's events were then made in the 1980s. For more on this topic, see Sylva Poláková's essay in this volume.

[58] For more on Adéla Babanová's work on the borders between the film industry and the art world, see Matěj Forejt, "Možná že se nic z toho nikdy nestalo – rozhovor s Adélou Babanovou" [Perhaps None of it Ever Happened – An Interview with Adéla Babanová], *ART ANTIQUES* 18, no. 10 (2019), pp. 52–64.

changes in the style of an artist, whilst also broadening the possibilities of these new works for presentation outside the art world – at cinemas and film festivals. Instead of the *migration* Gass criticises, then, what we are seeing in the Czech Republic is more akin to an *expansion*.

Terminological Maturation. The Construct of the Moving Image and Its Resonance in Czech Artistic Periodicals

Eva Krátká

The term "moving image" only became fully established in the Czech context with the publication of a translation of a key chapter from a book by the American film theorist Noël Carroll. Using a reference to a common cinematic term, he explained why the construct he put forward could be of help when classifying an important component of many artworks whilst also disrupting or even denying the specificity of the medium to which it is tied.[59] This line of thought, casting doubt on previous claims that every art form has a specific medium that corresponds to it, was published in Czech in 2001, five years after it first came out in English in *Iluminace: Journal for Film Theory, History, and Aesthetics*, which was established at the very end of the 1980s and currently serves as the central platform of Czech film studies.[60] The term "moving image" has since undergone several academic revisions and is only slowly making its way to greater popularity in Czechia. This has less to do with its excessively "general denotation" than with its general "underuse".[61] The position expressed by one of the co-authors of this publication, art theorist and historian Tomáš Pospiszyl, therefore seems characteristic (and also cynical): "No one has come up with a term so far that would fit all of it".[62]

The paradox of this terminological construct, which is accepted – as we will see below – in expert circles but often bypassed in common practice, "allows for borderline works on the boundaries of film, visual art, and other visual forms to become free of constricting, established terms such as film or video that are derived from specific media"[63] and thus mediates the possibility of tracing through the following sample of textual "narratives" which contribute to the Czech framework of conceptualising art

[59] The text was published as the fourth chapter of Noël Carroll, *Theorizing the Moving Image* (Cambridge – New York – Oakleigh: Cambridge University Press, 1996), in Czech, see Noël Carroll, "Definování pohyblivého obrazu" [Defining the Moving Image], *Iluminace* 13, no. 2 (2001), pp. 5–32; see also Sylva Poláková – Martin Mazanec, "Editoriál" [Editorial], in *Katalog událostí českého pohyblivého obrazu Jiné vize 2000–2010, II.* [Catalogue of the Events of the Czech Moving Image Other Visions 2000–2010, II], eds. Martin Blažíček – Alexandr Jančík – Martin Mazanec – Sylva Poláková (Olomouc: PAF Edition, 2011), pp. 9–11; Ray Privett – James Kreul, "Podivný případ Noëla Carrolla. Rozhovor s kontroverzním filosofem filmu" [The Strange Case of Noël Carroll], *Iluminace* 14, no. 1 (2002), pp. 89–113, especially pp. 105–106.

[60] Ivan Klimeš, "Filmová studia v předsálí svých zdejších dějin" [Film Studies in the Antechamber of their Local History], *Slovo a smysl* [Word & Sense] 17, no. 35 (2020), pp. 139–147, on the magazine, see especially pp. 144–147, accessed 2 Apr 2022, https://wordandsense.ff.cuni.cz/wp-content/uploads/sites/18/2021/02/Ivan_Klimes_139-147.pdf or https://www.iluminace.cz/index.php/cz/about-iluminace.

[61] Sylva Poláková, "'Současný český videoart' jako výzva filmovým studiím" ["Contemporary Czech Video Art" as a Challenge to Film Studies], in *Současný český a slovenský film – pluralita estetických, kulturních a ideových konceptů* [Contemporary Czech and Slovak Film – A Plurality of Aesthetic, Cultural, and Ideological Concepts], ed. Luboš Ptáček (Olomouc: Palacký University, 2010), pp. 111–125, especially p. 123.

[62] Pavlína Míčová, "Balet, nebo tancovačka? S Tomášem Pospiszylem o blízkých setkáních a vizuálním umění" [Ballet or a Village Dance? An Interview with Tomáš Pospiszyl on Close Encounters and Visual Art], A2 5, no. 6 (2009), p. 24.

[63] From an interview with Lenka Střeláková and Viktor Takáč on the exhibition *Jiné vize CZ* (2007–2015) [Other Visions CZ (2007–2015)] (Galerie AMU, Prague, 2016). Kateřina Nechvílová, "O jiných vizích pohyblivého obrazu, Lenka Střeláková a Viktor Takáč" [On the Other Visions of the Moving Image, Lenka Střeláková and Viktor Takáč], *Literární noviny* [Literary Newspaper] 27, no. 8 (2016), pp. 4–5, accessed 2 Apr 2022, https://artycok.tv/29890/pohyblive-obrazy-2. See also Martin Mazanec, *Pohyblivý obraz filmu a videa 1. Studijní text pro kombinované studium* [The Moving Image of Film and Video, 1st Text for Combined Course of Study] (Olomouc: Palacký University, 2014).

of the moving image in the past twenty years. What follows is an attempt to map this diverse field[64] using both primary and secondary textual sources from a corpus of Czech (and occasionally Slovak) periodical media focused on art (primarily printed, later also electronic), which are aimed at either purely academic[65] or otherwise narrowly defined audiences,[66] or at a broader group of readers that nevertheless share a set of related interests.[67] The selection of texts I mention most often relate to an artistic lineage in a discipline rooted in the technologies of analogue or digital video, whose artistic and aesthetic activity are thus closely connected with the opening and gradual maturation of the Czech discourse of the moving image in the last two decades.

From Technologies to Terminology

Reading through periodicals published over time, we learn that the entry of this topic into public media that are focused on visual art did not progress in a systematic fashion, but rather developed by degrees. We could say that this progression corresponds – to some extent – with the well-known concept of paradigm shift, which posits that periods of normal science alternate with profound change in research by the introduction of a new theory.[68] In our case, this process was significantly influenced by what artist, theorist, curator, and media archaeologist Miloš Vojtěchovský aptly

[64] Compare the Public Database of Periodicals, content section – radio and film magazines, accessed 2 Apr 2022, https://www.mkcr.cz/databaze-periodickeho-tisku-pro-verejnost-978.htmll#seznam. Surveys of period film studies and film magazines are part of an introductory note to a publication on Czech live action film, see "Úvodní poznámka, České a slovenské filmové časopisy" [Introductory Note, Czech and Slovak Film Magazines] in Eva Urbanová et al., *Český hraný film VI, 1981–1993* [Czech Live Action Film VI, 1981–1993] (Prague: Národní filmový archiv, 2010), p. 13. See also (mšt), the entry "Kritika filmová a televizní" [Film and TV Criticism] in *Slovník žurnalistiky* [A Dictionary of Journalism], eds. Jan Halada – Barbora Osvaldová (Prague: Karolinum, 2017), pp. 133–135; Radomír D. Kokeš, "Stav filmových časopisů v Česku a na Slovensku" [The State of Film Magazines in the Czech Republic and Slovakia], *Pandora* 8, no. 20 (2010), pp. 199–203; Briana Čechová, "*Kino-Ikon* č. 2/1999 – *Iluminace* č. 3/1999" [Kino-Ikon no. 2/1999 – Iluminace no. 3/1999], *Literární noviny* 11, no. 4 (2000), p. 13.

[65] The Czech periodicals that could be described as academic are *Iluminace* and *Sešit pro umění, teorii a příbuzné zóny* [Notebook for Art, Theory, and Related Zones], whose articles are characterised by terminological precision and undergo peer review before publication.

[66] Meaning visually oriented magazines, such as: *Ateliér* [Studio], *Cinepur*, *25fps.cz*, *Film a doba* [Film and Our Times], *Flash Art* Czech & Slovak Edition, *Fotograf*, *Kino-Ikon: časopis pre vedu o filme a "pohyblivom obraze"* [Kino-Ikon: a journal for the sciences of the moving image and cinema], *Labyrint revue*, *PROFIL* súčasného výtvarného umenia [PROFILE Contemporary Art Magazine], *Prostor Zlín* [Space Zlín], *3/4 Revue*, *Umělec* [Artist], *Výtvarné umění* [Magazine for Contemporary Art], and others.

[67] This primarily refers to culturally critical periodicals and reviews such as *A2*, *Literární noviny* [Literary Newspaper], the *Nový Prostor* [New Space] magazine *(a Czech street paper analogous to The Big Issue in the UK or Street News in New York City – translator's note)*, and some cultural sections in general publications, such as the weekly *Respekt* [Respect], or – exceptionally – the cultural sections of some dailies such as *Hospodářské noviny* [The Economic Newspaper], *Lidové noviny* [The People's Newspaper], and the like.

[68] Thomas S. Kuhn, *The Structure of Scientific Revolutions* (Chicago: University of Chicago Press, 1996).

called our "relative isolation and targeting of our own diaspora",[69] which led to an extended stagnation that took the form of a community project. More than thirty years have passed since we needed to quickly find our way within a flood of confusing terms that aimed to defend new technologies. In the 1990s, the media philosopher of Czech origin Vilém Flusser became one of the most influential theorists on the Czech scene, having recognised the revolutionary power of the technical image in comparison with the traditional image, and the illusions that film can therefore achieve.[70] Even so, reflections on the moving image played a subservient if not negligible role in his own writing.[71] In addition to the historically perceived hybrid-intermedia framework, which film historian Petr Szczepanik later ascribed to him,[72] Flusser's new media framework always provided the narrowest relational field in which to acquire more detailed knowledge about the nature of technical perspectives on the image.[73] Radek Pilař, pioneer and promoter of video art, described it emotionally as "so immaterial and so trustworthy, so liberated and so enslaved, the image in motion, fragile and strong, existent and non-existent [...]. We can enter into it, be inside it, move in the image, we can ourselves become the image, composed of points of light" [74]. His text "Viva video, video viva", which contains this quote, has been reprinted several times in various magazines after it was first published in 1992 and is today considered an artistic manifesto.[75] The referential framework of

[69] Miloš Vojtěchovský, "Poznámky k současnému českému videoartu" [Notes on Contemporary Czech Video Art], *Film a doba* 52, no. 2 (2007), pp. 95–99, here p. 99.

[70] Flusser's essential essay "Moc obrazu" [The Power of the Image] was published in a selection of his philosophical texts from the 1980s and '90s. See Milena Slavická – Jiří Fiala, eds., *Výtvarné umění, čtvrtletník pro současné umění* [Fine Art, Quarterly for Contemporary Art] 20, no. 3/4 (1996), pp. 131–138.

[71] Nevertheless, Flusser repeatedly stated that film is a contemporary artistic medium in the true sense of the word; see also Vilém Flusser, *Komunikológia* [Communicology] (Bratislava: Media Institute, 2002), especially chapter 3, "Co sú technické obrazy?" [What Are Technical Images?] (pp. 120–164), with sections on film (p. 132), video, (p. 137), television, (p. 140) and the cinema (p. 143).

[72] A new perspective on the intermediality of video art as "a media hybrid or intermedia *par excellence*" is explicated by Petr Szczepanik in "Intermedialita. Pojem" [Intermediality. The Term], *Cinepur* 11, no. 22 (2002), p. 56, accessed 2 Apr 2022, http://cinepur.cz/article.php?article=5. See also Petr Szczepanik, "Keiko Sei rozhovor" [An Interview with Keiko Sei], *Cinepur* 11, no. 23/24 (2002), pp. 16–19; Petr Szczepanik – Jakub Kučera, "Rozhovor s Davidem Normanem Rodowickem" [An Interview with David Norman Rodowick], *Iluminace* 15, no. 2 (2003), p. 94; Petr Szczepanik, *Nová filmová historie. Antologie současného myšlení o dějinách kinematografie a audiovizuální kultury* [New Film History. An Anthology of Contemporary Thought on the History of Cinematography and Audiovisual Culture] (Prague: Herrmann & synové, 2004).

[73] See Miloš Vojtěchovský, "Předpoklady budoucnosti: Mediální archeologie. Archeologie a budoucnost pohyblivého obrazu (de-archivace paměťových složek)" [Assumptions of the Future: Media Archaeology. The Archaeology and the Future of the Moving Image (De-archiving Memory Components)], accessed 2 Apr 2022, https://agosto-foundation.org/cs/predpoklady-budoucnosti-medialni-archeologie.

[74] See Radek Pilař, "Viva video, video viva", in *České umění 1980–2010, texty a dokumenty* [Czech Art 1980–2010, Texts and Documents], eds. Jiří Ševčík – Pavlína Morganová – Terezie Nekvindová – Dagmar Svatošová (Prague: VVP AVU, 2011), pp. 495–497, here p. 495.

[75] Ibid., p. 494.

this newly developed art which is based on the dematerialised reality of technology was also confirmed in a topical issue of the contemporary art journal *Ateliér* [Studio][76] that was published in 1995 on the occasion of the first Czech exhibition to contextualise technological developments in art – Orbis Fictus (National Gallery, Wallenstein Riding School, Prague, 1995).[77] This moment, however, also marked the start of a temporary pause in scholarly articles focusing on video art as such. The dire situation regarding the conceptualisation[78] and description[79] of video art – not to mention its long-term storage and maintenance[80] – continued. It developed into an uncommonly overripe inertia in how we use the term "video art" (or "video"), which has served remarkably well as a generalising *pars pro toto*. This state, however, also presaged a necessary turning point in the process of revising the nomenclature.

[76] Thematic articles in *Ateliér* 8, no. 26 (1995): Blanka Jiráčková, "Videoart" [Video Art], p. 2; Michael Bielický, "Nová média nebo Dematerializace umění" [New Media or the Dematerialisation of Art], p. 2; Vlasta Čiháková-Noshiro, "Virtuální realita – od malby po video" [Virtual Reality – From Painting to Video], p. 4; Jaroslav Vančát, "Úvahy nad (českým) obrazem elektronickým" [Reflections on the (Czech) Electronic Image], p. 5; Jana Tichá, "Rozhovor s Jiřím Příhodou" [An Interview with Jiří Příhoda], p. 5; Jaroslav Pavelka, "K dějinám českého videoartu" [On the History of Czech Video Art], p. 6; Jana Tichá, "Rozhovor s Petrem Skalou" [An Interview with Petr Skala], p. 6; Radek Horáček, "Brno na cestě k video a elektronickým médiím" [Brno on the Way to Video and Electronic Media], p. 12; "Orbis Fictus", p. 16. Compare the section "Technický obraz" [The Technical Image], in *České umění 1980–2010*, pp. 463–548.

[77] Ludvík Hlaváček – Marta Smolíková, eds., *Orbis Fictus: nová média v současném umění* [Orbis Fictus: New Media in Contemporary Art] (Prague: Sorosovo centrum současného umění, 1995).

[78] Jakub Effenberger, "Vandám, vandáš, vandáme aneb osamělý dav před bednou" [Vandamming, or the Lonely Crowd in Front of the Box], *Film a doba* 40, no. 3 (1994), pp. 148–151.

[79] As early as 1989, Jaroslav Vančát predicted that assessing video art would be difficult without the establishment of "specific categories that would capture not only the emerging specificities of video art, but that could 'help us attain the deeper shared regularities of the visual aspect of all the media concerned'". Jaroslav Vančát, "Video a výtvarná tvorba" [Video and Visual Art], *Film a doba* 35, no. 12 (1989), pp. 708–709; see also Eva Strusková, "O pořádání žánrového názvosloví" [On the Arrangement of Genre Terminology], *Film a doba* 36, no. 12 (1990), p. 719.

[80] E.g., Martin Blažíček, "Trable s Rumcajsem aneb co počít s českým videoartem 90. let" [Troubles with Rumcajs, or, What to Do with Czech '90s Video Art], *Cinepur* 20, no. 86 (2013), pp. 12–13.

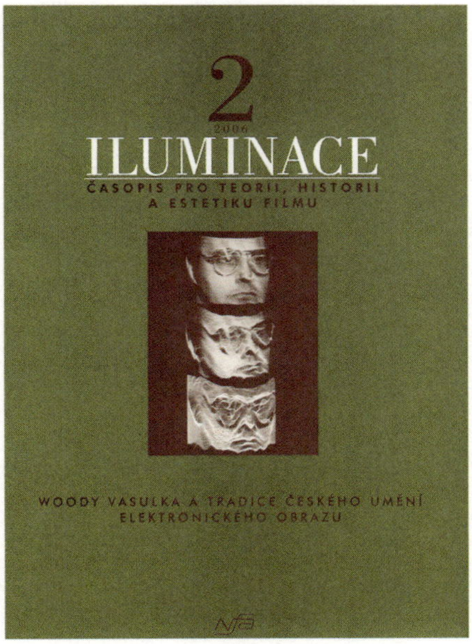

Covers of the thematic issues of the Iluminace journal.

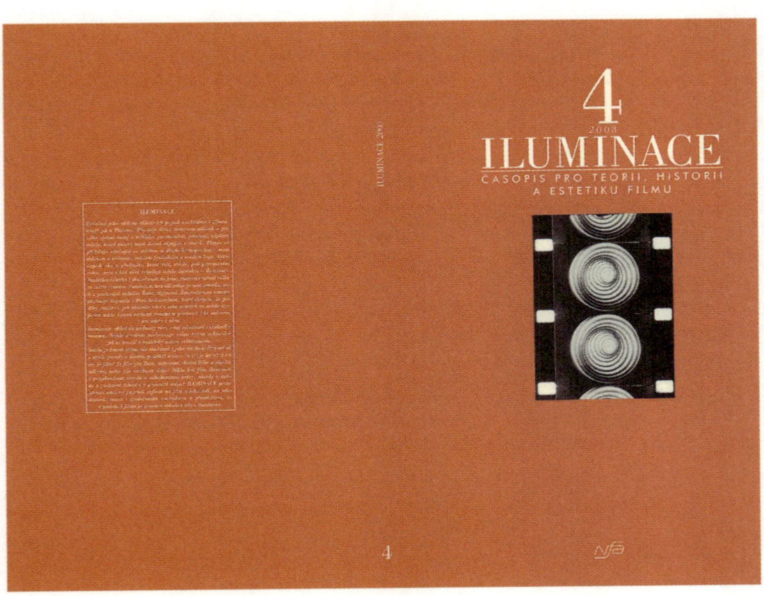

The Moving Image as Heterogeneous Practice

Despite the ongoing scholarly interest in the tradition of artistic styles and forms in the categories of experimental,[81] amateur,[82] or short film[83] and animation,[84] it was only between 2002 and 2008 that stimulating historical-theoretical essays began appearing in academic journals that opened up the themes arising from the heterogeneous character of the moving image to other layers of examination. These include studies by the theorists mentioned above – Petr Szczepanik[85] and Miloš Vojtěchovský[86] – and art historian Lenka Dolanová. One of her first academic papers titled "The Entry of 'Moving Images' into the Gallery",[87] in which she referenced not only fine art but also the history and theory of film and media, mostly focused on video installations from the 1960s and '70s, but in it the author also managed to update the case for dealing with the particular "intermedia paradigm"[88] that brought about the material and virtual fusion of contemporary art disciplines and experiences.

However, the topic that Dolanová identifies – the exhibition and presentation of art of the moving image in the context of fine art[89] – would only be further explored by other Czech critics with greater focus a few years later. Dolanová was also a long-term collaborator of Woody

[81] The categories of experimental film were discussed, for instance, in thematic issues of *Iluminace* 11, no. 2 (1999) (Nepředmětnost obrazu [The Immateriality of the Image]) and no. 3 (1999) (Strukturální film [Structural Film]); in the thematic issue titled "Současný český experimentální film" [Contemporary Czech Experimental Film], in *Cinepur* 10, no. 17 (2001), Helena Bendová presented an overview of the essential features of experimental film (pp. 18–19), "Obsah" [Contents], accessed 2 Apr 2022, http://cinepur.cz/list.php?issue=16&view_all=1; see also Martin Blažíček, "Spontánní film" [Spontaneous Film], *Cinepur* 14, no. 46 (2006), pp. 32–33.

[82] See *Iluminace* 16, no. 3 (2004) or *Iluminace* 28, no. 2 (2016).

[83] E.g., Čestmír Lang, "Krátký film jako intenzivní forma komunikace" [Short Films as a Concentrated Form of Communication], *Film a doba* 51, no. 4 (2005), pp. 194–198.

[84] E.g., the thematic issues of *Film a doba* 39, no. 3 (1993); *Cinepur* 12, no. 27 (2003); Jiří Pavlovský, "Comics ve filmu" [Comics in Films], *Živel* 8, no. 20 (2002), pp. 52–57; *Iluminace* 21, no. 4 (2009), theme: Současné myšlení o animovaném filmu [Contemporary Ideas on Animated Film]; or *Kino-Ikon*, 19, no. 2 (2015).

[85] See "doc. Mgr. Petr Szczepanik, Ph.D.", accessed 2 Apr 2022, https://kfs.ff.cuni.cz/cs/katedra/pedagogove/doc-mgr-petr-szczepanik-ph-d/ and footnote 15.

[86] In addition to his numerous contributions to *Umělec* or the *A2* cultural bi-weekly, see also Miloš Vojtěchovský's "Umění a elektronické technologie" [Art and Electronic Technologies], in *Dějiny umění 12* [The History of Art 12], ed. Lenka Bydžovská (Prague: Balios – Knižní klub – Euromedia Group, 2002), pp. 255–281.

[87] Lenka Dolanová, "Vstup 'pohyblivých obrazů' do galerie" [The Entry of "Moving Images" into the Gallery], *Iluminace* 15, no. 4 (2003), pp. 85–99.

[88] Ibid., p. 89.

[89] The author also returned to this topic in another text: Lenka Dolanová, "Video na výstavě, nebo v Multikině? Cinepur Choice dělá průřez světovým videem" [Videos in Galleries or at Multiplexes? Cinepur Choice Presents a Global Survey of Video], *A2* 4, no. 49 (2008), p. 11.

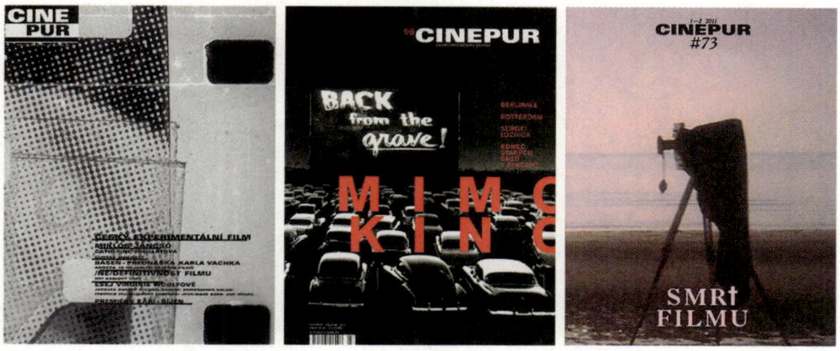

Covers of the thematic issues of Cinepur magazine.

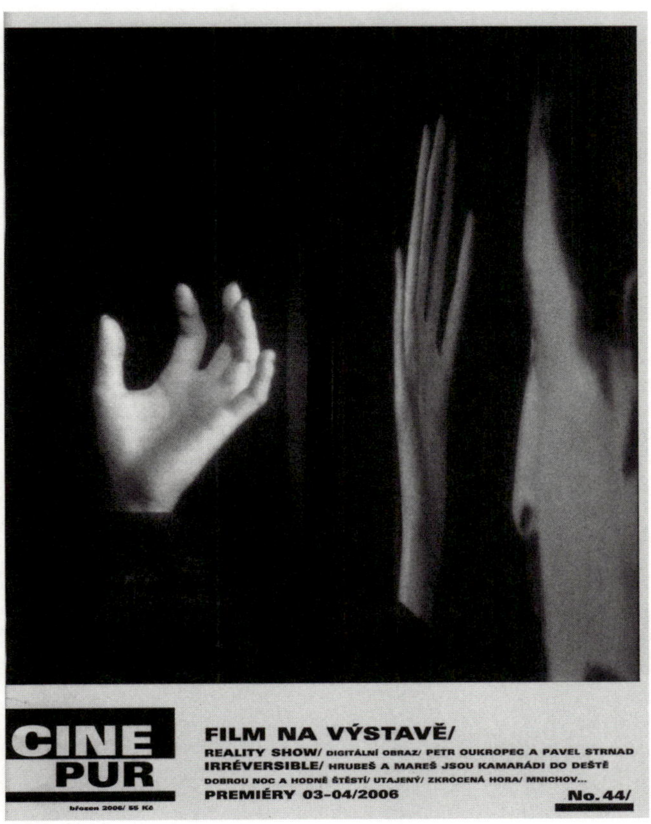

and Steina Vasulka[90] and she assessed their essential importance for the formation of art of the moving image (particularly video art), both internationally and in the Czech Republic, in several publications.[91] With her selection of translated essays and original Czech research texts collected in a special 2006 issue of *Iluminace*,[92] she wanted in part to confront the "somewhat unconvinced" responses (which she mentions in her editorial) "with which the art of this creative duo (and electronic art in general) is accepted".[93]

Following these initial studies, the topic of the bilateral interpenetration between fine art and film practice and theory as mediated by the moving image slowly began filling the pages of other, less academically focused periodicals. This was a necessary reaction to the fact that opportunities to encounter this process were multiplying.[94] Within the tradition of

[90] Similarly, Bohdana Kerbachová devoted her attention to Petr Skala or Radek Pilař, see Bohdana Kerbachová, "Experimentální filmy Petra Skaly ve sbírkách NFA" [Petr Skala's Experimental Films in the NFA Collection], *Iluminace* 26, no. 3 (2014), pp. 103–109; Bohdana Kerbachová, *Alchymie světla. Experimentální tvorba Petra Skaly* [Alchemy of Light. The Experimental Art of Petr Skala] (Písek: Prácheňské muzeum v Písku – Nakladatelství Vltavín, 2017); Josef Brukner – Bohdana Kerbachová – Jan Kříž – Jiří Kubíček – Radek Pilař – Blanka Stehlíková – Jaroslav Šedivý, *Radek Pilař: obrazy, ilustrace, animovaný film, video* [Radek Pilař: Paintings, Illustrations, Animated Films, Videos] (Prague: Slovart, 2003).

[91] See Lenka Dolanová, *Dialog s démony nástrojů* [A Dialogue With the Demons of Tools] (Prague: NAMU – Jihlava: JSAF, 2011); Miloš Vojtěchovský, ed., *Vašulkova kuchyňská kniha #1, texty k médiím: první & poslední* [Vasulka Kitchen Cooking Reader #1 Texts Beyond Media: First & Last] (Brno: Vašulka Kitchen Brno, 2020); Lenka Dolanová, *A Dialogue with the Demons of the Tools: Steina and Woody Vašulka* (Brno: Vašulka Kitchen Brno, 2022).

[92] "Woody Vasulka a tradice českeho uměni elektronickeho obrazu" [Woody Vasulka and the Tradition of Czech Art of the Electronic Image] (guest editor Lenka Dolanová), *Iluminace* 18, no. 2 (2006). The issue also included a DVD, *Virtuální houbaření* [Virtual Mushroom Hunting]. Contents of the issue: Lenka Dolanová – Woody Vasulka, "Editorial", 5–8; Gerald O'Grady, "Sférické poznání Woodyho Vasulky. Od dírkové kamery k otvorům v pinballu" [The Spherical Knowledge of Woody Vasulka. From the Pinhole Camera to Pinball Apertures], pp. 9–30; John Minkowsky, "Několik poznámek k videu Vasulkových v letech 1973–1974" [Several Notes on Videos by the Vasulkas 1973–1974], pp. 31–39; Peter Weibel, "Vládci kódů" [Rulers of Code], pp. 41–47; Maureen Turim – Scott Nygren, "Číst nástroje, psát obraz" [Reading Tools, Writing the Image], pp. 49–70; Yvonne Spielmann, "Video a počítač. Estetika Steiny a Woodyho Vasulkových" [Videos and Computers. The Aesthetics of Steina and Woody Vasulka], pp. 71–86; Vít Janeček, "A my jsme byli modernisti. Moravské a české počátky Woodyho Vasulky" [And We Were Modernists. The Moravian and Bohemian Beginnings of Woody Vasulka], pp. 87–101; Lenka Dolanová, "Co to tam vařili? Kuchaři, jejich Kitchen a chuť čerstvého videa" [What Were They Cooking? Cooks, Their Kitchen, and the Taste of Fresh Video], pp. 103–131; Bohdana Kerbachová, "Počátky českého videoartu" [The Beginnings of Czech Video Art], pp. 133–157; "Rozhovor. Woody Vasulka – Charles Hagen: Syntax binárních obrazů" [Interview. Woody Vasulka – Charles Hagen: The Syntax of Binary Images], pp. 159–178; Erkki Huhtamo, "Rozhovor s Woodym Vasulkou. Druhého března 1998, v jeho ateliéru v Santa Fe v Novém Mexiku" [Interview with Woody Vasulka. March 2nd 1998 in his studio in Santa Fe, New Mexice], pp. 179–188; Bohdana Kerbachová, "První schůzky naplňovalo snění. Rozhovor s Petrem Skalou" [The First Meetings Were Filled With Dreams], pp. 189–198; "Edice a materiály: Woody Vasulka, Technocentrický determinismus" [Editions and Materials: Woody Vasulka, Technocratic Determinism], pp. 199–203; Woody Vasulka, "Divadlo hybridních automatů" [The Theatre of Hybrid Automatons], pp. 205–208; Woody Vasulka,, "The Commission", pp. 209–216; "Projekty: Lenka Dolanová, Aspekty elektronické avantgardy: Steina a Woody Vasulkovi" [Projects: Lenka Dolanová, Aspects of the Electronic Avant-garde: Steina and Woody Vasulka], pp. 217–218.

[93] Dolanová – Vasulka, "Editorial", pp. 5–8, here p. 5.

[94] See e.g., Martin Blažíček – Alexandr Jančík – Martin Mazanec – Sylva Poláková, eds., *Katalog událostí českého pohyblivého obrazu. Jiné vize 2000–2010, I–II.* [Catalogue of the Events of the Czech Moving Image, Other Visions 2000–2010, II] (Olomouc: PAF Edition, 2011), cf. Poláková, "'Současný český videoart' jako výzva filmovým studiím", pp. 119–121.

"expanded cinema",[95] the moving image, situated at the borders between fine art, film, and performance, slowly began gaining importance in galleries both in Czechia and abroad,[96] as well as in public spaces. The growing number of pieces created by artists with a background in both the film and fine art communities (with varying degrees of experience and working in different technical conditions) forced both exhibition curators and film festival dramaturgs to confront this new phenomenon. Audiovisual works were everywhere:[97] spectators watched them on projection screens, digital screens, in cinemas or its gallery variation known as a blackbox, in clubs, on the street, or anywhere on the internet... The moving image even went camping for the first time![98]

This media relocation[99] caused a terminological "schism"[100] in the community of researchers, a schism that had to be dealt with. The

[95] See e.g., Martin Blažíček, "Stručný průvodce Expanded Cinema" [A Brief Guide to Expanded Cinema], *Cinepur* 14, no. 39 (2005), pp. 8–11; Lenka Dolanová, "Gene Youngblood / Pokud diskurz není utopický, není dostatečně radikální" [Gene Youngblood / If Discourse Is Not Utopian, It Is Insufficiently Radical], *Umělec* 10, no. 2 (2006), pp. 12–15, accessed 2 Apr 2022, http://www.divus.cc/london/cs/article/life-in-counterculture; or Lenka Dolanová, "Umělec jako metanávrhář. Gene Youngblood a jeho dílo" [The Artist as Meta-designer. Gene Youngblood and His Work], Artalk.cz, accessed 2 Apr 2022, https://artalk.cz/2021/04/16/umelec-jako-metanavrhar-gene-youngblood-a-jeho-dilo/.

[96] Especially in the Anglo-American gallery context, the omnipresent use of the moving image was labelled with many different terms, such as "other cinema" (Raymond Bellour, "D'un autre cinéma", *Trafic* 10, no. 34 (2000), pp. 5–21), "projected image" (Malcolm Turvey – Hal Foster – Chrissie Iles – George Baker – Matthew Buckingham – Anthony McCall, "Round Table: The Projected Image in Contemporary Art", *October* 29, no. 104 (2003), pp. 71–96, see also Tamara Trodd, "Introduction: Theorising the Projected Image", in Tamara Trodd, ed., *Screen/Space: The Projected Image in Contemporary Art* (Manchester: Manchester University Press, 2011), pp. 1–22), "gallery film" (Catherine Fowler: "Remembering Cinema 'Elsewhere': From Retrospection To Introspection in the Gallery Film", *Screen* 45, no. 4 (2004), pp. 324–343), "artists' cinema" (Maeve Connolly, *The Place of Artists' Cinema: Space, Site and Screen* (Bristol: Intellect Books, 2009)), "moving-image art" (Tanya Leighton, ed., *Art and the Moving Image: A Critical Reader* (London: Tate Publishing, 2009)), or "post-cinema" (Miriam De Rosa – Vinzenz Hediger, eds., "Post-what? Post-when? Thinking Moving Images Beyond the Post-medium/Post-cinema Condition", *Cinéma & Cie* XVI, no. 26/27 Spring/Fall (2016)).

[97] See Markéta Jonášová's contribution in this volume.

[98] Videokemp, a one-day festival of contemporary video art from the Czech art scene, took place more or less regularly between 2005 and 2015. "Videokemp 2005", accessed 2 Apr 2022, https://arthasnohistory.com/2005/07/31/videokemp-2005/; see also Lenka Sýkorová, "Jedná se o nekonečný den. S Viktorem Čechem o přehlídce Videokemp" [It's an Infinite Day. With Viktor Čech on the Videokemp Festival], *A2* 9, no. 17, 2013, accessed 2 Apr 2022, https://www.advojka.cz/archiv/2013/17/jedna-se-o-nekonecny-den.

[99] Themed issue of *Iluminace* 23, no. 1 (2011), Film je jinde / Mimo prostor kina [Film Is Elsewhere / Outside the Cinema], block editor Lucie Česálková.

[100] Martin Mazanec, "Výzkumný projekt: Český videoart: Od programu k formě" [Research Project: Czech Video Art: From Programme to Form], *A2* 4, no. 49 (2008), p. 1, pp. 16–17, here p. 16. Comp. Tereza Klečková: "Today, the Use of the term 'video art' has spread to virtually all areas in which the moving image is used." Tereza Klečková, "Generování pojmu 'videoart'" [Generating the Term "Video Art"], *25fps.cz*, accessed 2 Apr 2022, http://25fps.cz/2011/videoart/, or Sylva Poláková: "The survival of inadequate terms – though of course, mutual interpenetration commonly takes place both at the level of intermediality and interdisciplinarity – attests to a certain rigidity (academics), nostalgia (art critics), and indolence (curators), as well as pragmatism (the introduction of new terminology usually brings a temporary confusion that negatively impacts marketing strategies)." Poláková, "'Současný český videoart' jako výzva filmovým studiím", pp. 111–125, especially pp. 111–112.

general public could in turn see that the interest of editorial boards and contributors in the presentation of the moving image only grew slowly in comparison to its increasing prevalence. In 2003, in response to "the effect of 'institutional' blur that partially obscures the border between film (screened in a cinema) and video installations (shown in galleries)",[101] the editorial staff (led by editor-in-chief Helena Bendová) of the specialised, originally cinephile-focused magazine *Cinepur* announced the establishment of a special new segment in the review section[102] that was to "mark the provoking and inspiring border (or intersection) of video art and cinematography".[103] The phenomenon brought up a number of questions: What does film mean to fine art if the two forms are sometimes indistinguishable? What does the process of intersection described above consist of? What means does it use? And what do we call them? Video? Film?[104] Audio-vision? Where are the borders? Is it always simply dependent on the context in which they are presented?

[101] Helena Bendová, "Editorial no. 27", *Cinepur* 12, no. 27 (2003), p. 1, accessed 2 Apr 2022, http://cinepur.cz/article.php?article=15.

[102] The *per se* section gradually merged with the criticism and themes section, later transforming into a column titled Mimo kino [Outside the Cinema] and into the sections Český talent [Czech Talent] or Portrét [Portrait], which explored all segments of audiovisual art. Temporary sections aiming to review current developments in the fields of video art, TV series, and computer games, were again announced in the 51st edition (2007) in response to the thematic issues.

[103] Helena Bendová, "Editorial č. 30 / Podzimní počítání" [Editorial no. 30 / Autumn Counting], *Cinepur* 12, no. 30 (2003), p. 1, accessed 2 Apr 2022, http://cinepur.cz/article.php?article=50.

[104] Compare mentions of the media status of artists' own works, e.g., Tomáš Pospiszyl, "Pěchoučkovy filmogramy" [Pěchouček's Filmograms], *Film a doba* 54, no. 2 (2008), pp. 94–96, especially p. 94; or Lenka Střeláková, "Ein Film von Mark Ther" [A Film by Mark Ther], *ART ANTIQUES* 11, no. 12 (2012), 103–104; or the Přátelský film [Friendly Film] project (Pěchouček, Mazanec), see "Přátelský film" [Friendly Film], accessed 2 Apr 2022, https://www.kviff.com/cs/program/film/11/3556-pratelsky-film.

The (De)Stabilising of the Discursive Field

With the aim of answering some of these questions, the editors of *Cinepur* prepared a themed issue titled "Film at an Exhibition three years later" (2006).[105] Collaborators included external authors such as active art theorists, curators, and artists (e.g. Zbyněk Baladrán, Filip Cenek, Anetta Mona Chişa, Radim Labuda, Pavlína Míčová, Michal Pěchouček, Tomáš Pospiszyl, Pavel Ryška, Petr Strouhal, Mark Ther, Miloš Vojtěchovský, and Martin Zet). A related issue of the cultural bi-weekly magazine *A2*, subtitled "Film Outside the Cinema" (2009), was created in a similar manner.[106] With the editorial contribution of film critic Kamila Boháčková, this issue extended and complimented the Video(art) topic, explored in an issue only a few weeks earlier (2008).[107] The need for a revision of historical-critical research was also manifested by *Film a doba* [*Film and Our Times*], a journal that has established a strong reputation over a period of decades, which in its 52nd (2007)[108] and 53rd (2008)[109] volumes provided space for a section titled "Videoart dnes"

[105] *Cinepur* 14, no. 44 (2006), accessed 2 Apr 2022, http://cinepur.cz/list.php?issue=42. Selection of contents relating to the theme: Helena Bendová, "Film na výstavě" [Film at the Exhibition], pp. 14–15; Tomáš Pospiszyl, "Film x výtvarné umění" [Film x Fine Art], pp. 16–18; Miloš Vojtěchovský, "Poezie a poetika elektronického těla. Garry Hill a film" [The Poetry and Poetics of the Electronic Body. Garry Hill and Film], pp. 19–21; Jan Krsňák, "Nam June Paik / 'Nikdy se nedívám na video'" [Nam June Paik / I Never Watch Videos], pp. 22–23; Miloš Vojtěchovský, "David Lamelas, simulakra světelného kužele" [David Lamelas, Simulacra of a Cone of Light], pp. 24–25; Tomáš Pospiszyl, "Andy Warhol uvádí" [Andy Warhol Presents], p. 24; (survey prepared by Pavlína Míčová) "Stavy a souvislosti současného českého umění videa" [The States and Contexts of Contemporary Czech Video Art], pp. 26–29; Zbyněk Baladrán – Martin Mareček, "V obraze" [In the Picture], pp. 29–33; Radim Labuda, "[in da] re:mix", pp. 34–35. See also Martin Mazanec, "Neléčená schizofrenie mezi filmem a videem, mezi kanálem a galerií" [The Untreated Schizophrenia Between Film and Video, Between the Channel and the Gallery], *Cinepur* 16, no. 56 (2008), p. 6.

[106] *A2* 5, no. 6 (2009). Selections relating to the theme: Kamila Boháčková, "Warholovy pohyblivé obrazy. Proč film vychází z kina a kinosály z módy?" [Warhol's Moving Images. Why Is Film Leaving the Cinema and Cinemas Coming Out of Fashion?], p. 11; Miloš Vojtěchovský, "Broadcast Yourself. Film a YouTube databáze" [Broadcast Yourself. Film and the YouTube Database], p. 12; Lenka Dolanová, "Návrat Magalhãese. Framptonova cesta kolem filmu" [The Return of Magellan. Framptons Journey Around Film], p. 13, see "editorial", accessed 3 Apr 2022, https://www.advojka.cz/archiv/2009/6.

[107] *A2* 4, no. 49 (2008). Theme prepared by Kamila Boháčková and Petr Vaňous. Selections relating to the theme: Martin Mazanec, "Výzkumný projekt: Český videoart. Od programu k formě" [Research Project: Czech Video Art. From Programme to Form], p. 1, pp. 16–17; Lenka Dolanová, "Video na výstavě, nebo v Multikině?" [Videos in Galleries or at Multiplexes?], p. 11; Sylva Poláková, "Méně tvořit a více makat. S Michalem Pěchoučkem o 'kulátolství' a kolektivní terapii" [Creating Less, Working More. With Michal Pěchouček on "Culatolship" and Collective Therapy], pp. 14–15; see "editorial. VIDEO(ART)", accessed 2 Apr 2022, https://www.advojka.cz/archiv/2008/49.

[108] Thematic contents of *Film a doba* 52, no. 2 (2007): Javier Duero, "Videoart ve věku dospělosti" [Video Art in its Age of Maturity], pp. 88–89; Stanislav Ulver – Radana Ulverová, "LOOP is LOOP is LOOP (Smyčka je smyčka)" [LOOP is LOOP is LOOP (A Loop is a Loop)], pp. 90–94; Miloš Vojtěchovský, "Poznámky k současnému českému videoartu" [Notes on Contemporary Czech Video Art], pp. 95–99; Radek Stavěl, "Globální občanství v rámci vizuálního slovníku (YouTube)" [Global Citizenship Within the Framework of a Visual Dictionary], pp. 99–100.

[109] Thematic contents of *Film a doba* 53, no. 2 (2008): Stanislav Ulver – Radana Ulverová, "Hlavní město videoartu (LOOP)" [The Capital City of Video Art (LOOP)], pp. 88–92; Radana Ulverová, "Ruiny, bílý dům a kinematické rituály Lidy Abdulové" [Ruins, The White House, and the Cinematic Rituals of Lida Abdul, pp. 92–94; Tomáš Pospiszyl, "Pěchoučkovy filmogramy" [Pěchouček's Filmograms], pp. 94–96; Andrea Chreňová, "Extensions of Man", pp. 96–97; outside the theme section: Miloš Vojtěchovský, "DIAL H-I-S-T-O-R-Y (Johan Grimonprez)", pp. 85–87.

[Video Art Today]. Since this time, the journal has also included detailed reports or reviews from festivals (e.g., PAF Olomouc)[110] or trade fairs (e.g. LOOP in Barcelona).[111] The generational change, which took place in parallel to this process and is also related to the logics of new causal interests, led to the establishment in 2007 of *25fps.cz*, a structured internet student magazine "on film, new media, and more" created by students at the film studies department in Olomouc.[112] The contributions published on this website, grouped under the historicising tag "#experimentální film" [experimental film][113] present perspectives on various (often subcultural) themes relating to the moving image, from monographically conceived profiles of artists and analyses of particular pieces or exhibitions to broader considerations of VJing, animation, computer games, or post-internet art.

Despite numerous endeavours by visual artists and curators in this field, periodicals focused on fine art did not reflect the acceptance of various forms of moving images with more systematic analyses. The contributions from the generally unchanging group of collaborating authors capable of bridging the gap between the perspectives of film and art criticism and subjecting them to a more continuous analysis mostly consisted only of sidesteps in critical thinking. Compared to the intensity that accompanied discussions such as the theme of the death of the medium in relation to traditional painting as one of the lineages of the post-media rhetoric of artists, theorists, and critics,[114] an interest in the fact that, at the intersection of fine art and film, not even the artist must necessarily consider (in the words of artist Ján Mančuška) "the limitation of the image to the projection surface"[115] only began manifesting itself very tentatively through smaller journalistic

[110] E.g., Ester Nagyová, "Jiné vize animace" [Other Visions of Animation], *Film a doba* 55, no. 1 (2010), pp. 47–48; Ester Nagyová, "Instalace animace" [Installing Animation], *Film a doba* 56, no. 1 (2011), p. 46; Pavel Bednařík, "Oživování (živé) animace: PAF Olomouc 2008" [Reviving (Live) Animation: PAF Olomouc 2008], *Film a doba* 54, no. 1 (2009), pp. 40–42; or Lenka Střeláková, "Expanded animation. Pohyblivá audiovizuální fascinace" [Expanded Animation. Mobile Audiovisual Fascination], ART ANTIQUES 13, no. 2, (2014), pp. 34–39.

[111] These were usually written by Radana Ulverová and Stanislav Ulver. Matěj Strnad later began reporting on festivals on the 25fps.cz platform.

[112] "25fps means 25 frames per second. That's how many need to pass in front of our eyes for us to have a perfect illusion of movement." Jiří Kuruc, "Lukáš Gregor o 25fps: volný čas se mi stal cizím termínem (rozhovor)" [Lukáš Gregor on 25fps: Free Time Has Become Foreign Terminology (interview)], accessed 2 Apr 2022, https://www.filmovamista.cz/clanek/17-Lukas-Gregor-o-25fps–volny-cas-se-mi-stal-cizim-terminem–rozhovor-. In contrast, the internet revue Artalk.cz, established in 2008, has a different focus, and only marginally discusses art of the moving image, mostly in connection to its institutionalisation.

[113] "Experimentální film" [Experimental Film], 25fps.cz, accessed 2 Apr 2022, http://25fps.cz/category/experimentalni-film/. Compare Jiří Neděla, "Experimentální film I.-V." [Experimental Film I – V], 25fps.cz, accessed 2 Apr 2022, http://25fps.cz/author/jiri-nedela/. See also Martin Blažíček, "Experiment, nová dobrodružství v digitální kvalitě" [Experiment, New Adventures in Digital Quality], Cinepur 16, no. 60 (2008), pp. 21–23.

[114] Compare the Konec malby? [The End of Painting?] section in Ševčík – Morganová – Nekvindová – Svatošová, eds., *České umění 1980–2010* [Czech Art 1980–2010], pp. 411–462.

[115] Vít Havránek, "Ján Mančuška: Chtěl jsem se soustředit na možnosti vyprávění" [I Wanted to Focus on the Possibilities of Narration], *Flash Art Czech & Slovak Edition 1*, no. 1 (2006), pp. 40–43, here p. 42.

texts such as reviews. In magazines such as the quarterly *Flash Art Czech & Slovak Edition*, on which I participated for years as an editor, or *Umělec* [Artist], the theme of the coexistence of various media operating within the conception of the moving image was more often in tune with issues of the present discursive framework of art-making, whether this meant the documentary turn,[116] post-production,[117] forms of collaboration and collaborative strategies[118] or entries into public space.[119] An important role, of course, was played by artistic reflections on cinematic language,[120] which, over the years, framed a number of thematic issues, including the "Film" (2012) issue of *Fotograf Magazine*,[121] the 31st issue of *Flash Art Czech & Slovak Edition* (2014),[122] the 22nd issue of *Sešit pro umění, teorii a příbuzné zóny* [Notebook for Art, Theory and Related Zones] (2017)[123] or "Výtvarník ako filmár" [The Artist as Film-Maker] in the Slovak magazine *Kino-Ikon*

[116] E.g., David Kulhánek, "Praxe, teorie a expozice Zbyňka Baladrána" [The Practice, Theory, and Exhibitions of Zbyněk Baladrán], *Umělec* 8, no. 3 (2004), pp. 68–69; Mariana Serranová, "Zbyněk Baladrán", *Fotograf* 8, no. 14 (2009), p. 107; Zbyněk Baladrán, "Ruiny, archeologie a mezera mezi obrazy" [Ruins, Archaeology, and the Gap Between Images], *Labyrint revue* 16, no. 23/24 (2008), pp. 109–110; Kateřina Svatoňová, "Život v obrazech a odchylující se vidění" [Life in Images and Divergent Seeing], *Sešit pro umění a příbuzné zóny* 11, no. 22 (2017), pp. 83–106.

[117] E.g., Pavlína Míčová, "Přibližuji Double Brno" [Bringing Double Brno Closer], *Flash Art Czech & Slovak Edition* 3, no. 11/12 (2009), p. 57.

[118] E.g., Estelle Artus, "Prostory společné práce: film a video" [Spaces of Collective Labour: Film and Video], *Umělec* 8, no. 4 (2004), pp. 85–89. The Monoskop project since 2004: "About Monoskop", accessed 2 Apr 2022, https://monoskop.org/About_Monoskop.

[119] E.g., Mirjam Struppek, "Přísně veřejné / Když videoart proniká do vizuální sféry městského prostoru" [Strictly Public / When Video Art Invades the Visual Sphere of Urban Space], *Umělec* 9, no. 3 (2005), pp. 60–63; Sylva Poláková, "Relokace filmového obrazu / Svět mediálních fasád" [The Relocation of the Cinematic Image / A World of Media Facades], *Cinepur* 18, no. 62 (2009), pp. 23–25; Sylva Poláková, "Kážu decentralizaci: světlo do ulic: pohyblivý obraz ve veřejném prostoru" [I Preach Decentralisation: Light in the Streets: Moving Images in Public Spaces], *A2* 11, no. 3 (2015), p. 9 (the first of a series of six articles focused on Czech artists working with the moving image in public spaces, with the following articles all appearing in the Film sections of issues no. 7, 11, 15, 22, and 25/26); Sylva Poláková, "Konvergence filmu a architektury v pražských ulicích" [The Convergence of Film and Architecture in the Streets of Prague], *Sešit pro umění a příbuzné zóny* 4, no. 8 (2010), pp. 7–21; Sylva Poláková, "'Expanded' Pešánek", *Flash Art Czech & Slovak Edition* 6, no. 31 (2014), pp. 29–31; Sylva Poláková, "Videomapping. Světlo do ulic – pohyblivý obraz ve veřejném prostoru" [Video Mapping. Light in the Streets – the Moving Image in Public Spaces], *A2* 11, no. 15 (2015), p. 9; Kateřina Krejčová – Eric Rosenzveig – Vladimír Turner, "Směry pospolitosti: umělecká tvorba ve veřejném prostoru (on-line rozhovor)" [Directions of Solidarity: Art in Public Spaces (online interview), *Film a doba* 59, no. 3/4 (2013), pp. 135–138. The relocation of the medium also concerns animated art; see Václav Mílek, "Objekt animace. Třetí smysl. Rozhovor s kurátory" [The Object of Animation. The Third Sense. An Interview with the Curators], *Prostor Zlín* 16, no. 4 (2009), pp. 6–9; Eliška Děcká, "Animace ve veřejném prostoru / Všudypřítomná, využívaná i zneužívaná" [Animation in Public Spaces / Omnipresent, Exploited, Abused], *Cinepur* 24, no. 98 (2015).

[120] E.g., Martin Mazanec, "Zbyněk Baladrán", *Labyrint revue* 16, no. 23/24 (2008), pp. 86–88; Ján Mančuška, "Inscenovaná realita" [Staged Reality], *Flash Art Czech & Slovak Edition* 5, no. 15 (2010), pp. 28–31; Marika Kupková, "Mark Ther. O lomítku mezi videem a filmem" [Mark Ther. On the Bracket Between Video and Film], *Flash Art Czech & Slovak Edition* 6, no. 31 (2014), pp. 26–28.

[121] *Fotograf* 11, no. 19 (2012), theme: Film, accessed 2 Apr 2022, https://fotografmagazine.cz/magazine/film/.

[122] *Flash Art Czech & Slovak Edition* 6, no. 31 (2014), accessed 2 Apr 2022, https://flashart.cz/issue/flash-art-czech-slovak-edition-no-31-volume-vi/.

[123] *Sešit pro umění, teorii a příbuzné zóny* 11, no. 22 (2017), accessed 2 Apr 2022, https://vvp.avu.cz/sesit/archiv.

(2019).[124] At the same time, discussions about a number of controversies regarding taboo began to pick up steam. These socially unresolved themes gave this form of art an unprecedented, occasionally tabloid-like media space in the field of more popularly oriented cultural sections,[125] occasionally exacerbated by the attractive mythical status of art awards.[126]

In the case of the periodicals mentioned above, the most thematically relevant were blocks or contributions dedicated to entirely different aspects that helped shape the discourse of the moving image in the long term. In addition to the activities of artists, curators, dramaturgs, theorists, and critics, the pages of these magazines also discussed the transformation of Czech art universities[127] or the indisputable importance of institutions focused on amassing collections or working with historical memory.[128] An

[124] *Kino-Ikon: časopis pre vedu o filme a "pohyblivom obraze"* 23, no. 2 (2019), accessed 2 Apr 2022, http://www.sfu.sk/uploads/ckeditor/attachments/1903/OBSAH_SK-GB_2–19.pdf.

[125] See the telling titles of the following articles: Jan H. Vitvar, "Pomoč to a natoč to" [Piss on It and Film It], *Respekt* 18, no. 13 (2007), p. 20; Jan H. Vitvar, "Tajemství citlivého kluka" [The Mystery of the Sensitive Boy], *Respekt* 19, no. 7 (2008), p. 52; or "Jak pochopit výstavu Autovize? Přes lízání zadku" [How to Understand the Autovize Exhibition? Through Anilingus], iDNES.cz, accessed 2 Apr 2022, https://www.idnes.cz/kultura/vytvarne-umeni/jak-pochopit-vystavu-autovize-pres-lizani-zadku.A070305_160636_vytvarneum_off. Compare e.g., Michal Pěchouček, "Ondřej Brody", *Fotograf* 4, no. 6 (2005), pp. 88–89; or Tomáš Pospiszyl, "Ondřej Brody je normální" [Ondřej Brody is Normal], *Umělec* 15, no. 1 (2011), accessed 2. 4. 2022, http://88.208.121.86/praha/cs/article/ondrej-brody-is-normal; David Kořínek – Adam Malý, "Mark Ther", *Živel* 12, no. 30 (2009), pp. 140–147.

[126] For the first time in the history of the Jindřich Chalupecký Award, a prize for artists under 35, the laureate was a graduate of AVU, who as rewarded for his work in video. This news was shared by most dailies and magazines, see Marie Meixnerová, "MARK THER: Ther v etheru a taky hlavně Ther medailonek" [MARK THER: Ther in the Ether and a Ther Biography], *25fps.cz*, accessed 2 Apr 2022, http://25fps.cz/2012/mark-ther/; see also Jan H. Vitvar, "Můj divák se musí kochat. Mark Ther se stal výtvarníkem roku díky dvacetiminutovému videu" [My Spectator Must Feast Their Eyes. Mark Ther Became Artist of the Year Thanks to a Twenty-Minute Video], *Respekt* 22, no. 49 (2011), p. 72, accessed 2 Apr 2022, https://www.respekt.cz/tydenik/2011/49/muj-divak-se-musi-kochat; Matěj Nytra, "Das wandernde Sternlein / Na okraj vítězného filmu Marka Thera" [Das wandernde Sternlein / On the Margins of Mark Ther's Award-winning Film], *Cinepur* 21, no. 78 (2012), p. 22, accessed 2 Apr 2022, http://cinepur.cz/article.php?article=2214; Lenka Dolanová, "ARTEFAKTY. Cena Jindřicha Chalupeckého 2011" [ARTEFACTS. The Jindřich Chalupecký Award 2011], *A2* 7, no. 25 (2011), accessed 2 Apr 2022, https://www.advojka.cz/archiv/2011/25/artefakty. See also Lenka Střeláková's contribution to this volume.

[127] The conception for FAMU was a topic of debate on the pages of *Cinepur* magazine, e.g., *Cinepur* 11, no. 20 (2002); *Cinepur* 25, nos. 106, 107, 110 (2016); the individual departments were introduced in *Film a doba*, e.g., "FAMU dnes" [FAMU Today], *Film a doba* 45, no. 1 (1999), pp. 23–24; "FAMU dnes II" [FAMU Today II], *Film a doba* 45, no. 2 (1999), pp. 81–85; "FAMU dnes III", *Film a doba* 45, no. 3 (1999), pp. 139–141; Radana Ulverová, "Oba stejně, každý ve svém monitoru, dotkli jsme se obrazovkou. Rozhovor s Tomášem Kepkou" [Both the Same, each in Our Own Monitor, We Touched Through the Screen. An Interview with Tomáš Kepka], *Film a doba* 46, no. 4 (2001), pp. 199–203; "Centrum audiovizuálních studií FAMU" [The Center for Audiovisual Studies at FAMU], *Film a doba* 58, no. 3/4 (2013), pp. 133–142; while the institutional history was mostly explored in *Iluminace*: *Iluminace* 27, no. 4 (2015). *A2* 5, no. 16 (2009) searched for answer to the following questions: how to educate artists and how to teach students how to think about art in an age of permeable disciplines – the theme of Umělci a výzkumníci [Artists and Researchers] was prepared by Lenka Dolanová. The field of film studies was the subject of *Iluminace* 21, no. 1 (2009), with its theme of Film v době vizuálních studií [Film in the Times of Media Studies], guest editors Petra Hanáková – Václav Hájek; compare the discussion stirred up by Zdeněk Holý's essay "Ve věži ze slonoviny. Nad současným stavem oboru filmová věda v ČR" [In an Ivory Tower. On the Contemporary State of Film Studies in the Czech Republic], *Cinepur* 18, no. 63 (2009), p. 9, accessed 2 Apr 2022, http://cinepur.cz/article.php?article=1716. Art education was also included in *Flash Art Czech & Slovak Edition* 13, no. 46 (2018) (Kurátorství [Curatorship]) and no. 48 (Edukativní obrat [The Educational Turn]). For more, see Tomáš Pospiszyl's study in this volume.

[128] See Matěj Strnad's study in this volume. I would also like to draw attention to a recent discussion focused primarily on the issue of acquisitions by collecting institutions, accessed 2 Apr 2022, https://artalk.cz/tag/pohyblivy-obraz/.

emphasis of the culturally-societal and material aspects of these forms of art led to the publication of essays dedicated to audiovisual archiving, including empirical archival strategies specific to the materials' basic technological parameters, as well as academic essays on the borders of (poly) historical and theoretical studies[129] that are paralleled by the research focus known as media archaeology.[130]

Unfocused on the Spectator

Theoretically focused reflections also indirectly influenced the moment when attention shifted from the artist, the institution, or the medium to the spectator. This turn can thus be somewhat symbolically compared to some of the other endlessly discussed interpretive paradigm shifts (such as the death of the author, the death of film, etc).[131] This focus on the spectator, however, opened a space in which to analyse the moving image at the intersection of interests of contemporary theoretical-critical practice in the field of fine art and cinematic interpretive journalism. Although "today's generation of spectators is ideally adapted to the form of narration found in film and television, reading it automatically with all its conventions and meanings",[132] the transformed perceptual experience of the cinematic spectator and the gallery visitor necessarily demand different processes of observation. The polarisation of this reception – either through a need for deep immersion in the work on the one hand, or the transformation of a passive recipient into an active participant of the installation on the other[133] – was suggested by the brief but precise characteristic of Marika Kupková's exhibition project.

[129] Theoretical discussions about the establishment of a film archive were mostly presented on the pages of *Iluminace*, with contributions by film historians and historiographers (e.g., Ivan Klimeš, Jiří Rak, Pavel Zeman), theorists (e.g., Petr Sczcepanik, Tomáš Dvořák, Kateřina Svatoňová), and archivists, see e.g. *Iluminace* 9, no. 3 (2005), theme: Archiv – Databáze – Edice filmů na DVD [Archive – Database – DVD Editions]; or Adéla Kudlová, "Dělat odvážná rozhodnutí: Rozhovor s Dušanem Barokem" [Making Bold Decisions: An Interview with Dušan Barok], *Iluminace* 31, no. 4 (2019), pp. 85–89.

[130] See *Iluminace* 23, no. 2 (2011), theme: Archeologie médií v postmediální době [Media Archaeology in a Post-media Age] (guest editor Kateřina Svatoňová); Petra Skřiváčková, "Variantologie: polyhistorický přístup k myšlení o umění nových médií" [Variantology: A Poly-historical Approach to Thinking About New Media Art], Ezin TIM 4, no. 1/2 (2014), accessed 2 Apr 2022, https://www.phil.muni.cz/journals/index.php/tim/article/view/917/1052.

[131] Roland Barthes, "Smrt autora" [The Death of the Author], *Aluze* 10, no. 3 (2006), pp. 75–77. Compare with the theme Smrt filmu [The Death of Film] in *Cinepur* 20, no. 73 (2011), accessed 2 Apr 2022, http://cinepur.cz/list.php?theme=95; Petra Hanáková, "Digitální revoluce a podoby 'smrti filmu'" [Digital Revolution and Forms of the "Death of Film"], in *Kultura a totalita III. Revoluce* [Culture and Totalitarianism III – Revolution], eds. Ivan Klimeš – Jan Wiendl (Prague: Faculty of Arts Press, 2015), pp. 470–481; Alexandra Moralesová, "Experimentální film: Vstup do filmové laboratoře a setkání s tělem" [Experimental Film: Entering the Film Lab and Encountering One's Body], *Sešit pro umění a příbuzné zóny* 12, no. 24 (2018), pp. 61–91. See also *Iluminace* 19, no. 2 (2007), theme: Filmový divák a jeho (estetický) prožitek [The Cinematic Spectator and Their (Aesthetic) Experience].

[132] Tomáš Pospiszyl, "Film x výtvarné umění", pp. 16–17.

[133] Another form of polarisation, in the sense of the experience of the cinematic spectator, is described by Jenny Schlenzka, "The Cinematic OD BÍLÉ KOSTKY PO BLACK BOX" [The Cinematic FROM THE WHITE CUBE TO THE BLACK BOX], *Flash Art Czech & Slovak Edition* 6, no. 31 (2014), pp. 13–15. See also Martin Blažíček, "Live Cinema", *Film a doba* 55, no. 3/4 (2009), pp. 184–185; or Matěj Nytra, "Das wandernde Sternlein", p. 22.

Kupková is a curator and historian of film and media whose long-term research into audiovisual art addresses historical-cultural, institutional, and aesthetic considerations, among others. Her exhibition Bad Filming (Galerie U Dobrého pastýře, Brno, 2009) was in the curt assessment of one reviewer characterised as "a game with the spectator's expectations, i.e., a confirmation or subversive disruption of the expected".[134] Even this short, out-of-context extract suggests the recent radical transformations of the strategies of curating in the art world, namely the adoption of a critical approach to the layout of the gallery space and specific installation arrangement (both are among the crucial elements of any exhibition, which also include social, economic, and production elements), which, in the case of the moving image, was also connected to an emphasis on the position of the spectator. In this context, however, a critique of these particular frameworks[135] does not correspond merely to a thematisation of solutions to particular problems in the operation of galleries, it also approximates current trends in film studies.[136] The form of the cinematic experience, which

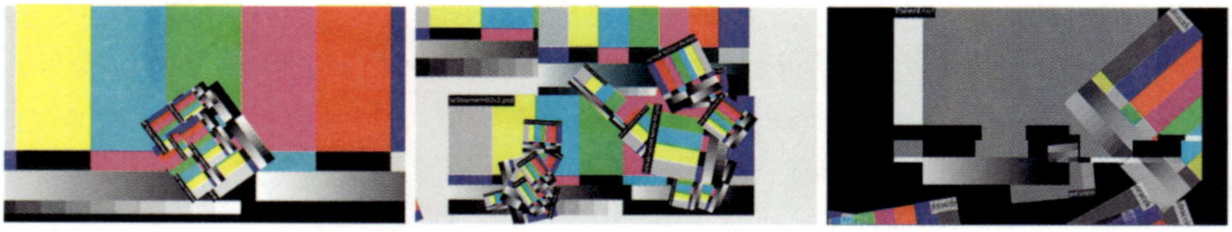

Martin Búřil *Monoskop no. 3 – Monkeyking legend* (2011), video, 6 min 52 s

can take on characteristics of a light game or a visual composition, with its affective, romanticising captivation in the sense of "We watch, we are moved"[137] (Viktor Takáč), also approximates the interest of media researchers for what is known as haptic criticism. This form of criticism does not place as much emphasis on subjective emotional experiences, focusing instead on a critical reflection of the artwork; on the changes that are effected by a disruption of the traditional distance and hierarchy between the spectator–critic and the aesthetic object itself.[138]

[134] Pavlína Míčová, "Bad Filming", *Flash Art Czech & Slovak Edition* 4, no. 14 (2009), p. 56.

[135] Cf. Petra Hanáková, "Aparát. Pojem" [Apparatus. Term], *Cinepur* 10, no. 17 (2001), p. 53, accessed 2 Apr 2022, http://cinepur.cz/article.php?article=109.

[136] See e.g., Jan Zálešák, "Rámec jako figura. Vystavovatel a jeho diváci v brněnském Domě umění" [The Framework as Figure. The Exhibitor and His Spectators in the House of Arts in Brno], *ART ANTIQUES* 10, no. 6 (2011), pp. 66–67, accessed 2 Apr 2022, https://www.artantiques.cz/ramec-jako-figura; Silvie Šeborová, "Bezpředmětný film" [Subjectless Film], *Flash Art Czech & Slovak Edition* 6, no. 27 (2013), p. 60, accessed 2 Apr 2022, https://flashart.cz/2013/06/11/bezpredmetny-film/; Klára Peloušková, "Mazancova galerie v Galerii mladých" [Mazanec's Gallery in the Galerie Mladých], Artalk.cz, accessed 2 Apr 2022, https://artalk.cz/2012/02/22/mazancova-galerie-v-galerii-mladych/.

[137] "TZ: Další film" [PR: Another Film], Artalk.cz, accessed 2 Apr 2022, https://artalk.cz/2013/03/05/tz-dalsi-film/. I am quoting here from a curatorial text for the exhibition by Kryštof Pešek, Martin Búřil, Roman Štětina, and Tomáš Moravec, Bezpředmětný film [Subjectless Film], Galerie U Dobrého pastýře, Brno, 6 Mar – 3 Apr 2013, curator Viktor Takáč.

[138] Jiří Anger, "Médium, které myslí sebe sama: Audiovizuální esej jako nástroj bádání a vyústění akademických trendů" [The Medium That Thinks Itself: The Audiovisual Essay as a Tool of Research and a Culmination of Academic Trends], *Iluminace* 30, no. 1 (2018), pp. 5–26, especially pp. 10–11.

The pressing need to "change entrenched institutional constellations", related to the "transformation of the cinematic spectator as passive 'voyeur' into an active 'attraction visitor'"[139] is responsible for a categorical shift in the current development of the media sphere. Given how incessantly connected we all are today, with digital tools at hand and in coexistence with truly virtual spaces, the intensive sharing of the present moment transforms both the way our subjectivity is formed and the way our entire society is perceived. These factors contribute to the massive rise of streaming platforms,[140] as these can be easily adapted to everyday thinking. On the other hand, we must also consider the contradiction hidden inside these platforms. The antagonistic tension between the tendency to collect data and the tendency to share creates a new combination of political-economical, cultural-social, and also (increasingly pressing) ecological concerns, which also doubtless have their place in the broader discussion on the construct of the moving image in all its forms (from the mechanical to the digital, from the static to the mobile, from the real to the virtual). When preparing this text, I wanted to capture all of these perspectives and their context, but the constantly expanding spectrum of topics does not always succeed in generating a balanced reflection in the Czech media. Furthermore, this reflection is influenced by many factors, not only by differences between cinephile or art-theory criticism and the academic writing for the public, suggested by the list of periodicals that fell within the scope of my research. It is also manifested in the form of approaches and surveys that are included in these texts. This aspect is mostly influenced by the communities that, over the years, form these platforms of reflection. The questions they pose mirror not only the shifts in the relationships between related contexts, but also the reality of the period. Hopefully, despite the somewhat fragmentarily captured chain of these narratives, this text will help illustrate the dimension of space and time in which the discourse of art of the moving image resonates.

[139] Marika Kupková, "Divák vs. návštěvník: proměny diváckých režimů" [Spectator vs. Visitor: Changes in Modes of Viewing], *Cinepur* 20, no. 73 (2011), pp. 75–79, here p. 75, p. 78; Tereza Klečková, "Přehlídky a výstavy – Hledisko pozorovatele" [Festivals and Exhibitions – The Spectator's Perspective], *25fps.cz*, accessed 2 Apr 2022, http://25fps.cz/2011/prehlidky-a-vystavy/. Cf. Tom Gunning, "Film atrakcí: raný film, jeho diváci a avantgarda" [Cinema of Abstractions: Early Film, Its Spectators, and the Avant-garde], *Iluminace* 13, no. 2 (2001), pp. 51–57.

[140] Matěj Nytra, "Aerovod", *Cinepur* 20, no. 85 (2013), p. 51, accessed 2 Apr 2022, http://cinepur.cz/article.php?article=2429; Hana Šilařová, "VOD distribuce, uvádění a sledování filmů / Kinematografie online" [VOD Distribution, Presenting and Watching Films / Cinematography Online], *Cinepur* 24, no. 98 (2015), accessed 2 Apr 2022, http://cinepur.cz/article.php?article=3258; Jindřiška Bláhová, "Editorial 126 / NETFLIX", *Cinepur* 28, no. 126 (2019), accessed 2 Apr 2022, http://cinepur.cz/article.php?article=4769; Ondřej Pavlík, "Netflix, chill a korona. Internetová televize v době pandemie" [Netflix, Chill, and Corona. Internet Television During the Pandemic], *A2* 16, no. 12 (2020), accessed 2 Apr 2022, https://www.advojka.cz/archiv/2020/12/netflix-chill-a-korona.

Competition Cages and Enclosures for the Moving Image

Lenka Střeláková

The gallery world, scholarly and journalistic articles, competitions, and collections of art of the moving image – the thematic outlines of this section of the book – refer directly to the environments, events, and discourses that anchor various forms of the moving image both theoretically and practically, in a sense normalising them. It is competitions organised within the world of film or art that, through their selection – or rather through the very conditions of participation, the rules of selection, and the ensuing evaluation, as well as the terminology they use – necessarily and markedly co-determine general positions on the kind of work that is considered interesting, timely, and relevant, as well as how it is interpreted. In this sense, competitions send messages both inwards, to the art scene, and outwards, to the general public, the critical community, and various distributors, producers, collection curators, or collectors. The competition format thus naturally represents a significant step towards valorising art of the moving image. This is unchanged by the intense and polarising discussions and attempts to reorganise the definition of competitions that have recently taken place in the art world.[141] Each of the competitions explored below, whether it is focused directly on the moving image, film, and video (Other Visions; Fascinations: Exprmntl.cz; Theatre Electrique), or contains art of the moving image to a significant degree (the Jindřich Chalupecký Award; the StartPoint Prize), naturally works with somewhat different pre-selection criteria. It is true in all cases, however, that these internal criteria (articulated to a greater or lesser degree), along with the specific selection of finalists, always realistically influence and critically define the potential shape and form of these notable works in a more complex manner than the ensuing announcement of the winner.[142]

Events and Places

Awards given to new types of artworks at competitions are, of course, preceded by a focused presentation of these works, whereby they are generally characterised – named and contextualised – for the first time. Art of the moving image has links both to "classical" experimental film and to video art, artists' cinema or artistic videos in general, as well as to new digital art or net art, which attests to the different formative environments and contexts in which we must search for creative self-realisation and affinity. In the Czech environment, this contextualisation of art of the moving image in terms of film and video takes place neither within the context of traditional festivals and competitions of amateur film, whose approach has become relatively settled through years of repetition, nor in the later-developed territory of presentation of (new) media art, where the contents are, contrastingly, often too fluid and disparate.[143] It was particularly the specific "events" of

[141] On the Czech scene, more focused discussions of the importance of art prizes and competitions – which, for reasons listed above, will not be the focus of this reflection – have taken place since 2017. At the time, the finalists of the Oskár Čepan Award, the most significant Slovak award for young visual artists, decided to respond to the competition's form of organisation by appearing as a collective and thus becoming collective winners. 2019, in turn, marked the beginning of a transformation of award-giving at the Jindřich Chalupecký Award, and was probably the last edition to have a single laureate. It is precisely the events surrounding the continual and clearly felt transformation of the Jindřich Chalupecký Award in the context of the debate described above that are still the strongest source of questions, proposals, declamations, disagreements, and understanding in which both experts and the general public take part.

[142] This is regardless of how many winners there ultimately are, whether the competition was marked by a competitive or a collaborative atmosphere, and whether this form of selected presentation will or will not continue to be called a competition. For a contextualisation of the complex causes and consequences of recent questions and developments in relation to art competitions, see Palo Fabuš, "Súťaže v umení a slabé gestá" [Art Competitions and Weak Gestures], *Artalk.cz*, accessed 5 Apr 2022, https://artalk.cz/2021/01/25/sutaze-v-umeni-a-slabe-gesta.5. 4. 2022, https://artalk.cz/2021/01/25/sutaze-v-umeni-a-slabe-gesta.

[143] As Martin Mazanec, long-term dramaturg, and present artistic director of the PAF Olomouc festival, put it so succinctly in a comment on digital culture festivals: "I often struggle with an insufficient understanding of the manner of presentation, which [festivals of digital culture and similar projects] often distribute across dance floors, theatres, galleries, and conference halls. I rarely understand what they are aiming for, whether the pieces work with sound and image, or film and video, or virtual reality, or record players..." Martin Blažíček, "Za hranicí animace / Rozhovor s Martinem Mazancem, dramaturgem Přehlídky animovaného filmu Olomouc" [Beyond the Borders of Animation / An Interview with Martin Mazanec, dramaturg of PAF Olomouc], *Cinepur*, accessed 7 Apr 2022, http://cinepur.cz/article.php?article=1968.

the moving image[144] that created the necessary conditions for discussion, evaluation, and awarding prizes to this form of art, and which took place in several parallel dimensions in front of different audiences.

In addition to these events, which were accessible to a broader audience and "collected" retrospectively with a view towards historical relevance and presented in the two-volume *Catalogue of Events of the Czech Moving Image*[145] from 2011, there were also more subtle stories and influences. These lineages of contextualisation, which are no less important, include teaching at art schools and film studies departments as well as introductory lectures and programming for (university) film clubs or festival selections, all of which significantly influenced both the creation and reception of moving image and video works in the Czech Republic.

The most important – and still operating – competitions of art of the moving image were created in locations where both these factors (related dramaturgical interests and an open and informed audience) were present, crystallising from guided tours and screenings of experimental films, art videos, or other audiovisual works outside the context of classical cinematography. In 2007, the PAF Festival in Olomouc introduced a new competition section, with its name being taken from a term established here and used by profile lectures and screenings led by Martin Čihák: Other Visions (Jiné vize).[146] A year later, the Ji.hlava International Documentary Film Festival (IDFF) presented the first – initially non-competitive – edition of its survey of Czech experimental film, whose title – Exprmntl.cz – refers to a portrait by Alice Růžičková and Martin Čihák of three Czech experimentalists both in life and film living in exile in Denmark.[147] Ten years later, the semantic nuance in choosing what seems at first like a synonymous name seems all the more significant in terms of establishing certain

[144] Specifically, presentations outside the standard gallery or cinematic context (though not necessarily outside the gallery or cinema), organised in the Czech Republic especially since the second half of the 2000s (e.g., the regular Audiovisual series at the Světozor cinema in Prague, which ran from 2005 to 2008). See also Markéta Jonášová's essay in this publication and Martin Mazanec – Sylva Poláková, eds., *Katalog událostí českého pohyblivého obrazu I a II. Jiné vize 2000–2010* [Catalogue of Events of the Czech Moving Image I, II. Other Visions 2000–2010] (Olomouc: Pastiche Filmz, 2011).

[145] See previous note.

[146] In 2002, the festival included the screening blocks "Other Visions – Vít Pancíř" (featuring a profile of this Czech experimental filmmaker and animator) and "Other Visions – Martin Čihák" (where Čihák introduced the work of the American experimental animator Robert Breer). A year later, this was followed by a programming block titled "Other Visions (Martin Čihák Lectures on Animation in Experimental Film)", which introduced Larry Jordan and Stan Vanderbeek. Further editions, which preceded the Other Visions competition, presented profiles of Marcus Bergner by Martin Čihák (2004) or David Možný by founding dramaturg of PAF Jiří Neděla (2006) among others.

[147] *Exprmntl KBH* (Alice Růžičková, Martin Čihák). Prague: Czech Television – Antonín Trš and Markéta Štinglová Creative Group, 2001, 16mm, 38 min. One of the artists portrayed in this documentary is Martin Klapper, who once made pirate copies of a number of avant-garde and experimental films at a club in Copenhagen and passed these video cassettes on to Martin Čihák. Čihák was then able, in the offline environment of the mid to late 1990s, inform an entire generation of audiences about experimental cinematography and share the spectatorial experience with them (see footnote no. 6). Martin Čihák interviewed by Lenka Střeláková, 26 May 2021.

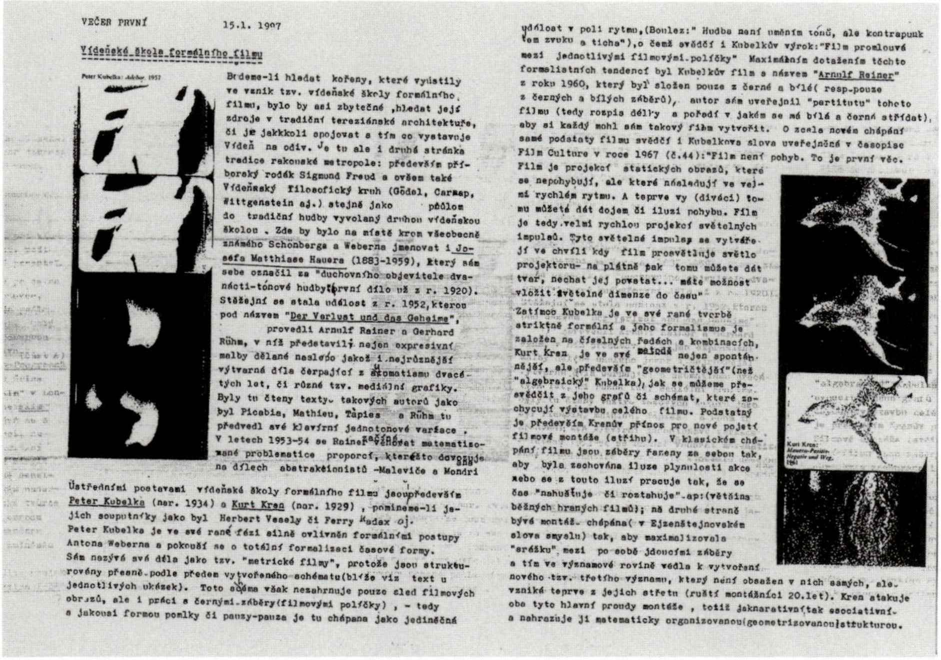

VEČER PRVNÍ 15.1. 1997

Vídeňská škola formálního filmu

Peter Kubelka: *Adebar*, 1957

Budeme-li hledat kořeny, které vyústily ve vznik tzv. vídeňské školy formálního filmu, bylo by asi zbytečné hledat její zdroje v tradiční tereziánské architektuře, či je jakkoli spojovat s tím co vystavuje Vídeň na odiv. Je tu ale i druhá stránka tradice rakouské metropole: především příborský rodák Sigmund Freud a ovšem také Vídeňský filosofický kruh (Gödel, Carnap, Wittgenstein aj.) stejně jako předělem do tradiční hudby vyvolaný druhou vídeňskou školou. Zde by bylo na místě krom všeobecně známého Schönberga a Weberna jmenovat i Josefa Matthiase Hauera (1883-1959), který sám sebe označil za "duchovního objevitele dvanácti-tónové hudby" (první dílo už z r. 1920). Stěžejní se stala událost z r. 1952, kterou pod názvem "Der Verlust und das Geheime", provedli Arnulf Rainer a Gerhard Rühm, v níž představili nejen expresivní malby dělané naslepo jakož i nejrůznější výtvarná díla čerpající z automatismu dvacátých let, či různé tzv. mediální grafiky. Byly tu čteny texty takových autorů jako byl Picabia, Mathieu, Tàpies a Rühm tu předvedl své klavírní jednotónové variace. V letech 1953-54 se Rainer začíná věnovat matematizované problematice proporcí, kterážto dovozuje na dílech abstrakcionistů -Maleviče a Mondriana.

Ústředními postavami vídeňské školy formálního filmu jsou především Peter Kubelka (nar. 1934) a Kurt Kren (nar. 1929), pomineme-li jejich souputníky jako byl Herbert Vesely či Ferry Radax aj. Peter Kubelka je ve své rané fázi silně ovlivněn formálními postupy Antona Weberna a pokouší se o totální formalizaci časové formy. Sám nazývá svá díla jako tzv. "metrické filmy", protože jsou strukturovány přesně podle předem vytvořeného schématu (blíže viz text u jednotlivých ukázek). Toto schéma však nezahrnuje pouze sled filmových obrazů, ale i práci s černými záběry (filmovými políčky), - tedy s jakousi formou pomlky či pauzy-pauza je tu chápana jako jedinečná událost v poli rytmu, (Boulez:" Hudba není uměním tónů, ale kontrapunktem zvuku a ticha"), o čemž svědčí i Kubelkův výrok: "Film promlouvá mezi jednotlivými filmovými políčky" Maximálním dotažením těchto formalistních tendencí byl Kubelkův film s názvem "Arnulf Rainer" z roku 1960, který byl složen pouze z černé a bílé(resp. pouze z černých a bílých záběrů), autor sám uveřejnil "partituru" tohoto filmu (tedy rozpis délky a pořadí v jakém se má bílá a černá střídat), aby si každý mohl sám takový film vytvořit. O zcela novém chápání samé podstaty filmu svědčí i Kubelkova slova uveřejněná v časopise Film Culture v roce 1967 (č.44): "Film není pohyb. To je první věc. Film je projekcí statických obrazů, které se nepohybují, ale které následují ve velmi rychlém rytmu. A teprve vy (diváci) tomu můžete dát dojem či iluzi pohybu. Film je tedy velmi rychlou projekcí světelných impulsů. Tyto světelné impulsy se vytváří ve chvíli kdy film prosvětluje světlo projektoru- na plátně pak tomu můžete dát tvar, nechat jej povstat... máte možnost vložit světelné dimenze do času"

Zatímco Kubelka je ve své rané tvorbě striktně formální a jeho formalismus je založen na číselných řadách a kombinacích, Kurt Kren je ve své metodě nejen spontánnější, ale především "geometričtější" (než "algebraický" Kubelka), jak se můžeme přesvědčit z jeho grafů či schémat, které zachycují výstavbu celého filmu. Podstatný je především Krenův přínos pro nové pojetí filmové montáže (střihu). V klasickém chápání filmu jsou záběry řazeny za sebou tak, aby byla zachována iluze plynulosti akce nebo se z touto iluzí pracuje tak, že se čas "nahušťuje či roztahuje" ap: (většina běžných hraných filmů); na druhé straně bývá montáž chápána (v Ejzenštejnovském slova smyslu) tak, aby maximalizovala "srážku" mezi po sobě jdoucími záběry a tím ve významové rovině vedla k vytvoření nového tzv. třetího významu, který není obsažen v nich samých, ale vzniká teprve z jejich střetu (ruští montážníci 20.let). Kren atakuje oba tyto hlavní proudy montáže, totiž jak narativní tak asociativní a nahrazuje ji matematicky organizovanou (geometrizovanou) strukturou.

Kurt Kren: *Mauern-Positiv-Negativ und Weg*, 1961

Martin Čihák's materials for lectures and screenings on avant-garde and experimental film Roxy, Prague, 1997.

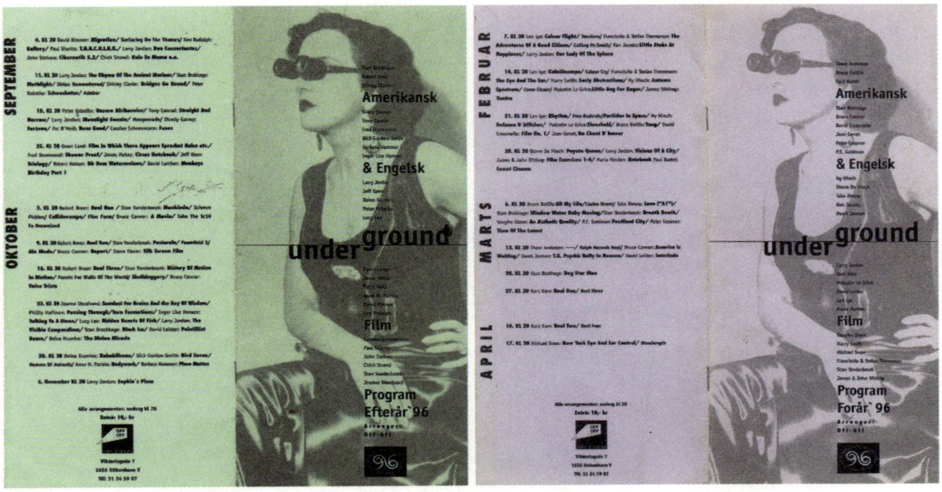

1996 programme of the Copenhagen cinema Off – Off, co-organised by Martin Klapper.

interpretive boundaries within which the curatorship/dramaturgy of both of these competitions operate.

As art of the moving image becomes an increasingly standard form of artistic expression, the (competition) contexts in which it appears are also becoming broader. The remainder of this text mostly explores the competitions in Olomouc and Jihlava, which have an extended and particular history of focusing on the moving image of film and video and on experimental film. In the sub-chapters that explore the support and award system of art of the moving image, I also follow other events and environments that have an indisputable position and/or ambition within this infrastructure of support.[148]

Other Visions

At the sixth edition of PAF, in 2007, Other Visions was presented as the logical outcome of the festival's dramaturgy, placing an emphasis on continuity as well as addressing the global needs and lack of reflection of a particular kind of work.[149] Other Visions was defined as "a competition of new forms of the moving image of film and video. It is a competition focused on works that make inventive use of animation methods and techniques. The Other Visions competition cycle extends the traditional programming blocks of the Olomouc festival that consistently provided space for artists stepping beyond limitations of genre and technology in classical animation (experimental film, computer animation, video art, etc.). The Other Visions competition aimed to reward works that influence both the art and film scenes in fresh ways, and to make them accessible".[150]

Since its establishment, Other Visions was introduced as a curated competition with clearly determined participation criteria that are *de facto* still valid today: "Every year, the selection of ten competition films and videos made in the Czech Republic in the last eighteen months will depend on the curatorial selection of figures of authority in the Czech art and film environment, with the curator changing every year along with the three-member international jury".[151] The concept of Other Visions was created by then-dramaturg of the PAF Olomouc festival, Martin Mazanec, and it speaks both to a conscious need for the contextualisation of works from

[148] The manuscript was created in the first half of 2021, so in the case of all the surveyed events, it could only take into account their (non-standard) form in the first year of the pandemic (2020).

[149] "Another developmental transformation that arises from a knowledge of the insufficient scope of Czech festivals is the creation of a new curated competition, Other Visions. A cycle with the same name has been part of PAF since the beginnings of the festival, and through this transformation into a competition section, our aim is to emphasise works that have no clearly definable genre: works on the borderlines of animation, video art, and experimental film". Pavel Bednařík, "Úvodní slovo ředitele přehlídky" [Festival Director's Introduction], in *Katalog PAF 2007* [PAF 2007 Catalogue] (Olomouc: Pastiche Filmz, 2007), p. 5.

[150] Veronika Klusáková – Pavel Bednařík, "Projekce soutěžních videí I., II. Jiné vize 007" [Competition Videos Screening I, II. Other Visions 007], in *Katalog PAF 2007* (Olomouc: Pastiche Filmz, 2007), p. 14.

[151] Ibid.

various environments and to a related vision for a firmer theoretical grasp of contemporary art – including erudite terminological care[152] – through curated selections, which offer one possible form of orientation in the growing pool of audiovisual production.[153]

The curator of the first edition of Other Visions was Přátelský film [Friendly Film], a curatorial and performing duo composed of Martin Mazanec and Michal Pěchouček, an artist and lecturer. During this time (ca. 2006–2008), they were active as curators and guides through the world of art videos and other works of art of the moving image, which they decided to screen primarily in movie theatres, with a thematic emphasis on the possibilities and meanings of modes of presentation. For that period, this was far outside the norm and often aroused resentment and a lack of understanding. At the same time, however, some visual artists were already entering the cinema and the movie theatre in more conceptual ways.[154]

Today, when artists use screening in a black box as one of the natural possibilities for the presentation of their work – in addition to more immersive installations or the explicit use of everyday screens (notebooks, tablets, phones, often complemented by various physical artefacts) – PAF and Other Visions still maintain a knowledge of the particular character of these works. Specifically, this means every year sees the creation not only of a screening block including all ten selected works,[155] which PAF distributes through commentated presentations at various festivals and other cultural events both in the Czech Republic and abroad,[156] but also an exhibition concept initiated by the curator of the edition in question and realised at PAF Olomouc as a gallery installation. One of the conditions for participating in Other Visions (apart from being non-commercial and being created in the

[152] PAF was the first entity in the Czech Republic to join the international discourse (including, for example, the Filmmuseum in Vienna or documenta in Kassel) in systematically writing about the moving image and its curation. See also Lenka Střeláková, "Expanded animation. Pohyblivá audiovizuální fascinace" [Expanded Animation. Moving Audiovisual Fascination], ART ANTIQUES 13, no. 2 (2014), pp. 34–39.

[153] The curators of Other Visions so far have been: Přátelský film (Martin Mazanec and Michal Pěchouček) (2007), Martin Fišr (2008), Lenka Dolanová (2009), Sylva Poláková (2010), Pavel Ryška (2011), Dušan Zahoranský (2012), David Kořínek (2013), Marika Kupková (2014), Lenka Střeláková (2015), Karel Císař (2016), Michal Novotný (2017), Rado Ištok (2018), Laura Amann (2019) and Tina Poliačková and Lumír Nykl (2020).

[154] E.g. Ján Mančuška, *Jestli je na mě něco dobrého, jsem to jen já, kdo to ví* [If There Is Something Good About Me, It Is Only I Who Knows It] (Kino Světozor, great hall, Prague, 2007), see "*Jestli je na mě něco dobrého, jsem to jen já, kdo to ví*", accessed 7 Apr 2022, https://jlbjlt.net/jelito/xqay8tQMMr7hoa7vE; Tomáš Svoboda, *Den nezávislosti* [Independence Day] (Kino Světozor, small hall, Prague, 2008), see "Den Nezávislosti, Tomáš Svoboda, Kino Světozor", accessed 7 Apr 2022, https://artycok.tv/1357/den-nezavislostiindependence-day.

[155] The curators of Other Visions usually consider this form of presentation and reception when selecting and arranging the individual works. At least three screening blocks were thus created with the overt intention of weaving a meta-narrative out of these ten works, or a feature-length film (Jiné vize 2015: *Kosmologická antropologie* [Other Visions 2015: Cosmological Anthropology], L. Střeláková; Jiné vize CZ 2016, K. Císař; Jiné vize CZ 2017, M. Novotný).

[156] Around the year 2010, PAF also began presenting Other Visions beyond the scope of the festival itself, e.g., with regular presentations at the Luhovaný Vincent "multi-genre festival" in Luhavočice or the Anilogue International Animation Festival in Budapest.

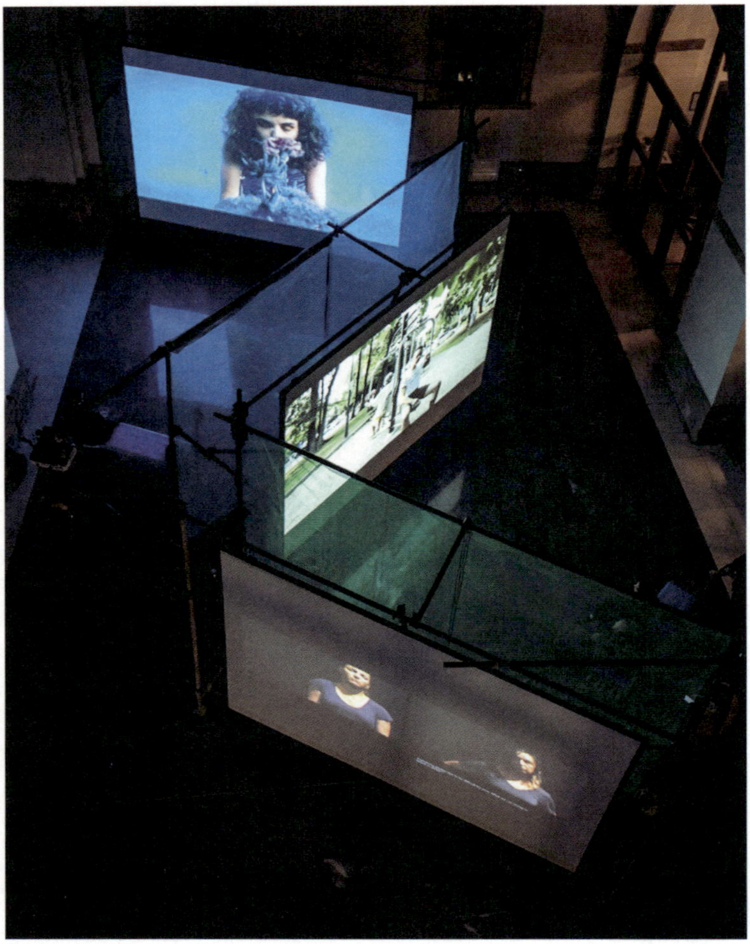

Other Visions CZ, competition section of the PAF Olomouc festival, exhibition in the attic and atrium of the Artistic Centre of Palacký University in Olomouc, (top) 2018, (left to right) 2009, 2011, 2013, 2014, 2015, 2016, 2017, 2018, 2019.

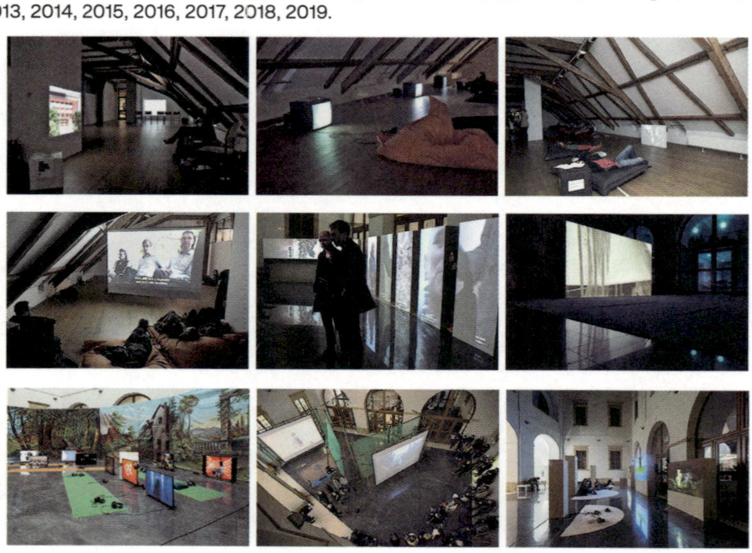

Czech Republic no more than a year and a half before the deadline) is the fact that the pieces must be presentable both in cinemas and galleries. The Other Visions exhibition is notable not only as a formal reminder of the broad range of art under scrutiny, but also for the profile of its finalists. From the very beginning, competitors have hailed mostly from the professional art scene and from art schools (along with the group of students and graduates of the Center of Audiovisual Studies at FAMU), and this trend is only becoming stronger over time.[157]

Exprmntl.cz

At its twelfth edition, in 2008, the Ji.hlava IDFF first introduced an (international) section of experimental films, Fascinations (Fascinace). Festival director Marek Hovorka wrote the following in his introduction to the catalogue: "[Jihlava festival] features a section named 'Fascination for Experimental Films', which is the result of our production and editing efforts characterised by openness to new film shapes and bold experiments – a sidestep from the ever-repeating cycle."[158]

In that year's catalogue, the Fascinations section is characterised thus:

> Experimental films are both in the centre and on the edge of cinema as they enter the festival whirl through the section entitled FASCINATION, which offers the audiences an opportunity to wonder at adventurous aesthetic renderings of images created at the time of a technology craze and under the spell of editing and numerous possibilities opened up by camera and optics, providing them with an opportunity to explore all the seemingly blind alleys, which, however, always constitute a source of renewal for the documentary film since they often work with documentary material and take a documentary point of view, the only difference being the use of experimental techniques.[159]

[157] In his 2016 curatorial text, Karel Císař notes: "If we can follow a certain process of emancipation in the previous years of the festival, it is to be found in the growing number of participants who used various forms of projected image to express them without having studied film. The most recent editions were completely dominated by such artists. We can ascribe this to the unprecedented availability of technology and the speed with which works created using this technology are disseminated". Karel Císař, "Jiné vize 2016 CZ", in *Katalog PAF 2016* (Olomouc: Pastiche Filmz, 2007), p. 24. Winners of Other Visions include (chronologically): Viktor Takáč, Martin Kohout, Daniel Pitín, David Možný, Alexandra Moralesová, Akile Nazli Kaya, Petr Šprincl and Marie Hájková, Barbora Kleinhamplová and Kristýna Bartošová, Janek Rous, Lucie Rosenfeldová, David Přílučík, Valentýna Janů and Kryštof Hlůže, Zbyšek Semelka, and, in the latest edition of the competition (2020), Štěpán Krahulec, Fanny Chaiyarach, and David Střeleček from the Academy of Art, Architecture and Design in Prague.

[158] Marek Hovorka, "Entry", in *12. katalog Mezinárodního festivalu dokumentárních filmů Ji.hlava 2008* [12th Catalogue of the Ji.hlava International Documentary Film Festival], p. 10.

[159] 12. katalog Mezinárodního festivalu dokumentárních filmů Ji.hlava 2008, p. 111.

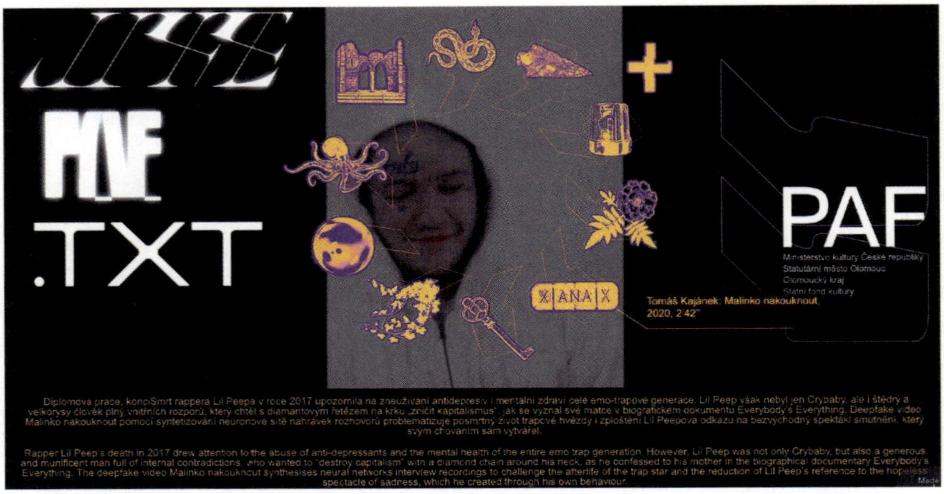

Other Visions CZ, competition section of the PAF Olomouc festival, screenshot from the online exhibition, 2020.

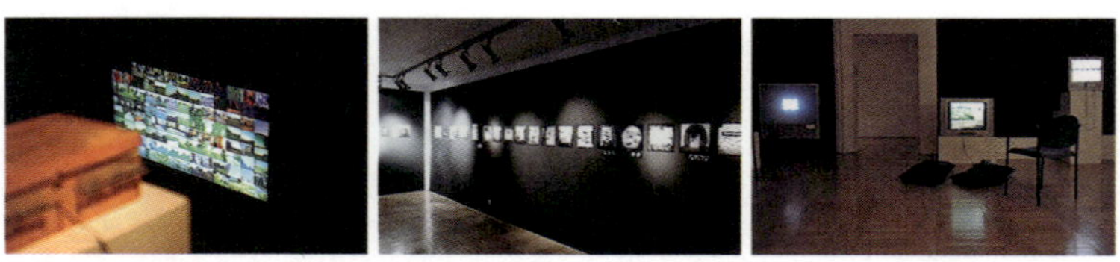

Laboratorium, exhibition off-screen program at the Ji.hlava International Documentary Film Festival, Vysočina Regional Gallery, Jihlava, 2011.

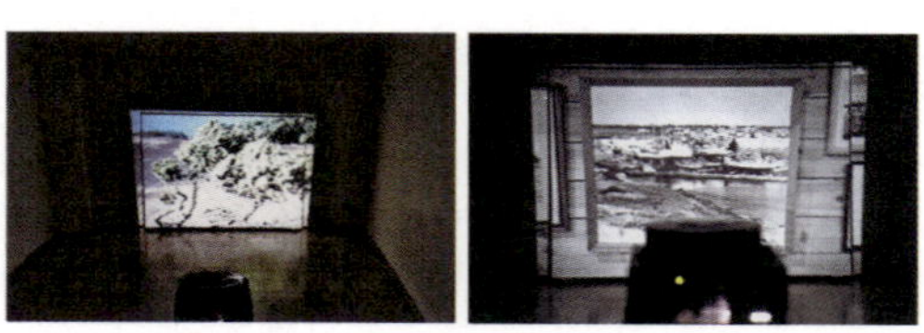

Over the course of the following years, the following brief characterisation established itself:

> The Fascinations section is a huge factory of experimental cinema, which rids film based in reality of everything that weighs it down, thus significantly deepening the possibilities of cinematic perception.[160]

Similarly to the situation with PAF Olomouc, the Fascinations section at Ji.hlava IDFF represents a logical culmination of tendencies that the festival doubtless reflected much sooner – experimental films made both in the Czech Republic and abroad represented a significant and natural component of the programming at Ji.hlava from the very beginnings of the festival, but they were never part of a comprehensive section or competition. The richly branching dramaturgy of Fascinations is the work of film historian and documentary film-maker Andrea Slováková. The section presented several programmes, one of which was competitive (an international competition for best experimental documentary), others non-competitive, profile-based, thematic, etc.[161] In 2008, the focus was on British avant-garde cinema of the 1960s and '70s, as well as the Exprmntl.cz programme, which was non-competitive at the time (it only entered the competition section in 2015 under the title Fascinations: Exprmntl.cz).

Every year, the jury judging both the international and Czech competition sections of Fascinations is composed of a "cinematic" family, at least one member of which is somehow connected to experimental audiovisual art – a refreshing and courageous concept that is often in resonance with the nature of the works presented. In 2008, the jury was composed of film historian and author of *Západní filmová avantgarda* [The Western Cinematic Avant-Garde] Stanislav Ulver, who was joined by his wife and son (a year earlier, Ulver had also been part of the first Other Visions jury). In following years, the winning films were decided by families of filmmakers that included Jan Daňhel, Martin Ježek, Alice Růžičková, Petr Skala, Martin Čihák, and Zbyněk Baladrán. The first edition of the Exprmntl.cz competition was judged by the French experimental film-maker Emmanuel Lefrant and his partner, the multimedia

[160] With "perception" replacing the earlier "expression". It is still true that the festival predominantly uses the phrase "experimental film" to describe the production presented there. Ji.hlava IDFF, accessed 8 Apr 2022, https://www.ji-hlava.cz/programove-sekce/fascinace.

[161] Fascinations includes or included the following events and competitions: Fascinations (competition for the best international experimental documentary film), Fascinations: Exprmntl.cz (competition for the best Czech experimental documentary film), Laboratorium (formerly the Fascinations off-screen programme for experimental documentaries), Conference Fascinations (a conference for distributors, gallerists, curators, and festivals of experimental film) and the related annual introduction of "the experimental scene of a particular region" (with an emphasis on Eastern European experimental and underground work under totalitarian regimes, e.g., the Balkan Peninsula and the Baltic states, Ukraine or Poland), and finally thematic (eroticism, home, garden, eternity, the factory, etc.) or biographical non-competition profiles (Jan Jedlička, Lumír Hladík).

artist Elene Gui, and the jury of the most recent edition of Fascinations (which took place online due to the pandemic), in 2020, consisted of Filip Cenek and Markéta Lisá, partners and both audiovisual artists.[162]

In contrast to the curated Other Visions with a selection of ten competing works selected by a different figure each year, the dramaturgy of Exprmntl.cz has – for years – characterised itself only in general terms claiming that it is a festival (or, later, competition) "of the latest Czech experimental films that touch upon reality and never cease in their search for new ways of expressing reality through classical and digital film". The relatively undefined criteria used for the selection (or rather the collection), together with the standardised presentation format for the competing works in the form of several screening blocks, mark the limits of Ji.hlava's renowned motto of "thinking through film", which is the festival's unofficial subtitle. Or rather: they draw attention to the problematic grasp of the "experimental" work that is increasingly created outside the context of cinema through the dispositif of the traditional film festival, adjusted for another form of production (a taxonomic system of film descriptions, the politics of premieres, the fixed conditions of cinema screenings, and the terminologically much more rigid conception of a much more fluid area of contemporary art).[163]

The question of the unclear boundary between a collection and an unspecified yearly selection of works[164] would seem to be more debatable in the context of the contemporary art world, where curators – with their critical perspective as well as their personal interests and modes of working – enter the spotlight with greater clarity than festival dramaturgs. At the same time, Exprmntl.cz (much more than Other Visions) has ambitions of introducing each of the works individually, ideally also

[162] The jury of Other Visions at PAF Olomouc is mostly composed of international festival guests, both artists and theorists. The curator never participates in choosing which of the ten works they selected will become the winner.

[163] Fascinations: Exprmntl.cz, for instance, does not put out a separate open call that could – like the Other Visions open call – inform more proactively within the art scene. The process of submission, for instance, a three-minute piece of video art, is done through the same interface used to submit feature-length documentary films produced internationally. Even these seemingly banal conditions shape the form of the competition, with more frequent appearances by artists tied to the cinematic context, students and graduates of film schools, or visual artists with a broader artistic scope and connections. Nevertheless, the participation of artists has increased in recent years, which is also a result of the increasingly rich and confident production of art of the moving image in this profession.

[164] The most frequent participants at Exprmntl.cz throughout the existence of the festival/competition are artists connected to CAS – the Center for Audiovisual Studies at FAMU (e.g., Martin Blažíček, Michal Cáb, Michal Kindernay, Dalibor Knapp, Anna Kryvenko, Adéla Kudlová, Franz Milec, Alexandra Moralesová, Kryštof Pešek, Vladimír Turner, Ondřej Vavrečka, and others). Since 2015, when the section became competitive, winners have included Anna Kryvenko, Ondřej Vavrečka, Lucie Navrátilová, and Diana Cam Van Nguyen. FAMU's hegemony over the awards was only interrupted in the last two editions, which were won by visual artists Marie Lukáčová (2019) and Zbyněk Baladrán (2020) – the works of the latter artist appear in the Exprmntl.cz section with considerable regularity.

inviting the author.[165] The missing articulation of the overall dramaturgical conception of these qualitatively diverse selections – which has long been incomprehensible both to spectators and to artists whose works have been repeatedly rejected despite meeting all the criteria – is all the more palpable in this respect.[166]

It is also hard to understand the premiere imperative mentioned above (of a presentation of the work in the context of cinema) as a condition for participation in the competition, later transformed by the festival into the "World Premiere" tagline, which represents, in the context of the small and close-knit Czech environment, a needlessly autocratic gesture on the part of the festival.[167] The festival argues that if this were not so, important figures including producers and distributors would not travel to Jihlava,[168] which is understandable from the perspective of the festival's management and their politics. With regard to Czech "experimental" production, however – most of which is created with minimal financial support – this argument seems rather exaggerated; a manifestation of the festival's lack of confidence and the limited sensitivity of the "factory" towards the situation in which most of these works (as well as their audiences) find themselves.[169]

The example of Ji.hlava is an apt demonstration of the fact that while works of the moving image themselves can no longer be easily

[165] In 2020, when the festival migrated online due to the pandemic, this agreeable effort, fulfilled for years, "spilled" over (due to the use of the video call format to interview artists) into an otherwise unthinkable situation (and one highly demanding for spectators) where these individual interviews took up more time in the programme than the competition pieces. Even so, this discipline, doubtless exhausting to organise, represents a welcome contrast to the presentation of Other Visions, which – barring several editions with more structured content (e.g., the 8th, in 2014, curated by Marika Kupková) – usually involves the curators speaking for the competing works.

[166] I did an extensive interview with Andrea Slováková about Ji.hlava's Fascinations in November 2019 at the behest of Kunsthalle Praha, one of the partners and sponsors of Conference Fascinations in 2018 and 2019. An abridged version of the interview was published in English in *Kunsthalle Conversations* ("Andrea Slováková in conversation with Lenka Střeláková", in *Kunsthalle Conversations*, eds. Ivana Goossen – Christelle Havranek (Prague: Kunsthalle Praha, 2020, pp. 38–53). Responding to a question about the selection and dramaturgy, Slováková said: "There are always a lot of selection criteria and it couldn't be described as some sort of trivial mathematical process. Creative methods and procedures adapted in the film play a role, as do critical and innovative ways of working with resources such as technology and media, character connections, and narrative – there are really a lot of aspects I look for when analysing each work. And that's also why layered essayistic works by experienced artists and simple student exercises might end up side by side – but each of them brings a perspective on reality that's powerful, inventive or surprising in some way." Ibid., p. 43.

[167] Also considering how negligible and lacking in foresight the festival's funding of the Exprmntl.cz prize seems to be (see footnote no. 38). Premiere politics might traditionally be connected to competitions at film festivals, but there are also gradations and adaptations (e.g., a premiere at a category A festival). Ji.hlava could certainly afford to make such a decision, but it would mean changing direction. i.e., instead of attempting to form a local, specific environment through adopted criteria, trying to adapt these in accordance with local needs and beginning to ask how activity in this environment could be supported.

[168] Ibid.

[169] For instance, the winning work of Fascinations: Exprmntl.cz in 2019 was Marie Lukáčová's *Moréna Rex*, which was presented as a "World Premiere". However, the work was created in co-production with the Center for Contemporary Arts Prague, where most interested spectators had already seen it (in its original, gallery installation form) long before Ji.hlava.

classified and allowed to take part in competitions on the basis of the medium used, the work's screening or installation demands, or the artist's degree, there are fundamental differences in how these works are treated. These differences arise from the diverging practices of gallery and cinematic institutions (and the competitions they organise) – and it is ultimately these practices that significantly contribute to the resultant form of the work.

Presentation, Support, and Awards in the Context of Film Events

Moving image competitions do not only codify specific, more or less clearly formulated criteria of evaluation – and, in consequence, criteria for the valorisation of the art in question. Along with exhibitions and other festivals, they also set the standard in matters of presentation, that is, they formulate the conditions under which the moving image of film and video can be presented and received.

Here, too, the works competing in Exprmntl.cz and Other Visions are subject to radically different treatments, mirroring the media scope and practice of each of the festivals. An individual approach to the presentation of moving image works arising from the context of contemporary art is always close to home for Other Visions – particularly considering the initial link to Martin Mazanec and Přátelský film discussed above. Various types, possibilities, and semantic associations of presentation were always thematised at PAF: works in Other Visions were shown both in a screening block in a traditional cinema situation as well as in variously composed shorter loops on television screens. Beginning in 2009, these were regularly installed in the attic spaces of the Jesuit convent where the festival takes place. A little later, these presentation modes were supplemented by screening onto walls or double-sided projection onto a hanging screen (Other Visions 2014, curator: Marika Kupková). The overall atmosphere, however, was not even vaguely reminiscent of an exhibition – rather, the space served as a relaxing lounge zone, which the works of Other Visions merely complemented, as sort of ornaments in passing. In 2015, when PAF symbolically confirmed a closer connection to the art scene through its name, which changed from the original Přehlídka animovaného filmu (Festival of Animated Film) to Přehlídka filmové animace a současného umění (Festival of Film Animation and Contemporary Art), Other Visions was installed for the first time as a fully-fledged exhibition in the atrium of the Jesuit convent,[170] which has since been devoted to an installation of the competing works.

[170] Differentiated Visions, exhibition of the 9th edition of Other Visions, 3–6 Dec 2015, Atrium of the Jesuit convent (curator: Lenka Střeláková, exhibition architecture: Matěj Al-Ali and Tomáš Moravec). The following exhibitions in this space were curated by Karel Císař, Michal Novotný, Rado Ištok, and Laura Amann. The latest exhibition of Other Visions – realised online due to the pandemic – was developed by Lumír Nykl and Tina Poliačková in 2020.

In contrast, the films competing in Fascinations: Exprmntl.cz are traditionally screened in several competition blocks, with the order of the screenings influenced by various factors including technical parameters, i.e., the screening formats of the individual works. The possibility of other forms of presentation and reception is virtually undiscussed, despite the fact that as early as 2011, Ji.hlava was progressive in presenting an "off-screen programme of the Fascinations section for experimental documentaries" called Laboratorium. Located in several galleries (Oblastní galerie Vysočiny – Vysočina Regional Gallery; Galerie Půda – Attic Gallery) and other festival spaces (DKO – Dům kultury – House of Culture; Dělnický dům – Labourers' House), over the years, the concept of the Laboratorium offered thematically conceived installations and screenings of various works, neighboured the game zone, and crossed over into interactive and VR installations, i.e., "audiovisual formats stepping beyond the projection screen", with references to reality always highlighted during the selection process.[171] However, these developments, undertaken as part of the Laboratorium, a kind of enclosure for art of the moving image, did not influence the format of the Exprmntl.cz competition, but instead unwittingly emphasised the awkwardness surrounding the competition's definition, the selection of Czech "experimental documentaries", and the fact that competition criteria and scoring are clipped onto normalised cages even in this – indeed, *particularly* in this – field.

The Exprmntl.cz competition nevertheless remains a crucial forum for presenting current Czech art of the moving image in film and video as well as experimental film. The Marienbad Film Festival once harboured similar ambitions, partly in response to the activities of the Czech Film Fund (CFF), which has, since 2015, put out a specialised call for the support of experimental films. The first edition of Marienbad took place in 2015, and its programme director at the time, Tereza Czesany Dvořáková (also a member of the Board of the Czech Film Fund in 2012–2015 and 2019–2022, and substantially responsible for the creation of this support programme), summarised the history of "other", avant-garde, and experimental films in the Czech Republic in the festival catalogue, where she also discussed the difficulties in this field of artistic production and the newly created CFF support programme: "I believe that the greatest challenge in the years to come is the need to get

[171] "The space of the Laboratorium is open to projections of the real into explosive forms of visual and audiovisual works searching for original aesthetic paths without losing reference to the everyday physical world we live in, to its documentation or archival representation. On the premises of the Vysočina Regional Gallery on Masarykovo náměstí, there is one room that serves as an alchemist's space for experiments with representations of the real." 15th Ji.hlava IDFF, 2011, accessed 8 Apr 2022, http://intermedia.ffa.vutbr.cz/mrizka-grid-diafilm; "The Laboratorium is a space for visual and sonic imprints of the real, this year stretching out across the Galerie Půda exhibition spaces. [...] The Laboratorium, which offers visual, sonic, and audiovisual works that enter into unusual forms of interplay with documentary material, archival images, documentation of both the present and the past, is the off-screen programme of the Fascinations section for experimental documentaries." 16th Ji.hlava IDFF, 2012, accessed 8 Apr 2022, http://archiv.protisedi.cz/article/jihlava-mezinarodni-festival-dokumentarnich-filmu-letos-posestnacte.

these films to other potential spectators. [...] And that is part of the reason that the Marienbad Film Festival was created".[172] In an interview made the following year, when asked "What is the Marienbad Film Festival all about?", festival director Zuzana Stejskalová agreed:

> It's about experimental film, which never had an independent platform in the Czech Republic. It would occasionally 'butt in' at established film festivals, where it would sometimes have its own section, but there was never a separate festival for experimental film – not until last year. It has been two years since the Czech Film Fund put out a separate call for experimental films and began supporting this type of art. And in order to provide a space to present these films collectively, the Marienbad Film Festival was established.[173]

The first edition of the Marienbad festival, however, presented its conception of experimental film with a strange combination of experimental and classical cinema, as well as new mainstream products of world cinema – an illegible dramaturgical orientation and profile, which did not become any clearer in the years to come. By the second edition, the notion of a collective presentation of the films transformed into Theatre Electrique, a competition for best Czech experimental film. Here, again, work with the classical medium of film was highlighted, implicitly rejecting parallel experiments and movements in the field of fine art. This was another variation on a well-known schism: visual artists working with the moving image do appear at film festivals – but only as part of the accompanying programme; in the shadow of cinema, whose position is ensured by the outdated definition consisting of the medium of film and screening: "Our subtitle claims that we are the last film festival".[174] It is no coincidence that this corresponds to the approach of the Czech Film Fund, which, while not explicitly stating the condition that works are created with film material (though that much is clear from the projects supported), does demand a compliance with "cinematographic requirements". Among other things, this means that the work must be presented in a cinematic situation, in an environment (even a site-specific one) intended for concentrated, shared, one-time reception. Projections primarily intended for fine art or gallery installations – even at renowned biennials of fine art and similar events – are

[172] Tereza Czesany Dvořáková, "Bylo, nebylo" [Once Upon a Time], in *Katalog Marienbad Film Festival 2016* [Marienbad Film Festival 2016 Catalogue] (Marienbad Film z. s., 2016), p. 8.

[173] "Marienbad Film Festival", *Všudybyl* 05/2017, 23 Oct 2017, p. 43, accessed 9 Apr 2022, https://www.e-vsudybyl.cz/archiv/marienbad-film-festival-4161. In addition to the festivals mentioned in this text, the "established film festivals" she references might also include the Karlovy Vary International Festival, which, in 2013, newly introduced Imagina, an international, non-competitive section for experimental and art films "with an unconventional approach to narration and style, original and radical visions of cinematic language". In 2015, the section included, among others, Roman Štětina's *Ztracený případ* [Lost Case].

[174] Ibid.

not relevant for CFF, as they exist beyond the formal limits of the field from within which the financial support is allocated.[175] In any case, the competition for best Czech experimental film at Marienbad was quietly cancelled after two years, as was the generous plan to support the winning works.[176] Unlike the other festivals discussed here, the stable form of the award,[177] publicly declared since the outset, also bore a symbolic meaning, intentionally referring to the context of making this type of art in the Czech Republic:

> Winners receive financial support – 10,000 CZK [ca €400]. By choosing this value, the festival draws attention to the fact that a proposal for the support of even a short, independent experimental film by the Czech Film Fund, which is the only institution in the Czech Republic to systematically support the creation of experimental film, is qualified by having to pay this relatively high entrance fee.[178]

Marienbad's management, whose changes in programming also reflect the festival's needs and its intention to operate on the local level, is planning to focus on profiles of experimental film producers in the future – a category that could also include established authorities in the art world who are their own producers.[179] Ideally, then, Marienbad would support, over the coming years, experimental art through both directed and spontaneous synergies, and all without a priori stratification by profession.

Connecting artists and industry professionals is a type of support long promoted by the Ji.hlava IDFF, which, in addition to screenings and other events for the general public, also traditionally organises an extensive

[175] From a seminar by Tereza Czesany Dvořáková and Monika Bartošová, "Jak žádat o podporu na výrobu experimentálního filmu?" [How to Request Funding to Produce an Experimental Film?] prepared for the etc. gallery (etc. galerie, Prague, 10 June 2021).

[176] Several artists – mostly film-makers – were awarded prizes in the two competition years: in 2017, the award for best Czech experimental film went to Ondřej Vavrečka (*De Potentia Dei*), Jan Kulka (*Pramítačka* [Archeoscope]), and Květa Přibylová (*Stopy, střepy, kořeny* [Traces, Fragments, Roots]), in 2018, it was Michaela Režová (*Štvanice* [Chase]), Michal Kindernay (*Transformace / Výpary / Melanosis* [Transformation / Vapours / Melanosis]), and František Týmal (*Taran*). The selection of three very different projects might at first seem confused, but it was intentional. The supportive system of the award was intended to affirm the diversity in what can be understood to be experimental (a particular form of narration, the use of special apparatuses to create or present the work, etc.).

[177] In the last few years, PAF has counterbalanced this deficit, adding to the variable material prizes from their own production and/or related to the festival's partnerships a fixed financial reward of ten thousand crowns for the winner. Ji.hlava IDFF, by contrast, does not publish the actual award neither at the award ceremony, nor in its final reports (the exception being the year 2019, when the award was sponsored – or rather paid for – by the 8smička gallery in Humpolec, a city near to Jihlava), so the prize is unknown even to competitors themselves. The festival management did not ultimately share information about the prize money even for the purposes of this text.

[178] Press release from 4 Sep 2018, accessed 9 Apr 2022, https://www.marienbadfilmfestival.com/docs/TZ_04092018.pdf.

[179] With the "experimental" category conceived very broadly, including connections to new waves or the debuts of directors such as Lucas or Spielberg. Jakub Felcman, guarantor of the Marienbad Film Festival programming, interviewed by Lenka Střeláková, 29 Jun 2021.

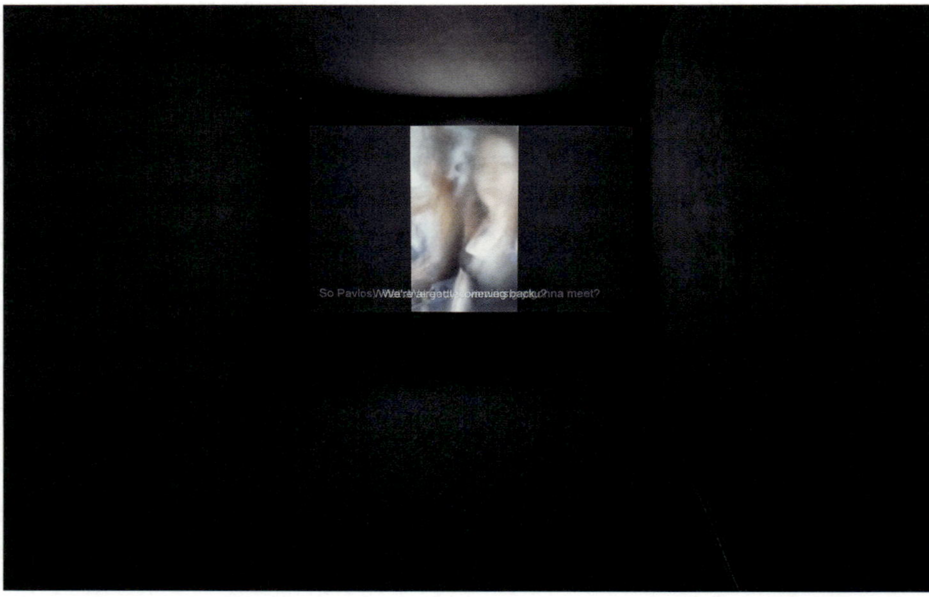

Tomáš Kajánek *Automatizovaný Youtubeový klik #1: Demokratizovaná zkušenost smrti přeložená v obraz na cestě za katarzí* [Automated YouTube Click #1: Democratized Experience of Death Translated into an Image on the Way towards Catharsis] and *Automatizovaný Youtubeový klik #2: Zastavte války, finanční násilí, krve prolívání* [Automated Youtube Click #2: Stop War, Financial Violence, Shedding Blood] (2018), installation at the exhibition of the finalists of the Jindřich Chalupecký Award, Trade Fair Palace, National Gallery, Prague, 2018.

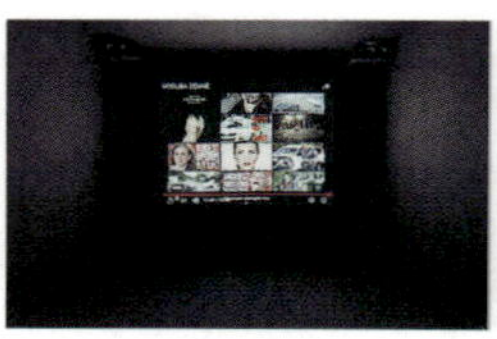

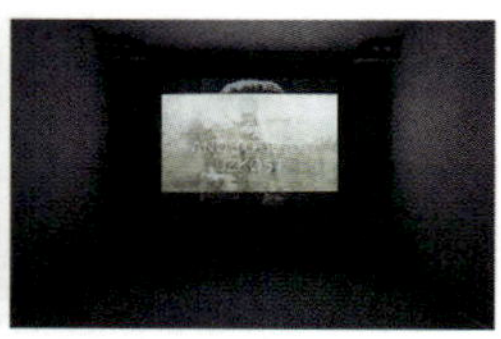

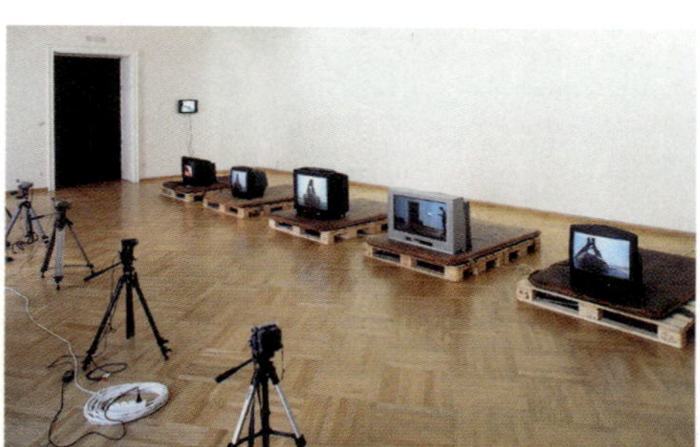

Radim Labuda *Tihle – Sociální situace: pět svázaných mužů* [These – Social Situation: Five Men Tied-Up] (2008), installation at the exhibition of the finalists of the Jindřich Chalupecký Award, Dům pánů z Kunštátu, House of Arts, Brno, 2008

“industry program” that includes the Conference Fascinations. In connection with this conference, Ji.hlava emphasises the festival’s ambition to “aid the international dissemination of Eastern European and Czech works and allow for cooperation with experienced international distributors, galleries, and festivals”,[180] also offering particular artists short one-to-one meetings with active participants in the festival including curators and distributors of collections or festival and other presentations of art of the moving image. Furthermore, the Conference Fascinations has a particular theme each year, and has already addressed topics such as distribution, curatorship, or the presentation and promotion of experimental film production, including particular aspects and examples of institutional and economic environments. Given the relative inaccessibility of this event, which is only available to accredited film professionals (or film students), it is difficult to responsibly assess its impact and declared support. Additionally, there are only very few conference outputs that communicate with the broader creative and professional community.

Presentation, Support, and Awards in the Context of the Art Scene

Organisers at competitions whose range of media is much broader (i.e., generally fine art competitions) have also had to confront the issues connected to the presentation and evaluation of art of the moving image existing outside the cinema and the traditional film industry. Among the most important of these is the Jindřich Chalupecký Award thanks to both its rich history (it was first awarded in 1990) and its focus on the younger generation (up to the age of thirty-five), in which new tendencies in art and the use of media are, naturally, most apparent. By contrast, even younger competitors and a stronger contingent of art of the moving image have always been a hallmark of the StartPoint Prize for best diploma works at art universities. This competition, originally limited to students of Czech art schools, was established in 2003, but starting with its fourth edition has broadened its scope to include other European countries.

It is true of both competitions that any current focus they might have on art of the moving image is determined by external conditions, i.e., the momentary focus of young artists. With regard to awards given to art of the moving image in the art world, the year 2008 was certainly significant,[181] with Radim Labuda receiving the Jindřich Chalupecký Award for his two connected works, *Tihle* [These] and *Ten druhý* [The Other]. In the spatial installation of the piece, video played a key role, presenting a record of a “social situation” initiated by the artist at a show opening, and

[180] Konference Fascinace, MFDF Ji.hlava, accessed 1 Jul 2023, https://www.ji-hlava.cz/konference-fascinace.

[181] E.g., Zbyněk Baladrán, Barbora Klímová, Ján Mančuška, Michal Pěchouček, Dušan Skala, Tomáš Svoboda, and others.

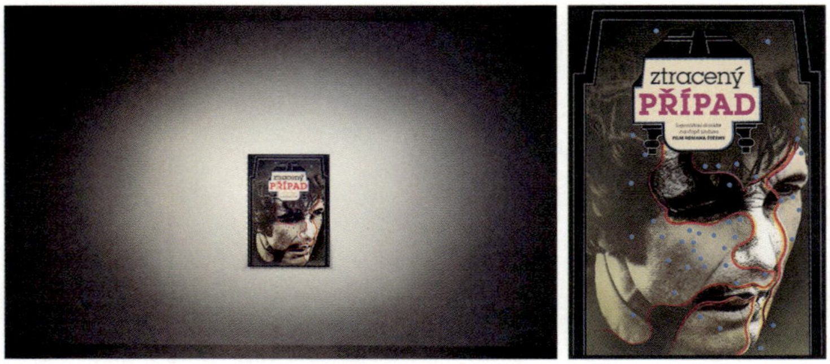

Roman Štětina *Ztracený případ* [Lost Case] (2014), installation at the exhibition of the finalists of the Jindřich Chalupecký Award, Trade Fair Palace, National Gallery, Prague, 2014

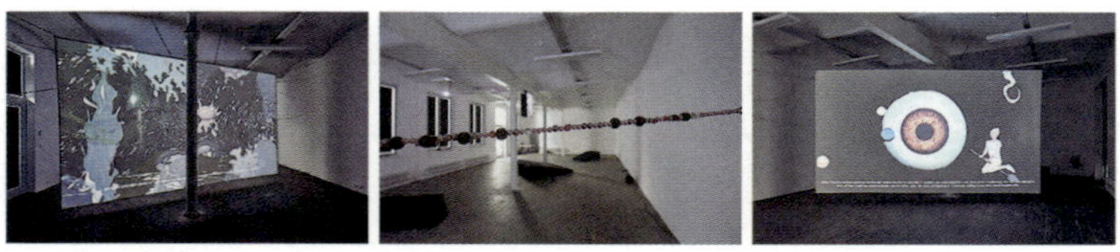

Marie Lukáčová *Moréna Rex* [Moraine Rex], 2019, installation at Cursor Gallery, Centre for Contemporary Arts Prague, 2019

Artur Magrot *Global Illumination* (2020), video, 5 min 36 s

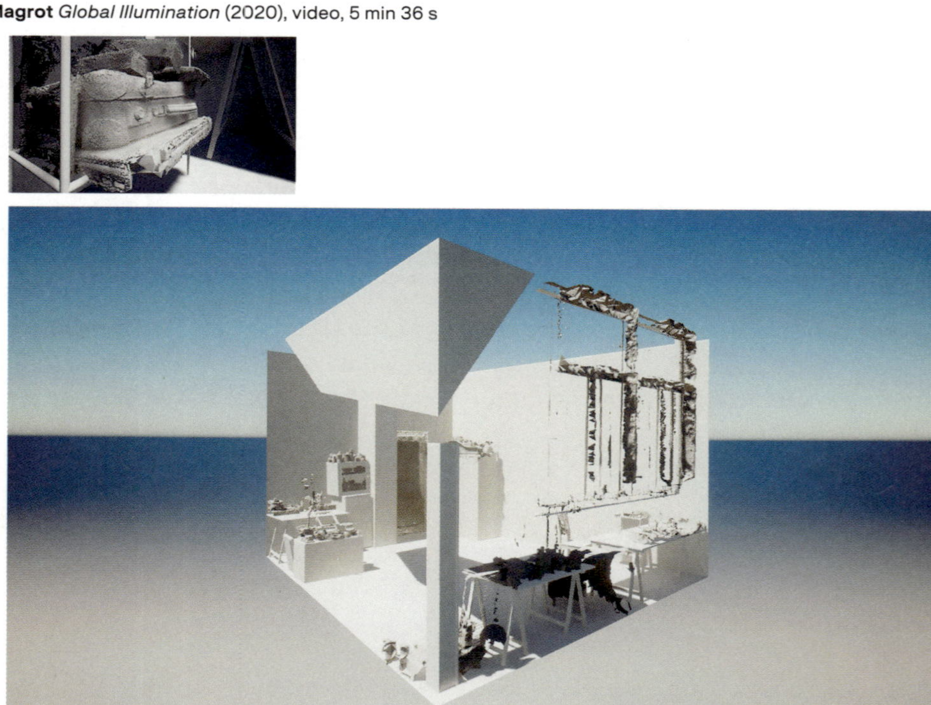

shown on classic CRT televisions, a mode closely tied to presentations of video art.[182] However, the first laureate to receive the award directly for an artistic video was Mark Ther in 2011 for his *Das wandernde Sternlein* [The Wandering Star], a controversial film featuring aestheticised paedophilic subject matter that was screened inside a black box. One of the competitor's to Ther's work was Filip Cenek's multi-channel slide projection titled *Vratké kino* [Wonky Cinema]. Since then, the medium of the moving image has made more or less regular appearances at the competition, both individually or as part of installations or environments (e.g., Adéla Babanová, 2012; Daniela Baráčková, 2013; Richard Loskot, 2014; Roman Štětina, 2014; Tereza Velíková, 2014; Barbora Kleinhamplová, 2015; Aleš Čermák, 2016; Dominik Gajarský, 2017; Martin Kohout, 2017; Alžběta Bačíková, 2018; Tomáš Kajánek, 2018; Marie Lukáčová, 2019; Jiří Žák, 2020, or Pracovní skupina pro výzkum mimosmyslové estetiky [Extrasensory-Aesthetics Research Working Group], 2020).

A particular sensitivity in relation to the presentation of art of the moving image was displayed by Tomáš Kajánek at the 2018 finalists' exhibition. The artist – who has a long-standing interest in topics such as the phenomenon of prosumerism, i.e., the merging of cultural consumption and production through user-generated content (UGC) on social platforms whose parameters and content he examines, reflects, and recontextualises – exhibited videos as ready-mades at the National Gallery. Two UGC videos were thus transported into the context of the art world, screened in gallery black boxes – other than this movement, the author made no encroachment on these videos. In accordance with this concept, he did not even download the videos in order to arrange them in a projection loop. Instead, as part of this thorough realisation, he streamed both selected videos directly from YouTube using a programmed, automated mouse click.[183] 2014 laureate of the Jindřich Chalupecký award, Roman Štětina, made the decision – which was radical in a different sense – to address the topic of the galleristic and cinematic contexts for presenting art of the moving image. At the finalists' exhibition at the National Gallery, Štětina exhibited "only" a poster to his film *Ztracený případ* [*Lost Case*], whose creation he initiated, entrusting Zdeněk Ziegler (graphic designer and creator of

[182] CRT televisions served as material, spatial artefacts with recordings of bound male figures that took the place of the actors who were present on the same mattresses on the day of the show opening, when the footage was filmed. Labuda connected the installation *Tihle* [These], subtitled *Sociální situace: Pět svázaných chlapů* [Social Situation: Five Men Tied Up] with his work *Ten druhý – Sociální situace: daniel.heart12* [The Other – Social Situation: daniel.heart12], which allowed visitors to interact with a young Filipino student (who made extra money by providing sexual services online) through a webcam and chat.

[183] Kajánek also accented his selected format of presentation in the title of both installations: *Automatizovaný Youtubeový klik #1: Demokratizovaná zkušenost smrti přeložená v obraz na cestě za katarzí* [Automated YouTube Click #1: Democratized Experience of Death Translated into an Image on the Way towards Catharsis] and *Automatizovaný Youtubeový klik #2: Zastavte války, finanční násilí, krve prolévání* [Automated Youtube Click #2: Stop War, Financial Violence, Shedding Blood].

legendary Czechoslovak film posters) with the realisation. The film itself was then screened weekly throughout the duration of the exhibition in Ponrepo, a traditional movie theatre space and cinema run by the Národní filmový archiv [National Film Archive].[184]

As one would expect, the StartPoint Prize is even more progressive in terms of the media range of the graduates' presentations. An installation featuring a video recording of an event by the artist was featured in the very first edition through the work of Ondřej Langr from the Department of Visual Arts Education at the Faculty of Education at the University of Ostrava, while the following year, art of the moving image (complemented by digital prints on polyester) even won the competition. The prize went to Pavel Ryška from the Faculty of Fine Arts at the Brno University of Technology for his *Ursonáta, stará švýcarská legenda* [Ursonate, An Old Swiss Legend] (DVD-video, 5:18, 2004). In the most recent edition of the StartPoint Prize (2020), three of the eight finalists submitted either a video or video installation related to topical social and cultural themes: Oskar Helcel from FAMU in Prague (deep fake technologies and developerism in public space), Ondřej Houšťava from the Academy of Fine Arts and Design in Bratislava (identity and queer theory), and Artur Magrot from the Academy of Fine Arts in Prague (lockdown, personal space, and alienation).

The more frequent and focused appreciation of art of the moving image logically entails a consolidation of its position on the Czech scene of art and culture, which is also favourable for the artists. In addition to a symbolic acceptance of their work, terminology is also developing as a tool to achieve not only a better and more sensitive grasp of the works within the specialised critical debate, but also for higher quality public presentations, which in turn conditions the possibilities of support. Support, after all, need not necessarily take the form of rewarding a winning work *ex post*, or, at most, offering further presentations or acquisitions – it can also take place during the creative process itself, e.g., in the form of consultations or equipment loans.

A specific example of such support and "institutional" care has been established by the Jindřich Chalupecký Society over the course of the last few years, namely since Karina Kottová came to lead the organisation. In addition to providing a basic budget for the work of art and the finalists'

[184] Štětina's edit-based film processes material from the renowned television series *Columbo*, primarily following the detective – and thus his actor – over the course of four decades (Columbo and Peter Falk chronologically from the late 1960s to the beginning of the 21st century). This study of a single genre and multiple temporalities develops as a kind of low-definition detective story, which sees the juxtaposition of the detective character – trapped in the mise-en-scene and the changeless attributes, coats, and gestures – and the ageing actor trapped again by this figure, whose internal world here merges into a single quiet, lonely, hour-long adventure. The combination of a running time bordering between medium-length and feature-length film and the intertwined, sophisticated narration means that *Lost Case* is predestined for concentrated viewing under conditions that can only be ensured by a screening in a cinema, while the regular Sunday repetitions enforce other semantic levels of the work.

exhibition, it also aims to provide ad hoc aid during production – in the sense of arranging filming locations, materials, and equipment – which is a relatively generous offering in the fine art context, made possible by the Society's partnership with the Biofilms rental company. "Softer", less visible – but similarly important – support is then provided by the Jindřich Chalupecký Society in the form of consultations on the work in progress or the offer of providing contacts and connections with other professionals. This production activity takes place both during the Award and in the Society's other curatorial initiatives that lead to the creation of co-productions and new commissioned works including audiovisual art productions.[185]

From Experiments to Visions

The approach of the Jindřich Chalupecký Society and the development of their Award is, after all, a clear reflection of the transformation that has taken place over the past twenty years in terms of the production, dissemination, and valorisation of art of the moving image within the world of fine art, as well as in the field of the ideological reconstruction of art institutions and their relationship to (educated, represented) artists. The professionalisation of both the creative process and its theoretical background results in experiments regarding modes of leadership, support, and evaluation that attempt to instil alternatives to the unidirectional, strictly hierarchical modus vivendi. In this light, activities connected to the cinematic (generally more conservative) environment operate in more closed, gradually changing structures that are shaped by – among other factors – economic flow (see the above-mentioned Czech Film Fund's arguments relating to the support of a particular form of audiovisual works).

Today, the boundary between experimental film and what's known as artists' cinema is much more permeable, the production of art of the moving image has gained confidence over the years, broadening its scope and professional context, mastering technologies, networking, garnering the attention of a broader audience, and adopting more precise and nuanced terminology. Now, it is again this artistic production that challenges others to experiment and dream of new visions: producers, organisers, critics, curators, dramaturgs, and other professionals. For it has become apparent that while there are established projects on the Czech scene devoted to the presentation of new Czech works of art of the moving

[185] Karina Kottová, director of the Jindřich Chalupecký Society, interviewed by Lenka Střeláková, 29 June 2021.

image of film and video,[186] there is also still plenty of space available for an initiative that would do a better job of harmonising and communicating the needs of artists, film-makers, and audiences; meaningfully overseeing the presentation; and offering a more structured perspective. Alternatively, it would be beneficial to open up events to interested parties who, for various reasons, did not make it into the competition programme but would still like to present their works, like the International Short Film Festival Oberhausen allows (to a degree and under the condition of personal presentation). The festival would ideally be linked to a multimedia library (or another form of distribution or archiving of the collected works ensuring their availability outside the space-time of the given event[187]). This is, of course, a relatively complex task, highly difficult in terms of technological, legality, and in other respects, all of which is already the territory of the following chapter by Matěj Strnad.

[186] In addition to those mentioned in the text, this also means much older festivals mostly connected to the tradition of amateur film: Mladá kamera Uničov [Uničov Young Camera] (an international festival of short films by film-makers under thirty with a history spanning almost fifty years and a preponderance of live-action, narrative content) and especially Brněnská 16 – Mezinárodní filmový festival krátkého filmu BRNO16 [International Short Film Festival BRNO16], one of the oldest short film festivals in the world, first organised in 1960. In addition to its international competition, the BRNO16 festival also started the Československá 16 [Czechoslovak 16] competition in 2019. The competition sections of both festivals present audiovisual works with a running time of under thirty minutes.

[187] Ji.hlava has its own multimedia library, and thanks to the 2020 online "covid" edition, the festival also extended and intensified its already established relationship with the DAFilms.cz portal, where the programme essentially migrated in October 2020. Neither the festival's multimedia library nor DAFilms.cz, however, offer a complete selection of the films competing in the Fascinations: Exprmntl.cz section. PAF, on the other hand, as part of its currently hibernating platform PAF Aport, organised several screening blocks of Other Visions, but for various reasons, this activity was not brought to a more systematic form and practice. A series of Other Visions was also published twice as a supplement to the Slovak magazine *Kinečko* (2013 on DVD, 2014 on a USB disk).

A Collection is Not a Project (Epilogue). On Attempts to Collect and Preserve Art of the Moving Image in the Czech Context

Matěj Strnad

The ways in which art of the moving image (including film and video) made itself at home in the Czech art world are suggested by the preceding chapters of this publication. But where exactly does video reside?

Where is it hidden away, who stores it? Is it supported by art museums? Why is it possible to attest to the importance and prevalence of the existence of art of the moving image through exhibition catalogues rather than collection catalogues? In this essay, the question "Where is Czech video?" will be considered from a practical and materialist perspective. We are not asking where it takes place, or where its development has led – we are interested only in where it is and where we can find it. Before attempting to respond, I must first briefly summarise why this question is so pertinent in the case of art of the moving image and why it has no clear answer.

Caring for Art of the Moving Image

The specific needs of care for art of the moving image in the context of visual art were first systematically thematised in the 1990s, especially in the United States and later also in Canada, the United Kingdom, the Netherlands, Germany, and France.[188] While problems related to the storage and playback possibilities of video were already the subject of discussions in the 1980s in expert and technically minded essays,[189] an awareness of these issues in the context of museums and fine art only spread gradually. In 1991, New York's MoMA (Museum of Modern Art) organised a symposium titled Video Preservation: Securing the Future of the Past.[190] Crucial for establishing a dialogue between traditional areas of preservation and the issues of video and magnetic media was the Playback conference,[191] organised in San Francisco in 1996, while the late 1990s saw the establishment of the Variable Media Initiative. This initiative brought together a number of museum and expert agents who gave rise to the broadly used concept of variability, i.e., a perspective on artworks (particularly technology-dependent ones) as at once fixed and variable, to various degrees and in various aspects. Part of their output is the still-inspiring Variable Media Questionnaire – an overview of tools for the digital preservation of works surviving on obsolete media.[192] This questionnaire can serve to record those variable characteristics of the work, if possible, as part of an active dialogue between artists and preservationists.

During the 2000s and 2010s, specialised workplaces were gradually established, as were courses and study programmes focused on

[188] E.g., the Solomon R. Guggenheim Museum (New York), the Daniel Langlois Foundation / DOCAM (Montréal), Montevideo / The Netherlands Media Art Institute (NIMk, Amsterodam), ZKM (Karlsruhe).

[189] Jim Wheeler. "Long-term Storage of Videotape", in *Special Issue of the FIAT Newsletter*, January 1986 (International Federation of Television Archives, 1986), pp. 66–75.

[190] Deirdre Boyle, *Video Preservation: Securing the Future of the Past* (New York: New York State Council on the Arts, 1993).

[191] Its importance is attested to by the fact that it was supported both by the Getty Foundation and the Andy Warhol Foundation for the Visual Arts.

[192] Variable Media Questionnaire, accessed 10 Feb 2022, https://variablemediaquestionnaire.net/.

conserving and restoring[193] media artworks. This discipline is now taught and researched at universities[194] and practised in museums. Working with video[195] can be considered a necessary and logical foundation, although this field is usually conceived quite broadly, presuming a readiness to address challenges relating to net-art or interactive media. Historically more established media of technically reproducible images, such as photography and cinematography, operate in somewhat more stable frameworks and apparatuses, i.e., the confluence of the practices of production, presentation, reception, and reflection. The volatility of the moving image as an artistic medium presents many non-trivial challenges. If we consider the standard (or indeed preferred) mode of presenting art of the moving image to be

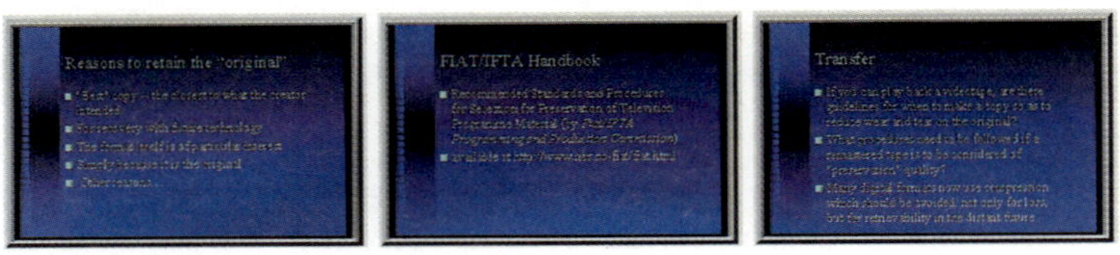

Screenshots from the website of the Playback conference organised by The Bay Area Video Coalition, 1996.

a gallery situation,[196] we cannot, for instance, reduce the given work only to its "content" or documentation. In order to understand it, and even to perceive its historicity, the content itself will not do. We must also take an interest in how the work was reproduced (presented, installed), to what extent this was the artist's intention, and why. We do not necessarily need to ask these questions of future audiences, but in our curatorial and conservational roles, we must be ready to answer them and, wherever necessary, prevent automatic reductions of the "work" to its "contents". An indelible component of caring for media art is an attempt at thorough documentation, including documentation of various iterations of the works, authorial intention, and the limits present during repeated presentations. To what extent is the chosen visual display unit (data projector, television screen, digital screen)

[193] I use these two terms in accordance with local practice, even though colloquial use today tends towards the simple description of "(time-based) media (art) conservator". Comp. Christine Frohnert – Hannelore Roemich, "Time-based Media Art Conservation Education Program at NYU: Concept and Perspectives", *Electronic Media Review* 5, vol. 5 (2017–2018).

[194] University of Amsterdam, New York University, Berner Fachhochschule, Staatliche Akademie der Bildenden Künste Stuttgart.

[195] I choose the term "video" to distinguish the conservators-restorers of media art from those who work on film as part of related but independent programmes situated in the cinematographic and film-historical context. Comp. Academic Courses on Film Archiving, Curating, and Programming, accessed 10 Feb 2022,https://www.fiafnet.org/pages/Training/Other-Film-Preservation-Courses.html.

[196] Of course, we do so with the knowledge that for many artists, the main ambition was to use their own moving images to replace those that were commonly available through television, appropriating or democratising the medium of television fully, not simply as an object. Even in Czechoslovakia and the Czech Republic; comp. e.g., the activities of the Nadace pro zpřístupnění médií [Foundation for Accessible Media]: Ivana Richterová, "Veřejně přístupná televize už letos?" [Publicly Accessible Television – This Year?], *Video + film* 3, no. 2 (1993), p. 6; Alena Kučerová – Stanislav Miler, "Také nenávidíte ohlupující televizi?" [Do You Also Hate Stultifying Television?], *Video + film* 3, no. 10 (1993), pp. 5–6.

an essential component of the work, and, by extension, how do we approach its unavailability or transformation, both of which we might have to face in the future? Can the work be presented in a loop? What do we do about the sound component?

There are numerous questions relating to forms of presentation. The notional whole of the discipline described here therefore has at its disposal methods through which these components, which are certainly not self-evident, can be addressed and described.[197] At the most advanced stages of this practice, it is not only the observation of these "variable" characteristics that takes place,[198] but also planning for the entire process of maintenance and conservation, including budgeting for costs connected to repeated presentations of the work in question. This planning can then form part of the acquisitional assessment – a process during which the acquisition under consideration is evaluated.[199]

Although I have stated my position against the automatic reduction of the "work" to simple content and attempted to suggest the problems related to the administration of the broader presentation context of the work, it is, of course, true that the content itself (i.e., the moving image and sound) also demands adequate care. Both classical film and – particularly – the easier to copy[200] formats of analogue video share the same double-edged problem. The more copies we make from the original matrix (the original negative in the case of film, a master tape in the case of video), the more it will be worn out and therefore at risk. At the same time, if we wish to preserve this original as a reference and create duplicate material which is then used to make copies, we introduce what's known as generation loss. In film and video, generations are what we mean by the results of every step of duplication or copying: the further we are generationally in terms of copies made of other copies of the original copy, the more optical and acoustic quality we lose and the more noise and lack of sharpness we gain. In an ideal world, these losses could be minimised, but more and more often, we

[197] Comp. The Metropolitan Museum of Art, Identity Report for Video Artworks, accessed 10 Feb 2022, https://www.metmuseum.org/-/media/files/about-the-met/conservation-and-scientific-research/time-based-media-working-group/artist-identity-report.pdf.

[198] Comp. the Variable Media project mentioned above.

[199] Comp. section 10.2 Collection Care in the Tate Acquisition and Disposal Policy, 2020, accessed 23 May 2022, https://www.tate.org.uk/documents/1685/acquisition_and_disposal_policy_2020.pdf.

[200] The process of classical film duplication (copying) usually requires professional photo-chemical treatment in a film lab (for instance, a positive master is copied through optic or contact copying, transferred to a negative duplication material, which is then "illuminated" by the master, after which it must be processed and developed so that it can then serve as a matrix with which to make other copies, etc.). Video duplication, on the other hand, could be carried out under relatively modest conditions and at significantly lower costs. All that is needed to make a new copy from a master are two recorders and the process can be scaled for purely amateur or home video needs. The easy copyability of analogue video was, after all, one of the revolutionary promises of all radical movements connected to this medium (comp. e.g., the Ant Farm collection and others).

are faced with a situation in which the work survives only thanks to a more or less expertly produced exhibition copy,[201] or even a copy of this copy, and so on. In theory, digital media do not suffer from these ailments, but only if ideal (and therefore rarely attainable in practice) conditions are achieved.[202] After all, even the physical media containing optical and sonic information represent a challenge, much greater in the case of analogue video than with classical film material. In simplified terms, films can, to a certain extent, be maintained passively (by ensuring adequate temperature, air humidity, and an ideal inert state). The binding agents that ensure the operation of a magnetic recording, however, are considerably less stable, as is the greater dependence of the entire analogue video system on the appropriate playback and display equipment that ensure reproduction (video players, etc.).

A generally accepted solution to the problem of obsolescence of analogue video is digitisation – which is now a truly urgent matter.[203] But even this process must be taken to task with regard to its parameters and subsequent sustainability. The first step is to determine the correct source for digitisation, followed by effecting the process in a manner that prevents the creation of further or new qualitative loss. The fulfilment of these maxims is certainly not the rule, and although the standards for the correct digitisation of analogue materials are well known,[204] they are not always adhered to (nor is this always possible). Generally speaking, in the case of digitisation, institutions were (and are) dependent on external financing, with the corresponding subsidy schemes generally designed on the basis of volume (the more digitised items the better). In practice, the actual digitisation parameters were thus generally defined by the aim of quick and easy availability rather than long-term conservational considerations. In contrast to popular belief, the process of care does not end with the act of digitisation. Quite the opposite – this step marks the beginning: the beginning of an unending process of digital storage using the appropriate codecs and formats, adequate storage, with regular checks and inevitable migrations.

Problems related to the identification of an adequate source (master) are also present in the case of born-digital works that have no limits concerning copying and sharing. The seeming availability is

[201] Comp. some of the works of early Czech video art, which survive only thanks to exhibition copies on Ivan Tatíček's tapes, e.g. *Větev – Prorážení televize větví* [Branch – Smashing Through a Television with a Branch] (Petr Váša, Marian Palla, 1994) (https://videoarchiv.nfa.cz/katalog/vetev, accessed 24 May 2022) or *Kytka* [Flower] (René Slauka, 1994) (https://videoarchiv.nfa.cz/katalog/kytka, accessed 24 May 2022).

[202] Nevertheless, in a standard workflow involving digital media, "lossless reproduction" is only rarely possible. In practice, it only really occurs in areas directly related to digital storage.

[203] Comp. the joint statement by UNESCO and IASA (the International Association of Sound and Audiovisual Archives) calling for the immediate digitisation of magnetic analogue media – Magnetic Tape Alert Project, accessed 10 Feb 2022, https://www.iasa-web.org/magnetic-tape-alert-project.

[204] IASA-TC 06 Guidelines for the Preservation of Video Recordings, accessed 10 May 2022, https://www.iasa-web.org/tc06/guidelines-preservation-video-recordings.

counterbalanced by necessary compression that only leads to greater degradation during future migrations. Generally, we can state that the price for the increasing availability of media of the moving image is the necessarily "consumerist" character of these technologies (in both analogue and digital media), reflected in the complexity of appropriate approaches to conservation. Since technological innovations are strongly influenced by the need to constantly offer consumers new and "better" products, it comes as no surprise that backward compatibility or sustainability are not quite in the interest of the tech industry.

Collections

In this section, after a brief introduction to selected problems in conservation and restoration, I will sketch out several attempts at addressing these problems in the Czech historical context. It must also be emphasised that for a long time, these problems were not identified *as* problems. In the Western context, the first systematic initiatives date back to the second half of the 1990s and were closely tied to museum institutions.[205] It was primarily museums that were capable of (and partly forced to by circumstance) working out sophisticated care systems for art of the moving image.

The fact that, for a long time, Czech memory institutions played virtually no role in caring for art of the moving image has a relatively simple, structural explanation: the long-term resignation of public institutions to purchase any contemporary art, closely connected to the lack of financing for such acquisitions. In this respect, there have been some positive developments, such as the establishment of the acquisition fund at the Ministry of Culture in 2017.[206] These developments can ultimately be explained by the increasing interest of experts and museum workers in this area. This is why, in the following examples, I examine *collecting* activities that only rarely aspire (or aspired) to serve as long-term preservation, this despite the fact that Czech museum law presumes and prescribes such preservation in the case of formally established museum collections.[207]

The landscape of collections and archives of Czech art of the moving image is disjointed, so a cursory sketch can hopefully be of assistance in helping the community of academics realise the pressing need for primary research. We can also hope that it will serve to support more focused arguments on why care for art of the moving image must be approached more systematically. The inflation of words such as *collection*,

[205] See above; the Solomon R. Guggenheim Museum initiated the Variable Media Initiative, Tate and MoMA proposed Matters in Media Art, etc.

[206] Comp. Collective of authors, *Sbírat umění* [Collecting Art] (Prague: Institut umění, 2017), accessed 10 Feb2022, https://www.culturenet.cz/coKmv4d994Swax/uploads/2018/01/sbirat_umeni_fin_11.1.pdf.

[207] "The owner of a collection listed in the central directory must [...] ensure the preparation, conservation, and restoration of the collection if these are necessary for its permanent preservation [...]." Act no. 122/2000 Sb., § 9.

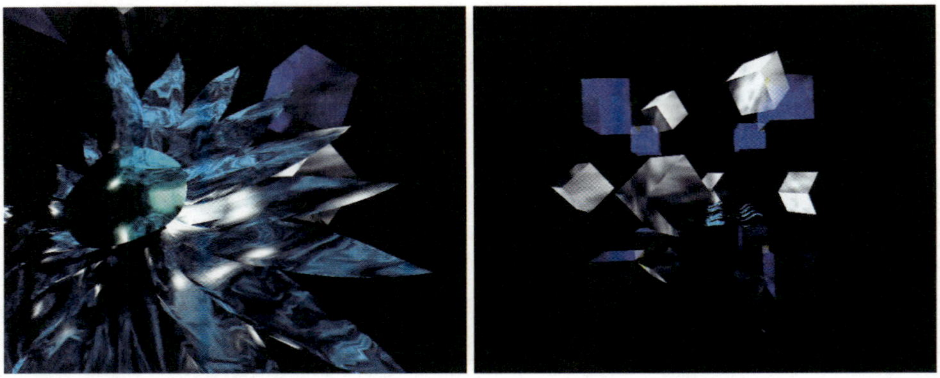

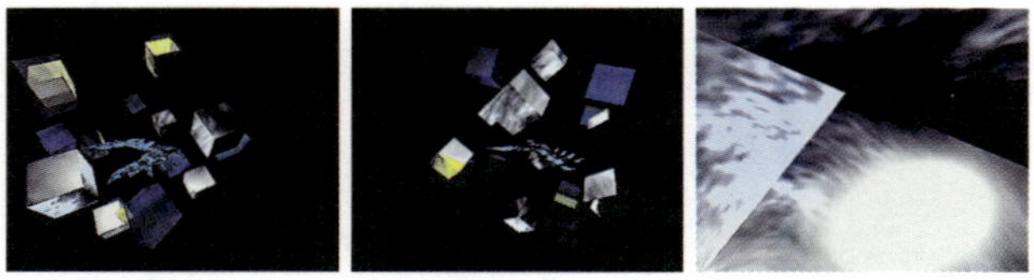

René Slauka *Kytka* [Flower] (1994), video, 2 min

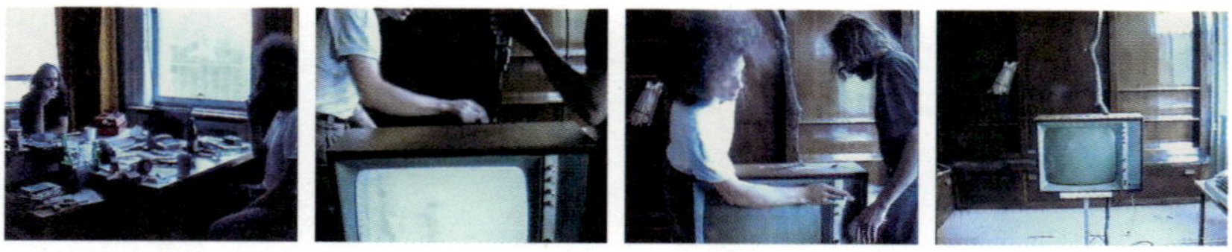

Petr Váša, Marian Palla *Větev – Proražení televize větví* [Branch – Smashing Through a Television with a Branch] (1994), video, 11 min

curator, or *archive* unfortunately does little to help differentiate sustainable initiatives from those that are unavoidably temporary. Although the final – or rather momentary – balance can seem unflattering, we must also remember the legitimate motivations of all participating agents. They did not present their activities as something they were not, and even if they spoke of collections and archives, we should not judge them using today's optics. After all, just as in the case of similar emerging fields, they focused primarily on production and exhibition.

In the context of collections and archives, we can mention the Media Archiv project. Symptomatically, and in contradiction to its name, this 1990s project focused less on archiving and more on presenting media art, particularly from abroad. The collection of Petr Vrána, a video artist who was active as both an artist and a lecturer first in emigration and later in Czechoslovakia and the Czech Republic, was closely connected with the ambition for a "media laboratory" and the activities of Nadace pro zpřístupnění médií [Foundation for Accessible Media].[208] In the early 2010s, there was an attempt to reframe this collection towards a broader presentation of art created in exile, and Petr Vrána (under the heading of the Media Archiv) began striving for the establishment of a multimedia Památník československého exilu [Czechoslovak Exile Memorial].[209] This was to include a number of film and video recordings made abroad under a broader narrative on "Czechoslovaks in exile".

Another 1990s attempt at collecting is that of Miloš Vojtěchovský and Jaroslav Anděl during their tenure at the National Gallery in Prague. Their efforts ranged from a proposal to establish a Laboratoř nových médií [New Media Laboratory] in 1996[210] to the establishment of a new media department as part of the Collection of Modern and Contemporary Art in the year 2000.[211] Almost immediately, however, internal managerial instability in this most significant of Czech art museums forestalled practically all activity in this regard for many years to come.

The case of the otherwise highly successful Moving Image Department, which ran at the National Gallery from 2015 to 2020, mostly directed by then head curator Adam Budak and Jen Kratochvíl, is somewhat deceptive. The name of this exhibition series seems to suggest the existence

[208] See footnote no. 636.

[209] Památník československého exilu [Czechoslovak Exile Memorial], accessed 8 May 2022, http://www.ceskoslovensky-exil.info/htmll/hlavni_stranka.htmll.

[210] NÁRODNÍ GALERIE: Nová média budou mít svoji laboratoř [THE NATIONAL GALLERY: New Media Will Get Their Own Laboratory], accessed 16 May 2022, https://archiv.hn.cz/c1–890592-narodni-galerie-nova-media-budou-mit-svoji-laborator.

[211] For more detail, see Anna Pogranová, "Nová média a české umělecké instituce v 90. letech 20. století" [New Media and Czech Art Institutions in the 1990s] (Diploma thesis, Prague: Faculty of Social Sciences, Charles University, 2016), accessed 10 Feb 2022, https://dspace.cuni.cz/bitstream/handle/20.500.11956/81578/DPTX_2013_2_11230_0_419998_0_152831.pdf?sequence=1&isAllowed=y.

of a separate department, but in fact, it was simply an exhibition cycle without other connections to the National Gallery's collection as such. According to the collection documentation, the National Gallery's current sub-collection dedicated to contemporary art and new media currently consists of about eight hundred items, with "art of the moving image" representing about a tenth of these.[212] For reasons of capacity, however, the National Gallery – along with other agents and collection administrators – currently makes only a limited effort to preserve art of the moving image.[213] The same is true for the second largest art museum in the Czech Republic, the Moravian Gallery, which has at its disposal several dozen works of a media nature, such as an extensive gift of works by Michal Pěchouček or the estate of Dalibor Chatrný, which also includes original 16mm films.

Given the demanding nature of responsible care for art of the moving image, it comes as no surprise that if the National Gallery or the Moravian Gallery lack a conservation system comparable to that which exists at selected Western institutions – we would, of course, also be hard pressed to find such a system at smaller galleries. Those that do have video in their collection include Galerie Klatovy/Klenová, Oblastní galerie Vysočiny [Vysočina Regional Gallery], or Galerie hlavního města Prahy [Prague City Gallery].[214] In 2020, a new player entered the field of collecting Czech video and media art – with considerable publicity:[215] Galerie moderního umění v Hradci Králové [Gallery of Modern Art in Hradec Králové]. Yet, at the time of writing, this gallery also lacks a corresponding storage infrastructure. The increasing representation of art of the moving image in public collections is, nevertheless, a fact, regardless of whether such acquisitions were made randomly or haphazardly, or – especially in recent years – systematically. The logical decentralisation of such activities, however, is also an implicit challenge for cooperation on methodology and conservation. Private collections and galleries, of course, are also interested in art of the moving image. In the local context, Sbírka Marek [the Marek Collection] is unique. Established in 2000, the collection began focusing on new media in

[212] I am proceeding from materials provided by Michal Novotný, director of the Collection of Modern and Contemporary art of the National Gallery, to the Národní filmový archiv as part of preparations for a collaboration on the NAKI Videoarchiv project in 2020.

[213] It must be said that during the time I spent writing this text, I was invited to provide external assessments on the state of several videos which the National Gallery is planning to exhibit at the Trade Fair Palace in the autumn of 2022.

[214] Comp. Magdalena Juříková, "Vyjádření GHMP k akvizicím pohyblivého obrazu" [The Prague City Gallery's Position on Acquisitions of Art of the Moving Image], Artalk.cz, accessed 10 Feb 2022, https://artalk.cz/2021/12/10/vyjadreni-ghmp-k-akvizicim-pohybliveho-obrazu/.

[215] Anežka Bartlová – Anna Remešová, "František Zachoval: Pohyblivý obraz se sbírá jen minimálně" [František Zachoval: Art of the Moving Image is Collected Only Minimally], *Artalk.cz*, 8 Mar 2021, accessed 1 May 2022, https://artalk.cz/2021/03/08/frantisek-zachoval-pohyblivy-obraz-se-sbira-jen-minimalne/; "Hradecká Galerie moderního umění rozšiřuje sbírku pohyblivého obrazu" [The Hardec Králové Gallery of Modern Art Broadens Its Collection of Art of the Moving Image], *Artalk.cz*, 25 Nov 2021, accessed 1 May 2022, https://artalk.cz/2021/11/25/hradecka-galerie-moderniho-umeni-rozsiruje-sbirku-pohybliveho-obrazu/.

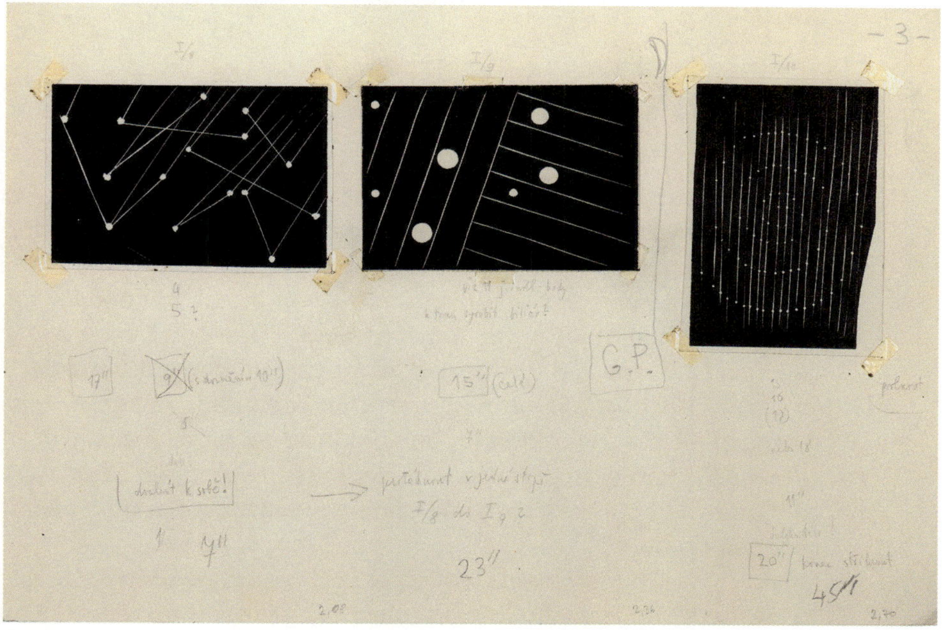

Dalibor Chatrný, graphic score for opto-acoustic compositions (1969–1970)

Alois Piňos *Geneze* [Genesis] (1969–1970), score

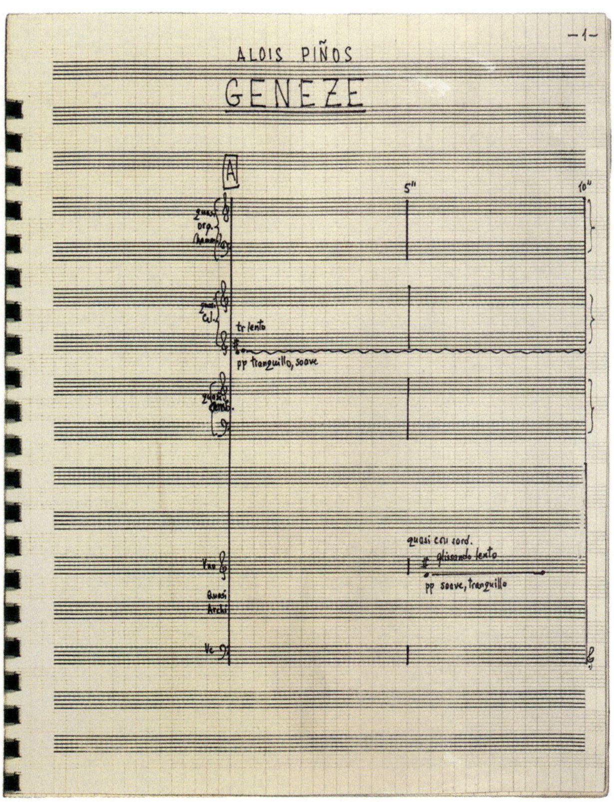

2007 and currently contains dozens of videos by Czech artists.[216] Given the common and matter-of-course use of the moving image, independent galleries also encounter the problems under discussion here. The etc. galerie, for instance, has worked extensively on the conditions for the creation and distribution of art of the moving image.[217] Several Czech commercial galleries also deal with the art of the moving image, but generally only as part of the portfolio of the artists they represent, not specifically and purposefully. This is understandable considering the virtually non-existent secondary market for moving image works.[218] For these same reasons, we only rarely encounter the theme of care and storage in the case of private galleries abroad.[219]

Concerning collecting or even archiving ambitions, two projects rooted in the university context took on more important roles than museums. The first is the Multimediální archiv [Multimedia Archive], whose beginnings at the Faculty of Fine Arts of the Brno University of Technology date back to 1994 and which covers a specific circle of artists, or rather events and initiatives mostly tied to the Brno art world and the figures that initiated the project. Also known as MAP (Media Archive Presents), this collection is an exception in that the administered works are available online,[220] but its processes of technical realisation and maintenance are highly dependent on ad hoc support from its host institution.

The second relevant collection, which declares itself to be "the only systematic collection of Czech video art and art video documentation",[221] is the Videoarchiv of the Academic Research Centre of the Academy of Fine Arts in Prague (VVP AVU). Beginning in 2007, this workplace gradually established itself as a central collection point for many artists connected to AVU or the art scene in Prague (and, by extension, the Czech Republic). Given its dependence on a department primarily devoted to research, its capacity for preservation tasks was severely limited, or else dependent on the momentary situation. Despite these conditions, artist

[216] A focus on fields including art of the moving image thus became a defining feature of the collection, comp. Michaela Banzetová, "Současní čeští sběratelé umění. Marika Kupková: nebylo možné ignorovat videoart" [Contemporary Czech Art Collectors. Marika Kupková: It Was Impossible to Ignore Video Art], *Czech Television*, 26 Oct 2020, accessed 16 May 2022. https://art.ceskatelevize.cz/360/soucasni-cesti-sberatele-umeni-marika-kupkova-nebylo-mozne-ignorovat-videoart-MiGlf.

[217] Comp. "Manuál pro zacházení s pohyblivým obrazem" [Manual for Handling the Moving Image], accessed 10 Feb 2022, https://etcgalerie.cz/cs/manual/.

[218] Loop Barcelona, eds., *I Have a Friend Who Knows Someone Who Bought a Video, Once: On Collecting Video Art* (Milano: Mousse Publishing, 2016).

[219] The neugerriemschneider gallery in Berlin, for instance, employs its own archivist (comp. Christin Pommert, "Between Creation and Preservation – The Position of a Gallery in Preserving Multimedia Art for the Future", paper at the Artworks from the Digital Era in Galleries and Museums colloquium,22–23 Oct 2019, accessed 10 Feb 2022, https://www.vasulkakitchen.org/en/umelecke-sbirky-digitalni-epochy-v-galerii-a-muzeu.

[220] Media archive presents, accessed 10 Feb 2022, http://media-archiv.ffa.vutbr.cz/.

[221] O videoarchivu [On the Video Archive], accessed 10 Feb 2022, https://vvp.avu.cz/videoarchiv/o-videoarchivu/.

Sláva Sobotovičová, art historian Terezie Nekvindová, and others[222] managed to arrange a collection unique both in volume (1170 entries) and time frame. In 2019, the collection of the Videoarchiv was placed in the care of the Národní filmový archiv [National Film Archive] while VVP AVU continues to focus on documenting exhibitions and other art events. The historical Videoarchiv is still available where it was created, but VVP AVU no longer develops or processes it.

The final aspect of the hypothetical solution are research and outreach activities. Although these activities cannot resolve the collection situation by themselves, they do contribute to raising awareness of the issue and can, perhaps, bring adequate strategies to light. Problems related to the unsystematic and insufficient care for art of the moving image have been debated at round table discussions hosted by the PAF Olomouc festival.[223] Meanwhile, 2019 saw an international colloquium hosted by the recently established Vašulka Kitchen Brno,[224] which has since that time run a project to process its own (i.e., the Vašulkas') archive. The last recent significant initiative is the New Media Museums international project under the patronage of the Olomouc-based CEAD / Olomouc Museum of Modern Art. Its aim is to focus on possibilities for collecting and taking care of new media art, but it must necessarily also address the absence of any background or safety barriers for video collecting.

But it too, like many of the examples described above, including the Národní filmový archiv's "Videoarchiv", is *a project*. Many institutions abroad specialising in issues related to the preservation and archiving of media art, such as the WRO Art Center, C3 in Budapest, or LIMA, were also dependent on projects. Although all these institutions have extensive collections, only the latter operates at a similar level of technical infrastructure as that exhibited by the Tate media labs or the Solomon R. Guggenheim Museum. Polish colleagues from WRO and Hungarian colleagues from C3 admit that long-term storage of the collections they administer is somewhat uncertain, or rather a challenge, and is unambiguously dependent on – project-based – financing. As LIMA offers its specialised services and infrastructure to a number of Dutch museums, it has somewhat more

[222] Barbora Vavrová – Sylva Poláková, "Videoarchiv jako obraz doby – Rozhovor se Slávou Sobotovičovou o Videoarchivu VVP AVU" [A Video Archive as an Image of the Times – An Interview with Sláva Sobotovičová on VVP AVU's Videoarchiv], *Filmový přehled* [Film Survey], accessed 10 Feb 2022, https://www.filmovyprehled.cz/cs/revue/detail/videoarchiv-jako-obraz-doby-rozhovor-se-slavou-sobotovicovou-o-videoarchivu-vvp-avu.

[223] Comp. the roundtable Pohyblivé archivy, průzkum praxe a situace [Mobile Archives – A Survey of the Practice and Situation] (Olomouc, 2015); the roundtable Situace distribuce [The Distribution Situation] (Olomouc, 2016); the roundtable Veřejné sbírky [Public Collections] (Prague, 2016), accessed 10 Feb 2022, https://artycok.tv/29890/pohyblive-obrazy-2, and Den videa [Day of Video] (Prague, 2018), accessed 10 Feb 2022, https://artycok.tv/41639/den-videa.

[224] Comp. Miloš Vojtěchovský, ed., *Vasulka Kitchen Reader* (Vasulka Kitchen Brno: Brno 2020), accessed 10 Feb 2022. https://www.vasulkakitchen.org/sites/default/files/document/01_vasulka_kitchen_reader_web.pdf.

stable structural foundations and can serve as an inspiration for a particular form of shared and networked care, also for the Czech context. Nevertheless, the current project-based precariousness of (not only) the cultural scene clearly leads to a constant and systematic marginalisation of the challenges related to care for what is currently one of the most common forms of creative expression. Strictly speaking, museums should be forced to take new media works in their collections just as seriously as works in traditional media, but in realistic terms, they do not have the conditions to do so. Dozens of works processed by the Národní filmový archiv with the maximum possible diligence and as part of a robust infrastructure (that is also used to store digital cinematography) will change little about the situation in itself – it is necessary, also in direct relation to a number of the activities described above, to search for a stable and institutionalised solution. This is a demanding but not impossible task – one which must begin with the realisation that *long-term care* cannot be addressed and supported as a *project* – it has to be a commitment.

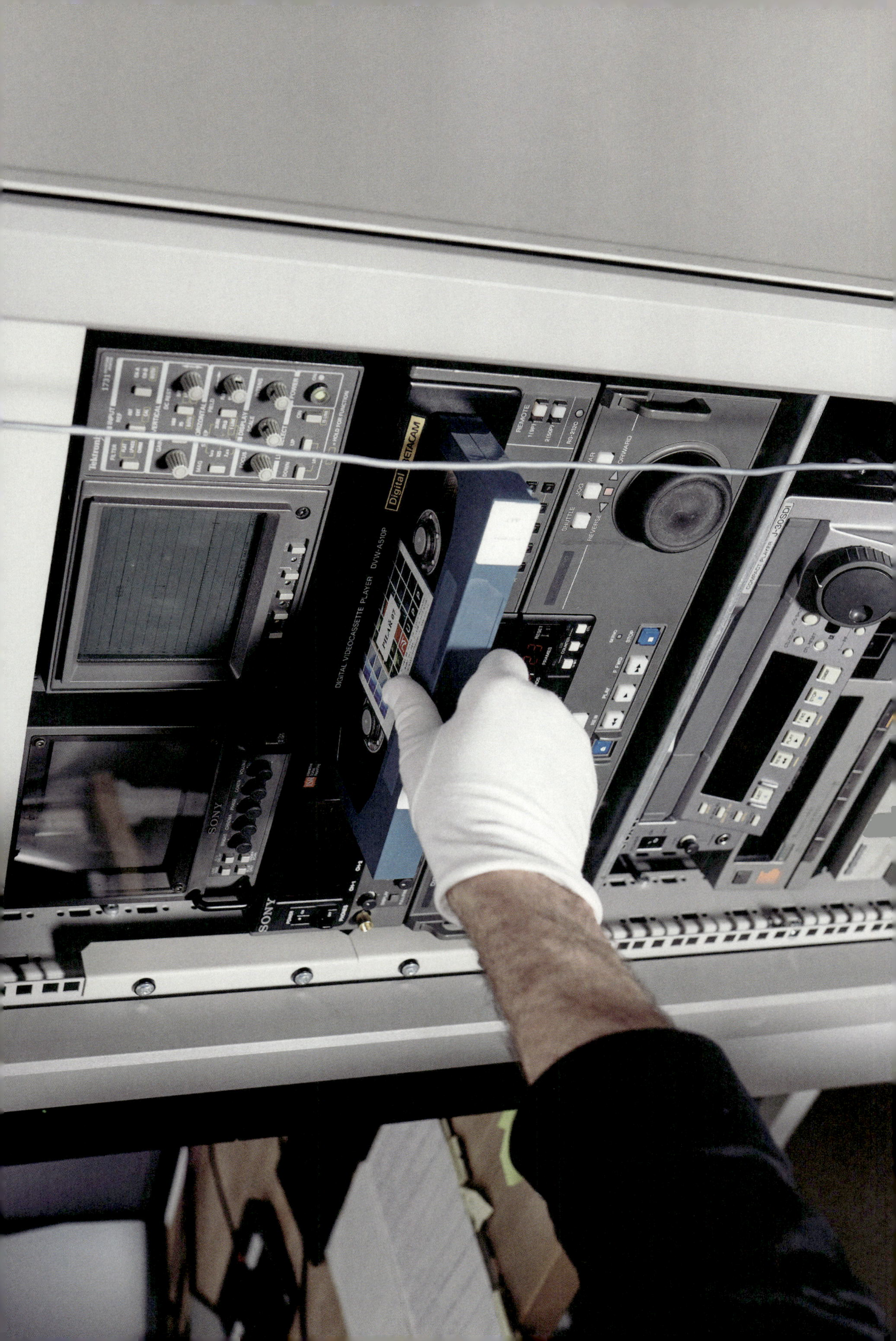
Digital BETACAM
DIGITAL VIDEOCASSETTE PLAYER DVW-A510P
SONY
REMOTE
SHUTTLE
JOG
REVERSE
FORWARD
J-30SDI

Martin Blažíček
is a media artist, curator, and pedagogue. His practice includes short films, video, live performance in both sound and image, programming, and design. His research focuses on code-oriented art and the beginnings of Czech avant-garde and experimental film. He has published writing on music, film, and media art in both specialised and academic journals. He has taught at the Center for Audiovisual Studies at FAMU since 2011, and in 2022, he became the head of the department.

Matěj Forejt
is a film journalist and theorist. His work explores animation, the exhibiting of art of the moving image, and the culture of the former Eastern Bloc countries, especially the German Democratic Republic. He has degrees in the theory and history of modern and contemporary art from the Academy of Art, Architecture and Design and film studies from the Faculty of Arts of Charles University, and also studied at the University of Hamburg. He worked at Národní filmový archiv from 2015 to 2019 and is currently at Czech Television. He is also an editor of the academic journal Iluminace and collaborates as a journalist and critic with Czech Radio Vltava and several periodicals.

Eva Krátká
is an art historian. Her long-term focus is Czech art of the 20th and 21st centuries. During her tenure at VVP AVU (the Research Centre of the Academy of Fine Arts in Prague) in 2003–2012, she participated in several research projects and conferences. She spent several years as editor-in-chief of the Czech & Slovak Edition of Flash Art magazine, where she also published numerous texts about contemporary art and the art world, including interview with artists, curators, and collectors.

Markéta Mansfieldová
is a curator and researcher. She has a master's degree in Exhibition Studies from the University of the Arts in London and in Arts and Heritage from Maastricht University. She worked as a curator at the Národní filmový archiv and etc. galerie, where she explored both historical and contemporary forms of audiovisual art. As an independent curator and critic, she has worked on art projects in both the Czech Republic and abroad. Her other research topic is the construal of identity in the context of Central Europe.

Martin Mazanec
is a curator and pedagogue. He has a degree in sociology and film studies from the Faculty of Arts at the Palacký University in Olomouc, and did his doctoral studies at FAMU. His focus is the curatorship and mediation of art of the moving image in the context of the gallery and the cinema. He has been the principal curator of the PAF platform since 2007, where he focuses on the role of the moving image in the context of animation, contemporary art, and music. Since 2017, he has led the Video Studio at FaVU in Brno along with Jan Šrámek. He has edited several monographic catalogues and anthologies and occasionally publishes in various periodicals.

Marie Meixnerová
is a graduate of English philology, film science, and communication studies at the Faculty of Arts of Palacký University in Olomouc. In 2017 and 2018, she studied at the Teachers College at Columbia University in New York. Her research and curating activities have long focused on the communicational and interpretive strategies of internet art and the history and theory of the moving image and animation in relation to digital art. As a curator, she works at PAF and ScreenSaverGallery, among others. She teaches curating of internet art at the Faculty of Arts at Masaryk University in Brno.

Sylva Poláková
is a film historian and curator. She works at the Národní filmový archiv, where she focuses on experimental film and art of the moving image from an interdisciplinary perspective. From 2020 to 2022, she directed the research project The Audiovisual Work Outside the Context of Cinema: Documentation, Archiving, and Accessibility and continues her work in long-term care for art of the moving image. She is also active as an educator, collaborates with galleries, museums, and festivals, and contributes to specialised and academic journals.

Tomáš Pospiszyl
is an art historian, curator, and pedagogue. He has examined the relationship between art of Eastern Europe and the West or high art and popular culture. He has published articles about official artistic life in Czechoslovakia and has a long standing interest in the relationship between film and visual art. He taught at the Center for Audiovisual Studies at FAMU from 2003 to 2018. He currently leads the Department of Theory and History of Art at the Academy of Fine Arts in Prague.

Matěj Strnad
is an audiovisual archivist and curator. He leads the curator's department at the Národní filmový archiv, where he is in charge of developing the collecting conception and special acquisitional, restorational, and curatorial projects. He is the chairman of the committee for the accessibility of collections at FIAF, the International Federation of Film Archives. He has a master's from the Center for Audiovisual Studies at FAMU. He writes, lectures, and teaches about topics related to care for audiovisual heritage and media art.

Lenka Střeláková
is a historian of contemporary art, curator and critic, a graduate of the Academy of Arts, Architecture and Design in Prague. Her domain is art of the moving image on the borders of the cinema, the gallery, and the database. Since 2011, she has been editor-in-chief of the cultural service jlbjlt.net. Between 2013 and 2020, she was an editor of the Artyčok.tv online platform, and since 2016, she has worked at an editor of the database of contemporary Czech art, Artlist.cz, and publications published by the Center for Contemporary Arts Prague.

Kateřina Svatoňová
is a film and media theorist. She has been at the Film Studies Department of the Faculty of Arts at Charles University since 2009, and has led the department since 2015. She has a long-standing interest in the theory, history, and philosophy of media, media-archaeological research into (Czech) modernity, transformations of (the perception of) space and time in visual culture, the parallel history of cinema, and the relationship between film and other media. She is a member of the editorial board of the academic journal Iluminace, a curator and co-curator of several exhibitions from the history of film and media, and the author of various texts and books.

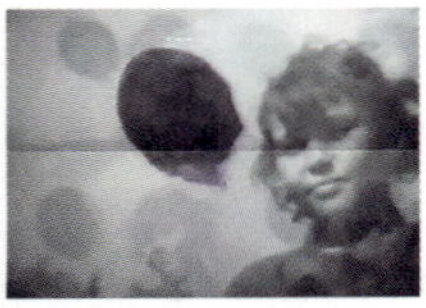

p. 70

Malování do vzduchu [Painting in the Air]
(Radek Pilař, 1965–1990)
→ https://id.nfa.cz/malování-do-vzduchu

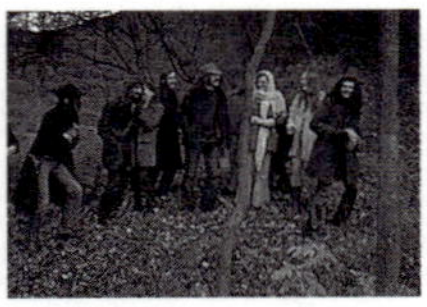

pp. 98, 99, 101–102

Pocta Fafejtovi [A Homage to Fafejta] (Jan Ságl, 1972)
→ https://id.nfa.cz/pocta-fafejtovi

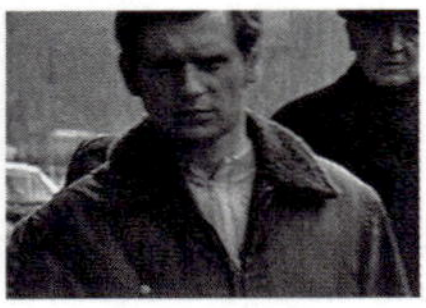

p. 52

Underground (Jan Ságl, 1972)
→ https://id.nfa.cz/underground

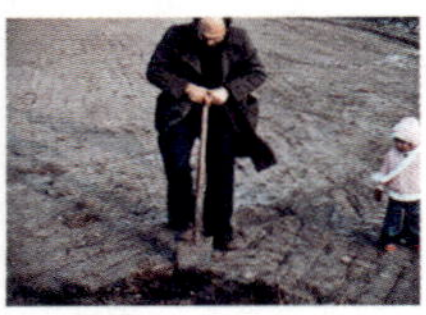

p. 105

Zmenšil jsem průměr Země
[I Reduced the Diameter of Earth] (Lumír Hladík, 1977)
→ https://id.nfa.cz/prumer-zeme

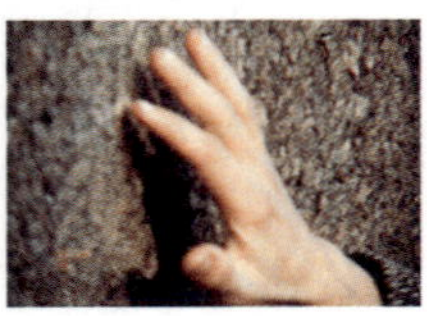

p. 106

Už nikdy tenhle balvan [The Never Boulder]
(Lumír Hladík, 1978)
→ https://id.nfa.cz/balvan

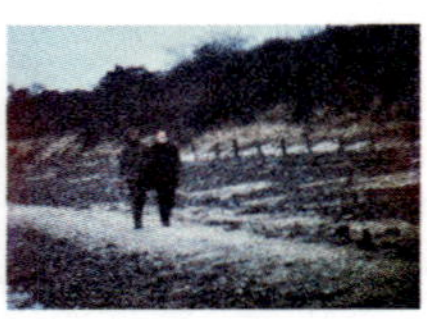

pp. 21, 104–106

Moře v zrcadle [The Mirrored Sea]
(Lumír Hladík, 1980)
→ https://id.nfa.cz/more-v-zrcadle

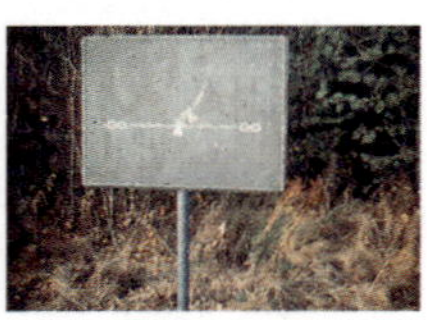

pp. 104, 106

Můj osobní „nekonečný“ vektor
[My Personal "Infinite" Vector]
(Lumír Hladík, second half of the 1970s)
→ https://id.nfa.cz/osobni-nekonecny-vektor

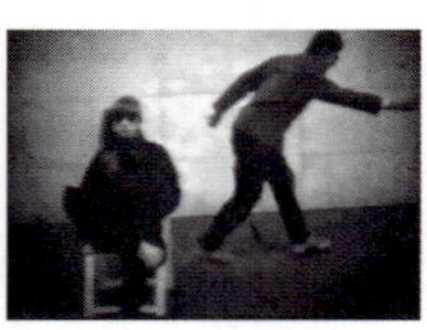

pp. 40, 42, 47

Metrofilm (Ivan Tatíček, 1984)
→ https://id.nfa.cz/metrofilm

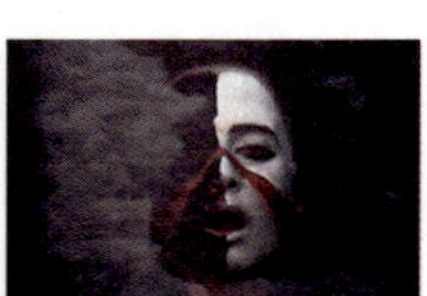

pp. 21, 48, 52

Pohádka pro šílence
[A Fairy-Tale for Madmen] (Pigi, 1985)
→ https://id.nfa.cz/pohadka-pro-silence

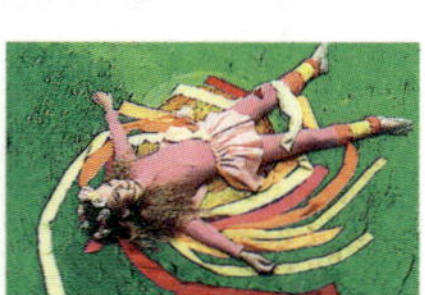

p. 56

Musica Picta – Čas radování
[Musica Picta – Time of Mirth] (Radek Pilař, 1985–91)
→ https://id.nfa.cz/cas-radovani

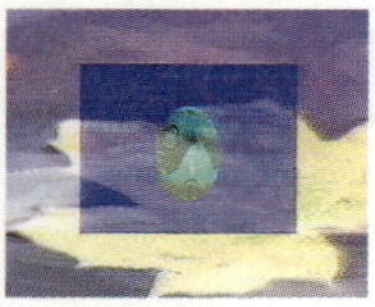

pp. 71, 75

Zrcadlo času [The Mirror of Time] (Radek Pilař, 1985–92)
→ https://id.nfa.cz/zrcadlo-casu

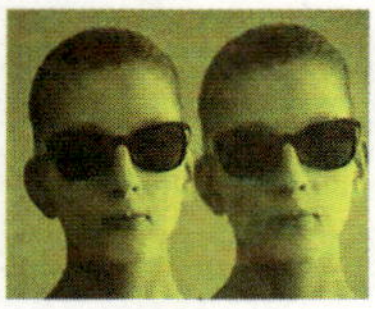

p. 74

Motýl v tunelu [Butterfly in the Tunnel] (Ivan Tatíček, 1989)
→ https://id.nfa.cz/motyl-v-tunelu

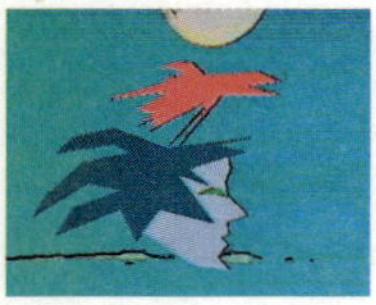

pp. 74, 212

Obrázky [Pictures] (Lucie Svobodová, 1989)
→ https://id.nfa.cz/obrazky

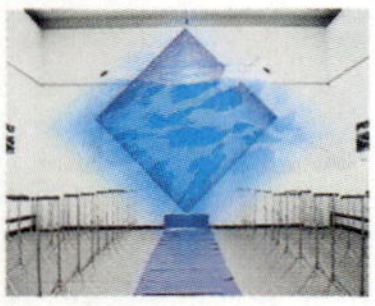

book cover (1/2)

Yes No Yes (Radek Pilař, 1992)
→ https://id.nfa.cz/yes-no-yes

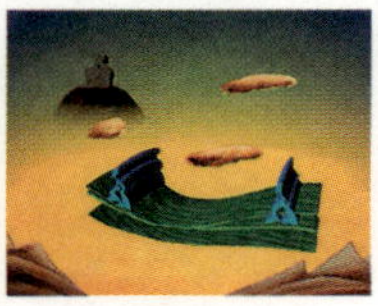

pp. 235, 239

Cesta [*Journey*] (Lucie Svobodová, 1993)
→ https://id.nfa.cz/cesta

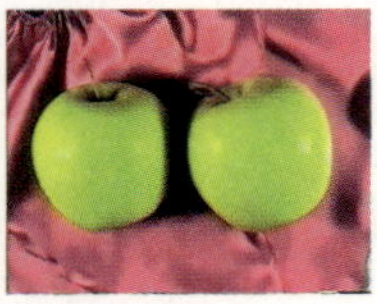

p. 144

Wet Video (Elen Řádová, 1993)
→ https://id.nfa.cz/wet-video

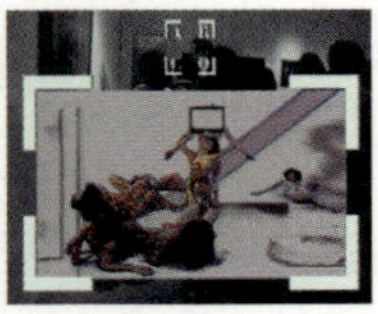

p. 165

ARCO – Aneb český videoart proniká do světa [ARCO – Or Czech Video Art Penetrates the World] (Ivan Tatíček, 1993)
→ https://id.nfa.cz/arco

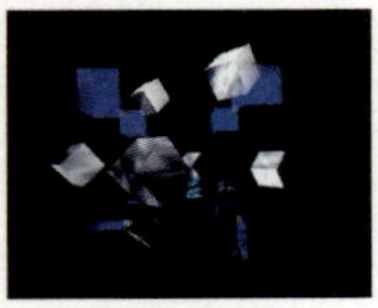

pp. 294, 296

Kytka [Flower] (René Slauka, 1994)
→ https://id.nfa.cz/kytka

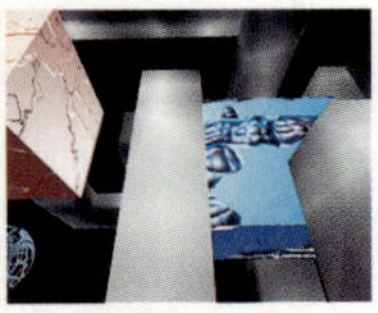

p. 212

Hlavolam [Brain Teaser] (René Slauka, 1994)
→ https://id.nfa.cz/hlavolam

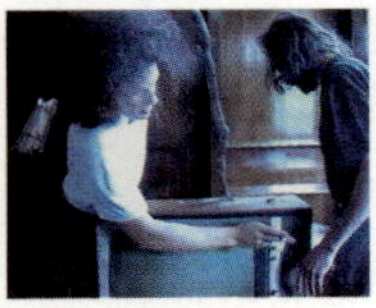

pp. 212, 294, 296

Větev – Proražení televize větví [Branch – Smashing Through a Television with a Branch] (Marian Palla a Petr Váša, 1994)
→ https://id.nfa.cz/vetev

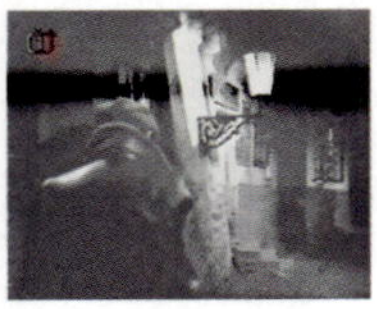

p. 173

13. revír [13th District] (Zdeněk Mezihorák, 1998)
→ https://id.nfa.cz/13-revir

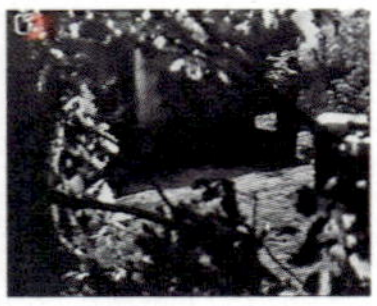

p. 173

Po stopách krve [On the Trail of Blood] (Zdeněk Mezihorák, 1998)
→ https://id.nfa.cz/po-stopach-krve

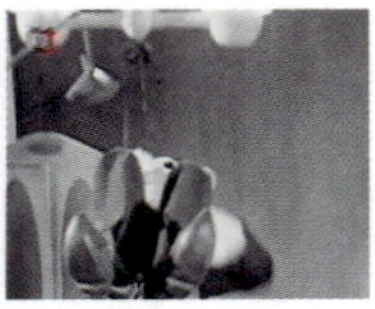

p. 173

Spejbl a Hurvínek [Spejbl and Hurvínek] (Zdeněk Mezihorák, 1998)
→ https://id.nfa.cz/spejbl-a-hurvinek

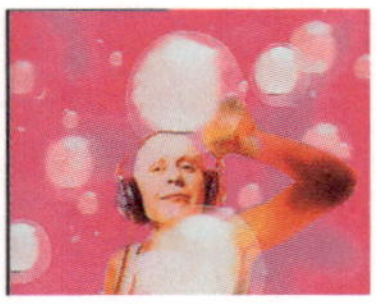

pp. 144, 167

Polednice [The Noonday Witch] (Niké Papadopulosová, 1999)
→ https://id.nfa.cz/polednice

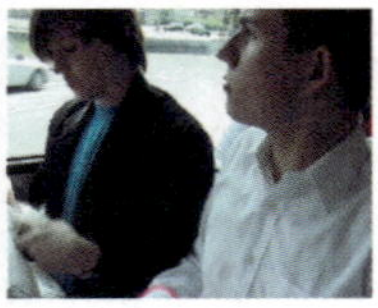

p. 117

MHD – Bus (Mark Ther, Ondřej Brody, 2002)
→ https://id.nfa.cz/mhd

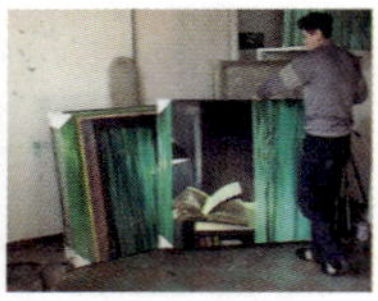

pp. 144, 208, 210

Sběratel [The Collector] (Michal Pěchouček, 2003)
→ https://id.nfa.cz/sberatel

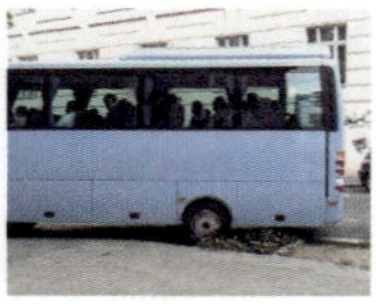

pp. 144, 174

360° (Eva Jiřička, 2006)
→ https://id.nfa.cz/360

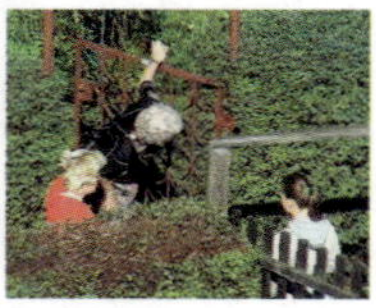

pp. 21, 209–210

Kapusta [Sauerkraut] (Pavla Sceranková, 2006)
→ https://id.nfa.cz/kapusta

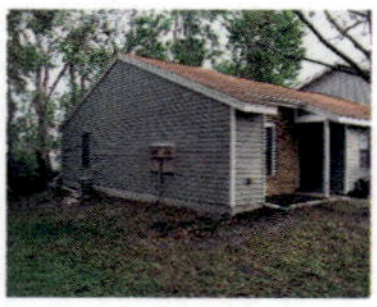

p. 212

Rozhovor se Sylvií Plath [Interview with Sylvia Plath] (Adéla Babanová, 2006)
→ https://id.nfa.cz/sylvie-plath

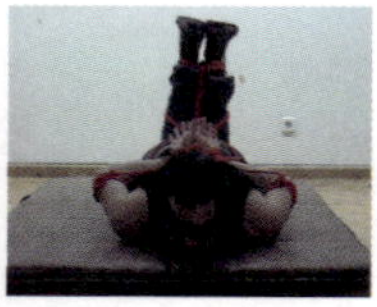

pp. 117, 282

Tihle – Sociální situace: pět svázaných mužů [These – Social Situation: Five Men Tied-Up] (Radim Labuda, 2008)
→ https://id.nfa.cz/tihle

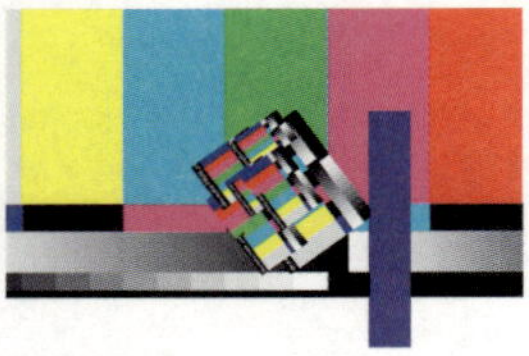

p. 264

Monoskop no. 3 – Monkeyking legend (Martin Búřil, 2011)
→ https://id.nfa.cz/monoskop-no-3

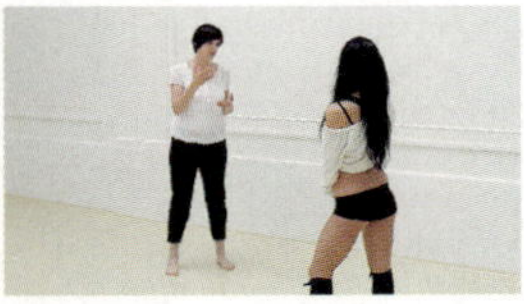

p. 212

Talk & Twerk (Alžběta Bačíková, 2014)
→ https://id.nfa.cz/talk-twerk

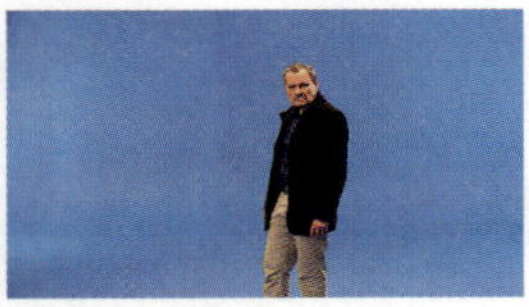

pp. 21, 246

Jako z filmu [Like in a Film] (Tomáš Svoboda, 2016)
→ https://id.nfa.cz/jako-z-filmu

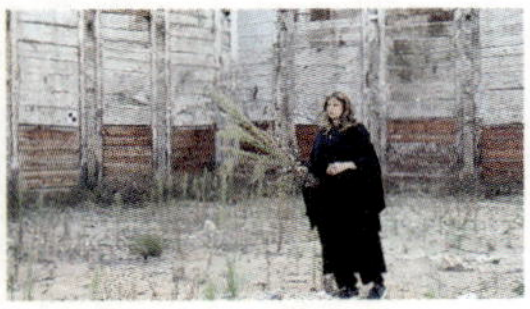

p. 212

It is Buildable (Oskar Helcel, 2020)
→ https://id.nfa.cz/it-is-buildable

"#19 Film", *Fotograf* 11, no. 19 (2012), accessed 2 Apr 2022, https://fotografmagazine.cz/magazine/film/.
"8.8.88", *Videoarchiv VVP AVU*, accessed 6 Apr 2022, http://vvp.avu.cz/videoarchiv/2476/?table=artvideoarchiv.
"10 let Nadace Open Society Fund Praha", 2002, accessed 20 May 2022, https://osf.cz/wp-content/uploads/2015/08/OSF_10let.pdf.
"16. MFDF Ji.hlava", *Protišedi.cz*, 2012, accessed 8 Apr 2022, http://archiv.protisedi.cz/article/jihlava-mezinarodni-festival-dokumentarnich-filmu-letos-posestnacte.

A

"About Monoskop", *Monoskop*, accessed 2 Apr 2022, https://monoskop.org/About_Monoskop.
"Academic Courses on Film Archiving, Curating, and Programming", *fiafnet*, accessed 10 Feb 2022, https://www.fiafnet.org/pages/Training/Other-Film-Preservation-Courses.html.
"Aleš Záboj (režisér): O Galerii-Drogerii Zlevněné zbcží", *Artyčok TV*, accessed 6 Apr 2022, https://artycok.tv/19695/o-galerii-drogerii-zlevnene-zbozi-1987.
"Andrea Slováková in conversation with Lenka Střeláková", in *Kunsthalle Conversations*, eds. Ivana Goossen – Christelle Havranek (Praha: Kunsthalle Praha, 2020), 38–53.
Anger, Jiří. "Médium, které myslí sebe sama: Audiovizuální esej jako nástroj bádání a vyústění akademických trendů", *Iluminace* 30, no. 1 (2018), 5–26.
Anon., "Experiment", *Informátor*, no. 2 (únor–březen 1985).
Artusová, Estelle. "Prostory společné práce: film a video", *Umělec* 8, no. 4 (2004), 85–89.

B

Bačić, Toma. "Tema Roma u suvremenoj umjetnosti", *Zarez*, accessed 20 Apr 2022, http://www.zarez.hr/clanci/tema-roma-u-suvremenoj-umjetnosti.
Bächlin, Peter. *Der Film als Ware* (Basel: Burg-Verlag, 1945).
Baladrán, Zbyněk. "Ruiny, archeologie a mezera mezi obrazy", *Labyrint revue* 16, no. 23/24 (2008), 109–110.
Baladrán, Zbyněk – Martin Mareček. "V obraze", *Cinepur* 14, no. 44 (2006), 29–33.
Balsom, Erika. *After Uniqueness: A History of Film and Video Art in Circulation* (New York: Columbia University Press, 2017).
Balsom, Erika. *Exhibiting Cinema in Contemporary Art* (Amsterdam: Amsterdam University Press, 2013).
Balsom, Erika. "Original Copies: How Film and Video Became Art Objects", *Cinema Journal* 53, no. 1 (2013), 100.
Baňková, Markéta. *Maličkost* (Praha: Argo, 2015).
Baňková, Markéta. *Straka v říši entropie* (Praha: Petr Prchal, 2010).
Banzetová, Michaela. "Současní čeští sběratelé umění: Marika Kupková: nebylo možné ignorovat videoart", *Česká televize*, 26. 10. 2020, accessed 16 May 2022, https://art.ceskatelevize.cz/360/soucasni-cesti-sberatele-umeni-marika-kupkova-nebylo-mozne-ignorovat-videoart-MiGlf.
Barry, Nora. "Rozprávanie príbehov na obrazovkách: dejiny webového filmu", in *V toku pohyblivých obrazov: Antológia textov o elektronickom a digitálnom umení v kontexte vizuálnej kultúry*, ed. Katarína Rusnáková (Bratislava: Vysoká škola výtvarných umení, Afad Press, 2005), 165–179.
Barthes, Roland. "Smrt autora", *Aluze* 10, no. 3 (2006), 75–77.
Bartlová, Anežka – Anna Remešová. "František Zachoval: Pohyblivý obraz se sbírá jen minimálně", *Artalk.cz*, 8. 3. 2021, accessed 28 Sep 2021, https://artalk.cz/2021/03/08/frantisek-zachoval-pohyblivy-obraz-se-sbira-jen-minimalne/.
Bartlová, Milena. *Naše, národní umění: Studie z dějin dějepisu umění* (Praha: Společnost pro odbornou literaturu – Barrister & Principal, 2009).
Baudry, Jean-Louis – Alan Williams. "Ideological Effects of the Basic Cinematographic Apparatus", *Film Quarterly* 28, no. 2 (Winter, 1974–1975), 39–47.
Bednařík, Pavel. "Oživování (živé) animace: PAF Olomouc 2008", *Film a doba* 54, no. 1 (2009), 40–42.
Bednařík, Pavel. "Úvodní slovo ředitele přehlídky", in *Katalog PAF 2007* (Olomouc: Pastiche Filmz, 2007), 5.
Bellour, Raymond. *Between-the-Images* (Zurich: JRP/ Ringier, 2012).
Bellour, Raymond. "D'un autre cinéma", *Trafic* 10, no. 34 (2000), 5–21.
Bellour, Raymond. "The Film Stilled: Unspeakable Images", *Camera Obscura* 8, č. 3 (1990), 98–124.
Bellour, Raymond. "The Power of Words, The Power of Images", *Camera Obscura* 8, no. 3 (1990), 7–10.
Belton, John. "Digitální technologie ve filmu: Nepravá revoluce", *Iluminace* 19, no. 4 (2007), 43–59.
Benda, Václav. "Paralelní polis", in *Noční kádrový dotazník a jiné boje: Texty z let 1977–1989*, ed. Patrik Benda (Praha: Agite/Fra, 2009), 56–66.
Bendová, Helena. "Editorial no. 27", *Cinepur* 12, no. 27 (2003), 1, accessed 2 Apr 2022, http://cinepur.cz/article.php?article=15.
Bendová, Helena. "Editorial no. 30 / Podzimní počítání", *Cinepur* 12, no. 30 (2003), 1, accessed 2 Apr 2022, http://cinepur. cz/article.php?article=50.
Bendová, Helena. "Film na výstavě", *Cinepur* 14, no. 44 (2006), 14–15.
Benjamin, Walter. *Výbor z díla I.: Literárněvědné studie* (Praha: Oikoymenh, 2009).
Bergeijk, Jeroen van – Geke van Dijk – Karel Koch – Bas Raijmakers, eds. *The Next Five Minutes: Zapbook* (Amsterdam: Paradiso, 1993).
Bernard, Jan. *Filmaři disentu – Michal Hýbek v paměti archivů a přátel* (Praha: Nakladatelství AMU, 2020).
Bey, Hakim. *Dočasná autonomní zóna* (Praha: tranzit. cz, 2004).
"Bez názvu", *Artyčok TV*, accessed 29 Mar 2022, https://artycok.tv/28697 krizovnicka-skola-cisteho-humoru-bez-vtipu.
Bielický, Michael. "Nová média nebo Dematerializace umění", *Ateliér* 8, no. 26 (1995), 2.
Bielický, Michael. "PRAHA, – NOVÁ MÉDIA, – AKADEMIE VÝTVARNÝCH UMĚNÍ / PRAGUE, – NEW MEDIA, – THE ACADEMY OF FINE ARTS", in *Orbis Fictus: nová média v současném umění / new media in contemporary arts*, eds. Ludvík Hlaváček – Marta Smolíková (Praha: Sorosovo centrum současného umění, 1995), 157–159.
Binarová, Alena. "Svaz výtvarných umělců v českých zemích v letech 1956–1972: Oficiální výtvarná tvorba v proměnách komunistického režimu" (Doctoral thesis, Palacký University, Olomouc, 2016).
Binarová, Alena. *Svaz výtvarných umělců v českých zemích v letech 1956–1972* (Olomouc: Vydavatelství FF UP, 2017).
Bláhová, Jindřiška. "Editorial 126 / NETFLIX", *Cinepur* 28, no. 126 (2019), accessed 2 Apr 2022, http://cinepur.cz/article. php?article=4769.
Bláhová, Jindřiška. "Teorie kontra řemeslo: Akademický senát navrhuje odvolání děkana Holého", *Respekt*, 26. 5. 2018, accessed 8 Jun 2021, https://www.respekt.cz/tydenik/2018/22/ teorie-kontra-remeslo.
Blažíček, Martin. "Čarodějné filmy pro lid: K československému filmovému undergroundu 80. let", *Iluminace* 29, no. 4 (2017), 5–29.
Blažíček, Martin. "Experiment, nová dobrodružství v digitální kvalitě", *Cinepur* 16, no. 60 (2008), 21–23.
Blažíček, Martin. "Klášter videoartu / Videokemp 2013", *Flash Art* 6, no. 28–29 (2013), accessed 30 Aug 2021, https://flashart.cz/2013/10/11/klaster-videoartu-videokemp-2013/.
Blažíček, Martin. "Live Cinema", *Film a doba* 55, no. 3/4 (2009), 184–185.
Blažíček, Martin. "Mediální pohyby v experimentální animaci Radka Pilaře", in *PAF Reader Nr. 1*, eds. Alexandr Jančík – Nela Klajbanová – Martin Mazanec (Olomouc: PAF, 2021), 90–94.
Blažíček, Martin. "Miloš Šejn: V mé práci jde v podstatě o vytržení", *Filmový přehled*, 31. 1. 2020, accessed 6 Apr 2022, https://www.filmovyprehled.cz/cs/revue/detail/milos-sejn-v-me-praci-jde-v-podstate-o-vytrzeni.
Blažíček, Martin. "Spontánní film", *Cinepur* 14, no. 46 (2006), 32–33.
Blažíček, Martin. "Stručný průvodce Expanded Cinema", *Cinepur* 14, no. 39 (2005), 8–11.
Blažíček, Martin. "Trable s Rumcajsem aneb co počít s českým videoartem 90. let", *Cinepur*, 6. 6. 2017, accessed 10 Jul 2022, http://cinepur.cz/article.php?article=2479.
Blažíček, Martin. "Za hranicí animace / Rozhovor s Martinem Mazancem, dramaturgem Přehlídky animovaného filmu Olomouc", *Cinepur*, 1. 11. 2010, accessed 7 Apr 2022, http://cinepur.cz/article.php?article=1968.
Blažíček, Martin – Alexandr Jančík – Martin Mazanec – Sylva Poláková, eds. *Katalog událostí českého pohyblivého obrazu: Jiné vize 2000–2010, I–II* (Olomouc: PAF Edition, 2011).

Blažíček, Martin – Sylva Poláková. "Ivan Tatíček – od amatérského filmu k profesionální videotvorbě", *Iluminace* 32, no. 1 (2020), 77–92.
Blažíček, Martin – Sylva Poláková. "Ivan Tatíček: Pravda je jinde, to jsme všichni věděli: Rozhovor s Ivanem Tatíčkem", *Filmový přehled*, 2019, accessed 10 May 2022, https://www.filmovyprehled.cz/cs/revue/ detail/ivan-taticek-pravda-je-jinde-to-jsme-vsichni-vedeli.
Bobčíková, Radka. "Brněnské přehlídky a festivaly digitálního umění v 90. letech" (Bachelor thesis, Masaryk University, Brno, 2015).
Boháčková, Kamila. "Úvod k tématu: animovaný film", *Cinepur* 13, no. 27 (2003), accessed 10 Jun 2022, http://cinepur.cz/article.php?article=16.
Boháčková, Kamila. "Warholovy pohyblivé obrazy: Proč film vychází z kina a kinosály z módy?", *A2* 5, no. 6 (2009), 11.
Bonitzer, Pascal. "Odrámování", *Iluminace* 15, no. 4 (2003), 31–34.
Bourriaud, Nicolas. *Postprodukce: kultura jako scénář: jak umění nově programuje současný svět* (Praha: tranzit.cz, 2004).
Boyle, Deirdre. *Video Preservation: Securing the Future of the Past* (New York: New York State Council on the Arts, 1993).
Brabec, Jiří. *Panství ideologie a moc literatury: Studie, kritiky, portréty (1991–2008)* (Praha: Akropolis, 2009).
Brukner, Josef – Bohdana Kerbachová – Jan Kříž – Jiří Kubíček – Radek Pilař – Blanka Stehlíková – Jaroslav Šedivý. *Radek Pilař: Obrazy, ilustrace, animovaný film, video* (Praha: Slovart, 2003).
Buddeus, Hana. "Fotografické podmínky happeningu", *Sešit pro umění, teorii a příbuzné zóny* 8, no. 16 (2014), 17–37.
Buddeus, Hana. *Zobrazení bez reprodukce: Fotografie a performance v českém umění sedmdesátých let 20. století* (Praha: UMPRUM, 2017).
Bühler, Melanie, ed. *No Internet, No Art: A Lunch Bytes Anthology* (New York: Onomatopee 102, 2015).
"Bulletin Board System", *Wikipedie*, 16. 7. 2020, accessed 20 May 2022, https://cs.wikipedia.org/wiki/Bulletin_Board_System.

C

Canudo, Ricciotto. "Teorie sedmi umění", *Iluminace* 4, no. 1 (1992), 19–21.
Carroll, Noël. "Definování pohyblivého obrazu", *Iluminace* 13, no. 2 (2001), 5–32.
Carroll, Noël. *Engaging the Moving Image* (New Haven – London: Yale University Press, 2003).
Carroll, Noël. *Theorizing the Moving Image* (Cambridge: Cambridge University Press, 1996).
Cartwright, Lisa – Marita Sturken. *Studia vizuální kultury* (Praha: Portál, 2010).
Casetti, Francesco. "The relocation of cinema", *Necsus* 1, no. 2 (2012), 5–34.
Cavell, Stanley. *The World Viewed: Reflections on The Ontology of Film* (Cambridge, Massachusetts – London, England: Harvard University Press, 1979).
"Centre for Contemporary Arts Prague, Annual report 2000", accessed 17 May 2022, https://cca.fcca.cz/fileadmin/user_upload/ CENTRUM/O_centru/Vyrocni_ zpravy/2000.pdf.
"Centrum audiovizuálních studií FAMU", *Film a doba* 58, no. 3/4 (2013), 133–142.
Císař, Karel. "Jiné vize 2016 CZ", in *Katalog PAF 2016* (Olomouc: Pastiche Filmz, 2007), 24.
Clayton, Sue – Laura Mulvey, eds. *Other Cinemas: Politics, Culture and Experimental Film in the 1970s* (London: Bloomsbury Academic, 2021).
Connolly, Maeve. *The Place of Artists' Cinema: Space, Site and Screen* (Bristol: Intellect Books, 2009).
Connor, Michael – Aria Dean – Dragan Espenschied, eds. *The Art Happens Here: Net Art Anthology* (New York: Rhizome, 2019).
"Conversations", *YouTube*, accessed 22 May 2022, https://www.youtube.com/watch?v=tqdjbXovLqM.
Coufalík, Pavel – Lada Hubatová-Vacková. "Neonová záře: Elektrická světelná reklama, kinetické a reflektorické hry", in *Divadlo ulice: Reklama a aranžérství výkladních skříní v kontextu modernismu 1918–1938*, ed. Lada Hubatová-Vacková (Praha: UMPRUM, 2021), 235–304.
Czesany Dvořáková, Tereza. "Bylo, nebylo", in *Marienbad Film Festival 2016* (Marienbad Film z.s., 2016), 8.
Čech, Viktor. "Videokemp 2007", *Videokemp*, 11. 8. 2007, accessed 10 Jul 2021, https://videokemp.wordpress.com/2007-2/.
Čechlovská, Magdalena. "Markéta Baňková: ‚Žádné technologie nenahradí mejdan'", *Hospodářské noviny*, 21. 1. 2005, accessed 4 Sep 2015, http://kultura.ihned.cz/index php?p=J00000_d&article[id]=15529680.
Čechová, Briana. "Kino-Ikon no. 2/1999 – Iluminace no. 3/1999", *Literární noviny* 11, no. 4 (2000), 13.
Česálková, Lucie – Kateřina Svatoňová, eds. *Diktátor času: (De)kontextualizace fenoménu Laterny magiky* (Praha: Národní filmový archiv, 2019).
Česálková, Lucie – Kateřina Svatoňová. "Laterna magika jako experiment v socialistické společnosti", in *Diktátor času: (De)kontextualizace fenoménu Laterny magiky*, eds. Lucie Česálková – Kateřina Svatoňová (Praha: Národní filmový archiv a Univerzita Karlova – Filozofická fakulta, 2019), 20–31.
Česálková, Lucie – Kateřina Svatoňová. "Na světelné křižovatce: Vzájemné zrcadlení města a filmu jako reklamní strategie", in *Divadlo ulice: Reklama a aranžérství výkladních skříní v kontextu modernismu 1918–1938*, ed. Lada Hubatová-Vacková (Praha: UMPRUM, 2021), 149–184.
"České umění kolem roku 1980 jako pole kulturní produkce", *Sešit pro umění, teorii a příbuzné zóny* 4, no. 9 (2010), 35.
Čihák, Martin. *Ponorná řeka kinematografie* (Praha: NAMU, 2013).
Čihák, Martin – Michal Bregant. "Skutečnější než realita", in *Alternativní kultura: Příběh české společnosti 1945–1989*, ed. Josef Alan (Praha: Nakladatelství Lidové noviny, 2001), 421–441.
Čiháková-Noshiro, Vlasta. "Virtuální realita – od malby po video", *Ateliér* 8, no. 26 (1995), 4.
"Články z tématu: Smrt filmu", *Cinepur* 20, no. 73 (2011), accessed 2 Apr 2022, http://cinepur.cz/list.php?theme=95.

D

Daniels, Dieter – Gunther Reisinger, eds. *Net Pioneers 1.0. Contextualizing Early Net-Based Art* (Berlin – New York: Sternberg Press, 2010).
"Databáze periodického tisku pro veřejnost, obsahové zaměření – rozhlasové a filmové časopisy", *MK ČR*, accessed 2 Apr 2022, https://www.mkcr.cz/databaze-periodickeho-tisku-pro-verejnost-978.html#seznam.
de Certeau, Michel. *L'invention du quotidien, 1: Arts de faire* (Paris: Union générale d'éditions, 1980).
De Los Santos, Luis Artemio. "Manifest Galerie Plevel", *PAF Olomouc*, accessed 20 Jun 2022, https://www.pifpaf.cz/cs/manifest-galerie-plevel.
De Rosa, Miriam – Vinzenz Hediger, eds. "Post-what? Post-when? Thinking Moving Images Beyond the Post-medium/Post-cinema Condition", *Cinéma & Cie* XVI, no. 26/27 Spring/Fall (2016).
Děcká, Eliška. "Animace ve veřejném prostoru / Všudypřítomná, využívaná i zneužívaná", *Cinepur* 24, no. 98 (2015).
"Den Nezávislosti, Tomáš Svoboda, Kino Světozor", *Artyčok TV*, accessed 7 Apr 2022, https://artycok.tv/1357/den-nezavislostiindependence-day.
di Lenardo, Jana. "Historie a současnost", *FaVU*, accessed 20 May 2022, https://www.favu.vut.cz/fakulta/historie-soucasnost.
Doaneová, Mary Ann. *Zrození kinematografického času: Modernita, nahodilost, archiv* (Praha: Karolinum, 2021)."doc. Mgr. Petr Szczepanik, Ph.D.", *kfs.ff.cuni*, accessed 2 Apr 2022, https://kfs.ff.cuni.cz/cs/katedra/pedagogove/doc-mgr-petr-szczepanik-ph-d/.
documenta 6 – Band 2: Fotografie, Film, Video (Kassel: Paul Dierichs KG & Co., 1977).
Dolanová, Lenka. *A Dialogue with the Demons of the Tools: Steina and Woody Vašulka* (Brno: Vašulka Kitchen Brno, 2022).
Dolanová, Lenka. "ARTEFAKTY: Cena Jindřicha Chalupeckého 2011", *A2* 7, no. 25 (2011), accessed 2 Apr 2022, https://www.advojka.cz/archiv/2011/25/artefakty.
Dolanová, Lenka. "Aspekty elektronické avantgardy: Steina a Woody Vasulkovi", *Iluminace* 18, no. 2 (2006), 217–218.
Dolanová, Lenka. "Co to tam vařili? Kuchaři, jejich Kitchen a chuť čerstvého videa", *Iluminace* 18, no. 2 (2006), 103–131.
Dolanová, Lenka. *Dialog s démony nástrojů* (Praha: NAMU – Jihlava: JSAF, 2011).
Dolanová, Lenka. "Gene Youngblood / Pokud diskurz není utopický, není dostatečně radikální", *Umělec* 10, no. 2 (2006), 12–15, accessed 2 Apr 2022, http://www.divus.cc/ london/cs/ article/life-in-counterculture.

Dolanová, Lenka. “Návrat Magalhãese: Framptonova cesta kolem filmu”, *A2* 5, no. 6 (2009), 13.
Dolanová, Lenka, ed. *Nejedna rodina: Jirousovi, Padrtovi, Ságlovi* (Humpolec: Nadační fond 8smička, 2020).
Dolanová, Lenka. “Umělec jako metanávrhář: Gene Youngblood a jeho dílo”, *Artalk.cz*, accessed 2 Apr 2022, https://artalk.cz/2021/04/16 umelec-jako-metanavrhar-gene-youngblood-a-jeho-dilo/.
Dolanová, Lenka. “Video na výstavě, nebo v Multikině? Cinepur Choice dělá průřez světovým videem”, *A2* 4, no. 49 (2008), 11.
Dolanová, Lenka. “Vstup ‚pohyblivých obrazů‘ do galerie”, *Iluminace* 15, no. 4 (2003), 85–100.
Dolanová, Lenka – Woody Vasulka. “Editorial”, *Iluminace* 18, no. 2 (2006), 5–8.
“Dopis Josefu Pecákovi” (18. 6. 1990), archive of the heirs of Radek Pilař.
Duero, Javier. “Videoart ve věku dospělosti”, *Film a doba* 52, no. 2 (2007), 88–89.

E

“editorial”, *A2*, no. 6 (2009), accessed 3 Apr 2022, https://www.advojka.cz/archiv/2009/6.
“editorial”, *A2*, no. 49 (2008), accessed 2 Apr 2022, https://www.advojka.cz/archiv/2008/49.
Effenberger, Jakub. “Vandám, vandáš, vandáme aneb osamělý dav před bednou”, *Film a doba* 40, no. 3 (1994), 148–151.
“Experimentální film”, *25fps.cz*, accessed 2 Apr 2022, http://25fps.cz/category/experimentalni-film/.

F

“FACEBOOK SCULPTURE”, 2013, accessed 20 Jul 2022, https://sites.google.com/site/facebooksculpture/.
Fajkusová, Eliška. “Výstavy a symposia ‚Hi-Tech umění‘ v Brně v letech 1992–1997” (Diploma thesis, Masaryk University, Brno, 2012).
“Fascinace: Exprmntl.cz”, *Ji.hlava*, accessed 8 Apr 2022, https://www.ji-hlava.cz/programove-sekce/ fascinace-exprmntl-cz.
“Festival digitálního obrazu In Out v Praze”, *iREPORT*, 30. 12. 2006, accessed 30 Aug 2021, https://www.ireport.cz/ 352-festival-digitalniho-obrazu-in-out-v-praze.
Filipová, Marta – Mathew Rampley. *Možnosti vizuálních studií* (Brno: Barrister & Principal, 2008).
Filipovic, Elena. “When Exhibitions Become Form: On the History of the Artist as Curator”, in *The Artist as Curator Issue #0*, ed. Elena Filipovic (Milano: Mousse Publishing, 2013), 3–20.
Fischer, Joachim – Dana Giesecke. “Umění distinkce a umění inkluze – K sociologii umělecké komunikace v SRN a v NDR”, in *Umění z NDR: Dědictví na obtíž?*, ed. Matěj Forejt (Praha: Galerie Rudolfinum, 2021), 20–35.
Flusser, Vilém. *Komunikológia* (Bratislava: Mediálny Inštitút, 2002).
Forejt, Matěj. “Možná že se nic z toho nikdy nestalo – rozhovor s Adélou Babanovou”, *ART ANTIQUES* 18, no. 10 (2019), 52–64.
Forejt, Matěj. “O kině po kině”, *Iluminace* 30, no. 3 (2018), 130–135.
Forej, Matěj, ed. *Umění z NDR: Dědictví na obtíž?* (Praha: Galerie Rudolfinum, 2021).
Fowler, Catherine. “Remembering cinema ‚elsewhere‘: from retrospection to introspection in the gallery film”, *Screen* 45, 4 (2004), 324–343.
Friedberg, Anne. *Window Shopping: Cinema and the Postmodern* (Berkeley, CA: University of California Press, 1993).
Frohnert, Christine – Hannelore Roemich. “Time-based Media Art Conservation Education Program at NYU: Concept and Perspectives”, *Electronic Media Review* 5, no. 5 (2017–2018).

G

Gass, Lars Henrik. *Film and Art After Cinema* (Zagreb: Multimedijalni institut, 2019).
Gass, Lars Henrik. *Film und Kunst nach dem Kino* (Köln: Strzelecki Books, 2017).
Gass, Lars Henrik. “Vom Markt zur Marke”, *Schnitt* 14, no. 2 (2009), 44.
Gelencsér, Gábor. “Continuing the Deviating Tradition of Hungarian Experimental Film Art: András Jeles’s *Joseph and his Brothers – Scenes from a Peasant Bible*”, *Alphaville: Journal of Film and Screen Media*, no. 9 (2015), 23–37.
Groys, Boris. “Kunst im Zeitalter der Biopolitik: Vom Kunstwerk zur Kunstdokumentation”, in *Documenta 11 Plattform 5: Ausstellung. Katalog*, eds. Heike Ander – Nadja Rottner (Ostfildern-Ruit: Hatje Cantz, 2002), 107–113.
Groys, Boris. “Umění ve věku biopolitiky: Od uměleckého díla k dokumentaci umění”, *Sešit pro umění, teorii a příbuzné zóny* 2, no. 4–5 (2008), 116.
Gunning, Tom. “Film atrakcí: raný film, jeho diváci a avantgarda”, *Iluminace* 13, no. 2 (2001), 51–57.

H

Hagener, Malte. “Kde je (dnes) film? Film ve věku imanence médií”, *Iluminace* 23, no. 1 (2011), 79–88.
Hagener, Malte. “Where Is Cinema (Today)? The Cinema in the Age of Media Immanence”, *Cinéma & Cie* 11, no. 3 (2008), 15–22.
Hall, David. “Video Art – The Significance of an Educational Environment”, in *Video Positive*, ed. Lisa Haskel (London: Foundation for Art and Creative Technology, 1989), 47.
Halter, Ed – Lauren Cornell, eds. *Mass Effect: Art and the Internet in the Twenty-First Century* (Cambridge, Massachusetts – London: The MIT Press, 2015).
Hanáková, Petra. “Aparát: Pojem”, *Cinepur* 10, no. 17 (2001), 53, accessed 2 Apr 2022, http://cinepur.cz/article. php?article=109.
Hanáková, Petra. “Digitální revoluce a podoby ‚smrti filmu‘”, in *Kultura a totalita III: Revoluce*, eds. Ivan Klimeš – Jan Wiendl (Praha: FF UK, 2015), 470–481.
Harvard Art Museums, accessed 29 Jun 2021, https:// harvardartmuseums.org/art/219479.
Havel, Ivan M. – Jarmila Poláková – Jana Semerádová – Pavel Smetana – Markéta Uhlířová. *entermultimediale* (Praha: ENTER multimediale, 2000).
Havel, Václav. “Šest poznámek o kultuře”, in *České umění 1938–1989*, eds. Jiří Ševčík – Pavlína Morganová – Dagmar Dušková (Praha: Academia, 2001), 377–382.
Havránek, Vít. “Český kinetismus 1956–1970 a skupina Syntéza” (Diploma thesis, Charles University, 1997).
Havránek, Vít. “Ján Mančuška: Chtěl jsem se soustředit na možnosti vyprávění”, *Flash Art Czech & Slovak Edition* 1, no. 1 (2006), 40–43.
Heathfield, Adrian. *LIVE Art and Performance* (London: Tate Publishing, 2004).
Hein, Birgit. *Film im Underground* (Frankfurt a. M.: Verlag Ullstein, 1971).
Hill, Chris. “Attention! Production! Audience! Performing Video in its First Decade, 1969–1980”, *VDB*, 1996, accessed 10 Jul 2022, www.vdb.org/sites/default/files/ attention.pdf.
“Historie nadace”, *Vzdělávací nadace Jana Husa*, accessed 6 Apr 2022, https://www.vnjh.cz/o-nadaci/ historie-od-1980/.
Hlaváček, Ludvík. “Postmoderna a neoexpresionismus”, in *Dějiny českého výtvarného umění VI/2*, eds. Rostislav Švácha – Marie Platovská (Praha: Academia, 2007), 715–728.
Hlaváček, Ludvík. “Sorosovo centrum současného umění”, *Atlas transformace*, 2008–2010, accessed 20 May 2022, http://www.monumenttotransformation.org/ atlas-transformace/html/s/sorosovo-centrum/ sorosovo-centrum-soucasneho-umeni.html.
Hlaváček, Ludvík. “Umění, technika a otevřená společnost: Komunikace jako transcendence / Arts, Technology, and Open Society: Communication as Transcendence”, in *Orbis Fictus: nová média v současném umění / new media in contemporary arts*, eds. Ludvík Hlaváček – Marta Smolíková (Praha: Sorosovo centrum současného umění, 1995), 8–12.
Hlaváček, Ludvík – Marta Smolíková, eds. *Orbis Fictus: nová média v současném umění / new media in contemporary arts* (Praha: Sorosovo centrum současného umění, 1995).
Hlaváčková, Jitka, ed. *Tomáš Ruller: Performe-Made – Udržitelné záblesky* (Praha: GHMP, 2018).
Hoffmann, Jens. “The Dirty Dozen: Twelve Issues of The Exhibitionist”, in *The Exhibitionist: Journal of Exhibition Making: The First Six Years*, ed. Jens Hoffmann (New York: Artbook, 2017), 9–15.
Holý, Zdeněk. “Ve věži ze slonoviny: Nad současným stavem oboru filmová věda v ČR”, *Cinepur* 18, no. 63 (2009), 9, accessed 2 Apr 2022, http://cinepur.cz/article. php?article=1716.

Horáček, Radek. "Brno na cestě k video a elektronickým médiím", *Ateliér* 8, no. 26 (1995), 12.
Horáček, Radek. "Výstava videoartu s lidskou tváří dorazila do Brna", *Mladá fronta*, 22. 12. 1994.
Horrigan, Bill. "Five Years Later", in *Art and the Moving Image: A Critical Reader*, ed. Tanya Leighton (London: Tate – Afterall, 2008), 293–294.
Hovorka, Marek. "Úvod", in *12. katalog Mezinárodního festivalu dokumentárních filmů Ji.hlava 2008* (Jihlava: 12. Mezinárodní filmový festival dokumentárních filmů Jihlava, 2008), 11.
Howes, Seth. *Moving Images On The Margins: Experimental film in the late socialist East Germany* (Rochester, New York: Camden House).
Hrabal, Bohumil. "Automat svět", *Literární noviny* 12, č. 24 (1963), 7.
"Hradecká Galerie moderního umění rozšiřuje sbírku pohyblivého obrazu", *Artalk.cz*, 25. 11. 2021, accessed 1 May 2022, https://artalk.cz/2021/11/25/hradecka-galerie-moderniho-umeni-rozsiruje-sbirku-pohybliveho-obrazu/.
Hubatová-Vacková, Lada. "Siluety plátěných nevěst: Aranžérství výkladních skříní v kontextu modernismu", in *Divadlo ulice: Reklama a aranžérství výkladních skříní v kontextu modernismu 1918–1938*, ed. Lada Hubatová-Vacková (Praha: UMPRUM, 2021), 17–148.
Huhtamo, Erkki. "Rozhovor s Woodym Vasulkou: Druhého března 1998, v jeho ateliéru v Santa Fe v Novém Mexiku", *Iluminace* 18, no. 2 (2006), 179–188.

CH

Chalupecký, Jindřich. "Experimentální umění: Happeningy, events, dekoláže", *Výtvarná práce* 14, č. 9 (1966), 1–7.
Chalupecký, Jindřich. "Umění, šílenství, zločin", *Sešity pro mladou literaturu* 2, č. 11 (květen 1967), 47.
Cherchi Usai, Paolo – David Francis – Alexander Horwath – Michael Loebenstein. "Curatorial Values: Two Case Studies", in *Film Curatorship: Archives, Museums, and the Digital Marketplace*, eds. Paolo Cherchi Usai – David Francis – Alexander Horwath – Michael Loebenstein (Vienna: SYNEMA, 2008), 132.
Chreňová, Andrea. "Extensions of Man", *Film a doba* 53, no. 2 (2008), 96–97.
Chvojková, Barbora – Karel Rada. "FAMU dnes", *Film a doba* 45, no. 1 (1999), 23–24.
Chvojková, Barbora – Karel Rada. "FAMU dnes II", *Film a doba* 45, no. 2 (1999), 81–85.
Chvojková, Barbora – Karel Rada. "FAMU dnes III", *Film a doba* 45, no. 3 (1999), 139–141.

I

"IASA-TC 06 Guidelines for the Preservation of Video Recordings", *IASA*, accessed 10 Feb 2022, https://www.iasa-web.org/tc06 guidelines-preservation-video-recordings.
"Identity Report for Video Artworks", *The Metropolian Museum of Art*, accessed 10 Feb 2022, https://www.metmuseum.org/-/media/files/about-the-met/conservation-and-scientific-research/time-based-media-working-group/artist-identity-report.pdf.
"Infermental 9 (1989)", *zkm*, 1989, accessed 10 Jul 2022, https://zkm.de/de/infermental-9-1989.
Internet Archive, accessed 30 Aug 2021, https://web.archive.org/web/20030807145619/http://www.inout.cz/indexFrame-a.htm>.
"InterVision Lab", *ABART*, accessed 20 May 2022, https://cs.isabart.org/group/4665/members.

J

"Já bych ty post-internety zakázala", *Facebook*, accessed 20 Jul 2022, https://www.facebook.com/events/499236446870532/.
Jančová, Veronika. "Poloprofesionál, nebo ‚profesionální amatér'? Filmová tvorba mezi amatérismem a profesionalismem", *Iluminace* 28, no. 2 (2016), 45–60.
Janeček, Vít. "A my jsme byli modernisti: Moravské a české počátky Woodyho Vasulky", *Iluminace* 18, no. 2 (2006), 87–101.
Janeček, Vít. "FAMU jako zážitková agentura", *Cinepur*, no. 106, 107 (2017).
Jarvie, I. C. *Movies and Society* (New York – London: Garland Publishing, Inc., 1986).
Jedličková, Alice. "Jak Perseus osvobodil Andromedu nebo osvobození Andromedy?", in *Vybrané kapitoly z intermediality*, eds. Lenka Krausová – Jan Schneider (Olomouc: Univerzita Palackého, 2008), 67–68.
Jedličková, Petra. "Kyberfeminismus tady a teď'", in *Nové čtení světa. 1. / feminismus devadesátých let českýma očima*, eds. Marie Chřibková – Josef Chuchma – Eva Klimentová (Praha: Marie Chřibková, 1999), 260–272.
Jedličková, Petra. "Ženy na drátech aneb český kyberfeminismus / Women on the Wires, or Czech Cyberfeminism", *Jedním Okem / One Eye Open* 1, zvláštní vydání (1998), 95–102.
Jenkins, Henry. *Convergence Culture: Where Old and New Media Collide* (New York – London: New York University Press, 2006).
Jiráčková, Blanka. "Videoart", *Ateliér* 8, no. 26 (1995), 2.
Jirous, Ivan M. *Zpráva o třetím českém hudebním obrození*, samizdat, 1975, *Moderní-Dějiny.cz*, 2013, accessed 12 May 2022, https://www.moderni-dejiny.cz/clanek/ivan-m-jirous-zprava-o-tretim-ceskem-hudebnim- obrozeni.
Jirousová, Věra. "Příklad post-moderny", *Výtvarná práce* 18, no. 5 (1970), 1–6.
Jirousová, Věra. "Velký malý králík Zorky Ságlové", *Výtvarné umění* 17, no. 1 (1993), 25.
"Jitro kouzelníků? (Umění věda společnost na přelomu tisíciletí)", *Agosto Foundation*, accessed 10 Jun 2022, https://www.agosto-foundation.org/cs/jitro-kouzelniku-umeni-veda-spolecnost-na-prelomu-tisicileti.
Jonášová, Markéta. "Globalizované krajiny českého audiovizuálního umění: Studie výstavního projektu Frisbee", *Sešit pro teorii, výtvarné umění a příbuzné zóny* 15, no. 30 (2021), 94–125.
Jones, Amelia. *Body Art / Performing the Subject* (Minneapolis: University of Minnesota Press, 1998), 16.
Juříková, Magdalena. "Vyjádření GHMP k akvizicím pohyblivého obrazu", *Artalk.cz*, 10. 12. 2021, accessed 2 Mar 2022, https://artalk.cz/2021/12/10/vyjadreni-ghmp-k-akvizicim-pohybliveho-obrazu/.

K

"Kalendář", *tranzit.cz*, accessed 8 Apr 2022, https://cz.tranzit.org/cz/.
Katalog událostí českého pohyblivého obrazu I., II. (Olomouc: Pastiche Filmz, 2011).
Kemp-Welch, Klara. *Networking the Bloc: Experimental Art in Eastern Europe 1965–1981* (Cambridge: The MIT Press, 2018).
Kerbachová, Bohdana. *Alchymie světla: Experimentální tvorba Petra Skaly* (Písek: Prácheňské muzeum v Písku – Praha: Nakladatelství Vltavín, 2017), 24–27.
Kerbachová, Bohdana. "Experimentální filmy Petra Skaly ve sbírkách NFA", *Iluminace* 26, no. 3 (2014), 103–109.
Kerbachová, Bohdana. "Počátky českého videoartu", *Iluminace* 18, no. 2 (2006), 133–158.
Kerbachová, Bohdana. "První schůzky naplňovalo snění: Rozhovor s Petrem Skalou", *Iluminace* 18, no. 2 (2006), 189–198.
Kholeif, Omar, ed. *You Are Here: Art After the Internet* (Manchester: Cornerhouse and SPACE, 2014).
Klečková, Tereza. "Generování pojmu ‚videoart'", *25fps.cz*, accessed 2 Apr 2022, http://25fps.cz/2011/videoart/.
Klečková, Tereza. "Přehlídky a výstavy – Hledisko pozorovatele", *25fps.cz*, accessed 2 Apr 2022, http://25fps.cz/2011/prehlidky-a-vystavy/.
Klimeš, Ivan. "Filmová studia v předsálí svých zdejších dějin", *Slovo a smysl* 17, no. 35 (2020), 139–147.
Klimeš, Ivan. "Filmová studia v předsálí svých zdejších dějin", *Slovo a smysl* 17, no. 35 (2020), 139–147, accessed 2 Apr 2022, https://wordandsense.ff.cuni.cz/wp-content/uploads/sites/18/2021/02/Ivan_Klimes_139-147.pdf.
Klimeš, Ivan – Jan Wiendl, eds. *Kultura a totalita III: Revoluce* (Praha: FF UK, 2015).
Klivar, Miroslav. *Nová umění v Čechách* (Praha: Regulus, 2001).
Klusáková, Veronika – Pavel Bednařík. "Projekce soutěžních videí I., II.: Jiné vize 007", in *Katalog PAF 2007* (Olomouc: Pastiche Filmz, 2007), 14.
Kluszczyński, Ryszard W. "The Mechanical Imagination – Creativity of Machines: Film Form Workshop 1970–1977", in *The Struggle for Form: Perspectives on Polish Avant-Garde Film, 1916–1989*, eds. Kamila Kuc – Michael O'Pray (New York: Columbia University Press, 2014), 117–136.
Knížák, Milan. *Akce, po kterých zbyla alespoň nějaká dokumentace 1962–1995* (Praha: Gallery, 2000).

Knížák, Milan. "Performance jako vývoj i jako degenerace", *Vokno* 3, no. 4 (1981), 44.
Lokeš, Radomír D. "Stav filmových časopisů v Česku a na Slovensku", *Pandora* 8, no. 20 (2010), 199–203.
"Konference Dokumentace umění", *Performanceart*, accessed 10 Feb 2022, https://performance.ffa.vutbr.cz/konference-dokumentace-umeni/.
Kontová, Helena. "Czechoslovakia: Information", *Flash Art* 10, no. 66–67 (1976), 18–22.
Kořínek, David – Adam Malý. "Mark Ther", *Živel* 12, no. 30 (2009), 140–147.
Košuličová, Ivana. "Animovaný film v kyberprostoru" (Diploma thesis, Masaryk University, Brno, 2001).
Kowolowski, František. "Talíř, který přilétne a zase odlétne", *Literární noviny* 17, no. 8 (2006), 15.
Krejčová, Kateřina – Eric Rosenzveig – Vladimír Turner. "Směry pospolitosti: umělecká tvorba ve veřejném prostoru (online rozhovor)", *Film a doba* 59, no. 3/4 (2013), 135–138.
"KRISTÝNA LUTZOVÁ: supermedia sculptor", *www.loginlogout.cz*, accessed 25 May 2022, http://www.kristynalutzova.cz/wwwloginlogoutcz.
Kršňák, Jan. "Nam June Paik / ‚Nikdy se nedívám na video'", *Cinepur* 14, no. 44 (2006), 22–23.
Krtička, Jan – Jan Prošek, eds. *Dokumentace umění* (Ústí nad Labem: Fakulta umění a designu Univerzity Jana Evangelisty Purkyně v Ústí nad Labem, 2013).
Krtilová, Kateřina – Kateřina Svatoňová. "Česko-německý, Medienwissenschaft'", *Iluminace* 26, no. 2 (2014), 155–159.
Křipač, Jan. "Petr Skala", *Filmový přehled*, 5. 5. 2017, accessed 24 Jul 2021, https://www.filmovyprehled.cz/cs/revue/detail/petr-skala.
Kučerová, Alena – Stanislav Miler. "Také nenávidíte ohlupující televizi?", *Video + film* 3, no. 10 (1993), 5–6.
Kudlová, Adéla. "Dělat odvážná rozhodnutí: Rozhovor s Dušanem Barokem", *Iluminace* 31, no. 4 (2019), 85–89.
Kuhn, Thomas Samuel. *Struktura vědeckých revolucí* (Praha: OIKOYMENH, 1997).
Kulhánek, David. "Praxe, teorie a expozice Zbyňka Baladrána", *Umělec* 8, no. 3 (2004), 68–69.
Kúnová, Eva. "Československý listopad 1989", *Ateliér* 2, no. 26 (1989), 7.
Kupková, Marika. "Divák vs. návštěvník: proměny diváckých režimů", *Cinepur* 20, no. 73 (2011), 75–79.
Kupková, Marika. "Mark Ther: O lomítku mezi videem a filmem", *Flash Art Czech & Slovak Edition* 6, no. 31 (2014), 26–28.
Kupková, Marika. "‚Zakázaná' sexualita v českém meziválečném filmu" (Diploma thesis, Masaryk University, Brno, 2001).
Kuruc, Jiří. "Lukáš Gregor o 25fps: volný čas se mi stal cizím termínem (rozhovor)", *Filmová místa*, accessed 2 Apr 2022, https://www.filmovamista.cz/clanek/17-Lukas-Gregor-o-25fps-volny-cas-se-mi-stal-cizim-terminem-rozhovor-.
Kurzor_gallery, accessed 15 Apr 2022, https://www.facebook.com/kurzorgallery/.
Kurzor_kolektiv, accessed 15 Apr 2022, https://kurzorkolektiv.wordpress.com/.
"Kytka", *Videoarchiv NFA*, accessed 24 May 2022, https://videoarchiv.nfa.cz/katalog/kytka.

L

"Lab SCSU'98", *Galerie Jelení*, accessed 22 May 2022, https://www.galeriejeleni.cz/1999/lab-scsu98/.
Labuda, Radim – David Kořínek, eds. *Supernova, katalog Ateliéru supermédií* (Praha: UMPRUM, 2019).
Labuda, Radim. "[in da] re:mix", *Cinepur* 14, no. 44 (2006), 34–35.
Lang, Čestmír. "Krátký film jako intenzivní forma komunikace", *Film a doba* 51, no. 4 (2005), 194–198.
Lang, David M. – David M. Switzer – Brandon J. Swartz "DVD sales and the R-rating puzzle", *Journal of Cultural Economics* 35, no. 4 (2011), 269.
"Legenda o Galerii PLEVEL", *Vimeo*, 5. 12. 2014, accessed 20 Jul 2022, vimeo.com/140757688.
Leighton, Tanya, ed. *Art and the Moving Image: A Critical Reader* (London: Tate Publishing, 2009).
Lialina, Olia. "All that Glitters", *Guggenheim*, 14. 9. 2010, accessed 16 Jun 2022, www.guggenheim.org/blogs/the-take/all-that-glitters.
Lialina, Olia. "Early Experiments Online", *Guggenheim*, 22. 7. 2010, accessed 16 Jun 2022, www.guggenheim.org/blogs/the-take early-experiments-online.
Lialina, Olia. "My Boyfriend Came Back From the War", *Net Art Anthology*, 2019, accessed 20 May 2022, https://anthology.rhizome.org/my-boyfriend-came-back-from-the-war.
Lialina, Olia. "Ubiquitous Minicinema", *Guggenheim*, 20. 8. 2010, accessed 16 Jun 2022, www.guggenheim.org/blogs/the-take/ubiquitous-minicinema.
Lindaurová, Lenka, ed. *MEZERA: Mladé umění v Česku 1990–2014* (Praha: Společnost Jindřicha Chalupeckého, Yinachi, 2014).
Lindaurová, Lenka. "Naše elektronická budoucnost", *Lidové noviny*, 2. 8. 1994, 11.
Liška, Pavel – Robin R. Mudry. *MEDA – Ambasadorka umění* (Praha: Museum Kampa, 2019).
LOOP Barcelona, eds. *I Have a Friend Who Knows Someone Who Bought a Video, Once: On Collecting Video Art* (Milan: Mousse Publishing, 2016).
Lustigová, Petra. "Umění nových médií v České republice do roku 2000" (Diploma thesis, Masaryk University, Brno, 2014).

M

Macek, Václav – Jelena Paštéková. *Dejiny slovenskej kinematografie 1896–1969* (Bratislava: Slovenský filmový ústav, 2016).
"Magnetic Tape Alert Project", *IASA*, accessed 10 Feb 2022, https://www.iasa-web.org/magnetic-tape-alert-project.
Macharáčková, Marcela, ed. *Brněnská osmdesátá* (Brno: TT klub výtvarných umělců v Brně, 2010).
"Malamut", *VVP AVU*, accessed 8 Apr 2022, https://vvp.avu.cz/archivy/i-datum/54/?table=vystavy.
Mančuška, Ján. "Inscenovaná realita", *Flash Art Czech & Slovak Edition* 5, no. 15 (2010), 28–31.
Manovich, Lev. *The Language of New Media* (Cambridge: The MIT Press, 2001).
"Manuál", *etc.galerie*, accessed 10 Feb 2022, https://etcgalerie.cz/cs/manual/.
MAP: Media archive presents, accessed 10 Feb 2022, http://media-archiv.ffa.vutbr.cz/.
Marek, Diviš. "2x o jednom: Jaká byla Mladá kamera", *Amatérský film* 17, no. 6 (1985), 127.
"Marienbad Film Festival", *Všudybyl* 5/2017, 23. 10. 2017, 43, accessed 9 Apr 2022, https://www.e-vsudybyl.cz/archiv/marienbad-film-festival-4161.
Matějová, Alina. "GIF art: Od grafického formátu až po etablované umění" (Diploma thesis, Masaryk University, Brno, 2014).
Mazanec, Martin. "Neléčená schizofrenie mezi filmem a videem, mezi kanálem a galerií", *Cinepur* 16, no. 56 (2008), 6.
Mazanec, Martin. *Pohyblivý obraz filmu a videa 1: Studijní text pro kombinované studium* (Olomouc: Univerzita Palackého v Olomouci, 2014).
Mazanec, Martin. "Video art, umění pohyblivého obrazu" (Diploma thesis, Palacky University, Olomouc, 2006).
Mazanec, Martin. "Výzkumný projekt: Český videoart: Od programu k formě", *A2* 4, no. 49 (2008), 1, 16–17.
Mazanec, Martin. "Zbyněk Baladrán", *Labyrint revue* 16, no. 23/24 (2008), 86–88.
Meigh-Andrews, Chris. *A History of Video Art* (London: Bloomsbury Academic, 2014).
Meixnerová, Marie. "MARK THER: Ther v etheru a taky hlavně Ther medailonek", *25fps.cz*, accessed 2 Apr 2022, http://25fps.cz/2012/mark-ther/.
Meixnerová, Marie. "Martin Kohout (Pash*)", *Mediabaze.cz*, 12. 10. 2013, accessed 22 May 2022, https://web.archive.org/web/20161029082628.
Meixnerová, Marie, ed. *#mm net art – internetové umění ve virtuálním a fyzickém prostoru prezentace* (Olomouc: Pastiche Filmz, 2014).
Meixnerová, Marie. "ScreenSaverGallery (2013–Present)", in *The Art of Screensaver*, ed. Marie Meixnerová (Olomouc: PAF & BUT, 2020).
Meixnerová, Marie. "Web 1.0", in *#mm net art – internetové umění ve virtuálním a fyzickém prostoru prezentace*, ed. Marie Meixnerová (Olomouc: Pastiche Filmz, 2014), 12.
Merhaut, Vladislav. "Explozionalista Vladimír Boudník očima kamery", *Kritická příloha Revolver Revue* 4, č. 14 (1999), 133–136.
Mersch, Dieter. "Tertium datur: Úvod do negativní mediální teorie", in *Medienwissenschaft: Východiska a aktuální pozice německé filozofie a teorie médií*, eds. Kateřina Krtilová – Kateřina Svatoňová (Praha: Academia 2016), 336–355.
Míčová, Pavlína. "Bad Filming", *Flash Art Czech & Slovak Edition* 4, no. 14 (2009), 56.

Míčová, Pavlína. “Balet, nebo tancovačka? S Tomášem Pospiszylem o blízkých setkáních a vizuálním umění”, *A2* 5, no. 6 (2009), 24.
Míčová, Pavlína. “Přibližuji Double Brno”, *Flash Art Czech & Slovak Edition* 3, no. 11/12 (2009), 57.
Míčová, Pavlína. “Stavy a souvislosti současného českého umění videa”, *Cinepur* 14, no. 44 (2006), 26–29.
“Michal Pěchouček – Sběratel”, *Moravská galerie*, accessed 10 Jul 2021, http://www.moravska-galerie.cz/moravska-galerie/vystavy-a-program/aktualni-vystavy/2003/michal-pechoucek-sberatel.aspx.
“Milan Knížák Lying Ceremony from Performance Files 1968”, *MoMA*, accessed 4 Apr 2022, https://www.moma.org/collection/works/178953.
Mílek, Václav. “Objekt animace: Třetí smysl: Rozhovor s kurátory”, *Prostor Zlín* 16, no. 4 (2009), 6–9.
Miller, Simone. “Never Ending Story: Zum musealen Umgang mit wiederholbarer Kunst”, in *Art Handling: Partituren der Logistik*, eds. Lucie Kolb – Christoph Lang – Wolfgang Ullrich – Judith Welter (Zürich: JRP – Ringier / Migros Museum für Gegenwartskunst, 2016), 51–58.
“Miloš Vojtěchovský, Umění a elektronické technologie”, in *Dějiny umění 12*, ed. Lenka Bydžovská (Praha: Balios – Knižní klub – Euromedia Group, 2002), 255–281.
Minkowsky, John. “Několik poznámek k videu Vasulkových v letech 1973–1974”, *Iluminace* 18, no. 2 (2006), 31–39.
Mirzoeff, Nicholas. *Jak vidět svět* (Praha: Artmap, 2019).
Mirzoeff, Nicholas. *Úvod do vizuální kultury* (Praha: Academia, 2012).
Moralesová, Alexandra. “Experimentální film: Vstup do filmové laboratoře a setkání s tělem”, *Sešit pro umění a příbuzné zóny* 12, no. 24 (2018), 61–91.
Morganová, Pavlína. *Lumír Hladík* (Praha: Galerie SVIT, 2011).
Morganová, Pavlína – Terezie Nekvindová – Sláva Sobotovičová, eds. *České akční umění: Filmy a videa 1956–1989* (Praha: Akademie výtvarných umění v Praze, Vědecko-výzkumné pracoviště, 2015).
“Moře v zrcadle”, *Artyčok TV*, accessed 6 Apr 2022, https://artycok.tv/20466/more-v-zrcadle-1980.
Moss, Ceci. *Expanded Internet Art: Twenty-First-Century Artistic Practice and the Informational Milieu* (New York: Bloomsbury, 2019).
“Mřížka | Grid (MFDF Jihlava)”, *Intermedia*, 2011, accessed 8 Apr 2022, http://intermedia.ffa.vutbr.cz/mrizka-grid-diafilm.
(mšt), “Kritika filmová a televizní”, in *Slovník žurnalistiky*, eds. Jan Halada – Barbora Osvaldová (Praha: Karolinum, 2017), 133–135.
Mugaas, Hanne. “The Year Video Art was Born”, *The Take*, 15. 7. 2010, accessed 24 Jul 2022, https://www.guggenheim.org/ blogs/the-take/the-year-video-art-was-born.

N

Nagyová, Ester. “Instalace animace”, *Film a doba* 56, no. 1 (2011), 46.
Nagyová, Ester. “Jiné vize animace”, *Film a doba* 55, no. 1 (2010), 47–48.
“NÁRODNÍ GALERIE: Nová média budou mít svoji laboratoř”, *Hospodářské noviny*, 10. 10. 1996, accessed 16 May 2022, https://archiv.hn.cz/c1-890592-narodni-galerie-nova-media-budou-mit-svoji-laborator.
Neděla, Jiří. “Experimentální film I.–V.”, *25fps.cz*, accessed 2 Apr 2022, http://25fps.cz/author/jiri-nedela/.
Nechvílová, Kateřina. “O jiných vizích pohyblivého obrazu, Lenka Střeláková a Viktor Takáč”, *Literární noviny* 27, no. 8 (2016), 4–5, accessed 2 Apr 2022, https://artycok.tv/29890/pohyblive-obrazy-2.
“Nejnovější články”, *Artalk.cz*, accessed 2 Apr 2022, https://artalk.cz/tag/pohyblivy-obraz/.
Nešlehová, Mahulena. “Informelní projevy”, in *Dějiny českého výtvarného umění VI/1*, eds. Rostislav Švácha – Marie Platovská (Praha: Academia 2007), 127.
Novitskova, Katja. *Post Internet Survival Guide 2010* (Berlin: Revolver Publishing, 2011).
Nytra, Matěj. “Aerovod”, *Cinepur* 20, no. 85 (2013), 51, accessed 2 Apr 2022, http://cinepur.cz/article.php?article=2429.
Nytra, Matěj. “Das wandernde Sternlein / Na okraj vítězného filmu Marka Thera”, *Cinepur* 21, no. 78 (2012), 22, accessed 2 Apr 2022, http://cinepur.cz/article.php?article=2214.

O

“O centru”, *FAMU*, accessed 12 Jul 2021, https://www.famu.cz/cs/katedry/centrum-audiovizualnich-studii/.
“O časopise”, *Iluminace*, accessed 2 Apr 2022, https://www.iluminace.cz/index.php/cz/about-iluminace.
“O mně”, *Zdeněk Svejkovský*, accessed 25 May 2022, http://www.zdeneksvejkovsky.name/cv/.
“O nás”, *CESNET*, accessed 16 Jun 2022, https://www.cesnet.cz/sdruzeni/.
“O videoarchivu”, *Videoarchiv VVP AVU*, accessed 10 Feb 2022, https://vvp.avu.cz/videoarchiv/o-videoarchivu/.
O’Dell, Kathy. “Performance, Video, and Trouble in the Home”, in *Illuminating Video: An Essential Guide to Video Art*, eds. Doug Hall – Sally Jo Fifer (New York: Aperture/Bay Area Video Coalition, 1990), 135–151.
O’Grady, Gerald. “Sférické poznání Woodyho Vasulky: Od dírkové kamery k otvorům v pinballu”, *Iluminace* 18, no. 2 (2006), 9–30.
O’Toole, Frani. “The New Museum Hits ‚Save‘ on Net Art”, *Hyperallergic*, 20. 2. 2019, accessed 20 May 2022, https://hyperallergic.com/485466/the-new-museum-hits-save-on-net-art/.
“Obsah”, *Cinepur* 10, no. 17 (2001), accessed 2 Apr 2022, http://cinepur.cz/list.php?issue=16&view_all=1.
“Obsah”, *Cinepur* 14, no. 44 (2006), accessed 2 Apr 2022, http://cinepur.cz/list.php?issue=42.
“Obsah”, *Kino-Ikon: časopis pre vedu o filme a “pohyblivom obraze”* 23, no. 2 (2019), accessed 2 Apr 2022, http://www.sfu.sk/uploads/ckeditor/attachments/1903/OBSAH_SK-GB_2-19.pdf.
“Obsah, News”, *Flash Art Czech & Slovak Edition* 6, no. 31 (2014), accessed 2 Apr 2022, https://flashart.cz/issue/flash-art-czech-slovak-edition-no-31-volume-vi/.
off, “Jak pochopit výstavu Autovize? Přes lízání zadku”, *iDNES.cz*, accessed 2 Apr 2022, https://www.idnes.cz/kultura/vytvarne-umeni/jak-pochopit-vystavu-autovize-pres-lizani-zadku.A070305_160636_vytvarneum_off.
Oplatková, Martina. “Filmařem a fotografem může být každý, kdo má co říci – rozhovor s Mgr. Tomášem Kepkou, filmařem a provozovatelem kursů pro dospělé”, *EPALE*, accessed 2 May 2021, https://epale.ec.europa.eu/cs/blog/filmarem-fotografem-muze-byt-kazdy-kdo-ma-co-rici-rozhovor-s-mgr-tomasem-kepkou-filmarem.
“Orbis Fictus”, *Ateliér* 8, no. 26 (1995), 16.
Orišková, Mária, ed. *Curating “Eastern Europe” and Beyond: Art Histories through the Exhibition* (Frankfurt am Main: Peter Lang – Bratislava: Veda, 2013).
Oriškova, Maria. *Dvojhlasné dejiny umenia* (Bratislava: Petrus, 2002).
“Otevřené sbírky: Zpráva o digitalizaci a zpřístupňování kulturního dědictví v České republice”, *Otevřené sbírky*, accessed 26 Sep 2021, http://www.otevrenesbirky.cz/.

P

“Památník československého exilu”, *Media Archiv*, accessed 8 May 2022, http://www.ceskoslovensky-exil.info/html/hlavni_stranka.html.
Pavelka, Jaroslav. “K dějinám českého videoartu”, *Ateliér* 8, no. 26 (1995), 6.
Pavlík, Ondřej. “Netflix, chill a korona: Internetová televizev době pandemie”, *A2* 16, no. 12 (2020), accessed 2 Apr 2022, https://www.advojka.cz/archiv/2020/12/netflix-chill-a-korona.
Pavlovský, Jiří. “Comics ve filmu”, *Živel* 8, no. 20 (2002), 52–57.
Pazdera, Zdeněk. “Elektronický štětec” (Neoznačený časopisecký výstřižek, po roce 1987), archive of the heirs of Radek Pilař.
Pěchouček, Michal. “Ondřej Brody”, *Fotograf* 4, no. 6 (2005), 88–89.
Peloušková, Klára. “Mazancova galerie v Galerii mladých”, *Artalk.cz*, accessed 2 Apr 2022, https://artalk.cz/2012/02/22/ mazancova-galerie-v-galerii-mladych/.
Pešánek, Zdeněk. *Kinetismus* (Praha: Česká grafická unie, 1941).
“Peter Bächlin”, *Historisches Lexikon der Schweiz*, 20. 11. 2012, accessed 29 Jun 2021, https://hls-dhs-dss.ch/de/articles/009131/2012-11-20.
Peterka, Jiří. “Historie naší liberalizace – I”, *eArchiv*, 8. 10. 2001, accessed 16 Jun 2022, www.earchiv.cz/b01/b1008002.php3.

Peterka, Jiří. "Historie naší liberalizace, díl III: Liberalizace Internetu v ČR", *eArchiv*, 23. 10. 2001, accessed 16 Jun 2022, www.earchiv.cz/b01/b1023001.php3.
Petříček, Miroslav. *Myšlení obrazem: Průvodce současným filosofickým myšlením pro středně nepokročilé* (Praha: Herrmann & synové, 2009).
PH – VH [Petra Hanáková – Václav Hájek]. "Editorial: Film v době vizuálních studií", *Iluminace* 21, no. 1 (2009), 37–39.
Pilař, Radek. "Bez názvu" Typewritten copy, 1989, archive of the heirs of Radek Pilař.
Pilař, Radek. "Bez názvu [průvodní text k výstavě oboru videa]" Typewritten copy, 1989, archive ofthe heirs of Radek Pilař.
Pilař, Radek. "Bez názvu [text o průběhu výstavy Československý listopad 1989]" Typewritten copy, 1989, archive of the heirs of Radek Pilař.
Pilař, Radek. "Do Prahy a Brna přijeli ze Santa Fe Steina a Woody Vasulkas, zakladatelé světového videoart" Typewritten copy, 1989, archive of the heirs of Radek Pilař, 2.
Pilař, Radek. "Dopis vedení Československé televize" Typewritten copy, undated, archive of the heirs of Radek Pilař.
Pilař, Radek. "Historie výtvarné elektroniky v České zemi" Typewritten copy, 1990, archive of the heirs of Radek Pilař, 1.
Pilař, Radek. "Nástin osnov" Typewritten copy, undated, archive of the heirs of Radek Pilař, 1.
Pilař, Radek. "Plán oboru video" Typewritten copy, undated, archive of the heirs of Radek Pilař. 1.
Pilař, Radek. "Podmínky pro vznik videa v Čechách" Typewritten copy, 1990, archive of the heirs of Radek Pilář.
Pilař, Radek. "Viva Video", *Ateliér* 2, no. 26 (1989), 7.
Pilař, Radek. "Viva video, video viva", in *České umění 1980–2010, texty a dokumenty*, eds. Jiří Ševčík – Pavlína Morganová – Terezie Nekvindová – Dagmar Svatošová (Praha: VVP AVU, 2011), 495–497.
Placáková, Marianna. "Jedna rodina: Ludmila Padrtová, Zorka Ságlová, Věra Jirousová, Juliana Jirousová", in *Nejedna rodina: Jirousovi, Padrtovi, Ságlovi*, ed. Lenka Dolanová (Humpolec: Nadační fond 8smička, 2020), 132–141.
"Pocta Fafejtovi", *dafilms*, accessed 5 Apr 2022, https://dafilms.cz/film/10190-pocta-fafejtovi.
Pogranová, Anna. "Nová média a české umělecké instituce v 90. letech 20. století" (Diplomová práce, Fakulta sociálních věd Univerzity Karlovy, 2016), accessed 10 Feb 2022, https://dspace.cuni.cz/bitstream/handle/20.500.11956/81578/DPTX_2013_2_11230_0_419998_0_152831.pdf?sequence=1&isAllowed=y.
"Pohyblivé obrazy a Jiné vize", *Artyčok TV*, accessed 1 Mar 2022, https://artycok.tv/29890/pohyblive-obrazy-2.
Pokorný, Marek. "Film / animace / umění", in *Filmy bez kina: Princip animace a současné umění*, Marek Pokorný – Radim Peško (Brno: Dům umění města Brna – Praha: Kant, 2003), 50.
Pokorný, Marek. "Po jitru kouzelníků nastává úplně banální den", *Mladá fronta Dnes*, 14. 12. 1996, 19, accessed 10 Jul 2022, https://www.agosto-foundation.org/cs/jitro-kouzelniku-umeni-veda-spolecnost-na-prelomu-tisicileti.
Poláková, Sylva. "‚Expanded' Pešánek", *Flash Art Czech & Slovak Edition* 6, no. 31 (2014), 29–31.
Poláková, Sylva. "Kážu decentralizaci: světlo do ulic: pohyblivý obraz ve veřejném prostoru", *A2* 11, no. 3 (2015), 9.
Poláková, Sylva. "Konvergence filmu a architektury: Případ Prahy" (Doctoral thesis, Charles University, Prague, 2015).
Poláková, Sylva. "Konvergence filmu a architektury v pražských ulicích", *Sešit pro umění a příbuzné zóny* 4, no. 8 (2010), 7–21.
Poláková, Sylva. "Méně tvořit a více makat: S Michalem Pěchoučkem o ‚kulátolství' a kolektivní terapii", *A2* 4, no. 49 (2008), 14–15.
Poláková, Sylva. "Relokace filmového obrazu / Svět mediálních fasád", *Cinepur* 18, no. 62 (2009), 23–25.
Poláková, Sylva. "‚Současný český videoart' jako výzva filmovým studiím", in *Současný český a slovenský film – pluralita estetických, kulturních a ideových konceptů*, ed. Luboš Ptáček (Olomouc: Univerzita Palackého, 2010), 111–125.
Poláková, Sylva. "Tomáš Svoboda: Dekonstrukce a (re) imaginace", *Fotograf* 11, no. 19 (2012), 68–71.
Poláková, Sylva. "Videomapping: Světlo do ulic – pohyblivý obraz ve veřejném prostoru", *A2* 11, no. 15 (2015), 9.
Poláková, Sylva. "Ztratit hlas, abych dostal nohy: Rozhovor s Lumírem Hladíkem", *Dok.revue*, 1. 11. 2020, accessed 17 May 2022, www.dokrevue.cz/clanky/ztratit-hlas-abych-dostal-nohy.
Poláková, Sylva – Martin Mazanec. "Editoriál", in *Katalog událostí českého pohyblivého obrazu: Jiné vize 2000–2010, II.*, eds. Martin Blažíček – Alexandr Jančík – Martin Mazanec – Sylva Poláková (Olomouc: PAF Edition, 2011), 9–11.
Pommert, Christin. "Between Creation and Preservation – the Position of a Gallery in Preserving Multimedia Art for the Future", příspěvek na kolokviu Artworks from the Digital Era in Galleries and Museums, *Vasulka Kitchen Brno*, 22.–23. 10. 2019, accessed 10 Feb 2022, https://www.vasulkakitchen.org/en/umelecke-sbirky-digitalni-epochy-v-galerii-a-muzeu.
Pospiszyl, Tomáš. "Andy Warhol uvádí", *Cinepur* 14, no. 44 (2006), 24.
Pospiszyl, Tomáš. *Asociativní dějepis umění: Poválečné umění napříč generacemi a médii (koláž, intermediální a konceptuální umění, performance a film)* (Praha: tranzit.cz, 2014).
Pospiszyl, Tomáš. "Film x výtvarné umění", *Cinepur* 14, no. 44 (2006), 16–18.
Pospiszyl, Tomáš. "Ondřej Brody je normální", *Umělec* 15, no. 1 (2011), accessed 2 Apr 2022, http://88.208.121.86/praha/cs/article/ ondrej-brody-is-normal.
Pospiszyl, Tomáš. "Pěchoučkovy filmogramy", *Film a doba* 53, no. 2 (2008), 94–96.
Pospiszyl, Tomáš. "Úkoly pro dějiny umění východní Evropy doby socialismu", *Sešit pro umění, teorii a příbuzné zóny* 13, no. 27 (2019), 17–24.
Pospiszyl, Tomáš, ed. *Vladimír Ambroz: Akce / Action* (Praha: BiggBoss, 2017).
Pospiszyl, Tomáš – Eric Rosenzveig, eds. *CAS: Co je to?* (Praha: Nakladatelství AMU, 2013).
Pospíšilová, Hana. "Galerie Drogerie Zlevněné zboží: Neoficiální prezentace výtvarného umění v 80. letech v Brně" (Bachelor's thesis, Masaryk University, Brno, 2012).
Press, Jan. "Výroční zpráva Moravské galerie za rok 2014", *NUŠL*, accessed 20 Oct 2021, https://invenio.nusl.cz/record/200696/files/nusl-200696_1.pdf.
Privett, Ray – James Kreul. "Podivný případ Noëla Carrolla: Rozhovor s kontroverzním filosofem filmu", *Iluminace* 14, no. 1 (2002), 89–113.
"Projects Archive", *Future Gallery*, accessed 22 May 2022, http://thefuturegallery.org/index.php?/ongoing/archive/.
"Projeďte se výstavou", *Artalk.cz*, 4. 10. 2009, accessed 10 Oct 2021, https://artalk.cz/2009/10/04 projedte-se-vystavou/.
"Projev Radka Pilaře na Ústředním plénu sekce Svazu výtvarných umělců" Typewritten copy, undated, archive of the heirs of Radek Pilař, 2.
"Přátelský film", *kviff.com*, accessed 2 Apr 2022, https://www.kviff.com/cs/program/film/11/3556-pratelsky-film.
"Před 25 lety do Česka oficiálně dorazil internet: Byl pomalý a drahý", *ČT24*, 13. 2. 2017, accessed 16 Jun 2022, www.ct24.ceskatelevize.cz/veda/2033584-pred-25-lety-do-ceska-oficialne-dorazil-internet-byl-pomaly-a-drahy.
"Příběh ateliéru", *Performanceart*, 2002, accessed 15 Apr 2022, https://performance.ffa.vutbr.cz/ARCHIV/CDROM/inner/sub/pribeh.htm.
Přichystalová, Denisa. "V zajetí světla: užití laseru v české scénografii a umění 20. století" (Bachelor's thesis, Masaryk University, Brno, 2020).

R

Rezek, Petr. *Tělo, věc a skutečnost v současném umění* (Praha: Jazzová sekce, 1982).
Richterová, Ivana. "Veřejně přístupná televize už letos?", *Video + film* 3, no. 2 (1993), 6.
Rodowick, David N. *The Virtual Life of Film* (London: Harvard University Press, 2007).
Rosenthal, Kathleen. "‚DDR-Stars' v Kasselu – Oficiální příspěvek NDR k výstavě documenta 6", in *Umění z NDR: Dědictví na obtíž?*, ed. Matěj Forejt (Praha: Galerie Rudolfinum, 2021), 92–97.
Ross, Christine. "The Temporalities of Video: Extendedness Revisited", *Art Journal* 65, no. 3 (Fall, 2006), 82–99.
Rousková, Pavla. "Sbírka Janiny Ojrzyńské – náhradní institucionální rámec českého umění v období sedmdesátých a osmdesátých let 20. století" (Diploma thesis, Academy of Art, Architecture and Design, Prague, 2019).
Rožánek, Filip. "Před 30 lety začala vysílat stanice OK3, přinesla nejen Tutti Frutti", *lupa.cz*, 14. 5. 2020, accessed 10 Jul 2022, https://www.lupa.cz/aktuality/pred-30-lety-zacala-vysilat-stanice-ok3-prinesla-nejen-tutti-frutti/.

"Rudolf Němec a Eugen Brikcius / Kuklení a sluneční hodiny", *Art for Good*, accessed 20 Feb 2022, https://www.artforgood.cz/cs/dalsi-dila/pakukleni-a-slunecni-hodiny.

Ruller, Tomáš. "Příběh ateliéru", *Performanceart*, 2002, accessed 20 May 2022, http://performance.ffa.vutbr.cz/ARCHIV/CDROM/inner/sub/pribeh.htm.

Ruml, Jan. "Originální videojournal – co mi uvízlo v paměti", *Paměť a dějiny* 9, no. 1 (2015), 92–94.

Rusnáková, Katarína. "Digitálne umenie na Slovensku v prvej dekáde 21. storočia: perspektívy a frustrácie, I. časť", *Profil súčasného výtvarného umenia* 19, no. 3 (2012), 8–25.

Rusnáková, Katarína. "Internetové umění a jeho formáty", in *#mm net art – internetové umění ve virtuálním a fyzickém prostoru prezentace*, ed. Marie Meixnerová (Olomouc: Pastiche Filmz, 2014), 13–24.

Růžičková, Alice. "Český dokumentární film v 80. letech: Originální Videojournal'" (Diploma thesis, FAMU, Prague, 2000).

S

Salón užitého umění, 89 pražských výtvarných umělců (Praha: Svaz českých výtvarných umělců, 1989).

"Sbírka Marek Collection: O sbírce", *marekcollection.cz*, accessed 29 Jan 2022, https://marekcollection.cz/cz/o-sbirce.

Sei, Keiko. "Jak lépe porozumět médiím reálného času", in *Video art '94 – Nature in Motion / Příroda v pohybu* (Praha: Mánes, 1994), 9.

Sei, Keiko. "Po stopách médií", in *Orbis Fictus: nová média v současném umění / new media in contemporary arts*, eds. Ludvík Hlaváček – Marta Smolíková (Praha: Sorosovo centrum současného umění, 1995), 148–149.

Sei, Keiko. "Solidity in Flux – Video Installation, Media Art and Media Landscape in Eastern Europe during the Transition", in *TRANSITLAND: Video art from Central and Eastern Europe after the fall of the Berlin Wall /1989–2009/*, ed. Alina Ignatova (Moskva: Centr kultury i isskustva "MediaArtLab", 2010), 43.

Sei, Keiko. "Za všetkými hranicami", in *video vidím ich sehe: slovenské, české a švajčiarske videoumenie*, eds. Esther Maria Jungo – Katarína Rusnáková – Maria Smolenická (Bern, 1994), 59–61.

Sellnerová, Veronika. "Post post-internet: Mapování vývoje české umělecké scény" (Magisterská diplomová práce, Filozofická fakulta Masarykovy univerzity, 2018).

Sellnerová, Veronika. "Reflexe českého post-internetového umění" (Bakalářská práce, Filozofická fakulta Masarykovy univerzity, 2016).

Serranová, Mariana. "Zbyněk Baladrán", *Fotograf* 8, no. 14 (2009), 107.

Sešit pro umění, teorii a příbuzné zóny 11, no. 22 (2017), accessed 2 Apr 2022, https://vvp.avu.cz/sesit/archiv.

Simonyi, Sonja. "Artists as Amateurs: Intersections of Nonprofessional Film Production and Neo-AvantGarde Experimentation at the Balázs Béla Stúdió in the Early 1970s", *Film History* 30, no. 1 (2018), 114–137.

Schlenzka, Jenny. "The Cinematic OD BÍLÉ KOSTKY PO BLACK BOX", *Flash Art Czech & Slovak Edition* 6, no. 31 (2014), 13–15.

Schneiderová, Alexandra. "Performance v rodinném filmu", *Iluminace* 16, no. 3 (2004), 69–82.

Skřiváčková, Petra. "Variantologie: polyhistorický přístup k myšlení o umění nových médií", *Ezin TIM* 4, no. 1/2 (2014), accessed 2 Apr 2022, https://www.phil.muni.cz/journals/index.php/tim/article/view/917/1052.

Slavická, Milena – Jiří Fiala, eds. *Výtvarné umění, čtvrtletník pro současné umění* 20, no. 3/4 (1996), 131–138.

Sloupová, Andrea. "Syntéza po Syntéze: české kinetické umění 60. let a pozdější tvůrčí postupy jeho protagonistů" (Diploma thesis, Charles University, Prague, 2008).

Sontag, Susan. "The Decay of Cinema", *The New York Times Magazine*, 25. 2. 1996.

Sontag, Susan. "Úpadek filmu", *Cinepur* 73, no. 1–2, 2011, 60–62.

Spielmann, Yvonne. *Video – The Reflexive Medium* (Cambridge, Massachusetts – London, England: The MIT Press, 2008).

Spielmannová, Yvonne. "Video a počítač: Estetika Steiny a Woodyho Vasulkových", *Iluminace* 18, no. 2 (2006), 71–86.

Stavěl, Radek. "Globální občanství v rámci vizuálního slovníku (YouTube)", *Film a doba* 52, no. 2 (2007), 99–100.

Stavová, Hana. "Role a možnosti filmového amatéra v letech 1960–1989" (Diploma thesis, Masaryk University, Brno, 2016).

Steyerl, Hito. "Too Much World: Is the Internet Dead?", *e-flux* 6, no. 49 (2013), accessed 10 Jul 2022, https://www.e-flux.com/journal/49/60004 too-much-world-is-the-internet-dead/.

Stöhr, Franziska. *endlos: Zur Geschichte des Film und Videoloops im Zusammenspiel von Technik, Kunst und Ausstellung* (Bielefeld: Transcript Verlag, 2016).

Struppek, Mirjam. "Přísně veřejné / Když videoart proniká do vizuální sféry městského prostoru", *Umělec* 9, no. 3 (2005), 60–63.

Strusková, Eva. "O pořádání žánrového názvosloví", *Film a doba* 36, no. 12 (1990), 719.

Střeláková, Lenka. "Ein Film von Mark Ther", *ART ANTIQUES* 11, no. 12 (2012), 103–104.

Střeláková, Lenka. "Expanded animation: Pohyblivá audiovizuální fascinace", *ART ANTIQUES* 13, no. 2, (2014), 34–39.

Svatoňová, Kateřina. *Mezi-obrazy: Mediální praktiky kameramana Jaroslava Kučery* (Praha: Národní filmový archiv, 2016).

Svatoňová, Kateřina. "Život v obrazech a odchylující se vidění: Úvahy nad medialitou pohyblivých obrazů v souladu s německou teorií/filosofií médií", *Sešit pro umění, teorii a příbuzné zóny* 10, no. 22 (2017), 83–106.

Sýkorová, Lenka. "Jedná se o nekonečný den: S Viktorem Čechem o přehlídce Videokemp", *A2* 9, no. 17, 2013, accessed 2 Apr 2022, https://www.advojka.cz/archiv/2013/17/jedna-se-o-nekonecny-den.

Szczepanik, Petr. "Filmy, které vidí vlastní vidění: Strategie intermediality a reflexivity v současné kinematografii" (Doctoral thesis, Masaryk University, Brno, 2002).

Szczepanik, Petr. "Intermedialita: Pojem", *Cinepur* 11, no. 22 (2002), 56, accessed 2 Apr 2022, http://cinepur.cz/article.php?article=5.

Szczepanik, Petr. "Média mezi kulturami a žánry: Rozhovor s Keiko Sei", *Cinepur* 12, no. 23–24 (2002), 16–19.

Szczepanik, Petr, ed. *Nová filmová historie: Antologie současného myšlení o dějinách kinematografie audiovizuální kultury* (Praha: Hermann & synové, 2004).

Szczepanik, Petr. "Videoklip – změna modelu diváka a elektronická tělesnost: Pragmatický obrat v teorii filmu a populární kultury" (Diploma thesis, Masaryk University, Brno, 1998).

Szczepanik, Petr – Jakub Kučera. "Rozhovor s Davidem Normanem Rodowickem", *Iluminace* 15, no. 2 (2003), 89–106.

Šeborová, Silvie. "Bezpředmětný film", *Flash Art Czech & Slovak Edition* 6, no. 27 (2013), 60, accessed 2 Apr 2022, https://flashart.cz/2013/06/11/bezpredmetny-film/.

Šedivá, Barbora. "Vlastně ani nevím, jestli se za tu dobu utvořil nějaký smysluplný způsob, jak novomediální umění učit", *Monoskop*, 2013, accessed 15 Apr 2022, https://monoskop.org/File:Rozhovor_s_Filipem_Cenkem.pdf.

Ševčík, Jiří – Pavlína Morganová – Terezie Nekvindová – Dagmar Svatošová, eds. *České umění 1980–2010, texty a dokumenty* (Praha: VVP AVU, 2011).

Ševčíková Lucie – Eva Žáková, eds. *Sbírat umění: Dílčí aspekty sběratelství a trhu se současným uměním v ČR* (Praha: Institut umění, 2017), accessed 10 Feb 2022, https://www.culturenet.cz/coKmv4d994Swax/ uploads/2018/01/sbirat_umeni_fin_11.1.pdf.

Šiklová, Jiřina. "The ‚Gray Zone' and the Future of Dissent in Czechoslovakia", *Social Research* 57, no. 2 (1990), 347–363.

Šilařová, Hana. "VOD distribuce, uvádění a sledování filmů / Kinematografie online", *Cinepur* 24, no. 98 (2015), accessed 2 Apr 2022, http://cinepur.cz/article.php?article=3258.

Šmejkal, František. *Vladimír Boudník* (Praha: Galerie na Karlově náměstí, 1965).

Šobáňová, Petra – Jana Jiroutová – José Rodrigo Delgadillo Blando. *Net art* (Olomouc: Universita Palackého v Olomouci, 2015).

Špirit, Michael. "K nedožitým narozeninám Jana Lopatky", *Bubínek Revolveru*, 2020, accessed 6 Feb 2022, https://www.bubinekrevolveru.cz/k-nedozitym-narozeninam-jana-lopatky.

T

"Tate Acquisition and Disposal Policy", *Tate*, 2020, accessed 23 May 2022, https://www.tate.org.uk/documents/1685/acquisition_and_disposal_policy_2020.pdf.

"Technický obraz", in *České umění 1980–2010, texty a dokumenty*, eds. Jiří Ševčík – Pavlína Morganová – Terezie Nekvindová – Dagmar Svatošová (Praha: VVP AVU, 2011), 463–548.
Tichá, Jana. "Rozhovor s Jiřím Příhodou", *Ateliér* 8, no. 26 (1995), 5.
Tichá, Jana. "Rozhovor s Petrem Skalou", *Ateliér* 8, no. 26 (1995), 6.
Tijen, Tjebbe van. "A context for collecting the new media", *Monoskop*, 1993, accessed 10 Jul 2022, https://monoskop.org/images/d/d9/Van_Tijen_Tjebbe_1993_A_Context_for_Collecting_the_New_Media.pdf.
"Tisková zpráva z 4. 9. 2018", *Marienbad Film Festival*, accessed 9 Apr 2022, https://www.marienbadfilmfestival.com/docs/TZ_04092018.pdf.
Trodd, Tamara. "Introduction: Theorising the Projected Image", in *Screen/Space: The Projected Image in Contemporary Art*, ed. Tamara Trodd (Manchester: Manchester University Press, 2011), 1–22.
Turvey, Malcolm – Hal Foster – Chrissie Iles – George Baker – Matthew Buckingham – Anthony McCall. "Round Table: The Projected Image in Contemporary Art", *October* 29, no. 104 (2003), 71–96.
Turimová, Maureen – Scott Nygren. "Číst nástroje, psát obraz", *Iluminace* 18, no. 2 (2006), 49–70.
"TZ: Další film", *Artalk.cz*, accessed 2 Apr 2022, https://artalk.cz/2013/03/05/tz-dalsi-film/.

U

Ulver, Stanislav – Radana Ulverová. "Hlavní město videoartu (LOOP)", *Film a doba* 53, no. 2 (2008), 88–92.
Ulver, Stanislav – Radana Ulverová. "LOOP is LOOP is LOOP (Smyčka je smyčka)", *Film a doba* 52, no. 2 (2007), 90–94.
Ulverová, Radana. "Oba stejně, každý ve svém monitoru, dotkli jsme se obrazovkou: Rozhovor s Tomášem Kepkou", *Film a doba* 46, no. 4 (2001), 199–203.
Ulverová, Radana. "Ruiny, bílý dům a kinematické rituály Lidy Abdulové", *Film a doba* 53, no. 2 (2008), 92–94.
"Úvodní poznámka: České a slovenské filmové časopisy", in Eva Urbanová et al., *Český hraný film VI, 1981–1993* (Praha: Národní filmový archiv, 2010), 13.

V

Valoch, Jiří. "Brněnský okruh: Památce Gerty Pospíšilové, bez níž by mnohé nebylo tak, jak bylo", in *Zakázané umění I*, eds. Milena Slavická – Marcela Pánková (Praha: Občanské sdružení pro podporu výtvarného umění, 1995), 162.
Vančát, Jaroslav. "Český obraz elektronický", in *Český obraz elektronický* "vnitřní zdroje", ed. Ivan Tatíček – Ivc Jebousek (Praha: DADA, s.r.o., 1994), 8–15.
Vančát, Jaroslav. "První kroky videoartu", *Panorama*, no. 2 (1991), 5.
Vančát, Jaroslav. "Stanovisko k plánu oboru video SČVU v souvislosti s uplatněním videotechniky v Národní galerii" Typewritten copy, undated, archive of the heirs of Radek Pilař.
Vančát, Jaroslav. "Úvahy nad (českým) obrazem elektronickým", *Ateliér* 8, no. 26 (1995), 8.
Vančát, Jaroslav. "Video a výtvarná tvorba", *Film a doba* 35, no. 12 (1989), 708–709.
Variable Media Questionnaire, accessed 10 Feb 2022, https://variablemediaquestionnaire.net/.
Vasulka, Woody. "Divadlo hybridních automatů", *Iluminace* 18, no. 2 (2006), 205–208.
Vasulka, Woody. "Galerie: místo pro pohyblivý obraz", in *Orbis Fictus: Nová média v současném umění / new media in contemporary arts*, eds. Ludvík Hlaváček – Marta Smolíková (Praha: Sorosovo centrum současného umění, 1995), 130–131.
Vasulka, Woody. "Technocentrický determinismus", *Iluminace* 18, no. 2 (2006), 199–203.
Vasulka, Woody. "The Commission", *Iluminace* 18, no. 2 (2006), 209–216.
Vasulka, Woody – Charles Hagen. "Syntax binárních obrazů", *Iluminace* 18, no. 2 (2006), 159–178.
Vavrová, Barbora – Sylva Poláková. "Videoarchiv jako obraz doby – Rozhovor se Slávou Sobotovičovou o Videoarchivu VVP AVU", *Filmový přehled*, accessed 10 Feb 2022, https://www.filmovyprehled.cz/cs/revue/detail/videoarchiv-jako-obraz-doby-rozhovor-se-slavou-sobotovicovou-o-videoarchivu-vvp-avu.
"Větev – Prorážení televize větví", *Videoarchiv NFA*, accessed 24 May 2022, https://videoarchiv.nfa.cz/katalog/vetev.
Videogram, accessed 17 Sep 2021, https://videogram.favu.vut.cz/archiv.
"Videokemp 2005", *Art Has No History*, 31. 7. 2005, accessed 2 Apr 2022, https://arthasnohistory.com/2005/07/31/videokemp-2005/.
"videokemp", *Videokemp*, 2006, accessed 30 Aug 2021, https://videokemp.wordpress.com/2006-2/.
"videokemp", *Videokemp*, 2011, accessed 20 Feb 2022, https://videokemp.wordpress.com/2011-2/.
Vitvar, Jan H. "Můj divák se musí kochat: Mark Ther se stal výtvarníkem roku díky dvacetiminutovému videu", *Respekt* 22, no. 49 (2011), 72, accessed 2 Apr 2022, https://www.respekt.cz/tydenik/2011/49 muj-divak-se-musi-kochat.
Vitvar, Jan H. "Pomoč to a natoč to", *Respekt* 18, no. 13 (2007), 20.
Vitvar, Jan H. "Tajemství citlivého kluka", *Respekt* 19, no. 7 (2008), 52.
"Vladimír Boudník – Akce v ulicích Prahy", *Videoarchiv VVP AVU*, accessed 20 Feb 2022, https://vvp.avu.cz/videoarchiv/2454/?table=artvideoarchiv.
Vodrážka, Miroslav. *Výtvarné umění a jeho subverzivní role v období normalizace: demytologizační a detektivní příběh* (Praha: Centrum pro dokumentaci totalitních režimů, 2019).
Vojtěchovský, Miloš. "Broadcast Yourself: Film a YouTube databáze", *A2* 5, no. 6 (2009), 12.
Vojtěchovský, Miloš. "David Lamelas, simulakra světelného kužele", *Cinepur* 14, no. 44 (2006), 24–25.
Vojtěchovský, Miloš. "DIAL H-I-S-T-O-R-Y (Johan Grimonprez)", *Film a doba* 53, no. 2 (2008), 85–87.
Vojtěchovský, Miloš. "Jitro kouzelníků: Umění, proutkaři a hrozivý konec milénia", *Vokno 2000* 1, no. 1 (1997), 34.
Vojtěchovský, Miloš. "Poezie a poetika elektronického těla: Garry Hill a film", *Cinepur* 14, no. 44 (2006), 19–21.
Vojtěchovský, Miloš. "Poznámky k současnému českému videoartu", *Film a doba* 52, no. 2 (2007), 95–99.
Vojtěchovský, Miloš. "Předpoklady budoucnosti: Mediální archeologie", *Agosto Foundation*, duben 2017, accessed 10 Jul 2022, https://agosto-foundation.org/cs/predpoklady-budoucnosti-medialni-archeologie.
Vojtěchovský, Miloš, ed. *Vasulka Kitchen Reader* (Brno: Vasulka Kitchen Brno, 2020), accessed 10 Feb 2022, https://www.vasulkakitchen.org/sites/default/files/document/01_vasulka_kitchen_reader_web.pdf.
Vojtěchovský, Miloš, ed. *Vašulkova kuchyňská kniha #1: texty k médiím: první & poslední = Vasulka kitchen cooking reader #1: beyond media texts: primal & final* (Brno: Vašulka Kitchen Brno, 2020).
"Vyhledávání", *Informační systém Masarykovy university*, accessed 5 Nov 2021, https://is.muni.cz/vyhledavani/?agenda=th&search=Teorie+interaktivn%C3%ADch+m%C3%A9di%C3%AD.

W

Wattenberg, Martin M. "IDEA LINE 2001", *Whitney Museum of American Art*, accessed 20 May 2022, whitney.org/exhibitions/idea-line.
"Web-projekty", *Performanceart*, accessed 20 May 2022, http://performance.ffa.vutbr.cz/ARCHIV/CDROM/inner/www.htm.
Weibel, Peter. "Vládci kódů", *Iluminace* 18, no. 2 (2006), 41–47.
Wheeler, Jim. "Long-term Storage of Videotape", in *Special Issue of the FIAT Newsletter*, January 1986 (International Federation of Television Archives, 1986), 66–75.
"Where technology meets art", *Institut intermédií*, accessed 15 Apr 2022, https://www.iim.cz/cs/.

Y

Yalkut, Jud. "Understanding Intermedia", *Arts Magazine* (květen 1967).
Youngblood, Gene. *Expanded Cinema* (New York: E. P. Dutton & Co., Inc., 1970).

Bibliography

Z

"Z rukopisu projevu Radka Pilaře k příležitosti otevření Media archivu" Typewritten copy, undated, archive of the heirs of Radek Pilař, 2.

"Z rukopisu projevu Radka Pilaře k příležitosti vzniku oboru video" Typewritten copy, undated (after 1987), archive of the heirs of Radek Pilař, 1.

"Zákon o ochraně sbírek muzejní povahy a o změně některých dalších zákonů", *Zákon no. 122/2000 Sb., § 9.*

Zálešák, Jan. "Rámec jako figura: Vystavovatel a jeho diváci v brněnském Domě umění", *ART ANTIQUES* 10, no. 6 (2011), 66–67, accessed 2 Apr 2022, https://www.artantiques.cz/ramec-jako-figura.

Zemánek, Jiří. "Od ideologie reality k pluralitním modelům: České umění elektronických médií v devadesátých letech", in *Dějiny českého výtvarného umění VI / 1, 2. 1958–2000*, eds. Rostislav Švácha – Marie Platovská (Praha: Academia, 2007), 910.

Zemánek, Jiří. "Od luminodynamismu k médiu videa", in *Dějiny českého výtvarného umění 1958–2000 VI / 2*, eds. Rostislav Švácha – Marie Platovská (Praha: Academia, 2007), 537–553.

"Zorka Ságlová – Pocta Fafejtovi", *Videoarchiv VVP AVU*, accessed 5 Apr 2022, https://vvp.avu.czvideoarchiv/2462/?table=artvideoarchiv.

"ZPRÁVA O ČINNOSTI Muzea města Brna, příspěvkové organizace za rok 2017", *Spilberk*, 2018, accessed 25 May 2022, https://www.spilberk.cz/wp-content/uploads/Vyrocni-zprava-2017–1.pdf.

Index of Cited Works

Editorial Note

The collective monograph *Mapping the Moving Image*, subtitled *Media, Agents, and Sites in the Czech Context*, is composed of eleven original essays divided into three sections for ease of orientation: History, Discourse, and Practice.

The illustrations used in the book emphasise the transformation of the media of the moving image of film and video and their forms of representation. Selected examples of works are most often illustrated, within the body of the text, through image sequences. Also used are period materials that relate to the circulation of moving images in the Czech context. These are examples of posters, invitations, photographs of published recordings, documentation of installations, exhibitions, and diverse events mentioned in the individual chapters. Each chapter is introduced by a transitional image. The archival sources and copyright information can be found in the list of illustrations.

As part of the academic and language review process, we decided to unify the names of organisations and institutions, which are written out in full when they are first presented in the publication and later identified only through acronyms. These can then be found in the index of terms and names. The names of studios at art universities whose names have changed over time are given in their current form, accurate to the date of .... The bibliography is complemented by the indexes of names, terms and works cited. Furthermore, the publication also includes a chronological list of works with a preview and QR code that links to an entry in the Videoarchiv catalogue, which makes available to the general public information about works that form part of the eponymous Národní filmový archiv collection (videoarchiv.nfa.cz/ katalog). The collection is gradually expanding and offers a historical, thematic, and generational cross-section through the history of Czech art of the moving image outside the context of cinematography.

Summary

The history of Czech experimental film, video art, net art, and other related disciplines on the boundaries of visual art and cinema spreads over a diverse field. We follow the art of the moving image from the late 1960s to the beginning of the third millennium, i.e., from a time when the amateur film scene began taking shape in Czechoslovakia, becoming one of the possible alternatives to the local film industry, and, particularly in the 1980s, contributed to the development of experimental films. For a short period in the 1960s, it was possible to develop publication activities, associations, and galleries and maintain relationships with the international art scene. The experiences gained from the development of international post-war art, which included an acceptance of non-material modes of artistic expression and an intensification of interest in new technologies, also transpired in artistic activities following the totalitarisation of society during the period known as normalisation, i.e., after the Prague Spring in 1968. The early 1970s saw the creation of the first moving image documentations of action art, at first made only on celluloid film. During the 1970s and '80s, on rare journeys abroad, some artists came into contact with video and, fascinated by the new technology, began exploring the possibilities of these media in solitary seclusion. It was only in the late 1980s that videoists – as artists working with video called themselves at the time – took a more systematic interest in standing up for their common interests and began negotiating an autonomous position among the disciplines of art. The period ubiquitously influenced by the totalitarianism established across society was characterised by a search for gaps in the system that would allow for free expression, for which strategy, caution, and courage were needed. The agents of unofficial culture therefore often found themselves on the fringes of the law. This was true of illicit access to the equipment at film studios at various state-run workplaces, of various ways of trying to find spaces to present art, and of the transport or posting of artworks or documentation abroad.

As a consequence of the socio-political changes in Czechoslovakia in the late 1980s and early '90s, cultural practice also saw a gradual transformation. Systemic changes in the organisation of art professionals, the opening up of the free market, access to new technology, and intensive contact with the world beyond our borders changed the atmosphere of society into a turbulent, enthusiasm-powered stream which was as easy to enter as it was surprisingly easy to drop out. All this concerns both the production of art and its public reflection. While tertiary art education was changing and opening up to the establishment of new studios, the autonomous position of art of the moving image within the art world had to be secured. Crucial in this process were curatorial activities that helped clarify and name works making use of the moving image, including them within the context of visual art (and the context of cinema, too). Exhibition concepts, as well as the themes of various new media festivals and other events, introduced the general public to manifestations of art that had had very limited possibilities in preceding decades. A sustained interest in the moving image began asserting itself on the pages of cultural periodicals and gradually entered academic curricula. The art of the moving image was also discovered as a cultural article that could operate within the system of the circulation of artworks or their conservation for future generations in the appropriate institutions.

It might seem that the process by which the discipline of art of the moving image was legitimised was thus concluded, but in order for this to truly take place, we must strive for the systematic documentation of works that are – by the nature of their media – highly ephemeral and fragile. These are the reasons behind this publication, which forms part of a complex research project by the Národní filmový archiv, focused on developing an archival methodology allowing collecting institutions and smaller workplaces alike to ensure care for this segment of fine art. The historical and theoretical research was based on primary sources and elaborated acquisition documentation, all available in the specialised database of the Národní filmový archiv's Videoarchiv in Prague, which can serve as an expansion of this volume.

Colophon

Mapping the Moving Image.
Media, Agents, and Sites in the Czech Context
Martin Mazanec, Sylva Poláková (eds.)

Authors of the essays:
Martin Blažíček, Matěj Forejt, Eva Krátká, Markéta Mansfieldová, Martin Mazanec, Marie Meixnerová, Sylva Poláková, Tomáš Pospiszyl, Matěj Strnad, Lenka Střeláková, Kateřina Svatoňová

The following individuals took part in the academic review process:
Jiří Anger, Petr Bilík, Palo Fabuš, Pavlína Míčová, Terezie Nekvindová, Miloš Vojtěchovský

English translation:
Ian Mikyska

Copy editing:
Megan Bedell (EN), Helena Černohorská (CZ)

Proofreading:
Kevin B. Johnson

Graphic design:
St. Anymade (Petr Cabalka, Filip Nerad)

Paper:
Fedrigoni Symbol Freelife Raster, Munken Print White

Typeface:
FK Grotesk Neue

Printing and binding:
Tiskárna Helbich, a.s.

Published by:
Národní filmový archiv, Prague
Závišova 502/5
140 00 Praha 4
www.nfa.cz

and

Spector Books
Harkortstraße 10
04107 Leipzig
www.spectorbooks.com

First edition: 2023
Printed in the EU

ISBN 978-3-95905-843-8

Distribution:
Germany, Austria: GVA, Gemeinsame Verlagsauslieferung Göttingen GmbH&Co. KG, www.gva-verlage.de
Switzerland: AVA Verlagsauslieferung AG, www.ava.ch
France, Belgium: Interart Paris, www.interart.fr
UK: Central Books Ltd, www.centralbooks.com
USA, Canada, Central and South America, Africa: ARTBOOK/ D.A.P., www.artbook.com
South Korea: The Book Society, www.thebooksociety.org

Národní filmový archiv

Covers
Radek Pilař *Yes No Yes* (1992), edit Anymade Studio,
Dominik Gajarský *Carausius morosus*, Dům U Zlatého prstenu, Galerie hlavního města Prahy [Prague City Gallery], 2016, Photo Tomáš Souček